London

timeout.com/london

Penguin Books

PENGUIN BOOKS

Published by the Penguin Group
Penguin Books Ltd, 80 Strand, London WC2R ORL, England
Penguin Books USA Inc., 375 Hudson Street, New York, New York 10014, USA
Penguin Books Australia Ltd, 250 Camberwell Road, Camberwell, Victoria 3124, Australia
Penguin Books Canada Ltd, 10 Alcorn Avenue, Toronto, Ontario, Canada M4V 3B2
Penguin Books (NZ) Ltd, cnr Rosedale and Airborne Roads, Albany, Auckland, New Zealand

Penguin Books Ltd, Registered Offices: Harmondsworth, Middlesex, England

First published 1989
First Penguin edition 1990
Second edition 1992
Third edition 1994
Fourth edition 1995
Fifth edition 1997
Sixth edition 1998
Seventh edition 1999
Eighth edition 2000
Ninth edition 2001
Tenth edition 2002
Eleventh edition 2003
10 9 8 7 6 5 4 3 2 1

Colour reprographics by Icon, Crowne House, 56-58 Southwark Street, London SE1 1UN
Printed and bound by Cayfosa-Quebecor, Ctra. de Caldes, Km 3 08 130 Sta, Perpètua de Mogoda, Barcelona, Spain

Edited and designed by
Time Out Guides Limited
Universal House
251 Tottenham Court Road
London W1T 7AB
Tel + 44 (0)20 7813 3000
Fax + 44 (0)20 7813 6001
Email guides@timeout.com
www.timeout.com

Editorial

Editor Will Fulford-Jones
Deputy Editor Simon Coppock
Listings Editor Cathy Limb
Proofreader Tamsin Shelton
Indexer Selena Cox

Editorial Director Peter Fiennes
Series Editor Ruth Jarvis
Deputy Series Editor Jonathan Cox
Guides Co-ordinator Anna Norman

Design

Group Art Director John Oakey
Art Director Mandy Martin
Art Editor Scott Moore
Senior Designer Lucy Grant
Designer Sarah Edwards
Scanning/Imaging Dan Conway
Ad Make-up Glen Impey
Picture Editor Kerri Littlefield
Deputy Picture Editor Kit Burnet
Picture Desk Trainee Bella Wood

Advertising

Group Commercial Director Lesley Gill
Sales Director/Sponsorship Mark Phillips
Sales Manager Alison Gray
Advertisement Sales Matthew Lennard, Terina Rickit,
Jason Trotman
Copy Controller Oliver Guy
Advertising Assistant Sabrina Ancilleri

Administration

Chairman Tony Elliott
Chief Operating Officer Kevin Ellis
Managing Director Mike Hardwick
Chief Financial Officer Rick Waterlow
Group Marketing Director Christine Cort
Marketing Manager Mandy Martinez
US Publicity & Marketing Associate Rosella Albanese
Group General Manager Nichola Coulthard
Guides Production Director Mark Lamond
Production Controller Samantha Furniss
Accountant Sarah Bostock

Contributors

Introduction Will Fulford-Jones. **History** Will Fulford-Jones (*London loves: Harry Beck* Tom Fulford-Jones; *Moving in* Laura Martz; *Stormy weather* Hugh Graham). **London Today** Hugh Graham. **Architecture** David Littlefield. **London on Song** Will Fulford-Jones. **The Gift of London** Simon Coppock. **Accommodation** Will Fulford-Jones, Hugh Graham; *additional reviews* Ismay Atkins, Jonathan Cox, Lily Dunn, Lesley McCave (*Dinner and a movie?* Ruth Jarvis; *The chain gang, See you at the bar?* Will Fulford-Jones; *Don't tell them we told you, but...* Gwen Cheeseman). **Sightseeing: Introduction** Will Fulford-Jones. **Central London** Will Fulford-Jones; *additional reviews* Lily Dunn, Sharon Lougher, Cath Phillips (*Hall or nothing, Many bridges to cross, London loves: The City on Sunday, A river runs through it, The wanderers: Bohemian Soho* Rhodri Marsden; *London loves: Routemasters* Ruth Jarvis; *Pepys show, The wanderers: Collegiate Bloomsbury, London loves: Speakers' Corner* Tom Fulford-Jones; *London loves: Animals, Shop around* Andrew Williams; *It's a man's world* Gwen Cheeseman; *Shake on it* Laura Martz; *The wanderers: Political Westminster* Simon Carter). **North London** Simon Coppock (*Might as well jump* Paul Mowat; *The wanderers: Rural Hampstead* Dan Gould; *London loves: The dead* Will Fulford-Jones). **East London** Simon Coppock; *additional reviews* Will Fulford-Jones (*Jack be nimble, Jack be quick* Will Fulford-Jones; *London loves: Iain Sinclair* Nicholas Royle; *EastBeginners* Hugh Graham). **South London** Hugh Graham (*London loves: The Woolwich Ferry* Will Fulford-Jones; *Dome alone* Rhodri Marsden). **West London** Isaac Davis (*Go west* Nicholas Royle; *London loves: The Blue Book* Laura Martz; *London loves: Ghosts* Andrew Williams). **Restaurants** Phil Harriss (*Vegging out; London loves: The Sunday roast; Late eats* Lily Dunn; *London loves: Gordon Ramsay* Simon Coppock; *London loves: Curry* Andrew Williams). **Pubs & Bars** Will Fulford-Jones (*London loves: Beer* Paul Mowat). **Shops & Services** Ros Sales (*The kinks* Laura Martz; *Pick up a picnic, Museum pieces, London loves: Car boot sales* Cathy Limb). **Festivals & Events** Simon Coppock. **Children** Ronnie Haydon. **Comedy** Sharon Lougher. **Dance** Donald Hutera. **Film** Will Fulford-Jones (*London loves: Singing along* Ruth Jarvis). **Galleries** Martin Coomer (*The graduates* Julia Hamilton). **Gay & Lesbian** Dan Gould (*Cruise control* Hugh Graham). **Music** Will Fulford-Jones. **Nightlife** Helen Gilchrist; *casinos* Simon Coppock (*Clubbed to death* Hugh Graham; *The naked truth* Will Fulford-Jones). **Sport & Fitness** Sam Le Quesne (*London loves: Darts* Will Fulford-Jones; *London loves: The dogs* Tom Fulford-Jones). **Theatre** Isaac Davis (*No great Shakes* Tom Fulford-Jones). **Trips Out Of Town** Simon Coppock. **Directory** Will Fulford-Jones (*Crime and the city solution* Hugh Graham).

Maps JS Graphics (john@jsgraphics.co.uk).

Photography by Hadley Kincade, except pages 7, 8, 10, 11, 13, 14, 15, 19 AKG London; page 9 London Transport Museum; page 17 PA Photos; page 20 Mirrorpix; pages 39, 40, 41, 42 Tony Gibson, page 163 Phill Pepper; page 262 Matt Carr; page 264 Steve Bardens; pages 267, 353 Amanda Edwards; page 304 Keith Saunders; page 341, 342 Alys Tomlinson; page 346 Jon Perugia; page 354 Paul Avis. The following images were provided by the featured establishments/artists: page 350 Hever Castle; page 351 Waddesdon, The Rothschild Collection (National Trust).

The Editor would like to thank Nyx Bradley, Julie Cook, Paul Fairclough, Sarah Guy, Malcolm Hay and Andrew Humphries. Also, thanks to contributors to previous editions of the *Time Out London Guide*, whose work forms the basis for parts of this book.

Contents

Introduction

First impressions are key. Which makes it kind of peculiar that London has lasted so long as a grade-A tourist destination. The slightly bleak and careworn state of our airports – Heathrow especially – is as nothing when compared to the tedium and grime that awaits you on your ride into London. The tube from Heathrow will take about a week to reach town (the Heathrow Express is far quicker, but also far less frequent, far less convenient and far more expensive). The overground rail train from Gatwick into town will be late arriving, if it shows at all. And don't even get us started on the laborious route to and from Luton (officially called, with quite splendid inaccuracy, London Luton). By the time you reach your accommodation, you'll be cursing this town through gritted teeth.

Other first impressions will be equally off-putting. Aren't these streets dirty, you'll ask yourself rhetorically as you stumble over yet another discarded fast-food wrapper. How do people put up with this five days a week, you'll quietly ponder while stuck between stations on an overcrowded tube train, or stuck stock-still atop a double-decker bus whose front-mounted destination sign seems less like intention and more like fantasy with each passing quarter-hour. *How* much, you'll wonder aloud when asked to fork out £3 for a beer, or £10 for a cinema ticket, or £15 for a compact disc.

But while first impressions are key, they're not – as cliché sometimes suggests they might be – everything. Or, at least, they shouldn't be. Those who come here and allow their first impressions to take them over are never going to get the most from the city. We mean visitors, sure, but also a surprisingly large number of residents, who are still allowing the (understandable) awe and horror at the sheer scale of the place they felt when they first moved to the big bad city to dominate them many years later.

The trick with London, as with any city of this magnitude, is to look between the cracks in the pavement. Explore the museums and the attractions, certainly, and rest assured that the city has plenty of impressive ones. Visit the picture-postcard sights, if only for fear of the despairing looks your friends will shoot your way if they found out you travelled all this way and didn't see Big Ben. But wander off the beaten track a little. Or a lot. Respond to the city's enormity not by hibernating into the safe and impeccably mapped tourist havens, but by going beyond them.

For it's here you'll find the real London. The London where history is not preserved in aspic but still living, breathing and having an influence. The London whose stories are unfamiliar and largely untold, and therefore worth hearing. The London not solely of the Circle line and within in, but of the evocatively named neighbourhood stations beyond it: Kennington, Belsize Park, Whitechapel, Kew Gardens, St John's Wood. The London of immigrant communities now every bit at home here as any dyed-in-the-wool Cockney. The London beyond the surface mess of the chip papers and the hassle-packed public transport. The London where you'll find the Londoners, both by birthright and adoption. Say hello; we won't bite.

For London is a challenge to which to rise, a game to play, a mystery to figure out, a monster you can't hope to pin down in a single visit… or, perhaps, a single lifetime. It's why we still make our homes here, and it's ultimately why you keep coming back to see us. First impressions? First impressions be damned. Have a great time.

ABOUT TIME OUT GUIDES

This is the 11th edition of the *Time Out London Guide*, one of the expanding series of *Time Out* guides produced by the people behind London and New York's successful listings magazines. Our guides are all written and updated by resident experts who have striven to provide you with all the most up-to-date information you'll need to explore the city or read up on its background, whether you're a local or a first-time visitor.

THE LIE OF THE LAND

Thanks to the chaotic street plan – or, rather, the lack of one – London is one of the most complicated of all major world cities to find your way around. To make it a little easier, we've included an area designation for every venue in this guide (such as Soho, Covent Garden, Westminster, et cetera), along with map references that point to our street maps at the back of the book (starting on page 394). However, for the sake of comprehensiveness,

we recommend that you follow the example of the locals and invest in a standard *A-Z* map of the city the minute you arrive.

ESSENTIAL INFORMATION

For all the practical information you might need for visiting the area – including visa and customs information, details of local transport, a listing of emergency numbers and a directory of useful websites – turn to the Directory chapter at the back of this guide. It starts on page 286.

THE LOWDOWN ON THE LISTINGS

We have tried to make this book as easy to use and practically useful as possible. Addresses, phone numbers, transport information, opening times and admission prices are all included. However, owners and managers can change their arrangements at any time. Before you go out of your way, we'd strongly advise you to phone ahead to check opening times and other particulars. While every effort and care has been made to ensure the accuracy of the information contained in this guide, the publishers cannot accept responsibility for any errors it may contain.

PRICES AND PAYMENT

In the listings, we have noted which of the following credit cards are accepted: American Express (AmEx), Diners Club (DC), MasterCard (MC) and Visa (V). Some venues will also accept other cards, such as Delta, Switch or JCB.

The prices we've listed in this guide should be treated as guidelines, not gospel. If prices vary wildly from those we've quoted, ask whether there's a good reason. If not, go

elsewhere. Then please let us know. We aim to give the best and most up-to-date advice, so we want to know if you've been badly treated or overcharged.

TELEPHONE NUMBERS

The area code for London is 020. All telephone numbers given in this guide take this code unless otherwise stated: add 020 to the numbers listed throughout the book if calling from outside London; otherwise, simply dial the number as written. For more details of phone codes and charges, *see p373*. The international dialling code for the UK is 44.

MAPS

The map section at the back of this book includes a trips out of town map, orientation and neighbourhood maps of the London area, and street maps of most of central London, with a comprehensive street index. The maps start on page 389.

LET US KNOW WHAT YOU THINK

We hope you enjoy the *Time Out London Guide*, and we'd like to know what you think of it. We welcome your tips for places to include in future editions and take note of your criticism of our choices. There's a reader's reply card at the back of this book for your feedback, or you can email us at guides@timeout.com.

Advertisers

We would like to stress that no establishment has been included in this guide because it has advertised in any of our publications and no payment of any kind has influenced any review. The opinions given in this book are those of *Time Out* writers and entirely independent.

There is an online version of this guide, as well as weekly events listings for 35 international cities, at **www.timeout.com**

In Context

MUSEUM OF LONDON
Discover a time when lions and hippos roamed Trafalgar Square!
Visit the new London before London gallery
FREE ADMISSION
Close to St Paul's
www.museumoflondon.org.uk

Charles I loses his head. *See p13.*

History

Murders, disasters, wars… and those were the quiet times.

London was founded by the Trojan prince Brutus and run by a race of heroic giants descended from the Celtic King Lud. Or so, at least, thought the 12th-century chronicler Geoffrey of Monmouth. However, the truth is rather more prosaic. Though Celtic tribes did live in scattered communities along the banks of the Thames prior to the arrival of the Romans in Britain, there's no evidence to suggest that there was a settlement on the site of the future metropolis before the invasion of the Emperor Claudius' legions in AD 43. During the Romans' conquest of the country, they forded the Thames at its shallowest point and, later, built a timber bridge here (near the site of today's London Bridge). Over the following decade, a settlement developed on the north side of this strategically vital crossing.

During the first two centuries AD, the Romans built roads, towns and forts in the area, and trade flourished. The first mention of London (Londinium), by the Roman historian Tacitus, was in AD 60, when he described it as being 'filled with traders…a celebrated centre of commerce'. Progress was brought to a halt in AD 61 when Boudicca, the fearsome widow of an East Anglian chieftain, rebelled against the Imperial forces who had seized her land, flogged her and raped her daughters. She led the Iceni in a savage revolt, destroying the Roman colony at Colchester and then marching on London. The inhabitants were massacred and the settlement was burned to the ground.

After order was restored, the town was rebuilt and, around AD 200, a two-mile (three-kilometre) long, 18-foot (six-metre) high defensive wall was constructed around it. Chunks of the wall survive today, and the names of the original gates – Ludgate, Newgate, Bishopsgate and Aldgate – are preserved on the map of the city. The street known as London Wall traces part of its original course.

By the fourth century, racked by barbarian invasions and internal strife, the Empire was in decline. In 410 the last troops were withdrawn and London became a ghost town. The Roman way of life vanished, their only enduring legacies being roads and early Christianity.

SAXON AND VIKING LONDON

During the fifth and sixth centuries, history gives way to legend. The Saxons crossed the North Sea and settled in eastern and southern England, apparently avoiding the ruins of London; they built farmsteads and trading posts outside the walls.

Pope Gregory sent Augustine to convert the English to Christianity in 596. Ethelbert, Saxon King of Kent, proved a willing convert, and Augustine was appointed the first Archbishop of Canterbury. Since then, Canterbury has remained the centre of the English Christian

Church. London's first Bishop, though, was Mellitus: one of Augustine's missionaries, he converted the East Saxon King Sebert and, in 604, founded a wooden cathedral dedicated to St Paul inside the old city walls. On Sebert's death, his followers reverted to paganism, but later generations of Christians rebuilt what is now St Paul's Cathedral.

London, meanwhile, continued to expand. The Venerable Bede, writing in 731, described 'Lundenwic' as 'the mart of many nations resorting to it by land and sea'. This probably refers to a settlement west of the Roman city in the area of today's Aldwych (Old English for 'old settlement'). During the ninth century, the city faced a new danger from across the North Sea: the Vikings. The city was sacked in 841 and, in 851, the Danish raiders returned with 350 ships, leaving London in ruins. It was not until 886 that King Alfred of Wessex – aka Alfred the Great – regained the city, soon re-establishing London as a major trading centre with a merchant navy and new wharfs at Billingsgate and Queenhithe.

Throughout the tenth century, the Saxon city prospered. Churches were built, parishes established and markets set up. However, the 11th century brought more Viking harassment, and the English were even forced to accept a Danish king, Cnut (Canute, 1016-40), during whose reign London replaced Winchester as the capital of England.

In 1042 the throne reverted to an Englishman, Edward the Confessor, who devoted himself to building the grandest church in England two miles (three kilometres) west of the City at Thorney ('the isle of brambles'). He replaced the timber church of St Peter's with a huge abbey, 'the West Minster' (Westminster Abbey; consecrated in December 1065), and moved his court to the new Palace of Westminster. A week after the consecration, Edward died and was buried in his new church. London now grew around two hubs: Westminster, as the centre for the royal court, government and law, and the City of London, as the commercial centre.

THE NORMAN CONQUEST

On Edward's death, there was a succession dispute. William, Duke of Normandy, claimed that the Confessor, his cousin, had promised him the English crown, but the English instead chose Edward's brother-in-law Harold. Piqued, William gathered an army and invaded; on 14 October 1066, he defeated Harold at the Battle of Hastings and marched on London. City elders had little option but to offer William the throne, and the conqueror was crowned in Westminster Abbey on Christmas Day, 1066.

Recognising the need to win over the prosperous City merchants by negotiation rather than force, William granted the Bishop and burgesses of London a charter – still kept at Guildhall – that acknowledged their rights and independence in return for taxes. But, 'against the fickleness of the vast and fierce population', he also ordered strongholds to be built alongside the city wall, including the White Tower (the tallest building in the Tower of London) and the now-lost Baynard's Castle at Blackfriars. The earliest surviving written account of contemporary London was written 40 years later by a monk, William Fitz Stephen, who vividly conjured up the walled city and, outside, pastures and woods for hunting, youths wrestling and fencing in Moorfields, and skating on frozen ponds.

THE MIDDLE AGES

In the growing city of London, much of the politics of the Middle Ages – the late 12th to the late 15th centuries – revolved around a three-way struggle for power between the king and the aristocracy, the Church, and the Lord Mayor and city guilds.

The king and his court frequently travelled to other parts of the kingdom and abroad in the early Middle Ages. However, during the 14th and 15th centuries, the Palace of Westminster became the seat of law and government. The noblemen and bishops who attended court built themselves palatial houses along the Strand from the City to Westminster, with gardens stretching to the river.

1066 and all that...

London loves Harry Beck

As London icons go, it remains largely unheralded. Not for it the picture-postcard cosiness of the red double-decker or the skyline-dominating magnificence of St Paul's Cathedral. Yet it is perused, studied and examined millions of times a day for guidance, reassurance and pleasure, and its influence can be seen in countless similar examples of the form throughout the world. You would, literally, be lost without it. It is the map of the London Underground, and its original author, some 70 years ago, was an unassuming gentleman from Finchley named Harry Beck.

An engineering draughtsman with the Underground Group in the 1920s, Beck fell victim to the large cullings of public sector workers at the time of the Depression and lost his job. While out of work, he decided to set about addressing one of the Underground's biggest problems: producing a clear, useable map of the complex tube network.

Soon, Beck was rehired as a draughtsman by the Underground, but continued to work on his map at home. When he eventually submitted it to London Transport's publicity department, it was rejected immediately. A year later, Beck sent it in again, and this time his design was accepted. The 28-year-old was paid five guineas for his work, and in January 1933, 750,000 card folder prints of his map

were released to the public. In one corner was planted, gingerly, the inscription 'HC BECK'.

London has never looked the same since. Dispensing with the literal geography employed by previous mapmakers, which had produced diagrams that were topographically accurate but cluttered and impenetrable, Beck reorganised the infrastructure of the tube cleanly and systematically. Utilitarian yet elegant, stylised and pleasing to the eye, it offered a new kind of order to a sprawling city's chaos. A grateful public brushed aside critics' grumblings that the reconfigured map was a misleading stunt. They loved its usefulness and its simplicity.

As the years went by, the map underwent minor alterations as lines got extended and stations were closed. Beck oversaw the changes himself, but was unceremoniously relieved of his duties by London Underground in 1960 amid wranglings over ownership of the map and payment for his work. Beck was devastated by the undignified end to his association with a work of classic design that had, thanks to its brilliance, outgrown its author. But the fact that the map found in every tube station (and, incidentally, on the back page of this book) has changed so little since Beck's day is, perhaps, a fitting tribute to his quietly revolutionary design.

vant ce vint le ven
dredy au matin ce
peuple qui estoit
logie en la place Sainte Kathe
rine sevant la tour du chastel

The **Archbishop of Canterbury** is murdered
during the Peasants' Revolt of 1381.

The Model Parliament, which agreed
the principles of government, was held in
Westminster Hall in 1295, presided over by
Edward I and attended by barons, clergy and
representatives of knights and burgesses. The
first step towards establishing personal rights
and political liberty – not to mention curbing
the power of the king – had already been taken
in 1215 with the signing of the Magna Carta
by King John. Later, in the 14th century,
subsequent assemblies gave rise to the House of
Lords (which met at the Palace of Westminster)
and the House of Commons (which met in the
Chapter House at Westminster Abbey).

Relations between the monarch and the City
were never easy. Londoners guarded their
privileges with self-righteous intransigence,
and resisted all attempts by successive kings to
squeeze money out of them to finance wars and
building projects. Subsequent kings were forced
to turn to Jewish and Lombard moneylenders,
but the City merchants were as intolerant of
foreigners as of the royals. Rioting, persecution
and the occasional lynching and pogrom were
all commonplace in medieval London.

CITY STATUS AND COMMERCIAL CLOUT
The privileges granted to the City merchants
under Norman kings, allowing independence
and self-regulation, were extended by the
monarchs who followed, in return for financial
favours. In 1191, during the reign of Richard I,
the City of London was formally recognised as

a commune – a self-governing community –
and in 1197 it won control of the Thames,
which included lucrative fishing rights that
the City retained until 1857. In 1215 King John
confirmed the city's right 'to elect every year
a mayor', a position of great authority with
power over the Sheriff and the Bishop of
London. A month later, the Mayor had joined
the rebel barons in signing the Magna Carta.

Over the next two centuries, the power and
influence of the trade and craft guilds – later
known as the City Livery Companies – increased
as trade with Europe grew, and the wharfs by
London Bridge were crowded with imports
such as fine cloth, furs, wine, spices and precious
metals. Port dues and taxes were paid to
Customs officials such as part-time poet Geoffrey
Chaucer, whose *Canterbury Tales* became the
first published work of English literature.

The City's markets, already established,
drew produce from miles around: livestock at
Smithfield, fish at Billingsgate and poultry at
Leadenhall. The street markets, or 'cheaps',
around Westcheap (now Cheapside) and
Eastcheap were crammed with a variety of
goods. As commerce increased, foreign traders
and craftsmen settled around the port; the
population within the city wall grew from about
18,000 in 1100 to well over 50,000 in the 1340s.

BLACK DEATHS AND
REVOLTING PEASANTS
However, perhaps unsurprisingly, lack of
hygiene became a serious problem in the city.
Water was provided in cisterns at Cheapside
and elsewhere, but the supply, which came
more or less direct from the Thames, was
limited and polluted. The street called
Houndsditch was so named because Londoners
threw their dead animals into the furrow that
formed the city's eastern boundary. There was
no proper sewerage system; in the streets
around Smithfield (the Shambles), butchers
dumped the entrails of slaughtered animals.

These appalling conditions provided the
breeding ground for the greatest catastrophe of
the Middle Ages: the Black Death of 1348 and
1349. The plague came to London from Europe,
carried by rats on ships. During this period,
about 30 per cent of England's population died
of the disease. Although the epidemic abated,
it was to recur in London on several occasions
during the next three centuries, each time
devastating the city's population.

The outbreaks of disease left the labour
market short-handed, causing unrest among
the overworked peasants. The imposition of a
poll tax of a shilling a head proved the final
straw, leading to the Peasants' Revolt of 1381.
Thousands marched on London, led by Jack

Straw from Essex and Wat Tyler from Kent. In the rioting and looting that followed, the Savoy Palace on the Strand was destroyed, the Archbishop of Canterbury was murdered and hundreds of prisoners were set free. When the 14-year-old Richard II rode out to Smithfield to face the rioters, Wat Tyler was fatally stabbed by Lord Mayor William Walworth. The other ringleaders were subsequently rounded up and hanged. But no more poll taxes were imposed.

CHURCHES AND MONASTERIES

Like every other medieval city, London had many parish and monastic churches, as well as the great Gothic cathedral of St Paul's. Though the majority of Londoners were allowed access to the major churches, the lives of most of them revolved around their own local parish places of worship, where they were baptised, married and buried. Many churches were linked with particular craft and trade guilds.

Monasteries and convents were also established, all owning valuable acres inside and outside the city walls. The crusading Knights Templars and Knights Hospitallers were two of the earliest religious orders to settle, though the increasingly unruly Templars were disbanded in 1312 by the Pope and their land eventually became occupied by the lawyers of Inner and Middle Temple.

He's **Henry VIII**, he is, he is...

The still-standing Smithfield church of St Bartholomew-the-Great (founded 1123) and the names of St Helen's Bishopsgate, Spitalfields and St Martin's-le-Grand are reminders of these early monasteries and convents. The friars, active social workers among the poor living outside the city walls, were known by the colour of their habits: the Blackfriars (Dominicans), the Whitefriars (Carmelites) and the Greyfriars (Franciscans). Their names are still in evidence around Fleet Street and the west of the City.

TUDORS, STUARTS AND DIVORCE

Under the Tudor monarchs (who reigned from 1485 until 1603) and spurred by the discovery of America and the ocean routes to Africa and the Orient, London became one of Europe's largest cities. Henry VII brought to an end the Wars of the Roses by defeating Richard III at the Battle of Bosworth and marrying Elizabeth of York. Henry VII's other great achievements included the building of a merchant navy, and the Henry VII Chapel in Westminster Abbey, the eventual resting place for him and his queen.

> ### 'Many Londoners drank vast amounts to escape the horrors of daily life.'

Henry VII was succeeded in 1509 by arch wife-collector (and dispatcher) Henry VIII. Henry's first marriage to Catherine of Aragon failed to produce an heir, so the King, in 1527, determined that the union should be annulled. As the Pope refused to co-operate, Henry defied the Catholic Church, demanding that he himself be recognised as Supreme Head of the Church in England and ordering the execution of anyone who refused to go along with the plan (including his chancellor Sir Thomas More). Thus England began the transition to Protestantism. The subsequent dissolution of the monasteries transformed the face of the medieval city with the confiscation and redevelopment of all property owned by the Catholic Church.

On a more positive note, Henry did manage to develop a professional navy in between beheading his wives, founding the Royal Dockyards at Woolwich in 1512 and at Deptford the following year. He also established palaces at Hampton Court and Whitehall, and built a residence at St James's Palace. Much of the land he annexed for hunting became the Royal Parks, including Hyde, Regent's, Greenwich and Richmond Parks.

Post-Henry, there was a brief Catholic revival under Queen Mary (1553-8), though her marriage to Philip II of Spain met with much opposition in London. She had 300 Protestants

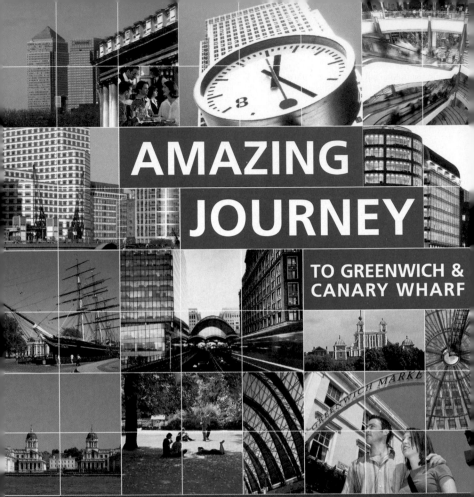

burned at the stake at Smithfield, earning her the nickname 'Bloody Mary'. However, this upturn in fortunes for Catholicism ended almost as soon as it had begun.

ELIZABETHAN LONDON

Elizabeth I's reign (1558-1603) saw a flowering of English commerce and arts. The founding of the Royal Exchange by Sir Thomas Gresham in 1566 gave London its first trading centre, allowing it to emerge as Europe's leading commercial centre. The merchant venturers and the first joint-stock companies (Russia Company and Levant Company) established new trading enterprises, and Drake, Raleigh and Hawkins sailed to the New World and beyond. In 1580 Elizabeth knighted Sir Francis Drake on his return from a three-year circumnavigation; eight years later, Drake and Howard defeated the Spanish Armada.

As trade grew, so did London. It was home to some 200,000 people in 1600, many living in dirty, overcrowded conditions; plague and fire were constant, day-to-day hazards. The most complete picture of Tudor London is given in John Stow's *Survey of London* (1598), a fascinating first-hand account by a diligent Londoner whose monument stands in the City church of St Andrew Undershaft.

The glory of the Elizabethan era was the development of English drama, popular with all social classes but treated with disdain by the Corporation of London, which went as far as to ban theatres from the City in 1575. Two theatres, the Rose (1587) and the Globe (1599), were erected on the south bank of the Thames at Bankside, and provided homes for the works of Marlowe and Shakespeare. Deemed 'a naughty place' by royal proclamation, Bankside was the Soho of its time: home not just to the theatre, but also to bear-baiting, cock-fighting, taverns and 'stewes' (brothels).

The Tudor dynasty ended with Elizabeth's death in 1603. Her successor, the Stuart King James I, narrowly escaped assassination on 5 November 1605, when Guy Fawkes and his gunpowder were discovered underneath the Palace of Westminster. The Gunpowder Plot had been hatched in protest at the failure to improve conditions for the persecuted Catholics, but only resulted in an intensification of anti-papist feelings in ever-intolerant London. To this day, 5 November is commemorated – and, a little incongruously, celebrated with fireworks galore – as Bonfire Night.

But aside from his unwitting part in the Gunpowder Plot, James I merits remembering for other, more important reasons. For it was he who hired Inigo Jones to design court masques, and what ended up as the first –

Elizabeth I.

and hugely influential – examples of classical Renaissance style in London, the Queen's House in Greenwich (1616) and the Banqueting House in Westminster (1619).

CIVIL WAR

Charles I succeeded his father in 1625, but gradually fell out with the City of London (from whose citizens he tried to extort taxes) and an increasingly independent-minded and antagonistic Parliament. The last straw finally came in 1642 when he intruded on the Houses of Parliament in an attempt to arrest five MPs. The country soon slid into a civil war (1642-9) between the supporters of Parliament (led by Puritan Oliver Cromwell) and those of the King.

Both sides knew that control of the country's major city and port was vital for victory. London's sympathies were firmly with the Parliamentarians and, in 1642, 24,000 citizens assembled at Turnham Green, west of the city, to face Charles's army. Fatally, the King lost his nerve and withdrew. He was never to seriously threaten the capital again; eventually, the Royalists were defeated. Charles was tried for treason and, though he denied the legitimacy of the court, he was declared guilty. He was beheaded outside the Banqueting House in Whitehall on 30 January 1649, declaring himself to be a 'martyr of the people'.

For the next 11 years the country was ruled as a Commonwealth by Cromwell. However, the closing of the theatres and the banning of the

Penny for the Guy? Mr Fawkes pays the price for the failed **Gunpowder Plot**. *See p13.*

supposedly Catholic superstition of Christmas, along with other Puritan strictures on the wickedness of any sort of fun, meant that the restoration of the exiled Charles II in 1660 was greeted with relief and rejoicing by the populace.

PLAGUE, FIRE AND REVOLUTION

However, two major catastrophes marred the first decade of Charles's reign in the capital. In 1665 the most serious outbreak of bubonic plague since the Black Death killed many of the capital's population. By the time the winter cold had put paid to the epidemic, nearly 100,000 Londoners had died. And on 2 September 1666, a second disaster struck. The fire that spread from a carelessly tended oven in Farriner's Baking Shop on Pudding Lane was to rage for three days and consume four-fifths of the City, including 89 churches, 44 livery company halls and more than 13,000 houses.

Despite the obvious tragic element, the Great Fire at least allowed planners the chance to rebuild London as a spacious, rationally planned modern city. Many blueprints were drawn up and considered, but, in the end, Londoners were so impatient to get on with business that the City was reconstructed largely on its medieval street plan, albeit in brick and stone rather than wood. The towering figure of the period turned out to be the extraordinarily prolific Sir Christopher Wren, who oversaw the work on 51 of the 54 churches that were rebuilt. Among them was his masterpiece, the new St Paul's, completed in 1711 and, effectively, the world's first Protestant cathedral.

After the Great Fire, many well-to-do former City residents moved to new residential developments that were springing up in the West End. In the City, the Royal Exchange was rebuilt, but merchants increasingly used the new coffee houses in which to exchange news. With the expansion of the joint-stock companies and the chance to invest capital, the City was emerging as a centre not of manufacturing, but of finance.

Anti-Catholic feeling still ran high, however. The accession of Catholic James II in 1685 aroused fears of a return to Catholicism, and resulted in a Dutch Protestant, William of Orange, being invited to take the throne with his wife, Mary Stuart (James's daughter); James later fled to France in 1688 in what became known – by its beneficiaries – as the 'Glorious Revolution'. One of the most significant developments during William III's reign was the founding of the Bank of England in 1694, initially to finance the King's wars with France.

GEORGIAN LONDON

After the death of Queen Anne, and in accordance with the Act of Settlement (1701), the throne passed to George, great-grandson of James I, who had been born and brought up in Hanover, Germany. Thus, a German-speaking king – who never learned English – became the first of four long-reigning Georges in the Hanoverian line.

During his reign (1714-27), and for several years afterwards, Sir Robert Walpole's Whig party had the monopoly of power in Parliament. Their opponents, the Tories, supported the Stuarts and had opposed the exclusion of the Catholic James II. On the King's behalf, Walpole chaired a group of ministers (the forerunner of today's Cabinet), becoming, in effect, Britain's first prime minister. Walpole was presented with 10 Downing Street as a residence; it remains the official home of all serving prime ministers.

During the 18th century, London grew with astonishing speed, in terms of both population and built-up area. New squares and streets of terraced houses spread all over Soho, Bloomsbury, Mayfair and Marylebone, as wealthy landowners and speculative developers who didn't mind taking a risk given the size of the potential rewards cashed in on the demand for leasehold properties. South London, too, became more accessible with the opening of the first new bridges for several centuries, Westminster Bridge (1750) and Blackfriars Bridge (1763). Until then, London Bridge had been the only bridge over the Thames. The old city gates, most of the Roman Wall and the remaining houses on Old London Bridge were demolished, allowing easier access to the City for traffic and people.

POVERTY AND CRIME

In the older districts, however, people were still living in terrible squalor and poverty, far worse than the infamous conditions of Victorian times. Some of the most notorious slums were located around Fleet Street and St Giles's (north of Covent Garden), only a short distance from streets of fashionable residences maintained by large numbers of servants. To make matters worse, gin ('mother's ruin') was readily available at very low prices, and many poor Londoners drank excessive amounts in an attempt to escape the horrors of daily life. The well-off seemed complacent, amusing

themselves at the popular Ranelagh and Vauxhall Pleasure Gardens or with organised trips to Bedlam to mock the mental patients. On a similar level, public executions at Tyburn – near today's Marble Arch – were among the most popular events in the social calendar.

The outrageous imbalance in the distribution of wealth encouraged crime: robberies in the West End took place in daylight. Reformers were few, though there were exceptions. Henry Fielding, author of the picaresque novel *Tom Jones*, was also an enlightened magistrate at Bow Street Court. In 1751 he and his blind brother John set up a volunteer force of 'thief-takers' to back up the often ineffective efforts of the parish constables and watchmen who were the only law-keepers in the city. This group of early cops, known as the Bow Street Runners, were the forerunners of today's Metropolitan Police (established in 1829).

Disaffection was also evident in the activities of the London mob during this period. Riots were a regular reaction to middlemen charging extortionate prices, or merchants adulterating their food. In June 1780 London was hit by the anti-Catholic Gordon Riots, named after ringleader George Gordon; the worst in the city's violent history, they left 300 people dead.

Some attempts were made to alleviate the grosser ills of poverty with the setting up of five major new hospitals by private philanthropists. St Thomas's and St Bartholomew's were already long established as monastic institutions for the

London's burning: Jan Luyken's impression of the **Great Fire** of 1666. *See p14.*

care of the sick, but Westminster (1720), Guy's (1725), St George's (1734), London (1740) and the Middlesex (1745) went on to become world-famous teaching hospitals. Thomas Coram's Foundling Hospital for abandoned children was another remarkable achievement of the time.

However, it wasn't just the indigenous population of London that was on the rise. Country people, who had lost their land because of enclosures and were faced with starvation wages or unemployment, drifted into the towns in large numbers. The East End became the focus for poor immigrant labourers with the building of the docks towards the end of the century. London's population had grown to almost a million by 1801, the largest of any city in Europe. And by 1837, when Queen Victoria came to the throne, five more bridges and the capital's first passenger railway gave hints that a major expansion might be around the corner.

THE VICTORIAN ERA

As well as being the administrative and financial capital of the British Empire, which spanned a fifth of the globe, London was also its chief port and the world's largest manufacturing centre, with breweries, distilleries, tanneries, shipyards, engineering works and many other grimy industries lining the south bank of the Thames. On the one hand, London boasted splendid buildings, fine shops, theatres and museums; on the other, it was a city of poverty, disease and prostitution. The residential areas were becoming polarised into districts with fine terraces maintained by squads of servants, and overcrowded, insanitary, disease-ridden slums.

The growth of the metropolis in the century before Victoria came to the throne had been spectacular enough, but during her reign, which lasted until 1901, thousands more acres were covered with housing, roads and railway lines. Today, if you pick any street within five miles (eight kilometres) of central London, chances are that its houses will be mostly Victorian. By the end of the 19th century, the city's population had swelled to in excess of six million.

Despite the social problems – memorably depicted in the writings of Charles Dickens – major steps had been taken to improve conditions for the majority of Londoners by the turn of the century. The Metropolitan Board of Works installed an efficient sewerage system, street lighting and better roads, while the worst slums were replaced by low-cost building schemes funded by philanthropists such as the American George Peabody and by the London County Council (created in 1888).

The Victorian expansion would not have been possible without an efficient public transport network with which to speed workers into and out of the city from the new suburbs. The horse-drawn bus appeared on London's streets in 1829, but it was the opening of the first passenger railway from London Bridge to Greenwich seven years later that heralded the London of the future. The first underground line, which ran between Paddington and Farringdon Road, opened in 1863 and proved an instant success, attracting more than 30,000 travellers on the first day. Soon thereafter, the world's first electric track in a deep tunnel – the 'tube' – opened in 1890 between the City and Stockwell, later becoming part of the present-day Northern line.

THE GREAT EXHIBITION

The Great Exhibition of 1851 captured the zeitgeist: confidence and pride, discovery and invention. Prince Albert, the Queen's Consort, helped organise this triumphant event, for which the Crystal Palace, a giant building of iron and glass – designed not by a professional architect but by the Duke of Devonshire's gardener, Joseph Paxton – was erected in Hyde Park. During the five months it was open, the Exhibition drew six million visitors from Great Britain and abroad, and the profits inspired the

Moving in

Sometimes, you can catch the air of the Caribbean wafting through certain London neighbourhoods. Brixton and Hackney in particular are rich with the smells of frying fish and the colours of the Jamaican flag. Life here has been shaped by people from the former colonies who came over on the 1950s and 1960s immigration wave, and by the boatload of newcomers that inspired them.

Just over half a century ago, on 22 June 1948, the troop ship *Empire Windrush* docked at Tilbury Dock, bringing 492 passengers and eight stowaways from Jamaica to a new life in England. Many had served in the war, and they came seeking better work opportunities in the capital of the country they'd been taught to love as their motherland. Each had paid £28 10/–, the price of three cows back home, for the passage. A few days before the ship docked, one of its passengers – calypso singer Lord Kitchener – wrote a song about how he was feeling. He called the simple eulogy 'London is the Place for Me'.

But was it? Perhaps not at first. Greeted by alien smoke, grime and stink, the *Windrush* passengers found jobs – as

Prince Consort to establish a permanent centre for the study of the applied arts and sciences: the result is the South Kensington museums and Imperial College. After the Exhibition, the Palace was moved to Sydenham and used as an exhibition centre until it burned down in 1936.

When the Victorians were not colonising the world by force, they had the foresight to combine their conquests with scientific developments. The Royal Geographical Society sent navigators to chart unknown waters, botanists to bring back new species, and geologists to study the earth. Many of the specimens that were brought back ended up at the Royal Botanic Gardens at Kew.

THE 20TH CENTURY
During the brief reign of Edward VII (1901-10), London regained some of the gaiety and glamour it lacked in the dour last years of Victoria's reign. A touch of Parisian chic came to London with the opening of the Ritz Hotel in Piccadilly; the Café Royal hit the heights of its popularity as a meeting place for artists and writers; and 'luxury catering for the little man' was provided at the Lyons Tea Shops and new Lyons Corner Houses

(the Coventry Street branch, which opened in 1907, could accommodate an incredible 4,500 people). Meanwhile, the first American-style department store, Selfridges, opened on Oxford Street in 1909.

Road transport, too, was revolutionised. Motor cars put-putted around the city's streets, before the first motor bus was introduced in 1904. Double-decked electric trams had started running in 1901 (though not through the West End or the City), and continued doing so for 51 years. In fact, by 1911 the use of horse-drawn buses had been abandoned.

London suffered its first air raids in World War I. The first bomb over the city was dropped from a Zeppelin near Guildhall in September 1915, and was followed by many nightly raids; bombing raids from planes began in July 1917. In all, around 650 people lost their lives as a result of Zeppelin raids.

BETWEEN THE WARS
Political change happened quickly after World War I. Lloyd George's government averted revolution in 1918-19 by promising (but not delivering) 'homes for heroes' for the embittered

post office workers, signpainters, musicians – but scarce housing and little acceptance. Signs reading 'No niggers' warned them away from rooming houses and pubs; racist taunts followed them down the street. So they created their own communities in the areas that would have them: poor, crime-ridden neighbourhoods such as Notting Hill, and pockets of south London.

On arrival, more than 200 of the *Windrush* passengers were housed in the deep wartime shelter beneath Clapham South tube station, convenient for the labour office in Brixton's Coldharbour Lane. (The shelter's two entrance-structures still stand on Clapham Common South Side, near The Avenue, and on Balham Hill's west side, opposite Gaskarth Road.) Many stayed in the area. Today, the descendants and successors of these *Windrush* pilgrims keep a little bit of the Caribbean alive in a London that's becoming ever more diverse.

returning soldiers. But the Liberal Party's days in power were numbered, and by 1924 the Labour Party, led by Ramsay MacDonald, had enough MPs to form its first government.

After the trauma of World War I, a 'live for today' attitude prevailed in the Roaring '20s among the young upper classes, who flitted from parties in Mayfair to dances at the Ritz. But this meant little to the mass of Londoners, who were suffering greatly in the post-war slump. In 1921 Poplar Council in east London refused to levy the rates on its impoverished population. The entire council was sent to prison but was later released, having achieved an equalisation of the rates over all London boroughs that relieved the burden on the poorest ones.

Still, things didn't improve immediately. Civil disturbances, brought on by an increased cost of living and rising unemployment, resulted in the nationwide General Strike of 1926, when the working classes downed tools in support of the striking miners. Prime Minister Baldwin encouraged volunteers to take over the public services and the streets teemed with army-escorted food convoys, aristocrats running soup kitchens and students driving buses. After nine days of chaos, the strike was called off by the Trades Union Congress (TUC).

'For all the changes, post-war life was drab, regimented and austere'

The economic situation only worsened in the early 1930s following the New York Stock Exchange crash of 1929; by 1931 more than three million Britons were jobless. During these years, the London County Council began to have a greater impact on the city's life, undertaking programmes of slum clearance and new housing, creating more parks and taking under its wing education, transport, hospitals, libraries and the fire service.

London's population increased dramatically between the wars, too, peaking at nearly 8.7 million in 1939. To accommodate the influx, the suburbs expanded quickly, particularly to the north-west with the extension of the Metropolitan line to an area that became known as Metroland. Identical gabled, double-fronted houses sprang up in their hundreds of thousands, from Golders Green to Surbiton.

All these new Londoners were entertained by the new media of film, radio and TV. London's first radio broadcast was beamed from the roof of Marconi House in the Strand in 1922, and families were soon gathering around enormous Bakelite wireless sets to hear the British Broadcasting

London suffered in **World War II**.

Company (the BBC; from 1927 called the British Broadcasting Corporation). Television broadcasts started on 26 August 1936, when the first telecast went out live from Alexandra Palace.

WORLD WAR II (1939-45)
Neville Chamberlain's policy of appeasement towards Hitler's increasingly aggressive Germany during the 1930s collapsed when the Germans invaded Poland, and on 3 September 1939 Britain declared war. The government implemented precautionary measures against the threat of air raids – including the digging of trench shelters in London parks, and the evacuation of 600,000 children and pregnant mothers – but the expected bombing raids did not happen during the autumn and winter of 1939-40, a period that became known as the Phoney War. In July 1940, though, Germany began preparations for an invasion of Britain with three months of aerial attack that came to be known as the Battle of Britain.

For Londoners, the Phoney War came to an abrupt end on 7 September 1940, when hundreds of German bombers dumped their

Stormy weather

Talking about the weather – or, more likely, moaning about it – is a great British pastime. It's how people make small talk here, and has been since time immemorial. Happily, London's meteorological history has given the locals plenty to talk about.

There have been mammoth floods in London roughly twice a century since 1099. On 6 January 1928 a northerly gale raised water levels in the Thames Estuary so much that water blew embankments in central London, rushing into the basements of houses and drowning 14 people. A mere 25 years later, on 31 January 1953, the greatest tidal surge on record for the North Sea killed 300 on the east coast before travelling up the Thames towards London, flooding factories and more than 1,000 homes in east London. Events such as these prompted the eventual construction of the Thames Barrier.

Londoners don't often have occasion to pray for rain, but during the summer of 1976 the capital simultaneously experienced its worst drought and heatwave in 300 years. From 22 June to 16 July, the temperature reached at least 27°C on a daily basis; it set a London record by topping 35°C on 26 june. Hosepipes were banned and reservoirs stood empty. Bowler-hatted City types went to work in shorts; school lessons were held outdoors; the government even appointed a Minister of Drought. With impeccable timing, though, the rain returned just in time for the August Bank Holiday weekend: on 31 August a rainstorm stopped play at Lord's. The crowd cheered.

loads of high explosives on east London and the docks. Entire streets were destroyed; the dead and injured numbered more than 2,000. The Blitz had begun. The raids on London continued for 57 consecutive nights, then intermittently for a further six months. Londoners reacted with tremendous bravery and stoicism, a period still nostalgically referred to as 'Britain's finest hour'. After a final massive raid on 10 May 1941, the Germans focused their attention elsewhere, but by the end of the war, a third of the City and the East End was in ruins.

From 1942 onwards, the tide of the war began to turn, but Londoners still had a new terror to face: the V1, or 'doodlebug'. Dozens of these explosives-packed pilotless planes descended on the city in 1944, causing widespread destruction. Later in the year, the more powerful V2 rocket was launched and, over the winter, 500 of them dropped on London, mostly in the East End. The last fell on 27 March 1945 in Orpington, Kent, around six weeks before Victory in Europe (VE Day) was declared on 8 May 1945. Thousands of people took to the streets of London to celebrate.

POST-WAR LONDON

World War II left Britain almost as shattered as Germany. Soon after VE Day, a general election was held and Churchill was heavily defeated by

London winters are invariably gloomy: take the month of December 1890, when not one minute of sunshine was recorded. Cheerier winters are pictured on quaint period Christmas cards that depict skaters on the Thames. Such Frost Fairs, as they were called, did occur during Britain's 'Little Ice Age' (1550-1850). During this stretch, the Thames froze over 14 times, the most recent in 1814. Not so picturesque was December 1852, when London's worst ever 'pea-souper' – a combination of fog and emissions from coal fireplaces and factories – reduced visibility to 12 inches: people couldn't see their own feet. Around 4,000 died from respiratory illnesses.

Of all the freak weather occurrences, the one everybody remembers is the hurricane of 16 October 1987, which caught even the Met Office by surprise. On the eve of the storm, BBC weather forecaster Michael Fish assured the nation they could sleep soundly. 'A woman rang to say she heard there was a hurricane on the way. Well, don't worry: there isn't.' Hours later, a great storm carved through London and the Home Counties, with winds gusting up to 115mph. Transport came to a halt, roads were blocked by fallen trees and tower blocks were wrecked. The Royal Botanic Gardens at Kew were stripped bare: 1,000 were uprooted, one of them dating from 1761. Hampstead Heath was left similarly barren. Eighteen people died across the south-east of England. And Michael Fish? He's Britain's longest-serving weather presenter.

the Labour Party under Clement Attlee. The new government established the National Health Service in 1948, and began a massive nationalisation programme that included public transport, electricity, gas, postal and telephone services. But for all the planned changes, life in London for most people was drab, regimented and austere.

In London, the most immediate problem faced by both residents and the local authorities was a critical shortage of housing. Prefabricated bungalows provided a temporary solution for some (though many of these buildings were still occupied 40 years later), but the huge new high-rise housing estates that

the planners began to erect were often badly built and proved to be very unpopular with their residents.

However, there were bright spots during this dreary time. London hosted the Olympics in 1948; three years later came the Festival of Britain (100 years after the Great Exhibition), a celebration of British technology and design. The exhibitions that took over land on the south bank of the Thames for the Festival provided the incentive to build the South Bank Centre.

FROM FUTURE TO NO FUTURE

As the 1950s progressed, life and prosperity gradually returned to London, leading Prime Minister Harold Macmillan in 1957 to famously proclaim that 'most of our people have never had it so good'. The coronation of Queen Elizabeth II in 1953 had been the biggest television broadcast in history, and there was the feeling of a new age dawning.

However, many Londoners were moving out of the city. The population dropped by half a million in the late 1950s, causing a labour shortage that prompted huge recruitment drives in Britain's former colonies. London Transport and the National Health Service were particularly active in encouraging West Indians to emigrate to Britain. Unfortunately, as the Notting Hill race riots of 1958 illustrated, the welcome these new emigrants received was rarely friendly. Yet there were areas of tolerance: among them was Soho, which, during the 1950s, became famed for its seedy, bohemian pubs, clubs and jazz joints, such as the still-jumping Ronnie Scott's.

By the mid '60s, London had started to swing. The innovative fashions of Mary Quant and others broke Paris's stranglehold on couture: boutiques blossomed along King's Road, while Biba set the pace in Kensington. Carnaby Street became a byword for hipness as the city basked in its newfound reputation as the music and fashion capital of the world. The year of student unrest in Europe, 1968, saw the first issue of *Time Out* (a fold-up sheet for 5p) hit the streets in August. The decade ended with the Beatles naming their final album *Abbey Road* after their studios in London, NW8, and the Rolling Stones playing a free gig in Hyde Park that drew around 500,000 people.

The bubble, though, had to burst – and burst it did. Many Londoners remember the 1970s as a decade of economic strife: inflation, the oil crisis and international debt caused chaos, and the IRA began its bombing campaign on mainland Britain. The explosion of punk in the second half of the decade, sartorially inspired by the idiosyncratic genius of Vivienne Westwood, provided some nihilistic colour.

THATCHERISM

History will regard the 1980s as the Thatcher era. When the Conservatives won the general election in 1979, Britain's first woman prime minister, the propagandist for 'market forces' and Little Englander morality, set out to expunge socialism and the influence of the 1960s and 1970s. A monetarist economic policy and cuts in public services savagely widened the divide between rich and poor. While professionals – particularly the new breed known as 'yuppies' (Young Urban Professionals) – profited from tax cuts and easy credit, unemployment soared.

In London, riots erupted in Brixton (1981) and Tottenham (1985); mass unemployment and heavy-handed policing were seen as contributing factors. The Greater London Council (GLC), led by Ken Livingstone, mounted spirited opposition to the Thatcher government with a series of populist measures, the most famous of which was a revolutionary fare-cutting policy on public transport. So effective was the GLC, in fact, that Thatcher decided to abolish it in 1986.

The spectacular rise in house prices at the end of the 1980s was followed by an equally alarming slump and the onset of a severe recession that only started to lift in the mid 1990s. The Docklands development – one of the Thatcher enterprise schemes, set up in 1981 in order to create a new business centre in the Docklands to the east of the City – has faltered many times, although it can now be counted a qualified success in terms of attracting business and a rapidly increasing number of residents to the Isle of Dogs and surrounding areas.

RECENT PAST AND NEAR FUTURE

The replacement of the by-now hated Margaret Thatcher by John Major as leader of the Conservative Party in October 1990 signalled an upsurge of hope in London. A riot in Trafalgar Square had helped to see off both Maggie and her inequitable Poll Tax.

Yet the early 1990s were scarred by continuing recession and an all-too-visible problem of homelessness on the streets of the capital. Shortly after the Conservatives were elected for another term in office in 1992, the IRA detonated a massive bomb in the City, killing three people. This was followed by a second bomb a year later, which shattered buildings around Bishopsgate, and by a Docklands bomb in February 1996, which broke a fragile 18-month ceasefire. The Good Friday agreement raised hopes for permanent peace in the province, and although disagreements about the decommissioning of weapons have given rise to sporadic violence in Northern Ireland,

these questions now appear to have been resolved, and the terrorist threat to the capital has been massively reduced.

In May 1997 the British people ousted the tired Tories, and Tony Blair's Labour Party swept to victory. However, initial enthusiasm from a public delighted to see some fresh faces in office didn't last. The government hoped that the Millennium Dome, built on a patch of Greenwich wasteland, would be a 21st-century rival to the 1851 Great Exhibition. However, it was badly mismanaged from the start, eventually eating nearly £1 billion of public money and becoming something of a national joke along the way.

It was not the government's only problem. A series of serious rail accidents (on a train network already on its knees), worsening crime, an epidemic of foot and mouth in 2001 and dissatisfaction with the National Health Service all led to Blair and Labour's approval rating dropping, amid mounting suspicion that the government was all style and no substance. However, the lack of a credible opposition meant Labour got re-elected with considerable ease in 2001.

A year earlier, Ken Livingstone, former leader of the ill-fated GLC, had become London's first directly elected mayor in circumstances that deeply embarrassed Labour. Despite evidence that the majority of London voters wanted to see Livingstone as the Labour candidate in the first ever mayoral elections, Blair, who'd long despised Livingstone's rebellious streak and lack of lapdog obeisance to the party line, all but imposed his own candidate on the party. Livingstone quit Labour in disgust and ran in the election as an independent, eventually winning in a landslide to head the new Greater London Assembly (GLA).

Almost three years on, the GLA is still finding its feet. And with another election not too far away, Livingstone and Labour still haven't kissed and made up, and few expect them to do so any time soon. The city is still beset by countless problems, insane property prices and appalling traffic and public transport chief among them. But while the city has its critics – the worst of whom, as always, tend to be its locals – people are still moving here. The city is as crowded, chaotic and popular as it's ever been, and it keeps right on changing and growing each year.

► For more on **Inigo Jones**, *see p30*.
► For more on **the Dome**, *see p172*.
► For more on **Ken Livingstone**, *see p24*.

Key events

AD 43	The Romans invade; a bridge is built on the Thames; Londinium is founded.
61	Boudicca burns Londinium; the city is rebuilt and made the provincial capital.
200	A city wall is built; Londinium becomes capital of Britannia Superior.
410	Roman troops evacuate Britain.
c600	Saxon London is built to the west.
604	St Paul's is built by King Ethelbert; Mellitus becomes Bishop of London.
841	The Norse raid for the first time.
c871	The Danes occupy London.
886	King Alfred of Wessex retakes London.
1013	The Danes take London back.
1042	Edward the Confessor builds a palace and 'West Minster' upstream.
1066	William I is crowned in Westminster Abbey; London is granted a charter.
1067	Work begins on the Tower of London.
1191	Henry Fitzalwin is the first mayor.
1213	St Thomas's Hospital is founded.
1215	The Mayor of London signs the Magna Carta, strengthening the City's power.
1240	First Parliament sits at Westminster.
1290	Jews are expelled from London.
1327	The first Common Council of the City of London.
1348-9	The Black Death devastates London.
1381	Wat Tyler and Jack Straw lead the Peasants' Revolt.
1397	Richard Whittington is Lord Mayor.
1476	The first ever printing press is set up by William Caxton at Westminster.
1512-3	The Royal Dockyards at Woolwich and Deptford are founded by Henry VIII.
1534	Henry VIII cuts off the Catholic Church.
1566	Gresham opens the Royal Exchange.
1599	The Globe Theatre opens on Bankside.
1605	Guy Fawkes fails to blow up James I.
1642	The start of the Civil War; Royalists are defeated at Turnham Green.
1649	Charles I is executed; Commonwealth is established under Cromwell.
1664-5	The Great Plague.
1666	The Great Fire.
1675	Building starts on the new St Paul's.
1692	Lloyd's first insurance market opens.
1694	The Bank of England is established.
1717	Hanover Square and Cavendish Square are laid out, signalling the start of the development of the West End.
1750	Westminster Bridge is built.
1766	The city wall is demolished.
1780	The anti-Catholic, anti-Irish Gordon Riots take place.
1802	The Stock Exchange is founded.
1803	The first public railway opens, horse-drawn from Croydon to Wandsworth.
1812	Prime Minister Spencer Perceval is assassinated at Parliament.
1824	The National Gallery is founded.
1827	Regent's Park Zoo opens.
1829	London's first horse-drawn bus runs from Paddington to the City; the Metropolitan Police Act is established.
1833	The London Fire Brigade is set up.
1835	Madame Tussaud's opens.
1836	The first passenger railway opens, from Greenwich to London Bridge; the University of London is founded.
1837	Parliament is rebuilt after a fire.
1843	Trafalgar Square is laid out.
1848-9	A cholera epidemic sweeps London.
1851	The Great Exhibition takes place.
1853	Harrods opens its doors.
1858	The Great Stink: pollution in the Thames reaches hideous levels.
1863	The Metropolitan line, the world's first underground railway, opens.
1864	The Peabody buildings, cheap housing for the poor, are built in Spitalfields.
1866	London's last major cholera outbreak; the Sanitation Act is passed.
1868	The last public execution is held at Newgate Prison.
1884	Greenwich Mean Time is established.
1888	Jack the Ripper prowls the East End; a London County Council is created.
1890	The Housing Act enables the LCC to clear the slums; the first electric underground railway opens.
1915-8	Zeppelins bomb London.
1940-1	The Blitz devastates much of London.
1948	The Olympic Games are held.
1951	The Festival of Britain takes place.
1953	Queen Elizabeth II is crowned.
1966	England win World Cup at Wembley.
1982	The last of London's docks close.
1986	The GLC is abolished.
1990	Poll Tax protesters riot.
1991	Riots in Brixton.
1992	Canary Wharf opens; an IRA bomb hits the Baltic Exchange in the City.
1997	Diana, Princess of Wales dies.
2000	Ken Livingstone is elected mayor; Tate Modern and the London Eye open.
2001	The Labour government is re-elected.
2002	Work begins on the reconstruction of Trafalgar Square.

London Today

Britain's capital is edging towards the future. But thanks to the appalling traffic, it might not make it there for a while.

London's a funny old place. The world flocks to the capital, both to work and play, and yet, in global 'quality of life' surveys, London always finishes near the bottom, somewhere around Brazzaville or Tijuana. The surveys have a point, too, but still the people come. In droves. According to the latest forecasts, in the next two decades, London's population will rise by almost ten per cent to 8.1 million.

Are we gluttons for punishment? London is dirty, expensive, crime-ridden and chaotic. Why doesn't the rest of the world flock to, say, Minneapolis or Helsinki, those perennial 'quality of life' winners? The answer is simple: because it's London. The city seduces the masses with its unparalleled ability to be all things to all people: traditional yet progressive, romantic yet modern, parochial but simultaneously global. The staunchly British London of *Yes, Minister* and *EastEnders* remains, but London's also a global village now: more than 300 different languages are spoken, and 30 per cent of Londoners are from ethnic minority groups.

Rather than shying away from London's complexity, urban planners are drawn to the city for the challenges it poses. Perhaps that's why London, despite the headaches, is still the belle of the ball: the ones that play hardest to get always have the most suitors. That said, there's a point at which complexity becomes a euphemism for chaos, and the flipside of being one of the most exhilarating cities on earth is that London often seems as if it's on the verge of falling apart.

MOTION SICKNESS

The doomsayers paint a bleak picture of transport in London, particularly the tube. It's expensive: a single inner-zone fare costs £1.60, compared with £1 in New York and 50p in Paris. It's inconvenient: unlike the 24-hour New York subway, London's tube network shuts at midnight. It's unreliable: last year, in one month alone, more than 1,000 peak-time trains were cancelled. And it's inefficient. It took just four years to build the entire Central line back in the 1890s. A century later, it took seven years to fix the escalators at Holborn station. During rush hour, the entire system is a claustrophobe's nightmare.

After decades of underinvestment, the Government finally decided the tube needs fixing, introducing the controversial Public-Private Partnership scheme (PPP). Under the scheme, private consortia are to be given 30-year leases to look after the tracks, while the trains will be publicly owned and maintained. Critics argue that the state will end up subsidising contractors' profits, and the scheme will create the same awkward division of labour that left the mainline railways in such a shambolic state.

'The flight to the suburbs has not resulted in a hollow, inner-city core.'

Above ground, things aren't much better. To alleviate traffic gridlock in the city centre, mayor Ken Livingstone is introducing a scheme he calls congestion charging: anyone entering central London in their car between 7am and 6.30pm will be charged £5 for the 'privilege'. Livingstone hopes that people will leave their cars at home in favour of public transport. Sceptics point out that public transport is already crowded enough, and that congestion charging will simply displace traffic problems to central London's perimeter.

All is not doom and gloom, however. Bus services have improved under Ken Livingstone. There are more night buses on the road than ever, and although the arrival of a new single-decker 'bendy' bus may sound the death knell for the classic double-decker (*see p86* **London loves**), the new vehicles can pack in more passengers. The mayor has also promised new tube lines and extensions, including the much-vaunted East London line that will finally connect such long-forgotten corners of the town as Hackney (to the east) and Forest Hill (in the south) to the tube network. London lives in hope.

LIVING IN A BOX

More than seven million people live in London. But with the ludicrous price of property, it's a miracle anyone can afford it. Horror stories abound about the exodus of nurses, teachers and policemen from the capital: last year, local paper the *Evening Standard* ran a piece about a fireman who commutes from Cardiff. It's easy to see why people are leaving: average

Londoners in their late twenties need a mortgage of 8.5 times their average salary of £26,000 to buy a home, and there's a waiting list of 180,000 for council housing.

As house hunters get pushed further out, the grottiest neighbourhoods become gentrified. Balham, Tooting and Streatham, for instance, have all been The New Clapham at various points over the last few years, at least according to estate agents. No matter how grim the neighbourhood, you can bet it's described as 'up and coming'. As if London weren't sprawling enough, developers are clamouring to build on green belt land to ease the housing shortage.

Necessity, though, is proving to be the mother of invention. Ken Livingstone has introduced a scheme whereby, in order to gain planning permission for building projects, developers will be required to allocate 50 per cent of the scheme to affordable homes. Other groundbreaking schemes include using dead space above supermarkets, car parks and petrol stations to provide affordable housing, while developers are considering proposals to build prefab, Portakabin-style flats on derelict land.

Housing woes aside, London is still a relatively healthy city from an urban planning perspective. The flight to the suburbs has not resulted in a hollow, inner-city core; the suburbs themselves are mini-cities in their own rights, with, by and large, excellent leisure facilities, parks, entertainment and transport links. And unlike many of the world's most populous cities, the gap between rich and poor is not a geographical one. London has no real slums. From Notting Hill to Brixton, from Bethnal Green to Battersea, the better off live side by side with poorer residents. The wealthy might not like it, but the mix means that London's problems can't be swept under the carpet.

POLICE AND THIEVES

London's citizens – and reputation – took a bruising last year, when the number of muggings soared to 232 a day and the capital's crime figures began to surpass New York's. The epidemic was partly attributed to the scourge of crack cocaine – use of the drug has risen 70 per cent in London in the last two years – which has triggered waves of gun crime between drugs gangs.

The Government has responded by putting more officers on the beat and imposing stricter sentences on muggers, while the opposition has called for a New York-style 'zero tolerance' approach to crime. But a more thoughtful experiment took place in Brixton, where police effectively decriminalised marijuana in order to spend their time tackling serious crime. The results were encouraging: street attacks in the

Pissing the night away

Amid the hoopla surrounding the Queen's Golden Jubilee celebrations, an equally important anniversary went largely unnoticed: the 150th birthday of the public toilet. This is a tragedy. The fate of London's public loos affects the everyday lives of locals far more than the state of the monarchy. Tourism is affected too. For many visitors, their first impression of London is not the gracious architecture, the double-decker buses or the splendid parks, but the all-pervading smell of piss.

These are sorry times for London's public toilets. The first public convenience was opened on 14 August 1852 opposite the Royal Courts of Justice in Fleet Street, in an effort to combat disease that spread through fouling. In the ensuing years, the civic-minded Victorians built thousands of them. And stunning structures they were, too, decked out with sparkling tiles, shiny copper pipes, wrought-iron fences and ornate pergolas.

But during the 1990s, 47 per cent of London's public toilets closed, leaving just one for every 20,000 inhabitants today. Politicians complained that the public WCs attracted unsavoury types. But the decline of the public toilet merely illustrates our transformation from a civic society to one beholden to the private sector. Nowadays, spending a penny has become a shameful affair: sneaking into a pub or fast-food restaurant, hoping to avoid the manager's beady eye. Who can blame people for peeing in the streets?

Waiting for a night bus at Trafalgar Square amid late-night drinkers has virtually become a water sport. When the National Gallery reported fairly recently that its stone walls were beginning to erode due to uric acid, Westminster council decided enough was enough. The solution? Mobile, open-air urinals. The council has introduced 14 of the pop-up pissoirs, used at weekends in Soho and Covent Garden.

These devices are of no use to women, but then the female of the species has always exhibited more self-control about these things. Critics also complain that it's uncouth to place urinals on the streets. But better to look at a man relieving himself from behind than having to ford through streams of his wee-wee. 'Provision of public toilets is as important an investment as a new airport,' said a spokesman for the British Toilet Association. 'We can either return to medieval days when people urinated in the streets or we can try to tackle the growing problem. Free and easy access to a public toilet is a fundamental human right.'

borough fell by 30 per cent in six months, arrests for Class A drugs rose 19 per cent, and an estimated 2,500 man hours were saved.

But the perception didn't match up to the reality. Middle England wasn't happy that Brixton was becoming a new Amsterdam, while locals complained that the 'softly, softly' approach had created a lawless atmosphere, attracting more, and increasingly brazen, drug dealers to the area. The police abandoned the experiment. And while the Government's efforts to reduce street crime seems to have paid off – overall, the number of muggings is down – the number of burglaries has risen.

REASONS TO BE CHEERFUL

There is, though, good news. Trafalgar Square is being dramatically remade, with the north side of it to be pedestrianised. Hungerford Bridge has been given the makeover of all makeovers. Urban planners have proposed a spectacular overhaul of the perpetually squalid King's Cross area. St Paul's Cathedral has received £5 million for a massive restoration, which will see 300 years of dirt and grime removed. The once-foul Thames is now so clean that 118 species of fish have returned. And citizens are fighting back against creeping corporatisation: in Streatham, locals rallied to prevent supermarket chain Tesco from ripping down their ice rink without building them a new and better one first.

None of these grand plans will go smoothly of course; this is London, after all. But with a little luck, the capital just might creep past Calcutta in those aforementioned 'quality of life' surveys. It'll never surpass Minneapolis or Helsinki; well, not unless everyone leaves, and, judging from the population trends of the last 2000 years, that's not likely to happen. And if it does, well, who'd want to live in London any more? Certainly not Londoners. They'd have nothing to moan about.

▶ For more on **Trafalgar Square**, see p128.
▶ For more on **traffic**, see p360.
▶ For more on **crime**, see p373.

Guildhall. *See p32.*

Architecture

If you build it, they will come.

The last couple of years have not been kind to London. Against a background of falling stock market values and less than impressive corporate performances, you'd be forgiven for anticipating an abrupt end to what has been a remarkable few years of reconstruction in the city. You'd be wrong. A combination of factors – London's dominance over British economic and cultural life, its decaying infrastructure, its position at the heart of Europe's architectural community – have managed to keep the cranes busy above the capital's skyline.

A rash of large millennial projects, which gave the city **Tate Modern** and an improved **British Museum**, left London with a swathe of world-class cultural centres. And the **Dome**. That was the fun stuff, but now the hard work is beginning: inner-city regeneration, tackling the chronic housing shortage, and having a go at improving the grossly inadequate public transport system. Borrowing the idea of arts-led regeneration from Bilbao, where Frank Gehry's extraordinary Guggenheim Museum has had a profound impact on the fortunes of that declining industrial town, London's councillors are hoping to lure private investment into what were once no-go areas.

Tate Modern has single-handedly marked out the traditionally poor borough of Southwark as a must-see destination, and plans are now afoot to use it as the focal point for a regeneration scheme stretching down to Elephant & Castle.

Similarly, the new **Laban Centre** on southeast London's Deptford Creek, due to open in early 2003, is seen as a magnet for private cash. Even slick commercial developments are being given a public face to keep them populated after hours: the giant scheme opposite the Tower of London, home to mayor Ken Livingstone's egg-shaped **GLA Building**, is greeting Tooley Street with a handsome new theatre.

The really big redevelopment projects are not so easily tackled, however, and are taking years to emerge. The most exciting is starting to materialise at King's Cross, where rail and tube facilities are in need of renewal and vast chunks of land lie empty to the north. Work to renew the tube has begun, and architects are trying to persuade the authorities to demolish the awkward 1970s extension to the front of the station and restore what was once a large public plaza. But don't hold your breath: delay and obfuscation are what the UK's planning and public funding regimes do best. Just look at the chaos affecting the **Wembley Stadium** rebuild, now a classic British embarrassment.

Progress at other regeneration hotspots is mixed. **Paddington Basin**, for example, is steaming ahead, and building work on this neglected and forgotten site is soon to provide west London with a cluster of first-class office towers. Orange and Marks & Spencer have already promised to occupy some of the buildings, and the developer wants to demolish

The new **GLA Building**. *See p27.*

part of the listed **Paddington Station** to expand rail capacity and free up extra building land. But heritage groups are actively opposing the idea, drawn up by architect Nicholas Grimshaw of Waterloo's **Eurostar Terminal**.

'The tide of history has given London no distinctive architectural style.'

Elephant & Castle is arguably most in need of good ideas and hard cash. Until recently, the council was planning a huge redevelopment of the area – new road system, office towers, better housing, the lot – in a multi-billion-pound building package that would take until 2013 to complete. But the borough's planning chief has retired, and there are questions about whether the local authority has the stomach for the scheme.

Unfortunately, most of the exciting building work is proceeding where London least needs it: in the centre. There has long been talk of developing the post-industrial landscape in the east of the city, and Livingstone has sworn that if London is ever to bid for the 2012 Olympics – which seems fanciful, given the mess made of its bid for the World Athletics Championships a year ago – then it is that part of the city that will host the event. But little has happened so far, and the impressive construction projects continue to be in the City and the West End.

Although opponents claim that cities like Barcelona and Berlin continue to be successful with low-rises, London's public authorities and corporate bodies are keen to build upwards (*see p30* **Tall storeys**). The controversial **Heron Tower** looks set to rise this year, but Norman Foster's **Swiss Re Tower**, now being built in the City and likened by many to a gherkin, is like nothing so much as a fat banker in a latticed body stocking. It is not an urban shape. No one can build close to it, or would want to: it clears space around itself because of its presence.

The Swiss Re Tower is an unexpected urban guest, a replacement for a building destroyed by an IRA bomb. And that is typical of London. Unlike many major cities, London has never been beautified or planned. It is a hotch-potch, the product of a gradual accumulation of towns and villages, adapted, renewed and disfigured by the changing needs of its population. The tide of history has given London no distinctive architectural style, being at once imperial, industrial, medieval and experimental.

LONDON'S BURNING

There are any number of events that have left their imprint on the buildings of the city, but the Great Fire of 1666 is a useful historical marker: it signals the end of medieval London and the start of the city we know today. Commemorated by Sir Christopher Wren's 202-foot-high **Monument** (*see p94*), the fire destroyed five-sixths of the largely wooden city, burning 13,200 houses and 89 churches.

After the three-day inferno, the authorities insisted on new building regulations. From now on, brick and stone would be the construction materials of choice, and key streets would be widened to act as the fire breaks of the future. Most of what can now be seen is a testament to the talents of Wren and his successors.

In a sense, though, the city of the Plague did not disappear. In spite of grand proposals from architects hoping to remodel the city along classical lines, London reshaped itself around its historic street pattern. And the buildings that had withstood the fire stood as monuments to earlier ages. One building that survived was the church of **St Ethelburga-the-Virgin** (68-70 Bishopsgate, the City, EC2), noteworthy as the city's smallest chapel. Sadly, where the fire failed, the IRA succeeded, destroying two-thirds of this 13th-century building with a 1993 bomb.

The Norman **Tower of London** (*see p95*), begun soon after William's 1066 conquest and extended over the next 300 years, remains the country's most perfect example of a medieval fortress. This is thanks to the Navy, which cheated the advancing flames of the Great Fire by blowing up the surrounding houses before the inferno could get to them six centuries later.

And then there is **Westminster Abbey** (*see p134*), begun in 1245 when the borough lay far outside London's walls and completed in 1745 when Nicholas Hawksmoor added the west towers. That said, though, cathedrals are never really finished: the statues set over the main entrance, with Martin Luther King taking centre stage, were added just a couple of years ago. Although the abbey is the most French of England's Gothic churches, deriving its geometry, flying buttresses and rose windows from across the Channel, the chapel, completed in 1512, is pure Tudor. 'Stone seems, by the winning labour of the chisel, to have been robbed of its weight and density, suspended aloft, as if by magic,' gushed American author Washington Irving centuries later.

The Renaissance came late to Britain, making its debut with Inigo Jones's 1622 **Banqueting House** (*see p131*). The addition

Holden on

Decades of under-investment, piecemeal additions and soaring passenger numbers mean that tube travel is something most people do with their heads down. More fools they: to do so is to be blind to the some of the finest and most daring architecture in London.

When the first underground line opened in 1863 – a four-mile stretch between Paddington and Farringdon – the stations assumed the strong warehouse aesthetic of the time. While fine pieces of work, they fail to capture the image of speed and efficiency for which the tube had been designed. The travelling public had to wait until after the Great War for that.

The tube system was crying out for expansion by the 1920s. Charles Holden (1875-1960), an establishment architect who had previously designed the Royal Artillery Memorial at Hyde Park, leapt at the chance to develop a new design typology for the network. He eventually designed more than 50 stations, as well as the asymmetrical ziggurat of London Underground's HQ at St James's Park.

Southgate and **Arnos Grove**, next to each other at the end of the Piccadilly line, are two of Holden's finest stations. Built in the '30s, they exhibit the clear, uncluttered geometry of good municipal architecture. Southgate (*pictured*) is the simpler and better of the two. Everything in the grand circular ticket hall, whose concrete roof appears to be held aloft by a single central column, contributes to the

sense of a coherent whole. Even the typeface on the shops announcing 'Newsagent' and 'Men's Fashion' adheres to the scheme.

Arnos Grove is more complex, the drum of the ticket hall sitting on a square plinth of a building. Contrast the overland platforms with their Victorian forebears: high-ceilinged ironwork has been replaced by lower, flat roofs, while window slots have been cast into the spartan concrete.

Holden's legacy can be seen in many of the new stations. Take **Westminster**, a vast essay in concrete that wouldn't be out of place in Fritz Lang's *Metropolis*. This is an architecture of steroid-fuelled strength: muscular concrete columns support giant steel cross-braces, creating a vast space for industrial stairs and escalators.

Southwark, on the other hand, is more polite: a gentler space where the concrete is smoother and clad in blue glass. But pause in the vast round ticket hall and experience the shock of recognition. This is Southgate, only shinier. Even the central roof-supporting column is there, piercing an information booth below. Good design doesn't date.

of a sumptuously decorated ceiling by Rubens in 1635, celebrating the benefits of wise rule, made the building a must-see for the public, who could watch from the balconies as Charles I dined. As it turned out, Chuck's wisdom was a trifle lacking: 14 years later, he provided the public with an even greater spectacle as he was led from the building and beheaded.

We have Jones to thank for **Covent Garden** (*see p122*) and Greenwich's **Queen's House** (*see p171*), but these are not his only legacies. Italian architecture, rooted in the forms and geometries of the Roman era, was all the rage by the turn of the 17th century. So, as a dedicated follower of fashion, Jones became proficient in the art of piazzas, porticos and pilasters. His work influenced the careers of succeeding generations of architects, but also introduced an unhealthy habit of venerating the past that would take 300 years to kick. Even today, London has a knack for glueing fake classical extras over the doors of cheap kit buildings in the hope it will lend them a little dignity.

RELIGIOUS ICONS

Nothing cheers a builder like a natural disaster, and one can only guess at the relish with which Wren and co began rebuilding in the aftermath of the Fire. Taking their cue from Jones, they brandished classicism like a new broom: the pointed arches of English Gothic were rounded off, Corinthian columns made an appearance and church spires became as multi-layered and complex as a baroque wedding cake.

'Sir John Soane shared the fascination with death that characterises freemasonry.'

Wren blazed the trail with daring plans for **St Paul's Cathedral** (*see p87*). The scheme, incorporating a Catholic dome rather than a Protestant steeple, was too Roman for the establishment and the design was rejected. The crafty Wren produced a redesign and gained planning permission by incorporating a spire, only to set about a series of mischievous u-turns once work had begun. His building – domed and heavily suggestive of an ancient temple – has survived to this day.

Wren's architectural baton was to be picked up by Nicholas Hawksmoor and James Gibbs, who were to benefit from an anxiety that London's population was becoming ever more ungodly. The 1711 initiative to construct an extra 50 churches was, then, a significant career opportunity. Gibbs became busy in and around Trafalgar Square, building the steepled Roman temple of **St Martin-in-the-Fields**

(*see p129*) and the baroque **St Mary-le-Strand** (Strand, WC2; now set against the monstrous **King's College**). Gibbs's work went down well, but the more experimental Hawksmoor had a rougher ride. His imposing **St Anne's** (Commercial Road, Limehouse, E14) proved so costly that the parish was left with insufficient funds to pay for a vicar, while **St George's** in Bloomsbury (*see p103*) broke the bank, costing three times its £10,000 budget.

St George's tries to evoke the spirit of the ancients. Rather than a spire, there is a pyramid topped by a statue of George I decked out in a toga, while the interior boasts all the Corinthian columns, round arches and gilding you'd expect from a man steeped in Antiquity. Many of these features are repeated in **Christ Church Spitalfields** (*see p155*), now undergoing restoration. Strangely, this dedication to his subject didn't extend to seeing the ancient sights at first hand: Hawksmoor never left the country.

Tall storeys

Like most European cities, London originated as a low-rise townscape punctuated by scores of church spires. The view began to change in the 1950s, when residential tower blocks began to sprout from war-damaged streets. The vogue for building high soon spread to office buildings; by the 1970s, London had acquired a ragged skyline that has been compared to a row of broken teeth.

Yet, despite protests that historic views are being trashed and that high-density complexes can be built without resorting to skyscrapers, London builds ever-upwards. Conservation body English Heritage has tried to resist tower-building, but has been opposed by mayor Ken Livingstone and government-sponsored quango the Commission for Architecture and the Built Environment. Livingstone is particularly keen on pressing ahead with 'clusters' of tall buildings that advertise London's economic strength. In all, he reckons London could accommodate around 20 new towers over the coming decade, in the City, Elephant and Castle, Docklands and Croydon.

The summer of 2002 proved a significant moment in the history of London's towers. A long-running and controversial public enquiry into a 677-foot (222-metre), 42-storey office block in the City, the **Heron Tower**, culminated in the

THE ADAM FAMILY AND BEYOND

Robert Adam, on the other hand, was a considerable traveller. One of a large family of Scottish architects, Adam found himself at the forefront of a movement that came to see Italian baroque as a corruption of the real thing. Architectural exuberance was eventually dropped in favour of a simpler interpretation of the ancient forms. In the interests of brevity (purists should look away now), the buildings became more Plain Jane than Big Hair.

The best surviving work of Adam and his brothers James, John and William can be found in London's great suburban houses **Osterley House** (*see p188*), **Syon House** (*see p187*) and **Kenwood House** (*see p150*), but the project for which they are most famous no longer stands. In 1768 they embarked on the cripplingly expensive Adelphi housing estate (after the Greek for 'brothers') off the Strand. Built over vaults used to store goods offloaded from river barges, most of the complex was pulled down in the 1930s and replaced by an office block, but part of the original development survives in what is now the **Royal Society for the Arts** (8 John Adam Street, Covent Garden, WC2).

Just as the first residents were moving into the Adelphi, a young unknown called John Soane was embarking on a tour of his own. In Rome, Soane met the wealthy Bishop of Derry who persuaded the 25-year-old to abandon his travels and accompany him to Ireland in order to build a house. But the project came to nothing and Soane dealt with the setback by working hard and marrying into money.

His loss is our gain, however, as he went on to build the Bank of England and the recently remodelled **Dulwich Picture Gallery** (*see p173*). The bank has been demolished, leaving nothing but the perimeter walls and depriving London of what is said to have been Soane's masterpiece. But a hint of what these ignorant

government giving the go-ahead to the development. There are plenty more developers waiting with towers of their own, and the Heron decision will give them confidence to make planning applications. Images of large residential towers for Southwark and Vauxhall have appeared in the architectural press, and a sleek 37-storey office building is being touted for St Botolph Street in the City.

Some schemes have already left the drawing board, however, and are close to completion. Norman Foster's 'erotic gherkin' for insurance firm **Swiss Re**, a stunningly curvaceous 549-foot (180-metre) structure, is due to open in 2003. And the 744-foot (244-metre) **Canary Wharf** building in Docklands is now flanked by a pair of heavies of almost the same height (*pictured*).

All these buildings are dwarfed by the world's really tall structures, which come in at twice the height. Yet even this state of affairs could eventually be remedied: Southwark council is considering a planning application for a monster 945-foot (310-metre) 'shard of glass' that would be the 18th tallest building in the world and the tallest in Europe. If built, it would dominate the city and become an instant London icon. Don't count on English Heritage offering its support.

The **Channel 4 Building** is one of numerous recent projects by Richard Rogers. *See p34.*

bankers might have enjoyed can be gleaned from a visit to Soane's house, now the **Sir John Soane Museum** (*see p100*), a collection of exquisite architectural experiments with mirrors, coloured glass and folding walls.

A committed freemason, Soane shared the fascination with death that characterise the organisation. The Dulwich Picture Gallery incorporates a dimly lit mausoleum containing the earthly remains of the building's benefactors, a rehearsal for the design of his own resting place. This is worth the quick walk north of King's Cross to the churchyard of **St Pancras Old Church**: just look for the square tomb with the gently curving roof – one of only two Grade I-listed tombs in the country, the other being that of Karl Marx – and you'll see where Sir Giles Gilbert Scott later got his inspiration for the traditional red phone box.

John Nash was less talented than Soane, a near-contemporary, but his contributions – among them **Buckingham Palace** (*see p130*), the **Haymarket Theatre** (Haymarket, W1) and **Regent Street** (W1) – have proved greater than those of any other individual. Regent Street began as a proposal to link the West End to the planned park further north, as well as, in Nash's words, 'complete separation between the streets and squares occupied by the nobility and gentry, and the narrow streets and meaner houses occupied by mechanics and the trading part of the community.' The areas to which he was referring are Mayfair and Soho.

THE 19TH CENTURY

By the 1830s the classical form had been established for 200 years, and a handful of upstarts began pressing for change. In 1834 the **Houses of Parliament** burned down, leading to the construction of Charles Barry's Gothic masterpiece (*see p133*). This was the beginning of the Gothic Revival, a move by the new romantics to replace what they considered to be foreign and pagan with a style that was not only native but Christian.

Barry would have preferred a classical design, but the brief was unambiguous and Gothic was to prevail. He needed help, and sought out a designer whose name alone makes him worthy of a mention: Augustus Welby Northmore Pugin. The result of Pugin's labours was a Victorian fantasy that, while a fine example of the perpendicular form, shows how the Middle Ages had become distorted in the minds of 19th-century architects. New buildings were constructed as a riot of turrets, towers and winding staircases that would today be condemned as the Disney-fication of history.

Even in renovating ancient buildings, architects would often decide that they weren't Gothic enough; as with the 15th-century **Guildhall** (*see p91*), which gained its corner turrets and central spire in 1862. Bombed by the Luftwaffe, the Guildhall was rebuilt largely as the Victorians had left it, apart from the interior statues of Gog and Magog, the protagonists in a legendary battle between ancient Britain and

Troy. In the post-war reconstruction of this stately building, these two ugly bastards got even uglier. There's also a good statue of Churchill, looking stereotypically grumpy.

The argument between the classicists and Goths erupted in 1857, when the government commissioned Sir George Gilbert Scott, a leading light of the Gothic movement, to design a new HQ for the Foreign Office. Scott's plans incensed anti-Goth Lord Palmerstone, then prime minister, whose diktats prevailed. But Scott exacted his revenge by building an office in which everyone hated working, and by going on to construct Gothic edifices all over the capital, among them the **Albert Memorial** (*see p139*) and **St Pancras Station** (*see p105*).

St Pancras was completed in 1873, after the Midland Railway commissioned Scott to build a London terminus that would dwarf that of its rivals next door at King's Cross. Using the project as an opportunity to show his mastery of the Gothic form, Scott built an asymmetrical castle that obliterated views of the train shed behind, itself an engineering marvel completed earlier by William Barlow. This 'incongruous medievalism' did not go unnoticed by critics, prompting one to write that company directors should go the whole hog and dress their staff in period costume. 'Their porters might be dressed as javelin men, their guards as beefeaters.'

Still, the Gothic style was to dominate until the 20th century, leaving London littered with charming, imposing but anachronistic buildings such as the **Royal Courts of Justice** (*see p97*), the **Natural History Museum** (*see p139*) and **Liberty** (*see p236*). World War I and the coming of modernism led to a spirit of tentative renewal, and the **Royal Institute of British Architects** (aka RIBA) and the BBC's **Broadcasting House** (Portland Place, Marylebone, W1) are good examples of the pared-down style of the '20s and '30s.

THIS IS THE MODERN WORLD

It must be evidence of the British love of animals that perhaps the finest example of between-the-wars modernism can be found at **London Zoo** (*see p109*). Built by Russian émigré Bethold Lubetkin and the Tecton group, the spiral ramps of the Penguin Pool were a showcase for the possibilities of concrete, which was also put to good use on the Underground: it enabled the quick and cheap building of large, cavernous spaces with the sleek lines and curves associated with speed. The Piccadilly line on the London Underground was a particular beneficiary (*see p29* **Holden on**).

However, there was nothing quick or cheap about the **Daily Express Building** (Fleet Street, the City, EC4). A black glass and chrome structure built in 1931, it's an early example of 'curtain wall' construction where the façade is literally hung on to an internal frame. Recently refurbished for a new occupant, the developers have, happily, not compromised the deco detailing of the original building, leaving the crazy flooring, snake handrails and funky lighting to dazzle passers-by.

WHAT IS IT GOOD FOR?

World War II left large areas of London ruined, providing another opportunity for builders to cash in. The destruction left the capital with a dire housing shortage, giving architects a chance to demonstrate the speed and efficiency with which they could house large numbers of families in tower blocks. Most were lamentable, partly because of poor build quality, partly due to ignoring the need for maintenance. Many have gone, but others – such as Sir Denys Lasdun's fabulous **Keeling House** 'cluster block' in Bethnal Green – have been reclaimed and offered to wealthy private tenants.

'The problem with being innovative, though, is that things can go wrong.'

The legacy of post-war architecture is viewed with anything from suspicion to horror by most Londoners, an experience that has both tempered the arrogance of the architectural profession and created a planning process that places so many hurdles in the way of developers that it's a wonder anything gets built at all. There are notable exceptions, however, including the **Royal Festival Hall** on the South Bank (*see p304*). The sole survivor of the 1951 Festival of Britain, the RFH was built to celebrate the war's end and the centenary of the Great Exhibition. In spite of its size, the Festival Hall can be a crowded and awkward space, but refurbishment is restoring what little grandeur the builders of post-war Britain managed to impart. The South Bank is currently the centre of the biggest planning question to face Londoners for a quarter-century: what to do with the **Hayward Gallery** (*see p76*) and **Queen Elizabeth Hall** (*see p304*). Rick Mather's scheme to overhaul the area is now mired in politics and his plans are unlikely to come to fruition for a few years, if at all.

But brutalism couldn't last forever. The 1970s and '80s offered up a pair of architectural replacements: postmodernism and high-tech. The former is represented by Cesar Pelli's **Canary Wharf** tower (Isle of Dogs, E14), an oversized obelisk that has become the archetypal expression of 1980s architecture and holds an ambiguous place in the city's affections. Its splendid isolation lent it star quality, but a current building boom is providing it with equally huge neighbours, opening up another part of the city's low-rise skyline to high-rise clutter.

Richard Rogers' **Lloyd's Building** (Lime Street, the City, EC3) is London's best known example of high-tech, where commercial and industrial aesthetics combine to produce arguably one of the most significant British buildings since the war. Mocked upon completion in 1986, the building still manages to outclass more recent projects, a fact not lost on **Channel 4** when it commissioned Rogers to design its new HQ in Horseferry Road, SW1, in the early 1990s.

Such projects are rapidly making London a showcase for brave and innovative buildings. Future Systems' **NatWest Media Centre** at Lord's cricket ground (*see p147*), perched high above the pitch like a giant bar of soap, is arguably London's most daring construction to date, especially given its traditional setting. And Will Alsop's multicoloured **Peckham Library** (171 Peckham Hill Street, Peckham, SE15) redefined community architecture so comprehensively that it beat the 443-foot (135-metre) high **London Eye** (*see p71*), already a national icon, and Norman Foster's **Canary Wharf Station**, on the recently extended Jubilee line, to RIBA's Stirling Prize in 2000.

The problem with being innovative, though, is that things can go wrong. And there's no better example of this than the daring pedestrian-only **Millennium Bridge** linking St Paul's with Tate Modern, designed by Foster and engineers Arup. After a lengthy delay, the bridge's opening descended into farce when it began to sway as soon as the public were allowed to cross it in mid 2000. It wasn't for two years that this steel and aluminium structure was finally able to offer a wobble-free crossing.

Canary Wharf Station.

THE SHOCK OF THE OLD

London's architecture is marked by the presence of a 'green belt', a slice of protected countryside that prevents the city from bursting its banks. In consort with a small but vocal army of conservationists, the green belt forces architects to work with old buildings rather than pull them down. Done well, the new is grafted on to the old in a way that is often invisible from street level; visitors will be surprised by the way contemporary interiors have been inserted into elderly buildings.

The best examples of this can be found in the assorted arts buildings that underwent millennial makeovers and expansions. The **National Portrait Gallery** (*see p129*) and the **Royal Opera House** (*see p305*) are good examples of architects adding modern signatures to old buildings, while the **British Museum** (*see p103*), the **National Maritime Museum** (*see p171*) and the **Wallace Collection** (*see p109*) have all gone one better, adding to their facilities by covering what were once external courtyards. Foster's exercise in complexity at the British Museum, where the £100 million Great Court created the largest covered square in Europe, is the most impressive.

It's this 'money for old rope' mentality that made possible the conversion of Sir Giles Gilbert Scott's power station into a premier-league art venue, **Tate Modern** (*see p79*), making a mockery of the architectural mantra 'form follows function'. This imposing edifice was dragged from obscurity by Swiss architects Herzog and de Meuron, who managed to preserve much of the original building while installing seven new floors of exhibition space. The sheer size of the place is a guarantor of the 'wow' factor, but the architects managed to squeeze some cosy little spaces from its bulk.

But none of these architectural gems counts for much if London's visitors can't actually get to them, or die from vehicle emissions on the way. Richard Rogers' plans for a Terminal 5 at Heathrow have finally been given the green light and Ken Livingstone is planning to charge drivers £5 for entering central London in an effort to scare them off. Other schemes are waiting in the wings, not least the east–west Crossrail programme that would run main-line trains under the city. Then there are plans to extend the DLR to London City Airport and even run the East London line into Hackney. A tip for planners: build the lot.

▶ For more on the redevelopment plans for **St Pancras**, *see p105*.
▶ For more on **City churches**, *see p84*.

The Clash

DIVINE **MADNESS**

London on Song

The city's dark soul has made for some capital records.

First, a disclaimer of sorts. This is not a comprehensive survey of London music. We have four pages, and such a history would take 100 times that. Instead, this chapter concentrates on the last four decades of pop music, taking a brief look at how contemporary London has been portrayed in contemporary song. But before we get on with our necessarily selective survey, it's worth devoting a word or two about what came earlier.

You'll find no mention here of nursery rhymes. That said, while we're here, it merits mention that the origins of 'London Bridge is Falling Down' lie in a Norse poem from almost 1,000 years ago. Meanwhile, as Cockney crooner **Anthony Newley** outlined in his jaunty take on it, 'Pop Goes the Weasel' is about the habit of London hat-makers to pawn (or 'pop') their equipment ('weasels') on Fridays in order to have some drinking money for the weekend.

We've passed on classical music, as – leaving aside pieces written for ceremonial occasions, such as coronations or state funerals – there's little that's genuinely evocative of London. **Elgar**'s *Cockaigne* overture is, perhaps, the most vibrant exception to this rule.

Countless London songs were written for and sung in music halls – what vaudeville was to America, music hall was to Britain – a century or so ago. Music hall songs are not without their jolly, knockabout charms, and we could have filled these four pages solely with the ones that mention London. But while it might be interesting to learn, for example, that the now-bleak Strand was once 'the place for fun and noise/All among the girls and boys' ('Let's All Go Down the Strand'), the truth is that the songs themselves are one-dimensional and tell us surprisingly little about London.

And there's also no mention in here of pre-war songs that have become standards, chiefly because a great many of them read as if their writers had never set foot in the city. In 'A Foggy Day', one of **Ira Gershwin**'s feeblest lyrics, the protagonist awakes to find a pea-souper enveloping the town – a lazier example of myth perpetuation you couldn't hope to find – which only lifts when he catches sight of his loved one. And in Briton **Eric Maschlitz**'s lyric to 'A Nightingale Sang in Berkeley Square', er, a nightingale – surely figurative; this traffic-packed square hasn't seen such exotic birdlife since the 17th century, when Mayfair was still largely rural – sings in Berkeley Square.

TERRY MEETS JULIE

So, instead, we start in the 1960s, not long after the arrival of rock 'n' roll in Soho hauled British pop from its easy-listening moorings. And we start with London's songwriter laureate.

Prior to **The Kinks**, London bands hadn't gloried in their origins: aping American blues acts was still the thing to do, thanks chiefly to

the Rolling Stones. But in Ray Davies, Muswell Hill-born and raised – a background affectionately detailed in 'Fortis Green' and gently mocked in 'Muswell Hillbilly' – the city found its greatest advocate.

Where to start? Davies has written the songbook of London, covering all its corners. Sometimes, he's personal: 'Lavender Hill' (it's in Clapham, and not as nice as Davies makes it sound) is pure romance; 'Berkeley Mews' (a quiet Marylebone street) is pure romance gone wrong; 'End of the Season', in which Davies mourns the end of summer (and gets 'no joy walking down Savile Row' in Mayfair), is pure romance on hold. At other times, he's detached: 'Denmark Street' offers a snapshot of the era when this street on the edge of Soho was home to countless music publishers, while the 'Dedicated Follower of Fashion', a swingin' London archetype, is sought in Regent Street and Leicester Square.

He does characters: 'Life on the Road' puts Davies in the position of a northerner moving to the city for the first time (dig out the **Smiths'** 'London' for a bleaker variation on the same theme). He does glib: 'London Song' is a funny, snarly shopping list of Londoners (from Dick Whittington to Charles Dickens, Thomas A'Becket to the Krays), landmarks (Highgate Hill, Streatham Hill, Leicester Square) and suburbs (Crystal Palace, Clapham, East Ham). And, of course, he does 'Waterloo Sunset', the closing track on the ace *Something Else by the Kinks* and the London song to end all songs. And that's before we've even gotten onto 'Holloway Jail', 'Willesden Green'…

Other 1960s acts used the city as a muse. The **Small Faces**, for example, whose 'Itchycoo Park' is reputed to be Little Ilford Park in the undistinguished east London suburb of Manor Park, E12: it was so nicknamed by singer Steve Marriott for the volume of stinging nettles in it. And, moving from the sublime to the ridiculous, Brit-Dylan **Donovan** often namechecked the city: 'Sunny Goodge Street' relates a stoner story on the tube, 'Sunny South Kensington' is a song in praise of swingin' London, and 'Hampstead Incident' is just plain baffling.

GO AHEAD, PUNK

It took punk, a decade or more later, for London to have such convincing chroniclers as the Kinks. This was a very different London to that delineated by Davies: from the boredom and lairiness found on its outskirts (the **Members'** classic 'Sound of the Suburbs', **Sham 69**'s altogether less appealing 'Hersham Boys') to the gritty, inner-city London pegged by **The Clash**. The latter's *London Calling* (1979) holds a place in many listeners' minds as a capital classic. Its title track is quite some battle-cry, but in truth, *London Calling* hasn't dated at all well: in 2002, it now sounds earnest, po-faced and surprisingly wet.

> ### 'Soho has been fertile ground for lyricists. Unsurprising: it's a pliant place.'

A couple of the Clash's contemporaries do better with their subject, primarily because they don't play it quite so straight. **Ian Dury** hailed from the end of District line, at the point where London melds into Essex. Pen-portraits are his strength, whether the lascivious 'Plaistow Patricia', who likes it best when she goes up west, or 'Billericay Dickie', a chirrupy elegy to an Essex chancer, though among his 'Reasons to Be Cheerful' are Piccadilly and the Hammersmith Palais. **Squeeze** had even less in common with punk, but their hummable, geezer-ish pop captured their home turf of south London to a tee: try the Clapham-set, baby-in-waiting yarn of 'Up the Junction' or the cheeky saarf Laahndan chic of 'Cool for Cats'.

BRITPOP AND BEYOND

London seeps from every grimy pore of **Blur**'s *Modern Life is Rubbish*. It starts with the inner sleeve, a caricature of the band sat stony-faced on the tube, clad in three-button suits and Dr Martens (bought, according to an in-character Albarn on 'Blue Jeans', on Portobello Road one Saturday). And it continues on the record itself, a bleak, grubby, cocksure hymn to a city that

draws romantics like moths to a flame but rarely delivers on its promise. It's never more so than on opening track 'For Tomorrow', whose singalong chorus belies the deep melancholy of its premise (two lovers clinging to their relationship because without each other they'd be swallowed up by the black hole of London, lost on the Westway, alone atop Primrose Hill).

Modern Life is Rubbish put London on the radar again. The following year, Blur issued *Parklife*, with its similarly iconic cover shot at Walthamstow dog track and set of 14 songs that picked up where *Modern Life is Rubbish* left off. This time, people got it: *Parklife* kicked off Britpop, all Union Jack T-shirts, cocky London attitude and ropey guitar bands.

For more, find **Stephen Duffy**'s 1995 single 'London Girls' (from the album *Duffy*), three verses of social observation on the wannabe Britpop royalty clogging up Camden pubs each night, then checking the music press each Tuesday lunchtime to see if stardom had come their way. 'I had no idea I was writing a period piece,' commented Duffy. But that's what it's become, its dry, detached perspective on youth culture aping **David Bowie**'s *The London Boys*. A B-side in 1967, the song focused on the original swingin' Londoners: the mid-1960s Soho set, popping pills and dressing dandy.

Britpop's apex was the May 1995 release of 'Common People', **Pulp**'s damning tale of middle-class students artlessly slumming their youth away in London. Its nadir came soon after, when the song was picked up by and became an anthem for all the middle-class students artlessly slumming their youth away in London. Unironically.

OH SO SOHO

Like Pulp's singer and lyricist Jarvis Cocker, the chief protagonist of 'Common People' studies at Central St Martin's School of Art on the Charing Cross Road. The college sits on the edge of Soho, a square mile that's long proven fertile ground for lyricists. Unsurprising: it's such a pliant place. It's romantic, as in the **Pogues**' glorious 'A Rainy Night in Soho' and **George**

Fame's 'Eros Hotel', taken from a poem by Fran Landesman about a seamy operation than no longer exists. It's lonely, as in **Dave Dee, Dozy, Beaky, Mick and Tich**'s 'Last Night in Soho', **Al Stewart**'s languid 'Soho (Needless to Say)', and **Phil Lynott**'s 'Solo in Soho'. It's seedy: Ray Davies inadvertently picked up a transvestite here in the Kinks' 'Lola', and much of **Soft Cell**'s debut album *Non-Stop Erotic Cabaret* is a paean to the place when it was overrun by peep shows and porn. It's violent: witness the righteous fury of **The Jam**'s '"A" Bomb in Wardour Street'. And it's where you get stood up: both **Kirsty MacColl** ('Soho Square') and **Jackie Leven** ('Alone in Soho Square') have written songs about their dates not showing up for meetings in the area's prettiest corner. Perhaps, in a parallel universe, they were waiting for each other.

Not that Soho's the only corner of London to have been chronicled in such detail. To the west, Chelsea's had chroniclers from punk act the **Members** ('Chelsea Nightclub') to jazzer **Billy Strayhorn** ('Chelsea Bridge'), new-waver **Elvis Costello** ('(I Don't Want to Go to) Chelsea') to exiled American **Jon Bon Jovi** ('Midnight in Chelsea'), wordy prog-rockers **Marillion** ('Chelsea Monday') to – of course – the Kinks' ('Did Ya'). Down south, Brixton's featured in songs by the Clash ('Guns of Brixton', the jail in 'Stay Free'), **Sugar Minott and Jah Son** ('Riot Inna Brixton') and **Eddy Grant** ('Electric Avenue').

Camden, too, has had multiple lives. It was pinned as Britpop Central by Stephen Duffy but, better still, it's where Sarah Cracknell and partner fall in love with the city and each other in **St Etienne**'s 'London Belongs to Me'. And NW1 features in countless songs by **Madness**. In 'One Better Day', two homeless people stagger the streets around Arlington House, a homeless shelter on Arlington Road. In 'Driving in My Car', they lurch from Camden to Muswell Hill in a 1959 Morris bought from a Brazilian in Primrose Hill. This is the same Primrose Hill from which **Eddi Reader** laments lost love (in the breathtaking, Mark Nevin-penned

RICHARD THOMPSON
MOCK TUDOR

THE STREETS

'Kiteflyer's Hill') and a homeless **Loudon Wainwright III** sits drinking viciously strong lager with just a scraggy dog for company ('Primrose Hill', on the lovely *Little Ship*).

ALMOST LOST

Some of the finest and most evocative London records fall between the cracks, and there are none finer than 1996 record *I Was the King, I Really Was the King* from Stoke Newington band **Animals that Swim**. It's a ragged, haunting album: shy, but still wearing its heart on its sleeve, chiefly because it doesn't know where else to put it. It treats the city with the mix of resignation and amazement with which almost all Londoners regard their home town, and does it with glorious, touching eloquence.

Simon Warner's first (and, so far, only) album *Waiting Rooms* (1997) is bolder, brasher and denser, a whirlygig epic of poverty and decadence. As with *I Was the King…*, London is more than just a location: it's as much a character as the fat, flirty fortysomething who moves in next door ('Mrs Zaniewski'), the flatmate who devours all the beans ('Kitchen Tango'), or the officious Underground staffer who catches Warner without a ticket on his way to see family at the end of the Metropolitan line ('Watford! Watford! I'd been to Watford!' he cries on 'Ticket Collector'). It's everything that **My Life Story**'s *Mornington Crescent* (1995), which can be neatly pinned as Anthony Newley Goes to Camden, could have been.

The characters on *Waiting Rooms* are, by and large, sympathetically drawn. Which is more than can be said of those painted by **Richard Thompson** on his magnificent 1999 set *Mock Tudor*. Like Animals That Swim and Warner, Thompson eschews obvious geographic inspirations. This is an album putatively about the dreary London suburbs in which Thompson was raised, though 'Sights and Sounds of London Town', a series of four verse-long character studies spat out by Thompson over an inappropriately jaunty major-key backdrop, moves into town with its King's Cross prostitute and Soho chancer.

DANCE THE NIGHT AWAY

Oddly, songs about London have never actually made up the city's soundtrack. In part, that's a function of the fact that so few London songs have been celebratory; those that are, 'Waterloo Sunset' chief among them, take on almost mythic status, but most paint a less endearing picture of a city that seems to eat its locals alive. We don't have a 'My Kind of Town' or 'I Left My Heart in San Francisco' here, much less a 'New York, New York'. Civic pride has never been cool here. Moreover, the sound of the city these days is not song-based rock, but dance music and, in 2002, garage.

Garage began as a London sound. As did jungle and drum 'n' bass, the musics from which it took its initial cues. As did rave and acid house, from which jungle eventually emerged a decade ago. But while **Scott Garcia** might have claimed garage for the capital on 'It's a London Thing', it's nothing of the sort. Sure, there are more outlets for it here – ratchet your radio dial down the FM band in some parts of town, and you'll find the array of pirate stations befuddling – and the music's most successful act (**So Solid Crew**, a 30-strong collective) hail from Battersea. And yet the majority of garage MCs spend too much tape aping the generic guns 'n' bitches braggadocio of their American hip hop heroes for this to ever be a London sound.

Mike Skinner's also from Birmingham, more or less: born in London and now living in Brixton but reared for the most part in the Midlands, he's joked that his London friends think he's a Brummie while his Birmingham pals pin him as a Cockney. Yet **The Streets**' 2002 debut *Original Pirate Material*, a loose-limbed, accessible garage/hip hop set, is perhaps the first great London album of the new millennium. This is not a romantic London of sunsets over the river: it's all about chasing girls, downing brandies, smoking weed and scoffing fry-ups. The beer, too, is now generic canned lager rather than draught ale. And yet London is as much a character as it's ever been. Ray Davies, you think, secretly approves.

Routemaster scale model
£5.99, London's Transport
Museum (*see p122*)

The Gift of London

Something to remember us by:
London souvenirs to appease your families and friends.

You tried your level best to avoid it this time – you really, really did. But somehow it happened anyway. The day before you left home, you accidentally promised your nearest and dearest that you'd bring them back something from London.

The choice is wide. London has countless landmarks that are known planet-wide: Big Ben, St Paul's Cathedral and the archetypal red double-decker London bus to name but three. And, British entrepreneurial spirit being what it is, many of them have found their way on to souvenirs ready for you, the full-walleted

visitor to our lovely city, to take home with you and disperse among your loved ones. (And, in some cases, your hated ones.)

How a city sees both itself and its visitors can be very revealing. Which is why we decided to blister our feet and batter our purses in search of some of the city's souvenirs. Some are lovely, covetable even, while others are less enticing. Either way – and remember that beauty being in the eye of the beholder, one person's junk is another's jewels – what you see on the next four pages is the tip of the iceberg. And what an iceberg it is.

St Paul's Cathedral souvenir teapot
£22.95, St Paul's Cathedral (*see p89*)

Tube shot glasses
£21.99, London's Transport Museum, (*see p122*)

Lousy T-shirt
£4.99, Tottenham Court Road souvenir stall

Jack the Ripper mug
£7.25, London Dungeon (*see p81*)

Miniature crown set
£39.95, Tower of London (*see p96*)

The Gift of London

Souvenir matches
£2.35, Southwark
Cathedral (*see p78*)

Phone box clock
£9.99, Oxford Street
souvenir shop

London A-Z jigsaw
£7.99, Museum of
London (*see p94*)

Policeman's helmet
£2.30, Traders
Gate gift shop

Decorative plate
£5.99, Terminus
Place souvenir stall

Map of old London
£2.99, Shakespeare's
Globe (*see p78*)

Metallised Tower Bridge model
£3, Tower Hill gift shop

Queen postcard
65p, Tower Hill
gift shop

Coloured pencils
£3.50, British Airways
London Eye (*see p72*)

Beefeater snowglobe
£1.99, Cromwell Place
souvenir shop

Accommodation

Accommodation

Atmospheric, beautiful and oh so classy... an ABC of where the city sleeps.

At a press conference in late 2002 to launch his new strategy for selling London to visitors, mayor Ken Livingstone mentioned that one of the city's major problems is its lack of good-quality, affordable accommodation. When asked how this situation could be rectified, Livingstone didn't appear to have any answers.

And herein lies the greatest challenge facing London in its bid to attract more visitors. We do deluxe hotels well here, whether traditional (the Dorchester and the Savoy, say) or modish (the Sanderson). We're pretty good at the expensive variety too. But for those travelling on a budget – say, £50-£120 a night – there's little choice of hotels. Or, at least, there's little choice of *good* hotels. Things are improving (the Travel Inn chain, while a bit bland, does offer clean, comfortable and safe accommodation at under £80 a night), but slowly.

London's greatest concentration of seriously plush hotels is in Mayfair. Further down the ladder, Bloomsbury brims with mid-priced hotels. For cheaper beds, try Ebury Street near Victoria (SW1), Gower Street in Bloomsbury (WC1) and Earl's Court (SW5). Bayswater (W2), Paddington (W2) and South Kensington (SW7) are worth exploring for small, budget hotels. For gay and lesbian accommodation, *see p295*.

INFORMATION AND BOOKING
If you haven't booked ahead, staff at a London Tourist Board centre (*see p374*) will look for a place within your area and price range for a £5 fee (if you book a few weeks in advance, a deposit may be required). You can also see what's available and make reservations on their website. The LTB also publishes *Where to Stay & What to Do* (£4.99), available at its centres or in good bookshops. Most hotels have their own booking websites as well.

London Tourist Board Hotel Booking Line
7604 2890/8759 3909/7802 5480/
www.londontown.com. **Open** 9am-6pm Mon-Fri;
9am-1pm Sat.

PRICES AND CLASSIFICATION
Though British hotels are classified according to a star system agreed by the English Tourism Council, the AA and the RAC, we don't list star ratings, which tend to reflect facilities rather than quality; instead, we've classified hotels, within their area headings, according to the price of the cheapest double room per night.

Despite the fact that VAT is included in the quoted price of almost everything in the UK, many high-end hotels sneakily quote room prices exclusive of the tax, presumably to soften the shock of the bill. Always ask whether the price you're being quoted includes tax or not; to help, all room rates listed here are inclusive of 17.5 per cent VAT (sales tax). After adding the VAT, we've rounded the rates to the nearest pound; to check rates without VAT, simply divide the quoted price by 1.175.

Be sure to ask about special rates and offers. Many hotels that draw a lot of business travel offer heavily discounted rates on weekends, and deals are often available throughout the year via hotels' websites. Always check online or ask when you call: what have you got to lose?

FACILITIES AND ACCESSIBILITY
We've listed the main services offered by each hotel, though many offer additional facilities, from screening rooms to in-room PS2s. Always check before booking if you require a particular facility. It's safe to assume that guestrooms in hotels listed as Deluxe, Expensive or Moderate will include a TV and a telephone; conversely, not all hotels in the Cheap bracket has en suite facilities.

The best Hotels

For style
Great Eastern Hotel. *See p46*.

For value
Any **Travel Inn**. *See p46*.

For classiness
The **Ritz** (*see p53*) or the **Savoy** (*see p51*).

For cosiness
Hampstead Village Guesthouse. *See p61*.

For comfort
Charlotte Street Hotel. *See p47*.

For opulence
The **Dorchester**. *See p51*.

For a party crowd
The **Generator**. *See p51*.

A place to perch at the **Rookery**. *See p47.*

We've tried to indicate which hotels offer rooms adapted for the needs of disabled guests, but always check the specifics with the hotel before booking. **Holiday Care** (01293 774535/ www.holidaycare.org.uk) has details of hotels in the UK that are accessible for the disabled and elderly.

EMERGENCY ACCOMMODATION
Shelter is a national charity that provides advice on housing and homelessness. If you get stranded in London without anywhere to stay, call its 24-hour helpline on 0808 800 4444.

The South Bank & Bankside

Cheap

London County Hall Travel Inn Capital
County Hall, Belvedere Road, SE1 7PB (0870 238 3300/fax 7902 1619/www.travelinn.co.uk). Waterloo tube/rail. **Rates** £74.95-£79.95 double. **Credit** AmEx, DC, MC, V. **Map** p401 M9.

This particular branch of the Travel Inn chain has three things going for it: location, location, location. Situated in County Hall, it's next to the London Eye, across the bridge from the Houses of Parliament and a short walk from the Eurostar terminal at Waterloo. The decor is generic, but the rooms are clean and comfortable. And in a city full of posey hotels, it's refreshing to find accommodation that is unabashedly tourist-friendly – there are Union Jack T-shirts in the lobby gift shop – and value for money. There are central branches at **Tower Bridge** (Tower Bridge Road, SE1; 0870 238 3303), **Euston** (1 Dukes Road, WC1; 0870 238 3301) and **Kensington** (11 Knaresborough Place, SW5; 0870 238 3304). **Hotel services** *Bar. Disabled: adapted rooms. No-smoking rooms. Restaurant.* **Room services** *Dataport.*

Mad Hatter Hotel
3-7 Stamford Street, SE1 9NY (7401 9222/fax 7401 7111/www.fullers.co.uk). Southwark tube/Waterloo tube/rail. **Rates** £79-£99.50 double. **Credit** AmEx, DC, MC, V. **Map** p404 N8.

The Mad Hatter offers one of London's best deals. True, it feels corporate, but this is no bad thing: the hotel combines the old-fashioned charm of a small English inn with the polish and comfort of an efficiently run business. Rooms are large and attractively decorated, Tate Modern and the South Bank are minutes away, and the attached Fuller's pub serves a decent selection of English ales. **Hotel services** *Bar. Disabled: adapted rooms. No-smoking floor. Restaurant.*

The City

Deluxe

Great Eastern Hotel
Liverpool Street, EC2M 7QN (7618 5000/fax 7618 5001/www.great-eastern-hotel.co.uk). Liverpool Street tube/rail. **Rates** £264 single; £311-£370 double; £394-£554 suite. **Credit** AmEx, DC, MC, V. **Map** p405 Q6.

So this is what £70 million buys? That's how much Sir Terence Conran and Wyndham International spent transforming this hotel from a crime-packed fleapit into one of London's very finest hotels. We think it was money well spent. The hotel plays on its location perfectly: businessfolk love its access to the City, while proximity to Shoreditch endears it to a clubbier crowd. And everyone loves the smart yet comfy, hip yet homely guestrooms. The attention to detail is a joy: power-points built into desks (no faffing with laptop cables), a porthole in the bathroom door (no losing your way in the dark), free DVD and CD hire. Downstairs sit five restaurants and a couple of other public spaces (one of which, the airy Gallery, is breathtaking). Our only grumbles are the vague signage and the lack of a late-opening residents' bar, but even these oversights look set to change in 2003. One of London's very finest hotels. **Hotel services** *Air-conditioning. Bar. Beauty salon. Business services. Concierge. Disabled: adapted rooms. Gym. No-smoking floor. Restaurant.* **Room services** *Dataport. Hi-fi. Minibar. Room service (24hrs). Turndown. TV: cable.*

Holborn & Clerkenwell

Deluxe

One Aldwych
1 Aldwych, WC2B 4RH (7300 1000/fax 7300 1001/www.onealdwych.com). Covent Garden or Temple tube/Charing Cross tube/rail. **Rates** £346-£423 single; £370-£446 double; £581-£1,086 suite. **Credit** AmEx, DC, MC, V. **Map** p401 M7.

One of a welter of terrific hotel conversions in the late 1990s – the 95-year-old building was built for the *Morning Post* newspaper – this handsome operation has garnered countless awards in the five years since it opened. It goes about its business stylishly but unshowily: even the oft-buzzing Lobby Bar, a vast, imposing space, pleasingly lacks flash. The rooms are modish and chintz-free, helped along by works of art by young artists and baby TVs in the bathroom, and hampered only by the bewildering array of light switches. There are two fine restaurants, Axis and Indigo, and a lovely screening room (see p50 **Dinner and a movie?**), but the hotel's jewel is the basement fitness centre, with a well-equipped gym, a steam room, a sauna and a gorgeous pool. **Hotel services** *Air-conditioning. Bar. Business services. Concierge. Disabled: adapted rooms. Gym. No-smoking floors. Parking. Swimming pool (indoor).* **Room services** *Dataport. Minibar. Room service (24hrs). Turndown. TV: cable/pay movies/VCR.*

Expensive

Rookery

Peter's Lane, Cowcross Street, EC1M 6DS (7336 0931/fax 7336 0932/www.rookeryhotel.com). Farringdon tube/rail. **Rates** £223-£241 single; £264 double; £323-£582 suite. **Credit** AmEx, DC, MC, V. **Map** p402 O5.
Located between the City and the West End, Clerkenwell makes a great base from which to explore London, but contains few places to stay. The quiet, discreet yet raffish Rookery offers 33 unique rooms in a row of converted 18th-century houses. Like sister hotel Hazlitt's (see p53), the decor could perhaps be described as Georgian minimalist, with artfully placed antiques, plaster busts and framed portraits, and massive oak beds with ornate headboards, sleek white lines and clawfoot baths. For a blowout, go for the Rook's Nest, a two-floor suite with a retractable roof and views towards St Paul's. **Hotel services** *Babysitting. Concierge. Garden. Laundry. Limousine service. No-smoking floors.* **Room services** *Dataport. Minibar. Room service (10am-10.30pm). TV: cable.*

Bloomsbury & Fitzrovia

Expensive

Academy Hotel

21 Gower Street, WC1E 6HG (7631 4115/fax 7636 3442/www.etontownhouse.com). Goodge Street tube. **Rates** £164 single; £192-£222 double; £252-£265 suite. **Credit** AmEx, DC, MC, V. **Map** p399 K5.
For an archetypal English experience, you can't go wrong with the Academy. Set in five Georgian townhouses, it has quite a cavernous feel with lots of corridors opening out to large and grand rooms. Decor is very *Country Life*: overstuffed armchairs, heavy, dark wood furniture and woven rugs fill the floor, while neutral walls give space to gold-framed mirrors, opulent floral curtains and botanical prints. The bar and dining room have a more modern touch with spot lighting and bright colour combinations.

Hotel services *Business services. Garden. No-smoking rooms.* **Room services** *Dataport. Hi-fi. Minibar. Room service (24hrs). Turndown.*

Blooms Townhouse

7 Montague Street, WC1B 5BP (7323 1717/fax 7636 6498/www.bloomshotel.com). Holborn or Russell Square tube. **Rates** £135 single; £180-£210 double; £225 suite. **Credit** AmEx, DC, MC, V. **Map** p399 L5.
The 26 rooms in this 18th-century townhouse are clean, airy and elegant, if utterly untrendy: prepare for plenty of dark wood, floral curtains and generic four-star flounciness. Blooms tends to attract a mature crowd who enjoy reading *The Times* to a soft classical soundtrack. Reasons for a visit: the charming patio garden backing on to the British Museum, the extensive and well-kept malt whisky 'library', and the stylish themed rooms including the Dickens, Theatre Royal or Lord's suites. The service is effective, if not overwhelmingly friendly; in fact, it's all terribly English and uninterfering. **Hotel services** *Bar. Business services. Concierge. Garden. No-smoking rooms. Restaurant.* **Room services** *Dataport. Minibar. Room service (24hrs). Turndown. TV: cable.*

Charlotte Street Hotel

15 Charlotte Street, W1P 1HB (7806 2000/fax 7806 2002/www.charlottestreethotel.com). Tottenham Court Road tube. **Rates** £217 single; £247-£347 double; £387-£699 suite. **Credit** AmEx, DC, MC, V. **Map** p399 J5.
The Union Jack hanging above the front door immediately pins this as a Tim and Kit Kemp hotel. Then again, so does the ineffable tastefulness of this fine operation. The decor in the guestrooms – which range from reasonably sized doubles up to a vast and homey penthouse suite – is along the same lines as the other Firmdale hotels: smartened-up English chic, inviting and chintz-free. Happily, another decidedly English characteristic missing from the place is stuffiness: this is a smart hotel, certainly, but it's also relaxed. The facilities include a small gym and a luxurious screening room (see p50 **Dinner and a movie?**), staff are friendly, and the restaurant, Oscar, is extremely agreeable. Most impressive, all told. **Hotel services** *Air-conditioning. Bar. Concierge. Gym. Restaurant.* **Room services** *Dataport. Hi-fi. Minibar. Room service (24hrs). Turndown. TV: cable/DVD/VCR.*

Montague on the Gardens

15 Montague Street, WC1B 5BJ (7637 1001/fax 7637 2516/www.redcarnationhotels.com). Holborn or Russell Square tube. **Rates** £205 single; £235 double; £405-£522 suite. **Credit** AmEx, DC, MC, V. **Map** p399 L5.
One of a raft of chintz-packed, purportedly trad-British hotels in this part of town, the Montague pulls off the schtick better than most. Certainly, there's not much wrong with the location: the hotel's on one of Bloomsbury's nicer streets, metres from

the British Museum. The decor's a little overbearing, a timeworn pastiche of English lordly living, but middle-aged Americans seem to love it. Rooms are not vast for these prices, but they're comfortable enough, and the staff are friendly and helpful.
Hotel services *Air-conditioning. Bar. Business services. Concierge. Disabled: adapted room. Garden. Gym. No-smoking rooms. Parking. Restaurant.* **Room services** *Dataport. Minibar. Room service (24hrs). TV: cable/pay movies.*

myhotel bloomsbury

11-13 Bayley Street, WC1B 3HD (7667 6000/fax 7667 6001/www.myhotels.co.uk). Tottenham Court Road tube. **Rates** £135-£199 single; £217-£294 double; £364-£1,175 penthouse. **Credit** AmEx, DC, MC, V. **Map** p399 K5.

When the boss describes himself as 'owner and visionary', as Andy Thrasyvoulou does in myhotel's brochures, you've every right to expect the worst. Happily, that's the only nauseating thing about this handsome hotel. The rooms are smart and designed according to feng shui principles; handy, as the singles aren't exactly palatial. However, the doubles are just fine, and on the top floors sit myplace, an apartment-style suite of suites that can be rented out separately or together. On the ground floor is a bar and a branch of Yo! Sushi; downstairs are meeting rooms, a gym and Jinja, which offers a variety of therapies. A couple of nice touches: the peaceful Library offers a pair of free internet terminals, and the mypreferences form, to be filled out before

Montague on the Gardens. *See p47.*

arrival, allows staff to leave a few of your favourite CDs and movies in your room ready for check-in. A new myhotel opened in **Chelsea** in November 2002 (35 Ixworth Place, SW3; 7225 7500).
Hotel services *Air-conditioning. Bar. Concierge. Beauty salon. Business services. Gym. No-smoking floors. Restaurant.* **Room services** *Dataport. Hi-fi. Room service (24hrs). Telephone. TV: cable/pay movies/VCR.*

Sanderson

50 Berners Street, W1T 3NG (7300 1400/fax 7300 1401/www.ianschragerhotels.com). Oxford Circus tube. **Rates** £229-£317 single; £258-£347 double; £441-£881 suite. **Credit** AmEx, DC, MC, V. **Map** p398 J5.

This former wallpaper factory, a Schrager/Starck operation, does a roaring trade. The capacious lobby, dotted with striking modern furniture, leads into the Long Bar; it's buzzing most nights, but we prefer the quieter, residents-only Purple Bar and its adjacent pool room. The bedrooms appeal: all white, of course, with bathrooms cheekily separated only by billowing sheer curtains and/or panes of glass (the building's listed status meant they couldn't add walls). This being a hotel full of Starck designs, there are occasional impracticalities – the alarm clocks, for example, are lovely and sleek, but with controls so small it takes tweezers to operate them – but it all looks divine. The stunning spa offers a variety of decadent treatments for those who book ahead.
Hotel services *Air-conditioning. Beauty salon. Business services. Disabled: adapted rooms. Garden. Gym. No-smoking floors. Parking.* **Room services** *Dataport. Room service (24hrs). TV: cable/DVD.*

Moderate

Harlingford Hotel

61-3 Cartwright Gardens, WC1H 9EL (7387 1551/ fax 7387 4616/www.harlingfordhotel.com). Russell Square tube/Euston tube/rail. **Rates** £72 single; £90 double; £100 triple; £108 quad. **Credit** AmEx, DC, MC, V. **Map** p399 L3.

Situated on a pretty Georgian crescent packed with budget hotels, the Harlingford has undergone a dramatic facelift. Formerly a humble family-run hotel, it's called in the designers: the freshly painted white walls are now adorned with postmodern art, and copies of *Wallpaper** are scattered just so around the modish purple lounge. The bedrooms themselves are modestly decorated, although cutting-edge bathrooms are promised for 2003. Visitors have access to the pretty gardens and tennis courts out front.
Hotel services *Business services. Garden.*

Jenkins Hotel

45 Cartwright Gardens, WC1H 9EH (7387 2067/fax 7383 3139/www.jenkinshotel.demon.co.uk). Russell Square tube/Euston tube/rail. **Rates** £52-£72 single; £85 double; £105 triple. **Credit** MC, V. **Map** p399 L3.

This small Georgian B&B has an informal, friendly feel: the check-in desk is in the owner's kitchen, and

Dinner and a movie?

The dutiful visitor to London will, of course, be out pounding the pavements, *Time Out London* in hand, day and night. The wise visitor knows when to stop. And we know where. Three contemporary-luxury hotels have contemporary-luxury screening rooms and run a regular programme of films. The schtick is that you can't just buy a ticket: dinner is part of the package. Which shouldn't be a hardship, since, hell, you've got to eat and – guess what – the attached restaurants are of the contemporary-luxury variety, all of them worth a visit in themselves.

The Film Club at the **Covent Garden Hotel** (*see p54*) runs on Saturday nights, offering a 6.30pm three-course dinner in Brasserie Max followed by an 8pm movie for £30 plus wine and service. On Sunday it's the turn of the **Charlotte Street Hotel** (*see p47*): same times, same deal but at the Oscar restaurant. Both offer a programme of light classics, such as *Moonstruck, Unforgiven* and – for Christmas – *It's a Wonderful Life*. **One Aldwych** (*see p46*) shows four films of a similar bent every weekend, at 2.30pm and 8pm on Saturday and Sunday. The earlier showing is preceded by brunch in Indigo, the later by dinner in the rated Axis (a particularly nice deal). Both are £35, drink included.

All screening rooms have big leather chairs and good sound, vision and sightlines. No popcorn, mind, and you might have to wait for the last people to finish their coffee, but it's a great way to escape for an evening. You don't have to be staying at the hotel: screenings are open to everyone. But then rooms at One Aldwych (*pictured*) are very tempting, and there's a special rate at both Covent Garden and Charlotte Street: it would be such a shame to have to start pounding those pavements back to your hotel afterwards...

---

a bookshelf full of London travel guides sits outside the breakfast room for your perusal. The handsome rooms are generally painted in soft hues – light yellow or cream – and are relatively tasteful in decor for this price range. Guests have access to the private gardens and tennis courts.
Hotel services *No-smoking throughout.* **Room services** *Minibar.*

Morgan Hotel

24 Bloomsbury Street, WC1B 3QJ (7636 3735/fax 7636 3045). Tottenham Court Road tube. **Rates** £60-£70 single; £88 double; £130 triple. *Flat* £90 1 person; £120 2 people; £165 3 people. **Credit** MC, V. **Map** p399 K5.

This atmospheric, family-run hotel is a little piece of *EastEnders* plopped down beside the grandeur of the British Museum: cockney staff, floral chintz and a delightfully old-school panelled breakfast room chock-full of London memorabilia. The rooms could use freshening up, but they are air-conditioned (which is a rarity in small London hotels) and the owners insist a refurbishment is in the works for 2003. There's a separate annexe of spacious flats (all of which are equipped with their own kitchenettes) that are much smarter: one of the better deals in central London.
Hotel services *Air-conditioning.*

Cheap

Arosfa

83 Gower Street, WC1E 6HJ (tel/fax 7636 2115). Euston Square or Goodge Street tube. **Rates** £39 single; £52 double; £70 triple. **Credit** MC, V. **Map** p399 K4.

Arosfa means 'place to stay' in Welsh, apparently, and it's an apt summary of this simple budget hotel. More cheap than cheerful, Arosfa still has plenty going for it: it's in a lovely Grade II-listed Georgian terrace house, it's spotless, and there's a pleasant walled garden. The rooms are spartan but cover the basics. At the moment, bathrooms are shared, but the owners are awaiting planning permission to make all the rooms en suite, and the hotel may have to close for a while in 2003 to allow for the work.
Hotel services *Garden. No-smoking floors.*

Ashlee House

261-5 Gray's Inn Road, WC1X 8QT (7833 9400/ fax 7833 9677/www.ashleehouse.co.uk). King's Cross tube/rail. **Rates** £34-£36 single; £22-£24 twin; £22 triple; £13-£19 dorm. **Credit** MC, V. **Map** p399 M3.

As youth hostels go, Ashlee House stands out from the crowd. For one thing, you don't have to be young to stay here: the oldest guest has been an 86-year-old

Japanese man. Secondly, there's none of that ridiculous curfew business – there's a 24-hour reception – and the rooms are clean and brightly coloured, from shocking pink to a cheery yellow. But the best thing about the place, besides the free luggage storage, the free historical London Walk and the central location, is the welcoming, good-humoured staff.
Hotel services *No-smoking rooms.*

Generator

37 Tavistock Place, WC1H 9SD (7388 7666/fax 7388 7644/www.the-generator.co.uk). Russell Square tube. **Rates** (per person) £40-£42 single; £23.50-£26.50 twin/double; £20-£22.50 multi; £10-£17 dormitory. **Credit** MC, V. **Map** p399 K4.
Grand Central Station for the backpackers' brigade, Generator is a veritable party machine. It's got the cool industrial look – steel, chrome, exposed pipes – mixed with that *Top of the Pops* aesthetic so popular with the kids: neon signs, coloured lights, video games. Then there's the bar, with its karaoke nights and happy hours, the 24-hour games room with pool tables, and the movie lounge. There's practical stuff: an internet room, a cafeteria-style restaurant, a travel agent. Oh, we almost forgot: there are beds, too – 837 of them – should you ever want to get some kip. Quiet rooms can be requested.
Hotel services *Air-conditioning. Bar. No-smoking rooms. Restaurant.*

St Margaret Hotel

26 Bedford Place, WC1B 5JL (7636 4277/fax 7323 3066). Holborn or Russell Square tube. **Rates** £52.50 single; £64.50-£97 double; £90.50-£105.50 triple. **Credit** MC, V. **Map** p399 L5.
This enormous townhouse hotel is a warm, bustling place. There are a couple of spacious lounges, one favoured by younger travellers, the other a more sedate affair where mature guests chat about their visit to the British Museum. The rooms are spotless, comfortable and all the beds have reading lights; some of the triples are huge. Bedrooms at the back overlook the Duke of Bedford's private garden and the hotel's own garden, to which guests have access.
Hotel services. *Garden. No-smoking rooms.*
Room services *TV: DVD/web TV.*

Marylebone

Moderate

Dorset Square Hotel

39 Dorset Square, NW1 6QN (7723 7874/fax 7724 3328/www.firmdale.com). Baker Street tube/ Marylebone tube/rail. **Rates** £115-£135 single; £164-£247 double; £282 suite. **Credit** AmEx, DC, MC, V. **Map** p384 F4.
Dorset Square was the first of Tim and Kit Kemp's hotels, and you can tell. That isn't necessarily a bad thing; the decor just tends towards straight-up traditional British, as opposed to the quieter and more refined designs found at, say, the Charlotte Street Hotel (*see p47*). Still, as always at a Firmdale oper-

ation, the rooms are all decorated invidually, which makes room selection like Forrest Gump's box of chocolates. There's not much to do around here at night, which is why the hotel's Potting Shed bar and restaurant seems to do a roaring trade.
Hotel services *Air-conditioning. Bar. Business services. Concierge. Garden. Restaurant. No-smoking rooms.* **Room services** *Dataport. Minibar. Room service (24hrs). Turndown. TV: cable/VCR.*

Mayfair & St James's

Deluxe

Claridge's

55 Brook Street, W1A 2JQ (7409 6444/ www.claridges.co.uk). Bond Street tube. **Rates** £315-£345 single; £395-£450 double; £565-£3,850 suite. **Credit** AmEx, DC, MC, V. **Map** p400 H6.
Claridge's has one of London's most talked-about restaurants as a feather in its cap: to dine at Gordon Ramsay at Claridge's (*see p200*), you have to book weeks ahead. Yet even if you don't land the Ramsay dinner, to stay at this frightfully English, determinedly unshowbiz spot is to experience the luxury end of the hotel trade at its most exemplary – and, perhaps surprisingly, unstuffy. The art deco foyer is notable for its period ornamentation, and a gargantuan central light fitting that looks like a giant pile of white glass noodles. Each of the 203 guest-rooms is decorated individually but traditionally, with a dash of transatlantic luxury in their coolly marbled and chromed bathrooms. Up on the sixth floor, the Olympus Suite spa has top-flight facilities.
Hotel services *Air-conditioning. Bar. Beauty salon. Business services. Concierge. Disabled: adapted rooms. Gym. No-smoking floor. Restaurant.* **Room services** *Dataport. Hi-fi. Minibar. Room service (24hrs). Turndown. TV: cable/pay movies.*

Dorchester

Park Lane, W1A 2HJ (7629 8888/fax 7409 0114/ www.dorchesterhotel.com). Hyde Park Corner tube. **Rates** £346-£370 single; £387-£452 double; £558-£2,496 suite. **Credit** AmEx, DC, MC, V. **Map** p400 G7.
The best feature of this Mayfair old-stager is right in front of you as you enter. The opulence of the hotel's vast lobby is unmatched in London, and the rooms just off it – among them the magnificent Oriental restaurant and a variety of ballrooms – are no less impressive. Not that the accommodations are in any way shabby, mind. A recent refit of all the well-proportioned guestrooms has smartened them up in tastefully opulent country-house style, but with high-end technology to boot: 42in flatscreen TVs with CD/DVD player, web access and a vast music jukebox of over 2,500 tracks from Mozart to Outkast. There are speakers in the bathroom, too, handy for a long soak in what staff claim are London's deepest tubs.
Hotel services *Air-conditioning. Bar. Beauty salon. Business services. Concierge. Disabled: adapted rooms. Garden. Gym. No-smoking floors. Parking.*

Restaurant. **Room services** *Dataport. Hi-fi. Minibar. Room service (24hrs). Turndown. TV: cable/DVD/pay movies/VCR.*

Metropolitan

Old Park Lane, W1Y 4LB (7447 1000/fax 7447 1147/www.metropolitan.co.uk). Green Park or Hyde Park Corner tube. **Rates** £323 single; £365 double; £570-£2,300 suite. **Credit** AmEx, DC, MC, V. **Map** p400 G8.

Londoners know two things about the Metropolitan. One, that in a cupboard in its (very fine) restaurant Nobu, tennis star Boris Becker knocked up a girl who wasn't his wife. And two, that the Met Bar is packed nightly with C-list starlets falling out of their minidresses and into the arms of some D-list pop idol. Happily, there's plenty more to this Park Lane operation than just that. The modern guestrooms are spacious and handsome, with extra marks for the effective lighting and Sony hi-fis. The health club is nicely kitted out, with a steam room and plenty of bookable treatments. And while the Met Bar at night is too frantic for some tastes, at least the welcoming pubs of Shepherd Market (or, if you're cheeky, the Hilton's Windows bar) aren't far away.

Hotel services *Air-conditioning. Bar. Beauty salon. Business services. Concierge. Gym. No-smoking rooms. Parking. Restaurant.* **Room services** *Dataport. Hi-fi. Minibar. Room service (24hrs). Turndown. TV: cable/pay movies/VCR.*

Ritz

150 Piccadilly, W1J 9BR (7493 8181/fax 7493 2687/www.theritzlondon.com). Green Park tube. **Rooms** 133. **Rates** £364 single; £429-£511 double; £593-£2,291 suite. **Credit** AmEx, DC, MC, V. **Map** p400 J8.

Still the epitome of traditional British luxury, the Ritz is nonetheless continuing to shake off its stuffy image. Standards are as excellent as ever, and attention to detail is a forte. Customers are mainly here for leisure: the doormen and concierges know the regulars by name. Decor is luxuriant: marble bathrooms (most with walk-in showers as well as a bath), heavy drapes, silk bedspreads, gold-leaf trimmings. Even if you get a room overlooking Piccadilly rather than Green Park, the traffic noise is virtually non-existent. Prices are sky-high, though deals can soften the blow. And if a night here is out of reach, at least treat yourself to tea in the glorious Palm Court.

Hotel services *Air-conditioning. Bar. Beauty salon. Business services. Disabled: adapted rooms. Garden. Gym. No-smoking floors. Parking. Restaurant.* **Room services** *Dataport. Hi-fi. Minibar. Room service (24hrs). Turndown. TV: cable/VCR.*

Expensive

No.5 Maddox Street

5 Maddox Street, W1S 2QD (7647 0200/fax 7647 0300/www.living-rooms.co.uk). Oxford Circus tube. **Rooms** 12. **Rates** £270-£381 double suite; £500 2-bedroom suite; £675 3-bedroom suite. **Credit** AmEx, DC, MC, V. **Map** p398 J6.

This suites-only boutique hotel is a great little secret. Decor is modern luxury – cream walls, blond wood floors, suede-effect sofas and leather pouffes – and space allocation in all 12 suites is generous: families and friends will feel at home in the two-bedroom suites. There's no restaurant or bar, but with Mayfair and Soho just outside the door, it's hardly an issue. Yet leaving your bolthole seems a crime given the in-room facilities. Why not light a fire, slip into your silk kimono and cook up your own feast in the kitchenette? Rooms have direct-dial phone and fax numbers, ISDN and voicemail, with DSL broadband net access coming soon.

Room services *Room service (7am-4.30pm). TV: cable/VCR.*

Trafalgar

2 Spring Gardens, SW1A 2TS (7870 2900/fax 7870 2911/www.thetrafalgar.hilton.com). Charing Cross tube/rail. **Rates** £158-£292 double; £380-£450 suite. **Credit** AmEx, DC, MC, V. **Map** p401 K7.

Not content with its major slice of the business market, Hilton opened its first 'lifestyle' hotel in July 2001 to try to tap into a younger, hipper, boutique hotel-loving crowd. The result is remarkably successful. The location is prime, the level of service is first-rate and the restrained good taste of the decor and furnishings creates the right balance between hipness and comfort. The Trafalgar's credentials have been boosted by its airy bar Rockwell winning a couple of major awards (its roof terrace offers wonderful views) and by the positive reviews garnered by restaurant Jago. Another plus mark goes for its status as the world's first Carbon Neutral hotel, meaning it arranges for an appropriate number of trees to be planted to balance its carbon dioxide emissions.

Hotel services *Air-conditioning. Bar. Business services. Concierge. Disabled: adapted rooms. Garden (rooftop). No-smoking rooms. Parking. Restaurant.* **Room services** *Dataport. Hi-fi. Minibar. Room service (24hrs). TV: cable/pay movies/web TV.*

Soho & Chinatown

Expensive

Hazlitt's

6 Frith Street, W1D 3JA (7434 1771/fax 7439 1524/www.hazlittshotel.com). Tottenham Court Road tube. **Rooms** 23. **Rates** £205 single; £229 double; £287 deluxe; £352 suite. **Credit** AmEx, DC, MC, V. **Map** p399 K6.

Hazlitt's is a home from home for its repeat customers (including many well-known authors), who love the hotel's sense of privacy in the heart of Soho. There's an atmospheric feel to the building, and decor includes antique furniture, clawfoot baths and four-poster or half-tester beds. The building's listed status means major alterations are forbidden (there's no lift), but the owners have made the most of the space: even in single rooms, there's a hidden-away

Try this for size: one of **Hazlitt's** luxurious half-testers. *See p53.*

sink and a bath behind a heavy drape. There's no restaurant on site, and the limited room service is unlikely to fill you up, but with Soho on your doorstep, you won't even notice.

Hotel services *Business services. No-smoking rooms.* **Room services** *Dataport. Minibar. Room service (24hrs). TV: cable/VCR.*

Covent Garden & St Giles's

Deluxe

Savoy

Strand, WC2R OEU (7836 4343/fax 7240 6040/ www.savoy.co.uk). Covent Garden or Embankment tube/Charing Cross tube/rail. **Rooms** 233. **Rates** £341-£376 single; £405-£441 double; £582-£1,469 suite. **Credit** AmEx, DC, MC, V. **Map** p401 L7.

Turn down Savoy Court (the only two-way street in Britain you drive on the right), walk past the quietly impressive Savoy Theatre (which predates the hotel) and head in through one of London's most iconic entrances (only the Ritz tops it)… there's nothing quite like walking into the Savoy, still one of the capital's classiest hotels 114 years after opening. The public spaces are exquisite: take tea in the Thames Foyer, sup a cocktail in the opulent American Bar, or chow down in the pricey Savoy Grill. Guestrooms vary in design: some are comfy, plush and English, while others are more in keeping with the beautifully maintained art deco theme elsewhere in the hotel. We prefer the latter. If you can, splash out on a room facing the river view: the hotel sits on the crook of the Thames, and the views both east and west are postcard-perfect.

Hotel services *Bar. Beauty salon. Business services. Gym. No-smoking rooms. Parking. Restaurant. Swimming pool (indoor).* **Room services** *Dataport. Hi-fi. Minibar. Turndown. TV: cable/pay movies/VCR.*

Expensive

Covent Garden Hotel

10 Monmouth Street, WC2H 9HB (7806 1000/fax 7806 1100/www.firmdale.com). Covent Garden or Leicester Square tube. **Rates** £229 single; £276-£381 double; £381-£816 suite. **Credit** AmEx, DC, MC, V. **Map** p399 L6.

One of six Tim and Kit Kemp hotels in London, the Covent Garden Hotel is most similar in style to their Charlotte Street operation (*see p47*). The formula is common to most of the Firmdale hotels, but it bears repeating: friendly staff, a nice restaurant and buzzy bar, a gym in the basement, a quiet drawing room with an honesty bar for residents to use after hours, and impressively proportioned guestrooms done out in a warm, English style. That there's little else to say is testament to the none-more-smooth way it's run. Touches unique to this fine operation include a plush screening room (*see p50* **Dinner and a movie?**) and a full-time, on-site masseuse who'll rub the day's stresses from your shoulders in minutes.

Hotel services *Air-conditioning. Bar. Beauty salon. Business services. Concierge. Gym. Restaurant.* **Room services** *Dataport. Hi-fi. Minibar. Room service (24hrs). Turndown. TV: cable/pay movies/VCR.*

St Martin's Lane

45 St Martin's Lane, WC2N 4HX (0800 634 5500/ 7300 5500/fax 7300 5501/www.ianschragerhotels. com). Covent Garden or Leicester Square tube. **Rates** £247 single; £270-£329 double; £493-£1,645 penthouse. **Credit** AmEx, DC, MC, V. **Map** p401 L7.

Its location on the fringes of Covent Garden makes it fashionable with the fashionable, yet the Corrs playing in the foyer and the two (count 'em) Beverley Craven CDs available to rent suggest the out-crowd are also welcome at this smart Ian Schrager hotel. St Martin's Lane is designed by Philippe Starck, whose finest flourish here is the neat gadget by each bed that lets guests change the colour of the lighting in

their minimally decorated rooms, adding pink or green or blue where otherwise there is only white (linen, walls, curtains, chairs). The floor-to-ceiling windows show off an unwitting checkerboard at night from the outside, as each guest picks a different hue to light their room. The theme continues in the Light Bar, a sea of colour and cocktails.
Hotel services *Bar. Business services. Disabled: adapted rooms. Garden. Gym. No-smoking floors. Parking. Restaurant.* **Room services** *Dataport. Minibar. Room service (24hrs). Turndown. TV: cable/VCR.*

Knightsbridge & South Kensington

Deluxe

Blakes

33 Roland Gardens, SW7 3PF (7370 6701/fax 7373 0442/www.blakeshotels.com). Gloucester Road or South Kensington tube. **Rates** £200 single; £299-£393 double; £640-£1,051 suite. **Credit** AmEx, DC, MC, V. **Map** p397 D11.
Blakes, the sumptuous hotel Anoushka Hempel opened in South Kensington in the 1970s, remains in fashion. The original boutique hotel, Blakes offers a discreet and luxurious hideaway for the beautiful and glamorous. Each room is a self-contained fantasy in extravagant colours, evoking oriental exoticism. The rooms spill over with antique treasures, silk embroidered cushions and lacquered chests.
Hotel services *Business services. Garden. No-smoking rooms. Parking.* **Room services** *Minibar. Room service (24hrs). Turndown. TV: cable/VCR.*

Expensive

The Gore

189 Queen's Gate, SW7 3EX (7584 6601/fax 7589 8127/www.gorehotel.com). **Rates** £182-£199 single; £223-£335 deluxe double; £346 suite. **Credit** AmEx, DC, MC, V. **Map** p397 D9.
For more than a century this delightful Victorian townhouse (in fact, two knocked together) has been a hotel. But while there's a 19th-century retro richness to the decor and furnishings (and the 5,000 prints and paintings on the walls), the vibe created by the cheery staff is entirely 21st-century. The presence of the popular Bistrot 190 and an appealingly dark, wood-panelled bar give the Gore a not-just-for-the-tourists buzz, while the bedrooms, varying in size from small to palatial, are kitted out with antiques and big, ultra-comfy beds. If money's no object, go for one of the individually themed deluxe rooms or, even better, the wonderful Tudor Room with its Thomas Crapper mahogany throne WC.
Hotel services *Bar. Business services. Concierge. Laundry. No-smoking floor. Restaurant.* **Room services** *Dataport. Minibar. Room service (7am-11pm). TV: cable.*

Knightsbridge Hotel

10 Beaufort Gardens, SW3 1PT (7584 6300/ www.firmdale.com). Knightsbridge tube. **Rates** £158-£176 single; £194-£287 double; £381-£440 suite. **Credit** AmEx, DC, MC, V.
The newest of the Firmdale chain, what the Knightsbridge lacks in facilities – there's no bar, restaurant or gym – it makes up for with its location. Situated around the corner from Harrods and Harvey Nicks, it's a shopper's paradise. Given the reasonable rates – you certainly won't find anywhere else this nice around here at these prices – guests have a bit

The chain gang

Many global chains have branches in London. Don't, as a rule, expect a great deal of individual character, but do rest assured that you'll get the standard of service and level of comfort you last found at the same chain's outlets in New York, Kuala Lumpur, Sydney, Paris... wherever, really.

● At the top end, there are **Four Seasons** at Canary Wharf (46 Westferry Circus, E14; 7510 1999) and Mayfair (Hamilton Place, Park Lane, W1; 7499 0888). See www.fourseasons.com for more.
● **Sheraton** hotels sit in Mayfair (Piccadilly, W1; 7499 6321), Belgravia (20 Chesham Place, SW1; 7235 6040) and Heathrow (Colnbrook and Bath Road, UB7; 8759 2424), with the more luxurious Sheraton Park Tower on Knightsbridge (No.101, SW1; 7235 8050). For full details, see www.starwood.com/sheraton.
● Among the innumerable London **Marriott** hotels (see www.marriott.com for a full list) are the branches in Belgravia (Grosvenor Square, W1; 7493 1232) and Mayfair (140 Park Lane, W1; 7493 7000), as well as at County Hall (Westminster Bridge Road, SE1; 7928 5200).
● See www.hilton.com for the full story on the range of **Hilton** hotels in London, or just go directly to Islington (53 Upper Street, N1; 7354 7700), Mayfair (22 Park Lane, W1; 7493 8000) or Paddington (225 Edgware Road, W2; 7402 4141).
● On a budget? Try **Holiday Inn**. The global chain has many hotels scattered around London, from Hoxton (275 Old Street, EC1; 7300 4300) to Hampstead (215 Haverstock Hill, NW3; 0870 400 9037) via Oxford Circus (57-9 Welbeck Street, W1; 7935 4442). You can consult www.holiday-inn.com for a full list.

of extra cash with which to go store crazy. Rooms are smart and English in feel, with the occasional curve-ball thrown to confuse the chintz lovers (check the glowing ladder in the drawing room).

Hotel services *Air-conditioning. Business services. Concierge.* **Room services** *Dataport. Hi-fi. Minibar. Room service (24hrs). Turndown. TV: cable/pay movies.*

Pelham

15 Cromwell Place, SW7 2LA (7589 8288/fax 7584 8444/www.firmdale.com). South Kensington tube. **Rates** £176 single; £211-£294 double; £529-£811 suite. **Credit** AmEx, DC, MC, V. **Map** p397 D10.
This Firmdale hotel's location, near South Ken tube and the major museums, means that the Pelham is to sightseeing what the Charlotte Street Hotel (*see p47*) is to nightlife, or what the Knightsbridge Hotel (*see p55*) is to shopping. The chain prides itself on ploughing more money than many of its competitors into maintaining and updating the decor in its guestrooms, and so it is here. The style – restrained, quietly modish British classicism, with the occasional quirky item or picture thrown in for fun – will be pleasingly familiar to anyone who's stayed at any of the chain's other operations.

Hotel services *Air-conditioning. Bar. Business services. Concierge. Restaurant.* **Room services** *Dataport. Minibar. Room service (24hrs). Turndown. TV: cable/pay movies/VCR.*

Moderate

Aster House

3 Sumner Place, SW7 3EE (7581 5888/fax 7584 4925/www.asterhouse.com). South Kensington tube. **Rates** £75-£99 single; £135-£180 double. **Credit** MC, V. **Map** p397 11D.
Sumner Place is one of South Ken's most elegant addresses and Aster House gamely attempts to live up to its prestigious location. The pink marble-effect lobby, with its elaborate gold chandeliers, is kitsch glam; the lush garden, with its pond and ducks, is truly sweet; and the palm-filled observatory, where guests eat breakfast and read the papers, is a lovely space. Traditional floral motifs dominate the comfy bedrooms, some of which come with fab marble bath-rooms; all are equipped with power showers.
Hotel services *Air-conditioning. Business services. Garden. Laundry. No-smoking throughout.* **Room services** *TV: cable.*

Cranley Gardens Hotel

8 Cranley Gardens, SW7 3DB (7373 3232/fax 7373 7944/www.cranleygardenshotel.com). Gloucester Road tube. **Rates** £79-£89 single; £109-£115 double; £135 triple. **Credit** AmEx, DC, MC, V. **Map** p397 D11.
Formerly a Hilton, this converted Victorian town-house still has the feel of an American chain, but mixed with the charm of a small English hotel. The faux-gentlemen's club lobby is the best bit, with fake Corinthian columns, plush couches and piped-in classical music, but the bedrooms are a bit bland. It's

The breakfast room at **Five Sumner Place**.

comfy enough, though, and the family who runs it keeps it from feeling too corporate. You can't fault the location, either: there's a wealth of museums nearby, plus King's Road and Knightsbridge for shopping.
Hotel services *Bar. Business services. Restaurant.* **Room services** *Room service (8am-midnight). TV: cable.*

Five Sumner Place

5 Sumner Place, SW7 3EE (7584 7586/fax 7823 9962/www.sumnerplace.com). South Kensington tube. **Rates** £100 single; £153 double. **Credit** AmEx, MC, V. **Map** p397 D11.
The much-lauded Five Sumner Place's location is second to none: a lovely row of white terraced houses in the heart of South Ken. The decor, while not the height of fashion, is more tasteful than in most faux-period hotels: a pleasant mix of soft greys, blues and pinks. The breakfast room, an airy glass observatory, is also pleasing; so is the presence of a lift, a rarity in townhouse hotels. But the hotel's real strength is the friendly and gentle manner of its long-time manager, Tom Tyranowicz.
Hotel services *Garden. No-smoking floors.* **Room services** *Dataport. Minibar. Room service (8am-8pm).*

Gainsborough Hotel

7-11 Queensberry Place, SW7 2DL (7957 0000/fax 7957 0001/www.eeh.co.uk). South Kensington tube. **Rates** £79-£102 single; £141-£170 double; £223-£258 suite. **Credit** AmEx, DC, MC, V. **Map** p397 D10.

The Gainsborough lives up to its role as part of the Elegant English Hotels mini-chain. Named after the celebrated English artist, the hotel's gracious lobby is adorned with a Gainsborough portrait of the Duchess of Richmond. The bedrooms have classy aspirations, with Louis XIV-style furniture, quality damask upholstery and Chinesesy porcelain lamps. The elegant Picasso bar, with its fabulous black and gold drapes, is a chic spot for breakfast. For the price, this is one of London's more luxurious hotels. **Hotel services** *Air-conditioning. Bar. Business services. Concierge. No-smoking rooms.* **Room services** *Room service (24hrs). TV: cable.*

Gallery Hotel

8-10 Queensberry Place, SW7 2DL (7915 0000/fax 7915 4400/www.eeh.co.uk). South Kensington tube. **Rates** £141-£170 double; £188 triple; £258 suite. **Credit** AmEx, DC, MC, V. **Map** p397 D10.
A middle-class Ritz? The flagship of the Elegant English Hotels mini-chain, this Victorian mansion hotel is a cut above its sister, the Gainsborough. The luxurious lobby bar is pure gentlemen's club (rich mahogany panelling, leather armchairs and a striking Jacobean-style fireplace), while the basement Morris lounge is more Arts-and-Crafts. While the plush bedrooms rather bravely combine classical English chintz with modern abstract art, the granite bathrooms are the essence of modern comfort. **Hotel services** *Air-conditioning. Bar. Concierge. Gym. Limousine service.* **Room services** *Dataport. Minibar. Room service (24hrs). Turndown. TV: cable/VCR.*

Hotel 167

167 Old Brompton Road, SW5 0AN (7373 0672/fax 7373 3360/www.hotel167.com). Gloucester Road tube. **Rates** £72-£86 single; £90-£99 double. **Credit** AmEx, DC, MC, V. **Map** p397 D11.
In a sea of period hotel clones, Hotel 167 is a quirky little gem. The lobby sets the stage for something different, with its art deco tiled floor and giant abstract paintings. Upstairs, the pot-pourri scented bedrooms are an eclectic mix of traditional and bohemian: antique wooden furniture and the odd Victorian painting, mixed with more contemporary touches (Mexican bedspreads, Klee prints). Everything's a bit rough around the edges, but that's part of the hotel's charm: its atmosphere has inspired both a song (an unreleased track by the Manic Street Preachers) and a novel (*Hotel 167*, by Jane Solomon). **Room services** *TV: cable.*

Swiss House Hotel

171 Old Brompton Road, SW5 0AN (7373 2769/fax 7373 4983/www.swiss-hh.demon.co.uk). Gloucester Road tube. **Rates** £74 single; £93-£109 double; £125 triple; £140 quad. **Credit** AmEx, DC, JCB, MC, V. **Map** p397 D11.
Formerly a private residence used by Swiss Air crews, this smart townhouse hotel has a crisp, country-fresh appeal. The lovely blue breakfast room, with its pine furniture and dark wood beams, is more Alpine cottage than standard B&B. The bedrooms

Upstairs, downstairs: the **Vicarage Hotel**.

are clean and serene: white walls, wooden furniture and classic navy bed linens, a far cry from the floral nightmare typical of most budget hotels. Dynamic manager Beatriz Lopera keeps the place ticking over smoothly and maintains good relations with the hotel's resident ghost (don't worry, it's friendly). **Hotel services** *Concierge. No-smoking rooms.* **Room services** *Dataport. TV: cable.*

Cheap

Abbey House

11 Vicarage Gate, W8 4AG (7727 2594/fax 7727 1873/www.abbeyhousekensington.com). High Street Kensington or Notting Hill Gate tube. **Rates** £45 single; £74 double; £90 triple; £100 quad. **No credit cards. Map** p394 B8.
Situated on a quiet Victorian square, this townhouse hotel offers affordable access to one of London's more exclusive neighbourhoods. The lobby is suitably swanky: chandeliers, greenery and a black-and-white tiled floor. The simply decorated rooms are more of a reality check, but they cover the basics and most have orthopaedic mattresses. Bathrooms must be shared, but are clean and prettily decorated.

Vicarage Hotel

10 Vicarage Gate, W8 4AG (7229 4030/fax 7792 5989/www.londonvicaragehotel.com). High Street Kensington or Notting Hill Gate tube. **Rates** £46 single; £76-£100 double; £93 triple; £100 quad. **No credit cards. Map** p394 B8.

The lobby of this Victorian townhouse is glitzy verging on tawdry: red and gold wallpaper, ornate gilt mirrors, ghastly carpet. But climb the stairs – and there are a lot of stairs – and you'll find extremely tasteful bedrooms. Decorated in pastels, the rooms have a lovely, fresh feel, furnished with wooden antiques, comfortable beds and muted floral patterns. The summery TV lounge is just as pretty. The hotel is currently in the process of converting several rooms to incorporate en suite bathrooms.

Belgravia & Pimlico

Deluxe

Lanesborough
Hyde Park Corner, SW1X 7TA (7259 5599/fax 7259 5606/www.lanesborough.com). Hyde Park Corner tube. **Rates** £335-£393 single; £464 double; £699-£6,213 suite. **Credit** AmEx, DC, MC, V. **Map** p400 G8.
This former hospital has garnered a reputation as one of London's most opulent hotels. The rooms combine elegant furnishings with space-age technology, and the range of facilities is excellent: in-room computers and software, internet access, private phone lines, digital movies and music libraries. The glass-roofed conservatory is a fantasy of chinoiserie, trickling fountains and exotic vegetation, and the Library bar, a gentleman's bolthole, comes complete with wall to wall books, a cocktail piano and impeccable service. **Hotel services** *Bar. Business services. Disabled: adapted rooms. Gym. No-smoking rooms. Parking. Restaurant.* **Room services** *Dataport. Room service (24hrs). Turndown. TV: cable/DVD/web TV.*

Moderate

Tophams Belgravia
28 Ebury Street, SW1W 0LU (7730 8147/fax 7823 5966/www.tophams.co.uk). Victoria tube/rail. **Rates** £115 single; £130-£150 double; £170 triple; £260 family room. **Credit** AmEx, DC, MC, V. **Map** p400 H10.
They don't come much cosier than Tophams. Run by the same family for more than 60 years, it's delightfully old-school: narrow, higgledy-piggledy corridors, low ceilings, creaky floors. The decor is evocative of granny's house: china cabinets, candlewick bedspreads, white wicker furniture. There's an enchanting crimson restaurant, with an adjoining bar, popular with the hotel's distinguished lady visitors. Service is personalised: one visitor returned so often the hotel's owners had a room decorated specifically to his tastes. Rooms at the back have a view of Margaret Thatcher's house.
Hotel services *Bar. Business service Disabled: adapted rooms. No-smoking room. Parking. Restaurant.* **Room services** *Dataport. Room service (24hrs). Turndown. TV: cable.*

Cheap

Woodville House & Morgan House
107 Ebury Street, SW1W 9QU (7730 1048/fax 7730 2571/www.woodvillehouse.co.uk) & 120 Ebury Street, SW1W 9QQ (7730 2384/fax 7730 8442/ www.morganhouse.co.uk). Victoria tube/rail. **Rates** £46-£74 single; £66-£88 double; £86-£110 triple; £122 quad. **Credit** MC, V. **Map** p400 H10.

Accommodation

Going potty for pewter: **Hampstead Village Guesthouse**. *See p61.*

Housed in neighbouring Georgian townhouses, these cosy B&Bs are cheap and cheerful personified. Apart from the differences in decor – the Woodville is traditional English, the Morgan has a more contemporary feel – the hotels have a lot in common: they're owned by the friendly husband-and-wife team of Rachel Joplin and Ian Berry, and both have lovely breakfast rooms and tiny walled gardens. The bedrooms are small but comfy, some equipped with orthopaedic mattresses. Family-sized rooms come complete with their own teddy bears, which is a pretty good indication of the homely atmosphere you'll find here.
Hotel services *Air-conditioning (selected rooms, Woodville). Garden. No-smoking rooms.*

North London

Moderate

30 King Henry's Road

30 King Henry's Road, Primrose Hill, NW3 3RP (7483 2871/fax 7209 9739/www.30kinghenrysroad. co.uk). Chalk Farm tube/Primrose Hill rail. **Rates** £80 single; £100 double. **No credit cards.**
Set in the home of Carole and Andrew Ingram, this plummy B&B is a piece of *Country Life* magazine in north London. The mid-Victorian house is decorated in a beautiful rustic style, and the resident greyhound, Joe, is a friendly mutt. The bedrooms are tasteful and homely. Breakfast is served in the country-style kitchen, and Primrose Hill – one of London's most romantic spots – is no more than a short walk away.
Hotel services *Air-conditioning. No-smoking throughout.*

Cheap

Hampstead Village Guesthouse

2 Kemplay Road, Hampstead, NW3 1SY (7435 8679/fax 7794 0254/www.hampsteadguesthouse. com). Hampstead tube/Hampstead Heath rail. **Rates** £48-£66 single; £72-£84 double; £90-£150 studio. **Credit** AmEx, MC, V.
The leafy village of Hampstead is a dream address for many Londoners; this welcoming B&B makes the fantasy an affordable reality. A short walk from the grassy splendours of Hampstead Heath, this lovingly restored Victorian pile is home to Annemarie van der Meer, her husband Jim and Marley the dog. The characterful interior is filled with books, knick-knacks and Delft earthenware, and each of the cosy bedrooms comes equipped with reading lamps, small fridges and phones. Full English breakfasts are served, weather permitting, in the lovely garden; meal times are flexible. There's also a separate cottage, with its own kitchenette, that sleeps five. You'll have to pay a 5% surcharge if you do decide to use the credit card.
Hotel services *Garden. No-smoking throughout. Parking.*

South London

Moderate

Riverside Hotel

23 Petersham Road, Richmond-upon-Thames, Surrey TW10 6UH (8940 1339/fax 8948 0967/ www.riversidehotelrichmond.co.uk). Richmond tube/rail. **Rooms** 22. **Rates** £65 single; £85-£90 double; £125 suite. **Credit** AmEx, DC, MC, V.
Perched on the banks of the Thames, this friendly family-run hotel is 20 minutes by train to Waterloo but feels worlds away. The advantages of staying out here are plenty: you get more room for the money, pastoral scenery and a host of country attractions within walking distance, including Ham House, Marble Hill House and Richmond Park. Rooms are pleasantly decorated, and many have river views, as does the cheery yellow dining room. The spacious suites offer great value.
Hotel services *No-smoking rooms. Parking.* **Room services** *Dataport. Room service (10am-11.30pm). TV: cable.*

West London

Moderate

Amsterdam Hotel

7 Trebovir Road, Earl's Court, SW5 9LS (7370 2814/fax 7244 7608/www.amsterdam-hotel.com). Earl's Court tube. **Rates** £78-£86 single; £88-£100 double; £112-£135 triple. **Credit** AmEx, DC, JCB, MC, V.** **Map** p396 B11.
With its elegant palm-filled lobby, Caribbean prints and tropical upholstery, the Amsterdam should have been named the Miami. The pastel rooms are all comfortable and modern, and the whole place screams Florida condo; even the breakfast room has wicker and bamboo touches. The hotel also has its own 24-hour internet room. Sadly, while we've previously received a warm welcome, our greeting this time failed to match the cheeriness of the rooms.
Hotel services *Business services. Concierge. Garden. No-smoking rooms.* **Room services** *Room service (7.30am-9.30pm).*

Colonnade Town House

2 Warrington Crescent, Little Venice, W9 1ER (7286 1052/fax 7286 1057/www.etontownhouse.com). Warwick Avenue tube. **Rates** £148 single; £173-£211 double; £270-£288 suite. **Credit** AmEx, DC, JCB, MC, V.
This sumptuous Victorian hotel pampers its guests and yet is, for London, moderately priced. The catch? Its slightly off-centre location, which is actually a bonus: the neighbourhood of Little Venice, with its pretty canals, is one of London's most picturesque. The classically decorated rooms, with Egyptian cotton sheets and crushed velvet bedspreads, are deliciously plush. There's history, too: the JFK suite has an enormous four-poster bed

Don't tell them we told you, but...

Every hotel likes to make a bit of a play when a celebrity comes to visit. Usually, it's a win-win situation: the hotel gets a publicity boost, the celeb keeps his or her name in the papers. But sometimes one or more parties would prefer their publicity to be a bit less, well, public.

Take Johnny Depp, for example. The Hollywood star is alleged to have filled his bathtub during a stay at the **Portobello Hotel** (*see p63*) with vintage champagne as a surprise for Kate Moss. Unfortunately, while he was enjoying supper, a chambermaid popped in to tidy up. Perturbed by the colour of the 'water' in which she presumed he was going to bathe, she pulled the plug.

Another celebrity rumoured to have been embarrassed in the bathroom is Leonardo DiCaprio. While staying in the penthouse at the **Metropolitan** on Park Lane (*see p53*) and wandering around *sans* clothing, he presumed the bathroom had a one-way window, as did the shower room. Alas, it

looks both ways... a red-faced Leonardo was reported to have unwittingly displayed his assets to the occupants of a passing bus.

That's nothing compared to the chambermaid who had to tidy up after Alice Cooper. Sent to clean room 16 of the Portobello Hotel, the poor unfortunate pulled back the duvet to find a boa constrictor nestling in the sheets, along with a five-pound note and instructions to buy some mice for the hungry monster. Jude Law and Sadie Frost, meanwhile, are far nicer types. On their wedding night, they filled their bed in the Loft Suite at the **Covent Garden Hotel** (*see p54*) with red roses.

Some stars use hotel rooms as a temporary refuge – Gareth Gates holed up at the **Leonard** on Seymour Street to avoid the paparazzi after *Pop Idol*, and Liz Hurley hid at the **Halkin** after Hugh Grant's dalliance with Divine Brown – but Richey Edwards of the Manic Street Preachers used his room to prepare to disappear forever. At 7am on

custom-built for the president's 1962 state visit; Sigmund Freud, a former guest, has a similarly opulent suite named after him; and Alan Turing, the genius who cracked the Enigma code, was born here. **Hotel services** *Air-conditioning. Business services. Concierge. Garden. No-smoking rooms. Parking.* **Room services** *Dataport. Minibar. Room service (24hrs). Turndown. TV: cable.*

London Elizabeth Hotel

Lancaster Terrace, Bayswater, W2 3PF (7402 6641/ fax 7224 8900/www.londonelizabethhotel.co.uk). Lancaster Gate tube. **Rates** £100 single; £115-£140 double; £180-£250 suite. **Credit** AmEx, DC, JCB, MC, V. **Map** p395 D6.
The Elizabeth has a glitzy, almost dowdy appeal: this was probably a glamorous spot in the 1970s. The lobby is filled with gaudy chandeliers and slightly shabby damask furniture, and the overwhelmingly pink Rose Garden restaurant, with its painted floral murals, verges on the kitsch. The adjacent bar, which opens on to a lovely terrace, is similarly theatrical. Upstairs, the standard rooms are comfortable enough, but, if you've got the cash, go for a suite. The Conservatory Suite is an opulent oval affair with stained-glass windows; the lavish Hyde Park Suite, with its elaborate furnishings and enormous mirrors, is straight out of *Dynasty*. Both are, by London standards, a bargain. **Hotel services** *Air-conditioning (deluxe rooms & suites). Bar. Business services. Concierge. Garden. Parking. Restaurant.* **Room services** *Dataport. Room service (24hrs).*

Mornington Lancaster Hotel

12 Lancaster Gate, Bayswater, W2 3LG (7262 7361/ fax 7706 1028/www.mornington.se). Lancaster Gate tube. **Rates** £125 single; £140 double; £165 triple; £175 suite. **Credit** AmEx, DC, MC, V. **Map** p395 D7.
At first glance, the Mornington is your typical smart-ish Victorian hotel: dignified stucco exterior; clubby, wood-panelled lobby and library bar. But listen closely to the surrounding conversations and you'll soon realise you're staying in an outpost of Stockholm. Swedish-run, the Mornington is a refreshing change from theme-park English. The staff couldn't be more helpful, and most of the rooms have a clean, contemporary Scandinavian feel, with polished wooden floors, bright contemporary bedspreads and no trace of chintz. **Hotel services** *Bar. Business services. Concierge. No-smoking rooms.* **Room services** *Dataport. Iron. Room service (7-10am, 4-11pm). Turndown. TV: cable/pay movies.*

Pembridge Court

34 Pembridge Gardens, Notting Hill, W2 4DX (7229 9977/fax 7727 4982/www.pemct.co.uk). Notting Hill Gate tube. **Rates** £125-£165 single; £160-£195 double. **Credit** AmEx, DC, MC, V. **Map** p394 A7.
This lovingly restored townhouse shows fine attention to detail: the hotel is adorned with Victorian and Edwardian accessories, including long gloves, fans and beaded purses that wouldn't look out of place in the V&A. The hotel cat Churchill, alone since the demise of his mate Spencer, roams the building at his leisure. Rooms are spacious (except for the 'small

1 February 1995, Edwards left room 516 of the **Embassy Hotel** on Bayswater Road and was never seen again.

HRH Crown Prince Alexander II, son of the exiled King Peter II of Yugoslavia, used a London hotel to make an entrance rather than an exit. He was born in suite 212 of **Claridge's** (*see p51*) on 17 July 1945, with Winston Churchill and George VI declaring the suite to be sovereign Yugoslav territory for the day so that the new prince would be born in his own country.

Diana, Princess of Wales, and Dodi Fayed are said to have enjoyed discreet liaisons at **Duke's Hotel** (35 St James's Place, SW1; 7491 4840/www.dukeshotel.co.uk), but you'll feel at home even if international espionage interests you more than international royalty: this is also where Ian Fleming, Sean Connery, George Lazenby, Roger Moore and Pierce Brosnan have all sampled what may be the world's best dry Martini, as mixed by Gilberto Preti.

single' rooms, which really are small) with huge sash windows accompanied by heavyweight, flamboyant curtains. Bathrooms, on the other hand, are the picture of modernity. Classy without being pretentious, casual without letting standards slip: Pembridge Court pitches it just right. Of course, it helps that the back door opens directly on to Portobello Road.
Hotel services *Air-conditioning. Bar. Business services.* **Room services** *Dataport. Room service (24hrs). Telephone. TV: cable/VCR.*

Portobello Hotel

22 Stanley Gardens, Notting Hill, W11 2NG (7727 2777/fax 7792 9641/www.portobello-hotel.co.uk). Notting Hill Gate tube. **Rates** £120 single; £160-£260 double. **Credit** AmEx, DC, MC, V. **Map** p394 A6.
A towering old house overlooking a private garden, converted slightly awkwardly into a hotel, eccentrically furnished with a raft of rock 'n' roll clients… This couldn't be anywhere but Notting Hill. The Portobello is the essence of west London shabby chic, and the idiosyncracies and inconveniences – it's not unusual to find the toilet wedged into a closet, or the bathtub in the bedroom – are part of its eccentric charm. Rooms vary wildly in size and style, from the pokey (such as the Moroccan-themed room 406) to the inviting (one room on the first floor has a circular bed and windows looking on to Stanley Gardens), helping the rock stars remember how many albums they've sold. In a word? Characterful.
Hotel services *Air-conditioning. Bar. Business services. Restaurant.* **Room services** *Dataport. Minibar. Room service (24hrs). TV: cable/VCR.*

Vancouver Studios

30 Prince's Square, Bayswater, W2 4NJ (7243 1270/fax 7221 8678/www.vienna-group.co.uk). Bayswater or Queensway tube. **Rates** £77 single; £97-£112 double; £132 triple. **Credit** AmEx, DC, MC, V. **Map** p394 B6.
In the hotel biz, 'home away from home' is a cringe-inducing cliché, but it rings true for Vancouver Studios. On one hand, it's a cosy Victorian hotel, situated in a Grade II-listed townhouse with a grandfather clock in the lobby and a fireplace for cold winter nights. On the other, it's young, funky and urban, perfect for independent living: each room comes with its own fully equipped kitchenette. The rooms are bang up to date, with bright contemporary bedspreads, Kandinsky prints on the walls and power showers. But the loveliest part of the hotel is the cutesy lounge, with its country casual decor, cacti and knick-knacks, opening on to a delightful walled garden. A rare gem.
Hotel services *Garden. Parking.* **Room services** *Dataport. Minibar.*

Westbourne Hotel

163-5 Westbourne Grove, Notting Hill, W11 2RS (7243 6008/fax 7229 7201/www.aliashotels.com). Notting Hill Gate tube. **Rates** £175-£225 double. **Credit** AmEx, MC, V. **Map** p394 A6.
Discreet and stylish, it's not just the location in the heart of 'bohemian' London that makes this such a trendy retreat: you'll spot the latest designs on the guests and may even see some fashion-house famous faces. The decor is loungey with stark white walls, 1950s coffee tables and low slung chairs. And while there have been changes since our last visit – they've done away with the bar and are introducing a private dining room – the minimalist air remains. Rooms are comfortable and quirky with individual features, such as an aluminium four-poster bed and interesting pieces of original art on the walls.
Hotel services *Air-conditioning. Bar. Business services. Garden. No-smoking rooms.* **Room services** *Dataport. Room service (24hrs). Telephone. Turndown. TV: cable/DVD.*

Cheap

Garden Court Hotel

30-31 Kensington Gardens Square, Bayswater, W2 4BG (7229 2553/fax 7727 2749/www.gardencourt hotel.co.uk). Bayswater or Queensway tube. **Rates** £39-£58 single; £58-£88 double; £72-£99 triple; £82-£120 quad. **Credit** MC, V. **Map** p394 B6.
From the moment you enter the airy lobby, with its giant Beefeater, Italianate marble busts and bonsai trees, it becomes clear that the Garden Court has a bit of panache. Run by the same family for 50 years, the welcoming atmosphere spills over into the agreeable lounge, which is decorated in oil paintings and greenery. The bedrooms are generally cheery, with comfy beds and pleasant wooden furniture. Guests have access to the pretty square out front.
Hotel services *Garden.* **Room services** *TV: cable.*

Space and flavour at **Pembridge Court**. *See p62.*

Kensington Gardens Hotel

9 Kensington Gardens Square, Bayswater, W2 4BH (7221 7790/fax 7792 8612/www.kensingtongardens hotel.co.uk). Bayswater or Queensway tube. **Rates** £40-£55 single; £75 double; £95 triple. **Credit** AmEx, DC, MC, V. **Map** p394 B6.

First, the good stuff. This small townhouse is situated in a lovely Victorian square, and guests have access to the private garden out front. The black and white tiled lobby is elegant, the front desk is manned 24 hours a day, and it's a short walk from Hyde Park and the newly hip Westbourne Grove. The rooms are clean and comfortable, if not particularly inspiring, and come with their own minibars. On our visit, the staff seemed pretty glum, but the hotel is nevertheless good value and, with its great location, you'll be too busy having fun elsewhere to notice.
Room services *Minibar. TV: cable.*

Mayflower Hotel

26-8 Trebovir Road, Earl's Court, SW5 9NJ (7370 0991/fax 7370 0994/www.mayflowerhotel. activehotels.com). Earl's Court tube. **Rates** £65 single; £79 double; £109 triple; £120 quad. **Credit** AmEx, JCB, MC, V. **Map** p396 B11.

Since our last visit, the Mayflower has had the makeover of all makeovers. Once run-of-the-mill, the rooms are now a gorgeous combination of minimalism and exoticism: crisp white bedlinen, stunning oriental wood furniture, colonial ceiling fans. All rooms come with sumptuous marble bathrooms, and unexpected luxuries such as hi-fis and modem points. The lobby, not yet completed in late 2002, promises to be a feng shui extravaganza, complete with a fountain, limestone flooring and Eastern-style fireplace. If the prices don't rise too much, this place

could give the big-name style hotels a run for their money. Ask about the adjoining Court Apartments, modern four-room suites that go for a song.
Hotel services *Business services. Concierge. Parking.* **Room services** *Dataport. Hi-fi. TV.*

Rushmore Hotel

11 Trebovir Road, Earl's Court, SW5 9LS (7370 3839/fax 7370 0274/www.rushmorehotel.co.uk). Earl's Court tube. **Rates** £55 single; £65 double; £85 quad. **Credit** AmEx, DC, JCB, MC, V. **Map** p396 B11.

For budget hotels, you don't get much more stylish this. Fresco-style paintings adorn the rooms, featuring scenes ranging from pastoral Tuscany to ocean views; some of the beds are draped stylishly with overhanging curtains and elegant satin bedspreads. The whole place has a chi-chi European feel, down to the wrought-iron chairs, glass tables and black granite surfaces of the elegant breakfast room. The staff are as sweet as pie, too. The Rushmore proves that, with a little imagination, cheap can be beautiful.
Hotel services *Business services. No-smoking rooms. Parking.* **Room services** *TV: cable.*

Youth hostels

Hostel beds are either in twin rooms or dorms. If you're not a member of the International Youth Hostel Federation (IYHF), you'll pay an extra £2 a night (after six nights you automatically become a member). Alternatively, join the IYHF for £13 (£6.50 for under-18s) at any hostel, or through www.yha.org.uk, which also allows you to book rooms. Always phone ahead for availability. The hostels listed take MasterCard and Visa; prices include breakfast.

City of London *36-8 Carter Lane, EC4V 5AB (7236 4965/fax 7236 7681). St Paul's tube/ Blackfriars tube/rail.* **Reception open** 7am-11pm daily; 24hr access. **Rates** £15-£30; £15-£24 under-18s. **Map** p404 O6.

Earl's Court *38 Bolton Gardens, Earl's Court, SW5 0AQ (7373 7083/fax 7835 2034). Earl's Court tube.* **Reception open** 7am-11pm daily; 24hr access. **Rates** £22.40; £20.50 under-18s. **Map** p396 B11.

Hampstead Heath *4 Wellgarth Road, Golders Green, NW11 7HR (8458 9054/fax 8209 0546). Golders Green tube.* **Reception open** 6.45am-11pm daily; 24hr access. **Rates** £20.40; £18 under-18s.

Holland House *Holland House, Holland Walk, W8 7QU (7937 0748/fax 7376 0667). High Street Kensington tube.* **Reception open** 7am-11pm daily; 24hr access. **Rates** £21; £18.75 under-18s. **Map** p394 A8.

Oxford Street *14 Noel Street, W1F 8GJ (7734 1618/fax 7734 1657). Oxford Circus tube.* **Reception open** 7am-11pm daily; 24hr access. **Rates** £22-£24; £17.75 under-18s. **Map** p398 J6.

Rotherhithe *Island Yard, Salter Road, Rotherhithe, SE16 5PR (7232 2114/fax 7237 2919). Rotherhithe or Canada Water tube.* **Beds** 320. **Reception open** 7am-11pm; 24hr access. **Rates** £24; £20 under-18s.

St Pancras *79-81 Euston Road, NW1 2QS (7388 9998/fax 7388 6766). King's Cross tube/rail.* **Beds** 152. **Reception open** 7am-11pm daily; 24hr access. **Rates** £24; £20 under-18s. **Map** p399 L3.

YMCAs

You may need to book months ahead to stay at a YMCA: many specialise in long-term accommodation. A few of the larger hostels are listed below (all are unisex), but you can get a full list from the National Council for YMCAs (8520 5599/www.ymca.org.uk). Prices are around £25-£30 per night for a single room and £40-£45 for a double.

Barbican YMCA *2 Fann Street, EC2Y 8BR (7628 0697/fax 7638 2420). Barbican tube.* **Map** p402 P5.

London City YMCA *8 Errol Street, EC1Y 8SE (7628 8832/fax 7628 4080). Barbican tube/Old Street tube/rail.* **Map** p402 F4.

Wimbledon YMCA *200 The Broadway, Wimbledon, SW19 1RY (8542 9055/fax 8540 2526). South Wimbledon tube/Wimbledon tube/rail/.*

Staying with the locals

These organisations can arrange accommodation in a Londoner's home (often more fun than an impersonal hotel); rates include breakfast.

At Home in London *70 Black Lion Lane, Hammersmith, W6 9BE (8748 1943/fax 8748 2701/www.athomeinlondon.co.uk).* **Open** *Phone enquiries* 9.30am-5.30pm Mon-Fri. **Rates** £29-£65 single; £52-£90 double. *Min stay* 2 nights. **Credit** AmEx, MC, V.

Bulldog Club *14 Dewhurst Road, Kensington, W14 0ET (7371 3202/fax 7371 2015/www.bulldog club.com).* **Open** *Phone enquiries* 10am-6pm Mon-Fri. **Rates** £85 single; £105 double. *Membership* £25/3yrs. **Credit** AmEx, MC, V.

Host & Guest Service *103 Dawes Road, Fulham, SW6 7DU (7385 9922/fax 7386 7575/www.host-guest.co.uk). Fulham Broadway tube.* **Open** 9am-5.30pm Mon-Fri. **Rates** from £17/person. *Students* from £95/wk. *Min stay* 2 nights. **Credit** MC, V.

London Bed & Breakfast Agency *71 Fellows Road, Swiss Cottage, NW3 3JY (7586 2768/fax 7586 6567/www.londonbb.com).* **Open** *Phone enquiries* 9am-6pm Mon-Fri; 10am-2pm Sat. **Rates** £20-£60. *Min stay* 2 nights. **Credit** MC, V.

London Homestead Services *Coombe Wood Road, Kingston-upon-Thames, Surrey KT2 7JY (8949 4455/8541 0041/fax 8549 5492/ www.lhslondon.com).* **Open** *Phone enquiries* 9am-7pm daily. **Rates** from £20 single; from £36 double. *Min stay* 3 nights. **Credit** MC, V.

See you at the bar...

... but which to choose? Well, let's see...
● It could be the glorious art deco American Bar at the **Savoy** (*see p54*), where the first Martini ever to be mixed in Britain is said to have been concocted. You'll pay through the nose, but the cocktails will be worth it.
● You may prefer the Windows bar atop the **Hilton** on Park Lane (7493 8000). The cocktails aren't up to much and neither is the pianist, but it's worth suffering both of them for the view – 28 floors above London, at night it's simply spectacular.
● Down at the **Dorchester** (*see p51*), there's no view to speak of. But you won't need one: the cocktails here are impeccable, the opulence is breathtaking (the piano is

covered in baby mirrors) and the service is suitably deferential.
● The Long Bar at the **Sanderson** (*see p49*) is jammed every night. Understandably so: it's a grand space that's perpetually buzzing with activity.
● There can be no doubt about the speciality of the Rockwell at the **Trafalgar** (*see p53*). Every imaginable variety of bourbon is sat there behind the bar looking at you.
● And you're after simpler pleasures, why not the **Columbia Hotel** (95-9 Lancaster Gate, W2; 7402 0021)? There are famous or semi-famous rock acts staying here every night of the year and, rockers being what they are, you can expect a little action in the 24-hour bar.

Self-catering apartments

It can be expensive to rent in London, but if you're in a group, you may save money by renting from one of the following. All specialise in holiday lets, though some have minimum stay requirements. **Accommodation Outlet** (*see p295*) caters for gay and lesbian flat-hunters.

Apartment Service *1st floor, 5-6 Francis Grove, Wimbledon, SW19 4DT (8944 1444/fax 8944 6744). Wimbledon tube/rail.* **Open** 9am-6.30pm Mon-Fri. **Rates** from £90 double studio. **Credit** AmEx, DC, MC, V.

Astons Apartments *31 Rosary Gardens, South Kensington, SW7 4NH (7590 6000/fax 7590 6060/ www.astons-apartments.com). Gloucester Road tube.* **Open** 8am-9pm daily. **Rates** £76.40 single studio; £105.75 double studio. **Credit** AmEx, MC, V. **Map** p396 C11.

Holiday Serviced Apartments *273 Old Brompton Road, Earl's Court, SW5 9JA (7373 4477/fax 7373 4282/www.holidayapartments.co.uk). Earl's Court tube.* **Open** 9.30am-5.30pm Mon-Fri. **Rates** from £80 single/double studio. **Credit** AmEx, MC, V. **Map** p396 C11.

Independent Traveller *Thorverton, Exeter, Devon EX5 5NT (01392 860807/fax 01392 860552/www.gowithit.co.uk).* **Rates** £250-£2,000/wk apartment. **Credit** MC, V.

Palace Court Holiday Apartments *1 Palace Court, Bayswater Road, Bayswater, W2 4LP (7727 3467/ fax 7221 7824/www.palacecourt.co.uk). Notting Hill Gate or Queensway tube.* **Open** 8.30am-11pm daily. **Rates** (plus 10% service) £65 single studio; £79 double studio; £86 triple studio. **Credit** MC, V.

Perfect Places *53 Margravine Gardens, Hammersmith, W6 8RN (8748 6095/fax 8741 4213/www.perfectplaceslondon.co.uk).* **Open** *Phone enquiries* 9am-7pm daily. **Rates** from £550/wk. **Credit** AmEx, MC, V.

University residences

During university vacations much of London's student accommodation is open to visitors, providing a basic but cheap place to stay.

Arcade Halls *The Arcade, 385-401 Holloway Road, Holloway, N7 ORN (7607 5415/fax 7609 0052/ www.unl.ac.uk/accommodation). Holloway Road tube.* **Rates** £20/night; £86/wk. **Available** 30 June-1 Sept 2003.

Goldsmid House *36 North Row, Mayfair, W1K 6DN (bookings 01273 207481/fax 7491 0586). Bond Street or Marble Arch tube.* **Rates** £23 single; £32 twin. **Available** 8 June-22 Sept 2003. **Map** p398 G6.

High Holborn Residence *178 High Holborn, Holborn, WC1V 7AA (7379 5589/fax 7379 5640/ www.lse.ac.uk/vacations). Holborn tube.* **Rates** £35 single; £57 twin; £67 triple. **Available** summer 2003. **Map** p399 M5.

International Students House *229 Great Portland Street, Marylebone, W1W 5PN (7631 8300/8310/fax 7631 8315/www.ish.org.uk). Great Portland Street tube.* **Rates** £12-£18 dormitory; £31 single; £25 twin. **Available** all year. **Map** p398 H5.

King's College Conference & Vacation Bureau *Strand Bridge House, 138-142 Strand, Covent Garden, WC2R 1HH (7848 1700/fax 7848 1717/www.kcl.ac.uk/services/conbro/vehelo.html). Temple tube.* **Rates** £18-£33 single; £33-£52 twin. **Available** summer 2003. **Map** p404 N8.

Passfield Hall *1-7 Endsleigh Place, Bloomsbury, WC1H 0PW (7387 3584/fax 7387 0419/ www.lse.ac.uk/vacations). Euston tube/rail.* **Rates** £25-£27 single; £46-£48 twin; £60-£62 triple. **Available** 22 Mar-27 Apr, 5 July-28 Sept 2003. **Map** p399 K4.

Walter Sickert Hall *29 Graham Street, Islington, N1 8LA (7040 8822/fax 7040 8825/www.city.ac.uk/ ems). Angel tube.* **Rates** £30-£40 single; £55-£60 twin. **Available** early July-mid-Sept 2003. **Map** p402 P3.

Camping & caravanning

None of these campsites is especially central and transport into town isn't what it might be, but all are conveniently cheap.

Crystal Palace Caravan Club Site *Crystal Palace Parade, SE19 1UF (8778 7155). Crystal Palace rail/3 bus.* **Open** *Office Mar-Oct* 8.30am-8pm daily. *Nov-Feb* 9am-8pm daily. **Rates** £16.75-£19 caravan pitch. **Credit** MC, V.

Lee Valley Campsite *Sewardstone Road, Chingford, E4 7RA (8529 5689/fax 8559 4070/ scs@leevalleypark.org.uk). Walthamstow Central tube/rail then 215 bus.* **Open** *Apr-Oct* 8am-10pm daily. *Nov-Mar* closed. **Rates** £5.60; £2.50 under-16s. **Credit** MC, V.

Lee Valley Leisure Centre Camping & Caravan Park *Meridian Way, Edmonton, N9 0AS (8803 6900/fax 8884 4975/leisurecentre@ leevalleypark.org.uk). Edmonton Green rail/W8 bus.* **Open** *Apr-Oct* 8am-10pm daily. *Nov-Mar* 8am-8pm daily. **Rates** £5.80; £2.50 5-16s; free under-5s. **Credit** MC, V.

Longer stays

If you're staying for months rather than weeks, it may be cheaper to rent a place. However, accommodation is still very expensive – £500 a month or more for a studio flat, £900 and up for a two-bed place, anywhere from £300 to £800 for a room in a shared house – and you'll normally have to pay a month's rent in advance and a further month's rent as a deposit.

The best source for places to rent is *Loot*, published daily. Capital Radio publishes a flatshare list, available from its foyer (30 Leicester Square, WC2) on Friday at around 5pm. Also, try the small ads in *Time Out* magazine (available from newsstands and newsagents from Tuesday in central London and Wednesday further out) and *Midweek* (free outside tube stations on Thursday).

Sightseeing

Introduction

Welcome to London.

Your main problem? Time. There's a reason why the Sightseeing section of this book stretches to a monumental 122 pages: there's an awful lot to see here.

If you're revisiting the city after four or more years away, you'll be in for a surprise. The turn of the millennium saw an unprecedented amount of building and rebuilding activity, with new sights and attractions opening all over the city at regular intervals. Many and varied they were, too, from the defiantly modish (the British Airways London Eye, Tate Modern, the Wellcome Wing of the Science Museum) to the more traditional (the Great Court at the British Museum, the refurbished Somerset House).

Happily, and perhaps a little surprisingly, the momentum hasn't been lost since the millennial celebrations died down. The year 2002 saw the opening of the stunning new Hungerford Bridge and the expansive Darwin Centre at the Natural History Museum, and work is continuing on making London a more attractive place for visitors: witness the refurbishment of the Museum of London and the pedestrianisation of Trafalgar Square, perhaps the two largest such projects scheduled for completion in 2003.

However, don't to limit yourself to only the biggest, boldest and brashest sights. Tucked between them are smaller, cosier museums that impress just as much, if not more so, than their headline-grabbing compadres. The Sir John Soane Museum, Dennis Severs' House and Highgate Cemetery pass many visitors by; try and squeeze them and others into your schedule. Which will, of course, be a busy one: did we mention there's a lot to see here?

LONDON PASS

The **London Pass**, which offers free entry to more than 50 attractions and free travel on public transport, is available for one, two, three and six days, priced at £26 (£16 child), £44 (£27 child), £58 (£37 child) and £91 (£50 child) respectively. Before you rush in, consider that many of London's major attractions, including the British Museum, the Natural History Museum and Tate Modern, are free to enter anyway. However, 'extras' include free mobile phone rental, commission-free currency exchange and discounted tickets for a couple of West End shows. The pass is also available without the travel thrown in, which represents better value if you're only planning to travel in zones 1 and 2.

For more information, and to buy online, go to www.londonpass.com, or call 0870 242 9988 for credit card bookings (9am-8pm Mon-Fri; 10am-4pm Sat). Passes are also available from Exchange International: there are 20 offices in London, including at the major train stations.

Trips & tours

Balloon tours

Adventure Balloons *Winchfield Park, London Road, Hartley Wintney, Hampshire RG27 8HY (01252 844222/www.adventureballoons.co.uk).* **Flights** *Apr-Oct* daily, weather permitting. **Fares** *Home Counties flights* £145 per person. *London* £165 per person. **Credit** MC, V.

Bicycle tours

See p361.

Bus tours

Big Bus Company *48 Buckingham Palace Road, Westminster, SW1 (0800 169 1365/7233 9533/ www.bigbus.co.uk).* **Open-top bus tours** three routes, 2hrs; all with live commentary. **Departures** every 15min from Green Park, Victoria & Marble Arch. *Summer* 8.30am-7pm daily. *Winter* 8.30am-4.30pm daily. **Pick-up** Green Park (near the Ritz); Marble Arch (Speaker's Corner); Victoria (outside Thistle Victoria Hotel, 48 Buckingham Palace Road, SW1). **Fares** £16 (£14 if booked online); £6 5-15s; free under-5s. Tickets valid for 24hrs, interchangeable between routes. **Credit** AmEx, DC, MC, V.

Sightseeing

The best · Sights & attractions

For beasts...
London Zoo (*p109*); the city farm at **Coram's Fields** (*p272*); **WWT Wetland Centre** (*p179*); **Natural History Museum** (*p140*).

... or for the beastly
London Dungeon (*p81*); the voodoo dolls at the **Horniman Museum** (*p173*).

For therapy...
Wellcome Wing at the **Science Museum** (*p140*); **Chelsea Physic Garden** (*p143*).

... or for retail therapy
Borough Market (*p256*); **Selfridges** (*p236*).

For spring...
Queen Charlotte's Cottage at the **Royal Botanic Gardens** (*p176*).

... or for summer...
Soho Square (*p119*); **St James's Park** (*p130*); swimming in **Hampstead Ponds** (*p148*).

... or for autumn...
Thames Barrier test closure (*p168*); the leaves in **Regent's Park** (*p109*).

... or for winter
Candlelit tours of **Sir John Soane's Museum** (*p100*); ice-skating at **Somerset House** (*p98*); Christmas at the **Geffrye Museum** (*p158*); cosy **Jerusalem Tavern** (*p221*).

For the ancient...
Tower of London (*p96*); holy books in the **British Library** (*p105*); **Hampton Court Palace** (*p178*); the **British Museum**'s bog man (*p102*).

... or for the (post)modern
Tate Modern (*p79*); **2 Willow Road** (*p150*); **Canary Wharf** (*p33*); **Swiss Re Tower** (*p28*).

For going underground...
The tube simulator at **London's Transport Museum** (*p122*); **Cabinet War Rooms** (*p132*); the crypt at **St Paul's Cathedral** (*p89*).

... or for going overground
British Airways London Eye (*p72*); **Primrose Hill** (*p146*); the **Monument** (*p94*).

Greenwich. *See p168.*

Original London Sightseeing Tour
8877 1722/www.theoriginaltour.com. **Departures**
Summer 9am-7pm daily. *Winter* 9.30am-5pm daily.
Pick-up Victoria Street; Marble Arch (Speakers'
Corner); Baker Street tube (forecourt); Coventry
Street; Embankment station; Trafalgar Square.
Fares £15; £7.50 concessions; £1 discount if
booked online. **Credit** MC, V.

Helicopter tours
Cabair Helicopters *Elstree Aerodrome,
Borehamwood, Hertfordshire WD6 3AW (8953
4411/www.cabair.com). Edgware tube/Elstree rail.*
Flights from 9.45am Sun. **Fares** £129. **Credit** MC,
V. **Map** p389.

Personal tours
Tour Guides *7495 5504/www.tourguides.co.uk.*
Tailor-made tours with Blue Badge guides for
individuals or groups, on foot, by car, coach or boat.

River tours
See p359.

Specialist tours
Gentle Journeys Garden Day Tours
*01935 815924/from USA 1-800 873 7145/
www.gentlejourneys.com.* **Departures** *May-Sept*
9am Tue-Thur, Sun (return approx 6.30pm).
Meeting point Victoria Coach Station.
Tickets £60/day.

Open House Architecture *39-51 Highgate Road,
NW5 (7267 7644/www.londonopenhouse.org).* Call
for details of tours and content. **Departures**
Summer 10.15am Sat; 10.45am Sun. *Winter* 10.15am
Sat. **Meeting point** in front of Royal Academy of
Arts, Piccadilly, W1 (Piccadilly Circus tube).
Duration 3hrs (& occasional one-day tours).
Tickets £18.50; £13 students; advance booking
advisable. **Credit** MC, V.

Taxi tours
Black Taxi Tours of London *7935 9363/
www.blacktaxitours.co.uk.* **Cost** £70.
A tailored two-hour tour for up to five people.

Walking tours
Arguably the best company running walks around
London is **Original London Walks** (7624 3978/
www.walks.com), which encompasses sorties on
everything from Sherlock Holmes to riverside pubs.

Other walks companies include **Citisights** (8806
4325/www.chr.org.uk/cswalks.htm), **Historical
Tours** (8668 4019/www.historicalwalksoflondon.
com) and **Stepping Out** (8881 2933). If you'd
prefer to do it yourself and at your own pace, the
excellent **Green Chain** walks connect a number of
green spaces in south-east London (8921 5028/
www.greenchain.com).

For more self-guided walks, see *Time Out London
Walks* volumes 1 and 2 (£9.99 and £11.99).

The South Bank & Bankside

Renovation, refurbishment, regeneration and other tales of the riverbank.

Maps p403, p406 & p407

To any local or visitor with two eyes and a modicum of common sense, it should be obvious that central London's greatest natural asset is the river that runs through it. Quite why it took the planning authorities so long to catch on, then, is a mystery. But catch on they eventually did. The Royal Festival Hall was built here for the Festival of Britain in 1951, and other arts venues – two more concert halls, a three-auditorium theatre complex, a cinema and a gallery – developed around it. But it's only been in the last half-decade that London's South Bank has grown into the status that it should have gained decades ago.

The stretch of river from Lambeth Bridge to Tower Bridge is now London's most approachable area. The arts venues still stand (more's the pity, in the case of the brutally unattractive buildings housing the Hayward Gallery and the Queen Elizabeth Hall), but around them have grown a welter of new attractions, some tilted squarely at visitors, others appealing chiefly to locals. To the west sits the **London Eye** (*see p72*) and the regenerated County Hall (*see p73* **Hall or nothing**). Further east are the all-conquering **Tate Modern** (*see p79*), the rebuilt **Globe Theatre** (standing as a reminder that even 400 years ago, the river was a cultural hotbed; *see p78*) and the glossy **Vinopolis** (*see p81*). All around sit flats and apartments worth at least five times what they would have sold for in the mid 1990s. There's a buzz here.

And yet, even without any of these glamorous new attractions, the pedestrian-friendly and car-free South Bank would still be a lovely place to come, if only for a walk. On summer mornings, the sun bouncing off the water and connecting with the buildings opposite gives the lie to the popular cliché of London as a grey city. At night in winter, when the air is crisp and fresh, it's as romantic as this matter-of-fact city ever gets. Be jealous of the lucky bleeders who live around here, whether in expensive loft apartments or in the pleasingly high number of community housing projects.

Lambeth Bridge to Hungerford Bridge

Embankment or Westminster tube/Waterloo tube/rail.

Just north of Lambeth Bridge huddle the red-brick buildings of **Lambeth Palace**, official residence of the Archbishops of Canterbury since the 12th century. It's closed to the public except for the occasional fête in the grounds and for London Open House (*see p267*). Next door is the **Museum of Garden History** (*see p75*) in the old church of St Mary-at-Lambeth. St Thomas's Hospital, containing the **Florence Nightingale Museum** (*see p72*), stands on one side of Westminster Bridge, but the dominant presence is the looming bulk of the

Museum of Garden History. *See p75*.

revamped **County Hall** and its myriad attractions both good and bad (*see p73* **Hall or nothing**). Outside it sits the stunning **British Airways London Eye** (aka the Millennium Wheel; *see below*), close by the not-so-stunning Jubilee Gardens.

The stretch between the London Eye and Hungerford Bridge will – touch wood – eventually be home to the BFI's **Film Centre**, a five-screen replacement for the current National Film Theatre (*see p286*). David Chipperfield, the designer responsible for the branch of the Wagamama (*see p199*) chain in Lexington Street, Soho, was awarded the commission in August 2001. However, an announcement in October 2002 that the new building would not, as planned, house a replacement for the much-loved but defunct Museum of the Moving Image caused a great deal of controversy. And in any case, it's still by no means certain that the plan will go ahead, much less that it will meet its proposed completion date of 2007.

British Airways London Eye

Riverside Building, next to County Hall, Westminster Bridge Road, SE1 (0870 500 0600/customer services 7654 0828/www.ba-londoneye.com). Westminster tube/Waterloo tube/rail. **Open** *Oct-Apr* 9.30am-8pm daily. *May-Sept* 9.30am-10pm daily. **Admission** £10.50; £8.50 concessions; £5 5-15s; free under-5s. **Credit** AmEx, MC, V. **Map** p401 M8.

After construction problems and an aborted opening due to safety concerns, this 450ft (137m) monster wheel has won its place in the hearts of Londoners and visitors. Indeed, so loved is the Eye that Lambeth council recently extended its lease by 20 years: it was originally planned to be only a temporary structure, hauled up for five years in celebration of the millennium.

The views from it are unparalleled in a city in which more or less the tall buildings that have in the past provided the public with views over London have been closed due to terrorism fears. You'll need to book in advance if you want to ensure a ride, especially at weekends and in school holidays; a particular drag given the laboriousness of the phone booking system. And despite the timed ticketing, the queues can be deeply irritating. But all will be forgotten when you finally clamber aboard one of the 32 capsules (each of which holds 25 people) for a 30-minute ride affording views of up to 25 miles (40kms) on clear days. Oh, and don't forget your camera: sure, it sounds obvious, but you'd be amazed how many people end up kicking themselves five minutes into the journey.

Dalí Universe

County Hall, Riverside Building, Queen's Walk, SE1 (7620 2720/www.daliuniverse.com). Waterloo tube/rail. **Open** 10am-5.30pm daily. **Admission** £8.50; £7.50 concessions; £4.95 10-16s; free under-10s. **Credit** AmEx, DC, MC, V. **Map** p401 M8.

This exhibition devoted to the extravagantly moustachioed Surrealist and expert self-publicist will barely take a half-hour: most of the artist's pieces are to be found at a museum in the Spanish town of Figueras, where Dalí was born. Still, it's time reasonably well spent. The wall mounted quotes by, and (silent) videos and photographs of, Dalí do well at introducing the extent of the artist's eccentricity, but stop short of filling in the details (perhaps so that you buy the £17.50 souvenir book on sale at the end). The exhibition itself includes over 500 pieces of painting and sculpture, grouped into the three concepts that most influenced Dalí's life: the hyper-surreal 'Dreams and Fantasy', where his oil painting *Spellbound*, created for the Hitchcock film of the same name, makes an appearance; the exotic and indulgent 'Femininity and Sensuality', which fetures the famous 'Mae West Lips' sofa; and the more thought-provoking 'Religion and Mythology', including an interesting series of Bible scenes by the atheist turned Catholic. The souvenir shop sells mainly prints, starting at around £600 a piece.

Florence Nightingale Museum

St Thomas's Hospital, 2 Lambeth Palace Road, SE1 (7620 0374/www.florence-nightingale.co.uk). Westminster tube/Waterloo tube/rail. **Open** 10am-5pm Mon-Fri (last entry 4pm); 11.30am-4.30pm Sat, Sun (last entry 3.30pm). **Admission** £4.80; £3.60 concession, 5-18s; free under-5s; £12 family. **Credit** AmEx, MC, V. **Map** p401 M9.

The brand new **Hungerford Bridge**. *See p75.*

Hall or nothing

As you're waiting in the queue for a trip up above the Thames on the London Eye, be sure to cast a glance to your left at the former seat of London government: **County Hall**. The London County Council was based there from 1922 until 1965, when the Greater London Council took over. Then, in 1986, the GLC was abolished by Margaret Thatcher's Conservative government, after a series of rows over how the high taxes of London's wealthy suburban population were being used to subsidise what were called 'Loony Left' schemes to benefit those on lower incomes in deprived areas of the city. The building seems proud of this political history: large golden letters still display the LCC/GLC dates on the side of County Hall facing the Houses of Parliament.

Since the GLC left, County Hall has undergone something of a personality crisis. For the first seven years it lay empty, then in 1993 it was bought by Japanese company Shiriyama Shokisan. Since then, portions of the building have been sold off piecemeal. The finest rooms and most scenic river views are now owned by the upmarket Marriott Hotel, which offers them to the well-heeled for between £150 and £800 a night. Around the back, you can stay in the considerably more austere Travel Inn on Belvedere Road for a more reasonable £80 with views of very little.

The 750-foot (229-metre) walkway between County Hall and the river features signs advising that 'the selling of merchandise is strictly prohibited'. However, the signs are hard to see behind the multitude of hot dog stands and souvenir stalls flogging their wares. This side of the building also provides a bizarre mishmash of attractions. The London Aquarium (*see p75*), with its tanks of gently gawping marine life, is flanked by the truly hideous Namco Station, which promises 'three floors of fun' and delivers three floors of bumper cars, bowling and burgers. Above it you'll find Flex'n'Fly, a bungee-cum-trampoline contraption around which bored parents gaze up at their screaming, bouncing youngsters, secretly hoping that the ropes will snap and send them sailing over County Hall. There's also a Chinese restaurant, a fitness centre, an empty room where the Football Hall of Fame briefly stood, the incongruous Dalí Universe (*see p72*), the offices of the Diana, Princess of Wales Memorial Fund and, from 2003, Charles Saatchi's new gallery of modern art (*see p75*).

The GLC was said to have failed because it couldn't be all things to all Londoners. The owners of County Hall seem to be trying, in this respect at least, to do what the GLC could not. Which means we're left with a magnificent, historic building that no longer has a clue what it's for.

Let us
on your
imaginary
forces work

Shakespeare's Globe
Bankside ~ London
Theatre Tour and Exhibition
TEL: 020 7902 1500   FAX: 020 7902 1515
www.shakespeares-globe.org   Bankside Marketing Group

A small museum with well-thought-out displays of personal mementoes, clothing, furniture, books, letters and portraits belonging to the famous nurse and social campaigner, as well as Crimean War relics and nursing materials. It was at St Thomas's that Nightingale set up the first nursing school in 1859. See the website or call for details of tours, talks, temporary exhibitions and children's events.

London Aquarium

County Hall, Riverside Building, Westminster Bridge Road, SE1 (7967 8000/tours 7967 8007/ www.londonaquarium.co.uk). Westminster tube/ Waterloo tube/rail. **Open** 10am-6pm daily (last entry 5pm). **Admission** £8.75; £6.50 concessions; £5.25 3-14s; £3.50 disabled; free under-3s; £25 family. **Credit** MC, V. **Map** p401 M9.

Assuming you can shut out the sound of screaming kids, there's something very calming about watching a school of fish swim in circles at this County Hall attraction. It's also rather fascinating seeing how ugly some of them are (the fish, not the kids). This is made possible by the fact that, as the name suggests, you'll be looking through the glass walls of extra-large fish tanks at a range of fish, from bright and beautiful yellow tangs to the rather small and ill-looking shark that flicks his eyes when he swims. Organised by geographical origin, there are explanatory notes beside each aquarium, but this is a place best appreciated by kids, who can gawk at – and, in the case of the rays, even touch – a wide range of water dwellers. If you want to avoid falling over little people in the dark, come outside of school holidays and avoid weekends.

Museum of Garden History

Church of St Mary-at-Lambeth, Lambeth Palace Road, SE1 (7401 8865/www.museumgardenhistory. org). Waterloo tube/rail/C10, 507 bus. **Open** Feb-mid-Dec 10.30am-5pm daily. **Admission** free. *Suggested donation* £2.50; £2. **Credit** AmEx, MC, V. **Map** p401 L10.

This cosy, enthusiastically run museum illustrates the development of the English passion for gardening, primarily through a selection of antique horticultural tools and photographic panels on famous garden designers and plant hunters. The tireless John Tradescant, gardener to James I and Charles I, is given particular prominence. A replica of a 17th-century knot garden has been created, using geometric shapes based on squares and whole or partial circles that incorporate the letter 'T' for Tradescant into four symmetrical positions. It also contains several dramatic examples of topiary. In the graveyard, one of the sarcophagi contains the remains of Captain Bligh, abandoned in the Pacific by his mutinous crew aboard HMS *Bounty*.

Saatchi Gallery

County Hall, Riverside Building, Westminster Bridge Road, SE1 (7823 2363). Westminster tube/ Waterloo tube/rail. **Open** *From Spring 2003* 10am-10pm daily. **Admission** phone for details. **Credit** phone for details. **Map** p401 M9.

If any one man can be said to have been responsible for the boom in modern British art over the last decade, it's Charles Saatchi. The advertising mogul and inveterate collector accumulated a who's who of Young British Artists in the 1990s; indeed, a Saatchi seal of approval became enough to catapult a young unknown into the big leagues almost overnight. Saatchi's moving his gallery from north London to County Hall this spring (the exact opening date was unconfirmed in late 2002), just a mile from Tate Modern. On display will be a permanent collection of Saatchi's holdings from the likes of Damien Hirst, Chris Ofili, Tracey Emin and Sarah Lucas, plus a series of temporary exhibits.

Hungerford Bridge to Blackfriars Bridge

Embankment or Temple tube/Blackfriars or Waterloo tube/rail.

Since its inception, the **South Bank Centre** arts complex (*see p304*) has represented London at its most self-consciously modern. The squat concrete mass of Sir Leslie Martin's **Royal Festival Hall** – built for the Festival of Britain as a showcase for the architectural and building skills of the time and dubbed the 'people's palace' – has been hailed as a triumph of democratic public design. However, it would be fair to say that none of the buildings along this stretch – with the possible exception of the striking new Hungerford Bridge (*see p78* **Many bridges to cross**) – is universally admired.

Things are changing, however, under a masterplan by architect Rick Mather. The long-term renovation of the Festival Hall began several years ago, but work scheduled for the next few years will bring better acoustics, the reinstatement of the original recital space, the restoration of the roof garden, new bars, cafés and backstage areas, a new staff office building, a dedicated education centre and an expanded Poetry Library. The work is scheduled for completion in 2006, but don't hold your breath.

The **Hayward Gallery** (*see p76*) sits next door to the Royal Festival Hall and its sibling venues the Queen Elizabeth Hall and the Purcell Room. A few admire it as an elegant modern building, but most see it for what it is: a brutalist concrete eyesore. The 48-foot (15-metre) Neon Tower that tops the building was designed by Phillip Vaughan and Roger Dainton, and celebrated its 30th birthday last year. No one sent it any cards. Assuming funding comes through as hoped – a decision was due to be taken by the Arts Council at the end of 2002 – the building will be closed for most of 2003 to allow for an extension, designed by Dan Graham, to be built atop the foyer, plus a new entrance and a new café.

Sightseeing

Further along the river sit two more cultural venues. The National Film Theatre enjoys – or, perhaps, endures – a rather grim location underneath Waterloo Bridge; arguably, it'll be the greatest beneficiary of Mather's plan for the South Bank redevelopment if it all goes ahead. And next door sits Sir Denys Lasdun's **Royal National Theatre** (*see p333*), whose recent programme of renovations (separate from the Mather scheme) transformed the Lyttelton Theatre and brought an array of new work into the cosy 100-seat Loft space.

Further east along the river, the beautifully restored **Oxo Tower Wharf** began life at the start of the 20th century as a power station for the Post Office before being bought by Oxo (who produced Oxo cubes and long eggs for pork pies here). The company incorporated its name into the design of the art deco tower to circumvent council rules against large-scale advertising. The building was earmarked for demolition in the 1970s, but local residents formed the non-profit-making Coin Street Community Builders to save it. In 1984 it purchased the tower and the swathe of derelict land between the tower and Waterloo Bridge and transformed it into a place to live, work and visit. The tower now contains flats, small crafts shops/workshops and a restaurant (*see p191*) with great views. On the ground floor there's an exhibition about the regeneration of the area (future plans include a floating Thames Lido, the 'Hothouse' community training and leisure centre and further co-operative homes).

Coin Street Builders also maintains the contrived **Gabriel's Wharf** (which, with its schmaltzy crafts shops and restaurants, is the only jarring point on the South Bank), and organises the annual Coin Street Festival, London's biggest free arts festival (*see p263*).

Hayward Gallery

Belvedere Road, SE1 (box office 7960 4242/ www.hayward.org.uk). Embankment tube/Charing Cross or Waterloo tube/rail. **Open** *During exhibitions* 10am-6pm Mon, Thur-Sun; 10am-8pm Tue, Wed. **Admission** varies. **Credit** AmEx, DC, MC, V. **Map** p401 M8.

One of London's finest venues for contemporary and historical art, partly because of the flexibility of its space, the Hayward can usually be counted on for an intriguing programme. After film artist Douglas Gordon's show finishes in January 2003, the gallery is hoping to close for redevelopment (*see p75*). Assuming this is the case, it will be reopening on 23 October with a blockbuster celebration of the centenary of the National Art Collections Fund, showing a wide range of works from public collections across the country. Assuming it isn't the case… well, it's anyone's guess. But there will definitely be exhibitions taking place: phone or check online for details.

Around Waterloo

Waterloo tube/rail.

A walkway links the Royal Festival Hall to **Waterloo Station**, where Eurostar trains arrive and depart from under Nicholas Grimshaw's glorious glass-roofed terminus. The roundabout outside Waterloo Station once provided shelter for some of London's lost souls, but since 1999 the £20 million **BFI London IMAX Cinema** (*see p287*) has occupied the site. Behind the station on the other side, **Lower Marsh** has a lively market on weekdays and contains a branch of the excellent Konditor & Cook café (*see p191*). It leads on to the Cut, home of the Young Vic theatre (*see p338*).

For a less savoury aspect of Waterloo, see the surviving entrance to the **London Necropolis Railway** at 121 Westminster Bridge Road. From 1854, after rapid population growth and cholera epidemics caused overcrowding in city cemeteries, this small station ferried coffins and funeral parties to a cemetery set up by the London Necropolis and National Mausoleum Company in Brookwood, Woking. The station was bombed in 1941 and never rebuilt.

Bankside

Borough or Southwark tube/London Bridge tube/rail.

With theatres, bear-baiting pits, bawdy houses and inns, the area between Blackfriars Bridge and London Bridge, known as **Bankside**, was London's pleasure zone for centuries. Far from condemning this depravity, the Church made a tidy sum from its regulation – it even controlled the local brothels – and if anyone got too unruly they could always be cast into the dank depths of the Clink Prison (now the **Clink Prison Museum**; *see p77*). Next door are the remains of **Winchester Palace**, though little is left beyond the rose window of the Great Hall.

Like Battersea Power Station upriver, Bankside Power Station was designed by Sir Giles Gilbert Scott; remodelled by Swiss architects Herzog and de Meuron, it makes a magnificent home for **Tate Modern** (*see p79*). Tiny in comparison, and a reminder of the Bankside of old, is its neighbour, the reconstructed **Shakespeare's Globe** (*see p78*). In its shadow is another old playhouse, the **Rose Theatre** (*see p78*), and next door is a ramshackle terrace containing the house in which Catherine of Aragon, the first wife of Henry VIII, took shelter on arriving in London in 1502, and where Christopher Wren is said to have lived during the construction of St Paul's. Further back from the river, Southwark Street is home to the **Bramah Museum of Tea and**

Tate Modern, one of London's major success stories of recent years. *See p79.*

Coffee (*see below*). St Paul's is now linked to Bankside – and, specifically, the Tate Modern – by Norman Foster's **Millennium Bridge** (*see p78* **Many bridges to cross**); further east is **Southwark Cathedral** (*see p78*).

Details of sights and attractions in the Bankside and Borough areas can be found at the **Southwark Information Centre** opposite London Bridge Station (6 Tooley Street; 7403 8299; 10am-6pm Mon-Sat, 10am-5.30pm Sun; closes 4pm Nov-Mar).

Bramah Museum of Tea & Coffee

40 Southwark Street, SE1 (7231 6197/ www.bramahmuseum.co.uk). London Bridge tube/rail. **Open** 10am-6pm daily. **Admission** £4; £3.50 concessions. **Credit** AmEx, DC, MC, V. **Map** p405 S9.

Former tea taster Edward Bramah set up this museum in the early 1990s to chart the history of tea and coffee drinking. In 2001 he moved away from Butler's Wharf, frustrated by the disinclination to put up signs there, and now he's further along the river towards Bankside. The displays document the role of tea and coffee in British society.

Clink Prison Museum

1 Clink Street, SE1 (7378 1558/www.clink.co.uk). London Bridge tube/rail. July-Sept 10am-6pm daily. *July-Sept* 10am-9pm daily. *Tours* hourly. **Admission** £4; £3 concessions, 5-15s; £9 family. *Tours* £1 extra. **Credit** AmEx, MC, V. **Map** p404 P8.

The private prison of the successive Bishops of Winchester, the Clink housed prostitutes, drunks, actors and other reprobates between the 12th and 16th centuries. Given this fascinating history, it's a shame that the exhibition devoted to it is a little shoddy. The few re-creations of prison scenes have seen better days, while the explanatory notes and displays are rather unilluminating.

Golden Hinde

St Mary Overie Dock, Cathedral Street, SE1 (0870 011 8700/www.goldenhinde.co.uk). Monument tube/London Bridge tube/rail. **Open** daily, times vary. **Admission** £2.75; £2.35 concessions; £2 4-13s; free under-4s; £8 family. **Credit** MC, V. **Map** p404 P8.

This full-size reconstruction of Sir Francis Drake's 16th-century flagship is impressively shipshape considering the quarter-century it's spent circumnavigating the world as a seaborne museum. The five levels have been recreated in minute detail (the diminutive proportions of the 14-cannon gun deck and hold feel painfully real), and the kid-friendly atmosphere on board is fleshed out by 'crew' in Elizabethan costume (kids' parties can be catered for with advance notice). There are separate 'Living History Experiences' (some overnight) in which participants dress in period clothes, eat Tudor fare and learn the skills of the Elizabethan seafarer.

HMS Belfast

Morgan's Lane, Tooley Street, SE1 (7940 6328/ www.iwm.org.uk). London Bridge tube/rail. **Open** *Mar-Oct* 10am-6pm daily (last entry 5.15pm). *Nov-Feb* 10am-5pm daily (last entry 4.15pm). **Admission** £5.80; £4.40 concessions; free under-16s (must be accompanied by an adult). **Credit** MC, V. **Map** p405 R8.

This 11,500-ton battlecruiser was built in 1938 and played a leading role in the Normandy Landings and supported UN forces in Korea before being decommissioned in 1965. Kids love exploring its seven decks, boiler and engine rooms and massive gun turrets. Call for details of Family Learning Weekends or to find out how to organise a children's party here.

Rose Theatre

56 Park Street, SE1 (7902 1500/www.rosetheatre. org.uk/www.shakespeares-globe.org). London Bridge tube/rail. **Open** by appointment for groups of 15+; phone for details. **Admission** £9.50; £8 concessions; £7.50 5-15s. **Credit** AmEx, MC, V. **Map** p404 P8.

Everyone has heard of the Globe (*see below*), but until excavations carried out by Museum of London archaeologists in 1989, few knew of the Rose. In fact, the theatre – built by Philip Henslowe and operational from 1587 until 1606; what the Globe is to Shakespeare, the Rose is to Christopher Marlowe – was the first playhouse to be built at Bankside; without it, the Globe would have ended up somewhere else, if it had been built at all. Long term, the Rose Theatre Trust hopes to fully excavate the site; in the meantime, it's being looked after by the folks at Shakespeare's Globe. Currently, only groups of 15 or more can book guided tours, though it's possible that regular weekend opening hours may be put in place during 2003; call or check online for details.

Shakespeare's Globe

21 New Globe Walk, Bankside, SE1 (7902 1500/ www.shakespeares-globe.org). Mansion House or Southwark tube/London Bridge tube/rail. **Open**

Tours & exhibitions May-Sept 9am-12.30pm daily. Oct-Apr 10am-5pm daily. Tours: late Sept-mid May half-hourly; 10am-5pm daily. Virtual (videoscreen) tours: mid May-late Sept 12.30-5pm Tue-Sun. **Admission** *Late Sept-mid May* £8; £6.50 concessions; £5.50 5-15s; free under-5s; £24 family. *Mid May-late Sept* £5; £4 concessions; £3.50 5-16s; free under-5s. **Credit** AmEx, MC, V. **Map** p404 O7.

The original Globe Theatre, where many of William Shakespeare's plays were first staged and which he co-owned, burned down in 1613 during a performance of *Henry VIII*. Nearly 400 years later, it was rebuilt not far from its original site under the auspices of actor Sam Wanamaker (who, sadly, didn't live to see it up and running), using construction methods and materials as close to the originals as possible. You can't help but feel that Shakespeare would be pleased with the reconstruction, which includes an impressive exhibition of memorabilia related to famous performances of his works. The centrepiece is a guided tour of the theatre itself; note that there are none in the afternoon from May to September, when historically authentic (and frequently very good) performances are staged (*see p333*). However, during this period, visitors still have access to the exhibition.

Southwark Cathedral

Montague Close, SE1 (7367 6700/tours 7367 6734/ www.dswark.org/cathedral). London Bridge tube/rail. **Open** 8am-6pm daily (closing times vary on religious holidays). *Services* 8am, 8.15am, 12.30pm, 12.45pm, 5.30pm Mon-Fri; 9am, 9.15am, 4pm Sat; 8.45am, 9am, 11am, 3pm, 6.30pm Sun. *Choral*

Many bridges to cross

Between Battersea Power Station and the Tower of London, there are 15 bridges spanning the River Thames. Some of the capital's finest views are to be seen while strolling across them. And, happily, strolling across the Thames has been made far more pleasurable by the addition of two pedestrian-only bridges, with another one in advanced planning stages.

The **Millennium Bridge** opened in the summer of 2000 as the first dedicated pedestrian bridge across the Thames. It then shut immediately in farcical circumstances, with the public blamed by the architects for walking in step with each other and causing the bridge to sway alarmingly from side to side. Some 18 months and £5 million of repairs later, it now carries flocks of tourists from St Paul's to the new London attractions of Tate Modern and the Globe Theatre. It's a sleek and slinky spectacle: nicknamed the Blade of Light because of its fibre-optic

enhanced sci-fi appearance at night, its only downside appears to be the alarming translucence of the walkway, which has led to clusters of teenage boys idly lingering underneath the southern end of the bridge and casually waiting for skirt-wearing girls to walk across above them.

The recently completed pedestrian crossings either side of the **Hungerford Railway Bridge** connect Charing Cross and the West End with the South Bank Centre. Anyone who made the trip in the mid 1990s will recall gingerly making their way down a series of planks attached by rusty bolts to a rusty iron frame. Despite the great views from it looking east down the Thames, it was the most hideous of the river's crossing points.

The new structure has been constructed with the purpose of completely obliterating the sight of the dilapidated railway bridge, which it does very successfully. It's sensitively lit at night in a way IKEA would

Evensong 5.30pm Tue, Fri, Sun (boys); 5.30pm
Thur (girls). **Admission** *Exhibition* £3; £2.50
concessions; £1.50 5-16s; free under-5s; £12.50
family. **Credit** AmEx, MC, V. **Map** p404 P8.
Originally the monastic church of St Mary Overie,
this building became an Anglican cathedral in 1905.
The first church on the site may date from as early
as the seventh century; the oldest parts of the present building are still more than 800 years old,
including the Retro-Choir, where the trials of several Protestant martyrs took place during the reign
of Mary Tudor.

After the Reformation, the church fell into disre-
pair and parts of it became a bakery and a pigsty.
These days, especially with the recent addition of a
visitors' centre that boasts state-of-the-art displays
on Southwark past and present and on London in
general, it's all looking rather splendid. Among its
treasures are the Stone Corpse, a grim 15th-century
effigy of an emaciated cadaver in a shroud; a bronze
of Shakespeare (whose brother Edmund was buried
in an unknown grave here in 1607 but is commemorated in a stone in the choir); and a tablet to Sam
Wanamaker, who oversaw the reconstruction of
Shakespeare's Globe (*see p78*). Outside, the lovely
lavender-scented grounds are packed with local
workers on sunny lunchtimes.

Tate Modern

*Bankside, SE1 (7887 8000/www.tate.org.uk).
Blackfriars tube.* **Open** 10am-6pm Mon-Thur, Sun;
10am-10pm Fri, Sat. *Tours* 11am, noon, 2pm, 3pm
daily. **Admission** free. *Temporary exhibitions*
prices vary. **Map** p401 O7.

That the most ambitious of London's millennial projects – build an accessible museum of contemporary
art in a gargantuan, long-deserted power station –
has received a measure of criticism from London's
famously self-regarding modern art establishment
is one of only many reasons to love it. And many do:
visitor numbers at Tate Modern since its 2000 opening have been beyond anyone's expectations, and
show few signs of slowing down.

The aforementioned criticism has been largely a
result of director Nicholas Serota's decision to organise the works thematically rather than chronologically: galleries come with titles such as History/
Memory/Society and Still Life/Object/Real Life. It's
a brave way to display art, and one that would work
in very few galleries. But it works here brilliantly,
drawing the viewer closer to the often challenging
works and setting them in a broader perspective
than would otherwise be the case. The gallery makes
the art more approachable to the casual viewer
without cheapening the former or patronising the
latter; and if that's not the point of an operation such
as this, then we don't know what is.

For six months of the year the vast Turbine Hall
hosts works from the Unilever Series of commissions; Anish Kapoor's *Marsyas*, a gigantic PVC
membrane, will be there until 6 April 2003. Other
temporary exhibitions this year include a retrospective of German painter Max Beckman (13
Feb-5 May) and a show of pieces by Sigmar Polke
entitled Printing Mistakes (from Oct). Guided tours
of the gallery are available, and both the restaurants
(*see p191*) and shop are fabulous.

be proud of, its white pylons complimenting
the nearby London Eye beautifully.

The proposed **Jubilee Bridge**, which will
distract attention from the nasty Alexandra
Bridge carrying trains south out of Cannon
Street Station, will be the only covered
bridge across the river, a futuristic tube-like
structure running alongside the existing
railway. On the face of it, it will have none of
the obvious functionality of its two sisters
further upstream, with no major tourist
attractions either north or south of the bridge
(the planned expansion of Borough Market at
Bankside may prove to be a draw, but that's
about it), and would seem mainly to be a
boon for the lazy City worker. Not only are
Southwark and London Bridges only a mere
two-minute walk away, but, should they
choose to use the new crossing, lifts are
planned to transport them up to bridge level.
There's no completion date for the bridge;
for more, see www.jubileebridgelondon.com.

Vinopolis, City of Wine

*1 Bank End, SE1 (0870 241 4040/
www.vinopolis.co.uk). London Bridge tube/rail.*
Open noon-9pm Mon, Fri, Sat; noon-6pm Tue-Thur,
Sun (last entry 2hrs before closing). **Admission**
£11.50; £5 5-14s; £10.50 concessions. *Art exhibition
only* £3. **Credit** AmEx, MC, V. **Map** p404 P8.
A visit to Vinopolis is a rather quiet and staid experience. The atmosphere isn't helped by the fact that
the exhibits are rendered useless without the audio
guide, so if you get fed up with Oz Clarke's ramblings,
you'll find yourself wandering among a bunch
of mysterious pictures with a herd of deadly silent
viewers. Exhibits are set up by country, with five
opportunities to taste wine from different regions.
Most of the displays are in the form of photographs
and videos, though there are some interesting artefacts at the beginning (such as ancient vine cuttings
encased in silver that were dug out of tombs). And if,
after a couple of tastings, you want a bit of fun, try
the virtual Vespa trip through a Chianti vineyard, or
the plane tour to the far reaches of Australia. Extras
include a a wine shop, a restaurant, a cheese counter
and tasting courses.

Borough

Borough or Southwark tube/London Bridge tube/rail.

Borough has a whole host of Dickensian
associations. The **George** pub, London's only
surviving galleried inn, is mentioned in *Little
Dorrit*, as is **St George-the-Martyr** church
(on the corner of Borough High Street and Long
Lane). **White Hart Yard** housed the White
Hart Inn, where Mr Pickwick meets Sam Weller
in *The Pickwick Papers* (it was pulled down
in 1889), and Little Dorrit herself is born in
Marshalsea Prison, which used to stand a
few doors away and in which Dickens' father
was jailed for debt in 1824. Another literary
landmark, the Tabard Inn where Chaucer's
pilgrims meet at the start of *The Canterbury
Tales*, used to stand in **Talbot Yard**.

Borough as a whole is enjoying something
of a renaissance after a long lull. Until 1750,
London Bridge was the only crossing point
into the City, and **Borough High Street**
became a stagecoach terminus. The 17th-
century poet Thomas Dekker described it as
'a continued ale house with not a shop to be
seen between'. Raucous Southwark Fair was
held here from 1462 until its suppression by
the spoilsport Corporation of London in 1763.

These days, the High Street is thriving again,
with old caffs, pubs and shops alongside
aromatic modern Turkish restaurants and bar
chains such as the Slug & Lettuce. But the
area's modern *succès fou* has been **Borough
Market**, which, having hosted fruit and
vegetable stalls since the 13th century, has been
given a new lease of life by the Friday and

Saturday gourmet food markets held here (*see
also p256*). For a while there have been fears
that the beautiful covered market building
and unique surrounding streets, little touched
this century and long popular for film sets
(it's here that a certain singleton can be seen
entertaining, shopping and romancing in
Bridget Jones's Diary), may be lost to a rail
improvement scheme. A definite decision has
still not been made, but while it looks hopeful
that the market will remain in some form, the
future of the surrounding streets is by no means
assured. Keep up to date on the scheme at
www.save-borough-market-area.org.uk.

Several attractions are clustered around
London Bridge Station: the **Old Operating
Theatre, Museum & Herb Garret** (*see
p82*), the gory **London Dungeon** (*see p81*)
and **Winston Churchill's Britain at War
Experience** (*see p82*). Architecture buffs
should visit the **Cromwell Buildings** at
Redcross Way. This striking colonial-looking
block, with its ironwork and plant-filled
verandas, is a historically significant example
of the low-cost housing for which this area is
renowned. Modelled after a pair of houses
designed by the Prince Regent for the Great
Exhibition of 1851, it was constructed in 1864 by
Sir Sydney Waterlow, who the previous founded
the Improved Industrial Dwellings Company,
one of the earliest providers of low-cost housing.
In 1889 he donated Waterlow Park, part of his
own estate, to the public; *see p147*.

London Dungeon

*28-34 Tooley Street, SE1 (7403 7221/
www.thedungeons.com). London Bridge tube/rail.*
Open *Oct-mid Mar* 10.30am-6pm daily. *Mid Mar-
mid July* 10am-5.30pm daily. *Sept-Nov* 10am-5.30pm
daily. *Mid July-early Sept* 9.30am-7.30pm daily.
Admission £10.95; £9.50 students; £6.95 5-14s,
concessions; free under-5s. **Credit** AmEx, MC, V.
Map p405 Q8.
Venture through the doors of the London Dungeon,
and you are immediately and atmospherically transported into a ghoulish world of disease, death and
torture. Blood-stained faces appear out of the shadows, guts spewing from their stomachs or projectile
vomit from their mouths. It is quite disgusting. The
constant hum of screams and moans adds to the fear
that every time you turn a corner you expect some
frightener to jump out brandishing a big medieval
nutcracker (and that's not for the type you eat).

The Wicked Women section follows the big, bad
names in history, such as Boudicca, Anne Boleyn,
Queen Elizabeth I and, er, Anne Robinson. Be prepared for the jailed skeleton who comes to life (and
be prepared for the screams it provokes). If you can
hack the queues, the torture chambers, where actors
demonstrate techniques to lucky participants, make
for an entertaining diversion.

Heads up! **London Dungeon**. *See p81.*

London Fire Brigade

94A Southwark Bridge Road, SE1 (7587 2894/ www.london-fire.gov.uk). Borough tube. **Open** 10.30am, 2pm Mon-Fri by appointment only. **Admission** £3; £2 7-14s, concessions; free under-7s. **Credit** MC, V. **Map** p404 O9.

This small museum traces the history of firefighting from the Great Fire of London in 1666 to the present. Exhibits include old firefighting appliances. All visitors have to pre-book on guided tours, which are tailored to different needs.

Old Operating Theatre, Museum & Herb Garret

9A St Thomas's Street, SE1 (7955 4791/ www.thegarret.org.uk). London Bridge tube/rail. **Open** 10.30am-5pm daily (last entry 4.45pm). **Admission** £3.75; £2.75 concessions; £2.25 6-16s; free under-6s. **No credit cards. Map** p405 Q8.

A relic of the days when the cure for an ingrowing toenail was amputation and when bodysnatching gangs such as the 'Borough Boys' roamed the area, the Old Operating Theatre, rediscovered in 1956, is the oldest surviving part of the original St Thomas's Hospital. Set, atmospherically, in the roof of an old medieval church (which was adjacent to the surgical ward and was extended into), it is accessed via a vertiginous wooden spiral staircase (sadly, there's no disabled access). Just inside is the pungent herb garret, where medicinal herbs were once stored and are now displayed again.

When you've marvelled at the labels describing the uses of eyebright, pennyroyal, heartease ('used in love charms and for diseases of the heart') and the like and the recipes against such ills as 'mental vacancy and folly', brace yourself for the operating theatre itself. Display cases include such delights as strangulated hernias, leech jars, wooden nipple shields, amputation knives, massive forceps and physicians' sticks used as biting gags. Photographs of the hospital, including the female ward (now occupied by Borough High Street post office), give a real sense of its history. Call for details of lectures and summer workshops for families and children.

Winston Churchill's Britain at War Experience

64-6 Tooley Street, SE1 (7403 3171/ www.britainatwar.co.uk). London Bridge tube/rail. **Open** *Apr-Sept* 10am-5.30pm (last entry 5pm) daily. *Oct-Mar* 10am-4.30pm daily (last entry 4pm). **Admission** £6.50; £4.50 concessions; £3.50 5-16s; £15 family; free under-5s. **Credit** AmEx, MC, V. **Map** p405 Q8.

Lots of fascinating memorabilia of London during the Blitz, including real bombs, rare documents and photos. However, the place is a bit shabby and homemade in feel. Topics covered include Army Girls and other 'women at war', and rationing. Children love the atmospheric reproductions of an Anderson shelter, a GI's club and a darkened bombsite.

Tower Bridge & Bermondsey

Bermondsey tube/London Bridge tube/rail.

The stretch of river from London Bridge to Tower Bridge is dominated by **HMS Belfast** (*see p77*), the soaring, glass-roofed Hay's Galleria (a former enclosed dock that's been turned into a tacky mall), and the new Norman Foster-designed GLA building (*see p27*). Mayor Livingstone and his crew moved into this vast glass ball in 2002. Inside, as you might expect, it's an impressive facility. But from the outside, it fails to convince. Granted, it looks quite striking from the other side of the river, from where you can't help but look at it head on. But from close up, especially from the sides or the rear, it's less impressive; it doesn't seem to have been built so much as dropped there by accident.

This is the start of **Bermondsey**, an area that was long a focus for Christianity – **Tooley Street** was once home to no fewer than three abbots, a prior and the church of St Olave's. Its near-namesake, **St Olaf House**, a fabulous art deco 1930s warehouse, is worth a look, as is the building that will house the **Zandra Rhodes Fashion & Textile Museum** (*see p83*).

East of the spectacular Tower Bridge (*see p95*), **Butler's Wharf** is home to a trio of Sir Terence Conran restaurants and the excellent **Design Museum** (*see p83*), which Conran, the man who did much to bring good household design to the ordinary punter, helped establish. The Conran company HQ itself is just round the corner, backing on to New Concordia Wharf.

Check out **St Saviour's Dock**, a muddy creek between towering warehouses, visible over a low parapet in Jamaica Road. This was a notorious haunt for pirates in the 18th century, who were hanged at its mouth. In Dickens' day, the streets around here formed a slum called Jacob's Island, where Bill Sikes gets his comeuppance in *Oliver Twist*. Indeed, much of the area still has a Dickensian feel to it.

But the times they are a-changing, and not all for the best. Though Bermondsey Square still has its superb antiques market, and though the old, listed warehouses are being sympathetically transformed into office blocks and posh flats whose names (the Vanilla & Sesame Building, Coriander Court, the Fennel Building) are evocative of their spice-storage days, much of the area is starting to feel a little fake, with its pristine cobbled streets, expensive art shops and twee delis, and the influx of chains such as Starbucks and All Bar One.

Up past the Design Museum, New Concordia Wharf is a calm marina-like backwater populated by swans and geese, with a gleaming new swing bridge in front of converted

GLA Building and **Tower Bridge**. *See p82.*

warehouses. Further up, past trendy offices affording glimpses of people hunched over laptops, is a lovely spot with old barges turned into floating gardens.

Design Museum

28 Shad Thames, SE1 (7403 6933/ www.designmuseum.org). Tower Hill tube/London Bridge tube/rail/15, 47, 188, 78, 100 bus. **Open** 10am-5.45pm Mon-Thur, Sat, Sun (last entry 5.15pm); 10am-9pm Fri (last entry 8.30pm). **Admission** £6; £4 concessions, 5-15s; free under-5s; £16 family. **Credit** AmEx, MC, V. **Map** p405 S9.

This white, 1930s-style building is a fine container for exhibitions devoted to design in all its forms. The Design Museum's main problem is (and has always been) lack of space: to counter this, director Alice Rawsthorn has dropped the permanent displays of 20th-century objects and current cutting-edge innovations to allow a more varied range of temporary shows. Exhibitions in 2003 cover the creations of shoe guru Manolo Blahnik (1 Feb-11 May), 1970s Italian group Superstudio (1 Mar-1 June), graphics supremo Peter Saville (23 May-14 Sept) and Dutch designer Hella Jongerius (5 July-12 Oct). The best European design projects, in all disciplines, of the past two years will feature in the European Design Biennial (23 Sept 2003-11 Jan 2004). The museum's own collection of 20th- and 21st-century items will appear in an annually changing series of themed displays; A Century of Chairs is on show until 12 Oct 2003. Outside, on the riverfront terrace, the small glass 'tank' will be used for a series of eight-week installations about living in a confined space.

The museum's main event for 2003 is the launch of a new national awards scheme covering all fields of design: Designer of the Year (to rival the Turner Prize for art and the Stirling Prize for architecture), with a purse of £25,000. Work by four candidates (nominated in Jan 2003) will be on show from 1 Mar to 29 June; the winner for 2002, chosen by the public and a jury of experts, will be announced in June.

Designed-out visitors can refresh themselves at the museum's very good ground-floor café run by Konditori & Cook, and tempting shop. Above the museum is the upmarket Blueprint Café (actually a restaurant) with a balcony overlooking the Thames.

Fashion & Textile Museum

83 Bermondsey Street, SE1 (7403 0222/ www.ftmlondon.org). London Bridge tube/rail. **Open** phone for details. **Admission** phone for details. **Map** p405 Q9.

This striking building in zany designer Zandra Rhodes's trademark colours of orange and pink is already a local landmark. It's scheduled to open in spring 2003 with an exhibition called 'My Favourite Dress', showcasing the creations of designers including John Galliano, Alexander McQueen and Christian Lacroix, after which time the museum will host three to four temporary exhibitions a year on fashion, textiles and photography alongside a permanent collection.

Sightseeing

The City

Money makes the world go round.

Maps p402-p405

This is real London. Everything around it and outside it is… well, not pretend. But certainly a latecomer to the party, and in many cases an uninvited guest at that.

London began here. Indeed, for many centuries, the area known as the City – an irregularly shaped square mile boundaried by Smithfield and Moorfields in the north, Tower Hill to the east, the Thames to the south and Temple Bar in the west – essentially *was* London. The Romans settled here in the first century AD, turning the place into a commercial hub. And though there were a few small settlements outside the City in the following years, it wasn't until the 17th century that any significant building activity occurred outside its boundaries.

Since then, London has expanded apace around the City, but the City has barely batted an eyelid. That's not to say it hasn't changed down the years, for it has. Over 13,000 houses were burned down in the Great Fire of 1666; barely half that many *people* live in the City today. Yet the area is still a world apart from its neighbours. Its ruling body, the Corporation of London, is arguably the most powerful local council in the country, and certainly the richest. And few areas anywhere in the world are as proud of its traditions as the City is, perhaps because few areas anywhere in the world have quite as many traditions of which to be proud.

Today, the City is dominated by the hifalutin' financial businesses that sit on every corner, driving the economies both of London and the country as a whole. Bankers and brokers, wide-boy dealers and bowler-hatted gents (nowhere near as commonplace as the stereotype has it, but there are still a few of them around); all turn the Square Mile into a heaving mass of activity between 8.30am and 6.30pm daily. But before the working day begins and as soon as it finally draws to a close, the City vanishes back into its shell. At night and on the weekend, there's no quieter corner of London than the one that, hours earlier, has been its noisiest.

It seems redundant to point out that London is a mixture of the old and the new; there's not a city on earth to which that particular cliché couldn't be applied. But nowhere in Britain do the ancient and the modern sit in such close proximity. You can almost hear the buildings arguing among themselves, jostling for superiority. At the moment, it seems as if the modern is winning out. Some of old London's most imposing buildings – the Monument chief among them – are being lost in a morass of new skyscrapers. Not demolished, certainly, but hemmed in and oppressed by glass and steel and the might of big business. Mind you, it's not the existence of such new buildings that's a problem; it's that with only a few exceptions – Richard Rogers' Lloyd's Building on Lime Street chief among them – they're either deeply ugly (the soon-to-be-completed Swiss Re Tower) or deeply bland (too many to mention).

No matter. Such 'progress' just makes looking for the history that much more of an adventure, each stumbled-upon discovery an exciting event. And there's plenty upon which to stumble. The City exists on its medieval streetplans, and away from the main drags, in the tiny passageways that thread between the grand old buildings, a real sense of dislocation can occur. Get lost for a while in the City's secret alleyways: the chances are you'll find a peaceful tavern, a half-forgotten church or a length of wall from ancient times waiting for you in the shadows.

City Information Centre

St Paul's Churchyard, EC4 (7332 1456/ www.cityoflondon.gov.uk). St Paul's tube. **Open** *Apr-Sept* 9.30am-5pm daily. *Oct-Mar* 9.30am-5pm Mon-Fri; 9.30am-12.30pm Sat. **Map** p404 O6. Information on sights, events, walks and talks in the Square Mile.

Along Fleet Street

Chancery Lane tube/Blackfriars tube/rail.

It's no coincidence that one of the arterial roads connecting Buckingham Palace to the Square Mile (or Queen to Commerce) is **Fleet Street**. 'Media' is the perfect word to describe the industry that was undertaken here, as the reporters mediated on the antagonism created between the two powers: the City of Westminster and the City. It was handy, for that matter, that the law courts were based nearby too.

Though the newspapers turned their backs on Fleet Street more than a decade ago, the place will always be associated with the age of hot metal and circulation wars. Wynkyn de

The view of **St Paul's Cathedral** is tainted as never before by construction cranes. *See p89*.

Worde introduced printing presses to Fleet Street in 1500, setting up at **St Bride's** church (still referred to as the printers and journalists' church, and purportedly to be the inspiration for the tiered wedding cake). Only Reuters, the press agency that started life in 1850 with a fleet of carrier pigeons, remains here; the rest of the newspapers that once dominated the locale have moved out, mostly to Wapping or Canary Wharf. Still, the ghosts of the rags still pervade the street in its buildings – the *Daily Telegraph* was at No.135 and the *Daily Express* at Nos.121-8, a building that still retains its glorious glass face and art deco staircase and foyer – and in its pubs and restaurants (many a boozy hack missed a deadline after a long lunch at El Vino, at No.47). It wasn't just newspapers that were based here: satirical magazine *Punch* was started on the street, an event celebrated at the Punch Tavern (No.99).

Fleet Street's tradition of journalism finds echoes in the names of those who frequented it even earlier. The City's literary talent drank here frequently, perhaps too frequently. At the long-gone Devil's Tavern at No.1, Pepys, Ben Jonson and Samuel Johnson all supped, the latter even making his home in the immediate neighbourhood (*see below*); Dickens, however, preferred Ye Old Cheshire Cheese (*see p221*).

The street takes its name from the largest of London's forgotten rivers. The Fleet flows into the Thames at Blackfriars Bridge, but is now totally submerged. However, it was once a major inlet for trade; the etymology of 'fleet' contains an Anglo-Saxon reference to 'inlet' or 'estuary'. In its heyday, the river was flanked by enormous docks that received visits from ships bearing coal, spice and fabrics. Pollution of the river at its upper reaches, however, put paid to its status as a trading post, and it's now buried beneath ground. *See also p98* **A river runs through it**.

Dr Johnson's House

17 Gough Square, off Fleet Street, EC4 (7353 3745/www.drjh.dircon.co.uk). Chancery Lane or Temple tube (both closed Sun)/Blackfriars tube/rail. **Open** *May-Sept* 11am-5.30pm Mon-Sat. *Oct-Apr* 11am-5pm Mon-Sat. *Tours* by arrangement; groups of 10 or more only. **Admission** £4; £3 concessions; £1 5-14s; free under-5s; £9 family. *Tours* free. *Evening tours* £5-£8 per head. **No credit cards. Map** p404 N6.

Samuel Johnson loved London as much, if not more, than he loved life, if we're to take him at his word – enough, anyway, to have had 17 different residences. This one alone remains intact. He lived here from 1748 to 1759, while working on the first of his English dictionaries in the garret with the help of his six amanuenses. In 1752, following the death of his wife, his Jamaican servant Francis Barber moved into 17 Gough Square, which has been restored to its original condition. Visitors can wander through a series of handsome panelled rooms bedecked with period furniture, prints and portraits.

London loves Routemasters

They're a symbol of London throughout the world, and without them no postcard or holiday album is complete. Beetling around Piccadilly Circus or sweeping past Big Ben, the open-backed Routemaster bus is as English as... well, not an awful lot else these days. Bright, red and somehow cuddly, their conductors the personal face of an impersonal city, Routemasters evoke a warmth shared by little else in London.

Their enduring success isn't only down to sentiment. One of the world's design classics, they do the job they were built to do nearly half a century ago better than anything that could replace them: with swift exit and entry via the broad back platform and no hanging around to pay the driver, they carry passengers comfortably and swiftly through the snarled city traffic.

Mechanically, Routemasters remain entirely unsurpassed for reliability and maintainability. Their superior efficiency means that their dwindling numbers tend to ply busy commuter routes unserved by tube. Londoners in the know actively choose to live in these usually scorned areas. There is no finer way to get to work than on the front seat of a Routemaster, the sun on your face, breezing past gridlocked traffic in the bus lane, then hanging off the pole as your stop approaches.

The tube might be simpler, but anybody who wants to learn a city should travel by bus and look out of the windows. On a Routemaster, they should look inside the windows, too. Look *at* the windows, even: the simple rivets that hold them in place, the handles that open them, burnished by decades of hot hands. Then look at the slatted, stable wooden floors; the compact, curving staircase, with maroon 'push once' bell at its top and bottom (one ring for 'stop', two for 'start' – this by the conductor only – and a carillon for 'whoa!'); the little tapping hammer the conductor uses to rap the front window as a start signal to the driver. And, if you're sitting in prime sightseeing territory in the seat at the front left on the bottom deck, look at the drivers themselves, yanking the power-unassisted steering wheel and heaving great levers that recall a steam train. No modish bendy bus will ever come close.

They may try, though. Undeniably, Routemasters are less safe than a bus with doors and broad steps that stops only at stops, and they are entirely hostile to wheelchairs, pushchairs and the mobility-impaired. They won't do in the 21st century and, if we choose to let sentiment blind us to that, European law will quickly enlighten us. It seems the quintessential London bus is destined to survive only in some

Around St Paul's

St Paul's tube.

When you look at the majestic dome of **St Paul's Cathedral** (*see p89*) rising out of the City's clamour, its cranes and facelifts, its traffic jams and security alerts, it's difficult not to feel a sense of peace and security. One thinks of the Blitz, and the famous photograph by Herbert Mason of Wren's masterpiece standing firm while the surrounding buildings burned. The dome is a serene curve in a concrete jungle of angles. At night, when it is underlit, there really isn't anything in London to touch it in terms of beauty. It draws the eye. As do the two baroque towers, one of which contains the largest bell in England, 'Great Paul', which weighs 17 tons and is tolled daily at 1pm.

There has been a cathedral dedicated to St Paul on this site since AD 604. The current building was designed by Christopher Wren, and it isn't difficult to see why this is his masterpiece. It was begun in 1675 and took 35 years to build. Unusually for architects, Wren was still around to admire his own creation when it had been completed.

Paternoster Square, once a forbidding arena of shadowy ginnels, grim pubs and boarded-up premises, lies alongside the cathedral and is in the process of being scrubbed up in one of the largest redevelopments currently being undertaken in the capital. Its new complex of buildings will be unveiled to the public in 2003.

There's a quaint little row of shops on **Bow Lane**, while bistros, champagne bars, restaurants and shops also huddle together, vying for your attention in this cosy alleyway. Further along is **St Mary Aldermary**, an attempt by Wren to hark back to the pre-Great Fire perpendicular style. Inside you'll find a little display containing oyster shells: a bit of a step up from the communion wafer, you might think, but the oysters are actually from the Thames and were a staple part of workmen's

Cole Abbey, are, unfortunately, usually closed.
Facing the former across scruffy **Queen
Victoria Street** is the unexpectedly neat
red-brick, 17th-century mansion of the **College
of Arms** (*see below*), which still examines and
records the pedigrees of those to whom such
things matter.

North of Blackfriars Station is Apothecaries'
Hall, one of the most charming of the livery
halls (though the most interesting one is
Fishmonger's Hall, for which *see p93*).
Close by on Ludgate Hill stands the church
of St Martin within Ludgate, its lead spire
still visible over the surrounding buildings as
Wren intended (which, alas, is more than can
be said for those of most of his other churches).
After reflecting on the works of God, ponder
upon the sins of man round the corner in the
most famous court in the land, the **Old Bailey**
(*see below*), built on the site of the infamous
Newgate Prison.

Central Criminal Court (Old Bailey)
*corner of Newgate Street & Old Bailey, EC4
(7248 3277). St Paul's tube.* **Open** *Public gallery*
10.30am-1pm, 2-4pm Mon-Fri. **Admission** free.
No under-14s; 14-16s accompanied by adults only.
Map p404 O6.
The Central Criminal Court, commonly known as
the Old Bailey, was built by Edward Mountford in
1907 on the site of the old Newgate Prison. The
bronze figure of Justice on the copper-covered dome
overlooks the area where convicts were once
executed. Many notorious criminals have been tried
at the Old Bailey, including Dr Crippen, Peter
Sutcliffe – aka the Yorkshire Ripper – and Jeffrey
Archer. Visitors can view trials from the public galleries, although children under 14 are not admitted;
bags, phones and cameras are also prohibited. If you
spot a judge carrying a posy of flowers into court,
it's not because he wants to liven the place up a
bit; traditionally, the flowers masked the stench
emanating from the jail.

College of Arms
*Queen Victoria Street, EC4 (7248 2762/
www.college-of-arms.gov.uk). Blackfriars tube/rail.*
Open 10am-4pm Mon-Fri. *Tours* by arrangement
6.30pm Mon-Fri; prices vary. **Admission** free.
Map p404 O7.
In medieval times, heralds' main role in society was
to organise tournaments. The knights who took part
were recognised by the arms on their shields and the
crests on their helmets. The heralds got to be such
experts at recognising the symbols that they became
responsible for recording arms, and, eventually, for
controlling their use. The practice continues within
the venerable college, the present building dating
from the 1670s. Only the wood-panelled entrance
room is accessible to the public, although tours can
be booked in order to view the Record Room and the
artists working on the intricate certificates.

emasculated, touristic rat-run form
or other. Meanwhile, hold on tight.
*The following routes use Routemasters:
6, 7, 8, 9, 10, 11, 12, 13, 14, 15, 19,
22, 23, 38, 137, 36, 73, 159. For more
information, see www.routemaster.org.uk
or www.routemasterwebsite.fsnet.co.uk.*

diets in the 17th and 18th centuries. Once
the oysters were consumed, the shells were used
as filling material in the buildings they were
erecting. The shells on display were discovered
in the church tower.

Over Queen Victoria Street is **Garlick Hill**,
its medieval name proving false the supposed
antipathy between the English and the pungent
bulb. At the bottom of the street is Wren's
church of St James Garlickhythe, which has
the highest roof in the City after St Paul's.
Its light-filled interior remains much as it
was in the 17th century, and has earned it the
nickname of 'Wren's Lantern'.

South of St Paul's lies a little explored but
delightful tangle of alleyways, concealing
shops, pubs and the dinky Wren church of
St Andrew by the Wardrobe. Built between
1685 and 1695, the church's curious name dates
from 1361, when the King's Wardrobe – the
ceremonial clothes of the Royal Family – were
moved to the adjoining building. Nearby, two
other Wren creations, St Benet and St Nicholas

Sightseeing

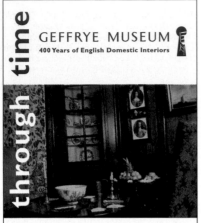

St Paul's Cathedral

Ludgate Hill, EC4 (7236 4128/www.stpauls.co.uk).
St Paul's tube. **Open** 8.30am-4pm Mon-Sat. *Galleries,*
crypt & ambulatory 9.30am-4pm Mon-Sat. Closed
for special services, sometimes at short notice.
Tours 11am, 11.30am, 1.30pm, 2pm Mon-Sat.
Admission *Cathedral, crypt & gallery* £6; £3 6-16s;
£5 concessions; free under-6s. **Audio guide** £3.50;
£3 concessions. **Credit** *Shop* MC, V. **Map** p404 O6.

It's now perhaps the most famous building in
London, but St Paul's almost never got built. Sir
Christopher Wren had to fight to get his plans for
the building approved (they were turned down in the
first place), and the building process was by no
means simple. However, be glad he persisted. It truly
is a stunning sight: impressive enough during the
day (the steps at the building's front are vast and
daunting), it's positively iconic at night, up-lit from
ground level, a brooding presence in the heart of the
City. From the outside, at least, it's many locals'
favourite London building, and we're not about to
argue with them.

Many come here as much for the views as anything, and well they might. It's a 530-step, 280ft
(85m) climb to the open-air Golden Gallery near the
top; walk around the gallery, taking in London in
all its magnificence (and marvelling at the sheer
volume and variety of construction cranes that surround you). En route, you'll pass the Whispering
Gallery (259 steps up), which runs around the
dome's interior and takes its name from the acousti-
cally implausible but absolutely true fact that if you
whisper into the dome's wall, someone at the other
side of the gallery can hear it perfectly.

That's not to suggest, though, that there's little to
see elsewhere in the building; there's plenty,
although this is one attraction where buying a guide-
book is imperative if you want to make the most of
what you're seeing. That said, some of the monuments are fairly easily explained, such as the one to
the Americans who died in Great Britain during
World War II, and the one to poet John Donne in the
south aisle, the only monument in the building to
have survived the Great Fire. The two most eye-
catching tombs in the crypt are of the Duke of
Wellington and Horatio Nelson, though many
notable figures from the arts are also buried here.
Among them are Henry Moore, JMW Turner, Joshua
Reynolds, Max Beerbohm, Arthur Sullivan… and
Wren himself.

North to Smithfield

Barbican or St Paul's tube.

Smithfield Market was once an unusually
open space – a 'smooth field' – in the middle
of a bustling community. Records from as far
back as 1173 refer to its use as a market selling
animals, but the large expanse of land meant
that it was also used for jousts and sporting
events, as well as less savoury activities
(executions were once held here).

The Monument. *See p94.*

Today's Londoners, though, know Smithfield
as London's meat market. It opened for business
in 1868, and trades on today. Or, rather, tonight.
Trucks begin to pull into the market from
around midnight, though the buying-and-selling
trade doesn't commence until around 3am.
Wander around here an hour or so later, and
it's a peculiar sight. Not so much because of the
carcasses being hauled indelicately around the
buildings, but because alongside this nocturnal
trading roam London's clubbers.

Night owls have long fled here for a fix of
heartstoppingly greasy food: there are a
number of all-night caffs in the general vicinity
of the market. But since the addition of Fabric
(*see p319*), the area's become even more popular
among the clubbing fraternity. The Tinseltown
diner serves hearty scran to the disco kids
24/7 (*see p216* **Late eats**), though the truckers
and market porters prefer the more traditional
greasy spoons opposite the market. The twain
only meet at **Fox & Anchor** on nearby
Charterhouse Street, which opens at 7am and
serves a mean Guinness with its monstrous,
pig-packed breakfasts.

An Augustinian gentleman named Rahere
was responsible for **St Bartholomew's**
Hospital. During a 12th-century pilgrimage
to Rome, he contracted and almost died from

malaria, and vowed to build a hospital on his return to London. This he did in the shape of St Bartholomew's, affectionately referred to these days as Bart's. In its grounds is **St Bartholomew's Hospital Museum** (7601 8152, 10am-4pm Tue-Fri), which charts the hospital's history and contains epic biblical murals by social commentator William Hogarth, who was baptised in the nearby **St Bartholomew-the-Great**, the oldest parish church in the capital (*see below*).

St Bartholomew-the-Great

West Smithfield, EC1 (7606 5171/ www.greatstbarts.com). Barbican tube/Farringdon tube/rail. **Open** *Mid Nov-mid Feb* 8.30am-4pm Tue-Fri; 10.30am-1.30pm Sat; 8.30am-1pm, 2.30-8pm Sun. *Mid Feb-mid Nov* 8.30am-5pm Tue-Fri; 10.30am-1.30pm Sat; 8.30am-1pm, 2.30-8pm Sun. **Admission** free; donations welcome. **Map** p402 O5. Although its nave was torn down during Henry VIII's monastic purge – it once extended the length of the churchyard to the 13th-century gateway, now the entrance from Smithfield – this is still a wonderfully evocative place; most of the Norman arches are original. Benjamin Franklin served a year as a journeyman printer in the Lady Chapel; Hugh Grant famously didn't get married here in *Four Weddings and a Funeral.*

Around Bank

Mansion House tube/Bank tube/DLR.

A triumphant triumvirate of buildings – the **Bank of England**, the **Royal Exchange** and **Mansion House** – stake their claim to being, if not the geographical centre of the Square Mile, then its symbolic heart. This trio of imposing buildings, made from the best Portland stone, are only let down by the architectural oddity at nearby **Number 1 Poultry**, which resembles the prow of a ship.

The Bank of England was founded in 1694 to fund William III's war against the French. Most of what you see today was the work of Sir Herbert Baker in the 1920s; John Soane's original building was shamefully demolished to make room for it, though a reproduction of his Stock Office was built a few years ago ostensibly to house the excellent **Bank of England Museum** (*see p91*).

The Lord Mayor of London's official residence, Mansion House (7626 2500; group visits only, by written application to the Diary Office, Mansion House, Walbrook, EC4, at least two months in advance), was designed by George Dance and completed in 1753. It's the only private residence in the United Kingdom to have its own court of justice, which comes complete with 11 prison cells. Its magnificent pediment by Robert

Guildhall. *See p91.*

Taylor depicts London defeating envy and bringing plenty in its exploitation of its Empire. How times change.

The current Royal Exchange, the third on that site, was built by William Tite and opened by Queen Victoria in 1844. Within a few years its design was seen to be somewhat outmoded in the face of a Gothic revival in the 1850s. Trading no longer takes place within its walls but plans are afoot to turn the building into a five-star shopping complex.

Next to the Royal Exchange, on Cornhill, keep a lookout for the statue of James Greathead who, in 1874, patented the 'Greathead Shield', a tunnelling device that enabled deep shafts to be constructed for the London tube network. Poetically, the statue incorporates a vent for one of those very same underground railways.

Further west is the centre of the City's civic life, **Guildhall** (*see p91*), base of the Corporation of London, as well as an excellent library, the **Clockmakers' Company Museum** (*see p91*), the church of **St Lawrence Jewry**, and the **Guildhall Art Gallery** (*see p91*), housing the Corporation of London's art collection.

Next to Mansion House stands one of the City's finest churches, **St Stephen Walbrook**, the trial run for St Paul's. Nearby is the heap of stones that was the Roman **Temple of Mithras** (*see below*). Other notable churches in the vicinity are Hawksmoor's idiosyncratic **St Mary Woolnoth** (*see below*) at the junction of King William Street and Lombard Street and Wren's exquisite **St Mary Abchurch** off Abchurch Lane.

Bank of England Museum
entrance on Bartholomew Lane, EC2 (7601 5545/ cinema bookings 7601 3985/www.bankofengland. co.uk). Bank tube/DLR. **Open** 10am-5pm Mon-Fri. *Tours* by arrangement. **Admission** free; £1 audio guide. *Tours* free. **Map** p405 Q6.
Surprise: what could have been a tedious puff piece on the brilliance of British money men (yawn) turns out to be a fascinating exposition on the history of the national bank. The museum tells its story in a series of exhibitions spread through several pristine, handsome rooms. Among the topics singled out for attention are the architecture of the buildings used down the years (the bank has partly made up for destroying Sir John Soane's 18th-century masterpiece by housing the museum in a gleaming replica of his Stock Office) and the way money is printed; not here, but in the drab Essex town of Loughton. Other highlights include a collection of old bank-notes – the image of Britannia that's graced every note has changed surprisingly little down the years – and some fun interactive displays. Admission is free, though the bank can probably afford it.

Clockmakers' Museum
Guildhall Library, Aldermanbury, EC2 (Guildhall Library 7332 1868/Clockmakers' Company 7236 0070/www.clockmakers.org). Mansion House or St Paul's tube/Bank tube/DLR/Moorgate tube/rail. **Open** 9.30am-4.45pm Mon-Fri. **Admission** free. **Map** p404 P6.
This timepiece museum reopened in 2002 in a crisp, well-ordered room in the Guildhall Library. The constant ticking noise may make you unconsciously rush through the displays, but if you linger, you'll find a nice, compact history of horology. Exhibits run from huge grandfathers to teensy pocket watches, but most fun is the small display of curios. One particularly odd clock has a mechanism controlled by a small metal ball rolling around on a constantly tilting plate. The ball travels 2,522 miles in a year, although the caption dryly remarks that 'the system is not conducive to accurate time-keeping'. An enjoyable diversion.

Guildhall
Gresham Street, EC2 (7606 3030/tours ext 1463/ www.corpoflondon.gov.uk). Bank tube/DLR. **Open** *May-Sept* 9.30am-5pm daily. *Oct-Apr* 9.30am-5pm Mon-Sat. Last entry 4.30pm. *Tours* by arrangement; groups of 10 or more people only. **Admission** free. **Map** p404 P6.

Guildhall has been the centre of the City's government for more than 800 years. The Great Hall fell foul of the Great Fire and the Blitz but has been restored: banners and shields of the 100 livery companies adorn the walls, while every Lord Mayor since 1189 gets a namecheck on the windows. Meetings of the Court of Common Council (the governing body for the Corporation of London, presided over by the Lord Mayor) take place monthly, though the Guildhall is mostly used for banquets and ceremonial events.

Guildhall Art Gallery
Guildhall Yard, off Gresham Street, EC2 (7332 3700/www.guildhall-art-gallery.org.uk). Mansion House or St Paul's tube/Bank tube/DLR/Moorgate tube/rail. **Open** 10am-5pm Mon-Sat (last entry 4.30pm); noon-4pm Sun (last entry 3.45pm). **Admission** £2.50; £1 concessions; free under-16s. Free to all after 3.30pm daily, all day Fri. **Credit** (over £5) MC, V. **Map** p404 P6.
Begun when it commissioned portraits of the judges assessing property claims after the Great Fire of 1666, the Corporation of London's art collection now runs to some 4,000 paintings. At any one time, around 250 are on display at this rather plain gallery near the Guildhall itself, although a large number of works can also be seen on computer terminals throughout the building. Painters whose works feature include Constable, Rossetti and Millais, but on the whole, the eclectic collection is of greater historical importance than artistic worth. Indeed, the main reason to come here is not for the art, but to see the Roman amphitheatre discovered by archaeologists in 1988 and opened to the public 14 years later.

St Mary Woolnoth
Lombard Street, EC3 (7626 9701). Bank tube/DLR. **Open** 9.30am-4.30pm Mon-Fri. **Admission** free; donations appreciated. **Map** p405 Q6.
Wulnoth, a Saxon noble, is thought to have founded this church on the site of a Roman temple to Concord. It was rebuilt often, most recently by Hawksmoor in 1716-17, and its interior, based on the Egyptian Hall of Vitruvius, is one of the architect's finest. Edward Lloyd, in whose coffee shop Lloyd's of London was founded, was buried here in 1713. When Bank station was built between 1897 and 1900, the church was undermined, the dead removed from the vaults and lift shafts sunk beneath the building.

Temple of Mithras
on raised courtyard in front of Sumitomo Bank/ Legal & General Building, Temple Court, 11 Queen Victoria Street, EC4. Mansion House tube. **Open** 24hrs daily. **Admission** free. **Map** p404 P6.
In the third century AD, the rival cults of Mithraism and Christianity were battling for supremacy. The worship of the macho Persian god Mithras appealed particularly to Roman soldiers, and the troops on the British frontier built the small temple to their champion near this spot (cAD 240-50). The reconstructed foundations aren't much to look at, but show the Roman influence on the later design of churches: rounded apse, central nave and side aisles.

Around the Tower of London

Tower Hill tube/Tower Gateway DLR.

Tourists flock here, of course. The businesses between Tower Hill tube and the **Tower of London** itself make an absolute killing each summer from passing trade. Not that you can blame the coach parties – the Tower is one sight that genuinely entertains – but you can't help but wish more of them would stop for a few seconds outside the tube to take in a part of London's history that, while less demonstrable, is just as fascinating to behold. It's a piece of London's original **Roman wall**, added to in medieval times but still, in essence, as it was two millennia ago. Should you not fancy the

Tower, you can follow the course of the wall to the **Museum of London** (*see p94*), a matter of just under two miles (three kilometres).

The City's most famous chronicler, Samuel Pepys (*see p95* **Pepys show**), is celebrated in **Seething Lane**. The diarist lived here – there's a bust of him in Seething Lane Gardens – and the church where he is buried, **St Olave Hart Street** (nicknamed by Dickens 'St Ghastly Grim', after the leering skulls at the cemetery's entrance) is nearby. Pepys watched London burn in 1666 from **All Hallows by the Tower** (*see p93*) at the bottom of Seething Lane.

Between here and London Bridge stand two reminders of London's great days as a port. David Lang built the **Custom House** in 1817,

London loves The City on Sunday

As detailed elsewhere in this chapter, London's financial district is also the city's oldest part: the Roman town of Londinium was founded in AD 50, with its initial settlements just east of what is now Bank tube station. Unfortunately, attempts to explore this historically rich area during the week are often hampered by frantic people in suits barking into mobile phones. Should you visit on a Sunday, however, you can treat yourself to some exquisitely peaceful strolling, with barely another soul in sight and eerily empty roads.

It's a delight for the flitting tourist, as there's an immense amount to see but,

because many things are shut, little to explore in depth. **St Paul's Cathedral** (*see p89*) is open for services but not sightseeing, so the adjoining Festival Gardens are virtually empty. From the cathedral, signposts will lure you through tiny side streets to such improbably named attractions as the ruins of the **Temple of Mithras** (*see p91*), the church of **St James Garlickhythe** and **Dr Johnson's House** (*see p85*). There is no area of London so keen on informing you what's around the next corner, what used to be situated in a particular place, who donated trees, who established the right of way under an archway, all documented on hundreds of

but the most appealing part of the building, its riverfront façade, was added by Robert Smirke a decade later. Next door is **Billingsgate Market**: for years London's fish market, trading closed here in 1982 and moved to a new building on the Isle of Dogs.

The lanes behind the waterfront are packed with churches: **St Magnus the Martyr**, **St Mary at Hill**, **St Margaret Pattens** and **St Dunstan in the East**, the latter boasting some lovely gardens. Near here is the **Monument** (*see p94*), from where it's a mere 202 feet to Pudding Lane. In Farryner's bakery here, in the early hours of 2 September 1666, a fire started that was to blaze for three days, destroying four-fifths of medieval London.

plaques, boards and signs. With no distractions or noise, it's easy to immerse yourself in history here.

Visitors are generally staggered by the variety of architecture in the space of a few yards, and nowhere is this more apparent than on Sunday. The green and maroon of deserted **Leadenhall Market** (*see p93*) makes a strange neighbour to the grim pipework of the imposing Lloyd's Building. The 30-odd churches in the area can slip by almost unnoticed: the **Church of the Holy Sepulchre**, for example, tucked round the back of the Central Criminal Courts.

You should bring some lunch with you – 99 per cent of the bars and cafés have chairs firmly on tables until Monday morning – but you'll be spoiled for beautiful settings in which to eat it: **Finsbury Circus** (*pictured*, during the week), the **Barber Surgeon's Herb Garden** at London Wall, **Postman's Park** off St Martin's Le Grand, the **Rose Garden** at Christchurch Greyfriars, and dozens more that you'll chance upon as you wander.

Should you wish to escape the solitude of your Sunday meander, nip over the Millennium Bridge to **Tate Modern** (*see p79*), wander through Aldgate to the colour and noise of the markets on **Brick Lane** and **Petticoat Lane** (*see p254-5*), or head south to the **Tower of London** (*see p96*). You can also explore the high walks of the Barbican and Moorgate en route to the chic bars of Hoxton. But for relaxation, space and time to yourself, it's a case of right time, right place.

Just north-east of Monument is one of the City's most delightful surprises. 'Foreigners' – meaning anyone from outside London – were allowed to sell poultry (and, later, cheese and butter) at **Leadenhall Market** from the 14th century. The current arcaded buildings, painted in green, maroon and cream with wonderful decorative detail, are the work of Horace Jones, who also built Smithfield Market.

The market today is a charming place. It helps that the buildings are beautifully maintained, of course: in summer, when the sun seeps through into the market, there are few more evocative places. But what makes the market special still is its range of shops. Sure, there's a Virgin selling records, a branch of the Jigsaw fashion chain and the requisite Body Shop, but alongside them sit florists and fruiterers, butchers and fishmongers, a shoeshine stall and a lovely pub (the Lamb).

Between Leadenhall and Liverpool Street rail station there are more churches: **St Helen Bishopsgate**, off Bishopsgate (*see p94*), **St Andrew Undershaft** on St Mary Axe, **St Botolph Aldgate** (*see p94*) and **St Katharine Cree** on Leadenhall Street. The latter, one of few churches built in England during the years preceding the Civil War, is an extraordinary hybrid of classical and Gothic styles. Nearby is the oldest synagogue in the country: the superbly preserved **Bevis Marks Synagogue**, located in a courtyard off Bevis Marks, was built in 1701 by Sephardic Jews who had managed to escape from the Inquisition in Portugal and Spain.

This area suffered considerable damage from the IRA bombs of April 1992 and April 1993. A great deal of restoration work has been undertaken, though the tiny pre-Fire church of **St Ethelburga-the-Virgin** (built 1390) on Bishopsgate was devastated.

All Hallows by the Tower

Byward Street, EC3 (7481 2928/www.allhallows bythetower.org.uk). Tower Hill tube. **Open** *Church* 9am-5.45pm Mon-Fri; 10am-5pm Sat, Sun. **Admission** free; donations appreciated. **Audio tour** £2.50 (suggested donation). **Map** p405 R7. Though just the walls and 17th-century brick tower were left standing after World War II attacks, post-war rebuilding at All Hallows has created a pleasingly light interior. A Saxon arch testifies to the church's ancient roots (seventh century). Other relics include Saxon crosses, a Roman tessellated pavement, Tudor monuments and a superb carved limewood font cover (1682) by Grinling Gibbons.

Fishmongers' Hall

London Bridge, EC4 (7626 3531/www.fishhall.co.uk). London Bridge tube/rail. **Open** tours only, by arrangement. **Admission** free; donations appreciated. **Map** p405 Q7.

The Barbican: 2,000 flats, one arts complex and no soul.

The most interesting of the remaining City guilds or livery companies (the union HQ of once-powerful trades), this 19th-century hall displays, amid a jumble of precious loot, the dagger used by fishmonger and mayor William Walworth to stab Wat Tyler in the back and put down the Peasants' Revolt of 1381.

St Botolph Aldgate

Aldgate, EC3 (7283 1670). Aldgate tube. **Open** 9.30am-3pm Mon-Fri; services only Sun. **Admission** free; donations appreciated. **Map** p405 R6.

The original St Botolph, built by the City's east gate, may date back to the tenth century. The galleried interior of the current plain brick, stone-dressed structure, built by George Dance in 1744, is notable for John Francis Bentley's highly original ceiling, lined with angels. Daniel Defoe was married here in 1683.

St Helen's Bishopsgate

Great St Helen's, EC3 (7283 2231/www.st-helens. org.uk). Bank tube/DLR/Liverpool Street tube/rail. **Open** 9am-5pm Mon-Fri; services only Sat, Sun. **Admission** free. **Map** p405 R6.

It survived the Great Fire and the Blitz, but St Helen's was badly damaged by IRA bombs in 1992 and 1993. Founded in the 13th century, the spacious building incorporates 15th-century Gothic arches and a 14th-century nuns' chapel. The unusual double nave demonstrates that this used to be two churches side by side, one belonging to a Benedictine nunnery. St Helen's is known as the 'Westminster Abbey of the City' because of its splendid collection of medieval and Tudor monuments to City dignitaries. **St Andrew Undershaft**, nearby, and **St Olave's**, on Hart Street, are also pre-Fire churches.

The Monument

Monument Street, EC3 (7626 2717). Monument tube. **Open** 9.30am-5pm daily. **Admission** £1.50; 50p 5-15s; free under-5s. **No credit cards**. **Map** p405 Q7.

When it was erected in 1671-7 to commemorate the Great Fire of 1666, Christopher Wren and Robert Hooke's 202ft (66m) Doric column towered over the City. These days, it's been hemmed in by huge offices; not just no longer dominant, but more or less ignored by those who work in the surrounding buildings. And while the exterior is smart, it seems a shame that the summit of this historic structure, 311 steps above the ground, should be awash with graffiti. Still, the views from atop it are worth the hike, especially if you don't plan on going up the taller, more central St Paul's (*see p89*). One side contains the relief of Charles II supervising the rebuilding of London; the carving was done by Caius Cibber in 1672, after he'd spent some time in jail for debt. His revenge was to perch the King's finger on the pert nipple of a woman's exposed breast.

Museum of London

150 London Wall, EC2 (7600 3699/recorded information 7600 0807/www.museumoflondon. org.uk). Barbican or St Paul's tube. **Open** 10am-5.50pm Mon-Sat; noon-5.50pm Sun. **Admission** free. **Credit** Shop AmEx, MC, V. **Map** p402 P5.

London's own museum deserves a better setting than the middle of a roundabout, accessible only via a scruffy and unprepossessing overhead walkway. Happily, this will change from mid 2003, when the museum's new ground-level entrance will open. And in any case, the museum's far better inside, where it tells the story of the city over an exhaustive and exhausting series of exhibit-packed rooms.

While a chronological walk through the museum, from the new London Before London gallery detailing life 450,000 years ago to the present-day exhibits, it's also time-consuming (pun intended) if you want to do it justice. Highlights en route include Roman London, which puts some welcoming visuals to a time most often detailed in dry historical tomes; the cute if low-tech Great Fire Experience show; a walk-through exhibit of recreated Victorian shops; and the oral histories in the World City galleries. If you're pushed for time, start downstairs, which is where you'll find the liveliest of the galleries. But in truth, there's little here to criticise. Stock your London library at the shop on your way out.

Tower Bridge Experience

SE1 (7403 3761/www.towerbridge.org.uk). Tower Hill tube/London Bridge tube/rail. **Open** 9.30am-6pm daily. Last entry 5pm. **Admission** £4.50; £3 5-15s, concessions; free under-5s; £14 family. **Credit** AmEx, MC, V. **Map** p405 R8.

There are exhibits here: photographs of the ground-breaking bascule bridge at various stages in its building, by architect Horace Jones and engineer

Pepys show

The years 1660 to 1669 form London's most extraordinary decade, containing three such landscape-changing events as might not happen in a century, let alone a mere few years. The Great Fire of London, the plague and the Restoration to the throne of Charles II after Oliver Cromwell's great experiment with republicanism seem era-defining occurrences, not least because of the way they were chronicled in the celebrated diaries of Samuel Pepys. Historical records show bald facts and sometimes more intimate truths, but it is through Pepys's accounts of this turbulent age that our eyes have truly been opened to Restoration London.

If it's fitting to start a summary of Pepys's life with the great events that framed it, it is also limiting. For the diaries themselves, which run almost perfectly through the decade from start to close, offer just what we've come to expect from the published journals of public figures in our time: a mix of current affairs and very private revealings.

Pepys was born in Salisbury Court, off Fleet Street, in 1633, and was to prove the most markedly able of his siblings. After receiving a degree in 1654 from Cambridge, he became secretary to Edward Mountagu, a family friend who became Councillor of State under Cromwell, at Whitehall Palace. Pepys married and moved to a house in Axe Yard, off King Street; on 1 January 1660 it was here that he began to keep a diary.

Pepys's diary pays as much heed to the social machinations of his time as it does to its author's innermost feelings. While the invaluable passages that catch the eye are often the all-encompassing affairs of state, it is quickly clear that Pepys's wonderfully informal, confessional style sets his work apart from mere fact recorders.

Of course, the diaries were never intended for publication, which perhaps makes their fluency and steadfastness all the more astonishing. Pepys in fact wrote in code, so fearful was he of having his infidelities discovered, and it wasn't until 1825, long after the events told within, that the journal found itself in print. The author's jealousies, rages and cheatings described without self-consciousness are still lifelike in their relevance, and it is the attention to detail and the unflinching honesty that are the most valuable characteristics: it is hard not to empathise at the very least with this gregarious, careless, sometimes tormented but always truthful soul.

But what of Pepys's London? Apart from the confessional tone, we find a pure and believable picture of a time now otherwise unknowable. Even the diarist's routine recordings bring home something of the atmosphere of his lifetime: aside from the Great Fire, for which Pepys is most often cited as a source, we have entries marking public executions at Tyburn, excursions to fashionable Kensington, descriptions of bear and bull baiting ('a very rude and nasty pleasure'), talk of church life (Pepys worshipped at St Olave Hart Street), trips to the theatre and the opera... detail on such a minute scale as to colour this city so it seems familiar to Londoners today.

For that is Pepys's art. His diary is a work of such conviviality, unrivalled certainly in its own time and probably in ours for its sheer scope. It is a vast portrait (the current, definitive edition runs to nine volumes) of a city at a remarkable juncture in its history. But it's also, perhaps unwittingly, a self-portrait of a fascinating man who holds his own in the legacy of great London writers.

John Wolfe-Barry, and a couple of films. However, they're diversions to the main attraction: the chance to walk inside this London landmark, and look down the Thames from the large picture windows. After this, the rather tedious elucidation of the bridge's mechanics will come as a bit of a disappointment.

Tower of London

Tower Hill, EC3 (information 0870 756 6060/tickets 0870 756 6060/www.hrp.org.uk). Tower Hill tube/ Fenchurch Street rail. **Open** *Mar-Oct* 9am-5pm Mon-Sat; 10am-5pm Sun. *Nov-Feb* 10am-4pm Mon, Sun; 9am-4pm Tue-Sat. **Admission** £11.50; £8.75 concessions; £7.50 5-15s; £34 family; free under-5s. **Credit** AmEx, MC, V. **Map** p405 R7.

The first trick is to arrive early; first thing, if possible. The ever-popular Tower is far more manageable early in the day, before the hordes descend; its lawns and buildings dappled with early-morning sunlight, it's also, more simply, a lovelier place. The second trick is to hook up with one of the free tours given by the 39 genial Yeoman Warders, more commonly known as Beefeaters, who live on site. Their retelling of the Tower's 900-year history may come with a little hokum attached, but it's a history worth relating – betrayal, torture and death are the three main themes, Richard III, Sir Walter Raleigh and William the Conqueror some of its key figures – and the whistlestop tours succeed in breaking down the stories behind the Bloody Tower, Traitor's Gate and the Tower's other highlights. Of the exhibitions, the best sits in the White Tower: a collection of equipment from the Royal Armouries (check the enormous armour that belonged to Henry VIII). The Crown Jewels display is strangely mundane, each excessively bejewelled trinket seeming less and less interesting the further down the exhibit you get. The daily costumed presentations are a nice touch.

North of London Wall

Barbican tube/Moorgate tube/rail.

Running close to the impressively redeveloped Liverpool Street Station and the rather blander Broadgate Centre next to it, **London Wall** follows the northerly course of the old Roman fortifications. Part of the wall, and the remains of one of the gates into the Cripplegate Roman fort, can be seen in **St Alfage Gardens**.

The area just to the north of here was levelled during the Blitz. Rather than encourage office developments, the City of London and London County Council purchased a large site in 1958 to build 'a genuine residential neighbourhood, with schools, shops, open spaces and amenities'. Unfortunately, we ended up with the **Barbican**, a vast and ugly estate of 2,000 flats and an arts complex (*see below*) that, altogether, exudes almost no warmth or sense of community. Some of those who live there defend it to the hilt, arguing chiefly that its

location is superbly convenient. They're right, too. But to the outsider, it's a truly bleak place, and few outside its walls would be all that sorry to see it razed to the ground and rebuilt from scratch.

Marooned amid the towering blocks is the only pre-war building in the vicinity: the heavily restored 16th-century church of **St Giles Cripplegate**, where Oliver Cromwell was married and John Milton buried. The Nonconformist connection continues further north-east: **Bunhill Fields** was set aside as a cemetery during the Great Plague, though it doesn't appear to have been used at that time. Instead, because the ground was apparently never consecrated, the cemetery became popular for Nonconformist burials, gaining the name of 'the cemetery of Puritan England'. Much of the graveyard is cordoned off these days, but it's still possible for visitors to stroll through it and take a look at the monuments to John Bunyan, Daniel Defoe and William Blake, that most unconformist of Nonconformists.

Opposite Bunhill Fields on City Road is the **Museum of Methodism** and **John Wesley's House** (*see below*). The founder of Methodism lived his last years in the Georgian house; upstairs, in 1951, Denis Thatcher married Margaret Hilda Roberts.

Barbican Art Gallery

Level 3, Barbican Centre, Silk Street, EC2 (box office 7638 8891/enquiries 7382 7105/ www.barbican.org.uk). Barbican tube/Moorgate tube/rail. **Open** 10am-6pm Mon, Tue, Thur-Sat; 10am-9pm Wed; noon-6pm Sun. **Admission** £7; £5 concessions. **Credit** AmEx, MC, V. **Map** p402 P5.

Once you've found your way into this impenetrable arts complex (which also contains a cinema, *see p283*, and a concert hall, *see p303*), you'll be rewarded with a generally interesting selection of temporary shows. In 2003 the gallery stages 'Exodus', Brazilian photographer Sebastião Salgado's first major show in London (13 Feb-1 June); it will then close for refurbishment until spring 2004.

Museum of Methodism & John Wesley's House

Wesley's Chapel, 49 City Road, Finsbury, EC1 (7253 2262). Moorgate or Old Street tube/rail. **Open** 10am-4pm Mon-Sat. *Tours* ad hoc arrangements on arrival. **Admission** free. **Credit** MC, V. **Map** p403 Q4.

John Wesley opened this chapel for worship in 1778, and in 1981 a museum of his work was created in the crypt. Highlights include the pulpit and a large oil portrait of the scene at his deathbed. His house next door has been restored to its original Georgian interior design. In the kitchen and study you can see his nightcap, preaching gown and personal experimental electric-shock machine.

Holborn & Clerkenwell

Where legal eagles sit side by side with loft-dwelling hipsters.

Holborn

Maps p399 & p401

Holborn tube.

First referred to as 'Holeburnstreete' in 1249 and named after the Holebourne river, a tributary of the now-vanished Fleet (*see p98* **A river runs through it**), Holborn (pronounced Hó-bun) was initially a major goods route into the City. Today, though it takes something from its neighbouring districts (the money-mad City, commercial Covent Garden and learned Bloomsbury), it derives most of its atmosphere from the four surviving Inns of Court, which were situated here to symbolise the law's role as mediator in the historical battle for power between the City and royal Westminster.

In the Inns of Court, members of the legal profession wander safely out of touch with reality. Amble **Lincoln's Inn** and **Gray's Inn**, and sample the joys of passing 'by unexpected ways, into its unexpected avenues, into its magnificent ample squares, its classic green recesses', as essayist Charles Lamb put it two centuries ago. The alleys and open spaces of the Inns remain a haven from the fumes of central London, but most of the buildings are open by appointment only (some just for group tours).

Aldwych

The western flank of modern Holborn is formed by the car-filled conduit of **Kingsway**, carved out of slum-lined streets in the early 1900s in an attempt to relieve traffic congestion, and culminating in the crescent of **Aldwych**. The handsome Meridien Waldorf hotel faces a trio of unashamedly Imperial buildings: India House, Australia House and Bush House, now home to the BBC World Service. Between here and the Thames lies **King's College**, its 1960s buildings sitting uncomfortably with Robert Smirke's graceful 1829-31 originals. Easier on the eye is **Somerset House** (*see p98*).

Two nearby curiosities are worth a glance. On **Temple Place** is one of a handful of still-functioning cabmen's shelters. These green-painted sheds are a legacy of the Cabmen's Shelter Fund, set up in 1874 to provide cabbies with an alternative to pubs in which to hide from the elements and get a hot meal and (non-alcoholic) drink. And back near King's

is the entrance to Aldwych, the most recently operational of London's ghost tube stations. It's hired out for special events and movie shoots.

Back on the Strand are the churches of St Mary-le-Strand (James Gibbs' first public building; 1714-17) and **St Clement Danes** (*see p98*). Just north loom the imposing neo-Gothic **Royal Courts of Justice** (*see below*), opened in 1882 by Queen Victoria. The stress of the commission was such that the architect GE Street's crowning achievement brought him to an early grave. The fearsome bronze griffin in the middle of the road near here marks the site of **Temple Bar** and the official boundary of the City, past which the Queen cannot stray without the Lord Mayor's permission. Just beyond is the church of **St Dunstan in the West** (*see p98*) and the 17th-century **Prince Henry's Room** (*see below*), while south of the Strand – just inside the City – are **Middle Temple** (Middle Temple Lane, EC4; 7427 4800) and **Inner Temple** (Inner Temple Treasury Office, EC4; group tours, mornings only, costing £10, can be booked on 7797 8241). Built around a maze of courtyards and passageways, they're especially atmospheric when gaslit after dark.

Prince Henry's Room

17 Fleet Street, EC4 (7936 4004). Temple tube (closed Sun). **Open** 11am-2pm Mon-Sat. **Admission** free; donations appreciated. **Map** p404 N6.

The oldest son of King James I of England and VI of Scotland, Henry was just 14 when he became Prince of Wales in 1610. In the same year, the house containing this beautiful oak-panelled room, used by the prince's lawyers, was built. Its magnificent plaster ceiling has the Prince of Wales's feathers at its centre, together with the initials PH. The rest of the building was the Prince's Arms, a tavern frequented by Pepys. Some of the items the diarist left there, including a letter, pictures and a quill, are on display.

Royal Courts of Justice

Strand, WC2 (7947 6000/www.open.gov.uk). Temple tube (closed Sun). **Open** 9.30am-1pm, 2-4.30pm Mon-Fri. No court cases during Aug & Sept. **Admission** free. **Map** p399 M6.

On the premise that justice must both be done and be *seen* to be done, anyone is free to take a pew in the 88 courts in this splendid Gothic building, where the High Court presides over the most serious civil trials in the country. Spectators can come and go as they please. Lists in the central hall bear the names of the parties in the cases being heard but don't give information about the proceedings; try asking the black-robed court ushers. Cameras, mobile phones and under-14s are not admitted.

St Clement Danes

Strand, WC2 (7242 8282). Temple tube (closed Sun)/Blackfriars tube/rail. **Open** 9am-4pm Mon-Fri; 9am-3pm Sat, Sun. **Admission** free; donations appreciated. **Map** p399 M6.

Though it's not the church that gave rise to the nursery rhyme (that was St Clement Eastcheap), this Wren-designed church behaves as if it were: its bells ring out the tune three times a day (9am, noon and 3pm). In 1941 the church burnt down in a German air raid, but was restored in the 1950s as a memorial to allied airmen; these days it's the central church of the RAF. Outside there's a controversial statue of Arthur Harris, famous for the bombing of Dresden.

St Dunstan in the West

186A Fleet Street, EC4 (7242 6027). Chancery Lane tube. **Open** 10am-2pm Tue; 5-8pm Fri; 2-6pm Sat; 9am-2pm Sun; some concerts on Fri. **Admission** free; donations appreciated. **Map** p404 N6.

St Dunstan was first mentioned in 1185, but the present early Gothic-revival building dates from 1831-3. John Donne was rector here (1624-31); Izaak Walton (whose *Compleat Angler* was published in the churchyard in 1653) held the posts of 'scavenger, questman and sidesman' (1629-44); and in 1667 a lecherous Pepys popped in to hear a sermon and unsuccessfully try to fondle a local girl ('at last I could perceive her to take pins out of her pocket to prick me if I should touch her again').

Somerset House

Strand, WC2 (7845 4600/www.somerset-house.org.uk). Covent Garden or Temple tube (closed Sun). **Open** 10am-6pm daily; extended hours for courtyard & terrace. *Tours* phone for details. **Admission** *Courtyard & terrace* free; charge for exhibitions. **Credit** *Shop* MC, V. **Map** p401 M7.

First a Tudor palace built by Edward Seymour, the first Duke of Somerset and brother of Henry VIII's third wife Jane, and later a royal residence, the original Somerset House was demolished by King

A river runs through it

As you stand at the north end of Blackfriars Bridge and look up towards Farringdon, it's hard to imagine that at one time you would have been standing bang in the middle of a sizeable canal. Designed by Sir Christopher Wren and built in the late 17th century, the New Canal formed part of the **Fleet**, at that time one of London's main rivers. The canal, though, is long gone, and the Fleet, which rises in Hampstead and flows down through Camden, King's Cross, Clerkenwell and the City before joining the Thames at **Blackfriars Bridge**, is now a totally submerged part of London's intricate network of underground tunnels.

Built in the aftermath of the Great Fire of London in 1666, the New Canal was said to have been inspired by the Grand Canal in Venice. It had four decorative bridges, including one at **Fleet Street** and another that now forms the **Holborn Viaduct**, and was a magnificent architectural spectacle. Unfortunately, Wren had not counted on the torrent of waste and offal that flowed downstream from the meat market at Smithfield. The canal was more like an open sewer, which impinged somewhat on gondola activity. The New Canal was in place for less than 100 years before it was covered over.

Further upstream, the river runs under what is now **Farringdon Road**, a section converted into a sewer when work began

on the Metropolitan line between King's Cross and Farringdon in the 19th century. Again, there are few hints that the river runs through this area, but hints there are: a road called **Fleet Square**, next to the Eastman Dental Hospital on Gray's Inn Road.

Our next clue is behind King's Cross Station: **Battle Bridge Road**, named after a bridge that originally crossed the Fleet. As Camden expanded, an anchor was discovered buried near here, suggesting that it was once possible to reach at least this far by boat. Further north, **Royal College Street** lies on top of another section of the river, and around **Kentish Town Road** it ran along a similar course to the Regent's Canal, excavations for which in 1812 relegated another section of the Fleet to sewer status.

North of Camden are two tributaries. One originates at the bathing pond in the south-east corner of **Hampstead Heath**, before flowing under Dartmouth Park and through Kentish Town; the other starts in the pond in the south of Hampstead Heath, runs under the train station, down **Fleet Road** and **Malden Road**, before meeting up with the first tributary at **Castlehaven Road**, just north of Camden Lock. Both stretches would have been pleasant babbling brooks, but suburban sprawl had encroached even on village Hampstead by the end of the 19th century.

While away the summer in **Lincoln's Inn Fields**.

Courtauld Gallery *Somerset House, Strand, WC2 (7848 2526/www.courtauld.ac.uk).* **Open** 10am-6pm daily (last entry 5.15pm). *Tours* phone for details. **Admission** £5; £4 concessions; free under-18s. Free to all 10am-2pm Mon. *Annual* £22. **Credit** MC, V.

The Courtauld collection is less broad and daunting than the National Gallery's, but it's still highly impressive. Happily, too, the Courtauld doesn't suffer anything like the crowds of the National Gallery, making a stroll around here a real pleasure. There are some world-famous works, led by Manet's plaintive *A Bar at the Folies Bergère* and Van Gogh's *Self-Portrait with a Bandaged Ear*, and others that aren't far behind: pieces by Cézanne, Modigliani and Toulouse-Lautrec are all standouts. Look out for Pissarro's *Lordship Lane Station*, and muse on just how much Dulwich has changed in the 130 years since it was painted.

Gilbert Collection *Somerset House, Strand, WC2 (7240 4080/www.gilbert-collection.org.uk).* **Open** 10am-6pm daily (last entry 5.30pm). *Tours* phone for details. **Admission** £5; £4 concessions; free students, under-18s. Free to all after 4.30pm daily. *Annual ticket* £10. **Credit** MC, V.

Only real estate money could buy a collection this garish. The realtor in question was Sir Arthur Gilbert, who spent half a lifetime amassing this £100 million spread of decorative art goodies. It'll not be to everyone's taste, that's for sure: the hardstone mosaics, many by the Montelatici family, are among the vilest pieces of art on display in London. Happily, there's plenty more to look at in the nicely laid out series of interlinked rooms, including a dazzling silver collection and a 200-strong array of intricately decorated snuff boxes, housed in an atmospherically lowlit space.

Hermitage Rooms *Somerset House, Strand, WC2 (information 7845 4630/Ticketmaster 7413 3398/ www.hermitagerooms.co.uk).* **Open** 10am-6pm daily (last admission 5.15pm). **Admission** £6; £4 concessions. **Credit** MC, V.

The Hermitage Rooms host rotating exhibitions from the world-famous State Hermitage Museum in St Petersburg. New exhibitions arrive twice a year, with everything from paintings and drawings to decorative art and jewellery liable to be presented. For each ticket sold, £1 goes to the State Hermitage.

George III, who approved the construction of William Chambers' neo-classical design. The new buildings became home to the Navy Board, to seats of learning such as the Royal Academy of the Arts and, eventually, to the Inland Revenue and the Register of Births, Marriages and Deaths.

Today, the tax office remains in the East and West wings, but after a magnificent millennial makeover, the **Courtauld Gallery**, **Gilbert Collection** and **Hermitage Rooms** have moved in. Also here is a display featuring artefacts from the first Somerset House found during excavation work, a café, a restaurant (the Admiralty; *see p204*), a river terrace, and the stunning Edmond J Safra Fountain Court, which gurgles away happily with special displays at 1pm, 6pm and 10pm most of the year. During the day, it's lovely; after dark, it's spectacular. Shocking to think that the courtyard in which it sits was, for years, a car park. There's a lovely open-air ice rink here each winter (*see p326*).

Lincoln's Inn & Gray's Inn

The winding streets to the west of the courts bear the names of several of the now-defunct Inns of Chancery, such as **New Inn** and **Clement's Inn**, and are home to the one-time cradle of left-wing agitation, the London School of Economics (LSE). Tucked away on **Portsmouth Street** is the Old Curiosity Shop, which purports to have been the inspiration for the Dickens novel of the same name.

The broad expanse of **Lincoln's Inn Fields** is London's largest square and Holborn's focal point. On the north side of the square is **Sir**

John Soane's Museum (*see below*); on the south side are the **Museums of the Royal College of Surgeons** (7869 6560), which hold a variety of anatomical and pathological specimens but are closed until 2004. To the east are the daunting buildings of the Inn itself.

Chancery Lane, running from the Strand to High Holborn, is home to the Public Records Office and the Law Society. At its northern end are the subterranean shops of the **London Silver Vaults** (7242 3844), selling everything from silver spoons to antique clocks. Around the corner, towards Holborn Circus, teeter the overhanging, half-timbered Tudor buildings of **Staple Inn**, one of the former Inns of Chancery. Across the road, by the ancient Cittie of Yorke pub, is an alley leading into the most northerly of the Inns of Court, **Gray's Inn**. The last Inn to be founded (in 1569), its hall – group tours of which can be arranged on 7458 7800 – contains a superb screen, said to be made from the wood of a galley from the Spanish Armada.

West of here, back towards Holborn tube, is **Red Lion Square**, an unprepossessing block notable for one crumpled old building. Just as radicalism has fallen out of fashion in these deeply conservative times, so the **Conway Hall**, built in 1929 and for years the cradle of the capital's campaigning left, has been all but forgotten. But though the spotlight is elsewhere these days, the hall still holds more than its share of free-thinkers and fundraisers. See www.conwayhall.org.uk or call 7242 8037 to find out what's on in town.

Sir John Soane's Museum

13 Lincoln's Inn Fields, WC2 (7405 2107/ www.soane.org). Holborn tube. **Open** 10am-5pm Tue-Sat; 6-9pm 1st Tue of mth. *Tours* 2.30pm Sat. **Admission** free; donations appreciated. *Tours* £3; free concessions. **Map** p399 M5.

One of London's most mind-boggling museum collections is crammed into the house of the man who amassed it. Sir John Soane was known in his lifetime as one of London's finest architects, most famous for the original Bank of England building. But he was also an inveterate collector, buying and hoarding an astonishing quantity of objects. The museum presents Soane's house as it was when he died in 1837: crammed to bursting with vases, statues, furniture, clocks, architectural models, works of art (including Hogarth's *Rake's Progress* series) and, downstairs, a 3,300-year-old Egyptian sarcophagus. It's the most wonderful kind of chaos; and beautiful, too, especially on the first Tuesday of the month, when the museum opens into the evening and is lit by candles. Tickets for the excellent tours go on sale at 2pm on a first-come first-served basis. The rest of the time entry is free, but give generously as the museum is planning to extend into the house next door, also owned by Soane. Restoration should begin in 2003.

Clerkenwell & Farringdon

Map p402

Chancery Lane or Farringdon tube.

The tidy little neighbourhood of **Clerkenwell**, which lies north and east of Holborn, has its origins in a hamlet that grew up in the 12th century around the religious foundations of the Priory of St John of Jerusalem, the long-gone St Mary's Nunnery and, from the 14th century, the Carthusian monastery of Charterhouse (now a posh OAP home). The original Clerk's Well, first mentioned in 1174 and long thought lost, was rediscovered in 1924, and can be viewed through the window of 14-16 Farringdon Lane.

Over the centuries, a strong crafts tradition grew up in Clerkenwell, as French Huguenots and other immigrants settled to practise their trades away from the City guilds. The area was thought 'an esteemed situation for gentry' until the early 19th century, when population pressure and dilapidation led to an influx of Irish, then Italian, immigrants. Radicals were also attracted; Lenin edited 17 editions of the Bolshevik paper *Iskra* from a back room (which has been preserved) in the Marx Memorial Library at 37A Clerkenwell Green. By the late 19th century, the district had become a 'decidedly unsavoury and unattractive locality'.

The fascinating enclave of **Ely Place** was once the site of the Bishop of Ely's London palace; all that remains is the delightful church of **St Etheldreda** (*see p101*). The private,

St Ethelreda. *See p101.*

gated road, now lined by Georgian houses, is crown property and remains outside the jurisdiction of the City of London. West of here, the no-nonsense **Leather Lane Market** sells clothes, food and pirate videos, and supports a number of cheap caffs. Running parallel is the centre of London's diamond trade, **Hatton Garden**, which doubled as a Greenwich Village street in Stanley Kubrick's *Eyes Wide Shut*.

Property developers finally wised up to the attractions of an area so close to the City and the West End in the 1980s, and Clerkenwell underwent a property boom. However, the craftspeople and artists haven't been driven out completely by the loft-dwelling financiers. That this is the case is down in no small part to the Clerkenwell Green Association, which provides affordable studios for artists and craftspeople at Pennybank Chambers in **St John's Square** and Cornwell House on **Clerkenwell Green**. Many sell their wares from their studios by appointment; see www.cga.org.uk for details.

Along with the property development has come a vast improvement in Clerkenwell's nightlife, non-existent a decade ago. **St John Street**, which links the Angel with Smithfield Market, is home to bloodthirsty restaurant St John (No.26; *see p193*) and hip bar Cicada (No.126), while the drab **Farringdon Road** offers pioneering gastropub the Eagle (No.159; *see p221*). The heart of the neighbourhood, though, is **Exmouth Market**, a chummy pedestrianised strip lined with record shops

(Clerkenwell Music at No.27), bars (football-themed Café Kick at No.43; *see p221*) and restaurants (Moro, at Nos.34-6; *see p195*).

Museum & Library of the Order of St John

St John's Gate, St John's Lane, EC1 (7324 4000/ www.sja.org.uk/history). Farringdon tube/rail. **Open** 9am-5pm Mon-Fri; 10am-4pm Sat. *Tours* 11am, 2.30pm Tue, Fri, Sat. **Admission** free; donations requested. **Map** p402 O4.

This was once the entrance to the Priory of St John of Jerusalem. Tucked away inside the door is a small museum with exhibits relating to the priory; you get the feeling there's an interesting story to be told here, but the shabby and unenthusiastic presentation doesn't do it justice. Better is the more modern exhibit, tucked down a corridor, relating to today's St John Ambulance Brigade, which uses interactive computer displays to tell the tale of this volunteer-led organisation.

St Etheldreda

14 Ely Place, EC1 (7405 1061). Chancery Lane tube. **Open** 7.30am-7pm daily. **Admission** free; donations appreciated. **Map** p402 N5.

Britain's oldest Catholic church (built in the 1250s) is the only surviving building of the Bishop of Ely's London residence. The simple chapel, lined with the statues of local martyrs, is London's sole remaining example, excepting parts of Westminster Abbey, of Gothic architecture from the reign of Edward I. The strawberries once grown in the gardens were said to be the finest in the city, receiving plaudits in Shakespeare's *Richard III*; every June the church holds a 'Strawberrie Fayre' in Ely Place.

Sightseeing

Bloomsbury & Fitzrovia

Where London learns.

Bloomsbury

Map p399

Chancery Lane, Holborn or Tottenham Court Road tube/Euston or King's Cross tube/rail.

Taking its name from 'Blemondisberi', or 'the manor of (William) Blemond' (he acquired the area in the early 13th century), Bloomsbury was mainly rural until the 1660s, when the fourth Earl of Southampton had Southampton (now **Bloomsbury) Square** built around his house. In the following century, the area to the north grew, with each successive street and square grander than the last. Check out **Bedford Square** (1775-80), London's only complete Georgian square, and huge **Russell Square**, laid out in 1800 and recently refurbished.

The area is less impressive today than it must have been two centuries ago, ravaged a little by time and traffic and a lot by some architecturally unsympathetic developments to the north (the ugly hotels on and around **Calthorpe Street** and **Woburn Place** in particular). Bloomsbury is also markedly less residential than it once was: most of the imposing townhouses are now used as offices. Still, the predominance of blue plaques on the buildings around here are reminders that this was once a prestigious neighbourhood.

Bloomsbury's western edges, along **Malet Street**, **Gordon Street** and **Gower Street**, are dominated by the **University of London** and its various associated institutions (*see p106* **The wanderers**), among them the **Percival David Foundation for Chinese Art** and the **Petrie Museum of Egyptian Archaeology** (*see p103*). Just south of the collegiate quarters is the impressive but troubled **British Museum**; don't attempt to see it all in a day.

But away from the grand institutions lie arguably Bloomsbury's most interesting pockets. To the south, linking **Bloomsbury Way** with **Southampton Row**, is **Sicilian Place**, a charming stretch of colonnaded shops. North-east of here is **Lamb's Conduit Street**, awash with quietly stylish new restaurants and decidedly old-school pubs; at the top of here, on **Guilford Street**, is **Coram's Fields**, a sweet kids' park handily close to the children's hospital on **Great Ormond Street**, and the faded grandeur of **Mecklenburgh Square**.

Head east and you'll soon reach Patrick Hodgkinson's **Brunswick Centre**. When it was completed in 1973, it was flagged as the future for community living: a shopping centre and cinema topped by sloped rows of flats, with a car park beneath. A wander around here is fascinating, and its Grade II listing is merited for curiosity value alone. Yet it's hard not to conclude that this angular slab must be a bleak place to live. Its incongruity is not all Hodgkinson's doing: he wanted to paint it cream to blend in with the surrounding Georgian stucco, but quit before it was finished and his wishes weren't honoured. The building remains grey and a far cry from **Woburn Walk**, a loveable stretch of shops and cafés to the north-west, near **The Place** theatre (*see p280*) and the traffic-clogged **Euston Road**.

British Museum

Great Russell Street, WC1 (7636 1555/recorded information 7323 8783/disabled information 7323 8299/textphone 7323 8920/www.thebritishmuseum. ac.uk). Holborn, Russell Square or Tottenham

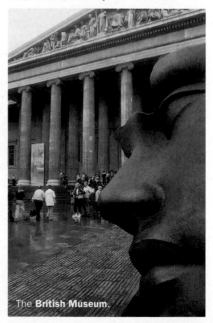

The **British Museum**.

Court Road tube. **Open** *Galleries* 10am-5.30pm
Mon-Wed, Sat, Sun; 10am-8.30pm Thur, Fri.
Great Court 9am-6pm Mon-Wed, Sun; 9am-11pm
Thur-Sat. *Highlights tours (90mins)* 10.30am,
1pm, 3pm daily. **Admission** free; donations
appreciated. *Temporary exhibitions* prices vary.
Highlights tours £8; £5 concessions, under-11s.
Map p399 K5.

Entering the world-class British Museum by the
main (south) entrance, you'll find yourself in the glorious light of the stunning, glass-roofed Queen
Elizabeth II Great Court, the largest covered public
space in Europe. There's a café and restaurant, but
the impatient will want to head straight to the
Rosetta Stone (Room 4) and Parthenon marbles
(Room 18) to the west. In the centre, the restored
Reading Room houses the Hamlyn library and a
state-of-the-art multimedia centre that offers virtual
tours and artefact searches. At the very least, you'll
be wanting to see the Egyptian mummies (Rooms
62-3), Sutton Hoo Ship Burial (Room 41) and Lindow
Man (Room 50), plus the various treasure hoards, the
working clocks (Room 44)... there's far too much for
one visit, so buy a souvenir guide (£6) and start with
your must-sees. For the indecisive, there are free
location-specific 'Eye Openers' tours, a 90-minute
general tour (£8; bookable at the information desk)
and three different audio tours (£3.50).

The museum began with royal physician Dr Hans
Sloane, who bequeathed his books, paintings, classical antiquities and stuffed animals to the nation in
1753. Imperial plunder gradually overwhelmed the
available space and, in 1847, the British Museum
was rehoused in the current neo-classical edifice.
Then, in 1998, the British Library (*see p105*) had to
be relocated to solve a new set of logistical problems
caused by the museum's steady expansion and huge
popularity. The move allowed the Sainsbury
African Galleries (Room 25) to open in 2001; it will
be joined by the Wellcome Gallery of Ethnography
in September 2003.

This year, the museum celebrates its 250th
anniversary with special temporary exhibitions
('The Museum of the Mind', 10 Apr-7 Sept; 'London,
1753', 23 May-23 Nov) and the reopening of the
King's Library in November. This will contain a
showcase permanent exhibition, 'Enlightenment:
Rethinking the World in the 18th Century', focusing
on how and why museums were created. Sadly,
many of the museum staff feel there's little to celebrate: 15% of them (mainly in the conservation
department, which bodes ill for the future) will lose
their jobs due to the museum's £6 million of debt.
Visitors rejoice, though: increased government funding will end gallery closures in early 2003.

Dickens' House
*48 Doughty Street, WC1 (7405 2127/
www.dickensmuseum.com). Chancery Lane
or Russell Square tube.* **Open** 10am-5pm Mon-Sat.
Tours by arrangement. **Admission** £4; £3
concessions; £2 5-15s; £9 family. *Tours* free.
Credit *Shop* AmEx, MC, V. **Map** p399 M4.

London's most famous author didn't really feel at
home until he left the city of his birth. Perhaps he
just never settled: London is scattered with plaques
commemorating the fact that the great man lived
here, from Devonshire Terrace near Paddington to
Camden's Bayham Street. This Georgian terrace,
though, is the only one of his homes to have survived
the years intact. Restored to its former state and
packed with Dickens ephemera, it's now a decent if
rather unexciting museum. On Wednesdays from
May to September, the one-man 'Sparkler of Albion'
shows bring the author and his characters to life.

Percival David Foundation of Chinese Art
*53 Gordon Square, WC1 (7387 3909/
www.pdfmuseum.org.uk). Euston Square, Goodge
Street or Russell Square tube/Euston tube/rail.*
Open 10.30am-5pm Mon-Fri. **Admission** free;
donations appreciated. **Map** p399 K4.

A University College London operation, the Percival
David Foundation holds what is reputed to be the
best collection of Chinese ceramics outside China:
stretching from the 10th to the 18th centuries, some
pieces are truly beautiful while others are chiefly
of historical value (and yes, this is a polite way of
saying that they're a bit ugly). It's named for the
professor who donated the collection to UCL in
1950 and, while academic in scope, is by no means
unwelcoming to the passer-by. Under-14s must be
accompanied by an adult.

Petrie Museum of Egyptian Archaeology
*University College London, Malet Place, WC1
(7679 2884/www.petrie.ucl.ac.uk). Goodge Street
tube.* **Open** 1-5pm Tue-Fri; 10am-1pm Sat.
Admission free; donations appreciated.
Map p399 K4.

It's a pity the Petrie sits so close to the British
Museum, whose own vast collection understandably
overshadows it. For this cosy museum, operated
under the auspices of UCL, holds one of the
world's finest collections of Egyptian and Sudanese
archaeology. This being a primarily academic establishment, the labelling of items could be a little more
involving, but the displays – the world's oldest piece
of clothing (from 2800 BC) sits among the requisite
hordes of mashed-up bits of pottery – still succeed
in holding the attention. Fascinating, all told.

St George Bloomsbury
*Bloomsbury Way, WC1 (7405 3044). Holborn or
Tottenham Court Road tube.* **Open** 9.30am-5.30pm
Mon-Fri; 10am-12.30pm Sun. **Map** p399 L5.

A classical portico leads from the smoke-blackened
exterior of this episcopal Hawksmoor church (1716-
31) into its flaking interior. If you want to see inside
it, you'll have to be quick: the church looks likely to
close during summer for an extensive and much-
needed programme of renovation work. If you make
it before it shuts (call ahead to check), try and time
your visit with one of the regular lunchtime concerts.

St Pancras Parish Church

*Euston Road (corner of Upper Woburn Place), NW1
(7388 1461). Euston tube/rail.* **Open** 12.45-2pm
Wed; noon-2pm Thur; 9.15-11am Sat; 7.45am-noon,
5.30-7.15pm Sun; occasional lunchtimes Tue, Fri.
Services 8am, 10am, 6pm Sun; 1.15pm Wed. *Recital*
1.15pm Thur. **Admission** free. **Map** p399 K3.
Built in 1822 at a cost of £89,296, this was London's
most expensive church since St Paul's. Its spectacular exterior – the doorway of which provides
shelter for many of the area's homeless people –
was inspired by the Ionic Temple of Erectheum in
Athens and its main features, the Caryatid porches,
are used as entrances to the burial vaults.

Somers Town & King's Cross

Where Bloomsbury is genteel and polite,
Somers Town, which sits on the other side
of Euston Road, is rough and rude. Three rail
stations dominate it, sitting back cockily on
the Euston Road and ferrying passengers to
and from the north. The furthest west of the
three is **Euston Station**, a bleak, characterless
1960s building erected after British Rail
was shamefully allowed to demolish Philip
Hardwick's glorious early Victorian 72-foot (22-
metre) portico and similarly grand Great Hall.
The furthest east is Lewis and Joseph Cubitt's
King's Cross Station, the impact of whose
fearsome façade has been all but eradicated by
the wretched modern frontage. In between the
two is **St Pancras Station**, a magnificent and
much-loved Victorian glass-and-iron train shed
fronted by Sir George Gilbert Scott's exuberant,
high Gothic Midland Grand Hotel, now known
as **St Pancras Chambers** (*see below*).

But between and beyond the rail termini,
Somers Town is a virtual wasteland. Towards
Euston sits a labyrinthine council estate
long riven by racial conflict. Around King's
Cross, drug dealers conduct their trade and the
occasional downcast hooker touts for business,
the police's persistent attempts to rid the area of
its cavalcade of sleazy characters having failed.
Behind the station, grim and shady stretches of
wasteland are being readied for the arrival of
the Channel Tunnel rail link in 2007. But until
it shows up – and possibly long beyond then –
it seems likely that King's Cross and Somers
Town will remain an uninviting area.

British Library

*96 Euston Road, NW1 (7412 7332/www.bl.uk).
Euston Square tube/Euston or King's Cross
tube/rail.* **Open** 9.30am-6pm Mon, Wed-Fri;
9.30am-8pm Tue; 9.30am-5pm Sat; 11am-5pm
Sun. **Admission** free; donations appreciated.
Map p399 K3.
Even fans of the red-brick British Library would
agree it's better inside than out, notwithstanding the
imposing portico and Paolozzi's grand reworking of

St George Bloomsbury. *See p103.*

Blake's Newton in the forecourt. With two cafés and
three exhibition spaces around a central glass tower
containing the King's Library, there's a diverting
morning to be spent here. The John Ritblat Gallery
is the draw for bookworms: here you can see the
Magna Carta, Beatles lyric sheets and the Gutenberg
Bible, listen to archive recordings of James Joyce or
Bob Geldof, or gawp at Beethoven's tuning fork. The
Pearson Gallery's temporary exhibitions begin in
2003 with 'Magic Pencil: Children's Book Illustration
Today', curated by kids' laureate Quentin Blake, and
downstairs, there's a pleasingly interactive history
of printing, binding and sound recording. Free access
to the library's 150 million items depends on getting
a Readers' Ticket (7412 7677), but if your research
needs aren't pressing, there are guided tours.

St Pancras Chambers

*St Pancras Station, Euston Road, NW1 (7304
3921). King's Cross tube/rail.* **Open** 11.30am-
3.30pm Mon-Fri. *Tours* 11am, 1.30pm Sat, Sun.
Admission free. *Tours* £5. **No credit cards.**
Map p399 L3.
This small exhibition about the history of the long-
deserted Midland Grand Hotel is limited, from
Monday to Friday, to a few displays on the ground
floor. However, the hour-long weekend guided tours
(no booking; it's first-come, first-served) afford
the opportunity to see a little more of the building's
magnificent interior. In 2004 work will begin on converting St Pancras Chambers into a hotel once more,
so see inside it while you still have the chance.

St Pancras Old Church & St Pancras Gardens

St Pancras Road, NW1 (7974 1693). King's Cross tube/rail. **Open** *Gardens* 7am-dusk daily. **Map** p399 K2.

St Pancras Old Church, set on one of the oldest sites of Christian worship in London (it may date back to the fourth century), has been ruined and rebuilt on a number of occasions, though it's now a handsome enough building. However, it's the surprisingly serene churchyard, beautifully restored a couple of years ago after an extended period of neglect, that merits the hike up the bleak St Pancras Road. Among those buried here are writer William Godwin and his wife, Mary Wollstonecraft; over this grave, daughter Mary Godwin (author of *Frankenstein*) declared her love for poet Percy Bysshe Shelley. However, the most famous grave is that of Sir John Soane: one of only two Grade I-listed tombs in Britain (the other is Karl Marx's, in Highgate Cemetery), its dome went on to influence Sir Giles Gilbert Scott's design of the classic British phone box.

Fitzrovia

Maps p398 & p399

Goodge Street, Great Portland Street, Oxford Circus, Tottenham Court Road or Warren Street tube.

Fitzrovia, squeezed in between Gower Street, Oxford Street, Great Portland Street and Euston Road, was named for Fitzroy Square in its north-western corner, which was itself named after Henry Fitzroy, the son of Charles II, and later the Earl of Euston. For a long time, it was the haunt of down-at-heel artists and writers, who drank away their talent in pubs such as the Fitzroy Tavern on **Charlotte Street**.

With the exception of the smoggy, mile-long **Tottenham Court Road**, dominated at its southern end by electronics shops and in its northern portion by stores hawking home furnishings, the area is quiet. Shoppers tend not to stray north of **Oxford Street**, and the lack of sights – the main one, the BT Tower on

The wanderers Collegiate Bloomsbury

Fashionable two centuries ago but now merely respectable, Bloomsbury's gaggle of venerated institutions form the most highly concentrated area of academia in London.
Start at Euston Square station and walk south along Gower Street.
On your right, its red-brick facade and turrets rising ominously above its surroundings, is the **University College Hospital** (UCH) building. Much groundbreaking work has been achieved in various medical fields, such as neurologist Sir William Gowers' still-revered 1880 textbook on the nervous system. Yet if you removed UCH from Bloomsbury, placed it on a dark hill and added some forked lightning, it could serve as a remarkably good house of horror.

Opposite sits **University College London** (UCL), founded in 1826 along radical lines: female students and non-Anglicans excluded by Oxford and Cambridge were admitted. Its grand frontispiece, a classical portico topped with a striking dome, was the work of architect William Wilkins, who also built the National Gallery. Inside lies one of the oddest exhibits in all of London: the preserved skeleton of Jeremy Bentham, whose utilitarian beliefs influenced the university's founding. Bentham's head used to lie in a box between his legs but was removed when authorities found it was being used as a football in the front quadrangle.

Continue south along Gower Street and turn left on to Torrington Place.
At this junction lies a large and textbook-heavy branch of **Waterstone's** bookshop. From the south side of UCL you can gain access to the **Petrie Museum** (*see p103*), an oft-overlooked collection of Ancient Egyptian artefacts.
Turn right onto Malet Street.
The **University of London Union** (ULU) is a draw for students from all London's affiliated colleges and universities, offering shops, bars and a gig venue (*see p311*). On Fridays, pick up second-hand bargains from the book fair.

Opposite lie two ill-fitting institutions: the smart, modernised front of the **Royal Academy for Dramatic Art** (RADA), and the greyer **School of Hygiene and Tropical Medicine** (ScHTM). The former's doors admit just 32 students a year, which seems miserly until you see its list of alumni: Anthony Hopkins, John Hurt, Kenneth Branagh... The ugly '50s building next to ULU is **Birkbeck College**, whose focus for 180 years has been on helping full-time workers obtain degrees.

Senate House, the tallest building in the area at 210 feet (64 metres), is the administrative centre of the University of London. Hitler reportedly liked the building and fancied setting up here had Germany won World War II. The massive library is worth the entry just for the archaic lifts that connect its

Howland Street, for a long time the tallest building in London, closed to the public years ago after bomb threats – mean it's off most tourists' maps. Office staff, many from the worlds of advertising and broadcasting, and students from Bloomsbury colleges and the University of Westminster on **New Cavendish Street** plug the pubs in the evening, with the former also making good use of Charlotte Street restaurants such as the Spanish **Navarro's** (No.67) and the French **Elena's L'Étoile** (No.30) during their lunch hour.

All Saints

Margaret Street, W1 (7636 1788/www.ucl.ac.uk/ ~ucgbmxd/allss.htm). Oxford Circus tube. **Open** 7am-7pm daily. *Services* 8am, 10.20am, 11am, 5.15pm, 6pm Sun. **Map** p398 J5.
Designed by William Butterfield around the time that Ruskin's *Stones of Venice* was published, this Victorian church embodies Ruskinian principles. It's noted for its structural polychromy (the use of highly coloured materials rather than surface decoration).

Pollock's Toy Museum

1 Scala Street (entrance on Whitfield Street), W1 (7636 3452/www.pollocksweb.co.uk). Goodge Street tube. **Open** 10am-5pm Mon-Sat. **Admission** £3; £1.50 3-16s; free under-3s. **Credit** *Shop* MC, V. **Map** p398 J5.
Shuffle through the small entrance and enter a veritable Tardis of a building, converted a little chaotically into an incomparably charming museum of children's toys. There are thousands of exhibits here in a multitude of themed cabinets: some you might expect (toy soldiers, teddy bears, board games, dolls' houses), others may surprise (the folksy toys from Mexico and India are lovely, while the penny dreadful comics will raise a smile). The museum's most impressive collection, however, is of toy theatres; call for details of regular puppet shows. It's all a long way from PS2s and Bob the Builder. Incidentally, the fact that there are three floors on the way up but four on the way down is explained by the fact that the museum sits in two house: one built in 1880, the other a century older. On street level sits a delightful little shop selling yo-yos, badges, puppets and other arcane goodies.

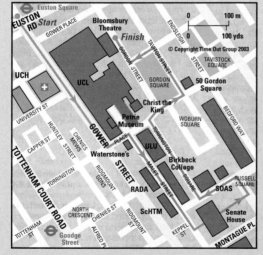

north-eastern corner of Russell Square is the Faber building, now part of SOAS but then the offices of the famous publisher; TS Eliot once worked here.
Continue through the campus to Byng Place.
Opposite is the stunning Gothic Revival church **Christ the King**, formerly used by 19th-century sect the Catholic Apostolic Church but now, like almost everything in Bloomsbury, part of the University of London.
Turn right and walk round Gordon Square.
Virginia Woolf and her acolytes founded the **Bloomsbury Group** at 50 Gordon Square. A self-absorbed clan of writers and artists, they counted among their number Lytton Strachey (who lived at No.51) and economist John Maynard Keynes (at No.46). Nearby is the **Percival David Gallery of Chinese Art** (*see p103*).
Up Gordon Street, itself in the north-west corner of the square, is UCL's **Bloomsbury Theatre** and the **UCL Student Union**. During term-time, the street is a hive of activity as students rush between lectures. Understandably, it's even noisier around closing time on a Friday night.

furthest reaches, though you may find its security guards less than welcoming.
*Walk through Senate House and on to Russell Square. If you turn right, you'll soon see the **British Museum** (see p102). Instead, though, we shall turn left up Thornhaugh Street.*
Behind Birkbeck is the **School of Oriental and African Studies** (SOAS). The main building was completed in the '40s, but there's an ugly '70s extension. Tucked into this

Marylebone

Fashionable shops, smart restaurants and unappealing attractions.

Maps p395 & p398

Baker Street, Bond Street, Edgware Road, Great Portland Street, Marble Arch, Oxford Circus or Regent's Park tube.

Hemmed in by the noisy thoroughfares of Oxford Street, Edgware Road, Marylebone Road and Great Portland Street, Marylebone was once made up of two ancient manors, Lileston (Lisson) and Tyburn (named after a stream that flowed through the area). By the 14th century, these manors were violent places; indeed, Tyburn was the site of a famous gallows until 1783, a spot marked by a plaque on the traffic island at Marble Arch.

After frequent ransacking of the parish church (which stood on what is now Oxford Street; large numbers of human bones were found marking the spot), it was demolished in 1400. A new church was built halfway up what has since become **Marylebone High Street**. It was called St Mary by the Bourne, a name that soon came to cover the entire village. This had been abbreviated to Marylebone by 1626.

Though nothing remains of the first two parish churches, you can see the foundations of the third – damaged in the war, demolished in 1949 – near the top of the High Street, in the **Memorial Garden of Rest**. Connected with many famed figures (Francis Bacon married here in 1606, William Hogarth painted the interior in 1735, and Lord Byron was baptised here in 1788), the garden is a lovely place to take stock of the area, its shops, restaurants and pubs centred around **Marylebone Lane** and Marylebone High Street.

Away from the shopping hub, Marylebone is a sedate world of orderly Georgian squares and streets. In the 16th century, its northern half – now **Regent's Park** – became a royal hunting ground, while the southern section was bought up by the Portman family. Two centuries later, the Portmans developed many of the elegant streets and squares that lend the locale its dignified air. Some, such as **Bryanston Square** and **Montagu Square**, have survived well; others, such as **Cavendish Square** (whose southern tip is marked by the rear of John Lewis, London's most approachable department store), are less impressive. One of the squares, laid out in 1761, still bears the Portman name; another, 1776's **Manchester Square**, is home to the **Wallace Collection** (*see p109*).

Harley Street and **Wimpole Street** have been renowned since the mid 19th century for their medical establishments. It was from No.50 that Elizabeth Barrett eloped with fellow poet Robert Browning in 1846; they were secretly married at the fourth **St Marylebone Parish Church**, on Marylebone Road. Dickens lived next door to the church at 1 Devonshire Terrace (demolished in 1959). Across the road, the **Royal Academy of Music** (*see p306* **School's in**), founded in 1822 and designed by John Nash, has a new glass recital building and a delightful little museum (7873 7373; open 12.30-6pm Mon-Fri; 2-5.30pm Sat, Sun).

Portland Place, leading up to Regent's Park, was the glory of 18th-century London. Though many of its houses have been rebuilt, its spacious proportions have been maintained. Where it links at **Langham Place** with Nash's **Regent Street** is the BBC's HQ, Broadcasting House. Next door is Nash's church **All Souls** (1822-4), with its slender spire. Over the road is the Langham Hilton, the first of London's grand hotels (it opened in 1865), while further north is the splendidly solid **Royal Insitute of British Architects** (*see p294*).

North of Marylebone Road, the landscape changes with the ugly '50s and '60s housing developments of **Lisson Grove**. One treasure is the plush Landmark Hotel, which opened as the Great Central Hotel in 1899 and was the last significant Victorian hotel to be built in the golden age of steam. After closing in 1939, it was used as offices, but in 1986 it was redeveloped as a hotel.

Slightly further west, **Church Street**, while a little rough around the edges, is a popular local food and general market that is rapidly gentrifying at its eastern end. Alfie's Antiques Market (*see p231*) and the clutch of designer homewares shops that have sprung up round it are being touted as the new Portobello.

St James's Spanish Place

Spanish Place, 22 George Street, W1 (7935 0943/ www.spanishplace.hemscott.net). Baker Street or Bond Street tube. **Open** 7am-6.45pm daily. *Services* 7.15am, 12.30pm, 6pm Mon-Fri; 10am, 6pm Sat; 8.30am, 9.30am, 10.30am, noon, 4pm, 7pm Sun. **Admission** free.

This early Gothic Roman Catholic church derives its name from an Iberian connection dating back to the restoration of Charles II, when a Spanish embassy was re-established in London, first in Ormond Street, then in Manchester Square. In 1791, just after the repeal of laws affecting Catholic worship, a chapel was built on the corner of Spanish Place and Charles Street (now George Street). Most of the holy objects in today's church came from this older building, mentioned by Thackeray in *Vanity Fair*. Official Spanish links ceased in 1827 but some items, including Alfonso XIII's standard, remain. The present church opened in 1890, directly opposite the first. Its Lady Chapel was designed by JF Bentley, architect of Westminster Cathedral. It was at St James's that 19-year-old Vivian Hartley, later known as Vivien Leigh, wed barrister Leigh Holman in 1932.

Wallace Collection

Hertford House, Manchester Square, W1 (7935 0687/www.the-wallace-collection.org.uk). Bond Street tube. **Open** 10am-5pm Mon-Sat; noon-5pm Sun. **Admission** free. **No credit cards. Map** p398 G5.
This sumptuously restored late 18th-century house belonged to Sir Richard Wallace, who, as the illegitimate heir of the Marquis of Hertford, inherited the furniture, paintings and Sèvres porcelain that the latter, a great Francophile, bought for safekeeping after the Revolution. Highlights include a Minton-tiled smoking room, rooms full of armour and weaponry and works by Titian, Velázquez, Gainsborough and Sir Joshua Reynolds. Franz Hals' *Laughing Cavalier* and Fragonard's *The Swing*, with its pink-cheeked lovers and complicit nymphs and statues, stand out. An extensive renovations programme in 2000 added several new galleries, which blend in beautifully with their historic surroundings, and the glass-roofed restaurant, Café Bagatelle, is among the best of all the London museums.

Regent's Park

Regent's Park (7486 7905, open dawn to dusk daily), laid out in 1817-28 by John Nash and named for his faithful patron, is central London's most well-mannered park. Originally part of Middlesex Forest, it's lively in summer, with a boating lake, tennis courts, music, a café and an open-air theatre (*see p338*). The **Outer Circle**, the road running around the park, is bordered to the south by Marylebone Road and Nash's sublime Park Crescent, completed in 1818 and originally intended to be a full circus. To the west of the park is the London Central Mosque, built in 1978; to the east are the splendid Palladian mansions of **Cumberland Terrace**, also by Nash. The northern edge of the park holds **London Zoo** (*see below*).

Just below Regent's Park, fronting out on to the perpetually congested Marylebone Road, are **Madame Tussaud's** (*see p110*) and the **London Planetarium** (*see below*). Nearby **Baker Street**, which leads to Oxford Street, is as alienating as Gerry Rafferty described it in his 1978 hit ('it's got so many people but it's got

The **BBC**.
See p108.

no soul'). Fictional 'tec Sherlock Holmes lived at No.221B, a fact celebrated at various museums (*see p110*), hotels and souvenir stands nearby.

London Planetarium

Marylebone Road, NW1 (0870 400 3000/ www.madame-tussauds.com). Baker Street tube. **Open** *June-Aug* 10am-5pm daily. *Sept-May* 12.30-5pm Mon-Fri; 10am-5pm Sat, Sun.
Admission (includes admission to Madame Tussaud's; *see p110*) £14.95; £11.70 concessions; £10.50 5-15s; £49 family. Under-5s not admitted.
Credit AmEx, MC, V. **Map** p398 G4.
The 20-minute show seems to be over very quickly. It's projected on to the dome's ceiling every 40 minutes, but you'd be hard pushed to fill a half-hour wait in the lobby: the zero-gravity weighing machine is briefly diverting, but conversations with the waxwork Stephen Hawking are a bit one-sided. The show itself has some great 3D motion effects, but the overenthusiastic narration irritates as much as it informs, and the supernova's a bit of a damb squib.

London Zoo

Regent's Park, NW1 (7722 3333/www.londonzoo. co.uk). Baker Street or Camden Town tube then 274, C2 bus. **Open** *Nov-Feb* 10am-4pm daily. *Mar-Oct* 10am-5.30pm daily. **Admission** £11; £9.30 concessions; £8 3-15s; free under-3s; £34 family.
Credit AmEx, MC, V. **Map** p398 G2.
In accordance with modern sensibilities, London Zoo, which celebrated its 175th birthday in 2001, lays heavy stress on its breeding programmes (of the more than 600 species that live here, 150 are on the International Union for the Conservation of Nature's Red List of the world's most threatened species), yet

P-P-P-Pick up a penguin at **London Zoo**. *See p109.*

it still manages to entertain. You'll need at least a day to make the most of it, with feeding times, reptile handling and the Web of Life exhibition in the Millennium Conservation Centre, where biodiversity is both explained and celebrated, among the more popular attractions. Elsewhere, the penguins parading like city gents in their famous modernist pool designed by Tecton and Lubetkin are perennial favourites, as is the children's petting zoo. If you come in spring (when, before the school holiday crowds descend, it can be a strangely romantic place) and summer, or on a winter weekend, you can reach the zoo by canalboat from Little Venice or Camden Lock (London Waterbus Company; 7482 2550); this has the not inconsiderable advantage of allowing you to circumvent the queues at the front.

Madame Tussaud's

Marylebone Road, NW1 (0870 400 3000/ www.madame-tussauds.com). Baker Street tube. **Open** *May-Sept* 9am-5.30pm daily. *Oct-June* 10am-5.30pm Mon-Fri; 9.30am-5.30pm Sat, Sun. Times vary during school holidays; phone for details. **Admission** (includes admission to London Planetarium; *see p109*) £14.95; £11.70 concessions; £10.50 5-15s; £49 family. **Credit** AmEx, MC, V. **Map** p398 G4.
Madame Tussaud's ticket hotline, which gives visitors timed entry slots, has made headway against the queues, but why people still flock here at all remains a mystery. Granted, some of the characters are astonishingly realistic and, until the novelty wears off, there's fun to be had as visitors bump into waxworks and half-apologise ('Oops, sorry… Buffy?!?'). But the voiceover scripts are dreadful, the selection of dummies eccentric (Yoshida Shigeru, anyone?) and, were it not for their clothes, the likes of James Dean, Elvis

and Brando would be unrecognisable. The Chamber of Horrors is as disappointing as it is tasteless, with an unconvincingly eviscerated Ripper victim and burning Joan of Arc. The nadir, though, is the 'Spirit of London' ride. 400 years of London history in as many seconds is pretty droll, but the Pudding Lane baker's stage-school Cockney brings the house down: 'Weren't *my* fault,' he tells the fleeing Mayor. Harrison Ford pursued by glitterball will please the mums; divorced dads like Kylie's bum 'n' boots and Darcey Bussell's interminable legs.

Sherlock Holmes Museum

221B Baker Street, NW1 (7935 8866/www.sherlockholmes.co.uk). Baker Street tube. **Open** 9.30am-6pm daily. **Admission** £6; £4 5-16s; free under-5s. **Credit** AmEx, DC, MC, V. **Map** p398 G4.
The amazing thing about this preposterous museum is that it nearly works: the burning candles, flickering grates, pipe, violin and hypodermic in the first-floor study are great. Then it all goes wrong. The waxworks on the top two floors are rubbish, the cases of curios seem to be there solely to prove someone's read the books, and the fascinating Conan Doyle conspicuous by his absence. In the author's place, the insistent it's-like-Holmes-really-existed hokum (the 'real' door key, Watson's handwritten notebook, the blue plaque outside) is just annoying. The Sherlock Holmes Collection of books, journals, photos and filmscripts (round the corner at Marylebone Library; 7641 1039, by appointment only) is a better bet for serious Sherlockians. Curiously, the nearby Sherlock Holmes Hotel (108 Baker Street, W1; 7958 5222/www.shh-w1.com) avoids the deerstalker schtick entirely: it's just a nice little boutique hotel.

Oxford Street & Marylebone High Street

Discreet Marylebone hits snooty Mayfair at **Oxford Street**, with **Marble Arch**, another Nash creation, marking its western extent. This unremarkable monument was intended to be the entrance to Buckingham Palace but, discovered to be too puny, was moved to this site in 1851. Only members of the Royal Family and some military types are allowed by law to walk through the central portal.

Oxford Street is London's most famous shopping street. It is also a scruffy, crowd-choked nightmare, lined with tatty clothes retailers. Selfridges (*see p236*) and the aforementioned John Lewis (*see p235*) are two of its few redeeming features.

More enticing shops can be found on **Marylebone High Street**: swanky clothes boutiques (for example, Agnès B at Nos.40-41), cosmetics retailers (such as Aveda, at Nos.28-9) and furniture shops (try Shaker, at Nos.72-3). It's here, too, that you'll find the area's best restaurants, among them Orrery (at No.55; *see p199*) and the Providores & Tapa Room (109 Marylebone High Street; *see p196*). The downside to this boom has been the inevitable arrival of chains such as Gap and Starbucks, which are starting to deprive the area of what has hitherto constituted its charm: its individuality.

Sisters are doing it for themselves

London is full of grand religious buildings. This isn't one of them. Indeed, while other churches, cathedrals and temples in the city are of record-breakingly large proportions, the only record held by the **Tyburn Convent** (8 Hyde Park Place, W2; 7723 7262/ www.tyburnconvent.org.uk) is that of London's smallest house: one of its buildings, is a mere three and a half feet wide (*pictured*).

The convent stands yards from what is now Marble Arch, but what was formerly Tyburn Tree, a public execution site from 1196 to 1783. When Henry VIII established the Church of England and declared himself its head in order that he might be allowed to divorce and remarry, he set about making Catholicism illegal. Between 1535 and 1681, 105 Catholics were martyred here.

The site became a place of pilgrimage for Catholics during the 19th century. However, it was not until 1903 that Tyburn Convent was established here by a group of Benedictine sisters, led by Mother Marie-Adele Garnier, who had been forced to flee France due to religious persecution. A link to the area's past can be found in the crypt, to which tours are offered daily at 10.30am, 3.30pm and 5.30pm (groups should call ahead to book). In a series of reliquaries are kept remains of some of those Catholics executed at Tyburn; assorted paintings commemorate their lives.

The area has changed immeasurably in the century since the convent was set up here. But life still goes on within its walls much as it always has. Just over 20 nuns live here now, in this oasis of peace. It's not grand. But regardless of your religious persuasion, it is a fascinating and moving place.

Sightseeing

Mayfair & St James's

Every street is millionaire's row in these classy, timeworn neighbourhoods.

Mayfair

Map p400

Bond Street, Green Park, Hyde Park Corner, Marble Arch, Oxford Circus or Piccadilly Circus tube.

Some London neighbourhood names are arcane. Others are peculiar. A few are downright mysterious. And Mayfair? Well, Mayfair is named after a fair that used to be held here in May. Rocket science this ain't.

The area, which is now contained between Oxford Street, Regent Street, Piccadilly and Park Lane, has belonged to the Grosvenor family since 1677. Back then, it was largely open land, though as the 18th century began, building work on it was well under way. The fair itself, an annual two-week binge, began in 1686, but local toffs forced its closure in the 1700s because they felt it was lowering the tone of the area.

The toffs are still in residence, and the tone of the area is still sky-high. Mayfair has arguably undergone the fewest changes, as regards social make-up, of all central London neighbourhoods. It's always been posh here: indeed, while the Duke of Wellington is its most distinguished former resident (he briefly lived at 4 Hamilton Place, before moving across the road to Apsley House in 1817), he has stiff competition. Benjamin Disraeli (29 Park Lane), Florence Nightingale (10 South Street), Percy Bysshe Shelley (29 Aldford Street), Sir Robert Peel (12 Great Stanhope Street), Handel and Jimi Hendrix (both at 25 Brook Street, though not at the same time), the Beatles (who lived in Flat L, 57 Green Street during 1963 and '64, and later set up the offices of Apple at 3 Savile Row)… the list is more or less endless.

And still they come. Mayfair's expansive, handsome architecture has long acted as a magnet to the wealthy. However, it's by no means unapproachable to the commoner. While a distinct whiff of exclusivity pervades its immaculate square, and its shops concentrate on goods few dare even to dream of affording – from designer clothes boutiques on **New Bond Street** and immaculate tailors on **Savile Row** to commercial art galleries on **Cork Street** – other pockets of the neighbourhood are more down to earth.

Three large squares dominate the north of Mayfair: **Hanover**, **Berkeley** and the immense **Grosvenor**, which contains the US Embassy and a grand statue of Franklin D Roosevelt. To the east lies Mayfair's commercial spread, the suitmakers, art retailers, couturiers and auctioneers (Phillips and Sotheby's both sit on New Bond Street); take time to visit Lawrence Holofcener's peculiar statues of Roosevelt and Winston Churchill that sit at either end of a bench on **Grafton Street**. To the north is the rather tattier Oxford Street and the neighbourhood's very own corner shop, Selfridges (*see p236*).

Walking south or south-east from Grosvenor Square will lead you through an assortment of imposing thoroughfares. You won't, sadly, hear any nightingales in **Berkeley Square**: the speeding couriers have scared them all away, though few are convinced there were any here to begin with. West on **Curzon Street** is one of London's nicest cinemas, the Curzon Mayfair (*see p284*), while the frontage of one of London's many lost tube stations has been preserved beautifully on **Down Street**.

However, it's the area around **Shepherd Market**, named for a food market set up here by architect Edward Shepherd in the early 18th

Handel House Museum. *See p113.*

Puttin' on **The Ritz** down on imposing Piccadilly.

century, that offers most for the visitor. Here you'll find a couple of fine, relaxed pubs (Ye Grapes at 16 Shepherd Market and the Shepherd's Tavern at 50 Hertford Street), several branches of Turkish eaterie Sofra, and, less salubriously, a handful of downmarket prostitutes, working from tatty apartment blocks whose accommodations probably bear little resemblance to the clutch of high-end hotels – the Hilton, the Dorchester, the Metropolitan and the Inter-Continental – mere moments away on **Park Lane**.

Faraday Museum

Royal Institution, 21 Albemarle Street, W1 (7409 2992/www.ri.org). Green Park tube. **Open** 10am-5pm Mon-Fri. *Tours* by arrangement. **Admission** £1. *Tours* £5. **Credit** MC, V. **Map** p400 J7.

This small museum in the building where Michael Faraday was professor features a re-creation of the lab where he discovered the laws of electromagnetics. It's probably of interest only to those of a scientific bent, but if you're at the Royal Institution, ask to see the prized possession, which isn't on public display: a silver cup presented to Humphry Davy by Tsar Alexander I in 1825 in gratitude for what Davy's famous lamp had done for the miners of Russia.

Handel House Museum

25 Brook Street (entrance at rear), W1 (7495 1685/ www.handelhouse.org). Bond Street tube. **Open** 10am-6pm Tue, Wed, Fri, Sat; 10am-8pm Thur; noon-6pm Sun. **Admission** £4.50; £3.50 concessions; £2 6-15s; free under-5s. **Credit** MC, V. **Map** p400 J7.

The fundraising battle was long and laborious, and the restoration painstaking. However, this only made the eventual opening in late 2001 of London's first classical music museum that much sweeter for the enthusiasts behind it. George Frideric Handel moved to Britain from his native Germany aged 25 and settled in this Mayfair house 12 years later, remaining here until his death in 1759. The house has been beautifully restored with original and recreated furnishings, paintings owned by the composer and a welter of scores. The programme of events is surprisingly dynamic for a museum so small: there are activities tilted at kids every Saturday and recitals most Thursday evenings, plus other less frequent events. Worth the wait, definitely.

Piccadilly & Green Park

Piccadilly, one of central London's grandest roads, links Hyde Park Corner with Piccadilly Circus. It's quintessentially British, too: en route down it, you'll pass the Apsley House (*see below*) and the stunning Wellington Arch (*see p115*), both at Hyde Park Corner; the Ritz Hotel (No.150); food emporium Fortnum & Mason (No.181); the Burlington Arcade (formerly a brothel, now a stuck-up shopping mall), and the **Royal Academy of Arts** (*see p114*).

But before any of those, you'll wander past **Green Park**. Originally used as a burial ground for London's lepers, it's the least glamorous and lovely of all central London's major parks: it can't match the views of St James's Park (*see p130*), the grandeur of Regent's Park (*see p109*) or the sheer scale of Hyde Park (*see p136*). However, it's not without its charms: in the autumn, the stroll down Queen's Walk from Green Park tube to Buckingham Palace is especially pleasant, and the gas lamps are a dusky treat all year round.

Apsley House: The Wellington Museum

149 Piccadilly, W1 (7499 5676/www.vam.ac.uk). Hyde Park Corner tube. **Open** 11am-5pm Tue-Sun. *Tours* by arrangement. **Admission** £4.50 (includes audio guide); £3 concessions; free under-18s, over-60s. *Tours* £2.50 per person (min 10). **Credit** AmEx, DC, MC, V. **Map** p400 G8.

London loves Animals

It's a truism – a cliché, even – that Britain is a nation of animal lovers. However, Londoners may lead the doting pack: witness the sculptural paeans erected to furry friends in the capital. The most recent is the statue of William Hogarth, best known as a painter but also a campaigner against animal cruelty. Appropriate, then, that he should be commemorated next to his pet pug **Trump**.

Cats are well celebrated here. **Hodge**, Dr Johnson's pet pussy, sits practically twitching its tail with alertness opposite the pioneer lexicographer's house in Gough Square (see p85), though he's nowhere near as famous as the lifesize **bronze feline** that's lurked halfway up Highgate Hill since 1964 to commemorate Dick Whittington's turning back (see p147).

The significance of lions and **unicorns** in the heraldic iconography of London ensures they are well represented in terms of statuary: take the stone set at the Kensington Road entrance to Kensington Palace (see p138), dating from the time of William III, or the 1897 pair, accompanied by Britannia, over the portico of Tate Britain (see p135). Another notable **lion** is to be found on the South Bank, by Westminster Bridge (see p71). Relocated from its original position by the now-demolished Red Lion Brewery, it's one of the largest remaining examples of Coade stone, an artificial stone whose secret formula died with its inventor, Eleanor Coade.

Some foreigners have got in on the act, parading their own iconic beasties. The American Embassy in Grosvenor Square (see p112) is topped by an **aluminium eagle** with a characteristically modest 35-foot (11-metre) wingspan, while South Africa House in Trafalgar Square (see p129) has Sir Charles Wheeler's 1934 **gilt springbok**.

For exotic beasts, try Crystal Palace. There you'll find David Wynne's black marble sculpture of **Guy the Gorilla** – London Zoo's star attraction before his premature death in 1978 – which some critics regard as the finest animal statue in Britain. Elsewhere in the grounds are 29 **brick, iron and stucco dinosaurs** (see p173), created in 1854 by Waterhouse Hawkins. They bear little anatomical resemblance to the prehistoric lizards with which we're familiar from Jurassic Park, but do serve as a charmingly bizarre testament to can-do Victorian enterprise.

Yet the dinosaurs pre-date London's most famous animals by 13 years. Designed by Sir Edwin Landseer, the **marble lions** in Trafalgar Square (see p129) – 20 feet long by 11 feet high (six by three-and-a-half metres) – were a late addition to the square, going up in 1867 (nearly three decades after Nelson's famous column) at the then-phenomenal cost of £17,183. So how shall we celebrate the projected pedestrianisation of the square? A bronze slowworm on the empty plinth...

Known, rather grandly, as No.1 London – it's the first building one encountered during a visit to London from the village of Kensington – Apsley House was built by Robert Adam in the 1770s and was the London residence of the Duke of Wellington from 1817 until his death in 1852. Though his descendants still live here, some rooms are open to the public and contain interesting trinkets: Goya's Wellington portrait shows the Iron Duke entering Madrid, hot on the heels of his defeat of the French in 1812. An X-ray of the painting in 1966 showed that Wellington's head had been brushed over that of Joseph Bonaparte, Napoleon's brother: Goya had been working on the portrait when he found out Wellington had been victorious. Having jumped the gun, he decided to curry favour with a quick repair.

Royal Academy of Arts

Burlington House, Piccadilly, W1 (7300 8000/ www.royalacademy.org.uk). Green Park or Piccadilly Circus tube. **Open** 10am-6pm Mon-Thur, Sat, Sun; 10am-10pm Fri. *Tours* vary. **Admission** varies. *Tours* free. **Credit** AmEx, MC, V. **Map** p400 J7.

Britain's first art school was founded in 1768 and moved to the extravagantly Palladian Burlington House a century later. It's best known these days for its galleries, which stage a roster of populist temporary exhibitions (there is a permanent collection, but only a fraction of it is on show at any time; make an appointment with the curator to see the rest). The must-see show for 2003 is 'Aztecs' (until 11 Apr), a survey of Aztec art and culture that includes many pieces on show for the first time outside Mexico. However, it'll do well to compete with the Summer Exhibition (June-Aug; call for exact dates), which for 235 years has drawn its exhibits from works entered by the public. Some 12,000 pieces are submitted each year, with 10% making it past the judges.

St James's Church Piccadilly

197 Piccadilly, W1 (7734 4511/www.st-james-piccadilly.org). Piccadilly Circus tube. **Open** 8am-7pm daily. *Evening events* times vary. **Map** p400 J7.
Consecrated in 1684, St James's is the only church Sir Christopher Wren built on an entirely new site. It was also one of the architect's favourites: 'I think

it may be found beautiful and convenient,' he said. It's a calming building without architectural airs or graces but not lacking in charm. It's also a busy building: along with its inclusive ministry, it runs a counselling service, stages regular classical concerts (*see p304*), provides a home for the William Blake Society (the poet was baptised here) and hosts markets in its churchyard: antiques on Tuesday, arts and crafts from Wednesday to Saturday.

Wellington Arch

Hyde Park Corner, W1 (7930 2726/www.english-heritage.org.uk). Hyde Park Corner tube.
Open *Apr-Sept* 10am-6pm Wed-Sun. *Oct* 10am-5pm Wed-Sun. *Nov-Mar* 10am-4pm Wed-Sun.
Admission £2.50; £1.90 concessions; £1.30 5-16s; free under-5s. **Credit** MC, V.
Built in the 1820s to mark Britain's triumph over Napoleonic France, Decimus Burton's Wellington Arch was moved from its original Buckingham Palace location to Hyde Park Corner in 1882. It was initially topped by a statue of Wellington, but since 1912, Captain Adrian Jones's *Peace Descending on the Quadriga of War* has finished it with a flourish. It was recently restored and opened to the public in 2001, with three floors of displays about the history of the arch. From the balcony, you can see the Houses of Parliament and Buckingham Palace, though trees may obstruct your view in summer.

Piccadilly Circus & Regent Street

Vast investment has improved the appearance of Leicester Square in recent years. No such luck with nearby Piccadilly Circus, mere metres away at the junction of Piccadilly, Regent Street, Shaftesbury Avenue and Coventry Street. Some have tried to pin it as London's Times Square, not altogether inappropriate given that it's nothing more than a filthy, chaotic traffic intersection, hemmed in by shops selling CDs and jeans, and stalls hawking scarcely edible fast food.

Piccadilly Circus is named for the stiff collars that were the speciality of tailor Robert Baker, who lived nearby in the 17th century. The advertising hoardings that overlook the maelstrom have been a fixture since 1910; the tired souvenir stalls and deafening videogame arcades at the nearby **Trocadero** (7439 1791/www.troc.co.uk) are more contemporary.

The centrepiece of Piccadilly Circus is the Shaftesbury Memorial Fountain; designed by Alfred Gilbert in honour of Lord Shaftesbury's philanthropy and completed in 1893, it depicts the Angel of Christian Charity. However, down the years, it's become known to all and sundry as Eros, its real meaning lost to all but a few. The story goes that the memorial was originally meant to face north-east, the pun being that if the archer were to fire his arrow, its shaft would bury itself in Shaftesbury Avenue. However, some nincompoop put it up the wrong way.

Connecting Piccadilly Circus to Oxford Circus to the north and Pall Mall to the south, **Regent Street** is a broad, curving boulevard that was conceived by John Nash in the early 1800s to separate the toffs of Mayfair from the working classes of Soho. The grandeur of the sweeping road is impressive, but while some of the shops have retained their aura – **Liberty** department store (*see p235*) and **Hamleys** toy emporium (*see p259*) among them – the chains have moved in of late and the retail choices down here are now more forlorn and generic.

Sightseeing

Eros. Kinda.

St James's

Maps p400 & p401

Green Park or Piccadilly Circus tube.

Not many visitors – nor many Londoners, for that matter – venture too far into St James's, which takes as its borders Piccadilly, Haymarket, the Mall and Green Park. And, that's just the way its habituées like it. For St James's is even posher than Mayfair, its comrade in swank north of Piccadilly. This is a London that has remained unchanged for centuries: charming in its way, but unreconstructed and snooty with it, never more so than in the gentlemen's clubs that line **St James's Street** and **Pall Mall** (*see below* **It's a man's world**).

The material needs of the venerable gents of St James's are met by the anachronistic shops and restaurants of **Jermyn Street** and **St James's Street**. Tourists make up most of the clientele today, but it's still a thrill to see the lovingly crafted goods and the timewarp shopfronts, among them cigar retailer JJ Fox (19 St James's Street) and upmarket cobbler John Lobb (No.9). A stroll around the alleys of this quiet locale is a lovely window to a London few see and even fewer get to live.

Around the corner from Jermyn Street is the Queen Mother's old gaff: **Clarence House**, on **Stableyard Road**. Its architect, John Nash, was also responsible for the remodelling of **St James's Palace** in the early 19th century. Built by Henry VIII on the site of St James's Hospital, it was one of the principal royal residences for more than 300 years and is still used by Prince Charles and various minor royals; indeed, tradition still dictates that foreign ambassadors to the UK are officially known as 'Ambassador(s) to the Court of St James'. Although the palace is closed to the public, it's possible to explore Friary Court on **Marlborough Road** and attend the Sunday services at the Chapel Royal (October to Good Friday; 8.30am, 11.30am).

Two other notable St James's mansions stand nearby and overlook Green Park. The neo-classical Lancaster House was rebuilt in the 1820s by Benjamin Dean Wyatt for Frederick, Duke of York, and impressed Queen Victoria with its splendour. Closed to the public, it's now used mainly for government receptions and conferences. A little further north, on **St James's Place**, is beautiful, 18th-century **Spencer House** (*see p117*), ancestral townhouse of Princess Diana's family and now open as a museum and art gallery.

It's a man's world

Rewind. It is the early 19th century, and you are walking through St James's of an evening. You idly peer in through the windows of a grand, palazzo-style building. Past the heavy brocade curtains and through the plumes of cigar smoke, you spy bewhiskered, ruddy-nosed octogenarians in tall leather armchairs perusing the newspapers and sipping port, with only the weighty ticking of a clock to disturb their peace.

Fast forward back to 2003, and you are walking through St James's of an evening. You idly peer in through the windows of a grand, palazzo-style building. Past the heavy brocade curtains and through the plumes of cigar smoke, you spy bewhiskered, ruddy-nosed octogenarians in tall leather armchairs perusing the newspapers and sipping port, with only the weighty ticking of a clock to disturb their peace...

The gentlemen's clubs of St James's began in the 18th centuries as societies that met in coffee houses, where those of like political persuasion could discuss the issues of the day. Men – always men – of similar rank and habits of mind whiled away the hours enjoying

rambunctious conversation. The societies evolved into permanent establishments, and many remain in St James's today.

The oldest of the gentlemen's clubs still in existence is **White's** (37-8 St James's Street, SW1), founded by Francis White in 1693. At first, efforts were made to keep membership non-elitist – 'class distinctions are waived in conversation' – but the upper-class dandies who frequented it proposed and implemented the elimination of those whose breeding wasn't quite up to scratch. Happily for them, Prince Charles felt sure enough of the place's pedigree to choose it for his stag party.

Across the road stands **Brooks's** (60 St James's Street, SW1), founded in 1764 and famous as a Whig haunt. Napoleon's death mask is kept on display in case you forget the Whigs' revolutionary past. And while the majority of clubs today have Tory leanings, the Conservatives' real stronghold is the **Carlton Club** (69 St James's Street, SW1). Founded in 1832 following the Reform win in the 1831 election, the club always has a portrait of the current Tory leader hanging over the stairs.

Across **Marlborough Road** lies the Queen's Chapel, which was the first classical church to be built in England. Designed by the mighty Inigo Jones in the 1620s for Charles I's intended bride of the time, the Infanta of Castile, the chapel now stands in the grounds of Marlborough House and is only open to the public during Sunday services (Easter to July; 8.30am, 11.30am). The house itself was built by Sir Christopher Wren.

Reached from the west via **King Street** or the Mall, **St James's Square** was the most fashionable address in London for the 50 years after it was laid out in the 1670s: some seven dukes and seven earls were residents by the 1720s. Alas, no private houses survive on the square today, though among the current occupants is the prestigious London Library, in the north-west corner. This private library was founded by Thomas Carlyle in 1841 in a demonstration of his disgust at the inefficiency of the British Library (a sentiment that many would have recognised until very recent times).

Further east, overlooking the Mall, is **Carlton House Terrace**, which was built by Nash in 1827-32 on the site of Carlton House. When the Prince Regent came to the throne as George IV, he decided his home was not ostentatious enough for his elevated station and levelled what Horace Walpole had once described as 'the most perfect palace' in Europe. No.6 Carlton House Terrace, now occupied by the Royal Society, was the Germany Embassy during the Nazi era; its interior was designed by Albert Speer, Hitler's architect.

Spencer House

27 St James's Place, SW1 (7499 8620/ www.spencerhouse.co.uk). Green Park tube. **Open** *House Feb-July, Sept-Dec* 11.45am-4.45pm Sun. *Restored gardens spring, summer* phone to check. **Admission** *Tour only* £6; £5 10-16s. No under-10s. **Map** p400 J8.

Designed by John Vardy – James 'Athenian' Stuart had a hand in the interiors, while the building was modified by Henry Holland and Philip Hardwick in later years – and built for John Spencer, who became Earl Spencer the year before his house was completed, this 1766 construction is one of the capital's finest Palladian mansions. The Spencers moved out just over a century ago and the lavishly restored building is used chiefly as offices and as a venue for corporate entertaining, hence the limited opening hours. However, the weekly guided tours are a splendid little Sunday diversion, especially if you get lucky and find your visit coinciding with a rare opening for the restful gardens.

The buildings that house these clubs are some of the most beautiful in London. Mostly palazzo-style, they contain magnificent staircases (particularly the **Athenaeum**, at 107 Pall Mall, SW1), priceless works of art and, in some cases, exceptional libraries. As well as lunch and dinner – usually soporific 'nursery food' favourites such as roast beef and Yorkshire pudding, followed by spotted dick and custard – most clubs offer rooms for members who wish to stay the night, ideal for those who have over-indulged on their favourite claret.

In the past, membership of gentlemen's clubs was a hereditary privilege. But in order to survive, traditionalists have had to relax the rules. In other words, it's not all bewhiskered, ruddy-nosed octogenarians these days. Some clubs now cater for both sexes, and such frightful modernities as television rooms and cocktail bars have been introduced to entice the younger generation. Generally, new members have to be proposed and voted in by long-standing members – which doesn't always work, as with the famous blackballing of Jeremy Paxman at the **Garrick Club** (15 Garrick Street, WC2) in 1995 – and there are waiting lists of up to six years at some establishments.

Of course, you won't be able to enter any of these incomparably exclusive haunts. Members guard their privacy with zeal, and while the doormen will be very polite in turning down your requests for access, turn you down they will. Instead, content yourself with ogling their imposing façades, trying to recognise their (self-)important members coming and going, and imagining a time when these clubs were the norm rather than the exception.

Sightseeing

Soho & Leicester Square

London at its liveliest.

Soho

Maps p398-p401

Leicester Square, Oxford Circus, Piccadilly Circus or Tottenham Court Road tube.

With few traditional sights, bohemian Soho is an attraction in its own right, the perfect locale for the urban *flâneur*. All human life is in Soho, in all its contradictions: the media types who work, drink and snort here co-exist with housing association residents, prostitutes, market traders, tailors, artists and junkies. Soho is home to 5,000 people, which is part of the reason why it hasn't suffered the tourist-led bastardisation of Covent Garden. There's a genuine sense of community, among both residents and those who work or drink here.

It's a far cry from the Middle Ages, when the area was used for farming, before becoming a hunting ground for London's aristocracy in the 16th and 17th centuries. It wasn't until the last quarter of the 17th century that it became residential, when, post-Great Fire, the City became too crowded. Among the first residents were Greek Christians (hence Greek Street) fleeing Ottoman persecution, and a larger wave of French Protestants (Huguenots) forced out of France by Louis XIV. However, despite the speed with which its pastoral history became swallowed up, the area's name at least retained some of its past identity: when the huntsmen who once frequented it spied their intended target, they would shout 'So-ho!'

Many early, well-to-do residents left their Soho Square mansions for Mayfair in the early 18th century. In their place came artists, writers, radicals and more foreign immigrants, particularly Italians. John Galsworthy, in *The Forsyte Saga*, summed up the Soho of the 19th century as 'untidy, full of Greeks, Ishmaelites, cats, Italians, tomatoes, restaurants, organs, coloured stuffs, queer names...'

As the resident population dropped in the 20th century, the area became known for its entertainments. Music came to Soho in the 1950s with Ronnie Scott's jazz club on Gerrard Street and the brief skiffle boom: Adam Faith and Cliff Richard were discovered at the 2 i's Coffee Bar at 59 Old Compton Street, now a Dôme brasserie. In 1962 Georgie Fame started his sweat-soaked residency at the Flamingo club (33-7 Wardour Street, these days a dreary

Irish pub); the nearby Marquee (90 Wardour Street, now part of Mezzo), hosted early gigs by Hendrix and Pink Floyd. Meanwhile, the sex industry, for which the area has been renowned for 150 years, expanded in the 1960s and '70s.

However, Soho began to turn the corner in the mid '80s and '90s, spurred on by a boom in gay business (the so-called 'pink pound'). Pubs such as the Golden Lion on Dean Street had long been the haunt of gay servicemen (as well as writer Noel Coward and murderer Dennis Nilsen, who picked up some of his victims in it), but the gay cafés, bars and shops that appeared along Old Compton Street injected some much-needed vitality into a district that had become the sole province of dirty old men.

That Soho is now more popular than ever is a cause for both celebration and concern. Old Compton Street is the closest London gets to a 24-hour culture. Yet the chains are moving in, bringing with them those faint hearts who used to find Soho too grimy. Pray it survives.

People-watch over a coffee in Soho.

The heart of Soho

The core of Soho is **Old Compton Street** and its surrounding avenues and alleys. This is Soho at its most heterodox and lively: gay bars and straight boozers, well stocked off-licences and continental delis, hifalutin' restaurants and low-rent strip joints. Grab a sandwich and a streetside table at Duke's Bar (No.27), featured in Michael Winterbottom's moving London flick *Wonderland*, and breathe it all in.

If Old Compton Street is Soho's heart, shady **Soho Square** is its lungs. This tree-lined quadrangle was built on land once known as Soho Fields and initially called King Square; a weather-beaten statue of the king in question, Charles II, stands in the centre. In summer, office workers munch sandwiches on benches – one of which bears a dedication to late singer Kirsty MacColl, who wrote a song about the square – or on the grass. London's one remaining French Protestant church and St Patrick's Catholic church provide spiritual nourishment in a square otherwise dominated by the advertising and film industries: the British Board of Film Classification and 20th Century Fox both reside here.

The two streets that link Soho Square to Old Compton Street are brimful of historical associations. The first of them, **Greek Street**, also offers the most evocative way to enter Soho: via the arch of the Pillars of Hercules pub leading from Manette Street to Greek Street. The sense of passing through a portal into a different world has entranced many Soho neophytes in the past. Casanova and Thomas de Quincey once lodged on Greek Street, and Josiah Wedgwood had his London showroom nearby. **Frith Street**, meanwhile, was home to John Constable, Mozart and William Hazlitt (at No.6, now a charming hotel; *see p55*), and John Logie Baird first demonstrated the wonder of TV above the Bar Italia (No.22).

Neighbouring **Dean Street** is also not without its stories, many of them relating to the bohemian crowd of serious drinkers who jollied around here in the 1950s (*see p120* **The wanderers**). Today's ever-thirsty creative and media types find solace and alcohol at the members-only Groucho Club (No.44) and with Soho House (40 Greek Street).

These days, Greek, Frith and Dean Streets are choc-a-bloc with bars and restaurants. Pricey old stagers such as the Gay Hussar (2 Greek Street) sit side by side with cheapie newcomers such as Café Emm (17 Frith Street); cocktail bars like Akbar (77 Dean Street; *see p223*) rub shoulders with old-style boozers such as the Crown and Two Chairmen (31 Dean Street); jazz clubs (Ronnie Scott's, at 49 Frith

Street, in Soho since 1959) jostle with strip clubs (Sunset Strip, at 30 Dean Street, opened the following year). West of here, though, work gets an equal billing with play. **Wardour Street** has long associations with the film industry and is home to several production companies. At the street's southern end is the churchyard of St Anne. Only the early 19th-century tower of the church survived the Blitz.

We're now in sex industry territory. Two tiny cut-throughs, **Tisbury Court** (linking Wardour and Rupert Streets) and **Walkers Court** (leading from Brewer Street to Berwick Street), are lined with insalubrious strip joints, which promise the earth but deliver only a hit to the wallet, and sex shops. Ignore the barkers out front and walk on, either to **Rupert Street** and its rash of grubby shops (Cheapo Cheapo Records, at No.53, is a treasure trove of cheap vinyl), or to the record shops and market stalls on **Berwick Street**. The City Gates Church Christian Fellowship, on **Greens Court**, attempts to provide a wholesome alternative to hand-scrawled signs in doorways advertising 'Model 1st Floor', or some variant thereof.

Branching off west is **Broadwick Street**, birthplace of William Blake and centre of a severe cholera outbreak in 1854. Local doctor John Snow became convinced that the disease was transmitted by polluted water and had the street's water pump chained up. That Snow was proved correct led to a breakthrough in epidemiology. The doctor is commemorated by a handleless replica water pump and in the name of the street's pub.

West Soho

Brewer Street is dotted with shops, among them the Vintage Magazine Store (Nos.39-43, 7439 8525) and Anything Left-Handed (No.57, 7437 3910). **Great Windmill Street**, which leads from Brewer Street to Shaftesbury Avenue, is also not without its sleazy charms. In 1932 the Windmill Theatre started its now-legendary 'revuedeville' shows; its centrepiece were 'erotic tableaux', which the law dictated could feature naked girls only if they stood stationary on stage. Some 70 years on, and the Windmill is a lap-dancing joint. Ho-hum.

But other than these two streets, and the roads and passageways around **Carnaby Street** – hip in the swingin' 1960s and now revitalised with fashion retailers and bars after a period of tawdry neglect – west Soho holds little of interest for the visitor. Walk west down **Beak Street** or **Brewer Street** and you'll reach **Regent Street**, which separates Soho from Mayfair; head south and, before long, you'll hit Piccadilly Circus.

Map p401

Leicester Square or Piccadilly Circus tube.

Shaftesbury Avenue, which wends its way down from New Oxford Street all the way down to Piccadilly Circus, was driven through slums in the 1880s. Over the next 20 years, seven theatres were built along the street; six still stand, and Shaftesbury Avenue is the heart of Theatreland. It also, though, has a brilliant cinema, the Curzon Soho (*see p284*), and a handful of Chinese opticians, herbalists, restaurants and travel agents that mark it

out as the northern edge of Chinatown, which extends south to Leicester Square.

In the 1950s many Chinese – mainly from Hong Kong and London's original Chinatown in Limehouse – were drawn to **Gerrard Street** and **Lisle Street** by cheap rents. Today, the ersatz oriental gates, stone lions and pagoda-topped phone booths suggest a Chinese theme park, yet Chinatown is still, despite recent rent hikes, a close-knit residential and working enclave: beyond the many restaurants, few concessions are made to tourism. Inevitably, the Chinese New Year celebrations see the place swamped by English revellers (*see p262*).

The wanderers Bohemian Soho

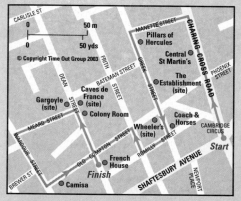

For a 20-year period after World War II, a small part of Soho was the centre of London's bohemian life, a refuge from the grey uniformity of the rest of the city. The overt sleaziness with which Soho became synonymous during the '70s had not yet taken hold; the excesses and outrages were instead being perpetrated by artists and intellectuals in the pubs and clubs, fuelled by alarming amounts of red wine, vodka, gin and champagne.

Walk up Charing Cross Road.
On your left is **Central St Martin's School of Art**, one of London's leading art colleges. From here, students such as the painter Frank Auerbach would frequently slip around the corner into this world of hedonism.
Turn the corner at Foyle's, down Manette Street and on to Greek Street.
On your left is one of London's oldest pubs, the **Pillars of Hercules** (7 Greek Street); like

most watering holes around these parts, it was frequented by the painter Francis Bacon. Further up Greek Street is the **Gay Hussar** restaurant (No.2; 7437 0973), longtime haunt of MPs and journalists. Here, homosexual Labour politician Tom Driberg tried to persuade Mick Jagger to become a Labour MP.
Head south down Greek Street.
Driberg was a regular member of the audience at Peter Cook's satirical comedy club the **Establishment**, which was housed at 18 Greek Street for a couple of years in the early '60s. Unconventional, irreverent and awash with alcohol, it was perfectly located in the heart of Soho. Today, it's a tedious bar called the **Boardwalk**.
Continue down Greek Street to Old Compton Street.
Wheeler's Fish Restaurant, at 19 Old Compton Street, was a favourite haunt of Francis Bacon. Here, at lunchtime, he would hold court for any number of painters, writers, musicians and gangsters. It closed in the 1980s, to be replaced by **Café Bohème**.
Continue down Greek Street to the junction with Romilly Street.
The **Coach and Horses** (No.29; *see p223*), run by the self-styled 'rudest landlord in London' Norman Balon, is an old-school Soho boozer of the first order. It was famously immortalised in Keith Waterhouse's play *Jeffrey Bernard Is Unwell*, a brilliant catalogue of anecdotes based on life in Soho and particularly that of the drunkard, gambler

Leicester Square

Map p401

Leicester Square or Piccadilly Circus tube.

Back in the 17th and 18th centuries, **Leicester Square** was a chic aristo hangout. However, by the 19th century, the attractions of the theatre and the flesh had taken over and the square gradually lost its grandeur. In the last few decades, it's become overrun with cinemas, some new and some long established. Indeed, the movies long proved the only draw here for locals; otherwise, it was used almost solely as a handily central meeting place by tourists.

In recent years, the square has undergone a transformation that, while aesthetically successful, hasn't improved the atmosphere here. The dazzling cinematic behemoths and globally popular stomach-fillers (burgers and ice-cream, natch) hardly make for an inspiring experience: without the buskers, dreadful even by London standards, you could be anywhere in Europe. Perhaps this is why tourists feel so at home here. **Leicester Place**, home to the cheap and cheerful Prince Charles cinema (*see p286*) and the French Catholic church of Notre Dame de France, which contains some murals by Jean Cocteau, offers the most interesting route out.

and writer Bernard, of whom there are cartoons hanging on the walls.

Turn right into Romilly Street, then head right on Frith Street to Old Compton Street. Take a left, and then the first right, up Dean Street.

After lunch in the 1950s, the action would move to a club. Pubs were then legally obliged to shut between 3pm and 5.30pm, and places such as Muriel Belcher's **Colony Room** (41 Dean Street) became the focal point. Artists such as Nina Hamnett and Lucian Freud, composers including Malcolm Arnold and Alan Rawsthorne, and poets like Louis MacNeice would be greeted by Muriel's 'Hello, cunty', and work towards the most biblical of hangovers. Dylan Thomas described his visits to Soho as 'a horrid alcoholic explosion that scatters all my good intentions over the saloon bars of the tawdriest pubs in London'.

Nearby were two other favourites: the **Caves de France**, and the opulent **Gargoyle**, on the corner of Dean and Meard Streets. In later years, it found fame of sorts as the first home of the Comedy Store (*see p278*).

Turn down Meard Street, left into Wardour Street, then right into Old Compton Street.

In the 1950s Old Compton Street was littered with shops selling exotic European groceries. Parmigianis, King Bomba and Roches have gone, sadly, but the fabulous smelling **Camisa** remains at No.61. A few doors down stood the **Swiss Pub** (No.53; now gay bar **Compton's**), a favoured haunt of Bacon et al; in between stood the **2 i's Coffee Bar**, the cradle of British rock 'n' roll (Nos.57-9, now a **Dôme** coffee bar).

Continue down Old Compton Street and then turn right into Dean Street.

Dylan Thomas once lost a manuscript of *Under Milk Wood* during a marathon drinking session at the York Minster on Dean Street. Back then, it was nicknamed the French Pub for its association with Charles de Gaulle and the Free French resistance movement, and for its French landlord Gaston Berlemont. It's now officially been recast as the **French House** (No.49; *see p223*), but remains defiantly old-school. Have a drink here. You've earned it.

Covent Garden & St Giles's

A shoppers' paradise, but plenty more besides.

Covent Garden

Maps p399 & p401

Covent Garden, Leicester Square or Temple tube.

The theatres are nice enough, and there's a measure of good food to be had in the restaurants. But 95 per cent of the visitors to Covent Garden come here simply to go shopping. For many, 'Covent Garden' means the area's pedestrianised piazza, where gift shops, market stalls and street entertainers vie for attention. The touristy nature of the area – it's hellishly busy most weekends – the influx of chain restaurants and shops, and the street entertainers are not to everyone's taste, yet Covent Garden works: even those locals who can't stand the place appreciate the need for it.

The neighbourhood's name is a corruption of the 'convent garden' of the Abbey of St Paul at Westminster, which originally stood on the site. In the 1630s would-be property speculator the

Earl of Bedford asked Inigo Jones to develop the centre of Covent Garden into an area 'fitte for the habitacions of *Gentlemen* and men of ability'. Influenced by the Italian neo-classicism of Palladio, Jones designed **St Paul's Covent Garden** (*see p123*); its main entrance facing on to the square beneath the portico has never been used, as William Laud, the Bishop of London, insisted the altar be in its traditional place against the east wall. The redundant portico now provides a stage-like area where jugglers and other street entertainers perform.

London's first planned square was a hit with the well-to-do, but as the fruit and vegetable market, founded in 1656, grew and newer, more exclusive developments sprung up west, Covent Garden's reputation slumped. Coffee houses, taverns and brothels thrived: John Cleland's archetypal tart-with-a-heart, Fanny Hill, lodged here. Later, the area's grandiose Victorian gin palaces acted as 'the lighthouses which guided the thirsty soul on the road to ruin'.

On the ropes in Covent Garden: street performers rule the Piazza. *See p123.*

Sightseeing

Yet, throughout these years, Covent Garden remained a fashionable venue for theatre and opera (as celebrated at the **Theatre Museum**; *see below*). From the time the first **Royal Opera House** (*see p305*) opened in Bow Lane in 1732, London's beau monde has gingerly picked its way through the filth and rotting vegetables to enjoy the glittering pleasures of the stage. The Theatre Royal in Drury Lane was the other main attraction; it was here that David Garrick revolutionised English theatre. With the Royal Opera, the area's theatrical reputation has been maintained to this day, though the fruit and veg market has long gone (in 1974, to Battersea).

Covent Garden Piazza

Once you negotiate the musicians, jugglers, comics and hucksters who roam the edge of London's largest pedestrianised public space, you'll find a mixed selection of goods. On Mondays, the south side's **Jubilee Market** is a chaotic treat, all silverware and watches, records and coins; the rest of the week, it's mostly given over to tatty tourist-oriented kit. The smarter **Apple Market** is one enormous gift shop, aimed squarely at visitors.

The jewel in the piazza's crown, however, is the stunning **Royal Opera House**, which stages ballet and opera more or less nightly. If neither are your cup of tea, or if you simply can't afford tickets (they're pricey if you want a decent view), take the time to pop into the open-all-day Amphitheatre Café for a drink or a snack: the views over the square are terrific.

London's Transport Museum

Covent Garden Piazza, WC2 (7379 6344/ www.ltmuseum.co.uk). Covent Garden tube. **Open** 10am-6pm Mon-Thur, Sat, Sun; 11am-6pm Fri. Last entry 5.15pm. **Admission** £5.95; £4.50 concessions; free under-16s when accompanied by an adult. **Credit** MC, V. **Map** p401 L6.

If London's buses, tubes and trains were run anywhere near as well as the museum devoted to them, you'd hear next to no complaints from the locals. This splendid operation offers a chronological survey of public transport in the city, which began with George Shillibeer's pioneering bus service in 1829. The museum then wends its way through the days of trolleybuses, trams and the building of the tube network, all the way to the 21st century. The exhibits here are engaging – especially the displays on London Transport design, from Harry Beck's seminal map (*see p9* **London loves**) to the creation of LT's own font, Johnston Sans Serif – and the captioning lucid, but the most enjoyable part of the museum's make-up is its interactivity, from the costumed actors who roam the museum to the open-backed buses into which adults and kids alike can't resist clambering. A refurbishment slated for 2004

The **Royal Opera House**.

will add more exhibition space (though the museum will have to close while the work is carried out). Real trainspotters will want to visit the Acton Town depot, which has 370,000 additional exhibits; see the website for details of occasional open days.

St Paul's Covent Garden

Bedford Street, WC2 (7836 5221). Covent Garden or Leicester Square tube. **Open** 9am-4.30pm Mon-Fri; 9am-12.30pm Sun. **Services** 1.10pm Wed; 11am Sun. *Choral Evensong* 2pm 2nd Sun of mth. **Admission** free; donations appreciated. **Map** p401 L7.

Known as the Actors' Church for its association with Covent Garden's Theatreland – lining its walls are memorials to stars from Ivor Novello to Hattie Jacques – this plain Tuscan pastiche was designed by Inigo Jones in 1631. Pepys's diary of 1662 contains the first recorded sighting of a Punch and Judy show under its portico, a fact commemorated in the Covent Garden May Fayre & Puppet Festival (*see p263*); it's also under the portico that George Bernard Shaw based the first scene of *Pygmalion*. The first known victim of the Great Plague, Margaret Ponteous, was buried in St Paul's churchyard.

Theatre Museum

Tavistock Street (entrance Russell Street), WC2 (7943 4700/www.theatremuseum.org). Covent Garden tube. **Open** 10am-6pm Tue-Sun. Last entry 5.30pm. **Admission** free. **Credit** AmEx, MC, V. **Map** p401 L6.

Not just 4 anoraks

...but 3 duffel coats
59 gorgeous models
5 Tube simulators
4 dead man's handles
3 mucky miners
and 1 brilliant time
had by all.

**London's Transport
Museum**
Covent Garden Piazza

... be *moved*
www.ltmuseum.co.uk

Walking into the Theatre Museum is a little like walking into a stage school, as people loll around on chairs and sofas watching performances and films of stage production techniques and productions from the National Video Archive. Regardless, it's great for kids: regular activities include hands-on crafts workshops, theatre make-up demonstrations (where you can be transformed into a toad or a cat), and quizzes.

However, there are plenty of static exhibits here, too. Walk down to the Main Gallery and spot the famous theatre hands and a few feet (although we were a little perplexed as to what Morrissey was doing there), and then take in the history of theatre in the form of paintings, theatre personality biographies, memorabilia, costumes and stage sets. There's also a section that traces the production of Wind in the Willows, from the book to the stage. Exhibitions for this year include Let Paul Robeson Sing! (until May 2003), exploring the singer, actor and film star's turbulent life; Rambert – 75 Years of Creativity (until October 2003), which features many photos and posters of beautiful people doing beautiful dance moves; and Drawn to Fame (until 23 November 2003), a show of theatrical caricatures by Gilbert Sommerlad that includes portraits of Bud Flanagan, Max Miller and Sir John Gielgud.

Elsewhere in Covent Garden

East of the Piazza, in **Bow Street**, stands the Magistrates' Courts. During the 1750s and 1760s, the courts were presided over by novelist and barrister Henry Fielding and his blind half-brother John ('the blind beak'), who was said to be able to recognise 3,000 thieves by their voices alone. It was Henry who, horrified by the lawlessness of Georgian London, set up the Bow Street Runners, precursors of the modern police. Nearby, on **Great Queen Street**, is the HQ of the United Grand Lodge of England, the **Freemasons' Hall** (*see p127* **Shake on it**).

Further along here is Browns members-only club (No.4; 7831 0802), at which assorted B-list celebs and toffs play out a tableau of sneering indulgence night upon night. Better to turn on your heels and head west: on the other side of Covent Garden are some nicer watering holes. Chief among them is the Lamb and Flag (33 Rose Street; *see p224*), one of central London's few surviving wooden-framed buildings, though the Salisbury (90 St Martin's Lane) is the best of the options nearer Leicester Square.

Near here sit a number of characterful little alleys. On the piss-drenched **Brydges Place**, linking **Bedfordbury** and **St Martin's Lane**, sits 2 Brydges Place, among the most discreet of London's members' clubs. **Goodwin's Court**, which runs parallel, contains a row of bow-fronted 17th-century houses lit by clockwork-operated gas street lighting. And

on **Cecil Court**, an anachronistic selection of shops trade on, untouched by fashion and awash with collectors of prints, stamps, tarot cards, theatrical playbills, cigarette cards, banknotes and coins. A stroll down here is one of central London's most charming pleasures.

It's all a far cry from the overbearing air of consumerist indulgence back near Covent Garden Piazza. Walk north from the market up **James Street** and you'll cross pedestrianised **Floral Street**, home to hip but increasingly mainstream stores such as Camper (No.39) and Paul Smith (Nos.40-44), and then **Long Acre**, dominated by the chains. Keep walking north and you'll hit **Neal Street**, whose stores run the gamut from kites to oriental tea sets and shoes. Lots of shoes.

After the Thomas Neal Centre, kind of a hipsters' Whiteley's, and the huge branch of Diesel, turn right into **Shorts Gardens** and immediately left into **Neal's Yard**. This hippie haven of health food and natural remedies (plus, incongruously, a shop dealing in wildly obscure indie music and skateboard ephemera) is a reminder of the 'alternative' scene that did so much, through its mass squats and demonstrations, to stop the brutal redevelopment of Covent Garden after the market moved to Battersea in 1974.

The consumer heaven continues up Shorts Gardens to **Seven Dials**, named for the seven roads coming off from it – be careful when crossing the street – and now a quaint little junction. There are more clothes shops up **Earlham Street**, plus a small street market most days, before you reach **Shaftesbury Avenue** and the end of Covent Garden.

The Strand

Skirting the southern edge of Covent Garden, the **Strand** was, until Victoria Embankment was constructed in the 1860s, a riverside bridle path. Built to link the City with Westminster and lined with the palatial homes of the aristocracy from the 13th century, it turns southwards at **Charing Cross**. In front of the station is an 1863 monument commemorating the original cross, erected near here by Edward I to mark the passing of the funeral procession of his queen, Eleanor, in 1290.

The Strand became as notorious for pickpockets and prostitution as Covent Garden (Boswell recalled how 'last night... I met a monstrous big whore in the Strand, whom I had a great curiosity to lubricate'), but within 100 years Disraeli thought it the finest street in Europe. The building of the **Savoy Hotel** in 1889 enhanced this reputation, although the adjoining Savoy Theatre, built by Richard

Sightseeing

Strung out on **Denmark Street**.

D'Oyly Carte to host Gilbert and Sullivan operas, predates it by eight years. It was reconstructed in its current art deco form in 1929, and restored in 1990 after a fire.

Today's Strand, brimming with traffic and lined with offices, shops, theatres, and the odd pub and restaurant, is a harsh and rather forlorn place, an impression that's heavily reinforced by the many homeless people who bed down in its doorways.

The Embankment

From the Strand, pedestrianised Villiers Street leads past Terry Farrell's monster-toy-brick **Embankment Place** and the characterful Gordon's wine bar (*see p224*) to **Embankment Gardens** and Embankment tube. All that remains of grand York House, which stood here from the 13th to the 17th century, is **York Watergate** on Watergate Walk, which once let on to the Thames.

Across from the gardens, between the river and the Embankment's constant traffic, is **Cleopatra's Needle**. Nothing to do with Cleopatra, this 60-foot (19-metre) granite obelisk dates from around 1475 BC. Presented to Britain by Egypt in 1819, it didn't make the journey here until 1878. Buried under the needle

are various objects, including photographs of 12 of the best-looking English women of the day. The sphinxes at the base were replaced facing the wrong way after being cleaned in the early 20th century.

From here, two new footbridges link the Embankment with the South Bank Centre. The old **Hungerford Bridge** was a shabby affair, but the genesis of its replacements, one either side of the rail bridge, were beset by delays and spiralling budgets. The huge New Adelphi building, with its giant clock, stands on the site of the Adam brothers' celebrated Adelphi, built in 1768-72. This terrace of 11 houses over arches and vaults was more of an architectural than commercial success, but it was mindless vandalism that it was pulled down in 1936.

St Giles's

This curious pocket of London has a tawdry history. A leper hospital was set up here by Queen Matilda, wife of Henry I, in 1101, when St Giles's was still a small village outside London. The hospital was dissolved by Henry VIII in 1539, but its chapel became the new parish church, **St Giles-in-the-Fields**. It was rebuilt in 1630, then replaced by a new church in 1730-4 after St George Bloomsbury (*see p103*) was built, creating a new parish carved out of the ancient parish of St Giles's. As well as being the area where the Great Plague started in 1665, it was here that prisoners on their way to be executed at the Tyburn gallows, which stood at Marble Arch from the 14th to the 18th century, were allowed to stop for one last drink in the Angel pub on **St Giles High Street**.

The 19th century saw St Giles's nosedive further with the emergence of the Rookeries: a small area bordered by St Giles High Street, Bainbridge Street and Dyott Street and overrun with criminals, prostitutes and vagrants. These days, a hostel for the homeless sits underneath Centre Point, the tall building on the corner of **Charing Cross Road** and New Oxford Street, and the top stretch of Charing Cross Road and the streets behind it are frequented by drug users, dealers and petty criminals.

Denmark Street, known as 'Tin Pan Alley', has a colourful musical history. At the Gioconda Café, the Small Faces signed up for their first recording, and Bowie met his first band, the Lower Third. At No.4, now the Helter Skelter music bookshop, was Regents Sound Studios, where the Stones laid down *Not Fade Away* and the Kinks recorded their first demo. And at No.6, now a guitar shop, the Sex Pistols wrote *Anarchy in the UK* in a dingy ground-floor room, and Bananarama squatted. The street is now dominated by musical instrument retailers, though London's most intimate music venue, the **12 Bar Club** (*see p313*), provides a reason to come here after the shops have shut.

Stacey Street, just to the south of here (but accessible only via Shaftesbury Avenue, or via Phoenix Street on Charing Cross Road, comes as a surprise. A small square lined with modern houses, it seems an odd place for a residential development, but a brilliant one. The grassy square in the middle, **Phoenix Gardens**, was set up by enterprising residents on the site of an old car park in the 1980s and is a lovely escape from the bustle mere metres away.

The remainder of the Charing Cross Road has long been dominated by bookshops: the modern Borders (No.120) faces up to the just-modernised Foyles, which celebrates its centenary next year (for both, *see p232*). Further down Charing Cross Road, south of

Shaftesbury Avenue, the books are mostly second-hand. Work up an appetite browsing, then sate it with a falafel or latka from the magnificent Gaby's Deli (No.30; 7836 4233).

St Giles-in-the-Fields

St Giles High Street, WC2 (7240 2532/www.giles-in-the-fields.org). Tottenham Court Road tube. **Open** 9am-4pm Mon-Fri. *Services* Sun. **Admission** free; donations appreciated. **Map** p399 K6.

There's been a house of prayer on this site for just over 900 years, though this Palladian building, designed by Henry Flitcroft (who went on to design Woburn Abbey), dates back to the early 1700s. Worthy of attention is the pulpit from the chapel in nearby West Street when John and Charles Wesley preached in the 18th century. Note also the allegorical medieval 'Pelican in her piety' image above the altar, in which a mother bird feeds her young with her own blood. Call for details of lunchtime recitals.

Shake on it

In Covent Garden, the crowds often get to be too much. In search of a pint, you head out of the bustle and into Holborn. Here, things are calmer, and there are several benevolent hostelries where you can wet your whistle: try the Freemasons' Arms (81-2 Long Acre, WC2; 7836 3115), the Sun (66 Long Acre, WC2; 7836 4520) and the Newton Arms (33 Newton Street, WC2; 7242 8797).

Wait a minute. The Freemasons' Arms is iffy enough, but the Sun isn't that a freemasonry symbol? And wasn't Newton, an early developer of the area, a freemason? Conspiracy theorists' antennae are twitching by now. And what's that big stone building with the tower looming over the middle of it all? Look closely at the edifice, which spans half a block, and you'll spot brass pentagrams embedded in the pavement and esoteric symbols like a compass and a sword carved into the façade. This is the **Freemasons' Hall** (Great Queen Street, WC2; 7831 9811/ www.grandlodge-england.org), headquarters of the United Grand Lodge of England.

The Freemasons have been the subject of conspiracy theories since at least the 1700s. *Plus ça change, plus c'est la même chose.* Rumblings persist today: the Freemasons are part of a secret elite that controls the economy, as demonstrated by the eye in the pyramid on the back of the US dollar bill; they practise Satanism; they are or have been associated with Nazism, the KKK, even the Mafia.

As unlikely as the many New World Order claims are, one thing's for sure: if the Freemasons did control the world, it might end up looking a lot like **Great Queen Street**. The street's bigger buildings all bear plaques with inscriptions like 'Masonic Housing Assocation' and 'Royal Masonic Benevolent Institution' (No.31), or the motto *audi vide tace*: 'hear, see and be silent'. Yet the Freemasons make no secret of the fact that they own a great deal of the street: even three centuries back, they were meeting at Covent Garden pubs.

Despite the outlandish stories, the Freemasons do a pretty convincing job of behaving like an old men's charity organisation, with secret handshakes to spice things up and honour tradition. The pocket watches, golf balls, cryptically decorated neckties and Toastmaster-y books in the windows of **Central Regalia** (23 Great Queen Street, WC2; 7405 0004/ www.centralregalia.com) and **Toye, Kenning & Spencer** (19-21 Great Queen Street, WC2; 7242 0471/www.toye.com) give a fair idea of the general demographic and the likely wildness levels.

For more on the Masons, visit the museum and library at Freemasons' Hall, and tour its temples during the week (call ahead to book; tours free Mon-Fri, £10 Sat). As part of their new policy of openness, they'll even sell you a CD-ROM of official documents for hours of decoding fun. If you're into that sort of thing.

Westminster

From the art of politics to the politics of art, this is the heart of England.

Maps p400 & p401

Embankment, Piccadilly Circus, Pimlico, St James's Park or Westminster tube/Charing Cross or Victoria tube/rail.

Westminster has been at the centre of matters both royal and religious for the best part of 1,000 years, since Edward the Confessor built his 'West Minster' and palace on marshy Thorney Island in the 11th century, while its political heart began beating in the 1300s, when the first Parliament met in the abbey. These days, political and royal landmarks make up most of the area's sights. Save for lifelong politicos (near Parliament) and cash-rich businessfolk (around Pimlico), few people live here and nightlife verges on the non-existent.

Trafalgar Square

Trafalgar Square remains exactly what it's been for as long as anyone can remember: a vast traffic island whose grandeur is wrecked by the constant roar and smell of cars, cabs, buses and bikes, and by the presence of hundreds of revolting pigeons. But, with any luck, this state of affairs will change in the next year. Mayor Ken Livingstone's battle to rid the square of its indigenous pigeon population has proved only partly successful: plenty of the buggers still remained in mid 2002, fed by gormless tourists with nothing better to do.

However, a grand redevelopment plan, part of the tweely named World Squares for All scheme, should have a far greater effect. The plan calls for the pedestrianisation of the entire north edge of the square, linking it with the **National Gallery** and quelling the barrage of traffic that has long irritated all and sundry. Mayor Ken Livingstone hopes that the newly beautified, pedestrian-friendly square will become a focal point for Londoners, and a regular venue for free entertainment events. An artist's impression of how it will look when improvements have been completed – all being well, in summer 2003 – are enticing; keep your fingers crossed that the planners employed a realist rather than a fantasist to paint them. Either way, pigeons are conspicuous by their absence from the image.

At the moment, the square's highlights are its statues. Sir Edwin Landseer's magnificent lions are still the focal point for tourists and intrepid climbers, while Nelson's Column remains a draw, despite its charmlessly phallic appearance. The empty fourth plinth in the north-west corner of the square is one of London's oddest attractions. Built in 1841, it was intended for a statue of William IV, but a lack of funds meant it was never completed, and for a century and a half, the plinth sat empty. From 1999 to 2002 three temporary works were commissioned for the plinth, from British artists Mark Wallinger, Bill Woodrow and Rachel Whiteread, but it's now empty again and will likely remain so for much of 2003.

National Gallery

Trafalgar Square, WC2 (7747 2885/ www.nationalgallery.org.uk). Leicester Square tube/Charing Cross tube/rail. **Open** (incl Sainsbury Wing) 10am-6pm Mon, Tue, Thur-Sun; 10am-9pm Wed. *Micro Gallery* 10am-5.30pm Mon, Tue, Thur-Sun; 10am-8.30pm Wed. *Tours* times vary. **Admission** free. *Special exhibitions* prices vary. **Credit** *Shop* MC, V. **Map** p401 K7.

Britain's National Gallery is also a national treasure. The collection, founded in 1824 with a mere 38 pictures but now 60 times that size, covers a span of over 650 years, from 13th-century religious paintings to a clutch of Van Goghs. In 2002 ambitious proposals for a £21-million development, involving the creation of a glass-roofed inner courtyard and two new entrances, were announced. These changes are principally to accommodate an expected flood of tourists from the pedestrianised Trafalgar Square.

Don't even think about seeing it all in a morning. Instead, check the floor plan and pinpoint a few areas of interest, or sign up to one of the worthwhile guided tours. Highlights are many and varied, and singling particular rooms out is, at least for the non-academic, partly a result of personal prejudice. However, among the early works especially worth seeking out are Leonardo's cartoon of *The Virgin and Child with St Anne and St John the Baptist* and Holbein's *The Ambassador*; there's a fine selection of pieces by Rembrandt and Vermeer in the North Wing; English painters represented in some depth include Constable (whose *Hay-Wain* is one of the most popular paintings), Gainsborough and Turner; and there is a rich choice of late 19th-century works from the likes of Van Gogh, Cézanne and Renoir.

Temporary shows held in the much-maligned Sainsbury Wing during 2003 will include the UK's first major exhibition of works by 16th-century artist Titian (19 Feb-18 May), and A Private Passion, a selection of 19th-century works by the likes of

Delacroix, Moreau, Rossetti, Renoir and Sargent accumulated by the American Grenville L Winthrop Collection and usually displayed only at Harvard University (25 June-14 Sept).

National Portrait Gallery

2 St Martin's Place, WC2 (7306 0055/ www.npg.org.uk). Leicester Square tube/Charing Cross tube/rail. **Open** 10am-6pm Mon-Wed, Sat, Sun; 10am-9pm Thur, Fri. *Tours* Aug free; times vary. **Admission** free. *Selected exhibitions* £5; £3 concessions. **Credit** AmEx, MC, V. **Map** p401 K7.
A far nicer place since its refurbishment a couple of years ago, the National Portrait Gallery attempts to tell the story of Britain – or, at least, a version of it – using nothing more than portraits of its more notable citizens. When put like that, it sounds like a pompous place; it's actually anything but. The exhibition is organised chronologically from top to bottom; ride the escalator to the second floor for portraits dating back five centuries, then work your way back down to ground level and the present day.

Highlights are many and varied. The top floor offers one of the many replicas Gilbert Stuart painted of George Washington; a fascinating room devoted to a variety of pictures of Mary, Queen of Scots; and an unattributed portrait of a young Henry VIII, looking far less imposing (and overweight) than in the more famous pictures of him. Dickens, Darwin and Disraeli (the latter painted by Millais) are among those featured on the first floor. The ground floor fares less well: check Paula Rego's clumsy portrait of Germaine Greer and a frankly smashable bust of fashion designer Zandra Rhodes

by Andrew Logan. But exhibits here seem to rotate more often than upstairs, and the programme of temporary exhibitions – which in 2003 include photographer Julia Margaret Cameron (6 Feb-18 May) and the annual BP Portrait Award show (5 June-14 Sept) – is worth keeping up with.

The NPG's collection runs to thousands of pieces, of which only a very small proportion can be displayed at any one time. However, computers in the IT Gallery are set up with the Woodward Portrait Explorer, a searchable database of the gallery's holdings. Access is free to all.

St Martin-in-the-Fields

Trafalgar Square, WC2 (7766 1100/Brass Rubbing Centre 7930 9306/box office evening concerts 7839 8362/www.stmartin-in-the-fields.org). Leicester Square tube/Charing Cross tube/rail. **Open** *Church* 8am-6pm daily. *Brass Rubbing Centre* 10am-6pm Mon-Sat; noon-6pm Sun. **Credit** MC, V. **Admission** free. *Brass rubbing* £2.90-£15. *Evening concerts* £6-£17. **Map** p401 L7.
A church has stood on this site since the 13th century, 'in the fields' between Westminster and the City; the Trafalgar Square redevelopments should finally give it a setting it deserves. Inside, dark woods and ornate Italian plasterwork greet visitors to this parish church for Buckingham Palace (note the royal box to the left of the gallery). The church holds regular concerts of classical music, for which *see p304*. The crypt, accessed on the south side of the building, holds a pleasant café, a small gallery, a gift shop and the wonderfully out-of-time London Brass Rubbing Centre.

Sightseeing

'Hurry up, lads: 'er Majesty went that way... ' Guards at **Buckingham Palace**. *See p130.*

The **Houses of Parliament**. *See p133.*

St James's Park & surrounds

From Trafalgar Square, the grand processional route of the **Mall** passes under Aston Webb's 1910 **Admiralty Arch** to the Victoria Memorial in front of **Buckingham Palace** (*see below*). En route, look out on the right for **Carlton House Terrace**: the last project completed by John Nash before his death, it was built on the site of Carlton House, George IV's home until he decided it wasn't grand enough for a king and built Buckingham Palace to replace it. Part of the terrace now houses the **Institute of Contemporary Arts** (*see p131*).

In the 17th century Charles II had the deer park of St James's Palace converted into a garden by French landscape gardener Le Nôtre, an area that was landscaped further by John Nash in the early 19th century. These days, many Londoners rate **St James's Park** as the loveliest of the capital's central green spaces. The view of Buckingham Palace from the bridge over the lake is wonderful, particularly at night when the palace is floodlit. The lake itself is now a sanctuary for wildfowl, among them pelicans (fed at 3pm daily) and Australian black swans. On the south side of the park, the Wellington Barracks, home of the Foot Guards, contains the **Guards' Museum** (*see p131*). Nearby are the fully intact Georgian terraces of Queen Anne's Gate and Old Queen Street.

Buckingham Palace & Royal Mews

SW1 (7930 4832/recorded information 7799 2331/credit card bookings 7321 2233/Royal Mews 7839 1377/www.royalresidences.com). Green Park or St James's Park tube/Victoria tube/rail. **Open** *State Rooms* early Aug-Sept 9.30am-4.15pm daily. *Royal Mews* Oct-July 11am-4pm; Aug-Sept 10.30am-4.30pm Mon-Thur. Last entry 45mins before closing. **Admission** £11.50; £9.50 concessions; £6 5-17s; free under-5s; £29 family. *Royal Mews* £5; £4 concessions; £2.50 5-17s; free under-5s; £12.50 family. **Credit** AmEx, MC, V. **Map** p400 H9.

Although Buckingham House, as it once was known, was built in 1703 for the Duke of Buckingham, it was purchased by George III and converted into a palace by his son George IV. It didn't become a royal residence until 1837, though, when Queen Victoria moved in. In August and September, while the Windsors are off on their holidays, the State Apartments – the rooms used for banquets and investitures – are open to the public. Once you've got past the thrill of *actually being inside Buckingham Palace*, though, it's not all that interesting, save for the Queen's Gallery, which features highlights of Liz's art collection.

Around the corner, on Buckingham Palace Road, the Royal Mews is home to the royal carriages that are rolled out for the Royals to wag their hands from on very important occasions. The Coronation Coach, the Glass Coach, the immaculately groomed horses and the sleek black landaus make the Mews one of the capital's better-value collections. Top banana, though, goes to Her Majesty's State Coach, a breathtaking double-gilded affair built in 1761. The Mews is closed during Royal Ascot and on state occasions.

Guards' Museum

Wellington Barracks, Birdcage Walk, SW1 (7414 3271). St James's Park tube. **Open** 10am-4pm daily (last entry 3.30pm). **Admission** £2; £1 concessions; free under-16s. **Credit** *Shop* AmEx, MC, V. **Map** p400 J9.

The British Army has five Guards regiments, whose history is recorded by this small museum founded in the 17th century under Charles II. It contains mainly uniforms and oil paintings, viewed to an accompaniment of martial music, but also houses a collection of curios, including the Guards' oldest medal (awarded by Cromwell to officers of his New Model Army at the Battle of Dunbar in 1651) and a bottle of Iraqi whisky captured in the Gulf War. The Guards can be seen in ceremonial action performing the change of guard at St James's Palace and at Buckingham Palace (*see p266* **Frequent events**).

ICA Gallery

The Mall, SW1 (box office 7930 3647/membership enquiries 7766 1439/www.ica.org.uk). Piccadilly Circus tube/Charing Cross tube/rail. **Open** *Galleries* noon-7.30pm daily. **Membership** *Daily* £1.50, £1 concessions Mon-Fri; £2.50, £1.50 concessions Sat, Sun; free under-14s. *Annual* £30; £20 concessions. **Credit** AmEx, DC, MC, V. **Map** p401 K8.

In February 2002 Ivan Massow, the chairman of the Institute of Contemporary Arts, resigned after calling much of the modern art championed by his institution 'pretentious, self-indulgent, craftless tat'. Certainly, the ICA is never far from controversy, which – whatever you think of the work within its walls – is just the way it should be. This arts centre, now approaching pensionable age but getting no less radical as it gets older, deals in challenging work, whether the arty and/or obscure films shown on its two screens, the events staged in its theatre – performance art to super-cool alt-rock – or the work exhibited in its gallery spaces. Henry Moore, Picasso and Max Ernst all had their first UK shows here; recent years have featured the likes of Damien Hirst and the Chapman brothers; and 2003 features shows from Jens Haaning, Matthieu Laurette & Aleksandra Mir (Feb-Mar), and Tom Burr and Cerith Wynn Evans (May-June). In between, the third annual Beck's Futures exhibition and art prize takes place, looking to promote the best of contemporary painting, sculpture, photography, installation and video.

Whitehall to Parliament Square

From Trafalgar Square, the long, gentle curve of **Whitehall** takes you into political Britain. Many of the big ministries that line the road maintain at least a façade of heart-of-the-empire solidity. Halfway down the street, the Horse

Guards building (try to pass by when the mounted scarlet-clad guards are changing; *see p266* **Frequent events**) faces the **Banqueting House** (*see below*), central London's first classical-style building. Nearby is Edwin Lutyens's ascetically plain memorial to the dead of both world wars, the **Cenotaph**, and, on **Downing Street**, the anonymous homes of the Prime Minister and Chancellor (closed off by iron security gates since 1990). At the end of King Charles Street sit the **Cabinet War Rooms** (*see p132*), the operations centre used by Churchill and his Cabinet during World War II air raids.

Parliament Square was laid out in 1868, and the architecture here is on a grand scale. **Westminster Central Hall**, with its great black dome, was built on the site of the old Royal Aquarium in 1905-11 and is used for conferences – the first assembly of the United Nations was held here in 1946 – as well as for Methodist church services. Following a lengthy facelift, **Westminster Abbey** (*see p134*) is now resplendent in its original pristine white. Similarly shaped but much smaller, **St Margaret's Westminster** (*see p134*) stands in its shadow, like a promising child next to an indulgent parent. Both Samuel Pepys and Winston Churchill were married here.

Few buildings in London genuinely dazzle, but the **Houses of Parliament** (*see p133*) are an exception. Built between 1834 and 1858 by Charles Barry and fancifully decorated by Augustus Pugin, their Disneyland Gothic chutzpah simultaneously raises a smile, a gasp and, perhaps, a chuckle. Although formally still known as the Palace of Westminster, the only surviving part of the medieval royal palace is **Westminster Hall** (and the **Jewel Tower**, just south of Westminster Abbey; *see p134*). Parliament's clock tower, popularly known as **Big Ben** (though it's the name of the bell rather than the tower itself), seems stumpy when viewed close up, especially with the London Eye (*see p72*) leering down on it from across the river. In the shadow of Big Ben, at the end of Westminster Bridge, stands a statue of Boudicca and her daughters gesticulating ambiguously towards Parliament.

Banqueting House

Whitehall, SW1 (7930 4179/www.hrp.org.uk). Westminster tube/Charing Cross tube/rail. **Open** 10am-5pm Mon-Sat (last entry 4.30pm). **Admission** £4; £3 concessions; £2.60 5-15s; free under-5s. **Credit** MC, V. **Map** p401 L8.

The only surviving part of the original Whitehall Palace (it was destroyed by fire in 1698), Inigo Jones's classically inspired Banqueting House (1619-22) was the first building in central London in the classical Renaissance style. There's a video and

Sightseeing

small exhibition in the undercroft, but the chief glory is the first-floor hall, designed for court ceremonials and magnificently adorned with ceiling paintings by Rubens that date from 1635. Charles I commissioned the Flemish artist and diplomat to glorify his less than glamorous father James I and celebrate the divine right of the Stuart kings. A bust over the entrance commemorates the fact that Charles was beheaded outside this building in 1649. The building is now chiefly used for corporate functions and occasionally will close especially to accommodate them: call ahead to check it's open before setting out.

Cabinet War Rooms

Clive Steps, King Charles Street, SW1 (7930 6961/ www.iwm.org.uk). St James's Park or Westminster tube. **Open** *Oct-Mar* 10am-6pm daily. *Apr-Sept* 9.30am-6pm daily. Last entry 5.15pm. **Admission** £5.80; £4.20 concessions; £2.90 disabled; free under-15s. **Credit** AmEx, MC, V. **Map** p401 K9.

The secret underground HQ of Churchill's World War II Cabinet has been preserved largely as it was left when it closed down on 16 August 1945. Every book, chart and pin in the Map Room occupies the same space now as it did on VJ day, and Churchill's bedroom still contains the BBC microphones with which he addressed the nation. It didn't often contain the prime minister himself, mind you: Churchill apparently found the room so unwelcoming that he preferred to catch up on his sleep at the bomb-damaged Savoy. You can also see the Cabinet Room and Transatlantic Telephone Room, and a collection of Churchill's private papers and speeches.

The wanderers Political Westminster

Start outside Westminster tube station.
As you come out of the tube, you'll see the **Houses of Parliament**, formally known as the New Palace of Westminster (*see p133*).
Turn left down Bridge Street.
On your right is the Clock Tower, commonly called **Big Ben** after the great bell it houses. Above the station is the **New Parliamentary Building**, home to MPs' offices and committee rooms. Completed in 2001, it was designed by Sir Michael Hopkins to echo the lines of the Houses of Parliament and their neighbouring buildings along the Embankment.
Cross over and view the river frontage of the Houses of Parliament, then walk back to the corner opposite the tube entrance.
You are now looking into **New Palace Yard**. It is dominated by the oldest part of the Palace: **Westminster Hall**, the gabled building on the south side of the courtyard. Begun in 1097 by William Rufus, it was enlarged between 1394 and 1399 by Richard II, who added its amazing hammerbeam roof. It's considered one of the finest medieval buildings in Europe.
Follow the road along Parliament Square to Abingdon Street, pausing outside the door marked 'St Stephen's Entrance'.
The small church opposite is **St Margaret's Westminster**, the official church of the House of Commons since 1614. When a new Speaker of the House is chosen, the bells are rung here. Above the doorway is a bust of Charles I, looking across the street at a statue of his old adversary, Oliver Cromwell.
St Stephen's Entrance is the door by which the public is allowed to enter the Houses of Parliament and watch the debating. The wait varies, but admission is free. A short distance from here, on 11 May 1812, Spencer Perceval was entering the lobby to the old House of Commons when he was shot by John Bellingham, a Briton who resented the government's failure to help him when he was imprisoned for debt in Russia. It remains the only assassination of a British prime minister.
Continue along Abingdon Street, then – after passing the Sovereign's Entrance at the base of the large square Victoria Tower – turn into Victoria Tower Gardens.
You're passing through **Old Palace Yard** where, in the 17th century, Guy Fawkes and his fellow gunpowder plotters were executed. The large statue, by Carlo Baron Marochetti, is of Richard the Lionheart. Further along is the Peers' Entrance to the **House of Lords**, and just inside the **Victoria Tower Gardens** is a statue of campaigning suffragette Emmeline Pankhurst, a cast of Rodin's glum-looking *Burghers of Calais* and a splendid Gothic Revival drinking fountain.
Leave the gardens the way you entered and cross to Great College Street.
Across **College Green** is the **Jewel Tower** (*see p134*), one of the few surviving parts of the old Palace of Westminster. The tower was the storehouse for parliamentary records from 1621 to 1864, when the records were transferred into the 395-foot (120-metre) **Victoria Tower** opposite. Britain's first skyscraper, it was the tallest tower in the world when it was built, but structural problems almost led to its collapse in the 1950s. The parliamentary records are still housed here, and can be consulted by any member of the public (for further details, phone 7219 3074).

Houses of Parliament

Parliament Square, SW1 (Commons information 7219 4272/Lords information 7219 3107/tours 7344 9966/www.parliament.uk). Westminster tube. **Open** (when in session) *House of Commons Visitors' Gallery* 2.30-10pm Mon; 11.30am-7pm Tue, Wed; 11.30am-6pm Thur; 9.30am-2.30pm Fri. *House of Lords Visitors' Gallery* from 2.30pm Mon-Wed; from 3pm Thur; from 11am occasional Fri. *Tours* summer recess only; phone for details. **Admission** *Public gallery* free. *Tours* £7; £3.50 concessions; free under-2s. *House of Lords tours* £7; £3.50 concessions, under-16s. **Map** p401 L9.

The first Parliament was held here in 1275, but Westminster did not become Parliament's permanent home until 1532, when Henry VIII upped sticks to Whitehall. Parliament was originally housed in the choir stalls of St Stephen's Chapel, where members sat facing each other from opposite sides; the tradition continues today. The only remaining parts of the original palace are Westminster Hall, with its hammerbeam roof, and the Jewel Tower; the rest burned down in a fire (1834) and was rebuilt in neo-Gothic style by Charles Barry and Augustus Pugin.

There are 1,000 rooms, 100 staircases, 11 courtyards, eight bars and six restaurants; none of them is open to the public, but anyone can watch the Commons or Lords in session from the visitors' galleries. A change in hours from January 2003 has brought the 'action' forward on Tuesdays, Wednesdays and Thursdays: previously, debating didn't start until mid-afternoon and often went on into the wee small hours. In truth, there's not much

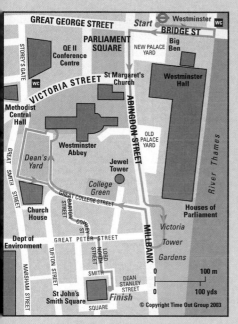

Return to Great College Street and walk west along it until it turns sharp left, then pass through the gateway into Dean's Yard.
The building at the corner of Great College Street is **Church House**. During World War II, the House of Lords found a temporary home here; the lords had relinquished their debating chamber to the House of Commons, whose own chamber was destroyed by bombing on 10 May 1941. As you pass through Dean's Yard, peer in some of the gateways on your right: these are private buildings occupied by Westminster School, founded by Henry VIII. It took over many of the monastic buildings vacated after the dissolution of the monasteries.

Continue to the corner closest to Westminster Abbey and find the doorway into the Cloisters (entrance should be free). Follow the Great Cloister around.
In the 14th and 15th centuries, the House of Commons met in the **Chapter House**, but the arrangement proved unpopular with the resident monks: then, as now, the MPs were boisterous trouble-makers. The Commons got its first permanent home when Edward VI gave them St Stephen's Chapel, the royal chapel in the Palace of Westminster. While you're here, don't miss the **Little Cloister** and **College Garden**, genuine havens of tranquillity in the heart of the metropolis.

Leave the abbey, head back down Great College Street and turn right into Barton Street (which becomes Cowley Street). Take Lord North Street opposite, into Smith Square.
These 18th-century streets have long been home territory for political plots and parliamentary career-building. All three political parties have their headquarters in the area: you'll pass the **Liberal Democrat HQ** at 4 Cowley Street, while **Conservative Central Office** is at 32 Smith Square. (The Labour Party is based a little further to the north on Old Queen Street.) Between the Liberal and Tory headquarters is **8 Lord North Street**, the former home of disgraced Tory MP Jonathan Aitken. There are also World War II signs here that indicate the location of public air raid shelters in the vaults under the street.

to see: most debates are sparsely attended and unenthusiastically conducted. The best spectacle is Prime Minister's Question Time at noon on Wednesdays, for which you need advance tickets (available through your MP or embassy). There's no minimum age but children must be able to sign their name in the visitors' book. Parliament goes into recess at Christmas, Easter and summer, at which times the galleries are open only for pre-booked guided tours.

Jewel Tower

Abingdon Street, SW1 (7222 2219/www.english-heritage.org.uk). Westminster tube. **Open** *Apr-Sept* 10am-6pm daily. *Oct* 10am-5pm daily. *Nov-Mar* 10am-4pm daily. Last entry 30mins before closing. **Admission** £1.60; £1.20 concessions; 80p 5-16s; free under-5s. **Credit** MC, V. **Map** p401 L9.
Together with Westminster Hall, this moated tower is a relic from the medieval Palace of Westminster. Built in 1365-6 to house Edward III's booty (*not* the Crown Jewels, as the notice outside would have it), it stored House of Lords records from 1621 to 1864. Today, it has an informative exhibition that includes a lively video on Parliament past and present.

St Margaret's Church, Westminster Abbey

Parliament Square, SW1 (7654 4840/ www.westminster-abbey.org). St James's Park or Westminster tube. **Open** 9.30am-3.45pm Mon-Fri; 9.30am-1.45pm Sun; 2-5pm Sun (times may change at short notice due to services). **Services** 11am Sun; phone to check. **Admission** free. **Map** p401 K9.
Founded in the 12th century but rebuilt in 1486-1523 and restored many times since, this historic church is dwarfed by the adjacent abbey. The impressive east window (1509) with its richly coloured Flemish glass commemorates the marriage of Henry VIII and Catherine of Aragon. Later windows celebrate Britain's first printer, William Caxton, buried here in 1491, explorer Sir Walter Raleigh, executed in Old Palace Yard, and writer John Milton (1608-74), who married his second wife here.

Westminster Abbey

20 Dean's Yard, SW1 (7222 5152/tours 7222 7110/www.westminster-abbey.org). St James's Park or Westminster tube. **Open** *Nave & royal chapels* 9.30am-3.45pm Mon-Fri; 9am-1.45pm Sat. *Chapter House* Nov-Mar 10am-4pm daily. Apr-Sept 9.30am-5pm daily. Oct 10am-5pm daily. *Pyx Chamber & Abbey Museum* 10am-4pm daily. *College Garden* Apr-Sept 10am-6pm Tue-Thur. Oct-Mar 10am-4pm Tue-Thur. Last entry 1hr before closing. **Admission** *Nave & royal chapels* £6; £3 concessions; £2 11-15s; free under-11s with paying adult; £12 family. *Chapter House, Pyx Chamber & Abbey Museum* £2.50; £1 with main entrance ticket; free with £2 audio guide. **Credit** MC, V. **Map** p401 K9.
Westminster Abbey has been bound up with British royalty since Edward the Confessor built his church to St Peter (consecrated in 1065) on the site of the Saxon original. With two exceptions, every king and queen of England since William the Conqueror

College Garden in **Westminster Abbey**.

(1066) has been crowned here, and many are also buried here: the royal chapels and tombs include Edward the Confessor's shrine and the Coronation Chair (1296). Of the original abbey, only the Pyx Chamber (the one-time royal treasury) and the Norman Undercroft remain; the Gothic nave and choir were rebuilt by Henry III in the 13th century; the Henry VII Chapel, with its spectacular fan vaulting, was added in 1503-12; and Hawksmoor's west towers completed the building in 1745.
The interior is cluttered with monuments to statesmen, scientists, musicians and poets. The centrepiece of the octagonal Chapter House is its 13th-century tiled floor, while the Little Cloister surrounding a pretty garden offers respite from the crowds, especially during free lunchtime concerts (call for details). Worth a look, too, are ten statues of 20th-century Christian martyrs in 15th-century niches over the west door. Come as early or late as possible or on midweek afternoons to avoid the tour groups.

Millbank

Millbank runs along the river from Parliament to Vauxhall Bridge. Just off here is Smith Square, home to two old-fashioned British institutions: **St John's Smith Square**, an exuberant baroque fantasy built as a church in 1713-28 but now a venue for classical music (*see p304*) with a nice basement bar/restaurant, and the Conservative Party (at No.32).
By the river, just north of Vauxhall Bridge, stood the Millbank Penitentiary, an attempt to build a prison based on the rather eccentric ideas of Jeremy Bentham. But in 1890, just 70 years after it was completed, it closed, being eventually replaced by the more enlightened Tate Gallery, now **Tate Britain** (*see p135*).

Overshadowing the Tate is the 387-foot (240-metre) **Millbank Tower**, home until recently to the Labour Party; over the river, the hideous toy-town-building-block bulk of **Vauxhall Cross** is the strangely conspicuous HQ of the internal security service, MI6.

Tate Britain

Millbank, SW1 (7887 8000/www.tate.org.uk). Pimlico tube/C10, 77A, 88 bus. **Open** *10am-5.50pm daily. Tours 11am, noon, 2pm, 3pm Mon-Fri; noon, 3pm Sat, Sun; free.* **Admission** *free. Special exhibitions prices vary.* **Credit** *MC, V.* **Map** *p401 K11.*

Tate Modern, its new young sibling, has garnered most of the publicity (and most of the visitors) in the last few years, with its exuberant displays of challenging modern art in its stunning regenerated building (*see p79*). But try not to leave Tate Britain behind. The increased space allowed it by the opening of Tate Modern and the transfer of some of its works downriver (incidentally, there are shuttle buses and boats between the two sites if you want to do both in a day) has allowed the Millbank gallery a little more space and comfort to accommodate its collection of British art from the 16th century to the present day.

The collection fills the 'something for everyone' remit that you'd hope from a gallery whose exhibits span five centuries, and does so in a way that engages most non-experts. The galleries are ordered more or less chronologically, taking in works by artists such as Hogarth, Blake (William and Peter), Gainsborough, Constable (who gets three rooms all to himself), Bacon, Moore and Hockney. The Clore Gallery extension, meanwhile, houses the Turner bequest. The shop is predictably well stocked and understandably popular, while the restaurant counters the deeply unattractive mural that lines its walls (it's by Rex Whistler, and is called *The Expedition in Pursuit of Rare Meats*) by serving up highly regarded meals.

Temporary exhibitions for 2003 include Constable–Delacroix: British Art and the French Romantics (6 Feb-11 May), exploring the influence of British painting on French art; work by Wolfgang Tillmans (7 June-14 Sept) and Bridget Riley (26 June-28 Sept); and the Turner Prize 2003 show (from 29 Oct), which nominates the work of four usually controversial British artists under 50 every year for a £20,000 prize awarded in a televised ceremony in December.

Victoria & Pimlico

Victoria Street, stretching from Parliament Square to Victoria Station, links political London with backpackers' London. **Victoria Coach Station** is a short distance away in **Buckingham Palace Road**; **Belgrave Road** provides an almost unbroken line of cheap and fairly grim hotels. The area has seldom stayed the same for long. In the 18th and early 19th centuries, it was dominated by the Grosvenor Canal, but in the 1850s much of this was buried

under the new Victoria Station. A century later, many of the shops and offices along Victoria Street were pulled down and replaced by the anonymous blocks that now line it.

Westminster Cathedral (*see below*) always comes as a pleasant surprise, coming into view only when you draw level with it. Built between 1896 and 1903, its interior has never been finished. Further down Victoria Street there is the grey concrete monstrosity that is the **Department of Trade and Industry** HQ.

Continuing along Victoria Street, you come to **Christchurch Gardens**, burial site of Thomas ('Colonel') Blood, the 17th-century rogue who nearly got away with stealing the Crown Jewels. A memorial is dedicated to the suffragettes, who held their first meetings at **Caxton Hall**, visible on the far side of the gardens. **New Scotland Yard** with its famous revolving sign is in Broadway. **Strutton Ground**, on the other side of Victoria Street, is home to a small market. At the other end, Richard Rogers' glorious **Channel Four Building** on the corner of **Chadwick Street** and **Horseferry Road** is worth a look.

Pimlico fills the triangle of land formed by Chelsea Bridge, Ebury Street, Vauxhall Bridge Road and the river. Thomas Cubitt built elegant streets and squares here in the 1830s, as he had in Belgravia, albeit on a less grand scale. The cluster of small shops and restaurants around Warwick Way forms the heart of Pimlico, but Belgrave Road, with its rows of solid white terraces, is its backbone. Nearby are many dignified, beautifully maintained townhouses.

Westminster Cathedral

Victoria Street, SW1 (7798 9055/tours 7798 9064/www.westminstercathedral.org.uk). Victoria tube/rail. **Open** *7am-7pm Mon-Fri, Sun; 8am-7pm Sat.* **Admission** *free; donations appreciated. Campanile £2; £1 concessions; £5 family. Audio guide £2.50; £1.50 concessions.* **Map** *p400 J10.*

A delightfully bizarre neo-Byzantine confection with candy-striped stone and brick bands, Britain's premier Catholic cathedral was begun in 1895 and completed in 1903 by John Francis Bentle. The site on which it was built, originally known as Bulinga Fen and forming part of the marsh around Westminster, was reclaimed by the Benedictine monks who owned Westminster Abbey and used as a market and fairground. After the Reformation, the land was used in turn as a maze, a pleasure garden, a ring for bull-baiting, and as the location for a prison, before being acquired by the Church in 1884.

Recent construction work has resulted in a new piazza at the front of the cathedral. The columns and mosaics (made from more than 100 kinds of marble) are magnificent; Eric Gill's sculptures of the Stations of the Cross (1914-18) are world-renowned; and the view from the 273ft (83m) bell tower is superb.

Sightseeing

Knightsbridge, Hyde Park & South Kensington

Shops and museums, museums and shops.

Sightseeing

Knightsbridge

Maps p395-p397, p400
Knightsbridge or South Kensington tube.

Knightsbridge was once notorious for its taverns and its highwaymen. These days, the majority of people who come to London's wealthiest neighbourhood are only too pleased to be parted from their cash. Chintzy **Harrods** (*see p137* **Shop around**) and the fash-mag heaven of **Harvey Nichols** (*see p235*) take in millions annually, but the smaller shops on and around **Brompton Road** are no less exclusive. **Beauchamp Place**, a favourite of the late Princess Diana, is lined with bijou boutiques, antiques shops and scruffy Portuguese eateries.

At night, this is a strange part of town. It takes a while to realise why, but then it'll hit you: the roads might be busy with traffic, but no one is walking around. *No one.* People who live in Knightsbridge don't walk because they don't need to walk. It simply doesn't occur to them as an option. They have large cars, often with chauffeurs. And when they don't take their large cars, they use black cabs. These people wouldn't know what a Travelcard looked like.

However, while a wander through the streets can be an eerie experience, it's also an enjoyably voyeuristic one. Perhaps because there are so few pedestrians, locals tend to leave their curtains open at night, allowing the stroller to stare in at how the other half live. Wander up **Montpelier Street** or **Ennismore Gardens** and have a gander in at early-evening cocktails, dinner parties or quiet nights by the fire.

Hyde Park & Kensington Gardens

Maps p394 & p395
High Street Kensington, Hyde Park Corner, Knightsbridge, Lancaster Gate or Marble Arch tube.

With an area of around 630 acres (one square mile), Hyde Park (5am-midnight daily; 7298 2100/www.royalparks.gov.uk) is the largest of London's royal parks and the first to have been opened to the public, in the early 17th century.

In the 1730s Queen Caroline dammed the Westbourne river – now one of the capital's hidden waterways – to create the **Serpentine**, the park's central feature and now one of the city's few boating lakes.

Each morning, soldiers of the Household Cavalry emerge from their (really ugly) barracks to ride through Hyde Park to Horse Guards Road for the **Changing of the Guard**. On royal anniversaries and other special occasions, a 41-gun salute is fired in the park, opposite the Dorchester Hotel on traffic-choked **Park Lane**. Further up near Marble Arch is **Speakers' Corner** (*see p140* **London loves**).

Merging into Hyde Park is **Kensington Gardens** (7298 2100/www.royalparks.gsi.gov. uk). Open from dawn until dusk, the gardens are part of **Kensington Palace** (*see below*), a royal residence since William III's asthma precipitated a search for a lung-friendly abode in 1689. The sunken garden and the Orangery built for Queen Anne are worth seeking out.

If you have kids with you, don't miss, in the north of the gardens, the new **Diana, Princess of Wales Memorial Playground** (*see p273*). Situated not far from the **Elfin Oak**, a gnarled, partly hollow stump carved with the figures of elves, fairies and animals, the playground will be part of a seven-mile (10.5-kilometre) walk designed to remember the life of the princess, who lived at Kensington Palace. It's hoped that the long-touted fountain in memory of the princess, designed by Kathryn Gustafson, will open by the Serpentine in August.

Kensington Palace

W8 (7937 9561/www.hrp.org.uk). Bayswater, High Street Kensington or Queensway tube. **Open** 10am-5pm (last entry) daily. **Admission** (includes audio guide) £10; £6.50 5-15s; £7.50 concessions; £30 family. **Credit** AmEx, MC, V. **Map** p394 B8.
Kensington Palace has known many royal residents since William and Mary moved here from Whitehall in 1689. The majority lived before George III became king in the 18th century and moved to Buckingham House, the precursor to Buckingham Palace, but in more recent times, it was home to Diana, Princess of Wales. It's a handsome, imposing building, more instantly appealing than the present

Shop around

Harrods may not have been the world's first department store: that much-contested honour is usually granted to Magasin au Bon Marché in Paris. However, that it is indisputably the world's best-known department store is down not just to sound management – 'omnia, omnibus, ubique', runs the store's motto, or 'all things, for all people, everywhere' – but to one of those right-place, right-time occurrences every business needs to thrive.

When Charles Henry Harrod acquired a Knightsbridge grocer's shop in 1849, the area was just a small village. Two years later, the Great Exhibition arrived, turning the neigbourhood on its head and setting the stage for the eventual growth of this humble establishment into the gargantuan behemoth that towers over Knightsbridge today. Business ticked over nicely enough to begin with. However, it wasn't until Harrod's son Charles Digby bought the store from his father in the 1860s and expanded it into a department store that business boomed.

While its reputation is now that of a store encumbered by tradition, Harrods became sucessful through innovation. Personal accounts were introduced in 1885, with Oscar Wilde and Lily Langtry among the first to sign up. Nine years later, new general manager Richard Burbridge – Harrod had

retired in 1889 – extended the shop's opening hours until 7pm, and in 1898 set up Britain's first escalator in the shop. Referred to as 'the moving staircase', it proved hugely popular, though attendants did have to stand by with smelling salts and brandy to soothe the nerves of some wary customers.

The innovation extended to the breadth of the stock. Woodman Burbridge (Richard's son) sold the store's first aeroplane in 1919, around the same time that Harrods gained a reputation for being able to sell any animal in the world. An alligator was bought as a gift for Noel Coward in 1955, while Prince Leka of Albania purchased a baby elephant for Ronald Reagan in 1967. Nowadays, sadly, you won't find anything more exotic than its dog coat fitting service.

Harrods has settled into old age relatively comfortably, as much tourist attraction as retail outlet under flamboyant owner Mohamed Al Fayed. When the shop first opened, it had a staff of three and had a weekly turnover of £20. Today, it employs 5,000 and takes in £1.5 million a day (and many times more than that during the sales). There are no wild animals or aeroplanes here now, but you're still likely to find something to loosen your purse strings in the shop's 25 acres of selling space.
For more on Harrods, see p235.

Sightseeing

Art in the park at the **Serpentine Gallery**.

royal residence. The most popular exhibit is the Royal Ceremonial Dress Collection, which displays gowns worn by the Queen alongside a selection of Diana's old threads. Tours of the State Departments take in the room where Queen Victoria was baptised (she was also born here) and the fine 17th-century paintings of the King's Gallery.

Serpentine Gallery
Kensington Gardens (nr Albert Memorial), W2 (7402 6075/www.serpentinegallery.org). Lancaster Gate or South Kensington tube. **Open** 10am-6pm daily. *Tours* free; 3pm Sat. **Admission** free. **Map** p395 D8.
A 1930s teahouse in London's grandest park has always seemed a slightly odd location for a cutting-edge gallery of contemporary art, but the Serpentine Gallery seems to thrive on the incongruity. It's been open as a gallery since 1970, since when it's shown works by the likes of Man Ray, Henry Moore and Damien Hirst (who won the Turner Prize here in 1994 for his infamous show *Some Went Mad, Some Ran*

Away); a late-1990s refurb improved the look and the flexibility of the space no end. During summer and autumn 2003, look out for shows from controversial photographer Cindy Sherman and New York-based painter John Currin. Admission is free.

Belgravia & Brompton

Maps p397 & p400
Hyde Park Corner, Knightsbridge, Sloane Square or South Kensington tube.

East of Sloane Street, west of Grosvenor Place and north of Eaton Square lies **Belgravia**. Until it was developed by Lord Grosvenor and Thomas Cubitt in the 1820s, the area comprised open fields and was popular as a site for duels. As soon as the first grand stucco houses were raised, Belgravia established a reputation as a highly exclusive, largely residential district, which it remains today. There's not much to see here, but tucked in among the apartment blocks, hotels and converted offices are some enticing little streets and mews holding some lovely pubs: **Wilton Row** offers the Grenadier, while the higgledy-piggledy Nag's Head (*see p224*) is on **Kinnerton Street**.

The area known as **Brompton**, meanwhile, sits across Sloane Street, otherwise bounded by King's Road, Sloane Avenue and Brompton Road. The area is similar to Belgravia, only without the nice pubs. Aside from the **London Oratory** (*see below*) and Arne Jacobson's eye-catching, incongruous **Danish Embassy** at 55 Sloane Street, it provides little in the way of sights, unless jealously ogling the beautiful houses of local rich folk is your idea of fun.

London Oratory

Thurloe Place, Brompton Road, SW7 (7808 0900/ www.brompton-oratory.org.uk). South Kensington tube. **Open** 6.30am-8pm daily. **Admission** free; donations appreciated. **Map** p397 E10.
The second largest Catholic church in the city – only Westminster Cathedral tops it – the London Oratory is an awesome, daunting spectacle whether you're a believer or not. Built in 1880-4 to the designs of little-known architect Herbert Gribble after an open competition, and known to locals (and Nick Cave, who wrote a suitably brooding song about a visit here) as the Brompton Oratory, it's a shameless attempt to imitate a florid Italian baroque church, both outside and in; indeed, many of the ornate internal decorations predate the building, including Mazzuoli's late 17th-century statues of the apostles, which once stood in Siena Cathedral. During the Cold War, the church was used by the KGB as a dead letter box.

South Kensington

Maps p396 & p397
Gloucester Road or South Kensington tube.

With the £186,000 profit of the 1851 Great Exhibition, and a matching government grant, Queen Victoria's husband Prince Albert oversaw the purchase of 87 acres of land for the building of institutions to 'extend the influence of Science and Art upon Productive Industry'. Although the prince didn't live to see the completion of 'Albertopolis', the scheme was an unqualified success. Concentrated in what's now known as South Kensington is Imperial College, the Royal Geographical Society, the Royal College of Art and the Royal College of Music, plus the museum triumvirate of the **Science Museum**, the **Natural History Museum** (for both, *see p140*) and the **Victoria & Albert Museum** (*see p141*). Albert's work was commemorated by the construction of the **Royal Albert Hall** (venue for the annual 'Proms' concerts; *see p303 and p306*) and the **Albert Memorial** (*see below*). Dwarfed by its neighbours, the **Royal**

College of Music Museum of Instruments (£1.50, £1 concessions; open Wed 2-4.30pm term-time; 7589 3643/www.rcm.ac.uk for tours) on Prince Consort Road is still worth a visit: the collection has instruments from Europe, Africa and Asia, dating back to the 1480s.

The deeply uninteresting residential part of South Ken stretches down to meet Chelsea around Fulham Road. Near its northern end, at No.81, stands the exuberant art nouveau **Michelin Building**, designed by Espinasse for the tyre manufacturers in 1905. It now houses book publishers, the pricey **Bibendum** restaurant and Sir Terence Conran's design shrine, the **Conran Shop** (*see p252*). Fulham Road, lined with swish antiques shops, bars and restaurants, continues down to Chelsea's football ground, **Stamford Bridge** (*see p329*), and on through Fulham towards Putney Bridge.

Albert Memorial
Hyde Park (opposite Royal Albert Hall), SW7 (tours 7495 0916/www.tourguides.co.uk). South Kensington tube. **Open** *Tours* call for details. **Map** p395 D8.
Designed by Sir George Gilbert Scott and finished in 1872, the Albert Memorial centres around a gilded Prince Albert holding a copy of the catalogue of the 1851 Great Exhibition. It's hard to believe that the

Embassies galore line **Belgrave Square.**

modest German Prince, who explicitly said, 'I would rather not be made the prominent feature of such a monument,' would have approved of the finished product. Anyone can see it from a distance, but the tours allow you to get closer to the memorial and examine the superbly crafted marble frieze of 168 leading literary and artistic figures.

Natural History Museum

Cromwell Road, SW7 (7942 5000/www.nhm.ac.uk). South Kensington tube. **Open** 10am-5.50pm Mon-Sat; 11am-5.50pm Sun. *Tours* hourly, 11am-4pm daily. **Admission** free. **Credit** AmEx, MC, V. **Map** p397 D10.

Your kids, as millions of kids before them have done, will head straight to the left upon entering this mammoth palace of learning and go directly into the dinosaur exhibit. And well they might, too: it's a splendid series of displays, although none quite tops the leering diplodocus in the main hall. However, there's plenty more for them than just a miniature *Jurassic Park*, and more than enough to intrigue grown-ups. The main body of the building is split into two sections, the Life Galleries and the Earth Galleries. The former is dominated by its displays on animal life. Some are terrific fun, the Creepy Crawlies exhibit in particular, but others are disappointing: the much-touted life-size model of a blue whale, the flagship exhibit in the Mammals galleries, is rather tatty and impressive only in size. The Earth Galleries are far more hit than miss – not least in Restless Surface, which examines how natural elements change the planet, and Earth's Treasury, an

artful exhibit of minerals and rocks – but curiously, it's again the most hyped exhibit, a lame re-creation of the Kobe earthquake, that falls the flattest.

Don't miss the shiny new Darwin Centre (opened October 2002), home to a staggering 22 million zoology specimens preserved in alcohol in glass jars, some hundreds of years old. The collection includes 170,000 'type' specimens, from which a species was first identified and named. Think of it as a gargantuan Noah's Ark. A small portion is on display on the ground floor, but it's best to take the free tour (every half-hour 10.30am-5pm daily, booking essential), which takes in some of the climate-controlled storage rooms and the Tank Room, containing the largest specimens – fish, snakes, monkeys – in huge jars and stainless steel tanks. Phase two of the centre, scheduled for 2007, will house the museum's entomology and botany collections: 28 million insects and six million plants.

Science Museum

Exhibition Road, SW7 (7942 4454/4455/ www.sciencemuseum.org.uk). South Kensington tube. **Open** 10am-6pm daily. **Admission** free. *Temporary exhibitions* prices vary. **Credit** AmEx, MC, V. **Map** p397 D9.

Like its two neighbours, London's Science Museum is too vast to get around in one go for all but the terminally enthusiastic. The museum was a sizeable space even before a 2000 expansion that added a whole new wing to the building; now it's gigantic. Stephenson's Rocket, a V2 missile and the Apollo 10 command module are among the most popular

London loves **Speakers' Corner**

During the 19th century, Hyde Park emerged as a favourite site for public demonstrations. However, the law forbade public assembly in the park, and all protests were deemed illegal. The Reform League defied the ban in 1866 and gathered thousands in the park to protest against it. The meeting proved the catalyst for change; the battle for the right of public assembly in Hyde Park was won in 1872. Among the changes was the establishment of Speakers' Corner, a small stretch of land at the north-eastern tip of the park where anyone is free to get up and talk about whatever they like to a crowd of curious observers.

Speakers' Corner remains more or less unchanged to this day: one of the great levellers of British society, and a beacon of free speech, both reasoned and borderline-insane. You can say just about anything here – only obscenity and blasphemy are forbidden, with religion and politics the two

hottest topics – but be wary. If the pen truly is mightier than the sword, then the spoken word can be yet more devastating. Some of the hecklers who gather to have their passions raised by the amateur orators who hold court 365 days a year would be turfed out of a Friday night Edinburgh Fringe comedy session for their sharp tongues.

But regardless of the merits (or otherwise) of its orators' arguments, Speakers' Corner also unwittingly succeeds in unlocking one of the city's great contradictions: the silence and loneliness you can feel even when surrounded on all sides by people. This is one man (or woman) against the world, a lone voice heard amid a din made by millions. It might seem that all the meaningless murmur of the Underground and uncontrolled chatter of the streets has been transposed to this remarkably active and organised communal area... and that it suddenly makes some kind of sense.

exhibits (the latter part of a display on space that includes a magnificently tatty old mock moon landscape), though our favourite has long been the enormous 1903 red mill engine that greets visitors as they pass through the main hall. Other high points include a display on medical history that gets a little neglected thanks to its fourth-floor location, and the kid-friendly basement, packed with interactive exhibits. The Wellcome Wing, which opened in 2000, is the museum's (expansive) concession to the 21st century, with an entertaining array of high-tech bits and pieces to be fiddled with. As with the permanent exhibits, temporary displays usually come with a populist twist: an exhibition of James Bond ephemera and gadgetry, which runs until 27 April 2003, has proven a huge draw at the box office.

Victoria & Albert Museum (V&A)

Cromwell Road, SW7 (7942 2000/www.vam.ac.uk).
South Kensington tube. **Open** 10am-5.45pm Mon,
Tue, Thur-Sun; 10am-10pm Wed. *Tours* daily; phone
for details. **Admission** free. *Temporary exhibitions*
prices vary. **Credit** AmEx, MC, V. **Map** p397 E10.
The galleries at the V&A, home to the world's greatest collection of decorative arts, reflect centuries of achievement in such varied fields as ceramics, sculpture, furniture making, jewellery, metalwork, textiles and dress, from Britain, Europe and Asia. The museum also contains the national collections of furniture, sculpture, glass, ceramics, watercolours and photography. Around four million objects are held here, including the finest collection of Italian Renaissance sculpture outside Italy.

The World Galleries span huge areas of the ground floor, each country marked clearly: look out for the Chinese Imperial robes and the huge Persian carpets taking up whole walls in the Islamic section. You'll find some of this country's cultural treasures in the British Galleries, such as Henry VIII's writing desk and James II's wedding suit. Design enthusiasts will love the 20th century Design Galleries, where you might see a copy of Blast, the Vortex manifesto, or the Dali-designed sofa modelled on Mae West's lips. Exhibits are incorporated into the architecture of the building, sometimes successfully and other times less so: a walk down the ceramic staircase is a gaudy affair after the equally verbose silver gallery. And as you won't be able to take the whole thing in on one visit, limit your stay to a couple of rooms and take a breather in the Pirelli Garden, where you'll get the best view of the red brick Victorian buildings.

The V&A has come under attack of late for the shameless populism of its temporary exhibitions, not least its show in late 2002 on gaudy fashion designer Gianni Versace. Its major shows for 2003 are a mixed bunch: Art Deco 1910-1939 (27 Mar-20 July), which will incorporate Cartier jewellery, Leger paintings and fashion by Jeanne Lanvin, Coco Chanel and Elsa Schiaperelli; a retrospective of designer Ossie Clark (from July 2003); and an exhibition entitled Gothic: Art for England 1400-1547 (from 9 Oct 2003), which will include tapestries, paintings, tombs and altarpieces. The opening of the Spiral, Daniel Libeskind's £75-million extension to the building, has been delayed until 2007.

Chelsea

Swingin' London swings no more, but charms regardless.

Maps p396 & p397
Sloane Square tube.

It's not what it used to be, poor old Chelsea. What it used to be is a highly impressive neighbourhood. Since the 16th century, when it was nicknamed a 'village of palaces', it's been the domain of the wealthy and the well bred: Sir Thomas More, the Duke of Norfolk, Henry VIII and Lord Howard of Effingham (conqueror of the Spanish Armada) all had homes here.

In later years, Chelsea became popular with artists and writers. Indeed, so numerous were these bohemian types that, in 1891, a group of them – including painters Whistler and Sickert – set up their own little hangout: the **Chelsea Arts Club**, originally at 181 King's Road but, since 1902, ensconced at 143 Old Church Street. The **King's Road** became a focal point for Swingin' London in the 1960s, with designers such as Mary Quant (whose shop, Bazaar, stood at No.138) and Ossie Clark daring passing hipsters to try their increasingly outlandish creations. A decade later, Vivienne Westwood's shop Sex was one of the cradles of punk: it's where John Lydon became Johnny Rotten and where his band, the Sex Pistols, got their name.

The rich remain in Chelsea to this day. However – crucially – the arty and hip types whose counterbalancing presence gave the area its character have gone, driven north to Notting Hill in the 1980s by skyscraping rent rises (and now being forced out of there for the same reason). Now, the King's Road is a shadow of its former self, lined not with pioneering boutiques but with dull chains, frequented not by the young and stylish, but by braying, Hackett-shirted Sloanes and daytrippers from the Kent suburbs. A few bright spots remain en route: a number of kids' shops (including Trotters at No.34 and Daisy and Tom at Nos.181-3), one of the better eateries in the portfolio of populist restaurateur Terence Conran (Bluebird, at No.350), the recently rejuvenated Peter Jones department store and buoyant **Royal Court Theatre** (*see p333*) in **Sloane Square**, and Westwood, who still holds her own at the World's End shop (No.430). But it's a mostly unexciting stretch.

The lack of enticing retail action means that the wanderer's attention can be turned to the sidestreets and squares off the main drag, and it's here that Chelsea is at its most charming. Sure, you can smell the money the second you venture out of the tube at Sloane Square, but a stroll around Chelsea's residential streets offers an intriguing glimpse at how the other half live.

By the river

Many of the aforementioned writers and painters who've called Chelsea their home have done so from the abundance of impressive houses on **Cheyne Walk**, parallel to the river. Pre-Raphaelite painter Rossetti lived at No.16 with a muster of peacocks, George Eliot called No.4 home, and JMW Turner resided at No.119. Hilaire Belloc, Mrs Gaskell, Thomas Carlyle (*see p143*) and James McNeill Whistler are others who've lived here; **Carlyle Mansions** has housed Ian Fleming, Henry James and TS Eliot over the years; and Oscar Wilde lived on **Tite Street**, in a house he had to abandon after his arrest for gross indecency at the Cadogan Hotel.

The saint and statesman Thomas More was placed in the Tower of London by King Henry VIII in 1535 for refusing to swear to the Act of Succession and the Oath of Supremacy, an act of treason that brought about his beheading. Although his manor house has long gone – it stood on an area of land that is now the site of Beaufort Street, and parts of the original orchard wall can still be seen bordering the gardens of the houses on the west side of Paultons Square – L Cubitt Bevis's statue of the 'man for all seasons' can be seen contemplating Chelsea Embankment outside **Chelsea Old Church** (*see p143*). It's from the Embankment that the stunning **Albert Bridge** arches over the Thames to Battersea.

Along Royal Hospital Road you'll find the **Chelsea Physic Garden** (*see p143*), where rock and herb gardens are cultivated in an attempt to measure their restorative properties. Further along is the **National Army Museum** and the **Royal Hospital** itself (for both, *see p143*). Part of the hospital's grounds were once the location of **Ranelagh Gardens**, celebrated during the 18th century as a favourite haunt of pleasure-seeking toffs. Canaletto's painting of the gardens, where the eight-year-old Mozart gave a concert in 1764, hangs in the National Gallery.

Chelsea Harbour's development from industrial wasteland into a swanky mixed-use area with opulent apartments, offices, high-class shops and restaurants, a hotel and a marina took just two and a half years. However, and in spite of its popularity with the rich and famous, including the late Princess of Wales and Michael Caine (who, for a while, had a restaurant venture here with Marco Pierre White), it's a bit of a ghost town.

Carlyle's House

24 Cheyne Row, SW3 (7352 7087/ www.nationaltrust.org.uk). Sloane Square tube/ 11, 19, 22, 39, 45, 49, 219 bus. **Open** *Apr-Oct* 2-5pm Wed-Fri; 11am-5pm Sat, Sun. **Admission** £3.60; £1.80 5s-16s. **Map** p397 E12.

In the care of the National Trust since 1930, this house was lived in by the great Victorian scholar from 1834 until his death in 1881. Jane, his wife, had a strong influence in the tasteful Victorian decor and the furniture, portraits and books, which are all still in place. Virginia Woolf, a friend of Carlyle's, made several references to him in her essays and novels, and the house itself may have served as the model for the Hilberrys' house in *Night and Day*. What struck her especially was the lack of running water. 'They were Scots,' she reported in her essay for *Good Housekeeping*, 'fanatical about cleanliness.'

Chelsea Old Church

Cheyne Walk, Old Church Street, SW3 (7352 5627/ www.domini.org/chelsea-old-church). Sloane Square tube/11, 19, 22, 49, 319 bus. **Open** 1.30-5.30pm Tue-Fri; 8am-1pm, 2-7pm Sun. **Admission** free; donations appreciated. **Map** p397 E12.

All Saints, as this church is known, dates back to the 13th century, though bomb damage means it's not entirely original. The chapel on the south side was rebuilt in 1528 by Thomas More for use as his private chapel. The church contains monuments to local families such as the Lawrences and the Cheynes, as well as local resident Henry James; rumour has it that heir-obsessed King Henry VIII wed Jane Seymour here before the state ceremony.

Chelsea Physic Garden

66 Royal Hospital Road (entrance in Swan Walk), SW3 (7352 5646/www.chelseaphysicgarden.co.uk). Sloane Square tube/11, 19, 22, 239, 319 bus. **Open** *Apr-late Oct* noon-5pm Wed; 2-6pm Sun. *Tours* times vary. **Admission** £4; £2 5-16s, concessions (not incl OAPs). *Tours* free. **Credit** *Shop only* MC, V. **Map** p397 F12.

Established in 1673 by the Worshipful Society of the Apothecaries of London, Chelsea Physic Garden's main objective was to provide medical students with the means to study plants used in healing. Sir Hans Sloane helped to develop the garden in the early 18th century (at the time, it was described as being three acres, one rood and 35 perches, plus greenhouse, stoves and bargehouses) and the grounds are still used today for research and education. Although

hours are limited, there are a couple of tours daily; it's worth calling ahead to time your visit to coincide with one. During these you'll be allowed to see such features as a garden demonstrating the history of medicinal plants; one of the oldest rock gardens in Europe, dating back to 1773; and greenhouses containing the types of yams from which modern contraceptives and steroids were synthesised.

National Army Museum

Royal Hospital Road, SW3 (7730 0717/ www.national-army-museum.ac.uk). Sloane Square tube/11, 19, 239 bus. **Open** 10am-5.30pm daily. **Admission** free. **Map** p397 F12.

The National Army Museum tends to be rather over-shadowed by the Imperial War Museum (*see p174*) and the new Firepower! exhibition devoted to the Royal Artillery (*see p167*), and understandably so: it hasn't benefited, as those two have, from millions of pounds' worth of recent investment and now comes across as a little shabby and careworn. However, assuming you have a level of enthusiasm for the subject – three floors on the history of the British Army – and can live without a whiz-bang computer display in every room, you'll go away satisfied.

The tale is told chronologically through an assortment of archive photographs, works of art (few of any great artistic worth, though Adolphe Yvon's 101sq ft (9.4sq m) portrayal of the Battle of Ulundi makes up in size what it lacks in quality), battle reconstructions and other militaristic ephemera. It's all a little bleak, though given its subject matter, perhaps that's only appropriate. Light relief comes with the board translating British Army slang on the third floor, which reveals an egg banjo to be a fried egg sandwich, donkey wallopers to be members of the cavalry, and a yellow handbag to be a 'ten-bottle case of Herforder Pils lager'. A programme of temporary exhibitions runs throughout the year.

Royal Hospital Chelsea

Royal Hospital Road, SW3 (7730 5282). Sloane Square tube/11, 19, 22, 137, 211, 239 bus. **Open** *Museum, chapel & hall* 10am-noon, 2-4pm Mon-Sat (May-Sept also 2-4pm Sun). **Admission** free. **Map** p397 F12.

Set up by King Charles (the inspiration came from Louis XIV's Hôtel des Invalides in Paris) and built by Wren, the Royal Hospital is today, as it was when it opened over three centuries ago, home to Army retirees known as the Chelsea Pensioners. Around 400 former servicemen call the site home, and they can feel privileged to be able to do so: it's an impressive sight, several cuts above your usual old folks' home and with an atmosphere all its own. Visitors are welcome to wander the recently smartened-up museum, which contains plans of how the museum used to look, an assortment of uniforms and a vast number of medals bequeathed to the museum by former residents. The Pensioners themselves are usually recognisable by their bright red uniform coats, though they'll likely be in plainer dress when you see them off duty here.

North London

Take your pick – history, greenery or *that* market...

Camden

Camden Town or Chalk Farm tube.

Stretching, approximately, from the statue of Victorian politician Richard Cobden at **Mornington Crescent** to the borders of **Chalk Farm** via **Camden High Street**, Camden Town filled up with cheap lodging houses from 1816, when the Regent's Canal and, later, the railway were laid out. It soon became known for its rough characters. Dickens's childhood home at 16 Bayham Street (no longer extant, but commemorated by a plaque) is believed to have been the model for the Crachits' house in *A Christmas Carol*.

This was a slum area until the late 1960s. Bohemian, too: the struggling actors in the film *Withnail & I* live here, following a Camden tradition of decadence established by Rimbaud and Verlaine a century earlier. However, like most bohemian enclaves, Camden has been taken over by the middle classes. Longtime locals such as Alan Bennett and Jonathan Miller, former *Beyond the Fringe* colleagues who still live a few doors from each other on one of Camden's most beautiful streets, have been joined by very 1990s celebs such as Blur's Graham Coxon. The architecture has grown more affluent with the residents: residents of the weatherbeaten Victorian terraces buy their provisions from Nicholas Grimshaw's high-tech 1988 Sainsbury's supermarket on **Camden Road**.

Camden is not to everyone's taste. Teenagers and students love it, but the rest of London is not so sure. The high street is awash with litter and framed by a host of drab shops and food vendors during the day; at night there's a slew of pubs and clubs with little in common save an NW1 postcode. And no matter the time of day, there'll be a rasta on a streetcorner trying to convince you the oregano he's selling is prime sensi, and a couple of punks by the Lock whose exquisite period detailing belies the fact they were born in the 1980s.

Come the weekend, Camden's enormously popular market (*see p255*) reaches fever pitch. Students and tourists jostle for position at stalls selling drugs paraphernalia (at the Bob Marley postcard end of the scale, rather than hypodermic-and-tourniquet sets), risqué bondage gear and other hippie tat you last saw at Glastonbury aeons ago. These visitors sadly miss the minority of worthwhile stalls: the collectibles in the Stables and the homewares in the main Market Hall. For Camden has become what Carnaby Street was a decade ago: an area defeated by its own popularity and erstwhile hipness. The family lunches in the glossy Wetherspoon's and steepling shop rents tell you in which direction we're heading here.

Fortunately, there's more to Camden than the market and its myriad down-at-heel music pubs. The **Roundhouse** on **Chalk Farm Road**, built as a tram turning point and then a prominent '60s music venue, is presently being redeveloped as a performance space and media centre (7424 9991/www.roundhouse.org.uk). The **Jewish Museum** (*see p146*), on **Albert Street** just off **Parkway**, is a gem; and a reflection, with many of the restaurants and bars, of the area's cultural diversity.

That said, you'll need to choose carefully: Camden has more indifferent pubs and restaurants than any neighbourhood so close

The **Regent's Canal**. *See p146.*

Might as well jump

Having discounted the home extinguishment solution (insufficiently public) and the tube self-flinging method (too messy), London's wannabe suicides have traditionally flocked to an unprepossessing neighbourhood in the north of the city to do the deed. Nestling among the rarified surrounds of Hampstead, Highgate, Crouch Hill and (ahem) Kentish Town is Archway, a mass of pleasant housing, dodgy estates, Junction Road's crummy-looking Quasar centre and the monolithic exercise in 1970s civic brutality known as Archway Tower.

However, the jewel of N19, and the destination of all north London's self-splatterers, is **Archway Bridge**, aka 'Suicide Bridge'. It rose phoenix-like over the remains of an 1809 tunnel through Highgate Hill that collapsed in 1812. The tunnel became a cutting for the Great North Road, one of the last London thoroughfares to levy a toll, and John Nash was commissioned to design the viaduct to carry Hornsey Lane, linking Highgate and Hornsey, over it. Alas, his original structure, designed to emulate a Roman aqueduct, was replaced in 1897 by Sir Alexander Binnie's vast cast-iron arch, today an impervious physical reminder of the 19th-century boundary of London.

From a lay perspective, there are two ways to take in the magnificence of Suicide Bridge. Drive through it from south to north, feeling the drag of the notoriously steep gradient and swiftly scanning the bridge from beneath for jumpers. Better, head for the Hornsey Lane: take in the glorious vista to the south and count the London landmarks rearing up before you. Reflect, if you will, on the human spirit's unfortunate predilection for flinging itself off tall monuments of great beauty: the Clifton Suspension Bridge in Bristol, San Francisco's Golden Gate Bridge and the Sydney Harbour Bridge have all suffered similar abuse. At least the jumpers' last conscious snapshot is aesthetically delicious, although pity the unfortunates driving underneath at the time.

The first recorded Archway Bridge suicide occurred in 1908, and not a year has passed without further unfortunates choosing the same way to die. If only they had decided to throw themselves off a one-storey bridge 40 times instead of once off a very tall one, just in case – *pace* Chris Morris – they changed their minds halfway through. And if only the spirit of actor-comic Peter Sellers saw fit to patrol the bridge in the wee small hours, salving pained souls. In 1969 Sellers and actor friend Wilfred Hyde-White were crossing the bridge on Hornsey Lane when they noticed a crowd gazing up at them. Looking over the parapet, they saw a fellow clinging to the outside of the iron structure. Sellers managed to talk down the would-be suicide, who was hauled to safety by rope.

Extra wire fencing now rings the bridge on either side. But this has so far proven no deterrent. The bridge continues to act as a beacon for jumpers, and the displays of heart-rending family farewell notices and melancholic drooping flowers will continue to proliferate on Archway's mighty monument.

London Canal Museum.

European Grand Tour. Audio-visual programmes provide information on Jewish festivals and Jewish life, while the regular temporary exhibitions begin in 2003 with By the Rivers of Babylon, on the unique culture of the Jews of Iraq.

Around Camden

North of Camden, green relief comes in the form of charming **Primrose Hill** and, at the edge of Hampstead Heath, **Gospel Oak**. Both locales have seen a steady influx of chain shops and cafés into their previously villagey enclaves, although in 2002 the good burghers of Primrose Hill successfully prevented a Starbucks opening on **Regent's Park Road**.

Tired-looking **Kentish Town** is merely a series of bargain stores and cheap eateries, linking Camden to **Highgate** and **Tufnell Park**, although the social elevation of its southern neighbour has led to the conversion of innumerable traditional London boozers into modern gastropubs. Travel along Highgate Road for nosh and a pint at the **Vine** (No.86) or the **Bull & Last** (No.168). The absolutely kitsch-tastic **Swiss Cottage** is a different kind of pleasure: go to the tube station of the same name, and there it is. The excitement stops at the entrance, sadly, but you can enjoy a table overlooking the road junction in summer.

South and east of Camden, **Camley Street Natural Park** offers bucolic charm amid the railway sheds and re-emerging gas works. The **Regent's Canal**, which runs along one side of the park, opened in 1820 to provide a working waterway to link east and west London; the nearby **London Canal Museum** (*see below*) fills in the details. The transportation of industrial materials along the canal ceased in the 1960s. But thanks to the efforts of the Inland Waterways, the towpath's in good shape for a stroll from Little Venice through Primrose Hill to Camden, and there's always the barge option for those who like holiday to mean holiday.

London Canal Museum

12-13 New Wharf Road, King's Cross, N1 (7713 0836/www.canalmuseum.org.uk). King's Cross tube/rail. **Open** 10am-4.30pm Tue-Sun. **Admission** (LP) £2.50; £1.25 8-16s, concessions; free under-8s. **Credit** MC, V. **Map** p399 L2.
Housed in a former ice warehouse, the Canal Museum traces the history of the ice trade, the Regent's Canal and the transportation industry the canal supported. Tracking ice from Norway by ship and then barge to the vast ice well that is open to view in the museum floor, there are also photos, videos and intricate models of boats upstairs (the 1920s archive documentary is a beauty), as well as a barge cabin to sit in. The 'authentic' boatman's conversation may be lame (think BBC northerners in an

to central London. Try the Caribbean fare at the Mango Room (*see p209*), cheap cakes and seafood pasta from the Portuguese caffs on Plender Street or top-notch pub food at the Engineer (65 Gloucester Avenue, NW1; 7722 0950), and then cool down with an ice-cream at Marine Ices (8 Haverstock Hill, NW3, 7482 9003), a north London institution since 1930.

Jewish Museum, Camden
129-31 Albert Street, NW1 (7284 1997/ www.jewishmuseum.org.uk). Camden Town tube. **Open** 10am-4pm Mon-Thur; 10am-5pm Sun. **Admission** £3.50; £2.50 OAPs; £1.50 5-16s, concessions; free under-5s. **Credit** MC, V.
One of a pair (its sister is in Finchley, at the Sternberg Centre, 80 East End Road, N3; 8349 1143), Camden's Jewish Museum provides a fascinating insight into one of Britain's oldest immigrant communities. Different aspects of six centuries of Jewish life are illustrated through oil paintings, artefacts from a tailor's 'sweatshop', silver and chinaware, and photographs and passports. The museum also has one of the world's finest collections of Jewish ceremonial art, including a collection of silver Hanukka candlesticks, spice boxes and an amazing 16th-century Italian synagogue ark, brought to Britain in the 19th century by an Englishman who had picked it up while doing his

afternoon radio play), but the fact that a married couple and their grown-up son actually lived in the tiny space is brought home with a decent thump.

St John's Wood

St John's Wood or Swiss Cottage tube.

The wealthy enclave west of Regent's Park contains the world's most famous cricket ground, **Lord's**, together with its **MCC Museum** (*see below*). From here, **Grove End Road** leads into **Abbey Road**, made famous by the Beatles when its recording facility was still officially called EMI Studios (No.3). The zebra crossing outside is always busy with tourists scrawling their names on the wall; if you're embarrassed to be seen with them, pretend you're here to peek at Sir Lawrence Alma-Tadema's gloriously ostentatious house on Grove End Road (No.44; closed to the public).

Lord's Tour & MCC Museum

Marylebone Cricket Club, Lord's, St John's Wood Road, NW8 (7432 1033/www.lords.org). St John's Wood tube/13, 46, 82, 113, 274 bus. **Open** *Tours Oct-Mar* noon, 2pm daily. *Apr-Sept* 10am, noon, 2pm daily. **Admission** *Tours* £7; £5.50 concessions; £4.50 5-15s; free under-5s. **Credit** MC, V.
Not renowned for being hospitable to innovation, the wearers of the famous tie have accepted the NatWest Media Centre, the stunning raised pod that dominates the self-proclaimed home of cricket. It joins the portrait-decked Long Room on the guided tour (you'll need to book), along with the expected collection of battered bats, photographs and blazers. There's plenty of WG Grace, a stuffed sparrow whose innings came to an abrupt end in 1936 and, holy of holies, the Ashes. No matter how often the Aussies win 'em, you can rest assured that cricket's holy grail – the entertaining story of whose creation is related with appealing dryness – will remain here.

Highgate

Archway or Highgate tube.

East of Hampstead Heath, perched on a hill of its own, graceful Highgate gets its name from a tollgate that used to stand on the site of the **Gate House** pub on the High Street; dinky shops now predominate. There are fine views from the top of **Highgate Hill**, at the foot of which legend has it that Dick Whittington, about to quit town, heard the Bow bells peal out 'Turn again Whittington, thrice Mayor of London'. For those who like their history apocryphal, the event is commemorated on the Whittington Stone near the eponymous hospital.

North of Highgate tube are shady **Highgate Wood** (*see below*) and the fairytale murk of **Queen's Wood**, though Highgate's most famous sight is **Highgate Cemetery** (*see*

p152 **London loves**). Adjoining it is beautiful **Waterlow Park** (7272 2825), donated to Londoners by low-cost housing pioneer Sir Sydney Waterlow in 1889. It has ponds, a mini-aviary, tennis courts, a putting green and, in 16th-century Lauderdale House, a garden café.

Further down Swain's Lane, peep through the Gothic entrance to **Holly Village**, a private village built in 1865. Hornsey Lane, on the other side of Highgate Hill, leads you to **Archway**, a Victorian viaduct offering vertiginous views of the City and the East End (*see p145* **Might as well jump**).

Highgate Wood

Oshobasho Café 8444 1505. Highgate tube. **Open** *Woods* dawn-dusk daily. *Café* 8.30am-6pm (dusk if earlier) Tue-Sun, bank hol Mon. **Admission** free.
Highgate Wood was mentioned (under another name) in the Domesday Book. Nowadays, it's a conservation area, with a nature trail, an excellent kid's playground, and plenty of space for picnics and ball games for those who like their time off to be busy; the more idle can simply saunter along the tranquil paths. Oshobasho Café is worth a visit in its own right, with healthy veggie fare to be enjoyed on its leafy terrace. Who needs Hampstead Heath?

Hampstead

Golders Green or Hampstead tube/ Hampstead Heath rail.

Long popular with the literati and chattering classes, Hampstead still insists on its village identity. Happily, its hilly geography has prevented the sort of urbanisation suffered by Camden, so it remains a haven for London's moneyed intelligentsia and literary bigwigs. They're in illustrious company. Pope and Gay took the waters here during its brief time as a spa; Thackeray and Dickens drank at Jack Straw's Castle on **North End Way**; Keats, Coleridge and Wordsworth wandered Hampstead Heath; and, in the 1930s, modernist and surrealist artists such as Barbara Hepworth and Henry Moore lived the village London idyll.

Hampstead tube stands at the top of the steep **High Street**, lined with opulent but unexciting shops and bars. Running north, and further uphill, is **Heath Street**. It also goes a short way south; important to know, for that's where you'll find great tea and sticky mittel-European cakes at Louis Pâtisserie (*see p209*). The twin lines of higgledy-piggledy terraces that make up **Church Row**, one of Hampstead's most beautiful streets, lead down to **St John at Hampstead** (*see p152* **London loves**). Close by, on **Holly Hill**, is Hampstead's nicest pub, the Hollybush (*see p225*). Another minute's climb brings you to the fine porcelain and paintings at **Fenton House** (*see p148*), while

Sightseeing

The wanderers Rural Hampstead

One of London's most cherished green spaces, Hampstead Heath brings city folk a taste of the country and much more besides.

Start with your back to the entrance of Hampstead Heath train station.

Look behind you to your right and you'll see the Magdala pub, outside which Ruth Ellis shot her former boyfriend in 1955 – the crime for which she became the last woman to be hanged in the UK. The bullet marks are still there, if you care to look.

Turn right up South End Road, with the heath looming before you on the right.

As the road winds upwards, two detours on your left are testimony to Hampstead's enduring artistic associations: **Keats House** (*see p149*) and **2 Willow Road** (*see p150*).

Enter the heath on your right.

This area is the location of a funfair on bank holidays. Any other time, the ponds and houses that back on to it on your right provide a peaceful backdrop. Fishing isn't allowed in this pond, but you can always feed the ducks.

Ignore the first pathway on your right and take the next one, which cuts between the second and third ponds.

On your left is the Mixed Bathing Pond. It's the smallest of the three bathing ponds, but still an incredibly idyllic place to swim in the summer. If you fancy a dip, the entrance is on the path up to the left after the pond.

Keep following the path you were on, then take the right fork.

On a relatively windy day, the kites will herald your arrival at Parliament Hill, so-called because this was the vantage point from which Guy Fawkes and his cronies hoped to watch the Houses of Parliament ablaze. The hill is a tobogganist's dream on London's rare snowy days.

Follow the path to the top of the hill.

Apart from the crowds that can gather, this is a perfect picnic spot. The view of London is wonderful (in summer, you can see even more by walking down in front of the trees that partially block the vista), but don't ignore the view behind you, topped by St Michael's Church in Highgate.

Continue down the path in the direction you've been heading, sticking to the lefthand forks, and take the sharp left by the pond.

The second pond on your right is the Men's Bathing Pond, entrance on the other side. It's popular with gay men in the summer and a few hardy old geezers in winter. Next along is the Model Boating Pond, after which the path splits. In front of you is the Sanctuary Pond, a haven for wildlife including ducks, mallards and great crested grebes.

Turn left, then take the first right after the mud track.

Sightseeing

the celestially inclined will want to potter round the corner to **Hampstead Scientific Society Observatory** (Lower Terrace, 8346 1056/ www.hampsteadscience.ac.uk).

East of Heath Street, a maze of attractive streets shelters **Burgh House** on New End Square, a Queen Anne house that now contains a small museum, and **2 Willow Road** (*see p150*), a residence built by émigré Hungarian architect Ernö Goldfinger for himself and his family in the 1930s. Nearby, off Keats Grove, is **Keats' House** (*see p149*), where he did most of his best work. If you're sated with all this loveliness, the Magdala pub on **South Hill Park** is where Ruth Ellis shot her former boyfriend in 1955, thus meriting the dubious distinction of becoming the last woman hanged in Britain.

Camden Arts Centre

Arkwright Road, corner of Finchley Road, NW3 (7604 4504/www.camdenartscentre.org). Finchley Road tube/Finchley Road & Frognal rail. **Open** phone to check. **Admission** free. **Credit** *Shop only* MC, V.

This innovative venue, dedicated to contemporary visual art and art education, is currently closed for refurbishment. The £4 million improvement scheme will create new galleries and studios, a café and re-landscape the garden. It's expected to reopen in autumn 2003; until then, call for details of Off-Centre, its series of off-site artistic collaborations.

Fenton House

3 Hampstead Grove, NW3 (7435 3471/information 01494 755563/www.nationaltrust.org.uk). Hampstead tube. **Open** *Mar* 2-5pm Sat, Sun. *Apr-Oct* 2-5pm Wed-Fri; 11am-5pm Sat, Sun. Bank hols 11am-5pm. Last entry 4.30pm. *Tours* phone for details. **Admission** (NT) £4.50; £2.25 5-15s; free under-5s. *Joint ticket with 2 Willow Road* £6.30. **No credit cards**.

Devotees of early music will be impressed by the collection of harpsichords, clavichords, virginals and spinets housed at this William and Mary house. The bequest was made on condition that qualified musicians be allowed to play them, so you may get to hear them in action (if not, phone for details of the fortnightly summer concerts). The porcelain collection won't appeal to everyone – the 'curious

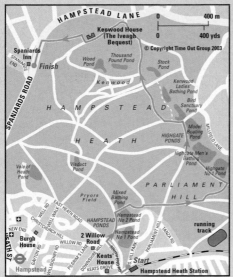

Reputed to be London's largest private residence – ironically, too big for anyone to take on – it recently served as the set for tedious BBC starmaking docusoap *Fame Academy*. When you reach the top of the hill, the entrance to Kenwood Estate is straight ahead.

Enter here, and keep to the righthand forks through the woods. When you get your first glimpse of the stuccoed south façade of **Kenwood House** (*see p150*), you can pop down to the water's edge to get a good look at the trompe l'oeil bridge. At the house itself, look back over the grounds. Concerts take place here in summer (*see p306*); you can either pay for entrance or sit on the hill with a picnic and listen from a distance for free.

From the north side of the house, take the exit north out of the heath, and go left along Hampstead Lane. In a quarter of a mile you'll reach the **Spaniards Inn** (Spaniards Road, NW3; 8731 6571). This evocative pub is still as popular as the day in 1780 when an anti-papist mob, on its way to apprehend Lord Mansfield, stopped for a drink and stayed so long they were caught by the military.

Admire the beautiful silver birches, but ignore the track (which leads to the secluded Ladies' Bathing Pond) and head uphill. A glance to your right from about halfway up and you'll see Witanhurst's neo-Jacobean façade.

grotesque teapot' certainly is, as are the poodles – but for fans there's Meissen and Rockingham work. The gardens are a delight (£1 unless visiting the house), with the small orchard coming into its own for September's Apple Day celebration. Out of season, enjoy the exterior: join the walking tours that begin in the '30s at 2 Willow Road (*see p150*) and go back in time through Georgian and Edwardian Hampstead to end up here (£6; 01494 755572).

Freud Museum

20 Maresfield Gardens, NW3 (7435 2002/ www.freud.org.uk). Finchley Road tube. **Open** noon-5pm Wed-Sun. **Admission** £5; £2 concessions; free under-12s. **Credit** MC, V.

Following Anna Freud's death in 1982, the house she and Sigmund shared for the last year of his life became a museum. You may feel a rush of excitement in the study (the analyst's couch! the round glasses! the uncomfortable chair!), chuckle at the cigar in its ashtray halfway up the stairs and ponder the copious library, but no effort's been made to provide intellectual or biographical context for the uninitiated. The 'explanatory' extracts from Freud's

writings might be fun to piece together, but if you're investing that kind of energy you might as well stay at home with the books. Upstairs, there's footage of the various branches of the Freud family, plus Anna's room (with another couch and handloom) and an elegantly lit gallery.

Keats House

Keats Grove, NW3 (7435 2062/www.keatshouse. org.uk). Hampstead Heath rail/Hampstead tube/ 24, 46, 168 bus. **Open** *Easter-Oct* noon-5pm Tue-Sun. *Nov-Easter* 10am-4pm Tue-Sun. *Tours* 3pm Sat, Sun. **Admission** £3; £1.50 concessions; free under-16s. **Credit** (over £5) MC, V.

Keats House, where the archetypal Romantic poet lived from 1818 to 1820, has been undergoing a programme of building maintenance: quite apart from the thousands of visitors this Grade I-listed building has hosted, it suffered bomb damage in the war and has a lingering problem with damp due to the nearby submerged River Fleet (*see p98* **A river runs through it**). The good news is that once it reopens in early 2003, more of the house will be accessible to the public (including Charles Brown's

Not your normal heritage property: **2 Willow Road**.

bedroom, a poetry reading room and new displays on Keats' girl-next-door sweetheart Fanny Brawne), although most visitors will be coming just to see the garden in which Keats wrote 'Ode to a Nightingale' and to smell the lavender growing by the front door.

2 Willow Road

2 Willow Road, NW3 (7435 6166/www.nationaltrust. org.uk). Hampstead tube/Hampstead Heath rail. **Open** *Mar, Nov* noon-5pm Sat. *Apr-Oct* noon-5pm Thur-Sat. Last entry 4pm. **Admission** (NT) *Guided tours* £4.50; £2.25 5-15s; free under-5s. *Joint ticket with Fenton House* £6.30. **No credit cards.**
The National Trust's only example of International Modernism, this is a strange and atmospheric building. The light pouring through the windows is a feature in itself, and the perfect functionalism of original fixtures and fittings a revelation. Designed and built by Austro-Hungarian architect Ernö Goldfinger in 1939 as a terrace of three houses (the two others are still occupied), it also contains works by Max Ernst, Bridget Riley and Henry Moore, and is lined with curios brought by guests. An introductory video and National Trust guide fill in the blanks.

Hampstead Heath

If you venture into the rolling woodland and meadows that make up Hampstead Heath, you'll feel you could be anywhere except in the bustling metropolis; small wonder this was the inspiration for CS Lewis's Narnia. For more on the heath, *see p148* **The wanderers.**

Nearby is **Kenwood House** (*see below*), whose Brew House restaurant serves one of the best breakfasts in London. There are lakeside concerts on Saturdays in summer (*see p306*), and band concerts on summer Sundays on Golders Hill Park and Parliament Hill. On the edges of the heath, historic pub the Spaniards Inn offers beer and decent nosh. You can pick up a diary of events at information points on the heath.

Kenwood House/Iveagh Bequest

Kenwood House, Hampstead Lane, NW3 (8348 1286/www.english-heritage.org). Hampstead tube/Golders Green tube then 210 bus. **Open** *Apr-Sept* 10am-6pm Mon, Tue, Thur, Sat, Sun; 10.30am-6pm Wed, Fri. *Oct* 10am-5pm Mon, Tue, Thur, Sat, Sun; 10.30am-5pm Wed, Fri. *Nov-Mar* 10am-4pm Mon, Tue, Thur, Sat, Sun; 10.30am-4pm Wed, Fri. *Tours by appointment only.* **Admission** (EH) free; donations appreciated. *Tours* £3.50; £2.50 concessions; £1.50 under-16s. **No credit cards.**
A majestic neo-classical house containing paintings by the likes of Rembrandt, Vermeer, Turner, Gainsborough and Reynolds. The original brick building was remodelled for Lord Mansfield by Robert Adam in 1764-73, with the richly decorated library a particular triumph. When developers attempted to buy Kenwood in 1922, the house and grounds were saved for the public by the 1st Earl of Iveagh, a brewing magnate, who bequeathed the estate to the nation in 1928. If more evidence were required of Lord Iveagh's good sense, the Old Masters he collected will provide it: Vermeer's *The Guitar Player*, of course, but also Rembrandt's self-portrait. There's an exquisitely restored Romany Buckland Caravan in a small building near the fine Coach House restaurant and café.

Islington

Map p402

Angel tube or Highbury & Islington tube/rail.

'Merry' Islington was first famous as an idyllic village – Henry VIII owned houses for hunting hereabouts – but by the 19th century it was known for its shops, theatres and music halls. From 1820, the arrival of Regent's Canal brought industrial slums, and Islington's decline into one of the poorest boroughs in London. However, like so much of London, its Georgian squares and Victorian terraces have been gentrified in the past 25 years, with rising property prices forcing poorer residents out. These days, despite pockets of poverty, this is a middle-class area, and a wealthy one at that.

Take Islington at a stroll. Start at Angel tube and walk along **Upper Street**, past the glass façade of the Business Design Centre (and, opposite, hoary old **Camden Passage** antiques market; *see p232*), along the side of the triangular Green and up towards Highbury. En route, you'll take in countless artsy and craftsy shops, the **Screen on the Green** cinema (*see p285*), the **Almeida Theatre** (*see p337*), a rash of mostly heaving yet mostly ordinary restaurants, the Victorian **Union Chapel** (*see p310*) and a disturbingly large number of estate agents.

Taking this route, you'll also avoid the new **N1 Centre** mall on Liverpool Road, near the Angel. Among its tenants are the gleaming new **Marquee** (*see p309*), a **Warner Village** cineplex (*see p285*) and a branch of **Borders**, none of which really excites. Still, this gleaming behemoth is but a symptom of the influx of chains into the area over the past half-decade or more, turning a formerly unique locale into something more nondescript. You might spy some cabbies nearby: **Penton Street**, at the end of **Chapel Market**, is where your chauffeur chewed down a pencil trying to pass the Knowledge (*see p186* **London loves**).

On the way along Upper Street, take a detour to **Canonbury Square**, a Regency square once home to George Orwell (No.27) and Evelyn Waugh (No.17A) and **Compton Terrace**. Worth a look is the **Estorick Collection of Modern Italian Art** (*see below*), while just to the east is the tranquil New River running beside the less than tranquil Marquess Estate. New River is neither new nor a river, but a 17th-century aqueduct made into a narrow park.

Just beyond the end of Upper Street is **Highbury Fields**, where 200,000 Londoners fled to escape the Great Fire of 1666. Highbury is a curious place, its housing a mix of the grand and the grubby. These days, it's best known for housing Arsenal FC's home ground, the compact, art deco Highbury Stadium. There's a museum here (Avenell Road, N5; 7704 4000/www.arsenal.co.uk; open 9.30am-4pm Fri) and very occasional guided tours, but if you want to see it, be quick: the team are moving to a large new ground in 2004.

Estorick Collection of Modern Italian Art

39A Canonbury Square, N1 (7704 9522/ www.estorickcollection.com). Highbury & Islington tube/rail/271 bus. **Open** 11am-6pm Wed-Sat; noon-5pm Sun. **Admission** £3.50; £2.50 concessions; free under-16s, students. **No credit cards.**

This beautiful Georgian townhouse in north London's Little Italy houses a fine collection of Italian Futurists, including Balla's *Hand of the Violinist* and Boccioni's *Modern Idol*, as well as pieces by Carra, Marinetti, Russolo and Severini. Eric Estorick was a US political scientist, writer and art collector whose interest in the Futurists began in the 1950s, four decades after the movement first threw itself at the world. The museum houses a library with over 2,000 books on modern Italian art, a shop, and a café with alfresco seating. Alongside the permanent collection runs a series of temporary exhibitions, which in 2003 includes the first showing of de Chirico's complete *Ariadne* series.

Sightseeing

Shop for books on **Church Street**. *See p153.*

London loves The dead

Like any city its size and age, London has long had more dead than it knows quite what to do with. But can any other city in Europe have three such marvellous cemeteries so close to each other as north London's famed trio? It's unlikely. All three were built in an eight-year span from 1832 to 1840, and are marked by their grand, over-the-top Victorian tombs and monuments. And despite the obviously rather gloomy *raisons d'être*, these are beautiful places, as idyllic and restful (pun not intended) as any park in the city.

Highgate Cemetery is London's most famous graveyard, marked by its dramatic tombs of towering angels and curling roses. Ghoulish celebrity spotters will be delighted with the Karl Marx and George Eliot memorials in the East Cemetery, but the West Cemetery is really the highlight. It is a breathtaking place: long pathways wind through tall tombs, gloomy catacombs and remarkably elaborate funerary architecture (plus the bones of poet Christina Rossetti and chemist Michael Faraday, if your appetite for the dead famous isn't sated). The cemetery closes during burials.

St John at Hampstead is less ostentatious than its near-neighbour, but just as restful and bucolic. Among those of note buried here are painter John Constable and his wife Mary; John Harrison, the inventor of the chronometer immortalised in Dava Sobel's book *Longitude* (later made into a movie); and, in an unmarked plot, comedian Peter Cook, who lived not far from here.

Abney Park Cemetery is a delightful, rambling old boneyard; not as striking or grandiose as Highgate Cemetery, perhaps, but then Stoke Newington itself isn't as grand as Highgate. These days, it's as much nature reserve as cemetery – plantlife flourished and animals and birds settled here during a period of neglect in the 1960s and '70s – and a stroll through it is gloriously other-worldly. Among the notables buried within are Salvation Army founder William Booth and painter Edward Calvert.

Kensal Green Cemetery, in north-west London, is more ordered and more severe. It's Victorian in origin, though the scale of the monuments – the great and the good in the 19th century clearly were desperate to be remembered – make that apparent from the off. William Makepeace Thackeray, Isambard Kingdom Brunel, Wilkie Collins and Anthony Trollope lie here, but many of the most eye-catching graves are of less famous people. Stroll at your leisure.

Abney Park Cemetery *Stoke Newington Church Street, Stoke Newington, N16 (7275 7557/www.abney-park.org.uk). Stoke Newington rail/73 bus.* **Open** *daylight hours daily. Tours 2pm 1st Sun of mth.* **Admission** *free.*

Highgate Cemetery *Swain's Lane, N6 (8340 1834/www.highgate-cemetery.org). Archway tube/C11, 271 bus.* **Open** *East Cemetery: Apr-Oct 10am-5pm Mon-Fri; 11am-5pm Sat, Sun. Last admission 4.30pm. Nov-Mar 10am-4pm Mon-Fri; 11am-4pm Sat, Sun. Last admission 3.30pm. West Cemetery tours: Apr-Oct noon, 2pm, 4pm Mon-Fri; hourly 11am-4pm Sat, Sun. Nov-Mar hourly 11am-3pm Sat, Sun.* **Admission** *EC £2. WC tours £3; £1 1st child 8-16 (others pay full price). Camera permit £1. No video cameras. No under-8s.* **No credit cards.**

St John at Hampstead *Church Row, NW3 (7794 5808). Hampstead tube.* **Open** *daylight hours daily.* **Admission** *free.*

Kensal Green Cemetery *Harrow Road, Kensal Green, W10 (8969 0152/ www.kensalgreen.co.uk). Kensal Green tube.* **Open** *Apr-Sept 9am-6pm Mon-Sat; 10am-6pm Sun. Oct-Mar 9am-5pm Mon-Sat; 10am-5pm Sun. Tours 2pm Sun.* **Admission** *free. Tours £5 donation; £4 concessions.*

Dalston & Stoke Newington

Dalston: Dalston Kingsland rail/30, 38, 56, 67, 149, 242, 243, 277 bus. Stoke Newington: Stoke Newington rail/73 bus.

Bishopsgate in the City passes through Shoreditch and becomes Kingsland High Street, otherwise known as the A10. This main road runs north through Dalston, Stoke Newington, past the Hassidic enclave of Stamford Hill, via Tottenham and out of London altogether.

Though scruffy and, at times, intimidating, **Dalston** is a vibrant place with kosher shops and bustling market stalls selling Afro-Caribbean vegetables. Lots of small cafés and all-night restaurants – forget New York, Dalston is the city that never sleeps – reflect the Turkish influx into the area.

Middle-class homebuyers started moving in to **Stoke Newington** in a big way after 1980, though the area remains raffish; it's been pinned, not inaccurately, as the neighbourhood people move to when they realise Islington's out of their price bracket. Attractive, villagey Stoke Newington Church Street has a number of good restaurants: **Rasa** (No.55), famed for its vegetarian south Indian cooking, was joined by **Rasa Travancore** (No.56) in 2001, while further up, the **Blue Legume** (No.101) has a nice, chilled vibe. For shoppers, there are second-hand bookstores and the joyful anarchy of **Cookson's Junk Yard** (121 Marton Road, N16; 7254 9941). Green spaces can be found in the shapes of **Clissold Park** (*see below*) and **Abney Park Cemetery** (*see p152* **London loves**).

Clissold Park

Stoke Newington Church Street, N16 (7923 3660). Bus 73. **Open** *Park* 7.30am-dusk daily. *Café* 10am-dusk daily.

Named for a 19th-century curate, Clissold Park dates back to earlier times; the nearby Queen Elizabeth Walk refers to a visit made by the young Elizabeth I. One of the park's more bizarre modern-day claims to fame is that one-time Baader Meinhof terrorist Astrid Proll worked here while she was on the run in the late 1970s (she was employed, under an assumed name, as a park warden). Nowadays, the only exotic species you're likely to find are the inhabitants of the small zoo, though the tennis courts, lake and tearooms offer an escape of a more refined kind.

Further north

Moving towards the northern perimeter of London, dull suburban streets are enlivened by the immigrant communities that have made them their home. **Golders Green**, **Hendon** and **Finchley** have large Jewish communities, the latter home to the **Jewish Museum** (*see p146*). Golders Green is also the focus of a growing population of Chinese and Japanese City workers, with the Oriental City shopping mall (399 Edgware Road; 8200 0009) supplying their shopping needs. There's been a Jewish cemetery on Hoop Lane since 1895; cellist Jacqueline du Pré is buried here, while **Golders Green Crematorium** numbers TS Eliot, Marc Bolan and Anna Pavlova among the hundreds of notable bodies it's sent up in smoke.

Tottenham and **Haringey** retain a Greek Cypriot and Turkish Cypriot identity. Both areas are fun for the sweet-toothed wanting to try a few honey-soaked pastries or the not-so-sweet-toothed drawn by the kebab shops of Green Lanes. **Muswell Hill**'s prime attraction, meanwhile, is the giant glasshouse of **Alexandra Palace** (*see below*).

Alexandra Park & Palace

Alexandra Palace Way, N22 (park 8444 7696/ information 8365 2121/boating 8889 9089/ www.alexandrapalace.com). Wood Green tube/ Alexandra Palace rail/W3, W7, 84A, 144, 144A bus. **Open** *Park* 24hrs daily. *Palace* times vary.

Hailed as 'the People's Palace' when it opened in 1873, with the aim of providing affordable entertainment for all, Alexandra Palace burned to the ground just 16 days later. Rebuilt, it became the site of the first TV broadcasts by the BBC in 1936, but in 1980 was destroyed by fire again. Proving that you can't put a good phoenix down, the born-again palace is back with us and still yields the best panorama of London. Its grounds provide a multitude of attractions – ice skating, boating, pitch-and-putt – while its entertainment and exhibition centre also hosts fairs and events, ranging from the Sailboat and Windsurf Show (1-2 Mar) to the Afro Hair and Beauty Show (25-26 May). There are also school holiday funfairs and a free and very popular fireworks display on or around Bonfire Night (*see p268*).

Royal Air Force Museum Hendon

Grahame Park Way, NW9 (8205 2266/www. rafmuseum.org.uk). Colindale tube/Mill Hill Broadway rail/32, 226, 292, 303 bus. **Open** 10am-6pm daily. *Tours* times vary. **Admission** free. **Credit** MC, V.

Claiming to be the birthplace of aviation in Britain, Hendon Aerodrome currently houses more than 70 aircraft, among them WWI Fokkers, WWII Spitfires and Cold War-era Valiants, together with all manner of aviation memorabilia. When redevelopment work finishes later this year – the grand opening is scheduled for 17 December 2003, the centenary of Orville Wright's first powered flight – the museum will boast a new barrel-vaulted, steel-clad building and exhibition that traces the history of aviation. There's an interactive show about the Battle of Britain and – hear the children whoop for joy – a Red Arrows flight simulator and 'touch and try' Jet Provost cockpit. The free Family Weekends are popular, with the next held on 30-31 Aug 2003.

Sightseeing

East London

EastEnders old and new maintain an uneasy truce.

Whitechapel & Spitalfields

Map p403 & p405

Aldgate, Aldgate East, Shoreditch or Whitechapel tube.

Although it's increasingly uppity, Whitechapel is still the City's poor relation. The green fields that surrounded the original St Mary Whitechapel were soon a suburb on the road to Essex, becoming just another part of town by the time of Defoe. Industries too noisy, smelly or dangerous for the financiers always went east: the **Whitechapel Bell Foundry** (*see p155*) on **Fieldgate Street** and Gunmakers' Company Proof House in **Commercial Road** give some vague yet tangible sense of the area's industrial longevity.

By Victorian times, the area was so wrecked by poverty and crime that missionaries sent to 'civilise' the area talked of it in the same terms as they used of their efforts in Africa. That Jack the Ripper should have remained undetected as he butchered the local population of prostitutes (*see p156* **Jack be nimble, Jack be quick**) is no surprise; neither, though, is the fact that the Salvation Army was established here.

Such problems have their benefits. Low rents attracted a steady influx of immigrants, whose influence has enriched the area. The Huguenots, French Protestant refugees, fled here in the 18th century. Irish and Germans came in the early 19th century, followed by Jewish refugees from eastern Europe from 1880 to 1914. And then, as the Jews prospered and moved north,

Spitalfields Market.
See p155.

Indians and Bangladeshis arrived. The textile businesses on Commercial Street and Commercial Road have simply passed from one group of immigrants to the next.

The best way to explore the heart of the East End is by bus and on foot. Take the 15 bus through the City and get off at **Aldgate East** at the stop between **Goulston Street** and **Old Castle Street**. Contrasts are visible from the off: Tubby Isaacs' jellied eel stall, established 1919, still hangs on by the Aldgate Exchange pub, with the new **Women's Library** on Old Castle Street itself. Opened in 2002 in a converted Victorian washhouse, the library holds a café and regular exhibitions, as well as the best women's history collection in the land (7320 2222/www.thewomenslibrary.ac.uk).

Commercial Street, which sweeps off to the left towards **Shoreditch**, is largely a wide swathe of Victorian warehouses. Halfway up is the covered **Spitalfields Market**, the western part of which is to be redeveloped as offices. An organic goods market is now held on Friday and Sunday where the old fruit and veg market used to be, and there's a booming Sunday trade in books, music, clothes, household accessories, and arts and crafts.

After dark, this stretch of road – highlighted by Hawksmoor's **Christ Church Spitalfields** (*see below*) opposite – has a Hell's Kitchen look about it, with prostitutes standing along the kerb. **Fournier Street**, running alongside Christ Church to link Commercial Street with Brick Lane, is more respectable: a reminder of the Huguenots, whose skill at silk weaving brought them prosperity here. Their tall houses, with distinctive shutters and ornate, jutting porches, line this and other nearby streets.

Time past, you could see inside one of these lovely homes: **19 Princelet Street**, a rare Grade II-listed, unrestored silk merchant's home built in 1719, with a hidden synagogue added in 1869. It's still trying to attract cash for repairs necessary to allow it to reopen as a museum of immigration; until then, call to get details for occasional openings or book a group tour (7247 5352/www.19princeletstreet.org.uk). Similar houses can found nearby in **Elder Street** and **Folgate Street**, where the unique, recreated Georgian residence, **Dennis Severs' House** (*see below*), is distinguished by the flickering gas flames over its front door.

Christ Church Spitalfields

Commercial Street, E1 (7247 7202). Aldgate East tube/Liverpool Street tube/rail/67 bus. **Map** p403 S5.
This might be the prolific Hawksmoor's finest monument. Built in 1714 as a place of worship for the Huguenot silk weavers, it's an impressive sight; especially so after dark, when its brooding outline looms scarily over Commercial Street. Restoration

work began in 2002 after years of neglect, with no one predicting an early completion. You can still stare at the outside: it's the best bit, after all.

Dennis Severs' House

18 Folgate Street, E1 (7247 4013/ www.dennissevershouse.co.uk). Liverpool Street tube/rail. **Open** 2-5pm 1st & 3rd Sun of mth; noon-2pm Mon (following 1st & 3rd Sun of mth); Mon eves (times vary). **Admission** £8 Sun; £5 noon-2pm Mon; £12 Mon eves. **No credit cards. Map** p403 R5.
With the possible exception of the John Soane Museum on its monthly candlelit opening nights in winter, no public building in London is as atmospheric as 18 Folgate Street. It was bought in the late 1970s by Californian exile Severs, and converted from its rundown state into the extraordinary series of spaces that remains today. The building is arranged as a 'still-life drama' encapsulating interiors from the early 18th century to Victorian times; the overall experience is like a piece of performance art, with the house the star: unfinished glasses of port stand on the table before a crackling hearth, the beds look like they've been slept in, cooking smells linger in the air… Approach with imaginations at the ready and leave your cynicism at the door.

Whitechapel Bell Foundry

32-4 Whitechapel Road, E1 (7247 2599/ www.whitechapelbellfoundry.co.uk). Aldgate East or Whitechapel tube. **Open** *Tours* by arrangement Sat. **Admission** (over-14s only) £8. **Credit** MC, V.
The Bell Foundry exemplifies the East End's move from outcast to multicultural treasure. Exiled by the City fathers from its original home in Houndsditch, the foundry was re-established in Whitechapel in 1570, where it cast Big Ben and America's Liberty Bell. Mindful of these associations, the Lord Mayor commissioned the foundry to make a new bell in 2001 that would be hung in Trinity Church in New York as part of the September 11 memorials. There are a few exhibits in the foyer, and a shop; if you want to take a tour, email ahead: places fill up quickly.

Brick Lane

Brick Lane's two main attractions have long been its cheap curry restaurants and its Sunday market. While the former are mostly uninspiring these days – notable exceptions are Sweet & Spicy (No.40) and Preem (No.120) – the latter is a more than diverting Sunday morning. Brick Lane's Jewish heritage survives in the 24-hour **Beigel Bake** at No.159, a wonderful London landmark (the bagels are terrific, too), while the Pride of Spitalfields on **Heneage Street** is one of the few old-fashioned pubs left in the area.

An artsier and more self-conscious Brick Lane has emerged since the Truman Brewery was opened up. Trendier brasseries, restaurants and bars are following the route marked out by the Vibe Bar (91 Brick Lane; 7377 2899) and Les

Trois Garçons restaurant (1 Club Row, E1; 7613 1924), and hip folk are still coming to catch the latest in designer furniture, clothing and art.

Whitechapel Road

Fieldgate Street, running behind the huge East London Mosque, is worth a detour for a look at the grim, derelict, Victorian bulk of **Tower House**, built as a hostel for the homeless. Stalin and Lenin stayed here during the Fifth Congress of the Russian Social Democratic Labour Party, as did Jack London when he called him to investigate the abject poverty of the East End. The Elephant Man, Joseph Merrick, was exhibited at what is now the Bombay Saree House, before Sir Frederick Treves, a surgeon at the **Royal London Hospital** opposite, spotted him and offered him a home in the hospital buildings. The hospital is now topped by a helipad, but there's still a museum there (*see p157*).

Crime has always thrived in this area. George Cornell was shot dead by Ronnie Kray in May 1966 at the Blind Beggar pub (No.337), while **Sidney Street**, which leads off Whitechapel Road opposite Cambridge Heath Road, was the site of a famous siege on 3 January 1911. Several anarchists barricaded themselves into a house and took potshots at the police and soldiers outside before the house caught fire. Two charred bodies were recovered but the gang's leader, a Russian enigmatically named Peter the Painter, was never found.

For decades, the alley at **Wood's Buildings** (down the side of the Bombay Saree House, across Whitechapel Road from the hospital) led to what was arguably the most desolate spot in the whole of the East End: an almost forgotten tract of land dominated by a huge, ruined Victorian school. It was here that Jack the Ripper claimed his first victim. The school may now have been converted into luxury flats, but the view back along the alley towards Whitechapel Road is still tinglingly Dickensian.

Back towards the City, the art nouveau **Whitechapel Art Gallery** (*see p157*) on Whitechapel High Street specialises in

Jack be nimble, Jack be quick

The facts are grisly. Everybody loves a murder story, and this one – five prostitutes are picked up off the streets and killed – is particularly juicy. The setting, too, is perfect: the killings took place in the smog-caked backstreets of Victorian London. So far, so thrilling. But still: if Jack the Ripper had ever been apprehended, there's no way his story would continue to hold such fascination.

Of course, he never was, and we're still no nearer knowing the identity of the world's first serial killer. Over a dozen movies and TV dramas have documented the case of the Ripper, as have countless books. Add the public's love of all things gory to a desire to play what amounts to a real-life game of Cluedo, and you have one of London's most ghoulish tourist attractions: Ripper-themed guided tours around the City and the East End.

Parts of the area where the Ripper plied his brutal trade have changed a great deal in the intervening 115 years. The streets near the City are now dominated by finance, impressively modern office blocks sitting erect on street corners. Mitre Square, where fourth victim Catherine Eddowes was murdered, is now hemmed in by such buildings.

But the closer you get to the East End, the more old-fashioned it gets. These streets – west of Bishopsgate and east of Vallance

Road – remain some of the most evocative in London. Some are grand and imposing, 1990s money having moved in and tarted up once-derelict buildings. Others are as grimy and downtrodden as in the Ripper's day. Most are safe, but there's an agreeable seaminess to them: unlike Wapping to the south and Islington to the north, the East End hasn't succumbed to Starbucks-supping, Gap-wearing gentrification just yet.

The murder sites have changed beyond recognition; the irony of the tours is that there's nothing to see. Mary Ann Nichols was hacked to bits on what is now Durward Street behind Whitechapel tube. Annie Chapman was killed on Hanbury Street, now the Truman Brewery. The Harry Gosling School on Henriques Street covers the site where Elizabeth Stride met her end. And Mary Kelly's home, where she was found splattered against the walls, is somewhere under Spitalfields Market.

Yet the Ripper tours are as much about atmosphere as anything, and here they deliver. The area is still sleazy. Prostitutes work the same avenues and alleyways they did over a century ago; the only difference is that they're working not to earn money for a gin fix, as then, but to appease their addictions to crack cocaine or heroin. Christ

contemporary art. The lobby of Whitechapel Public Library is adorned with a painted-tile depiction of the hay market that was held in the High Street for 300 years until its abolition in 1928. A modest market – clothes, veg, cheap radios, five lighters for a pound – continues to do well further along Whitechapel Road.

Royal London Hospital Archives & Museum

St Philip's Church, Newark Street, E1 (7377 7608/www.brlcf.org.uk). Whitechapel tube. **Open** 10am-4.30pm Mon-Fri (archives by appointment). **Admission** free; donations appreciated.

This small museum traces the hospital's history, from 18th-century voluntary institution through antisepsis, improved nursing and children's healthcare, to the adoption of cardiology and X-ray (a 1930s X-ray machine looks like something from Jules Verne). Norman Hartnell's jaunty designs for nurses' uniforms and George Washington's upper mandibular denture nestle among the requisite cases of grisly implements and bottles for outlandish pharmaceuticals, but the non-specialist will want more on the Elephant Man and forensics.

Whitechapel Art Gallery

80-82 Whitechapel High Street, E1 (7522 7888/ www.whitechapel.org). Aldgate East tube/15, 25, 253 bus. **Open** 11am-6pm Tue, Thur-Sun; 11am-8pm Wed. *Tours* 2.30pm Sun. **Admission** free. **Map** p405 S6.

The Whitechapel consistently puts on challenging and exhilarating shows of mostly modern art in its large ground-floor gallery and skylit upper gallery. That the Whitechapel has kept to its original remit of providing the people of East London with the best in modern art was demonstrated by its centennial retrospective in 2001. The gallery will begin this year spotlighting architect Mies van der Rohe.

Shoreditch & Hoxton

Map p403

Old Street tube/rail.

The intersection of two Roman roads (**Old Street**, running east–west, and **Kingsland Road**, which heads north–south) marked the beginnings of **Shoreditch**. Not quite the City or the East End, the place seems uncertain of its

Church Spitalfields still rises ominously on Commercial Street, though it's crumbling a bit these days. And the Ten Bells pub next door (*pictured*), where many of the victims drank, is still selling gin and beer, though it now supplements its drinkable stock with Ripperabilia: shirts, mugs, books and more.

But while the tour is entertaining, the guides don't pretend to know whodunnit, and nor do they mind. For the day this grisly case gets solved will also be the day the public obsession with it subsides, and the day the tour guides' cash cow runs out of milk. Don't count on it happening any time soon.
The best Ripper walk, from Original London Walks, leaves from Tower Hill station at 7.30pm nightly. For more information, call 7624 3978 or see www.walks.com.

Sightseeing

No place like the **Geffrye Museum**.

Sightseeing

identity, and its main focal point, around Old Street station, is dour and disorganised. But it has seen more cheerful times. James Burbage founded London's first theatre on the corner of **Great Eastern Street** and **New Inn Yard**. The same year, 1598, Ben Jonson, then Britain's foremost playwright after Shakespeare, fought actor Gabriel Spencer at Hoxton Fields (now **Hoxton Square**) and killed him. As he was a clergyman, Jonson escaped the gallows, but he had his left thumb branded.

Hoxton is the section of Shoreditch north of Old Street and west of Kingsland Road. From Victorian times until World War II, it was known for its overcrowded slums and its music halls. Both features have since disappeared under unappealing blocks of flats, but an influx of artists, musicians and other boho types has given the area an unexpected if arrogant chic. Centred around **Hoxton Square** are some cool bars (*see p227*), and many more that are trying hard to be cool, yet shops and other basic facilities remain conspicuous by their absence and the area is still pretty unpleasant.

Geffrye Museum

Kingsland Road, E2 (7739 9893/recorded information 7739 8543/www.geffrye-museum.org.uk). Liverpool Street tube/rail then 149, 242 bus/ Old Street tube/rail, then 243 bus. **Open** 10am-5pm Tue-Sat; noon-5pm Sun, bank hol Mon. **Admission** free; donations appreciated. **Map** p403 R3.
These beautiful almshouses, built in 1715, were converted into a museum of furniture and interior design in 1914. It consists simply of a series of rooms

that have been reconstructed in period style, but it amounts to an informative and atmospheric voyage through the ages of British domestic interiors from the Elizabethan era to the present day. The 20th-century rooms and exhibits are displayed in a 1998 extension to the almshouses, with Edwardian, 1930s and 1960s living rooms and a 1990s loft conversion arranged in a loop around a sinuous, skeletal staircase. This leads to the **Geffrye Design Centre**, a showcase gallery for contemporary designers and makers based locally in the East End, educational art rooms and a cosy temporary exhibition gallery.

A bright, airy restaurant separating the old and new sections looks out over the walled herb garden, which provides a pleasant 'outdoor room' in fine weather alongside the series of period garden rooms (open Apr-Oct). Family Sundays, held once a month, are popular for picnics on the front lawns and child-friendly activities. All in all, a delightful enterprise.

Bethnal Green & Hackney

Bethnal Green tube/rail/Hackney Central or Hackney Downs rail.

Known in Victorian times as the poorest area of London, **Bethnal Green** was targeted for wholesale slum clearance and the building of huge council estates during the 20th century but remains impoverished. The **Bethnal Green Museum of Childhood** (*see p159*), originally the east London branch of the V&A, opened in 1872. Almost as ancient is art deco-inlaid Anglo-Italian caff **E Pellicci** (332 Bethnal Green Road), run by the friendly Pellicci family for a century.

Hackney, to the north, was originally an extended village, popular in the 15th and 16th centuries with merchants who wanted to live near, but not too near, to the City. Hackney's oldest house, **Sutton House** (*see below*), dates from this period. It was something of a rural idyll until the 19th century, when the area's market gardens were buried under terraced houses and workshops, themselves to be replaced by housing estates after World War II.

While the borough of Hackney – the most incompetently governed in London, and that's saying something – stretches to Finsbury Park in the north-west and the edge of Stratford in the south-east, the area most people mean when they mention Hackney is centred around **Mare Street**. The redoubtable **Hackney Empire** (8510 4500/www.hackneyempire.co.uk), in its heyday one of London's great music halls, has stood here for years and is currently undergoing major restoration; expect it to open in early 2003. For years the only major entertainment venue in Hackney, it now has company almost directly opposite with plush new music venue **Ocean** (No.270; *see p309*). Also new to the area is the Technology Learning Centre, on the south side of the Town Hall Square, incorporating a Central Library, shops, restaurants, offices and the **Hackney Museum** (*see below*).

Bethnal Green Museum of Childhood

Cambridge Heath Road, E2 (8983 5200/ recorded information 8980 2415/ www.museumofchildhood.org.uk). Bethnal Green tube. **Open** 10am-5.50pm Mon-Thur, Sat, Sun. **Admission** free; donations welcome.
The refurbished second floor at this long-established museum is due to reopen late in 2003, but the main hall packs in plenty all by itself. The artistry and oddity of dolls is the main focus – displays range from macabre multi-faced dolls to beautiful and intricate dolls' houses – but there are also generous displays of puppets, clockwork and cuddly toys, boats and trains, magic lanterns and zoetropes and spinning tops. Kids can be deposited in the soft play area (weekends and school holidays only; £1.80) or distracted by the roaming art cart (weekends and school holidays only), and there are various activities for them around the museum. Nonetheless, the place may better suit the nostalgic adult than their offspring: for all the toys and gadgets on display, there isn't much that moves or can be played with. Under-8s must be accompanied by an adult. .

Hackney Museum

Hackney Technology & Learning Centre, 1 Reading Lane, E8 (8356 3500/www.hackney.gov.uk/ hackneymuseum). Hackney Central rail. **Open** 9.30am-5.30pm Mon, Tue, Fri; 9.30am-8pm Thur; 10am-5pm Sat. **Admission** free.

In typical Hackney council fashion, its museum moved from its old location five years before its new one was ready. But ready it now is, with £400,000-worth of gleaming new displays on the borough's history running alongside a changing programme of temporary exhibits that reflect the area's incomparably diverse ethnic make-up. A worthwhile diversion should you find yourself in the neighbourhood.

Sutton House

2 & 4 Homerton High Street, E9 (8986 2264/ www.nationaltrust.org.uk). Bethnal Green tube then 253, 106, D6 bus/Hackney Central rail. **Open** *Historic rooms* 1-5.30pm Fri, Sat; 11.30am-5.30pm Sun. *Café, gallery, shop* 11.30am-5pm Wed-Sun. **Admission** £2.20; 50p 5-16s; free under-5s; £4 family. *Tours* (1st Sun of mth) free. **Credit** MC, V.
The oldest house in the East End, this National Trust-owned red-brick Tudor mansion was built in 1535 for Henry VIII's first secretary of state. It opened as a community centre in the late 1980s after a fierce debate over its future that led to the superb restoration now on view. There are Tudor, Jacobean and Georgian interiors, as well as the Edwardian chapel and medieval foundations in the cellar. It also boasts what is possibly London's oldest loo: a 16th-century 'garderobe', and a protected wall of graffiti, believed to have been done by squatters in the early '80s. The café and shop are open all year, and on the fourth Sunday of the month (excluding January) there are free 'discovery days' with tours and workshops on aspects of Tudor life.

Mile End & Bow

Bow Church, Bow Road or Mile End tube.

Mostly common land until the 16th century, **Mile End** experienced a minor population explosion in the 1800s as industrialisation took hold. The area didn't suffer the ravages of poverty endured by neighbouring Whitechapel and Bethnal Green; nevertheless, it was here that the **Trinity Almshouses** were built for '28 decayed masters and commanders of ships' in 1695. East of the junction with Cambridge Heath Road, the cottages and tiny gardens are more village than metropolis, with dinky model galleons at the gate. In the 1860s William Booth founded the Salvation Army in Mile End. His statue here recently regained its exhortatory hand from vandals – fibreglass rather than bronze, as the original is in Denmark Hill.

To the south-west, **Mile End Park** borders Copperfield Road, home to the **Ragged School Museum** (*see p160*) and **Matt's Gallery** (*see p291*). Around £12 million from the Millennium Commission, matched by funding from a range of sponsors, saw the 1950s park remodelled by architects and planners Tibbalds TM2. It incorporates CZWG's award-winning bridge over Mile End Road. Now very near completion, it comprises a go-kart track (which is, in due course, to be solar-powered), a children's centre for under-tens, an Art Park and an Ecology Park. The two latter – energy-efficient, turf-covered buildings – serve as educational facilities and temporary exhibition spaces.

Further north, from where the Grand Union meets the Hertford Union Canals, **Victoria Park** (8533 2057) is a welcome slice of green stretching towards Hackney, a useful detour for those weary of all the cement planes. At the main Sewardstone Road entrance, look out for the deranged-looking Dogs of Alcibiades, which have stood here since 1912. The park's large ponds and tearooms give it an atmosphere reminiscent of Regent's Park.

Bow, to the east, has played a major role in the growth of London. In the 12th century the narrow Roman bridge over the River Lea at Old Ford was supplemented by a new bridge downriver. Its shape – in a bow – gave the area its name. Grain was transported by boat from Hertfordshire and unloaded at mills along the river: Three Mills (near Bromley-by-Bow tube) can still be visited, with Joseph Bazalgette's extraordinary Byzantine-Gothic Abbey Mill pumping station (built in 1868) nearby. The 19th century saw many new industrial works spring up, notably the Bryant & May match factory, scene of a bitter but ultimately successful match-girls' strike in 1888. A quarter of a century later, Bow struck another blow for women's rights when Sylvia Pankhurst, sister of Emmeline, launched the East London Federation of Suffragettes.

Ragged School Museum

48-50 Copperfield Road, E3 (8980 6405/ www.raggedschoolmuseum.org.uk). Mile End tube. **Open** 10am-5pm Wed, Thur; 2-5pm 1st Sun of mth. *Tours by arrangement; phone for details.* **Admission** free; donations appreciated.
Ragged schools were an early attempt at public education: here Dr Barnardo taught 900 shoeless East End urchins. This surprisingly good museum gives a history of each of the Tower Hamlets on the ground floor, touching on poverty, industry, wartime devastation and immigration through the centuries. There's a re-creation of a ragged classroom on the first floor (sometimes with modern schoolkids drilling the 3Rs for a 'teacher' in full Victorian fig), and the top floor is an early 20th-century kitchen. The museum's reliance on personal testimony provides a social history both eloquent and elegant.

Docklands

Various stops on the Docklands Light Railway.

The cradle of London, **Docklands** stretches east from Tower Bridge to the Isle of Dogs and beyond, its architecture alone telling pretty

Can you kick it? **Victoria Park**.

much the whole history of London. As the British Empire expanded in the 18th and 19th centuries, so did the traffic along the Thames, as ships arrived laden with goods from all corners. Different docks were built to specialise in various types of cargo: rum and hardwood at West India Docks on the **Isle of Dogs**; wool, sugar and rubber at **St Katharine's Dock** by Tower Bridge; ivory, coffee and cocoa at London Docks in **Wapping**.

During World War II, the docks suffered heavy bombing, but by the 1950s they had again reached full capacity. The recovery was to be short-lived: the collapse of the Empire and labour unrest were exacerbated by the docks' failure to modernise. Above all, the introduction of deep-water container ships led to the closure, one by one, of all London's docks from Tower Bridge to Barking Creek from 1967 to 1984.

Efforts were made to spruce up the area. In 1981 the Conservative government set up the London Docklands Development Corporation (LDDC), with a brief to regenerate the eight or so square miles of derelict land by building new offices and homes and attracting new businesses. Accused from the outset of favouring wealthy outsiders over local people, the LDDC came unstuck in the recession of the early 1990s, when developers found themselves with new buildings but no one to put in them. Since then, the situation has improved: the population of Docklands doubled to 77,000 in the 17 years to March 1998, when the LDDC disbanded, and the opening of the Docklands Light Railway and Jubilee line extension have made the area more accessible to Londoners than ever.

St Katharine's

Just east of Tower Bridge on the north bank of the Thames, St Katharine's once housed more than 1,000 cottages, a brewery and the 12th-century church of St Katharine, all of which were demolished (without compensation) to make way for a grandiose new docklands development scheme in 1828. **St Katharine's Dock**, which was built over the old settlement, remained open until 1968, re-emerging in 1973 as the first of the Docklands redevelopments. **St Katharine's Haven**, now a yacht marina, houses a squadron of russet-sailed, century-old barges in one corner, while restaurants and pubs pull in tourists by the coachload.

Wapping

Writing in 1598, London historian John Stowe saw **Wapping High Street** as a 'filthy strait passage, with alleys of small tenements or cottages… built and inhabited by sailors' victuallers'. Today, it's a quiet thoroughfare hemmed in on either side by warehouses (those in **Wapping Wall** are the most spectacular) and new flats.

The river at Wapping, to the east of St Katharine's, brims with history. Until well into the 19th century, convicted pirates were taken at low tide to **Execution Dock** (near the River Police station, at Wapping New Stairs), hanged, and left there in chains until three tides had washed over them. The **Captain Kidd** pub (108 Wapping High Street) commemorates one of the most famous recipients of this brand of rough justice: Kidd had been dispatched by the government to capture pirates in the Indian Ocean but decided to become one himself.

Another historic pub, the Town of Ramsgate (62 Wapping High Street), is where bloodthirsty Judge Jeffreys, who sent scores of pirates to Execution Dock, was himself captured as he tried to escape to Hamburg disguised as a sailor (he died in the Tower of London). 'Colonel' Blood was also caught here after attempting to steal the Crown Jewels in 1671. However, the **Prospect of Whitby** (*see p227*) is the oldest and most famous of the Wapping riverside pubs; Pepys, Dickens, Whistler and Turner were regulars before the days of coach parties.

The streets north of the **Highway** are working-class tenements with a colourful past. A large mural at St George's Town Hall on **Cable Street** commemorates the battle between local people and fascist blackshirts, led by Sir Oswald Mosley, on 4 October 1936. The march, meant to intimidate the local Jewish population, was abandoned and the blackshirts banished from the East End. The church of

St George-in-the-East, just off the Highway on **Cannon Street Road**, was built in 1714-29 to the designs of Nicholas Hawksmoor. Although the interior was rebuilt after the Blitz, the exterior and tower are typical of the architect.

Limehouse

Sandwiched between Wapping and the Isle of Dogs, Limehouse was named after the medieval lime kilns that once stood there. But, as with Wapping, its prosperity came from the sea: a 1610 census revealed that half the working population were mariners, and Limehouse later became a centre for shipbuilding. The straw-coloured **Sail Makers' & Ship Chandlers' Building** still stands at 11 West India Dock Road, despite the squatters and vandals.

The importance of Limehouse is reflected in the size of **St Anne's Limehouse** (corner of Commercial Road and Three Colt Street). Built between 1712 and 1724 in what were then open fields, it's probably Hawksmoor's most dramatic creation. The clock tower is the second highest in Britain after the one in which Big Ben is housed, and the church is the only non-HM ship in the world to have permission to fly the white ensign year-round.

Britain's first wave of Chinese immigrants, mainly seamen, settled in Limehouse in the 19th century. Their influence survives in street names like **Canton Street** and the few Chinese restaurants around **West India Dock Road** (the Old Friends at 659 Commercial Road is said to be the first Chinese restaurant in London). In Victorian times Limehouse was notorious for its gambling and drug dens – Oscar Wilde's Dorian Gray comes here to buy opium – and it features in stories by Sax Rohmer (creator of Fu Manchu) and Sir Arthur Conan Doyle. Dickens knew Limehouse well: he regularly visited his godfather in Newell Street and used the tiny, dark and still superb **Grapes** (*see p227*) as the model for the Six Jolly Fellowship Porters in *Our Mutual Friend* (1865).

Isle of Dogs

After two decades of intense development, the Isle of Dogs still bristles with cranes and the skeletons of yet more high-rise office blocks. The 800-foot (244-metre) rocket-shaped focal point, **Canary Wharf**, was designed by Cesar Pelli and has been the tallest building in the UK since it was finished in 1991. But it is no longer alone: in 2002 it was joined on Canada Square by the Citigroup Centre to the south-east and the HSBC tower to the north-east, and at least half a dozen other giants are already under construction. The sight of the tower through

Sightseeing

the glass-domed roof of Canary Wharf DLR station is spectacular and almost makes up for the disappointment at not being able to ride the elevator to sample the views from the top (closed to the public after an IRA bomb attack in February 1996, and since the events of September 11 unlikely to be reopened).

There's little about the Isle that isn't subject to dispute. Some insist it isn't an island at all but a peninsula (though the main section of West India Docks effectively splits it in two), and no one can agree on whether 'Dogs' refers to the royal kennels that were once kept here or whether it's a corruption of the dykes that were built by Flemish engineers in the 19th century. Above all, argument continues to rage over whether the Isle of Dogs shows the success of business-led regeneration or the failures of big business to consider local needs.

The best way to see Docklands is from the Docklands Light Railway (DLR). **Island Gardens**, at the very tip, offers a gorgeous view across the Thames towards Greenwich. There's also **Mudchute City Farm** (*see p274*), as well as one end of the 100-year-old pedestrian foot tunnel that surfaces on the South Bank by the *Cutty Sark* (lift service 7am-7pm Mon-Sat, 10am-5.30pm Sun; *see p168*). If the leaky wonders of Victorian subriverine engineering aren't your thing, you could get off instead in one of the most expansive (and

expensive) stations in the world: the Foster-designed **Canary Wharf** station, resplendent in glass and steel, is said to be as long as Canary Wharf Tower itself is high.

The **Museum in Docklands** (7001 9800/ www.museumindocklands.org.uk), nearby at West India Quay, was due to open in spring 2003, but call ahead before venturing there: the opening's been delayed countless times already. When (if?) it does open, it will plot the history of the docks and the Port of London from the Romans up to the 20th century.

Stratford, Leyton & Leytonstone

Stratford tube/DLR/rail/Leyton or Leytonstone tube.

Stratford ('street by the ford') was formed north of the 12th-century bridgehead. A wealthy Cistercian monastery, Stratford Langthorne Abbey, helped put it on the map. The abbey was dissolved by Henry VIII in 1538, but by then Stratford's prosperity was ensured, thanks to the development of industries such as gunpowder manufacture. In the mid 19th century, much of the area was covered by railway lines and marshalling yards, and it remains a busy transport nexus, boasting railway, tube and DLR stations and a decidedly odd-looking bus station. In due course, Eurostar trains will stop here too.

London loves Iain Sinclair

Peter Ackroyd may be London's biographer (*London: The Biography*, 2000) as well as the author of several notable London novels (try 1985's *Hawksmoor*, or *The House of Dr Dee* from 1993), but he has always acknowledged the inspiration of former parks gardener and second-hand book dealer Iain Sinclair. Born in Cardiff and educated in Dublin, Sinclair has been based in Hackney, east London, for over 30 years; in the 1970s he ran a small poetry imprint, Albion Village Press, from his home between Dalston and Haggerston.

Sinclair's self-published volumes of poetry such as *Lud Heat* (1975) and *Suicide Bridge* (1979) came to the attention of Ackroyd and others, but it wasn't until visionary independent publisher Mike Goldmark of Uppingham, Rutland, put out Sinclair's first novel, *White Chappell, Scarlet Tracings* (1987), about rare-book dealers and the Ripper murders, that news of his special talents began to spread beyond a specialist readership. His second novel, *Downriver*

(1991), won the Encore Award and the James Tait Black Memorial Prize and was followed by the extraordinary *Radon Daughters* (1994), a warped sequel to William Hope Hodgson's *The House on the Borderland* (1908) about an East End police informer with an addiction to X-rays (fed in the Royal London Hospital on Whitechapel Road).

Sinclair's fiction, a primordial soup of dark imaginings and invisible connections, is cooked up in language every bit as dense and intense as his poetry. Its feverish narratives and astonishing agglomeration of imagery are as rewarding as they are challenging; it's not an easy read. A major non-fiction work, *Lights Out for the Territory* (1997), in which speculations on the nature and reality of London were prompted by nine long walks through it, was equally stimulating while more accessible. This dialectical approach – the fiction is the Hard Stuff, non-fiction the Easy Option – has continued with the author's first short story collection, *Slow Chocolate*

Modern Stratford has a busy centre focused on Broadway, where an obelisk commemorates 19th-century philanthropist Samuel Gurney ('When the ear heard him then it blessed him' – baffling, frankly) and a small market sells clothes and knick-knacks. From there, the shopping centre leads to **Gerry Raffles Square,** where the shiny Stratford Picture House faces the venerable Theatre Royal Stratford East (*see p338*) and Stratford Circus, the latter living up to its claim to be 'East London's centre for all performing arts'.

Further out east, **Leyton** and **Leytonstone** lack the cohesion and charm of neighbouring Walthamstow to the north. Leytonstone was named after a milestone on the Roman road from the City to Epping Forest, and the whole area was originally marshy, fertile farmland. Leyton's newest attraction, the **Waterworks**, has reversed time by making water-filter beds, built to fight a cholera epidemic in the 1849, back into natural habitat. The visitor centre opened in August 2002 (8988 7566/ www.leavalleypark.com), so it's now easy for the human animal to drop in on the 900 species of plant and beast already there.

During the 18th century, this part of London was best known for its market gardening, but mid 19th-century industrialisation led to much of the land being covered by railways and gas works, with the population swelled by low-paid railway workers. Badly bombed in World War II, the area was redeveloped haphazardly. The petrol station on the corner of Leytonstone High Road is on the site of a greengrocer's shop where Leytonstone's most famous son, Alfred Hitchcock, spent his early childhood. Striking mosaics in Leytonstone tube depict the shop and various scenes from his films, while a hotel overlooking Epping Forest bears his name. The proliferation of discount supermarkets and second-hand furniture shops testifies to the fact that this remains one of London's poorest areas.

Walthamstow

Walthamstow tube/rail.

The name comes from the Old English word 'Wilcumestowe': a place where guests are welcome. It's a description that still applies today: Walthamstow is a friendly locale. Its borders are ancient ones: **Epping Forest** to the north, **Walthamstow Marshes** to the west. The first settlers lived here in the Bronze Age, when the whole area was thickly forested. In medieval times, much of it was cleared and replaced by farmland. Even now, most of its largely working-class population – though the middle classes are moving in apace, attracted by the relatively cheap property – has been spared the tenements and tower blocks that litter other parts of east London.

Sightseeing

Autopsy (1997) and fourth novel, *Landor's Tower* (2001), and his latest ambulatory volume of polemic and speculation, *London Orbital* (2002), in which Sinclair walks around the M25, the road that rings the city.

'In the novels,' Sinclair said in a *Time Out* interview to mark the publication of *Lights Out for the Territory*, 'I go straight into the magma. In *Lights Out* there's an element of light and clarification. I'm attempting to explain and make things clear. The tone is conversational.'

In *London Orbital*, Sinclair lingers in the Essex town of Purfleet with Dracula on his mind. He considers a passage from Stoker's novel in which the immortal one lies on a sofa consulting 'an English Bradshaw's Guide'. 'Sunk in reverie, on the couch in that dim library,' writes Sinclair, 'he resembles Peter Ackroyd, conjuring up mists and miasmas, busy streets and quiet courtyards, passages where time flows as sluggishly as the Exxon oil-seepage on the Thurrock foreshore.' Dracula's special subject is: doctored memory, describing the past in the excited prose of a contemporary observer.' The description may be of Ackroyd, but it fits Sinclair himself just as well.

EastBeginners

To millions of TV viewers worldwide, Albert Square is a quintessential slice of East End community life. The Queen Vic, the launderette, the street market, the Fowlers' house at No.45: all are real to devotees of *EastEnders*. Of course, Albert Square is but a televisual illusion, built (surprisingly flimsily) on a set at the BBC studios in Elstree, Hertfordshire, miles from the East End. But if it were not, where would it be?

Walthamstow is closest to Albert Square in postal code: E17 compared to Walford's fictional E20. Certainly the street market (*pictured*), London's longest, is packed with cheeky barrow boys and Mo Slater types flogging fruit and veg and dodgy gear. But further south, the area around **Mile End** and **Bow** has Roman Road Market, packed with caffs, chippies, launderettes and pubs. Nearby Tredegar Square is a classic East End square, albeit a little too posh for Walford. Its pub, the Morgan Arms (43 Morgan Street), comes close to emulating the Queen Vic on a Sunday, as Peggy Mitchell types in glitzy blouses down gins to a soundtrack of bellowed karaoke.

And then there's the square that's reputed to be the real-life inspiration for Albert Square. Fassett Square in **Dalston** (ironically, itself two miles from the real East End of London) was stumbled upon by a BBC location scout in 1983; several photographs and plaster casts later, it had been recreated in Elstree.

It certainly looks the part. Victorian yellow-brick terraced houses, built in the 1860s, surround a communal garden; their earliest occupants were clerks, merchants and master craftsmen, who could typically afford to keep a servant. Today, the houses are *EastEnders*-scruffy, with the requisite net curtains. And a train rumbling over a bridge in the background sounds just like the one on TV.

But it's by no means perfect. For one, there's a boxy block of flats on one side of the square. And for two, not only is the communal garden smaller than the one on TV, but fans can't get in to look for Arthur's bench as it's locked. Locked! Since when has Sharon stormed out of the Queen Vic for a good cry in the garden, only to stop and fumble with her keys? On the afternoon we visited, the only sign of life was a couple of boys playing cricket on the road, more reminiscent of the opening credits of *Neighbours* than a day in the life of Walford.

The soap's fictional neighbourhood, by the way, is reputed to have got its name from Walford Road in nearby **Stoke Newington**, an area far too gentrified for the Fowlers. Sometimes the truth hurts.

Walthamstow has two main thoroughfares. The narrow **High Street** contains the longest and, after Brixton, most varied market in London. **Walthamstow Market** stretches for more than a mile and is lined by inexpensive shops. The second thoroughfare is considerably drearier: undulating **Hoe Street**, which consists of a drab selection of kebab shops and mini-marts.

Lloyd Park contains the Waltham Forest Theatre and a variety of imported waterbirds. The aviary and manicured bowling green, frequented by white-clad locals, make it pleasant on a sunny summer's afternoon. The 18th-century building with its back imperiously turned to the park is the **William Morris Gallery** (*see below*). From here, a short walk up Forest Road will be rewarded by a dramatic view of the art nouveau **Walthamstow Town Hall**, one of the most startling pieces of municipal architecture in London. Its beautiful proportions, green and gold clock tower and circular reflecting pool have graced many a film and TV production; indeed, in pre-glasnost days, it was frequently called to stand in for Moscow or Leningrad.

The area's oldest buildings are in the well-concealed enclave of **Walthamstow Village**. Vestry Road is the site of the **Vestry House Museum** (*see below*) and the Monoux Almshouses, built in 1795 and 'endowed for ever... for the use of six decayed tradesmen's widows of this parish and no other'. Nearby St Mary's Church has a modest but tranquil interior. Timbered **Ancient House**, opposite the churchyard, was once a farmhouse. Restored in 1934, it sags like an unsuccessful fruit cake. The Village continues along Orford Road, with its Italian restaurants and cosy pub. Further north, just across the A406, lies **Walthamstow Stadium**, one of London's best-known greyhound racing tracks (*see p330* **London loves**).

Vestry House Museum

Vestry Road, E17 (8509 1917/www.lbwf.gov.uk). Walthamstow Central tube/rail. **Open** 10am-1pm, 2-5.30pm Mon-Fri; 10am-1pm, 2-5pm Sat. *Tours* groups only, by arrangement. **Admission** free.
This pint-sized museum was once a 19th-century police station (as evidenced by the still operational cell, into which visitors can be locked – at their request, of course). The main exhibition concentrates on the social history of the area, incorporating some fascinating photographs plus the original 1834 model of Frederick Bremer's motor car (Britain's first combustion-engine car). It does seem strange, however, that there's nothing about Britain's first powered flight, which was conducted by AV Roe over Walthamstow Marshes in 1909. Still, the costume and toy sections are well worth a look.

William Morris Gallery

Lloyd Park, Forest Road, E17 (8527 3782/ www.lbwf.gov.uk/wmg). Walthamstow Central tube/rail. **Open** 10am-1pm, 2-5pm Tue-Sat; 1st Sun of mth. *Tours* phone for details. **Admission** free; donations appreciated. **Credit** MC, V.
Opened to the public more than 50 years ago, this was the childhood home of influential late-Victorian designer, craftsman and socialist William Morris. In four rooms on the ground floor, Morris's biography is expounded through his work and political writings. Upstairs are galleries devoted to his associates – Burne-Jones, Philip Webb and Ernest Gimson – who assisted in contributing to the considerable popularity Morris's style retains today.

East of Blackwall

There's little to interest the visitor along the North Bank beyond Blackwall. Much of **Canning Town** was flattened by German bombers, and ugly post-war housing estates did nothing to revive its fortunes. Neighbouring **Newham** fared worse: the collapse of a tower block, Ronan Point, in 1968 caused several deaths. **London City Airport** was opened in 1987, south of Beckton, using the long, narrow quay between Royal Albert Dock and George V Dock as a runway for short-haul airliners.

Even here, though, there is something for the casual tourist. Near the Thames Barrier is London's first new park construction in recent history, **Thames Barrier Park** (North Woolwich Road, E16). A thickly covered sunken garden lined by walkways and overlooked by some quietly gorgeous riverside flats, it's a lovely and secluded spot for a summer's day idling. The only downer is that the visitors' centre for the Barrier itself, one of London's most stunning constructions, is on the other side of the Thames (*see p167*).

The view from **Thames Barrier Park.**

South London

Ignore narky north Londoners: there's plenty of charm south of the river.

Charlton, Woolwich & Eltham

This suburban corner of south-east London was once a wild and scary frontier. Just 200 years ago, a journey along the Old Dover Road from **Shooters Hill** to Charlton was a daunting one: the road was steep and bumpy, and the dense woodland sheltered fearsome highwaymen, Dick Turpin among them. The robbers were notoriously ruthless, but the law was equally merciless: convicted highwaymen were hanged at a gallows at the bottom of Shooters Hill, their bodies displayed on a gibbet at the summit.

Charlton village grew up around the splendid Jacobean manor, **Charlton House** (*see below*). The area's pretty unremarkable now, though **Maryon Wilson Park** hosted Antonioni's film *Blow-Up*. There's nothing unremarkable about the nearby **Thames Barrier** (*see p168*), however; the river path has majestic views of this engineering wonder.

Woolwich may be less glamorous than Greenwich (*see p158*), but its naval and military history is just as rich. The **Woolwich Arsenal** was established in Tudor times as the country's main source of munitions and had grown to colossal proportions by World War I, stretching 32 miles (52 km) along the river with its own internal railway system. When it closed in 1967, much of the land was used to build the ghastly **Thamesmead** housing estate.

Thankfully, the main section of the Arsenal, with its beautiful cluster of Georgian buildings, has been preserved. The atmospheric grounds, where Wellington and Marlborough drew up battle plans, are now open to the public, as is **Firepower!** (*see p167*). South of here, the Royal Artillery Barracks boasts the longest Georgian façade in the country; it's best seen from Woolwich Common or Grand Depot Road. The remains of the **Royal Garrison Church of St George**, hit by a bomb in 1944, stand as consecrated ground on the latter.

Henry VIII established the Royal Dockyard at Woolwich in 1512, initially so that *Great Harry*, his new flagship, could be built there. But Woolwich's maritime heritage isn't all glorious: Gallions Reach was the scene of the Thames' worst ever shipping accident in 1878, when a crowded pleasure steamer was struck broadside by a collier, with the loss of 700 lives.

Despite the bleak housing estates, this part of south-east London is blessed with a surprising number of green spaces. Many of them are connected by the **Green Chain Walk** (call 8921 5028 or see www.greenchain.com for maps), taking in pastoral meadows and ancient woodlands such as **Oxleas Wood** (accessible from Falconwood rail station).

Charlton House
Charlton Road, SE7 (8856 3951). Charlton rail/53, 54, 380, 442 bus. **Open** by appointment 9am-11pm Mon-Fri; 9am-5.30pm Sat. **Admission** free.
One of the best Jacobean buildings in Britain, Charlton House was built 1607-12, probably by John Thorpe, and occupied by Adam Newton, tutor to James I's eldest son Henry. The red-brick house looks like the grandest of stately homes, but now operates as a community centre. Highlights include the original oak staircase, marble fireplaces and ornate plaster ceilings. The grounds are scruffy, but a major redesign of the gardens has been approved, so the orangery (most likely by Inigo Jones) and 1608 mulberry tree should soon be back to their best.

Inside **Eltham Palace**. *See p167*.

London loves The Woolwich Ferry

You can't miss the silver streak of the Millennium Bridge, linking Tate Modern with St Paul's. A little further west, gleaming stylishly as it leads the way to the Festival Hall, is the new Hungerford Bridge. Plans are currently on the drawing board for a new covered bridge about halfway between these two new landmarks.

And yet, several miles to the east, a trio of diesel-powered boats chug back and forth across the river, taking south-east Londoners from North Woolwich to South Woolwich and back again. There is no bridge linking the two areas, and there are no tourists around here, which explains why no one is in any great rush to build one. But few mind.

They're a hardened lot around here, used to being ignored. Their football team moved out in 1915, dropped the 'Woolwich' from their name and went on to become Arsenal, one of the most successful teams in British history. The historic Woolwich Arsenal itself has gone, too, largely demolished to make way for the horrible Thamesmead housing estate. And while everyone else across the whole of London rests easy that the Thames Barrier will protect them in the unlikely event of flooding, Woolwich sits half a mile away from the protection, defenceless.

Across this stretch of Thames runs the **Woolwich Ferry**. It has existed since the 14th century, although it only took its present form – run by the local council, free to use – in 1889 after locals petitioned London's metropolitan authority for subsidised transport from one side of Woolwich to the other. The current three boats, each named for a local politician of some repute, have worked the route in rotation since the mid 1960s. And if their diesel engine seems a little dated, bear in mind the fact that the boats they replaced were paddle steamers.

In truth, there's not much to see here. Woolwich is shabby, and the Staten Island Ferry this ain't. But if you happen to be in the area – visiting any of the attractions detailed on pages 166 to 168, say, or taking a plane from or to nearby London City Airport – wander down to the water and hop on this gloriously scruffy, arcane and anachronistic service. A mess? Maybe. But it's our mess.

Eltham Palace

Court Yard, off Court Road, Eltham, SE9 (8294 2548/www.english-heritage.org.uk). Eltham rail. **Open** *Apr-Sept* 10am-6pm Wed-Fri, Sun. *Oct* 10am-5pm Wed-Fri, Sun. *Nov-Mar* 10am-4pm Wed-Fri, Sun. **Admission** *House & grounds (incl audio tour)* £6.20; £4.70 concessions; £3.10 5-16s; free under-5s; £15.50 family (2+3). *Grounds only* £3.60; £2.70 concessions; £1.80 5-16s; free under-5s. **Credit** MC, V.
Don't be fooled by the moat and medieval remains: Stephen Courtauld, a member of the textile family and patron of the arts (*see also p99* Courtauld Gallery), built this must-see art deco country house in the mid 1930s. In contrast to the neo-classical exterior, the interior is suave and sexy: all sensuous curves, polished veneer walls and modish abstract carpets, with the circular entrance hall housing Martini trays, simple white furniture and chunky glass cigarette boxes under a concrete and glass domed ceiling. The 15th-century great hall, the

second largest of its kind in England, is all that remains of the original palace, and is cleverly incorporated into the modern building.

Firepower!

Royal Arsenal, Woolwich, SE18 (8855 7755/ www.firepower.org.uk). Woolwich Arsenal rail. **Open** *Nov-Mar* 11am-5pm Fri-Sun (last entry 3.30pm); *Apr-Oct* 11am-5.30pm Wed-Sun (last entry 4pm). **Admission** £6.50; £5.50 concessions; £4.40 5-16s; free under-5s; £18 family. **Credit** MC, V.
This £15 million attraction is a toys-for-the-boys, whizzing and banging Imperial War Museum (*see p174*). Exhibits trace the evolution of artillery from primitive catapults to nuclear warheads: the History Gallery interprets wars in terms of weaponry, the noisy multimedia presentation Fields of Fire covers World War I through to Bosnia, the Gunnery Hall is full of howitzers and tanks, and the Real Weapon Gallery shows you how all the guns work.

North Woolwich Old Station Museum

*Pier Road, E16 (7474 7244/www.newham.gov.uk).
Beckton DLR/North Woolwich, Woolwich Arsenal or
Woolwich Dockyard rail, then foot tunnel to North
Woolwich Pier.* **Open** *Jan-Nov* 1-5pm Sat, Sun. *School
holidays* 1-5pm daily. **Admission** free. *Rides* £1.
This converted Victorian railway station is paradise
for trainspotters, using old engines, tickets and station signs, plus an authentic 1920s ticket office to
tell the story of the Great Eastern Railway. You can
also hop on the miniature railway – which runs
on the first and second weekends of each month,
weather permitting – or watch the Coffee Pot and
Pickett steam engines chuff past.

Thames Barrier Visitors Centre

*1 Unity Way, SE18 (8305 4188/www.environment-
agency.gov.uk). North Greenwich tube/Charlton rail/
161,177, 180 bus.* **Open** *Apr-Sept* 10.30am-4.30pm
daily. *Oct-Mar* 11am-3.30pm daily. **Admission**
£1; 75p concessions; 50p 5-16s; free under-5s.
Credit MC, V.
Completed in 1982, the Thames Barrier cost £535
million to build and is the world's largest adjustable
dam. A cross between giant metallic shark fins and
a fleet of Sydney Opera Houses, its nine piers anchor
massive steel gates that are raised from the riverbed
to protect London from devastating surge tides: the
barrier's already saved the city 67 times. The tiny
Visitors Centre on the south bank shows how the
barrier was built and how it works, and a map
shows the bits of London that would be submerged
if it stopped working. Time your visit to see the barrier in action: there's a partial test-closure monthly,
and a full-scale test each September (*see p266*).

Greenwich & Blackheath

Bustling riverside Greenwich is one of south
London's most charming locales. It's best
known for its maritime history and elegant
Georgian and Regency architecture, but it was
also a playground for Tudor royalty. Henry
VIII and his daughters Mary I and Elizabeth I
were all born here, and Greenwich Palace – in
those days, perfectly placed for hunting – was
Henry's favourite residence.

After the Tudors, the palace fell on hard
times. Under Oliver Cromwell, it became a
biscuit factory, then a prison. In 1660, however,
newly restored monarch Charles II embarked
on an ambitious scheme to return Greenwich to
its former glory. Work began on a new palace,
but only one riverside wing was built before
William and Mary succeeded Charles. They
preferred Hampton Court and Kensington, but
ordered Sir Christopher Wren to design another
wing so the unfinished building could house
the Royal Naval Hospital. He split it down the
centre, an inspired piece of design that provides
an unobscured view of the Queen's House
behind. The hospital is now known as the **Old
Royal Naval College** (*see p171*).

The most picturesque way of arriving is by
river to Greenwich Pier, where you'll disembark
in the shadow of the **Cutty Sark** (*see p169*).
The **Greenwich Tourist Information
Centre** (0870 608 2000), based in Pepys House
beside the *Cutty Sark*, provides full details on
sights and transport in the area. On the other

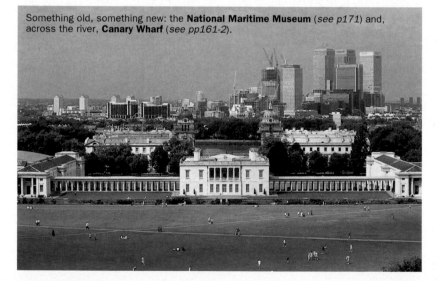

Something old, something new: the **National Maritime Museum** (*see p171*) and,
across the river, **Canary Wharf** (*see pp161-2*).

side of the historic ship lies **Greenwich Reach**. Due for completion in 2004, this complex will include a cinema, restaurants, flats and – continuing the maritime theme – London's first central cruise-liner terminal.

Greenwich would still pass for a gracious country town if it wasn't for its traffic-ridden centre. Each weekend, visitors flood in to sprawling **Greenwich Market** (*see p255*) to peruse the arts and crafts. For some peace and quiet, the Hawksmoor-designed church of **St Alfege Greenwich** (1712-18) on Greenwich High Road is usually open.

A lovely Thameside walkway by the *Cutty Sark* takes you past the Old Royal Naval College to the **Trafalgar Tavern**, built directly on the river and a favourite haunt of Thackeray, Dickens and Collins (Dickens set the wedding feast in *Our Mutual Friend* here). Tiny **Crane Street**, on the far side of the pub, leads to the bizarre, white, castellated Trinity Hospital, which in 1617 provided a home to '21 retired gentlemen of Greenwich'. The path continues as far as the **Cutty Sark Tavern**, dating from 1695. Seats outside the pub afford a view of the still-active wharfs downstream.

Greenwich Park (8858 2608) comes with a rich history: a Roman temple and 20 Saxon grave mounds have been identified here, and Henry VIII was born within at Greenwich Palace. In 1616 James I commissioned Inigo Jones to rebuild the Tudor palace, which became **Queen's House** (*see p171*), England's first Palladian villa. The park was later redesigned by André Le Nôtre, who landscaped Versailles for Louis XIV. At the southern end of the park is the 18th-century **Ranger's House** (*see p171*).

An energetic walk up the park's hill rewards you with a terrific view, taking in the verdant parkland and landmarks including St Paul's and the Dome, but the real attractions are the Wren-designed **Royal Observatory** (*see p171*) and Flamsteed House. Temporally speaking, you're now at the centre of the planet: Greenwich Mean Time, introduced in 1890, sets the world's clocks, and inside the museum's grounds you can straddle the Greenwich Meridian Line, one foot in each of the world's hemispheres. Those who don't fancy the walk uphill can take the royal blue Shuttle Bus (8859 1096; runs Apr-Sept: adults £1.50, children 50p, tickets valid all day). It meets boats at Greenwich Pier and provides a hop-on, hop-off service through the park, with stops at the Observatory and National Maritime Museum.

Maze Hill runs south from Trafalgar Road, forming the eastern boundary of Greenwich Park. At the top of the hill is a castle-like house built by architect and playwright John Vanbrugh, who lived here from 1719 to 1726;

Yachts and flocks at **Greenwich Market**

it has a superb view over the Old Royal Naval College towards the City. West of the park is the **Fan Museum** (*see below*), while to the north sits the still-controversial **Dome** (*see p172* **Dome alone**).

Cutty Sark

King William Walk, SE10 (8858 3445/ www.cuttysark.org.uk). Cutty Sark DLR/Greenwich DLR/rail. **Open** 10am-5pm daily (last entry 4.30pm). **Admission** £3.90; £2.90 concessions; free under-5s; £9.70 family. **Credit** MC, V.

Once one of the fastest ships on the ocean, Hercules Linton's 1869 vessel is now famous as the world's last surviving tea and wool clipper. The lower decks house an extensive exhibition on the *Cutty Sark*'s history, as well as paintings, models and the largest collection of carved and painted figureheads in the world. There's knot-tying and a hammock to keep younger visitors happy, plus shanty singers and costumed storytellers' sessions on summer weekends.

Fan Museum

12 Crooms Hill, SE10 (8305 1441/www.fanmuseum.org). Cutty Sark DLR/Greenwich DLR/ rail. **Open** 11am-5pm Tue-Sat; noon-5pm Sun. **Admission** £3.50; £2.50 concessions; free under-7s (free OAPs, disabled 2-5pm Tue). **Credit** MC, V.

Housed in two converted Georgian townhouses, this unexpectedly compelling museum is one of only two permanent exhibitions of hand-held folding fans in the world. The museum has some 3,000 fans, dating back to the 11th century, though only a fraction of the collection is on view at any one time because the

fans need to be rested to avoid damage. Exhibitions for 2003 will focus on contemporary fans (4 Feb-2 June) and Louis XIV fans (3 June-23 Sept).

National Maritime Museum

Romney Road, SE10 (8858 4422/information 8312 6565/www.nmm.ac.uk). Cutty Sark DLR/Greenwich DLR/rail. **Open** 10am-5pm daily. **Admission** free. **Credit** MC, V.

This gorgeous white neo-classical building is a lesson in symmetry and grace, and the museum inside offers a stunning mix of traditional exhibits and interactive presentations. Explorers is devoted to pioneers of sea travel, covering Columbus, the Vikings and the race to the Poles. Passengers is a paean to glamorous old ocean liners, Rank & Style traces the effects of climate and class on uniform styles, and Maritime London tells the capital's nautical history through old prints and model ships. Upstairs, Seapower covers naval battles from Gallipoli to the Falklands, while the Art of the Sea is the world's largest maritime art collection. Level 3 has kids' attractions: would-be sailors can learn to send Morse code, navigate Viking longboats or steer a modern passenger ferry. The big temporary exhibition for 2003 is dedicated to Queen Elizabeth I.

Old Royal Naval College

King William Walk, SE10 (8269 4747/ www.greenwichfoundation.org.uk). Cutty Sark DLR/ Greenwich DLR/rail. **Open** 10am-5pm daily (last entry 4.15pm). **Admission** free. **Credit** MC, V.

When the Royal Naval College left Portsmouth in 1873, it moved into Sir Christopher Wren's 1696 naval hospital. The elegant and majestic pair of neo-classical buildings, neatly framing Inigo Jones's Queen's House (*see below*), may look stunning from the river, but the view from behind is as striking: gold-topped domes frame the skyscrapers of Canary Wharf. The University of Greenwich settled here in 1998, but the public can still visit the chapel and the three ornately decorated rooms of the Painted Hall.

Queen's House

Romney Road, SE10 (8312 6565/www.nmm.ac.uk). Cutty Sark DLR/Greenwich DLR/rail. **Open** 10am-5pm daily. **Admission** free. **Credit** MC, V.

One of Britain's first truly classical buildings, the simple design of the Queen's House belies a more lavish interior. Designed by Inigo Jones in 1616 for James I's wife, Anne of Denmark, it was his first attempt at Palladian architecture. Inside, the Sea of Faces exhibition displays some 150 maritime portraits, with works by Hogarth and Gainsborough. A magnificent colonnade connects the building to the adjacent National Maritime Museum (*see above*).

Ranger's House

Chesterfield Walk, SE10 (8853 0035/www.english-heritage.org.uk). Blackheath rail/Greenwich DLR/rail. **Open** *Nov-Dec, Mar* 10am-4pm Wed-Sun; *Apr-Sept* 10am-6pm Wed-Sun; *Oct* 10am-5pm Wed-Sun (last entry 1hr before closing). **Admission** £4.50; £3.30 concessions. **Credit** MC, V.

Once a 'grace and favour' home to the Greenwich park ranger, by 1902 this pretty 18th-century, red-brick villa had been converted into council-owned changing rooms. After major refurbishment by English Heritage, it now houses the Wernher Collection, displaying crafts dating from 3 BC, Old Masters, 18th-century French furniture and Britain's largest private collection of Renaissance jewellery.

Royal Observatory

Greenwich Park, SE10 (8312 6565/www.rog.nmm. ac.uk). Cutty Sark DLR/Greenwich DLR/rail. **Open** 10am-5pm daily. **Admission** free. **Credit** MC, V.

The Royal Observatory was built by Wren in 1675 on the orders of Charles II, by then tired of losing his fleets at sea. The museum explains the remarkable search for longitude, from 45 years of celestial observation by Royal Astronomer John Flamsteed to John Harrison's creation of the first maritime clock. Other exhibits examine the origins of astronomy and the history of timekeeping from sundials to atomic clocks. The planetarium holds regular star-gazing shows: call ahead to book.

Blackheath

The dignified tree-lined avenue behind the Observatory leads you south to windswept **Blackheath**. Popular with kite-flyers, the heath is also home to some of Britain's earliest sports clubs: the Royal Blackheath Golf Club (1745), the Blackheath Hockey Club (1861) and the Blackheath Football Club (which actually plays rugby union; 1862).

Among the stately homes that surround the heath, the **Paragon** is special. Built in the late 18th century with the sole purpose of attracting the right sort of people to the area – Blackheath was then plagued by bandits – this beautiful crescent of prestigious colonnaded houses was left dilapidated after being bombed in World War II, but is now restored to its former glory as Blackheath's most desirable address.

Rotherhithe

West of Greenwich, **Rotherhithe** is most famous as the spot from which the Pilgrim Fathers set sail in the *Mayflower* (1620). Samuel Pepys referred to it as Redriffe, and both names probably come from the Anglo-Saxon 'redhra' and 'hyth', meaning 'mariner's haven'.

Rotherhithe was once home to the world's best shipbuilders, and its maritime past can be glimpsed in its atmospheric old warehouses, evocatively named docks and historic riverside pubs: the Mayflower (*see p228*) and the 17th-century Angel (101 Bermondsey Wall East; 7237 3608), which has a smuggler's trapdoor. The *Mayflower*'s captain, Christopher Jones, is buried in **St Mary's Rotherhithe** (*see p172*).

St Mary's Rotherhithe

St Marychurch Street, SE16 (7231 2465).
Rotherhithe tube. **Open** 7am-6pm Mon-Thur; 8am-6pm Sat, Sun. **Admission** free.

Local sailors and watermen built this beautiful parish church in 1715. The communion table in the Lady Chapel is worth attention: it's made from timber salvaged from the warship *Fighting Temeraire*, the subject of a famous Turner painting. Sadly, acts of burglary and vandalism in the 20th century mean the interior can now only be viewed through glass, under the watchful eye of a CCTV camera.

Camberwell, Peckham & Dulwich

Once a pretty country village, **Camberwell** is now one of London's most congested crossroads. There's a small park at the main intersection of Camberwell Grove and Denmark Hill (laughably still called Camberwell Green), and picturesque Georgian houses line the steep hill of **Camberwell Grove**, but the main draw is **St Giles Church**. St Giles is a typically grandiose early Victorian structure (its spire reaches 210 feet or 72 metres) by Sir George Gilbert Scott of St Pancras Station fame (*see*

p105). There are a number of hip bars here, too: try Redstar (*see p323*) or Funky Munky (25 Camberwell Church Street, SE5; 7277 1806).

Formerly a stopping place for cattle drovers on their way to market, the natural beauty of **Peckham** once inspired artists: William Blake saw a vision of angels on the Rye and, in *The Ballad of Peckham Rye* (1960), Muriel Spark refers without irony to 'the dusky scope of the Rye's broad lyrical acres'. Even the Victorian terraces of Spark's novel have now mostly been replaced by council estates and tower blocks, their bleakness alleviated somewhat by prize-winning **Peckham Library** (*see p34*).

Dulwich is only a short distance west of Peckham, but they're worlds apart. Dulwich Park is so pretty it could pass for one of the pastoral landscapes hanging in nearby **Dulwich Picture Gallery** (*see p173*), while the leafy village is lined with distinctive Georgian architecture and smart shops that cater to well-to-do young families. South of the village, you'll find **Dulwich Common** and palatial, red-brick **Dulwich College**, alma mater to PG Wodehouse, Raymond Chandler and Michael Ondaatje, plus the delightfully eccentric **Horniman Museum** (*see p173*).

Dome alone

The story of the **Millennium Dome** on the North Greenwich peninsula has been characterised by blame and counter-blame, bitterness and apathy. Constructed on the Thames' largest derelict site to celebrate the millennium in a style the government hoped would ape the Geat Exhibition of 1851, it came in at a cool £758 million and was open for exactly one year. It now stands as a monument to a 'once-in-a-liftetime experience' while it awaits news of its fate.

Part of the *raison d'être* of the Jubilee line extension from Charing Cross to Stratford was to connect the Dome with central London. Local residents are still grateful, but it does expose the site around the Dome as being little more than a glorified bus depot. The beautiful station at **North Greenwich** – designed by Will Alsop, the man behind the highly acclaimed Peckham Library (*see p34*) – still has posters informing tourists how they might reach other London attractions, but 90 per cent of people passing through it are merely using it as a gateway to homes in Thamesmead and Bexleyheath. The map of local information ominously excludes the Dome site as an area out-of-bounds, in the

same way that West Berlin used to be excluded from East Berliners' street maps.

The area is eerie in the extreme. The Dome looks as magnificent and imposing as it ever did, but it is now deserted: surrounded by kilometres of padlocked blue fencing and acres of red tarmac, and patrolled within by a Group 4 security vehicle manned by a bored individual clearly desperate to try some wheelspins. There's not a solitary skateboarder or in-line skater practising their moves, though the space is bigger than they'd ever get at a local park.

Skirting around the fencing to the south of the Dome, you reach the **Thames Cycle Route**, which hugs the river bend and allows you to walk right around the complex. As you sit on the deserted benches, you're reminded of London's past status as a busy port: the wharfs of **Silvertown** on the bank opposite, the small boats moored to buoys and the smell of the sea. Along the riverbank is the **Millennium Jetty**, also closed but containing an enormous sculpture by Antony Gormley; just around the corner at Blackwall Point there's another, by Richard Wilson. Standing here at dusk, your breath will be taken away

The TV transmitter may be the first bit of **Crystal Palace Park** you'll notice, but the legendary **Crystal Palace** is the park's *raison d'être*. Built in Hyde Park (*see p136*) to house the 1851 Great Exhibition, the spectacular all-glass edifice was then moved to Sydenham, where the grounds contained an amusement park, a tea maze and striking life-size model dinosaurs (now classed as listed buildings). The palace burned down in 1936, but the **Crystal Palace Museum** (8676 0700; open 11am-5pm Sun), in the former engineering school where John Logie Baird invented TV, helps bring it back to life. The **National Sports Centre** (*see p331*) is in the south-east corner of the park.

Dulwich Picture Gallery

Gallery Road, SE21 (8693 5254/www.dulwichpicture gallery.org.uk). North Dulwich or West Dulwich rail. **Open** 10am-5pm Tue-Fri; 11am-5pm Sat, Sun. **Admission** £4; £3 concessions; free under-16s. Free to all Fri. **Credit** MC, V.

That England's first public art gallery is small in no way reflects its importance. But before looking over the art, be sure to pay Sir John Soane's perfectly proportioned neo-classical building, which inspired the National Gallery's Sainsbury Wing and the Getty Museum in LA, due attention. The artists within are a roll-call of greats: Rubens, Van Dyck, Cuyp, Poussin, Rembrandt, Gainsborough, Raphael and Reynolds. The gallery's critically acclaimed revamp in 2000 added a lovely open-air café, educational facilities and a temporary gallery: 2003 exhibitions include a show on John Piper (1 Apr-22 June) and 'Shakespeare in Art' (16 July-10 Oct).

Horniman Museum

100 London Road, SE23 (8699 1872/www.horniman. ac.uk). Forest Hill rail/63, 122, 176, 185, 312, 352, P4 bus. **Open** 10.30am-5.30pm daily. **Admission** free; donations appreciated. **Credit** *Shop* MC, V.

The recent £13 million renovation should put the Horniman Museum on the visitor's map. Founded by Victorian tea-trader Frederick Horniman in 1901, the building looks like a quirky fairytale castle. Inside, it's no less eccentric: the Natural History gallery houses stuffed creatures, from the extinct (the dodo) to the endangered (the bittern); the Living Water Aquarium has simulated reef, swamp and river displays; the African Worlds gallery shows everything from Egyptian mummies to voodoo dolls; and the new Centenary Gallery has a Spanish Inquisition torture chair and ceremonial spears from the Solomon Islands. The new café and idyllic landscaped gardens are on hand to revive flagging spirits. The Music Gallery, due to open in early 2003, will choose its exhibits from a collection of 1,600 instruments, ranging from 3,500-year-old Egyptian clappers to 1937 Carlton jazz drums.

Stockwell, Kennington & Vauxhall

Stockwell was once a medieval manor but, like so much of London, rural life was forever transformed by the railway boom of the 1840s. Today, where once the cattle grazed on South Lambeth Common, there's a tube station, a war memorial and a clock tower; the manor house itself would now be in the middle of the notorious Stockwell Park housing estate. East of the station, 87 Hackford Road provides a cultural frisson: it was Vincent Van Gogh's home from 1873 to 1874. Further north, between Prima Road and Camberwell New Road, is **St Mark's Church**, built in 1824 on the site of a gallows: many of the Jacobite rebels of 1745 were hanged, drawn and quartered here.

Kennington Park is all that remains of the common where, during the 18th and 19th centuries, John Wesley and other preachers addressed large audiences; nowadays the Surrey faithful gather at the **AMP Oval** (*see p329*) to watch their team play cricket. North towards Lambeth is the **Imperial War Museum** (*see p174*), but a brief diversion on to Kennington Lane will uncover some of south London's most delightful streets. **Cardigan Street**, **Courtenay Street** and **Courtenay Square**

by the lights of three huge buildings on the opposite bank: **Canary Wharf**, flanked by the **HSBC** and **Citigroup** towers.

Drawdock Road takes you on to the station, past the Tunnel Avenue Industrial Estates and back to the dozen people still waiting for the bus. When environmentally friendly **Millennium Village** is complete, perhaps the area will feel more vibrant and deserving of the immense amount of money spent on it; right now it feels like the most enormous white elephant.

are lined with neat neo-Georgian terraced houses; across Kennington Road lies leafy and gorgeous **Cleaver Square**; while another gem, **Walcot Square**, lies further to the north-east.

Vauxhall, between Kennington and the Thames, won't detain you long. The small park bounded by Tyers Street, Goding Street and Glasshouse Walk offers a meagre remainder of the 18th-century **Vauxhall Pleasure Gardens**. The Real IRA chose to launch a missile at the nearby MI6 building from here; while the **Royal Vauxhall Tavern** (*see p301*), grande dame of gay pubs, sits in front of the park, quietly crumbling.

Imperial War Museum

Lambeth Road, SE1 (7416 5000/www.iwm.org.uk). Lambeth North tube/Elephant & Castle tube/rail. **Open** 10am-6pm daily. **Admission** free. **Credit** AmEx, MC, V. **Map** p404 N10.

Housed in a former lunatic asylum, the Imperial War Museum offers a gripping history of 20th-century warfare. The hardware in the lobby – Russian tanks, German rockets, a Mustang plane – may impress, but the sophisticated World War I and II galleries are the main attraction: the Trench and Blitz Experiences, along with the more familiar maps, film footage and artefacts, plunge you into the thick of hostilities. Conflicts Since 1945 is less popular but no less fascinating, explaining wars (such as the Korean War) that you're aware of but never really understood, while the Secret War deals with intrigue and espionage: exhibits range from a German

The exotic **Horniman Museum**. *See p173.*

Enigma Cipher machine to a dagger concealed in a pencil. Art of World War I and II, on the second floor, includes works by Henry Moore and Stanley Spencer. The recent five-storey £17 million extension includes a horrifying and moving permanent exhibition devoted to the Holocaust, with footage of Hitler's speeches, models of concentration camps and survivors' testimonials. Temporary exhibitions for 2003 include 'Women in Uniform'.

Brixton

Brixton was a marshy wasteland until the construction of Vauxhall Bridge in 1816 improved access to central London and planted the seeds for suburban development. Brixton Prison, which opened in 1820 off Jebb Avenue, soon gained a reputation as one of the harshest and unhealthiest in London: the first treadmill, invented by Sir William Cubitt, was used here to grind corn in 1921. **St Matthew's Church**, in the town centre, was consecrated in 1824 to serve the burgeoning community.

As the railways and trams of the 1860s turned the trickle of suburban commuters into a flood, **Electric Avenue** – later immortalised in Eddy Grant's song – became one of the first shopping streets lit by electricity. As wealthier residents moved out between the wars, their large houses were turned into cheap boarding houses that became popular with theatre folk: John Major, the former British prime minister, was raised here by his circus-performer father.

But Brixton's personality changed dramatically during the 1950s and 1960s with the arrival of immigrants from the West Indies. A generation later, tensions between blacks and police reached boiling point. The infamous riots of 1981, 1985 and 1995 centred on the area around Railton Road and **Coldharbour Lane**, which became known as the Front Line. Problems remain, particularly drug-related ones, contributing to the volatility of the area and occasional flare-ups. But Brixton's edginess has long been part of its charm.

Despite its troubles, the mood in Brixton is upbeat and the atmosphere buzzing. The area's gentrification – pop into **Trinity Gardens** for a glimpse of genteel Brixton – hasn't yet pushed out anarchists and artists who've been squatting here since the '70s, and the sizeable black population, almost a third of Brixton's residents, lives alongside a growing gay community. By day, Brixton's mixed-up craziness is best experienced by strolling chaotic **Brixton Market** (*see p255*). On your wanderings, pop into the Black Cultural Archives (378 Coldharbour Lane; 7738 4591), the friendly Brixton Art Gallery (35 Brixton Station Road; 7733 6957) or the Souls of the

Rock it in the daytime... **Electric Avenue**. *See p174.*

Black Folk Juice Bar (407 Coldharbour
Lane; 7738 4141). At night, it's a vibrant
neighbourhood: the Fridge, Mass (for both *see
p319*), Dogstar and the Bug Bar (for both, *see
p322*) all manage to tempt north Londoners
south of the river, though the punters taking
in the jazz at the atmospheric old Effra Hall
Tavern (Tue-Thur, Sat-Sun; 38A Kellett Road;
7274 4180) are mostly locals.

If you're after something calmer, **Brockwell
Park**, with its recently restored 1930s lido (*see
p327*) and pastoral views of south London, is
only 15 minutes' walk from the tube. The **Ritzy**
cinema (*see p286*), built on Coldharbour Lane
in 1911, is also a treat.

Clapham

When city dwellers fled the Great Plague and
then the Great Fire in the 17th century, many
ended up in **Clapham**: among the area's early
residents were Samuel Pepys and Captain Cook.
By the 20th century, the neighbourhood was in
decline, but gentrification in the '80s made it one
of the most upmarket areas south of the river.

The heart of the neighbourhood lies to the
north and east of **Clapham Common**;
anything west of there, even Clapham Junction
station, is considered part of Battersea (*see
below*). Despite being the main thoroughfare,
with a profusion of trendy bars and restaurants,
Clapham High Street is remarkably drab.
Head, instead, to the smart shops and cafés of
Abbeville Village south-east of the tube station.
Clapham Old Town, just north-east of the
common, centres on the Pavement and is home
to attractive 18th-century pubs and shops
too posh for the High Street. **Holy Trinity
Church** stands on the edge of the common; in

the 19th century it was home to the 'muscular
Christianity' of the Clapham Sect, a group of
wealthy Anglicans that included anti-slavery
campaigner William Wilberforce.

Walking west, **Clapham Common North
Side** boasts parades of tall, stately houses with
great views of the common itself. A cross
between a park and a wild place, the common's
bleak atmosphere was vividly evoked in
Graham Greene's *The End of the Affair*.
Popular with joggers and footballers by day,
after dark parts of the common become a gay
cruising ground (*see p297* **Cruise control**).

Battersea & Wandsworth

Battersea derives its name from Batrices Ege
(Badric's Island), the small Saxon settlement
that stood here more than 1,000 years ago.
Until the 19th century, the chief occupation here
was market gardening, but the coming of the
railways changed that: **Clapham Junction**
was soon the city's bustling transport hub (it's
still one of the busiest stations in the world),
and the fields became factories.

The industrial buildings have mostly given
way to luxury flats, notably Richard Rogers'
wedge-shaped glass tower Montevetro, but the
most distinctive piece of industrial architecture
is still here: **Battersea Power Station**. Yet
even Sir Giles Gilbert Scott's landmark (built
1929-33, closed 1983) is soon to be converted
into a vast riverside business and entertainment
complex, with 700 hotel rooms, a 2,000-seat
theatre, a multiplex cinema, office space and
residential accommodation. South of here is the
famous **Battersea Dogs Home** (4 Battersea
Park Road; 7622 3636), which has been rescuing
and rehabilitating strays since 1817.

West of the power station, **Battersea Park** (8871 7530) has a violent history: 'Colonel' Blood hid in the reeds here in 1671, waiting to shoot King Charles II as he bathed (Blood's nerve failed and Charles lived on), while in 1829 the Duke of Wellington fought a duel with Lord Winchilsea, who had accused him of treason for introducing the Catholic Emancipation Bill. The renowned **Festival Gardens**, created for the 1951 Festival of Britain, show the park's prettier side: subtropical gardens, a Thameside promenade, the Peace Pagoda (built by Japanese monks and nuns in 1985 to commemorate Hiroshima Day), and sculptures by Henry Moore and Barbara Hepworth.

Battersea has long been popular with artists and writers: Old Battersea Bridge was the subject of Whistler's moody *Nocturnes*, while Turner used to paint the river from **St Mary's Battersea**. St Mary's is also where Blake was married and Benedict Arnold buried.

To the south-west, **Wandsworth Common** – much nicer, frankly, than Clapham Common – is full of pretty parents with pretty dogs and children. The area's known as 'Nappy Valley', because of the proliferation of new families. To the east, you'll find smart shops, bars and restaurants of Northcote Road and Battersea Rise, while to the west lies an oddly shaped enclave of six streets, nicknamed the 'Toast Rack' (David Lloyd George used to live at 3 Routh Road). Off Trinity Road to the north is the Gothic Royal Victoria Patriotic Building. This extraordinary structure was built as an asylum for orphans of the Crimean War, but became a POW camp in World War II.

Putney, Barnes & Kew

Putney was effectively London's first suburb, with Thomas Cromwell and other Tudor courtiers commuting from homes in the village to jobs in the royal palaces of London. The busy High Street and the Land Rovers remind you it's the 21st century, but it remains a peaceful spot. Head west of the bridge, along the Embankment, to where the **Boat Race** (*see p263*) starts each year, or keep strolling along the towpath as far as Hammersmith Bridge.

East of Putney, Barnes has been home to the **WWT Wetland Centre** (*see p179* **Reeding corner**) since 2000. The other attraction is on **Barnes Common**, west of the bridge carrying the main road, Queen's Ride, over the railway line. Here stands the spindly tree, invariably decorated with flowers and other offerings, that put paid to rock star Marc Bolan in 1977.

Kew is famed for its gardens (properly known as the **Royal Botanic Gardens**; *see below*). North of the Kew Road entrance is the

Battersea Power Station. *See pp175-6.*

old-fashioned Maids of Honour tea shop (288 Kew Road; 8940 2752); **Kew Green**, its cricket ground surrounded by pubs, and elegant **St Anne's Church**, from 1714, are worth a visit.

Royal Botanic Gardens

Kew, Richmond, Surrey (8332 5655/information 8940 1171/www.kew.org). Kew Gardens tube/rail/ Kew Bridge rail/riverboat to Kew Pier. **Open** *End Mar-Aug* 9.30am-6.30pm Mon-Fri; 9.30am-7.30pm Sat, Sun. *Sept, Oct* 9.30am-6pm daily. *End Oct-beginning Feb* 9.30am-4.15pm daily. *Beginning Feb-end Mar* 9.30am-5.30pm daily. **Admission** £6.50; £4.50 concessions; free under-17s. **Credit** MC, V.

Developed in the 17th and 18th centuries in the grounds of Dutch-style Kew Palace (closed until at least 2004) and landscaped by 'Capability' Brown, Kew Gardens now cover 120 hectares (300 acres) and are filled with every imaginable variety of tree, shrub and flower. The foundation of its collections was laid by late 18th-century botanists who collated specimens from all continents, and Kew is now a world-renowned centre for horticultural research, boasting the world's largest orchid collection. First-time visitors would be wise to take the 'Kew Explorer' road train from the Victoria Gate for a 35-minute tour (£2.50; £1.50 concessions).

Among the highlights are the immense glasshouses. The most famous is the steamy Palm House (Decimus Burton and Richard Turner, 1848), while the Temperate House is the world's largest ornamental glasshouse. Specimens within are arranged geographically. Opposite the Palm House, the Plants & People exhibition explores our reliance on plants.

In addition, visit the Marianne North Gallery, which displays paintings by this extraordinary Victorian artist; the Great Pagoda (1762), by William Chambers near the Lion Gate; and the Japanese Gateway & Landscape. Make sure you stray from the main routes to enjoy the Riverside Walk or the secluded woods to the south-west. The grounds of Queen Charlotte's Cottage are a luxurious carpet of bluebells each May, and the brightly coloured Rhododendron Dell is well worth a look.

Highlights for 2003 include the Summer Festival's celebration of British biodiversity (22 May-28 Sept), an autumn harvest festival (11 Oct-2 Nov) and the colourful illuminations at Christmas (22 Nov-4 Jan).

Wimbledon

For two weeks every summer, Wimbledon seems the most glamorous place on the earth. Once the tennis tournament (*see p331*) is over, however, you're left with a pretty uneventful suburb. **Wimbledon Broadway**, the main drag, is dominated by the huge **Centre Court** shopping centre. Further east, **Wimbledon Theatre** is an entertainingly feverish example of Edwardian architecture.

For some, **Wimbledon Common** is a bigger attraction than the tennis – and big is the operative word. The immense, partly wooded expanse is crisscrossed with paths and horse tracks, and houses a museum (closed in winter) and tearoom. Baden-Powell lived here while writing his unfortunately titled handbook *Scouting for Boys* in 1908. On the east side of the common, the disused **Bluegate Gravel Pit** forms an idyllic lake. Cross the road at Parkside and walk down Calonne Road to discover the common's biggest surprise: the Thai Buddhist **Buddhapadipa Temple** (1-6pm Sat; 8.30-10.30am, 12.30-6pm Sun). Neighbouring **Wimbledon Park** has public tennis courts and a large boating lake.

Wimbledon Lawn Tennis Museum

Centre Court, All England Lawn Tennis Club, Church Road, SW19 (8946 6131/www.wimbledon.org/museum). Southfields tube/39, 93, 200 bus. **Open** 10.30am-5pm daily; spectators only during championships. **Admission** £5.50; £4.50 concessions; £3.50 5-16s; free under-5s. **Credit** MC, V.
This well-designed museum traces the history of the game from its birth on the lawns of Victorian England. Displays range from a mock-up of an Edwardian tennis party to highlights of the previous year's tournament, via a portrait gallery that includes a very fine caricature of John McEnroe. There are also men's and women's trophies, a view of centre court, and a treasure trove of tennis artefacts that includes Boris Becker's shoes and dresses worn by the Williams sisters.

Richmond

Despite the heavy traffic and constant roar of Heathrow-bound jets overhead, **Richmond** retains much of its villagey charm. Once known as Sheen, the area received its new name when Henry VII fell in love with it, acquired the local manor house and named it after his earldom in Yorkshire. Elizabeth I spent her last few summers at Richmond and died here in 1603.

All that remains of Richmond Palace now is a gateway on **Richmond Green**. Formerly a popular venue for jousting tournaments and pageants, the green is now best reached from between the pubs and antique shops of alley-like **Brewer's Lane**. The church of **St Mary Magdalene**, in Paradise Road, is a unique blend of architectural styles dating from 1507 to 1904, while elegant 18th-century **Richmond Bridge** is London's oldest surviving crossing. There's also impressive Georgian architecture on Old Palace Terrace and Maids of Honour Row, plus a Victorian town hall that now houses the **Museum of Richmond** (*see p178*).

The best reason to visit Richmond is to enjoy the Great Outdoors: **Richmond Park** is Britain's largest urban park and (with the exception of Epping Forest) the last vestige of the great oak forests that once surrounded London. Ideal for rambling, cycling, riding and all kinds of sport – there are football and cricket pitches, golf courses and ponds for anglers – the park also plays host to much wildlife, notably herds of red and fallow deer. Notable buildings include **Pembroke Lodge**, the childhood home of philosopher Bertrand Russell (now a café), and **White Lodge**, a fine Palladian villa. Don't miss the exquisite woodland haven that is **Isabella Plantation**, landscaped with a stream, ponds and gaudy floral displays, nor the impressive view from **Richmond Hill**, with the nearby **Terrace Gardens** descending steeply towards the river. This is the Thames at its most romantic: if it isn't flooding, follow the other lovestruck couples along the river to **Petersham** and **Ham**. It's impossibly pastoral in the early morning and evening, with brown cattle grazing water meadows by a misty river.

Kew Gardens. *See p176.*

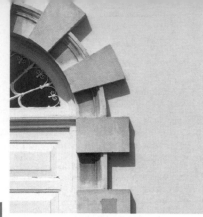

Knock, knock... **Marble Hill House**.

Museum of Richmond

Old Town Hall, Whittaker Avenue, Richmond, Surrey (8332 1141/www.museumofrichmond.com). Richmond tube/rail. Open May-Sept 11am-5pm Tue-Sat; 1-4pm Sun. *Oct-Apr* 11am-5pm Tue-Sat. **Admission** free.

Most exhibits in this small museum focus on Richmond's popularity as a royal resort, but it also celebrates the rich heritage of Kew, Petersham and Ham from prehistoric times – ancient weapons occasionally turn up in the river – to World War II.

Further south

A delightful walk or bike ride south along the Thames from Richmond takes you close to a clutch of fine country villas: **Orleans House** (*see p179*), **Ham House** and **Marble Hill House** (*see below*). Past **Twickenham** (home to the **Museum of Rugby**; *see below*), the river reaches the first substantial building of the Gothic Revival: Horace Walpole's idiosyncratic home **Strawberry Hill** (tours by appointment on Sundays, Apr-Oct; 8240 4224). Beyond, the Thames passes busy **Kingston** and curves around to **Hampton Court Palace** (*see below*).

Ham House

Ham, Richmond, Surrey (8940 1950/ www.nationaltrust.org.uk/hamhouse). Richmond tube/rail then 371 bus. Open House Apr-Oct 1-5pm Mon-Wed, Sat, Sun. *Gardens* 11am-6pm/dusk Mon-Wed, Sat, Sun. **Admission** £7; £3.50 5-15s; £17.50 family (2+2). *Garden only* £3; £1.50 5-15s; £7.50 family (2+2); free under-5s. **Credit** MC, V.

Built in 1610 for one of James I's courtiers, this sprawling red-brick mansion is all about spectacular gilt mouldings, ostentatious rococo mirrors and elaborate tapestries. There's the magnificent Great Staircase, damask-covered furniture and busy chinoiserie, and every object here – down to the flamboyant plant pots – are originals from the house, most from the 17th century. The formal gardens are being restored; until they're ready, you can take a lovely half-hour riverside stroll to Richmond.

Hampton Court Palace

East Molesey, Surrey (8781 9500/www.hrp.org.uk). Hampton Court rail/riverboat from Westminster or Richmond to Hampton Court Pier (Apr-Oct). Open Palace Apr-Oct 10.15am-6pm Mon; 9.30am-6pm Tue-Sun. Nov-Mar 10.15am-4.30pm Mon; 9.30am-4.30pm Tue-Sun (last entry 45mins before closing). *Park* dawn-dusk daily. **Admission** *Palace, courtyard, cloister & maze* £11; £7.25 5-15s; £8.25 concessions; £33 family (max 5 people); free under-5s. *Maze only* £3; £2 5-15s. **Credit** AmEx, MC, V.

Don't balk at the hefty admission charge: Hampton Court is like ten stately homes rolled into one. Cardinal Wolsey began building up the palace in 1514. Henry VIII then became enamoured with it, taking it over after Wolsey's fall from favour in 1529 and adding the staggering vaulted ceiling of the Chapel Royal (which took 100 men nine months to complete). Next, Oliver Cromwell fell in love with the place, recanting his puritanical vow to sell its treasures and wisely deciding to live here instead. Finally, as the Tudor style fell from fashion, Sir Christopher Wren was hired by William and Mary in the 1690s to rebuild the State Apartments in classical Renaissance style.

To simplify navigation, there are six bite-size tours. Highlights include Henry VIII's Great Hall, with hammer-beam roof and stained-glass windows depicting the crests of his wives; the Renaissance Picture Gallery (allegedly haunted by Henry's fifth wife, Catherine Howard) with works by Correggio, Parmigianino and Titian; and the Tudor kitchens, where period-dressed minions make 16th-century dishes. Outside, there's further costumed foolery in Clock Court plus the world-famous maze and 'Capability' Brown's Great Vine, planted in 1768 and still yielding 500-700lbs (230-320kgs) of grapes a year.

Marble Hill House

Richmond Road, Twickenham, Middx (8892 5115/ www.english-heritage.org.uk). Richmond tube/rail/ St Margaret's rail/33, 90, 490, H22, R70 bus. Open Apr-Sept 10am-6pm daily; *Oct* 10am-5pm daily. **Admission** £3.30; £2.50 concessions; £1.70 5-15s; free under-5s. **Credit** MC, V.

A textbook example of Palladian architecture, this elegant house was built in 1724 by George II for his mistress, Henrietta Howard. The opulent Great Room once welcomed Jonathan Swift, Horace Walpole and Alexander Pope, while the grand mahogany staircase almost led to war with Spain, after the British King ordered trees cut down in Spanish Honduras. In the grounds you'll find a sunken grotto and England's oldest black walnut tree. You can also get a ferry across the Thames to Ham House (*see p178*), or attend summer concerts in the park (call for details).

Museum of Rugby/ Twickenham Stadium

Twickenham Rugby Stadium, Rugby Road, Twickenham, Middx (8892 8877/www.rfu.com). Hounslow East tube then 281 bus/Twickenham rail. Open Museum 10am-5pm Tue-Sat; 11am-5pm Sun

Sightseeing

(last entry 4.30pm). *Tours* 10.30am, noon, 1.30pm, 3pm Tue-Sat; 1pm, 3pm Sun. **Admission** £6; £4 concessions; £19 family. **Credit** MC, V.

Twickenham is the home of English Rugby Union. The excellent tour of the stadium takes you into the dressing-rooms and players' tunnel, while the museum under the East Stand traces the sport's history. On show are the oldest jersey in existence, the Calcutta Cup, a scrum simulator, snippets of radio commentary and the world's greatest tries on video.

Orleans House Gallery

Riverside, Twickenham, Middx (8892 0221/ www.richmond.gov.uk/orleanshouse). St Margaret's rail. **Open** *Apr-Sept* 1-5.30pm

Tue-Sat; 2-5.30pm Sun. *Oct-Mar* 1-4.30pm Tue-Sat; 2-4.30pm Sun. **Admission** free. **No credit cards**.

Built in 1710 for James Johnston, Secretary of State for Scotland under William III, this Grade I-listed riverside building is named after the Duke of Orleans, who lived here from 1800 to 1817, during his exile from Napoleonic France (the Duke later became King Louis Philippe). Mostly demolished in 1926, the house retains James Gibbs's neo-classical Octagon Room. Noted for its ornate plasterwork and checked marble floor, the room contains the impressive Richmond upon Thames Art Collection, which ranges from 18th-century oils to contemporary crafts.

Reeding corner

Those relaxation CDs that use the soothing sounds of ocean surf and gurgling streams should incorporate a new noise into their repertoire: rustling reeds. It's the soundtrack to the WWT Wetland Centre, and quite possibly the most therapeutic noise in London. For while the Wetland Centre is just four miles from the West End, as soon as you pass through its gates you feel miles from London.

Nirvana is reached by a meandering sea of paths through lakes, ponds, rushes, reed beds and wildflower gardens, culminating in two raised lookout points from which to gaze at the centre's teeming bird life. London's wildlife equivalent of King's Cross Station, the Wetland Centre is home to 150 different species of bird, 300 varieties of moth and butterfly, 20 types of dragonfly, four species of bat and water vole, 300,000 aquatic plants and 27,000 trees.

It wasn't always this pretty. Until 1989 the site consisted of four huge concrete reservoirs owned by Thames Water. But when the reservoirs were made redundant in the '80s, naturalist Sir Peter Scott got permission from the water company to transform the 105 acres into wetland habitat. After the concrete boxes were transformed into a marshy oasis, the place became an avian five-star hotel and a twitcher's paradise: little ringed plovers, black-tailed godwits, kingfishers, willow warblers, herons and all manner of geese and swans, with the cast of characters changing by the season.

It's refreshing to visit a bit of central London where the appearance of a bittern causes the kind of excited frenzy usually reserved for a sighting of Kylie's bottom. Even if you have trouble identifying a sparrow, the

Wetland Centre – one of London's little miracles – is still a perfect spot for a bit of quiet contemplation and a healthy dose of natural Prozac. If the birdsong doesn't soothe your soul, the rustling reeds will.

WWT Wetland Centre

Queen Elizabeth's Walk, SW13 (8409 4400/ www.wwt.org.uk). Hammersmith tube then 283 bus/Barnes rail/33, 72 bus. **Open** *Mar-Oct* 9.30am-6pm daily (last entry 5pm). *Nov-Feb* 9.30am-5pm daily (last entry 4pm). **Admission** £6.75; £5.50 concessions; £4 4-16s; free under-4s; £17.50 family. **Credit** MC, V.

West London

A mix of scruffy, fashionable, bucolic and suburban neighbourhoods awaits.

Paddington & Bayswater

Maps p394 & p395

Bayswater, Lancaster Gate or Queensway tube/Paddington tube/rail.

Just north of Hyde Park, Paddington derives its name from the ancient Anglo-Saxon chieftain Padda. However, it's best known for its train station with its magnificent iron girder roof, designed by Isambard Kingdom Brunel in 1851. It was the building of the station, along with the Grand Junction Canal (1801), that precipitated the population boom in this area in the mid 19th century: the area was previously considered residentially off limits thanks to the location of the Tyburn gallows near present-day Marble Arch.

In the early 20th century there was another slump when the district became synonymous with prostitution and poverty. It's a reputation the area hasn't quite managed to shift in the intervening century. The area around Paddington is more than a little seedy: many of the once-grand white stuccoed houses have been converted into fleapit hotels or carved into warrens of bedsits. However, the establishment of the Heathrow Express (*see p356*), which provides a speedy link from the airport to Paddington Station, has started to turn things around in the neighbourhood, as has the huge and still-ongoing redevelopment of **Paddington Basin**, transforming the old Canal Basin and Goods Yard into a complex of flats, offices and other amenities. It'll take time, but the Paddington area is at least heading in the right direction.

Which is more than can be said for **Bayswater**, directly to the south. This is central London at its tattiest and least engaging, a slew of dreary hotels, touristy shops and crummy restaurants (the few honourable exceptions are mostly Chinese). This is a bleak part of town; not unsafe, just depressing and slightly unsavoury.

A left turn at the north end of Queensway opens up the richer pickings of trendy **Westbourne Grove**. As with Paddington and Bayswater, there isn't much to see here. But unlike those two neighbourhoods, Westbourne Grove does have some sense of residential community about it, some splendid restaurants (including some excellent Middle Eastern

options and the wild 'n' crazy Argentinian eaterie Rodizio Rico; *see p216*) and an increasing number of interesting shops. The Grove's western end, towards Portobello Road and Notting Hill (*see p181*), is markedly posher, with delis, antique shops and, particularly on Ledbury Road (which bisects Westbourne Grove), cool clothes boutiques.

Alexander Fleming Laboratory Museum

St Mary's Hospital, Praed Street, W2 (7886 6528). Paddington tube/rail/7, 15, 27, 36 bus. **Open** 10am-1pm Mon-Thur. By appointment 2-5pm Mon-Thur; 10am-5pm Fri. **Admission** £2; £1 concessions, 5-16s; free under-5s. **No credit cards. Map** p395 D5. Alexander Fleming made his momentous chance discovery of penicillin in this very room on 3 September 1928, when a Petri dish of bacteria became contaminated with a mysterious mould. His laboratory has now been recreated, while displays and a video offer insights into both his life and the role of penicillin in the fight against disease.

Portobello Road Market. *See p182.*

Maida Vale & Kilburn

Kilburn, Kilburn Park, Maida Vale or Warwick Avenue tube.

North of the roaring but atmospheric Westway (*see p182* **London loves**) lies much of Edgware Road, as well as Maida Vale and Kilburn. **Edgware Road** follows the course of ancient Watling Street, a traffic-clogged thoroughfare redeemed only by some of London's best kebab shops and Middle Eastern cafés.

Maida Vale, named after the British victory against the French at the Battle of Maida in southern Italy in 1806, is an affluent area characterised by Edwardian purpose-built flats, and prettified immeasurably by the locks around **Little Venice**. You can walk from here along the canals to **London Zoo**, or even take a boat (*see p109*). If you've time, swing by **Crocker's Folly** for a drink (24 Aberdeen Place, NW8; 7286 6608). This epic Victorian structure was built as a hotel by entrepreneur Frank Crocker, who'd received a sure-thing tip-off that a new rail terminus was to be built opposite it. Oops. The station was built a half-mile away in Marylebone. An understandably distraught Crocker then threw himself off the roof.

Kilburn High Road is well known for its pubs, patronised primarily by Irish expats. Kilburn is also a good place for bargain shopping, and its mainly Afro-Caribbean and Irish populations are well served by one of London's more enterprising local arts complexes, the Tricycle (*see p338*).

Notting Hill

Map p394
Notting Hill Gate or Westbourne Park tube.

There was little but piggeries in this area until a wave of white stuccoed buildings mapped out Notting Hill in the early and mid 1800s. After a period of prosperity, however, the district's fortunes declined again in the 20th century; it was solidly white and working class until the '50s, when there was an influx of West Indian immigrants, many of whom had little choice but to live in hideous properties owned by notorious landlord Peter Rachman. Riots, incited by white racists, followed in 1958, and it was only in the late 1980s that the area flourished once more.

Despite its sickly-sweet depiction in the Hugh Grant and Julia Roberts movie named after it and the concomitant increase in the tourist trade, Notting Hill is still a pleasant place for a weekend stroll. **Notting Hill Gate** itself is little more than a busy through road, although it does boast a perfectly serviceable little cinema named the Notting Hill Coronet (*see p286*). Around the corner on Pembridge Road

above the Prince Albert pub is the tiny Gate Theatre (*see p338*), one of the best pub theatres in town.

But when people talk about Notting Hill they really mean **Portobello Road**. This narrow, snaking thoroughfare, most famed for its market (*see p256*) and antique shops, forms the spine of the neighbourhood. There are cafés, bars, restaurants, curiosity shops and delis, many of which have been patronised by the same people for decades, the revamped Electric Cinema (*see p286*) and, towards its northern end, a flea market with modish used clothes, shoes and accessories on Fridays and Saturdays.

At the north end of Portobello Road, **Golborne Road** is a little less interesting, though it is redeemed in no small part by its great antiques shops and Portuguese pâtisseries: try the Lisboa (*see p215*). The other main feature of Golborne Road is Trellick Tower: built in 1973 by Ernö Goldfinger, it's seen by some as a hideous carbuncle and by others as a seminal piece of modern architecture.

Just east of Portobello Road, the Westbourne Park area is scruffy but perennially hip, especially around All Saint's Road, which has been colonised by quirky little boutiques over the last few years. Among the drinking options around here is Babushka (41 Tavistock Crescent, W11; 7727 9250), now a DJ bar specialising in vodka but, in a previous incarnation, the decidedly sleazy Black Cap pub from which Richard E Grant and Paul McGann are obliged to beat a very hasty retreat in the famous 'perfumed ponce' scene in the film *Withnail and I*. Up at the top of Ladbroke Grove, meanwhile, is **Kensal Green Cemetery**, a huge and beautiful resting place for Londoners including Thackeray, Trollope and Brunel (*see p152* **London loves**).

Kensington & Holland Park

Maps p394-p397
High Street Kensington or Holland Park tube.

No doubt to the delight of its heritage-conscious upper-class residents, Kensington is mentioned in the Domesday Book of 1086. In the 17th century the district grew up around Holland House (1606) and Campden House (1612), and was described by one historian in 1705 as a place 'inhabited by gentry and persons of note, with an abundance of shopkeepers and artificers'. This is still the case with both aspects of Kensington in evidence around the **High Street**. A lively mix of chain stores and individual shops stretches along the busy main road while the nearby streets and squares are lined by large townhouses. The most famous

Go west

In London, you're never exactly short of fun things to do in the middle of the night. But suppose, for a moment, that you've tired of late-night drinking clubs and had your fill of Hampstead Heath: how else might you entertain yourself while most Londoners are asleep? A midnight drive might not spring to mind, but the **Westway** is special and it's hard to guarantee it'll be empty of traffic at any other time.

In the late 1960s, communities in west London were ripped apart as the Westway squirmed unstoppably through North Kensington like some mutant sandworm. There's no doubt that the decision to construct a stretch of elevated motorway to link the end of the Western Avenue to the Marylebone Road was a controversial one, but nor is there any doubt, in the minds of regular Westway users, that it is a superb piece of engineering.

It's the sexiest two-and-a-half-mile drive you'll ever make. It may end too quickly, but the brevity of the experience takes nothing away from its visceral thrills. The

of the squares, **Kensington Square**, sports a generous display of plaques denoting residents of distinction, such as Thackeray (No.16) and John Stuart Mill (No.18).

Kensington Square is just behind the art deco splendour of Barker's department store (built 1905-13). Next door, on the sixth floor of the former Derry & Toms, is the Roof Gardens, a flashy restaurant/club. Over the road from here, at the foot of **Kensington Church Street**, is the church of St Mary Abbots, distinguished by the tallest steeple in London (250 feet, or 85 metres) and the secluded gardens to its rear.

Further west is **Holland Park**, one of London's most romantic parks. Beautiful woods and formal gardens surround the reconstructed Jacobean **Holland House**, named after an early owner, Sir Henry, Earl of Holland. The house suffered serious bomb damage during World War II and only the ground floor and arcades survived; the restored east wing contains the most dramatically sited youth hostel in town (*see p65*), while the summer ballroom has been converted into a stylish contemporary restaurant, the Belvedere. Open-air operas are staged in the park under an elegant canopy during the summer (*see p305*), and for children there's an adventure playground with tree-walks way you veer to the right as you pass the pneumatic headquarters of fashion chain Monsoon, formerly Paddington Maintenance Depot. The rollercoaster plunge that precedes your arrival in Marylebone Road. Or, heading out of town, driving into the sunset, racing the 747s easing down through the smog, left hand down on the wheel as Ernö Goldfinger's Trellick Tower slips by on the right.

In 2000, Transport For London inherited the M40 Westway from the Highways Agency as part of the deal over the creation of the Greater London Assembly and the Mayor's office, and downgraded it to A-road status. The view from the carriageways is changing, too. The M41 West Cross Route, which linked the Westway to Holland Park roundabout, has been transformed. Now the A3220, it boasts slip ramps to a shopping centre that hasn't yet been built.

At the Marylebone Road end, the former Paddington Goods Yard, once a forgotten retreat, glorious in its vast emptiness, is now Paddington Central. Great glass towers sprang up so swiftly they appeared to have been lowered from the clouds like the surveillance devices in JG Ballard's story 'The Watch-Towers'.

Ballard, indeed, wrote the key Westway novel: *Concrete Island* (1974), in which an executive's Jaguar spins, marooning its driver on an island that for years, in the real world, was home to an Astroturf pitch for Sunday league footballers. The Westway Sports Centre has now built indoor courts on the site. In film, Chris Petit accorded the Westway mythic status in his black-and-white road movie *Radio On* (1979), while novelist Will Self wrote admiringly of the road's curvaceous appeal in a classic piece of journalism collected in *Junk Mail* (1995).

The road signs may have changed colour and the speed limit come down, but the road still drives like a motorway. Indeed, as you approach Paddington Central from the west, you head straight for a gap between two towers. Align yourself correctly with the rising sun, floor the accelerator and you'll be learning to fly.

and rope swings, while tame rabbits, squirrels and peacocks patrol the grounds. The Kyoto Japanese Garden provides a tranquil retreat from the action. Among the historic houses worth a visit are **Leighton House** (*see below*), the 19th-century home of the painter Lord Leighton, and Linley Sambourne House, home of cartoonist Edward Linley Sambourne, which is scheduled to reopen in April 2003 (phone Leighton House for details).

Leighton House

12 Holland Park Road, W14 (7602 3316/ www.rbkc.gov.uk/leightonhousemuseum). High Street Kensington tube. **Open** 11am-5.30pm Mon, Wed-Sun. *Tours* noon Wed, Thur; by appointment other times (min group of 15). **Admission** free; donations appreciated. *Tours* £3 per person. **No credit cards.**

Situated on the edge of Holland Park, this stunning 19th-century building is the one-time residence and studio of Frederic, Lord Leighton (1830-96), an eminent Victorian artist. Hanging in its sumptuous interiors are paintings and drawings by both Leighton himself (among them *The Death of Brunelleschi* and *Clytemnestra From The Battlements Of Argos*) and some of his contemporaries, such as John Everett Millais and Edward Burne-Jones. The house was designed in 1864 by Leighton in collaboration with the architect George Aitchison, and the pair continued to improve and extend it until shortly before Leighton's death. In addition to the permanent displays and temporary exhibitions, there are talks and recitals; call for details or check online.

Earl's Court & Fulham

Maps p396 & p397

Earl's Court, Fulham Broadway or West Brompton tube.

Earl's Court changed from hamlet to built-up urban area with the arrival of the Metropolitan Railway in 1860, and from 1914 many of its imposing houses were subdivided into flats.

In the late '70s and '80s the neighbourhood became the gay centre of London, with the action centring on the Coleherne pub. One of England's more famous dominatrixes, Lindi St Clair (aka Miss Whiplash), set up parlour on Eardley Crescent until bankrupted by the Inland Revenue. Freddie Mercury also lived around here, at Garden Lodge, 1 Logan Place, and Earl's Court retains a strong gay vibe. The pleasantly laid-out **Brompton Cemetery** is sometimes exploited for sexual encounters (the proximity to graves presumably sharpening the experience), although an unmolested stroll in search of the grave of suffragette Emmeline Pankhurst is perfectly possible.

Earl's Court is also, though, known for its temporary populations. Cheap and cheerless hotels abound around here, as does an ever-changing Australian population. A decade or more ago, Earl's Court was known as Kangaroo Valley, after the sheer volume of Australian travellers who made the area their temporary home. There are less of them rooming around here now – high rents have driven them further west, chiefly to Shepherd's Bush – but the Prince of Teck (161 Earl's Court Road, SW5; 7373 3107) still flies the flag.

Neighbouring **Parsons Green** and **Fulham** are home to a more established and affluent population with aspirations of Chelsea living. Parsons Green is centred around a small green that once – of course – supported a parsonage.

It was considered the aristocratic part of Fulham even in 1705, when Bowack said it was inhabited by 'Gentry and persons of Quality'. Despite the proximity of Hurlingham Sports Club and the Queen's (Tennis & Rackets) Club, which hosts the Stella Artois pre-Wimbledon tournament, you can enter **Fulham Palace** (*see below*) without a huge bank balance. Next door, Bishop's Park offers pretty river walks.

Fulham Palace

Bishop's Avenue, off Fulham Palace Road, SW6 (7736 3233). Putney Bridge tube/14, 74, 220 bus. **Open** Museum *Mar-Oct* 2-5pm Wed-Sun. *Nov-Feb* 1-4pm Thur-Sun. *Tours* 2pm 2nd & 4th Sun of mth. **Admission** *Museum* free; under-16s must be accompanied by adult. *Tours* £3; free under-16s. **No credit cards.**

London loves The Blue Book

Only in London do taxis add to the charm of the tourist experience, as opposed to detracting from it. Elsewhere, harrowing tales of rip-offs, muggings and worse abound, but inside a licensed London taxi – still known as a 'black cab', despite increasing variations in colour thanks to on-vehicle advertising – you usually know you're being taken care of.

Life in the capital often involves crowds, chicanery, dirt and decay. But inside a cab, there's room to stretch your legs. The driver has a licence. The interior is clean. And most of all, you never need doubt you'll get where you want to go. You pay for it, yes, but that's London – and this is no small service you're getting. After all, becoming a legitimate London cabbie is no walk in the park. To win your stripes, you must prove you've got what's known, with admirable plainness of speech, as 'The Knowledge'.

What a lot of Knowledge there is. Everything prospective drivers need to know is contained in one tome: the *Guide to Learning the Knowledge of London*, known to all and sundry as the **Blue Book**. This 80-page volume, published by the Public Carriage Office, lists 320 runs – efficient routes for getting from A to B, say Clapham Junction to the Imperial War Museum – designed to help cabbies memorise the 25,000 London streets that surround Charing Cross in a six-mile radius. The runs also contain points of interest, from hospitals and railway stations to parks and pubs.

Guide to learning the 'Knowledge of London'
All London drivers' edition

The Blue Book is the cabbies' Bible, but it's also a tome to which every Londoner owes a great debt. Without the Blue Book, there'd be no Knowledge; without the Knowledge, cab drivers would probably follow the example of New York, where drivers have enough trouble finding the ignition, let alone the address to which you want to go.

Getting all this down pat takes at least two years, usually more; some describe it as like taking a degree. As with any body of knowledge, there are private schools that can help, but most hopefuls simply hire a moped and wear out its tyres learning the routes backwards and forwards before taking a written exam, a series of oral exams and a driving test. Made it that far? Welcome to the next level: it's time to learn the suburban Knowledge. The *A-Z* has never looked so big; cabbies have never seemed so smart.

Chiswick House. *See p186.*

The official residence of the Bishops of London from 704 until 1973, Fulham Palace is a chaos of periods and architectural styles; the oldest part dates from 1480, the most recent, William Butterfield's neo-Gothic chapel, from 1866. There's a quirky museum tracing its history, but to see the palace interior you need to join one of the informative Sunday tours. The beautiful grounds are open daily.

Shepherd's Bush & Hammersmith

Goldhawk Road, Hammersmith or Shepherd's Bush tube.

The approach to **Shepherd's Bush** from Holland Park Avenue is marked by Shepherd's Bush roundabout, with the Thames Water Tower springing out of its centre. The tower, which looks like a state-of-the-art toilet cistern, is a surge pipe for London's underground ring main. Designed by students at the Royal College of Art, it doubles as a huge barometer.

Shepherd's Bush Common once formed the centre of what was, 150 years ago, a 'pleasant village'. Now, however, it's a scruffy traffic island unsure even of its own name (the green space is very definitely the Common, but the road that surrounds it is Shepherd's Bush Green). Visitors descend here for two reasons, both of them cultural: the Bush theatre (*see p337*), a haven for new writing located above a pub, and the Shepherd's Bush

Empire (*see p310*), London's best mid-sized rock venue. Next door sits the Walkabout Inn, a monstrous Aussie theme pub that gives the transience of the local population away. Otherwise, there's little of interest save the new West 12 Shopping Centre on the Common, and the Afro-Caribbean-oriented Shepherd's Bush market, between Shepherd's Bush and Goldhawk Road tubes.

Shepherd's Bush and neighbouring White City are home to the **BBC Television Centre**, where you can take a backstage tour (*see p186*). The wide open spaces of Wormwood Scrubs to the north are marred by one of London's most famous and forbidding Victorian jails, but less than a mile down Goldhawk Road is **Ravenscourt Park**, a much more agreeable space with an adventure playground and a number of tennis courts.

South of Shepherd's Bush, Hammersmith is less depressing than its neighbour, but is still best known for its huge traffic interchange and the stone-clad corporate monstrosity of the **Broadway Centre**. Yet it's not without its architectural landmarks: the **Olympia Exhibition Centre** on Hammersmith Road, and the brown, ship-shaped curiosity called the London Ark, the city's first energy-saving, eco-friendly building. Knobbly Hammersmith Bridge, built in 1824, was London's first suspension bridge; Lower Mall, running along the river from the bridge, is a pleasant spot for a stroll or a pint at one of several riverside pubs, of which the Dove (*see p229*) is the pick. Culturally speaking, on the main shopping route of **King Street** stands the Lyric theatre (*see p338*), while the Riverside Studios (*see p282*) on **Crisp Road** is a three-theatre contemporary arts centre with a gallery and a repertory cinema.

BBC Television Centre Backstage Tours

Wood Lane, W12 (0870 603 0304/www.bbc.co.uk/ tours). White City tube. **Tours** By appointment only Mon-Sat. **Admission** *Tours* £7.95; £6.95 concessions; £5.95 10-16s, students; £21.95 family. No under-10s. **Credit** MC, V.

The BBC Experience in Broadcasting House having closed a couple of years ago, the best way to get a glimpse inside the Beeb is via one of the tours of these studios, responsible for thousands of shows a year. A typical tour will allow you glimpses into the news centre, various studios and a production gallery, but no two tours are ever the same: this is a working TV centre. Tours, which must be pre-booked and last 90 minutes, can be combined with tickets to sit in the audience of a BBC show; call for details.

Chiswick

Turnham Green tube/Chiswick rail.

A leafy suburb coveted by BBC execs, actors and minor celebs, Chiswick is in a world of its own. Turning your back on the tarmacked swoops of Hammersmith and walking west by the river from Hammersmith Bridge, **Chiswick**

Mall gives off a different vibe. Lining this mile-long riverside stretch is an assortment of grand 17th- to 19th-century townhouses with flowery, wrought-iron verandas. The nearby Fuller's Griffin Brewery on Chiswick Lane South has stood on the same site since the 17th century and offers tours and tastings (8996 2063; pre-booked tours at 11am, noon, 1pm, 2pm Mon, Wed-Fri; £5).

Chiswick Mall ends at the church of St Nicholas. Only the ragstone tower of the 15th-century building remains; the rest of the church is 19th century. Gravestones commemorate local painters Hogarth and Whistler, but they're buried elsewhere. Other Chiswick attractions include Palladian **Chiswick House** (*see below*) and **Hogarth's House** (*see p187*); further west is the **Kew Bridge Steam Museum** (*see p187*). The small but perfectly formed **Musical Museum** is presently moving to new custom-built premises and should reopen in 2004 (see www.musicalmuseum.co.uk for details).

South of here, overlooking Kew Gardens from the opposite side of the river, is **Syon House** (*see p187*). A cutesy riverside promenade, just east of Kew Bridge on the north side of the river, runs by the mini-village of Strand-on-the-Green, and takes in three of the best pubs in the area.

Chiswick House

Burlington Lane, W4 (8995 0508/www.english-heritage.org.uk). Turnham Green tube then E3 bus to Edensor Road/Chiswick rail/Hammersmith tube/rail

Living in a material world: the shops of **Southall**. *See p187.*

then *190 bus.* **Open** *Apr-Sept* 10am-6pm daily. *Oct* 10am-5pm daily. Last entry 30min before closing. **Admission** £3.30; £2.50 concessions; £1.70 5-16s; free under-5s. **Credit** MC, V.

The first and finest 18th-century Palladian villa in Britain, Chiswick House was designed by the third Earl of Burlington as a temple to hospitality: the glamorous events hosted by the Burlington dynasty attracted the cream of London society, from artists to politicians. It was Lord Burlington's passion for the fine arts that made the interiors here such a feast for the eyes: keen to create a house and garden of a kind found in ancient Rome, he employed William Kent to design sumptuous interiors to contrast with the restrained exterior. The extraordinary Domed Saloon is lit from the drum by windows derived from the Roman baths of Diocletian. The classical Italianate gardens with their temples, statues and lake are no less spectacular.

Hogarth's House

Hogarth Lane, Great West Road, W4 (8994 6757). Turnham Green tube/Chiswick rail. **Open** *Apr-Oct* 1-5pm Tue-Fri; 1-6pm Sat, Sun. *Nov, Dec, Feb, Mar* 1-4pm Tue-Fri; 1-5pm Sat, Sun. **Admission** free; donations appreciated. **No credit cards**.

This early 18th-century house was the country retreat of painter, engraver and social commentator William Hogarth. Fully restored in 1997, for the 300th anniversary of Hogarth's birth, it now functions as a gallery displaying most of his well-known engravings, including *Gin Lane, Marriage à la Mode, Harlot's Progress* and a copy of *Rake's Progress*, part of which depicts a scene in Bedlam lunatic asylum.

Kew Bridge Steam Museum

Green Dragon Lane, Brentford, Middx (8568 4757/ www.kbsm.org). Gunnersbury tube/Kew Bridge rail/ 65, 237, 267, 391 bus. **Open** 11am-5pm daily. **Admission** *Mon-Fri* £3.60; £2.70 concessions; £1.50 5-15s; free under-5s; £8 family. *Sat, Sun* £4.60; £3.70 concessions; £2.50 5-15s; free under-5s; £11.95 family. **Credit** MC, V.

This museum of water supply, housed in a Victorian riverside pumping station, looks at London's use and abuse of the world's most precious commodity. The highlight – or low point, depending on your take on it – is a walk-through sewer experience. On weekends at 3pm one of the biggest working steam engines in the world, a Cornish beam engine built in 1845 for use in the tin mines, stirs into motion.

Syon House

Syon Park, Brentford, Middx (8560 0883/ www.syonpark.co.uk). Gunnersbury tube/rail then 237, 267 bus. **Open** House *late Mar-early Nov* 11am-5pm Wed, Thur, Sun, bank hol Mon. Last entry 4.15pm. *Tours* by arrangement. **Admission** *House & Gardens* £6.95; £6.50 concessions; £5.95 5-15s; free under-5s; £15 family. *Gardens only* £3.50; £2.50 concessions, 5-15s; free under-5s; £8 family. *Tours* free. **Credit** AmEx, MC, V.

The London home of the Duke of Northumberland – it's been in the family for 400 years – Syon House was built on the site of a medieval abbey dedicated to the Bridgettine order (founded by Swedish mystic St Bridget) and is named after Mount Zion in the Holy Land. Brutally dissolved by Henry VIII, the monastery was remodelled as a house by 1517, though in 1547 it seems to have got its revenge when Henry's coffin, brought here en route to Windsor, burst open in the night, allowing the dogs to slobber on his remains. The fine Robert Adam neo-classical interior was created in 1761 for the 1st Duke of Northumberland. Among the many paintings on display inside are works by Gainsborough, Reynolds and Van Dyck. The gardens, which afford views of Kew Gardens (*see p176*) across the river, were modelled by 'Capability' Brown and now house a 19th-century conservatory, a miniature steam train, a garden centre, the London Butterfly House and the Aquatic Experience (all have separate admission charges to the house and gardens).

Further west

A couple of miles west of Chiswick is the suburb of **Ealing**, famous for Ealing Studios with its distinctive brand of anarchic comedy. The oldest site of continuous film production in Britain and the country's first studio built for sound, Ealing is undergoing a £70-million conversion to a state-of-the art facility geared to the digital age. Work, which is expected to be complete by 2004 and includes the renovation of the three original sound stages, is being carried out in phases so the studio can continue with TV and film production.

The area is a one-stop option for shopping (the Broadway Centre lies at its heart) and eating and drinking, plus it boasts a large selection of museums and parks. Worth a visit is **Walpole Park**, home to Pitshanger Manor (*see p188*) and the annual Ealing Jazz Festival. Further west still, in the middle of gigantic Osterley Park, is **Osterley House** (*see p188*), another Robert Adam revamp.

Just north of here are the colour and curries of **Southall**, which, like many previously sleepy parts of west London, has been given a new lease of life by Indian immigrants. The mainly Punjabi community offers authentic north Indian cuisine in countless cheap restaurants lining the Broadway. Visit on a Sunday, when the locals stroll among the market stalls and sari stores.

To the north, **Wembley** has been similarly enlivened by the mainly Gujarati community, although this district is better known as the home of the famous stadium. Plans to replace the 80-year-old structure – which ceased to be used for sporting events in October 2000 – have been in limbo now for years, and some doubt a replacement will ever be built. Certainly, the chaos, in-fighting and general inaction show up the much-discussed possible London bid for the 2012 Olympics as the pie-in-the-sky nonsense it indubitably is.

Nearby **Neasden** is another piece of sprawling suburbia, once satirised by the Monty Python team but now most famous for the multi-billion-rupee **Shri Swaminarayan Mandir** temple that was built here by a Hindu sect, replicating the Akshardam outside Ahmedabad in Gujarat, western India. Constructed in 1995, it required 5,000 tons of marble and limestone and the work of around 1,500 sculptors for an enterprise unprecedented in this country since cathedral-building in the Middle Ages. Visitors are welcome, but should dress discreetly.

Osterley House

Osterley Park, off Jersey Road, Isleworth, Middx (8232 5050/recorded information 01494 755566/ www.nationaltrust.org.uk). Osterley tube. **Open** *Park* 9am-dusk daily. House *end Mar-early Nov* 1-4.30pm Wed-Sun. **Admission** *House* £4.50; £2.25 5-15s; free under-5s; £11.20 family. *Park* free.
Now a National Trust property, Osterley House was built for Sir Thomas Gresham (the founder of the Royal Exchange; *see p90*) in 1576, but was transformed by Robert Adam in 1761. His quietly dramatic revamp is most prominent in the imposing colonnade of white pillars in front of the courtyard of the house's red-brick body. The splendid state rooms are worth a visit in themselves, but the still-used Tudor stables and the vast parkland walks add to Osterley's allure.

Pitshanger Manor & Gallery

Walpole Park, Mattock Lane, Ealing, W5 (8567 1227/www.ealing.gov.uk/pitshanger). Ealing Broadway tube/rail. **Open** 11am-5pm Tue-Sat. *Tours* by arrangement. **Admission** free.
Set in the beautiful surrounds of Walpole Park, Pitshanger Manor was largely rebuilt by Sir John Soane (for Sir John Soane's Museum, *see p100*), who transformed it into an idiosyncratic Regency villa, retaining only a wing designed in 1768 by George Dance the Younger. Painstakingly restored, the interior offers up the contrast between Soane's decorative schemes in his library, breakfast room and bedchamber and the formal rooms in the Dance wing, with their elaborate plasterwork. Tours include a short video, *A Day in the Death of John Soane*, that looks at Soane's use of Pitshanger to entertain friends and clients. The adjacent Gallery, which opened in 1996, is the biggest contemporary art gallery in west London.

London loves Ghosts

Scratch London's gleaming 21st-century surface and its murky, blood-spattered history is, almost literally, waiting to reach out and touch you. The capital is home to scores of ghosts, including a phantom stage coach that drives along **Bayswater Road** (*see p180*), the 'black nun' who roams the **Bank of England** (*see p90*) and a 'monkjester', Rahere, who haunts the church he founded in the 12th century, **St Bartholomew-the-Great** (*see p90*).

Of course, grander historical figures are the subject of better-documented after-death sightings. For a 'one-stop shop' of restless royals, look no further than the **Tower of London** (*see p96*). In the 13th century Archbishop of Canterbury Thomas à Becket was the first spectre spotted in the Tower, apocryphally tapping a wall with his cross and demolishing it. Henry VI, Sir Walter Raleigh and the 'Princes in the Tower' – Edward V and Richard, Duke of York – also make occasional visits from beyond the grave. Henry VIII's wives Anne Boleyn and Catherine Howard were both executed here, as was the 16-year-old Lady Jane Grey, the 'queen for nine days'. Their restless spirits are all still to be seen; Boleyn, for one, haunts the Green.

Theatres are also a magnet for supernatural shenanigans, with practically every London stage boasting its own ghost. The **Theatre Royal, Drury Lane**, leads the way with at least three ghosts: the Man in Grey who walks the back row of the upper circle, the clown Grimaldi, whose benevolent presence is indicated by the aroma of lavender, and the less helpful spirit of Charles Macklin. Maniacal Macklin murdered fellow actor Thomas Halam in 1735 following an argument over a wig. Why Macklin's ghost, rather than that of his victim, should be the one that haunts the theatre remains a mystery.

Alleged hauntings have been so often used as publicity stunts that when psychic Terry O'Sullivan found the genuine torture tools at the **London Dungeon** (*see p81*) attracted wandering spirits, no one was surprised... until he unearthed a tunnel in the back of the building used as an air-raid shelter during the Blitz, in which 61 people had been killed. O'Sullivan's subsequent 'psychic rescue' freed Tooley Street of its miserable spirits. Such a discovery just goes to show: you never know when you're a few feet away from a hot bed of the undead.

Eat, Drink, Shop

Restaurants

Bring an empty stomach with you: the choice of great eats here is spectacular.

Something incredible has happened to this city's restaurants over the past quarter-century. We don't exaggerate. If Londoners of the 1970s – well used to their national cuisine being the butt of the world's jokes, and overfamiliar with inferior ingredients, sledgehammer cooking methods and service from the Duke of Edinburgh's school of charm – could visit the restaurants in today's metropolis, they would not believe it. OK, the Prince Philip maître d' still crops up, imperiously directing customers, as do incompetent or ill-trained waiting staff. Prices, too, are often higher than they ought to be. Yet the range and quality of eating opportunities here is now better than ever.

Perhaps because of the national inferiority complex regarding their own cuisine, the British have long been open to new gastronomic influences. This, combined with the exciting cosmopolitanism of London and the inexorable rise of food as a fashion statement, has led to an explosive growth in the number of restaurants throughout the city.

London now has some of the best Indian restaurants outside the subcontinent: fans of the cuisines of India, Pakistan, Bangladesh and Sri Lanka should explore the districts of Southall, Wembley (Ealing Road) and Tooting. The city also contains some of Europe's best Chinese restaurants (centred on Chinatown), along with enticing enclaves of Turkish (Newington Green, N16), Middle Eastern (Edgware Road, W2), Korean (New Malden, Surrey), Jewish (Golders Green, NW11) and Portuguese (Vauxhall, SW8) restaurants and food shops. Dozens of other cuisines are also represented throughout the metropolis.

DOS AND DON'TS

For most people, eating out in London is an informal affair. It's rare that a restaurant enforces a dress code, although the pricier the restaurant, the smarter its clientele tends to be.

Not all London restaurants insist on reservations, but there's no harm in making them; we've indicated the places where booking is essential, but it's always best to book ahead where possible. While some London eateries are entirely non-smoking and others allow smoking anywhere, the most common arrangement is for staff to set aside sections of the restaurant for smokers. If you're passionate either way, mention it when you book.

Tipping is standard practice; ten to 15 per cent is usual. Some places add service automatically, so double-check the bill or you may tip twice. Be wary of places that include service in the bill but then leave the space for gratuities empty on your credit card slip. And always try to tip in cash, as some restaurants don't pass on credit card tips to their table staff.

We've listed a range of main course prices for each establishment, except for those that only serve set menu meals (where we've listed those prices instead). However, restaurants can (and often do) change their menus at any time, so these prices are only guidelines.

For the best places to eat with kids, *see p276*; for the best places to eat after hours, *see p216* **Late eats**. And for more information on all aspects of eating out in London, buy the annual *Time Out Eating & Drinking Guide* (£9.99).

People's Palace. *See p193.*

The South Bank & Bankside

Cafés & brasseries

Konditor & Cook
*10 Stoney Street, SE1 (7407 5100). London Bridge
tube/rail.* **Open** 7.30am-6pm Mon-Fri; 8.30am-4pm
Sat. **No credit cards. Map** p404 P8.
Part of the food revolution that has transformed
Borough Market, this high-quality bakery/food shop
has three pavement tables where you can sample
pizzas, sandwiches and mouth-watering cakes,
along with great coffee, teas and fruit juices.
Branches: throughout the city.

Manze's
*87 Tower Bridge Road, SE1 (7407 2985). Bus 1, 42,
188.* **Open** 11am-2pm Mon; 10.30am 2pm Tue Thur;
10am-2.15pm Fri; 10am-2.45pm Sat. **No credit
cards. Map** p405 Q10.
This is London's oldest (est. 1892) and most beautiful pie and mash shop. Eat jellied eels, mashed
potato and minced beef pie for about £5 and admire
the Victorian benches and tiling. Cockney ambrosia.

Southwark Cathedral Refectory
*Southwark Cathedral, Montague Close, SE1 (7407
5740/www.digbytrout.co.uk). London Bridge
tube/rail.* **Open** 10am-5pm daily. **Credit** MC, V.
Map p404 P8.
Housed in a smart modern wing at the back of
Southwark Cathedral (*see p78*), this is a peaceful
place in which to succumb to tempting cakes and
pastries. There are also hot lunches, soups, quiches
and sandwiches for its wide spectrum of customers.

Tate Modern Café: Level 2
*Tate Modern, Sumner Street, SE1 (7401 5014/
www.tate.org.uk). Southwark tube/London Bridge
tube/rail.* **Open** 10am-3pm Mon-Thur, Sun;
10am-3pm, 6-9.30pm Fri, Sat. **Main courses**
£4-£11 lunch; £6-£12 dinner. **Credit** AmEx, DC,
MC, V. **Map** p404 O7.
There's another café up a few floors, but we prefer
this sleek eaterie, which features great views of St
Paul's. Food – breakfasts (until 11.30am), brasserie
dishes, wraps, pastas – is less spectacular and wine
is costly, but the coffee and the burgers are good.

Fish

Livebait
*41-5 The Cut, SE1 (7928 7211/
www.santeonline.co.uk/livebait). Southwark
tube/Waterloo tube/rail.* **Open** noon-3pm, 5.30-
11.30pm Mon-Sat. **Main courses** £8.95-£28.50.
Credit AmEx, DC, MC, V. **Map** p404 N8.
This branch of the popular no-frills fish and seafood
chain is a safe bet for marine life of all descriptions,
served with a choice of sauces and accompaniments
(salads, chips and veg). The tiled floor and walls
make for swimming pool acoustics.
Branches: throughout the city.

The best | Restaurants

For breakfast in a hurry
Brick Lane Beigel Bake. *See p210.*

For a leisurely lunch
Pied à Terre. *See p195.*

For an afternoon cake
Pâtisserie Valerie. *See p201.*

For dinner in a room with a view
Oxo Tower Restaurant & Brasserie.
See p191.

For arguably the best food
in town
Gordon Ramsay. *See p209.*

Global

Baltic
*74 Blackfriars Road, SE1 (7928 1111/
www.balticrestaurant.co.uk). Southwark tube.*
Open noon-3pm, 6-11pm Mon-Sat; noon-3pm,
6-10.30pm Sun. **Main courses** £11-£12.50.
Credit AmEx, MC, V. **Map** p404 N8.
This glamorous east European venue comprises a
sleek modern bar (vodka's a speciality) fronting
an expansive restaurant with a huge atrium.
Attention to detail is evident in both service and
food: modern interpretations of classics such as
lamb sashlik with Georgian ratatouille. Set meals
are great value.

Tas
*33 The Cut, SE1 (7928 2111/
www.tasrestaurants.co.uk). Waterloo tube/rail.*
Open noon-11.30pm Mon-Sat; noon-10.30pm
Sun. **Main courses** £4.65-£14.45. **Credit** AmEx,
MC, V. **Map** p404 N8.
Kebabs, güveç stews, fish and vegetarian dishes are
served alongside an extensive wine list at this chic
Turkish restaurant. Musicians play in the roomy
main dining area every evening.
Branch: 72 Borough High Street, Bankside, SE1
(7403 7200).

Modern European

Oxo Tower Restaurant & Brasserie
*Oxo Tower Wharf, Barge House Street, SE1
(7803 3888/www.harveynichols.com). Blackfriars or
Waterloo tube/rail.* **Open** *Brasserie* noon-2.45pm,
5.30-11pm Mon-Sat; noon-3.45pm, 6-10.15pm Sun.
Restaurant noon-2.30pm, 6-11pm Mon-Sat; noon-
3pm, 6.30-10pm Sun. **Main courses** *Brasserie*
£10.25-£17. *Restaurant* £17.50-£26. **Credit** AmEx,
DC, MC, V. **Map** p404 N7.

Get the basics and more at **Smiths of Smithfield**. See p194.

The elegance of the architecture and the stunning views of the Thames make Oxo Tower one of the most exciting places in London to dine. The food lives up to the setting. Tables are usually offered for 6.30pm or 9.30pm in the evening.

People's Palace
Level 3, Royal Festival Hall, SE1 (7928 9999/ www.peoplespalace.co.uk). Waterloo tube/rail. **Open** noon-3pm, 5.30-11pm daily. **Main courses** £12.50-£17. **Credit** AmEx, DC, MC, V. **Map** p401 M8.
A suave dining room in the 1950s Festival Hall, where the highlight is a stage-like wall of picture windows on to the river. Assured, friendly service and a fashionable, Mediterranean-influenced menu (expertly prepared and in generous portions) make this one of London's best institutional restaurants.

The City

Cafés & brasseries

De Gustibus
53-5 Carter Lane, EC4 (7236 0056). St Paul's tube/ Blackfriars tube/rail. **Open** 7am-5pm Mon-Fri. **Credit** MC, V. **Map** p404 O6.
Bespoke sandwiches are the forte of this impressive café. Salads, a few hot dishes and sweet pastries are also offered to the throng of lunching office workers. **Branches:** 53 Blandford Street, Marylebone, W1 (7486 6608); 4 Southwark Street, Bankside, SE1 (7407 3625).

Japanese

City Miyama
17 Godliman Street, EC4 (7489 1937). St Paul's tube/Blackfriars tube/rail. **Open** noon-2pm, 6-9.30pm Mon-Fri; noon-2pm Sat. **Main courses** £9-£25. **Credit** AmEx, DC, MC, V. **Map** p404 O6.
A civilised if slightly staid venue where many Anglo-Japanese business deals have been discussed over the years. There's a sushi bar and teppanyaki table upstairs, but most diners congregate downstairs, perhaps to sample the interesting 'chef's specials' on the à la carte list. Prices are high.

Yokoso Sushi
40 Whitefriars Street, EC4 (7583 9656). Blackfriars tube. **Open** 11am-8pm Mon-Fri. **Main courses** *Sushi* £1.20-£3.20. **Credit** AmEx, MC, V. **Map** p404 N6.
Noted for the excellence of its fish, this two-year-old sushi bar is an unassuming, plainly attired place where excellent value, classic dishes include aji (horse mackerel), uni (sea urchin) and salmon.

Modern European

Bonds
5 Threadneedle Street, EC2 (7657 8088). Bank tube/DLR. **Open** noon-2.30pm, 6.30-10.30pm Mon-Fri. **Main courses** £17.95-£21. **Credit** AmEx, MC, V. **Map** p405 Q6.

It's part of a new luxury hotel development and its prices are hefty, but Bonds has, in Tom Ilic, an haute cuisine chef of the highest order. Dishes reflect a northern and central European influence, with offal, game and strong flavours to the fore. Somewhere to clinch that deal and enjoy yourself to boot.

1 Lombard Street
1 Lombard Street, EC3 (7929 6611/ www.1lombardstreet.com). Bank tube/DLR. **Open** *Brasserie* 7.30-11am, 11.30-3pm, 6-10pm Mon-Fri. *Restaurant* noon-3pm, 6-10pm Mon-Fri. **Main courses** *Brasserie* £12.50-£28.50. *Restaurant* £27.50-£29.50. **Credit** AmEx, DC, MC, V. **Map** p405 Q6.
This immense former bank is now split between an informal bar/brasserie (beneath a spectacular domed skylight) and a stately back restaurant. Here, chef Herbert Berger produces modern haute cuisine that shows thoughtful combination of flavours, textures and colours. Suits predominate at lunch, and dinners can be sparsely attended. Staff are punctilious.

Vegetarian & organic

The Place Below
St Mary-le-Bow, Cheapside, EC2 (7329 0789/ www.theplacebelow.co.uk). St Paul's tube/Bank tube/DLR. **Open** 7.30-10.30am, 11.30am-3.30pm Mon-Fri. **Main courses** £5.50-£7.50. **Credit** AmEx, MC, V. **Map** p404 P6.
Housed in the bright yet snug crypt of the famous 'Bow bells' church, this popular café produces soups, casseroles, quiches and scrumptious desserts. Snacks only are served after 2.30pm. An antidote to the more stuffy City eating venues.

Holborn & Clerkenwell

British

St John
26 St John Street, EC1 (7251 0848/4998/ www.stjohnrestaurant.co.uk). Farringdon tube/rail. **Open** *Bar* 11am-11pm Mon-Fri; 6-11pm Sat. *Restaurant* noon-3pm, 6-11pm Mon-Fri; 6-11pm Sat. **Main courses** *Bar* £3-£10. *Restaurant* £10-£16. **Credit** AmEx, DC, MC, V. **Map** p402 O5.
Chef Fergus Henderson ensures that no part of a pig is left unused. His first-class restaurant, an old smokehouse with bar and bakery attached, places offal on its deserved pedestal. Earthy starters such as snails in bacon precede equally robust main courses like venison liver with lentils. Able, informed staff add to the lively feel of the place.

Cafés & brasseries

Flâneur Food Hall
41 Farringdon Road, EC1 (7404 4422). Farringdon tube/rail. **Open** 8am-10pm Mon-Fri; 9am-10pm Sat; 9am-6pm Sun. **Main courses** £9-£11.90. **Credit** AmEx, DC, MC, V. **Map** p402 N5.

You'll find this excellent brasserie behind an upmarket deli. A meal might kick off with seared scallops with purple cauliflower and pink peppercorn beurre blanc; next could be roast cod with mash and mustard sauce. Wines are appealing too.

Goodfellas
50 Lamb's Conduit Street, WC1 (7405 7088).
Chancery Lane or Holborn tube. **Open** 8am-6.30pm
Mon-Fri; 10am-5pm Sat. **Main courses** £2.99-£4.25.
No credit cards. Map p399 M4.
It's the lunchtime buffet – pasta, cooked meats and salads – that rakes in punters to this cosy basement café, but the fine sandwiches pass muster, too.

French

Club Gascon
57 West Smithfield, EC1 (7796 0600). Barbican
tube/Farringdon tube/rail. **Open** noon-2pm, 7-11pm
Mon-Fri; 7-10.30pm Sat. **Main courses** *Tapas* £5-
£25. **Credit** MC, V. **Map** p402 O5.
The food of south-western France are served in tapas-sized portions at this much-loved restaurant. Prices can be high, but dishes such as organic salmon with wild herb sorbet show perfect balance. Three dishes should satisfy most appetites.

Modern European

Bank Aldwych
1 Kingsway, WC2 (7379 9797/www.bankrestaurants.
com). Holborn or Temple tube. **Open** 7.30-10.30am,
noon-3pm, 5.30-11.30pm Mon-Fri; 11.30am-3.30pm,

5.30-11.30pm Sat; 11.30am-3.30pm, 5.30-10pm Sun.
Main courses £8.95-£19.50. **Credit** AmEx, DC, MC,
V. **Map** p399 M6.
A clever makeover of a huge bank has produced this confident restaurant where roast cod cassoulet shares menu space with pastas, crustacea, meat (lamb with beetroot marmalade and sweet potato gnocchi) and desserts. Weekend brunches are child-friendly.

Smiths of Smithfield
67-77 Charterhouse Street, EC1 (7251 7950).
Farringdon tube/rail. **Open** *Bar meals* 7am-5pm Mon-
Fri; 10.30am-5pm Sat, Sun. *Dining Room* noon-2.45pm,
6-10.45pm Mon-Fri; 6-10.45pm Sat. **Main courses**
£10.50-£11.50. **Credit** AmEx, MC, V. **Map** p402 O5.
The Smiths complex – a converted warehouse with a ground-floor bar/café, first-floor cocktail bar and two restaurants on the next two floors – is like a megaclub. The Dining Room has an appealing menu where seared tuna with white bean salad might be followed by artichoke heart with fried ceps. The Top Floor is a more formal, British restaurant.

Spanish

Cigala
54 Lamb's Conduit Street, WC1 (7405 1717/
www.cigala.co.uk). Holborn or Russell Square tube.
Open noon-3pm, 6-10.45pm Mon-Fri; 12.30-3.30pm,
6-10.45pm Sat; 12.30-3.30pm Sun. **Main courses**
£13-£17. **Credit** AmEx, DC, MC, V. **Map** p399 M5.
Since opening in 2001, Cigala has attracted rave reviews. The service now comes close to matching the first-rate food: highlights are the modern

Vegging out

Among diehard carnivores, the word 'vegetarian' still conjures images of lentil pie and sweetcorn fritters. However, its meaning has moved with the times, pulled along by changing eating trends on a booming London restaurant scene. With concern over meat production growing and health a bigger issue than ever, more people are turning to the natural alternative. And it's not just about eating organic and feeling worthy: it's also to do with taste, quality and value for money.

Every year, London welcomes a new batch of vegetarian restaurants to join the thriving gang. And there are plenty out there from which to choose. Some are institutions that have been serving their local communities for so long they deserve museum status: the likes of **Food for Thought** (*see p205*), **Neal's Yard Bakery & Tearoom** (6 Neal's Yard, WC2; 7836 5199) and the charming **Bonnington Centre Café** (11 Vauxhall Grove, SW8; no

phone). Here, you'll find cheap and cheerful food of the wholemeal roll and beanburger variety, and you might even spot the dying fraternity of sock-and-sandal wearers puffing on a cup of Caro.

The likes of **Beetroot** (92 Berwick Street, W1; 7437 8591) and **Red Veg** (95 Dean Street, W1; 7437 3109) are far more modern. At Beetroot, Soho guys and gals discuss the latest twist in their Levi's over a box of all-veggie goodies; at Red Veg, they take away magnificent veggieburgers and falafel. There are also a number of gourmet veggie eateries: the **Gate** (*see p218*) keeps the local bohos happy with its minimalist interior and a menu annotated with words such as 'tartlet' and 'lavender brûlée', while **Manna** (4 Erskine Road, NW3; 7722 8028) serves excellent food in a wonderfully homey environment. Serious foodies can't get much better than the Modern European **Blandford**

Spanish wines and simple but immaculate dishes such as grilled sea bream with deep-fried courgettes and aïoli. Furnishings are modishly minimalist.

Moro

34-6 Exmouth Market, EC1 (7833 8336). Farringdon tube/rail. **Open** *Bar* 12.30-10.30pm Mon-Fri; 7-10.30pm Sat. *Restaurant* 12.30-2.30pm, 7-10.30pm Mon-Fri; 7-10.30pm Sat. **Main courses** £11-£15.50. **Credit** AmEx, DC, MC, V. **Map** p402 N4.

A terrific restaurant that deserves its fast-won fame, Moro has developed a cuisine that owes as much to North Africa and the Middle East as to Spain. Tapas are served at the long bar; the restaurant offers such delicacies as pot-roasted pork with sherry vinegar. Prices are fair given the quality; be sure to book.

Bloomsbury & Fitzrovia

Global

Archipelago

110 Whitfield Street, W1 (7383 3346). Goodge Street or Warren Street tube. **Open** noon-2.30pm, 6-11.15pm Mon-Fri; 6-11.15pm Sat. **Set meals** *Lunch* £26.50 3 courses. *Dinner* £32.50 2 courses; £38.50 3 courses. **Credit** AmEx, MC, V. **Map** p398 J4.

Menus don't get much weirder than this. Starters include warm monkey glands; marinated emu comes with nori sushi and gold leaf; pudding might be frazzled bee with honey. Bohemian decor and charming service don't prepare you for the sizeable bill.

Street (5-7 Blandford Street, W1; 7486 9696), where it won't matter if someone beside you is chewing on a bone while you're dribbling over a moist and tangy stilton soufflé.

For world food lovers, there's a swathe of restaurants that offer excellent vegetarian options. For creative Chinese, try **Ch'i** (8 Egerton Gardens Mews, SW3; 7584 7007); **Asakusa** has some great veggie Japanese dishes (265 Eversholt Street, NW1; 7388 8533); ever-popular Camden haunt **Bar Gansa** (2 Inverness Street, NW1; 7267 8909) is splendid for tapas; and you can go Greek at the quirky **Café Corfu** (7-9 Pratt Street, NW1; 7267 8008). Don't forget, too, that around half of India's population is vegetarian: both Drummond Street, NW1, and the Tooting area of south London are full to bursting with terrific south Indian restaurants.

Indian

Rasa Samudra

5 Charlotte Street, W1 (7637 0222/ www.rasarestaurants.com). Goodge Street tube. **Open** noon-3pm, 6-10.45pm Mon-Sat; 6-10.45pm Sun. **Main courses** £7.95-£14. **Credit** AmEx, MC, V. **Map** p398 J5.

Keralan seafood dishes, as well as the choice vegetarian food of the southern Indian state, are offered at this stylish restaurant, the priciest branch of the small Rasa chain. Couples should order a seafood feast (good value, despite its £30 price tag) and a vegetarian feast and settle back to enjoy some of London's best Indian food.

Branches: throughout the city.

Italian

Carluccio's Caffè

8 Market Place, W1 (7636 2228). Oxford Circus tube. **Open** 8am-11pm Mon-Fri; 10am-11pm Sat; 11am-10pm Sun. **Main courses** £4.85-£10.95. **Credit** AmEx, MC, V.

This branch of the innovative and rapidly proliferating new chain of Italian cafés – the winner of the *Time Out* Best Family Restaurant award in 2002 – tempts in shoppers with good, hearty food and terrific coffee at reasonable prices. Decor is modern, bright and minimal.

Branches: throughout the city.

Sardo

45 Grafton Way, W1 (7387 2521/ www.sardo-restaurant.com). Warren Street tube. **Open** noon-3pm, 6-11pm Mon-Fri; 6-11pm Sat. **Main courses** £8.90-£18. **Credit** AmEx, DC, MC, V. **Map** p398 J4.

Intriguing and expertly rendered specialities from Sardinia are the treasures to be found in these rustic Fitzrovia surroundings. Pleasant staff bring forth such delights as cured leg of lamb (gamy, intense), fregola (juicy beads of pasta) cooked in fish stock and served with seafood, and nearly 30 types of Sardinian wine.

Modern European

Pied à Terre

34 Charlotte Street, W1 (7636 1178/ www.pied.a.terre.co.uk). Goodge Street or Tottenham Court Road tube. **Open** 12.15-2.30pm, 7-11pm Mon-Fri; 7-11pm Sat. **Set meals** *Lunch* £19.50 2 courses; £23 3 courses. *Dinner* £35 2 courses; £43.50 3 courses; £55 8 courses. **Credit** AmEx, DC, MC, V. **Map** p398 J5.

Small, narrow and simply but stylishly decorated, Pied à Terre is a true gourmet's retreat. The set meals come with various add-ons (brilliant amuses bouches, divine petits fours), and throughout exhibit occasionally daring but invariably blissful combinations of ingredients.

Eat, Drink, Shop

Eat, Drink, Shop

Oriental

Hakkasan

8 Hanway Place, W1 (7907 1888). Tottenham Court Road tube. **Open** noon-2.30pm, 6-11.30pm Mon-Fri; noon-4.30pm, 6-11.30pm Sat, Sun. **Main courses** £5.90-£40, dim sum £3.50-£16. **Credit** AmEx, MC, V. **Map** p399 K5.

This capacious basement restaurant combines state-of-the-art design (featuring latticed wooden screens) with terrific interpretations of classic Chinese cooking. The dim sum are exquisite: yam dumplings come stuffed with prawns, wolfberries and sea moss. Dress smart-ish, and book for dinner.

Han Kang

16 Hanway Street, W1 (7637 1985). Tottenham Court Road tube. **Open** noon-3pm, 6-11pm Mon-Sat. **Main courses** £6.50-£28 (for 2). **Credit** MC, V. **Map** p399 K5.

Great value Korean food is produced behind this unprepossessing frontage. Lunch specials are especially cheap and attract many Korean students.

Silks & Spice

23 Foley Street, W1 (7636 2718/ www.silksandspice.co.uk). Goodge Street or Oxford Circus tube. **Open** noon-11pm Mon-Fri; 5.30-11pm Sat; 5.30-10.30pm Sun. **Main courses** £5.95-£21. **Credit** AmEx, MC, V. **Map** p398 J5.

A pleasing mix of spicy Thai and Malaysian food – including set menus, adventurous specials, deluxe lobster dishes and an express daytime set meal – continues to attract office workers to S&S. Ornate woodcarvings adorn its rather murky interior. **Branches**: throughout the city.

Marylebone

Fish & chips

Golden Hind

73 Marylebone Lane, W1 (7486 3644). Bond Street tube. **Open** noon-3pm, 6-10pm Mon-Fri; 6-10pm Sat. **Main courses** £5-£10.70. **Credit** AmEx, DC, MC, V. **Map** p398 G5.

Opened in 1914, this humble chippie may sport a classic caff-style interior (vintage fryer included), but you can order king prawns to start, then grilled haddock with herbs, as well as traditional battered cod.

Global

Original Tajines

7A Dorset Street, W1 (7935 1545). Baker Street tube. **Open** noon-3pm, 6-11pm Mon-Fri; 6-11pm Sat. **Main courses** £8.95-£11. **Credit** MC, V. **Map** p398 G5.

This attractive little Moroccan place delivers the goods, gastronomically, aesthetically and economically. A long menu contains several rare (to London) dishes, along with ridiculously tasty tagine stews. The Moroccan wine list deserves exploration.

Providores & Tapa Room

109 Marylebone High Street, W1 (7935 6175/ www.theprovidores.co.uk). Baker Street or Bond Street tube. **Open** *Providores* noon-2.45pm, 6-10.45pm Mon-Sat; noon-2.45pm, 6-10pm Sun. *Tapa Room* 9-11.30am, noon-10.30pm Mon-Fri; 10am-3pm, 4-10.30pm Sat; 10am-3pm, 4-10pm Sun. **Main courses** *Providores* £11-£15. *Tapa Room* £1.50-£9. *Cover* £1.50 (lunch Sat, Sun). **Credit** AmEx, MC, V. **Map** p398 G5.

Hakkasan. *See p196.*

Chef Peter Gordon and Anna Hansen preside over this two-floor operation. On the ground floor, the casual Tapa Room deals in globally inspired tapas. Upstairs is Providores, the smarter, bookable restaurant where spiced chicken breast might share a plate with quince aïoli. Dishes at both sound overly complex but work wonderfully well. This is fusion food at its best.

Six-13

19 Wigmore Street, W1 (7629 6133/ www.six13.com). Bond Street or Oxford Circus tube. **Open** noon-3pm, 5.30-11pm Mon-Thur, Sun; (prepaid only) from 7.30pm Fri (summer only); 8-11pm Sat (winter only). **Main courses** £19-£25. **Credit** AmEx, DC, MC, V. **Map** p398 G5.

The only truly sophisticated London restaurant serving kosher food, Six-13 offers a menu of Modern European cuisine combined with traditional Jewish dishes. Prices are high, but so is the quality. Smooth service, spacious pistachio-green surroundings and kosher wines are additional attractions.

Italian

Locanda Locatelli

8 Seymour Street, W1 (7935 9088/ www.locandalocatelli.com). Marble Arch tube. **Open** noon-3pm, 7-11pm Mon-Sat. **Main courses** £10-£28. **Credit** AmEx, MC, V. **Map** p395 F6.

Renowned chef Giorgio Locatelli's new restaurant is a fashionably retro, funky place. Despite sometimes slow service, tables are frequently booked up weeks in advance by punters eager to sample Locatelli classics such as duck with spelt and broccoli.

Middle Eastern

Fairuz

3 Blandford Street, W1 (7486 8108/8182). Baker Street or Bond Street tube. **Open** noon-11.30pm Mon-Sat; noon-10.30pm Sun. **Main courses** £9-£12. **Credit** AmEx, DC, MC, V. **Map** p398 G5.

Chatty staff and Mediterranean-style furnishings give a mellow feel to this popular Lebanese venue. The superb food includes a choice of 50 meze, and both meat and (unusually) vegetarian main courses. **Branch**: 27 Westbourne Grove, W2 (7243 8555).

Levant

Jason Court, 76 Wigmore Street, W1 (7224 1111/ www.levantrestaurant.co.uk). Bond Street tube. **Open** noon-11.30pm Mon-Fri; 5.30-11.30pm Sat, Sun. **Main courses** £12.50-£22.50. **Credit** AmEx, DC, MC, V. **Map** p398 G6.

An atmospheric basement with blaring music and lascivious belly dancing (both from 8.30pm each night) provides a fun setting for good food: spicy falafel, great mixed grills and Arabic ice-creams. Service is friendly.

Patogh

8 Crawford Place, W1 (7262 4015). Edgware Road tube. **Open** 1pm-midnight daily. **Main courses** £5-£9.50. **No credit cards**. **Map** p395 E5.

With just five tables on the ground floor and a similarly sized first floor, Patogh is frequently full ('Come back in half an hour,' staff will say). There's a brief no-frills menu of juicy kebabs, fluffy rice, huge flatbreads and traditional pickles. Smashing.

Modern European

Orrery

55 Marylebone High Street, W1 (7616 8000/ www.orrery.co.uk). Baker Street or Regent's Park tube. **Open** noon-3pm, 7-11pm Mon-Sat; noon-3pm, 7-10.30pm Sun. **Main courses** £14.50-£26. **Credit** AmEx, DC, MC, V. **Map** p398 G4.

The Conran Group's smallest, finest restaurant occupies a bright, skylit space. Its oft-changing Francophile menu is concise, its wine list renowned. Divine renditions of alluring dishes send diners into raptures. The French cheeses and the well-informed service are especially notable. Booking is essential.

Oriental

Selasih

114 Seymour Place, W1 (7724 4454). Edgware Road tube. **Open** noon-3pm, 6-10.30pm daily. **Main courses** £3.95-£17.95. **Credit** AmEx, DC, MC, V. **Map** p395 F5.

The weekday lunchtime buffet (£6.95) at this pretty Malaysian restaurant attracts everyone from Malay families to businessmen. Service can be slow, but the food is distinctive and authentic: fresh roti canai bread with moreish vegetable curry or spicy grilled mackerel in banana leaf. Be sure to book.

Wagamama

101A Wigmore Street, W1 (7409 0111/ www.wagamama.com). Bond Street or Marble Arch tube. **Open** noon-11pm Mon-Sat; 12.30-10.30pm Sun. **Main courses** £5.25-£8.50. **Credit** AmEx, DC, MC, V. **Map** p398 G6.

The much-imitated Wagamama chain of salubrious noodle bars continues to thrive across the city, and not least at this Marylebone outpost. It provides reliably generous portions of low-priced Sino-Japanese meal-in-one dishes, to be eaten at crowded, communal tables in minimalist surroundings. **Branches:** throughout the city.

Mayfair & St James's

British

1837

Brown's Hotel, 33 Albemarle Street, W1 (7408 1837/www.raffles-brownshotel.com). Green Park tube. **Open** 7-10.30am, noon-2.30pm, 7-10pm Mon-Fri; 8-11.30am, 7-10pm Sat; 8-11.30am Sun. **Set meals** *Lunch* £24 2 courses; £29 3 courses; £31 5 courses. *Dinner* £37-£45 grazing menu; £55 chef's selection. **Credit** AmEx, DC, MC, V. **Map** p400 G7.

Oozing that rare charm of effortless abundance, the dining room of this luxury hotel features armchairs and sofas, formal yet friendly staff, and a menu where seafood is a mainstay: lobster and asparagus salad, say, or Cornish crab open ravioli with black truffle and cognac sauce. A great place if you're looking to treat yourself.

Wiltons

55 Jermyn Street, SW1 (7629 9955). Green Park/ Piccadilly Circus tube. **Open** 12.30-2.30pm, 6.30-10.30pm Mon-Sat; 12.30-2.30pm, 6.30-10pm Sun. **Main courses** £15.90-£29.75. **Credit** AmEx, DC, MC, V.

Resolutely English, both in its furnishings (endless paintings, stuffed animals) and its menu (fish and game a speciality), Wiltons epitomises its St James's locale. Still, the food can be refreshingly inventive. Men must don jacket and tie to eat here; everyone must book from Monday to Thursday.

Cafés & brasseries

Victory Café

Basement, Gray's Antiques Market, South Molton Lane, W1 (7495 6860). Bond Street tube. **Open** 10am-6pm Mon-Fri. **No credit cards.** **Map** p398 H6.

The decor at the Victory is a curious blend of 1950s American diner (great jukebox) and post-war British adverts. Food is a mix of greasy spoon breakfasts and club sandwiches. A fun place for a cheap lunch.

Global

Gaucho Grill

19 Swallow Street, W1 (7734 4040). Piccadilly Circus tube. **Open** noon-3pm, 5-11pm Mon-Fri; noon-midnight Sat; noon-10.30pm Sun. **Main courses** £8.50-£32.50. **Credit** AmEx, DC, MC, V. **Map** p400 J7.

The cowhide upholstery leaves no doubts about the métier of this Argentinian steakhouse chain. The elegant, whitewashed restaurant provides a reverential atmosphere in which to devour sensational Argentinian steaks paired with decent side dishes. **Branches:** throughout the city.

Mô

23 Heddon Street, W1 (7434 4040). Piccadilly Circus tube. **Open** 11am-10pm Mon-Wed; noon-10pm Thur-Sat. **Main courses** £4-£8. **Credit** AmEx, DC, MC, V. **Map** p400 J7.

This North African teahouse is a cheaper, simpler option than its famous older sibling Momo next door. Furnished with sofas and Moroccan artefacts, it's an attractive place to enjoy the likes of harira (lamb and lentil soup) and great kofta meatballs.

Indian

Tamarind

20 Queen Street, W1 (7629 3561). Green Park tube. **Open** noon-3pm, 6-11.30pm Mon-Fri; 6-11.30pm Sat; noon-2.30pm, 6-11.30pm Sun. **Main courses** £10.50-£28.60. **Credit** AmEx, DC, MC, V. **Map** p400 H7.

Despite the departure of its star chef, Tamarind looks set to maintain its position in the top echelons of Modern Indian cookery. The excellent menu at the large, strikingly designed basement restaurant is strong on tandoori and north-west Indian dishes (beautifully presented and exquisitely spiced) but ranges across the whole subcontinent.

Eat, Drink, Shop

The extraordinary **Orrery**: Terence Conran's finest hour? *See p199.*

Italian

Cecconi's

5A Burlington Gardens, W1 (7434 1500). Green Park tube. **Open** noon-3pm, 7-11pm daily. **Main courses** £12-£23. **Credit** AmEx, DC, MC, V. **Map** p400 J7.
Sexy leather seating, low lighting and acres of white linen provide a suitable setting for Cecconi's accomplished interpretations of northern Italian cuisine. A meal of sea bass carpaccio followed by veal scallopine could be rounded off with luscious apricot tarte tatin. Staff are enthusiastic, and there's a great drinks list (wines and cocktails).

Middle Eastern

Al Sultan

51-2 Hertford Street, W1 (7408 1155/1166/www. alsultan.co.uk). Green Park or Hyde Park Corner tube. **Open** noon-midnight daily. **Main courses** £10-£12. **Credit** AmEx, DC, MC, V. **Map** p400 H8.
Just off Shepherd Market, this upmarket Lebanese is small and intimate, though formally decorated with linen, floral arrangements and mirrors. Staff are courtly. The attraction is the exemplary meze dishes: savoury sambousek pastries, flavourful loubieh (green beans) and succulent chicken wings.

Modern European

Gordon Ramsay at Claridges

55 Brook Street, W1 (7499 0099). Bond Street tube. **Open** 7-10am, noon-2.45pm, 5.45-11pm Mon-Fri; 8-10am, noon-3.30pm, 5.45-11pm Sat; 8-10am, noon-3.30pm, 6-11pm Sun. **Set meals** *Lunch, pre-theatre meal (5-7pm)* £25 3 courses. *Dinner* £50 3 courses; £60 6 courses. **Credit** AmEx, MC, V. **Map** p398 H6.
The stately art deco setting (surprisingly unstuffy) at Claridges has married well with the beautifully turned out, deliciously light cuisine of chef (and Ramsay protégé) Mark Sargeant. This sparkling pairing, plus keen-as-mustard staff, helped the place win *Time Out* Best New Restaurant in 2002.

Oriental

Kaya

42 Albemarle Street, W1 (7499 0622/0633). Green Park tube. **Open** noon-3pm, 6-11pm Mon-Sat; 6-11pm Sun. **Main courses** £7.50-£17. **Credit** AmEx, DC, MC, V. **Map** p400 J7.
Well considered and precise describes both the food and the service at this upmarket Korean restaurant. Raw cuttlefish and salmon (with rice, vegetables and lashings of raw garlic) is one of the more adventurous main courses. A serene atmosphere prevails.

Eat, Drink, Shop

Kiku

17 Half Moon Street, W1 (7499 4208). Green Park tube. **Open** noon-3pm, 6-10.30pm Mon-Sat; 6-10.30pm Sun. **Main courses** £3-£28. **Credit** AmEx, MC, V. **Map** p400 H8.
This harshly lit hangar of a Japanese restaurant holds some lovely treats for its mostly Japanese customers. You can't go wrong with the sushi or sashimi selection, but prices are high.

Nobu

Metropolitan Hotel, 19 Old Park Lane, W1 (7447 4747). Hyde Park Corner tube. **Open** noon-2.15pm, 6-10.15pm Mon-Thur; noon-2.15pm, 6-11pm Fri; 6-11pm Sat; 6-9.30pm Sun. **Main courses** £5-£27.50. **Credit** AmEx, DC, MC, V. **Map** p400 H8.
Settling down after a stint as the capital's sassiest destination restaurant, Nobu produces inventive Japanese food with Latin American flourishes (black cod in miso is a signature dish). Superb cocktails, sakes and views of Hyde Park add to the draw.

Soho & Chinatown

Cafés & brasseries

Bar Italia

22 Frith Street, W1 (7437 4520). Leicester Square or Tottenham Court Road tube. **Open** 24hrs daily; 7am-4am Sun. **Credit** (noon-3am only) AmEx, DC, MC, V. **Map** p398 K6.
Post-pubbers and pre-clubbers come to perch and preen at this Soho institution. The late drinks licence is a draw, but the coffee and the food – pizza, bagels, panini, cakes, croissants – are passable at best.

Maison Bertaux

28 Greek Street, W1 (7437 6007). Leicester Square or Tottenham Court Road tube. **Open** 8.30am-8pm daily. **No credit cards**. **Map** p399 K6.
Well over a century old, this tiny but congenial French café is one of London's top spots for a coffee and pastry. The croissants are fabulous.

Pâtisserie Valerie

44 Old Compton Street, W1 (7437 3466/ www.patisserie-valerie.co.uk). Leicester Square tube. **Open** 7.30am-8.30pm Mon-Sat; 9.30am-7pm Sun. **Credit** AmEx, MC, V. **Map** p399 K6.
Famous for its pastries and cakes, this venerable and attractive Franco-Belgian café can also provide English breakfasts (until 4pm), pastas and meat dishes, great coffee and (upstairs) wine and beer. **Branches**: throughout the city.

Star Café

22 Great Chapel Street, W1 (7437 8778). Tottenham Court Road tube. **Open** 7am-4pm Mon-Fri. **Main courses** £4.45-£6.90. **No credit cards**. **Map** p399 K6.
A caff with style, the Star is decked out in vintage advertising paraphernalia. Slick staff serve fresh sandwiches, pastas, daily lunch specials, plus a splendid array of breakfasts.

Chinese

China City

White Bear Yard, 25A Lisle Street, WC2 (7734 3388/www.chinacityrestaurant.co.uk). Leicester Square tube. **Open** noon-11.45pm Mon-Sat; 11.30am-10.15pm Sun; dim sum noon-5pm Mon-Sat; 11.30am-5pm Sun. **Main courses** £2-£22.50. *Dim sum* £1.80-£3.50. *Minimum* £10 dinner. **Credit** AmEx, MC, V. **Map** p401 K7.
Our favourite Chinatown dim sum venue is bright, spacious and reached through a courtyard off Lisle Street. Feast on delicate snacks such as char siu pork puffs, Japanese-style octopus and yin-yan cheung fun pasta. The full menu takes in most facets of Cantonese cuisine.

ECapital

8 Gerrard Street, W1 (7434 3838). Leicester Square tube. **Open** noon-11.30pm Mon-Thur, Sun; noon-midnight Fri, Sat. **Main courses** £6-£22. *Minimum* £10 dinner. **Credit** AmEx, MC, V. **Map** p401 K7.
Newly opened, ECapital has produced London's first real eastern Chinese menu. Head for the specials list to find rarities such as 'lion's head' pork meatballs (red-braised in sweetish soy sauce) and 'beggar's chicken' filled with mushrooms and pickles. Helpful staff run the simply furnished restaurant.

Mr Kong

21 Lisle Street, WC2 (7437 7341/9679). Leicester Square tube. **Open** noon-2.45am daily. **Main courses** £5-£26. *Minimum* £7 after 5pm. **Credit** AmEx, DC, MC, V. **Map** p401 K7.
A great place for novices to discover 'real' Chinese cuisine, Mr Kong has a specials list offering wonderful dishes that rarely appear on English-language menus. Braised belly pork with yam in hot-pot is quite delicious, as is 'deep-fried pig's intestine with spicy salt' (honest). The best of the three dining rooms is on the first floor. Staff are fairly congenial.

New Diamond

23 Lisle Street, WC2 (7437 2517/7221). Leicester Square tube. **Open** noon-3am daily. **Main courses** £5.80-£22. *Minimum* £10 from 5pm. **Credit** AmEx, DC, MC, V. **Map** p401 K7.
Like Mr Kong (*see above*), New Diamond makes proper Cantonese cuisine accessible to non-Chinese: from hot-pots to stir-fries (razor clams with asparagus in XO sauce, say). White walls together with trendy spotlighting produce a pleasing effect.

French

La Trouvaille

12A Newburgh Street, W1 (7287 8488). Oxford Circus tube. **Open** noon-3pm, 6-11pm Mon-Sat. **Main courses** £9.50-£17. **Credit** AmEx, MC, V. **Map** p398 J6.
'The Find' is that rare thing: a classy, cool yet utterly relaxed French restaurant with an exciting menu. Perhaps start with carpaccio of scallops with

Super noodles and other sturdy belly-fillers at **Melati**.

vanilla and pomegranate and move on to oxtail with mash topped with a crayfish, finishing with celery and green apple crème brûlée. Staff are delightful.

the exquisite cannelloni and the splendid carpaccio of pineapple. Bohemian-smart decor, charming staff and a huge wine list are added incentives.

Indian

Masala Zone

9 Marshall Street, W1 (7287 9966). Oxford Circus tube. **Open** noon-2.45pm, 5.30-11pm Mon-Fri; 3-5pm Sat (snacks only); 12.30-3.30pm, 6-10.30pm Sun. **Main courses** £5-£9.50. **Credit** MC, V. **Map** p398 J6.
Ignore the bleak concrete exterior: inside, this refectory-style venue mixes modern industrial design with enchanting Indian tribal art. The menu lists light bites and meal-in-one curries, including thalis. Gujarati vegetarian food is a highlight. Prices are low for the West End, staff are highly proficient and there's a real buzz to the place.

Italian

Quo Vadis

26-9 Dean Street, W1 (7437 9585/ www.whitestarline.org.uk). Leicester Square, Piccadilly Circus or Tottenham Court Road tube. **Open** noon-2.30pm, 5.30-11.30pm Mon-Fri; 5.30-11.30pm Sat. **Main courses** £10.75-£16.50. **Credit** AmEx, MC, V. **Map** p399 K6.
Part of Marco Pierre White's stable of thoroughbreds, Quo Vadis has been given a menu-makeover by chef Curtis Stone. Choice ingredients are handled with verve: witness the cappuccino of mushrooms,

Oriental

Kulu Kulu

76 Brewer Street, W1 (7734 7316). Piccadilly Circus tube. **Open** noon-2.30pm, 5-10pm Mon-Fri; noon-3.45pm, 5-10pm Sat. **Main courses** *Sushi* £1.20-£3. **Credit** MC, V. **Map** p400 J7.
This is the ideal Soho sushi joint: packed, popular and a little rough round the edges. The colour-coded dishes circulate on a conveyor (though you can also order directly from the chef). The selection is impressive, fresh and cheap, though portions are small. **Branch**: 39 Thurlow Place, South Kensington, SW7 (7589 2225).

Melati

21 Great Windmill Street, W1 (7437 2745). Piccadilly Circus tube. **Open** noon-11.30pm Mon-Thur, Sun; noon-12.30am Fri, Sat. **Main courses** £5.95-£7.85. **Credit** AmEx, MC, V. **Map** p401 K7.
A real old-stager, Melati has been dishing up Malaysian and Indonesian scran for years. Don't expect subtlety: this is basic stomach-lining food. But as basic, stomach-lining food goes, it's very good.

Ramen Seto

19 Kingly Street, W1 (7434 0309). Oxford Circus tube. **Open** noon-3pm, 6-10pm Mon-Sat. **Main courses** £4.50-£6.80. **Credit** MC, V. **Map** p398 J6.

Ramen is the forte at this pocket-sized eat-in and take-away joint: steaming bowls of egg noodles in soups, or plates of it fried and topped. Rice dishes, sashimi and sushi are also served by the friendly staff.

Saigon

45 Frith Street, W1 (7437 7109). Leicester Square tube. **Open** noon-11.30pm Mon-Sat. **Main courses** £3-£13.75. **Credit** AmEx, DC, MC, V. **Map** p399 K6.
A tranquil place, this Vietnamese venue is furnished in dark wood and bamboo. Food lacks a spicy punch, but the menu lists some interesting specials among the stir-fries. Young waitresses provide advice.

Sri Thai Soho

16 Old Compton Street, W1 (7434 3544). Leicester Square tube. **Open** noon-3pm, 6-11pm Mon-Sat; 6-10.30pm Sun. **Main courses** £7.50-£10.95. **Credit** AmEx, DC, MC, V. **Map** p399 K6.
The perfect place to sit back and soak up the funky vibe, sipping on a mango Margarita. The long menu includes good-value set meals, plus an extensive, pricier à la carte. Massaman curry oozes warm, meaty flavours. Staff are personable and friendly.
Branch: Bucklersbury House, 3 Queen Victoria Street, the City, EC4 (7628 5772).

Modern European

Alastair Little

49 Frith Street, W1 (7734 5183). Leicester Square or Tottenham Court Road tube. **Open** noon-3pm, 6-11pm Mon-Fri; 6-11pm Sat. **Set meals** *Lunch* £27 3 courses. *Dinner* £35 3 courses. **Credit** AmEx, MC, V. **Map** p399 K6.
Though Little no longer cooks here, his restaurant continues to defy Soho's flashy, cashy aesthetic. The daily changing set menu is imaginative, seasonal, eclectic and impressive. A summer's meal might start with roquefort and rosemary pizza, continue with wild salmon and broad beans with radish salad, and end with crème brûlée. Service is top rate.
Branch: 136A Lancaster Road, Notting Hill, W11 (7243 2220).

Andrew Edmunds

46 Lexington Street, W1 (7437 5708). Oxford Circus or Piccadilly Circus tube. **Open** 12.30-3pm, 6-10.45pm Mon-Fri; 1-3pm, 6-10.45pm Sat; 1-3pm, 6-10.30pm Sun. **Main courses** £7.95-£13. **Credit** AmEx, MC, V. **Map** p398 J6.
This bistro is all cosy corners and candles, and has managed to maintain an air of the well-kept secret (there's no name outside). A meal here is always a pleasure: it might begin with unadorned, thickly sliced smoked salmon, followed by braised rabbit in a white wine and tarragon sauce, then lemon tart.

Sugar Club

21 Warwick Street, W1 (7437 7776). Oxford Circus or Piccadilly Circus tube. **Open** noon-3pm, 5.30-10.30pm Mon-Sat; 12.30-3pm, 5.30-10.30pm Sun. **Main courses** £12-£24. **Credit** AmEx, DC, MC, V. **Map** p400 J7.

The plain decor at this two-floor restaurant (lively groundfloor, quieter basement) contrasts with the exotic menu: spicy kangaroo salad, anyone? Organic and wild produce are used where possible and the results can be thrilling, if costly (yet the £24 John Dory is worth every penny). Booking is essential.

Vegetarian & organic

Mildred's

45 Lexington Street, W1 (7494 1634). Oxford Circus or Piccadilly Circus tube. **Open** noon-11pm Mon-Sat. **Main courses** £4.90-£6.50. **No credit cards.** **Map** p399 K6.
Newly relocated from nearby Greek Street, Mildred's remains small, jolly and rammed. Customers know they can rely on substantial portions of the likes of ale pie (packed with marinated tofu and mushrooms) followed by double chocolate pudding. Delicious.

Covent Garden & St Giles's

Belgian

Belgo Centraal

50 Earlham Street, WC2 (7813 2233/ www.belgorestaurants.com). Covent Garden tube. **Open** noon-11pm Mon-Thur; noon-11.30pm Fri, Sat; noon-10.30pm Sun. **Main courses** £8.75-£17.95. **Credit** AmEx, DC, MC, V. **Map** p399 L6.
This flagship branch of the seafood, chips and beer chain – which also gave birth to the Bierodrome franchises – is themed as a monastic refectory. It occupies a vast post-industrial basement, reached by industrial lifts, and can get noisy, hot and stuffy when busy (which is often). Service is swift.
Branch: 72 Chalk Farm Road, Camden, NW1 (7267 0718).

British

Simpson's-in-the-Strand

100 Strand, WC2 (7836 9112/www.simpsons-in-the-strand.com). Charing Cross tube/rail. **Open** 7.15-10.30am, 12.15-2.30pm, 5.30-10.45pm Mon-Fri; 12.15-2.30pm, 5.30-10.45pm Sat; noon-3pm, 6-8.30pm Sun. **Main courses** £22.50-£23.50. *Minimum* £10 breakfast. **Credit** AmEx, DC, MC, V. **Map** p401 L7.
Grand, staunchly traditional and dating back to the early 19th century, Simpson's is famed for its roast meats, served flamboyantly at table from a trolley by cheerful staff. The splendid breakfasts offer a cheaper way of savouring the surroundings.

Cafés & brasseries

Zoomslide Café

Photographers' Gallery, 5 Great Newport Street, WC2 (7831 1772/www.photonet.org.uk). Leicester Square tube. **Open** 11am-5.30pm Mon-Sat; noon-5.30pm Sun. **No credit cards.** **Map** p401 K6.

Eat, Drink, Shop

London loves The Sunday roast

The British Sunday lunch is a ritual. The eating, of course, but also the planning, the shopping and cooking. It's got to be a big affair: why else would you spend half the day cooking something that's going to be devoured in less than 15 minutes?

Everyone has their say on how it should be done, and the arguments begin over the meat. If you pick chicken, it's relatively straightforward: no blood, and anyone who likes it dry and stringy hasn't been brought up properly. There's always the question of whether you're a breast, leg or thigh person, but the British aren't truly British if they have to fight over a bird. A joint of beef is a whole different story, though: well-cooked, rare or downright bloody?

Well, if you come to our house, this is what you'll get. Beef: a huge slab, roasted, bloody in the middle but brown at either end for the wimps. It's cut so fine that it'll melt on your plate beside the small crispy roast potatoes, which have little crunchy bits hanging off them for you to pick at while you politely wait for the real eating to begin. A cushion

of Yorkshire pudding (a mix of flour, eggs, milk and salt, baked and basted), frilly at the edges with a cute little dip in the middle. Carrots and broccoli in copious supply, boiled al dente. The whole lot topped with lashings of a light and thin gravy made with onions and a drop of Marsala to give it that extra kick. And, of course, lots of deep, rich red wine.

Failing that (and, let's be honest, we're not going to ask you around to ours no matter how nicely you ask)? You may get lucky in a pub, but you'll more than likely get something overcooked or underheated. Instead, try **Sonny's** in Barnes (94 Church Road, SW13; 8748 0393), which does an excellent slap-up three-course Sunday lunch for just £19; the **Butler's Wharf Chop House** (Butler's Wharf Building, 36E Shad Thames, SE1; 7403 3403), with its wonderful terrace view in the summer; and the mighty **Simpson's-in-the-Strand** (see p203), where you'll have the proper traditional British experience with waiters in penguin suits and a slab of meat wheeled in on a silver trolley. Sit back and pass the joint around.

A peaceful retreat from Leicester Square, this gallery café provides pastas, salads, rolls, cakes and a decent choice of coffees, teas and fresh juices.

Fish

J Sheekey
*28-32 St Martin's Court, WC2 (7240 2565).
Leicester Square tube.* **Open** noon-3pm, 5.30pm-midnight Mon-Sat; noon-3.30pm, 5.30pm-midnight Sun. **Main courses** £9.75-£24.50. **Credit** AmEx, DC, MC, V. **Map** p401 K7.
A discreet, intimate restaurant with oak-panelled walls, spacious seating, highly professional staff and superbly cooked fish. The menu is short and to the point, making the most of market-fresh fish, with classic or subtly unusual additions: anchovies with horseradish sauce, say. Seafood dining at its best.

Fish & chips

Rock & Sole Plaice
47 Endell Street, WC2 (7836 3785). Covent Garden tube. **Open** 11.30am-10pm Mon-Sat; noon-10pm Sun. **Main courses** £7-£13. **Credit** MC, V. **Map** p399 L6.
Decades old, this chippie manages to sell tasty, fairly priced cod, chips and mushy peas (as well as Dover sole and sardines) despite the touristification of Covent Garden. Eat outside in fine weather.

French

The Admiralty
*Somerset House, Strand, WC2 (7845 4646).
Charing Cross tube/rail.* **Open** noon-2.45pm, 6-10.45pm Mon-Sat; noon-2.45pm Sun. **Set meals** *Lunch, pre-theatre dinner (6-7pm Mon-Fri)* £25 3 courses. *Dinner* £28 2 courses; £33 3 courses; £37 5 courses (vegetarian); £42 5 courses (dégustation). **Credit** AmEx, DC, MC, V. **Map** p401 L7.
In the breathtaking setting of Somerset House (see p98), the Admiralty is adorned in rich colours and enhanced by beautiful chandeliers and preserved fauna. Food – foie gras terrine with Beaumes de Venise jelly, followed by roast partridge, say – is highly sophisticated, and staff serve it with panache.

Modern European

The Ivy
1 West Street, WC2 (7836 4751). Leicester Square tube. **Open** noon-3pm, 5.30pm-midnight Mon-Sat; noon-3.30pm, 5.30pm-midnight Sun. **Main courses** £8.75-£21.75. **Credit** AmEx, DC, MC, V. **Map** p399 K6.
Celeb-zone nonpareil, the Ivy is notoriously difficult for non-luminaries to penetrate (book six months in advance, choosing an unfashionable slot). Once

ensconced, you'll find courteous staff, smart but understated decor (behind stained-glass windows) and a menu offering sparkling renditions of French and British dishes, plus a scattering of fusion food.

Vegetarian & organic

Food for Thought

31 Neal Street, WC2 (7836 9072). Covent Garden tube. **Open** 9.30-11.30am, noon-8.30pm Mon-Sat; noon-5pm Sun. **Main courses** £3-£6.50. *Minimum* £2.50 (noon-3pm, 6-7.30pm). **No credit cards. Map** p399 L6.

The formula here hasn't changed much since it opened nearly 30 years ago: amiable service, cosy surroundings (shared tables) and a daily menu of low-priced tasty food: quiches, salads, stir-fries. Handy for Neal Street shopping, but queues form.

World Food Café

1st floor, 14 Neal's Yard, WC2 (7379 0298/ www.worldfoodcafe.com). Covent Garden tube. **Open** 11.30am-4.30pm Mon-Fri; 11.30am-5pm Sat. **Main courses** £4.65-£7.95. **Minimum** £5 (noon-2pm Mon-Fri; 11.30am-5pm Sat). **Credit** MC, V. **Map** p399 L6.

An open kitchen, three big shared tables and views over Neal's Yard create a pleasing, alternative environment in which to enjoy vegetarian 'world food': from Mexican platters to West African sweet potato stew. Standards vary, but the juices are superb.

Westminster

British

Shepherd's

Marsham Court, Marsham Street, SW1 (7834 9552). Pimlico or Westminster tube. **Open** 12.30-2.45pm, 6.30-11pm Mon-Fri. **Main courses** £18.50. **Credit** AmEx, DC, MC, V. **Map** p401 K10.

Pillars and partitions create intimate spaces for Westminster's political animals (MPs, journos, the odd peer) to plot in comfort at Shepherd's. The food is reliably good if unspectacular: grilled lemon sole, rump of lamb, calorific puds.

Cafés & brasseries

Café in the Crypt

St Martin-in-the-Fields, Duncannon Street, WC2 (7839 4342). Charing Cross tube/rail. **Open** noon-3pm, 5-7.30pm Mon-Wed; noon-3pm, 8.30-10.30pm Thur-Sat; noon-3pm Sun. **Main courses** £5.95-£7.50. **No credit cards. Map** p401 K7.

Wholesome good-value food, ranging from hearty casseroles to salads and British puds, is served by sociable staff from a cafeteria-style counter. The subterranean surroundings of the crypt are impressive, and the location – set back from Trafalgar Square – convenient if the National Gallery is on your day's agenda.

Indian

Cinnamon Club

Old Westminster Library, Great Smith Street, SW1 (7222 2555). St James's Park tube. **Open** 7.30-10am, noon-3pm, 6-11pm Mon-Fri; 6-11pm Sat; noon-3pm Sun. **Set meals** *Lunch* £15 2 courses; £18 3 courses. **Credit** MC, V. **Map** p401 K9.

Besuited power-brokers have taken to this formal, slightly old-fashioned place, although – perhaps surprisingly – there's nothing whatsoever staid about the food. Unusual (venison, tuna) and traditional ingredients appear in beautifully presented, sensitively spiced dishes, with especially inventive puddings. Booking is essential.

Quilon

St James's Court Hotel, 41 Buckingham Gate, SW1 (7821 1899). St James's Park tube. **Open** noon-2.30pm, 6-11pm Mon-Fri; 6-11pm Sat. **Main courses** £12.95-£21.95. **Credit** AmEx, DC, MC, V. **Map** p400 J9.

Run by India's Taj Hotel group, this upmarket Keralan restaurant is decked out in vibrant blue and orange. Service is exemplary. Own-made chutneys, complimentary rasam (peppery soup) in a glass and fine renditions of vegetarian, seafood, coconut and yoghurt-based dishes confirm Quilon's class.

Knightsbridge & South Kensington

Global

Jakob's

20 Gloucester Road, SW7 (7581 9292). Gloucester Road tube. **Open** 8am-10pm Mon-Sat; 8am-5pm Sun. **Main courses** £5-£8. **Credit** AmEx, MC, V. **Map** p396 C9.

This homespun, friendly Armenian café/restaurant makes a perfect lunchtime pre- or post-shopping stop. Choose from dozens of ultra-fresh salads, marinated kebabs, stuffed cabbage leaves and houmous at the salad counter, and accompany them with warm flatbread and splendid wine.

Modern European

La Tante Claire

The Berkeley, Wilton Place, SW1 (7823 2003). Knightsbridge tube. **Open** 12.30-2pm, 7-11pm Mon-Fri; 7-11pm Sat. **Main courses** £23-£35. **Minimum** £50 dinner. **Credit** AmEx, DC, MC, V. **Map** p400 G8.

London's best restaurant? La Tante must be in the running, as Pierre Koffmann stays diligently in the kitchen creating dishes of rare brilliance by elevating accepted flavour combinations to the heights. Menus are in French, though waiters are pleased to translate; expert sommeliers guide you through the substantial wine list. You'll need to book.

Eat, Drink, Shop

London loves Gordon Ramsay

It may soon be possible to mention Gordon Ramsay without using adjectives like 'aggressive' and 'foul-mouthed'. In 2002 he won the *Time Out* Special Award for Outstanding Achievement, along with the Perrier Award for Best New Restaurant for **Gordon Ramsay at Claridges** (*see p200*). Ramsay had taken on Claridges in September 2001, having become the only chef in London to hold a third Michelin star (for his restaurant **Gordon Ramsay**; *pictured*; *see p209*). Critics said standards would drop if he ran both places. Ramsay didn't agree. Ramsay was right.

Ramsay's biography is as interesting as it is becoming well known. He was a 17-year-old apprentice footballer for Glasgow Rangers before knee injuries led Rangers to let him go as a 19-year-old after only two brief first-team appearances. He then made rapid progress from an HND in Hotel Management to Marco Pierre White's kitchen, and thence via the best teachers in England (Albert Roux, Pierre Koffman) to France to hone his skills. Opening Aubergine at the age of 26, Ramsay had won his first Michelin star in two years and his second in only four. He then fell out with his backers, and founded his eponymous restaurant.

After his irascible turns on *Boiling Point*, a fly-on-the-wall TV documentary aired in 1998 in which he was filmed being spectacularly beastly to his staff, Ramsay's temper became as famous as his cooking. But he has also made it clear that he considers a great restaurant to be a team effort. Comparing his staff to Manchester United, he talks of how he's nurturing the culinary stars of the future; he demands the highest standards from his staff, but insists their efforts be acknowledged. Protegés Marcus Wareing at **Pétrus** (33 St James's Street, SW1; 7930 4272/www.petrus-restaurant.com) and Angela Hartnett at the **Connaught** (Carlos Place, W1; 7499 7070/www.savoy-group.co.uk) are showing the value of the Ramsay method. As he puts it: 'When people have been waiting two to three months, paying a hundred quid a head, I don't give a fuck what the public say. I want it perfect.'

Oriental

Vong
The Berkeley, Wilton Place, SW1 (7235 1010/ www.jean-georges.com). Hyde Park Corner tube. **Open** noon-2.30pm, 6-11.30pm Mon-Sat; 6-10.30pm Sun. **Main courses** £16-£32. **Credit** AmEx, DC, MC, V. **Map** p400 G8.
Despite the 1980s-style oriental decor, Vong exudes class. Its pan-oriental menu encompasses satays, lobster and daikon rolls, and sirloin steak in soy caramel sauce. Start with the sublime 'black plate' selection of starters. The high prices mean most customers are business diners. Service is first rate.

Spanish

Cambio de Tercio
163 Old Brompton Road, SW5 (7244 8970). Gloucester Road tube. **Open** 12.30-2.30pm, 7-11.30pm Mon-Sat; 12.30-2.30pm, 7-11pm Sun. **Main courses** £13.50-£15.50. **Credit** AmEx, MC, V. **Map** p396 C11.
The vivid colour scheme is no indication of the subtlety of Cambio's cuisine: witness the carpaccio of sliced monkfish scented with vanilla and served with salmorejo (aka gazpacho) sorbet. Wines include serious Spanish vintages. Staff don't speak much English, but people flock here for the food.

Belgravia & Pimlico

British

Boisdale
15 Eccleston Street, SW1 (7730 6922/ www.boisdale.co.uk). Victoria tube/rail. **Open** noon-2.30pm, 7-10.30pm Mon-Fri; 7-10.30pm Sat. **Main courses** £15-£25. **Credit** AmEx, DC, MC, V. **Map** p400 H10.
The Scottish-inspired food here includes Highland game terrine and offal, game or fish of the day. Boisdale has a small front dining room, a covered open space, a cosy back bar and a large open-plan restaurant/bar where jazz is played. Whisky and cigars are additional fortes.

Italian

Zafferano
15 Lowndes Street, SW1 (7235 5800). Knightsbridge tube. **Open** noon-2.30pm, 7-11pm Mon-Sat; noon-2.30pm, 7-10.30pm Sun. **Set meals** *Lunch* £19.50 2 courses; £24.50 3 courses; £28.50 4 courses. *Dinner* £29.50 2 courses; £37.50 3 courses; £41.50 4 courses. **Credit** AmEx, DC, MC, V. **Map** p397 F9.
Food verges on the stupendous at this deservedly popular spot, from the wonderful bread basket to the glorious desserts, via excellent meat and pasta dishes. Charming staff make for a relaxing atmosphere. Booking is essential.

Oriental

Hunan
51 Pimlico Road, SW1 (7730 5712). Sloane Square tube. **Open** noon-2.30pm, 6-11pm Mon-Sat. **Main courses** £7-£28. **Credit** AmEx, MC, V. **Map** p400 G11.
The trick at this smart little place is to phone ahead and opt for the 'leave it to us' feast, asking for typical Hunanese cuisine. Expect a long, delightful sequence of little dishes unknown at other London restaurants, and a merry dance of flavours.

Nahm
Halkin Hotel, Halkin Street, SW1 (7333 1234/ www.halkin.co.uk). Hyde Park Corner tube. **Open** noon-2.30pm, 7-10.30pm Mon-Fri; 7-10.30pm Sat; 7-10pm Sun. **Main courses** £24-£29. **Credit** AmEx, DC, MC, V. **Map** p400 G9.
The nuances and flavours of Thai cooking are perfectly captured by Aussie chef David Thompson. Dishes are imaginative, though the menu can be confusing and the prices high. Golden columns and marble flooring produce a classy if sterile ambience.

Chelsea

Cafés & brasseries

Top Floor at Peter Jones
Sloane Square, SW1 (7730 3434). Sloane Square tube. **Open** 9.30am-7pm Mon-Sat. **Main courses** £3.50-£13. **Credit** MC, V. **Map** p400 G11.
Perfectly sited to give your credit card a cooling-off period after a King's Road shopping spree, this self-service brasserie occupies a large, slightly impersonal space circling an open atrium looking down into the department store. The food (sandwiches, salads, divine desserts) is good and well priced.

Indian

Chutney Mary
535 King's Road, SW10 (7351 3113/ www.realindianfood.com). Fulham Broadway tube/ West Brompton tube/rail/11, 22 bus. **Open** 6.30-11pm Mon-Fri; 12.30-2.30pm, 6.30-11pm Sat; 12.30-3pm, 6.30-10.30pm Sun. **Main courses** £12.50-£24. **Credit** AmEx, DC, MC, V. **Map** p396 C13.
Newly redecorated with mirrorwork fabrics on walls, this split-level basement restaurant is dedicated to unearthing regional Indian culinary gems. These share the menu with modern Indian creations such as tandoori chops with avocado chutney. Anglo-Indian comfort-puddings are also highlights.

Modern European

Bibendum
Michelin House, 81 Fulham Road, SW3 (7581 5817/ www.bibendum.co.uk). South Kensington tube. **Open** noon-2.30pm, 7-11pm Mon-Fri; 12.30-3pm, 7-11pm

Eat, Drink, Shop

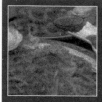

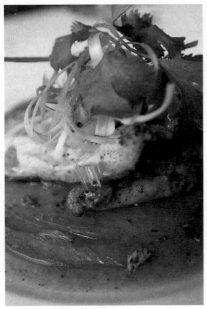

Camden's **Mango Room**.

Sat; 12.30-3pm, 7-10.30pm Sun. **Main courses**
Lunch £15.50-£26.50. **Credit** AmEx, DC, MC, V.
Map p397 E10.
Spacious and airy, with fantastic stained-glass windows, Michelin House makes a handsome venue; Matthew Harris's cooking, encompassing the likes of milk-fed lamb with garlic and mint gravy, is similarly sublime. Staff can be aloof, though, and the (massive) wine list is pricey. Book ahead.

Gordon Ramsay
*68-9 Royal Hospital Road, SW3 (7352 4441/3334/
www.gordonramsay.com). Sloane Square tube.*
Open noon-2pm, 6.45-11pm Mon-Fri. **Set meals**
Lunch £35 3 courses. *Meal* £65 3 courses; £80 7
courses. **Credit** AmEx, DC, MC, V. **Map** p397 F12.
You'll need to book months in advance to sample Ramsay's world-class cooking. The restaurant is square and elegant, the many-peopled service polite and attentive, the atmosphere surprisingly jolly for such hallowed turf. The food, though, stops you in your gustatory tracks.

North London

Cafés & brasseries

Louis Pâtisserie
*32 Heath Street, Hampstead, NW3 (7435 9908).
Hampstead tube.* **Open** 9am-6pm daily. **Main
courses** £1.60-£2.50. **No credit cards.**

There's a Hungarian slant to this old-fashioned tea-room, evident in the style of the splendid cakes and pastries, and in the provenance of the staff.
Branch: Louis Hungarian Pâtisserie, 12 Harben Parade, NW3 (7722 8100).

Global

Afghan Kitchen
*35 Islington Green, Islington, N1 (7359 8019). Angel
tube.* **Open** noon-3.30pm, 5.30-11pm Tue-Sat. **Main
courses** £4.50-£6. **No credit cards. Map** p402 O2.
Afghan home cooking – like Indian but with Persian influences – is reproduced in pre-prepared, pared-down form at this popular, bare-walled place. There are only two communal wooden tables downstairs and four upstairs, so expect to queue.

Bloom's
*130 Golders Green Road, Golders Green, NW11
(8455 1338).* **Open** noon-11pm Mon-Thur, Sun;
noon-3pm Fri. **Main courses** £6.50-£14.90.
Credit AmEx, MC, V.
Bloom's is an integral part of the London Jewish community's culinary experience. Food is a roll-call of classic (and very filling) Jewish dishes: chicken soup with kreplach, salt-beef sandwiches, chopped liver. Bright street scenes of Israel decorate the place.

Mango Room
*10 Kentish Town Road, Camden, NW1 (7482
5065). Camden Town tube.* **Open** 6pm-midnight
Mon; noon-3pm, 6pm-midnight Tue-Sat; noon-11pm
Sun. **Main courses** £9-£12. **Credit** MC, V.
Caribbean cuisine, both traditional and modern, is the stock-in-trade of this highly popular restaurant. Grilled goat's cheese with mango, pesto sauce and mixed-leaf salad might precede char-grilled pork loin with jerk sauce. Service can be slow, so grab a cocktail and admire the vibrantly coloured interior.

Mediterranean

Café Corfu
*7-9 Pratt Street, Camden, NW1 (7267 8088).
Camden Town tube.* **Open** noon-10.30pm Mon-Thur,
Sun; noon-11.30pm Fri, Sat. **Main courses** £7.95-
£14. **Credit** MC, V.
Trendy yet not pretentious, Café Corfu creates cutting-edge mainland and island Greek cooking including (unusually) plenty for vegetarians. The wine list is an added draw to this stylish place.

Iznik
*19 Highbury Park, Highbury, N5 (7354 5697). Arsenal
tube/Highbury & Islington tube/rail.* **Open** 10am-4pm,
6.30pm-midnight Mon-Fri; 6.30pm-midnight Sat, Sun.
Main courses £7.50-£9.50. **Credit** MC, V.
Iznik continues to produce outstanding northern Turkish bakes and stews. The Ottoman-inspired menu delivers strong, accomplished flavours; the room (decorated with Iznik- and Beykoz-style ceramics) is pretty; service is friendly and efficient.

Eat, Drink, Shop

Singapore Garden, the archetype of an excellent local restaurant.

Sariyer Balik

56 Green Lanes, Newington Green, N16 (7275 7681). Bus 141, 341. **Open** 5pm-1am daily. **Main courses** £6.50-£10. **No credit cards**.
Winner of the *Time Out* Best Turkish Restaurant award in 2002, this tiny venue specialises in marine life: mussels marinated in beer and deep-fried; lemony octopus salad; char-grilled bass. Fishing nets decorate the black-painted interior: you'll believe you're dining on the shore of the Bosphorus.

Oriental

Jin Kichi

73 Heath Street, Hampstead, NW3 (7794 6158). Hampstead tube. **Open** 6-11pm Tue-Fri; 12.30-2pm, 6-11pm Sat; 12.30-2pm, 6-10pm Sun. **Main courses** £5.30-£12.70. **Credit** AmEx, DC, MC, V.
This long-standing Hampstead favourite specialises in Japanese robatayaki cooking: a grill takes centre stage, with half a dozen wooden tables squeezed around the perimeter. There are many unusual dishes, plus great vegetable tempura and expertly prepared (if costly) sushi and sashimi.

Singapore Garden

83 Fairfax Road, Belsize Park, NW6 (7624 8233). Swiss Cottage tube. **Open** noon-2.45pm, 6-10.45pm Mon-Thur, Sun; noon-2.45pm, 6-11.15pm Fri, Sat. **Main courses** £6-£30. **Minimum** £10. **Credit** AmEx, DC, MC, V.

A pleasantly classy restaurant, featuring bright paintings, a jazz soundtrack and a menu that reflects Singapore's ethnic make-up: succulent chicken satay, Nonya beansprouts (paired with chewy dried fish), oyster omelette and, to drink, Tiger beer.

Vegetarian & organic

Heartstone

106 Parkway, Camden, NW1 (7485 7744). Camden Town tube. **Open** 9am-9pm Tue-Sat; 10am-4pm Sun. **Main courses** £8.50-£15. **Credit** MC, V.
A refuge of good living in Camden, this brasserie has a kind of 'brown rice with attitude' approach to organic food. Fresh tasting, simply cooked ingredients (including the occasional meat and fish dish) deliver masses of flavour. Prices are fair.

East London

Cafés & brasseries

Brick Lane Beigel Bake

159 Brick Lane, Shoreditch, E1 (7729 0616). Shoreditch tube. **Open** 24hrs daily. **No credit cards. Map** p403 S4.
The best bagels in Britain, served around the clock in characterful fashion by East End dahlins at magnificently low prices. A London institution; accept no substitute.

Jones Dairy Café

23 Ezra Street, Bethnal Green, E2 (7739 5372).
Bus 26, 48, 55. **Open** 9am-3pm Fri, Sat; 8am-3pm
Sun. **No credit cards. Map** p403 S3.
A great little café attached to an equally small shop.
Hot dishes include breakfast staples and poached
smoked haddock, or filling soup. Pastries and good
coffee could follow. During Columbia Road flower
market on Sundays, it's more of a takeaway place.

Global

Arkansas Café

Unit 12, 107B Commercial Street, Old Spitalfields
Market, Spitalfields, E1 (7377 6999). Liverpool
Street tube/rail. **Open** noon-2.30pm Mon-Fri;
noon-4pm Sun; dinner by arrangement.
Main courses £3.50-£13.50. **Credit** MC, V.
Map p403 R5.
Free-range pork ribs, Irish and US steaks, and
French corn-fed chicken all come under the grill at
this quirky American diner run by a gentleman
named Bubba. Rustic old chairs and beaten-up
tables soon fill at lunchtime with City workers (and
market-goers on Sundays) eager for juicy meats in
ample helpings.

Little Georgia

2 Broadway Market, London Fields, E8 (7249 9070).
Bus 26, 48, 55, 106, 236. **Open** 7-10pm Tue-Thur,
7-10.30pm Fri, Sat. **Main courses** £7.50-£12.
Credit MC, V.
This cosy modern Georgian restaurant in this newly
gentrified district provides excellent home cooking
in simple surroundings. Try the superb mixed meze
with khachapuri (Georgian cheesy flatbread), and
satsivi aubergine (with walnut sauce).

Indian

Café Spice Namaste

16 Prescot Street, Whitechapel, E1 (7488 9242/
www.cafespice.co.uk). Tower Hill tube/Tower
Gateway DLR. **Open** noon-3pm, 6.15-10.30pm Mon-
Fri; 6.30-10.30pm Sat. **Main courses** £9.95-£15.95.
Credit AmEx, DC, MC, V. **Map** p405 S7.
Top Indian chef Cyrus Todiwala has dressed up this
former magistrate's court in vibrant colours. His
food is equally inventive. Alongside traditional Parsi
dishes you'll find the likes of wild boar sausages and
duck tikka. The dhansaks (spicy meat and lentil
stews) are marvellous. Customers, mostly City workers, are tended to by highly efficient staff.

Eat, Drink, Shop

London loves Curry

The curry made its first appearance in London
in a coffee house in 1773, 150 years after
the East India Company first started importing
tea and spices. However, it took another
200 years for the dish to achieve national
ubiquity, with virtually every high street in
Britain now boasting a Taj Mahal of its own.
The British have taken the curry to their
heart: they spend £2.5 billion on Indian
food each year, and there are over 60,000
people employed in Indian restaurants.
MP Robin Cook, then the Foreign Secretary,
even commented in 2001 that the national
consumption of chicken tikka masala could
be taken as evidence that Britain is a truly
multicultural country.

Despite our fondness for the food, though,
the curry stereotype for close to two decades
has been that of the lager-loving lad and his
pals turning up at the local Indian after
closing time to continue boozing over a
few plates of chicken tikka masala – or the
hotter vindaloo for the more adventurous/
masochistic – nan bread, poppadoms and
onion bhajis, accompanied by the occasional
racist comment to the waiter. It's true that
the curry is still synonymous in many minds
with an after-pub, pre-home Friday night out,
but the entire industry is trying to drag itself
upmarket. Indeed, Cook's comments so
aggrieved restaurateur Iqbal Wahhab,
proprietor of London's exclusive, celeb-
friendly **Cinnamon Club** (*see p205*), that he
put his disdain for chicken tikka masala on
record, referring to it as 'a joke'. The dish is
one of several dozen that were invented by
the UK's curry houses to appeal to the spice-
shy English palate of the early '70s.

Whatever the details, it's clear that curry-
lovers are catered for now better than
ever, with many more up- and mid-market
restaurants serving authentic Indian dishes
from different areas of India. Try **Café Spice
Namaste** (*see p211*), the Michelin-starred
Zaika (*see p217*), the **Painted Heron** (112
Cheyne Walk, SW10; 7351 5232), **Tamarind**
(*see p199*) or **Yatra** (34 Dover Street, W1;
7493 0200), a restaurant in Mayfair that
offers both traditional and modern Indian
menus, plus a Bollywood-themed bar in the
basement. Enthusiasts of the traditional curry
house needn't panic, however: the 40-plus
frill-free and largely so-so establishments in
Brick Lane aren't about to go anywhere, and
should keep appetites sated with their blend
of Anglo-Indian cuisine for a while yet.

Mediterranean

Eyre Brothers

70 Leonard Street, Shoreditch, EC2 (7613 5346/ www.eyrebrothers.co.uk). Old Street tube/rail. **Open** noon-3pm, 6.30-11pm Mon-Fri; 6.30-11pm Sat. **Main courses** £10-£23. **Credit** AmEx, DC, MC, V. **Map** p403 Q4.

Charming staff, gently groovy premises and a menu of robustly flavoured Mediterranean dishes combine to much success here. Main courses might be grilled leg of lamb with moutabal and tabouleh, or baked salt cod with potatoes, tomatoes and olives.

The Real Greek

15 Hoxton Market, Hoxton, N1 (7739 8212/ www.therealgreek.co.uk). Old Street tube/rail/26, 48, 55, 149, 242 bus. **Open** noon-3pm, 5.30-10.30pm Mon-Sat. **Main courses** £9-£16.90. **Credit** MC, V. **Map** p403 R3.

The menu has been pared down and the capacity expanded at this highly popular Greek joint, which featured in the fighting scene in the film of *Bridget Jones's Diary*. Food is fun and inventive, including mezes of scallops on rice, and mackerel and crab cakes; the wine list is impressive but costly. Next door is a cheaper, 'Greek tapas' branch, Mezedopolio.

Oriental

Green Papaya

191 Mare Street, Hackney, E8 (8985 5486). Bus 48, 55, 253, 277, D6. **Open** 11am-midnight Mon-Sat; 11am-11.30pm Sun. **Main courses** £4.50-£8. **Credit** MC, V.

There's an understated but trendy look to this Vietnamese place. The conservatory at the back has a lovely glassed-in garden. The food is unusual, alluring and not to be missed: baked tilapia in banana leaf comes topped with garlic and fish sauce paste, marinated chicken comes with lime leaves.

Royal China

30 Westferry Circus, Canary Wharf, E14 (7719 0888). Canary Wharf tube/DLR/Westferry DLR. **Open** noon-11pm Mon-Thur; noon-11.30pm Fri, Sat; 11am-10pm Sun. *Dim sum* noon-5pm daily. **Main courses** £6-£40. *Dim sum* £1.90. **Credit** AmEx, DC, MC, V.

The Royal China chain's dim sum snacks are the best in London, but its full menu is also top-notch. This latest branch has a fabulous riverside location, with plate-glass windows offering views of the broad sweep of the Thames. The atmosphere is generally brisk and cheerful. Book for lunch. **Branches**: throughout the city.

Viet Hoa

70-2 Kingsland Road, Shoreditch, E2 (7729 8293). Bus 26, 48, 55, 67, 149, 242, 243. **Open** noon-3.30pm, 5.30-11pm Mon-Fri; 12.30-4pm, 5.30-11.30pm Sat, Sun. **Main courses** £3.50-£6.90. **Credit** MC, V. **Map** p403 R3.

Now firmly part of the hip Hoxton scene, this hugely popular Vietnamese venue is frequently packed. Service is consequently slow, but it's worth the wait in the newly spruced-up dining room for flavour-packed stir-fried and noodle dishes.

South London

Cafés & brasseries

The Lavender

171 Lavender Hill, Battersea, SW11 (7978 5242). Clapham Junction rail. **Open** noon-3pm, 7-11pm Mon-Fri; noon-4pm, 7-11pm Sat; noon-4pm, 7-10.30pm Sun. **Main courses** £7-£10.50. **Credit** AmEx, MC, V.

Solid and well-priced bistro cooking is the order of the day at this friendly, well-established brasserie. The surroundings are charmingly understated and unpretentious, and portions are big. **Branches**: 112 Vauxhall Walk, Vauxhall, SE11 (7735 4440); 24 Clapham Road, Clapham, SW9 (7793 0770); 61 The Cut, South Bank, SE1 (7928 8645).

Fish & chips

Brady's

513 Old York Road, Wandsworth, SW18 (8877 9599). Wandsworth Town rail/28, 44 bus. **Open** 6.30-10pm Mon; 6.30-10.30pm Tue, Wed, Sat; 6.30-10.45pm Thur, Fri. **Main courses** £6.35-£8.95. **No credit cards.**

One of London's very finest chippies, Brady's is a congenial old Wandsworth joint often packed with moneyed folk not used to takeaway queues. The tartare sauce is made in-house, and Dover sole and conger eel share menu space with cod. Crisp batter, flaky flesh: yum.

French

Chez Bruce

2 Bellevue Road, Wandsworth, SW17 (8672 0114). Wandsworth Common rail. **Open** noon-2pm, 7-10.30pm Mon-Thur; noon-2pm, 6.30-10.30pm Fri; 12.30-2.30pm, 6.30-10.30pm Sat; 12.30-3pm Sun. **Set meals** *Lunch* £21.50 3 courses (Mon-Fri); £25 3 courses (Sat, Sun). *Dinner* £30 3 courses. **Credit** AmEx, DC, MC, V.

Bruce Poole's beacon of excellence offers set meals with seven or eight choices at each course. The dining room is a relaxed, convivial place, detracting nothing from the earthy, no-nonsense, perfectly executed food and globally sourced wines.

Global

Bamboula

12 Acre Lane, Brixton, SW2 (7737 6633). Brixton tube/rail. **Open** 11am-11pm Mon-Fri; noon-11pm Sat. **Main courses** £5.95-£7.50. **Credit** MC, V.

Breakfast as only they know how: the **Brick Lane Beigel Bake**. *See p210.*

Lilting reggae accompanies good, fairly priced food at this small green Jamaican restaurant. Soups can precede jerk fish or 'rundown' chicken, to be followed by rum-laced bread pud.

O Cantinho de Portugal

135-7 Stockwell Road, Stockwell, SW9 (7924 0218). Stockwell tube/Brixton tube/rail/2, 322, 325, 355 bus. **Open** *Restaurant* noon-midnight daily. **Main courses** £4-£9.50. **Credit** MC, V.
This lively, welcoming Portuguese bar/restaurant is a focal point for the neighbourhood's large west Iberian population. Charming waiters serve well-priced, simply prepared dishes: seafood, pork, chicken and traditional Portuguese desserts.

Canyon

Tow Path, Richmond Riverside, Richmond, Surrey (8948 2944). Richmond tube/rail. **Open** noon-4pm, 6-11pm Mon-Fri; 11am-4pm, 6-11pm Sat; 11am-4pm, 6-10.30pm Sun. **Main courses** £9-£16. **Credit** AmEx, MC, V.
Few restaurants can better the riverside location, which makes this classy American restaurant – the modernist building is like a slice of California – a great spot for alfresco dining. Food is adventurous, staff are friendly, and brunch is served at weekends.

Indian

Lahore Karahi

1 Tooting High Street, Tooting, SW17 (8767 2477). Tooting Broadway tube/133 bus. **Open** noon-midnight daily. **Main courses** £3.95-£4.95. **No credit cards**.
The best of several Tooting Pakistani caffs, Lahore Karahi is constantly busy with local Asians and others enjoying lamb and chicken dishes cooked in the tandoor or the wok. Also good are 'vegetarian sizzlers' such as karahi karela (bitter gourd).

Radha Krishna Bhavan

86 Tooting High Street, Tooting, SW17 (8767 3462). Tooting Broadway tube. **Open** noon-3pm, 6-11pm Mon-Thur, Sun; noon-3pm, 6pm-midnight Fri, Sat. **Main courses** £1.95-£6.95. **Credit** AmEx, DC, MC, V.
Kathakali dance costumes and south Indian tourist posters adorn this keenly priced, high-quality Keralan eating house. Food encompasses a few chicken and meat dishes as well as seafood and vegetarian specialities. The tomato curry is sublime.
Branch: Sree Krishna Inn, 332 Kingston Road, Ewell, Surrey (8393 0445).

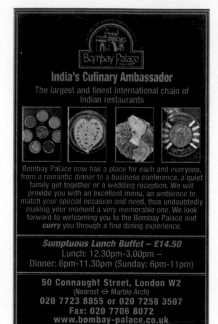

Italian

Enoteca Turi

28 Putney High Street, Putney, SW15 (8785 4449).
East Putney tube/Putney rail/14 bus. **Open** 12.30-
2.30pm, 7-11pm Mon-Sat. **Main courses** £9.50-
£14.50. **Credit** AmEx, DC, MC, V.
Putney's premier Italian restaurant is a bright, modern, noisy place that's renowned for its fine wine list.
Food from the seasonal menu might include a beautifully presented antipasti platter, pasta specials and
seafood risotto. Service can be slow.

Modern European

The Glasshouse

14 Station Parade, Kew, Surrey (8940 6777).
Kew Gardens tube/rail. **Open** noon-2.30pm,
7-10.30pm Mon-Thur; noon-2.30pm, 6.30-10.30pm
Fri, Sat; 12.30-2.45pm, 7.30-10pm Sun. **Set meals**
Lunch £17.50 3 courses (Mon-Sat); £25 3 courses
(Sun). *Dinner* £30 3 courses. **Credit** AmEx, MC, V.
An airy, wedge-shaped restaurant by Kew Gardens
station, the Glasshouse provides a modern,
stylish setting for its adventurous, French-inspired
cooking. The set-price menu has many choices, perhaps including rabbit with mascarpone sauce and
chorizo, followed by apricot and almond tart.

Inside

19 Greenwich South Street, Greenwich, SE10
(8265 5060/www.insiderestaurant.co.uk).
Greenwich rail/DLR. **Open** 6-11.30pm Tue; noon-
2.30pm, 6-11.30pm Wed-Fri; 11am-1pm, 6.30-11.30pm
Sat; 11am-3pm Sun. **Main courses** £10-£16.
Credit MC, V.
Greenwich's best restaurant is a little gem, with a
calm, relaxing interior, an extensive wine list and
impeccable service. Halibut might share a plate with
shallot purée and lemon thyme sauce, chocolate tart
with lavender ice-cream. Brunch is timed for
Greenwich market-goers at weekends.

Thyme

14 Clapham Park Road, Clapham, SW4 (7627
2468/www.thymeandspace.com). Clapham Common
tube. **Open** 6.30-10.30pm Mon-Sat; 7-10pm Sun.
Main courses £5-£10. **Credit** AmEx, MC, V.
Portions only come in starter sizes at this innovative
little restaurant. Graze on the likes of creamed cauliflower soup with truffle butter tortellini, and squid
stuffed with oxtail and risotto, or have a blow-out
with the five-course 'greatest hits' compilation.
Decor is plain, service is sussed, and food is thrilling.

Oriental

Tsunami

5-7 Voltaire Road, Clapham, SW4 (7978 1610).
Clapham North tube. **Open** 6-11pm Mon-Thur;
6-11.30pm Fri, Sat. **Main courses** £7.95-£16.50.
Credit AmEx, MC, V.

Winner of the *Time Out* Best Japanese Restaurant
award in 2002, Tsunami is an oasis of sleek design,
subtle lighting, efficient service and sublime dining.
As well as cheap bento meals, there's an exciting set
menu (including tea duck in sweet honey miso) and
interesting twists such as oysters in ponzu.

West London

Cafés & brasseries

Lisboa Patisserie

57 Golborne Road, Notting Hill, W10 (8968 5242).
Ladbroke Grove or Westbourne Park tube/23, 52 bus.
Open 8am-8pm daily. **Credit** MC, V.
The Lisboa would be a perfect pitstop for Portobello
market-goers who've staggered this far north, were
it not always crowded out. First-rate, low-priced coffees and delectable Portuguese pastries are the draw.

Lucky 7

127 Westbourne Park Road, Westbourne Park,
W2 (7727 6771). Royal Oak or Westbourne Park
tube. **Open** 7am-11pm Mon-Sat; 9am-10.30pm Sun.
No credit cards. Map p394 A5.
London's take on the classic US diner is maybe a little too archly done, but the quality of the food
silences most critics in a hurry. Top burgers.

Fish & chips

Geales

2 Farmer Street, Notting Hill, W8 (7727 7528).
Notting Hill Gate tube. **Open** noon-3pm, 6-11pm
Mon-Sat; 6-10.30pm Sun. **Main courses** £7.25-
£11.50. **Credit** AmEx, MC, V. **Map** p394 A7.
Posh for a chippie, Geales is an attractive neighbourhood place. Though you can get the trad cod,
chips and mushy peas (eat-in or takeaway), you can
also order grilled goat's cheese salad and calamares.

French

La Trompette

5-7 Devonshire Road, Chiswick, W4 (8747 1836).
Turnham Green tube. **Open** noon-2.30pm, 6.30-
10.30pm Mon-Sat; 12.30-3pm, 7-10pm Sun. **Set meals**
Lunch £19.50 3 courses (Mon-Sat); £23.50 3 courses
(Sun). *Dinner* £30 3 courses. **Credit** AmEx, MC, V.
This self-assured but unpretentious restaurant won
the *Time Out* Best Local Restaurant award in 2002.
Its earth-toned dining room is usually packed with
enthusiastic Chiswickites sampling such delights as
stuffed rabbit leg with apricots and cider.

Global

Dumela

42 Devonshire Road, Chiswick, W4 (8742 3149).
Turnham Green tube. **Open** 6.30-11pm Mon-Sat.
Main courses £9.50-£23.50. **Credit** MC, V.

Eat, Drink, Shop

Late eats

Ever staggered out of a bar at closing time spinning from alcohol-on-empty-stomach syndrome? Ever had to press your knees into your belly to stop the rumbling as the second half of a theatre performance rolls on for hours? A decade ago, this would have been a problem in London. But while late dining is still not quite the norm, then central London at least has more late-opening eateries than ever: the options are no longer limited merely to McDonald's or room service.

As London's beating heart 24/7, Soho's got its fair share of late-night eating haunts. Dark and candlelit but with a happy crowd of Soho regulars, **Café Boheme** (13 Old Compton Street, W1; 7734 0623; meals 8am-2.30am Mon-Sat; 8am-11pm Sun) is simultaneously romantic and upbeat, and the steak frites isn't bad either. Downstairs from the Soho Theatre is **Café Lazeez** (21 Dean Street, W1; 7434 9393; brasserie 11am-12.30am Mon-Sat), whose brasserie serves a global mix of chilli burgers and chicken jalfrezi. Conran's **Mezzonine** (100 Wardour Street, W1; 7314 4000; dinner 5.30pm-1am Mon-Thur; 5.30pm-3am Fri, Sat) serves a Thai-infused menu to a noisy and buzzy crowd; **New Diamond** (see p201) is one of the best of many late-opening eateries with its menu among the best in Chinatown; and no late night in Soho is complete without a visit to **Bar Italia** (see p201).

Outside Soho, the choices are patchier. For grills, meze and great juices, head to Edgware Road, W2 for **Al-Dar** (Nos.61-3; 7402 2541; meals 8pm-1am daily) and **Ranoush Juice Bar** (No.43; 7723 5929; meals 9am-3am daily). If you go late to **Maroush** (No.21; 7723 0773; meals noon-2am daily), you might even get to see belly dancing and a lounge-singing Arab Peter Stringfellow. Over in Dalston and Stoke Newington are a multitude of Turkish restaurants that serve until the early hours. And for a look at what London's clubbers look like after a night on the tiles, you can't go wrong with basement diner **Tinseltown** (33-6 St John Street, EC1; 7689 2424) and the classier **Vingt-Quatre** (325 Fulham Road, SW10; 7376 7224), London's two most worthwhile 24-hour diners.

Formerly the Springbok Grill, this little South African venue has been smartened up. The menu still majors in barbecues: crocodile and lamb sosatie, grilled bushpig with garlic mash, say. Prices can be steep, but the South African wines are good value.

Mandalay

444 Edgware Road, Paddington, W2 (7258 3696). Edgware Road tube. **Open** noon-2.30pm, 6-10.30pm Mon-Sat. **Main courses** £3.90-£6.90. **Credit** AmEx, DC, MC, V. **Map** p395 E4.

London's sole Burmese restaurant is a humble venue, with walls decked out in bunting. Charming staff serve good-value food that blends Indian, Thai and Chinese influences. You'll need to book.

Mandola

139-41 Westbourne Grove, Notting Hill, W11 (7229 4734). Notting Hill Gate tube/23 bus. **Open** noon-11.30pm Mon-Sat; 1-4.30pm, 6.30-11pm Sun. **Main courses** £6.50-£10.50. **Credit** MC, V. **Map** p394 A6.

An air of crowded intimacy pervades this popular Sudanese restaurant. Salata daqua (onions and cabbage in peanut sauce) could be followed by fried tilapia fish, and accompanied by gamardeen (dried apricot juice).

Rodizio Rico

111 Westbourne Grove, Bayswater, W2 (7792 4035). Bayswater tube. **Open** 6.30-11.30pm Mon-Fri; 12.30-4.30pm, 6.30-11.30pm Sat; 1-11.30pm Sun. **Set buffet** £17.90 (£11.50 vegetarian) 2 courses. **Credit** MC, V. **Map** p394 B6.

A giant open grill is the centrepiece of this Brazilian eat-all-you-want carvery. Load up on buffet salads, black bean stew and chips, then catch one of the waiters who patrol wielding metre-long skewers laden with chicken hearts, pork, lamb or (occasionally) rump steak. There's little joy for vegetarians.

Indian

Gifto's Lahore Karahi

162-4 Broadway, Southall, Middx (8813 8669). Southall rail. **Open** noon-11.30pm Mon-Thur; noon-midnight Fri-Sun. **Main courses** £2.50-£8.90. **Credit** AmEx, MC, V.

The biggest and possibly the best of Southall's many Punjabi restaurants, Gifto's has a long and enticing menu of tandoori and karahi dishes, plus pungent stews and Bombay-style snacks. Local Muslims and Sikhs often fill the bright dining room. Chefs in the large open kitchen exhibit mesmerising skill.

Karahi King

213 East Lane, North Wembley, Middx (8904 2760/4994). North Wembley tube/245 bus. **Open** noon-midnight daily. **Main courses** £3.50-£12. **No credit cards.**

Local north Indian families treasure this congenial temple to Punjabi cuisine. Behind its drab façade is a light, modern interior where wok-brandishing chefs star in the open kitchen. Great for tandoori food, breads and karahi (balti) dishes at low prices.

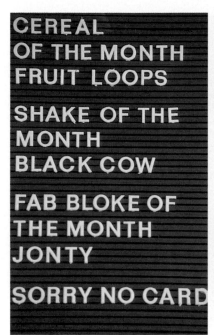

CEREAL
OF THE MONTH
FRUIT LOOPS

SHAKE OF THE
MONTH
BLACK COW

FAB BLOKE OF
THE MONTH
JONTY

SORRY NO CARD

American dining the West London way at Tom Conran's **Lucky 7**. *See p215.*

Zaika

*1 Kensington High Street, Kensington, W8
(7795 6533). High Street Kensington tube.*
Open noon-2.45pm, 6-10.45pm Mon-Fri; 6-10.45pm
Sat; 6.30-9.45pm Sun. **Main courses** £12.50-£31.50.
Credit AmEx, MC, V. **Map** p394 C8.
Vineet Bhatia is one of a select band of talented chefs
who have created Modern Indian cuisine in London.
His latest restaurant, a former bank impressively
decorated with expensive artefacts, produces
dishes that incorporate pan-Asian and Modern
European influences, as well as offering innovative
takes on Indian street food. Book ahead.

Italian

Assaggi

*Chepstow, 39 Chepstow Place, Notting Hill, W2
(7792 5501). Notting Hill Gate tube.* **Open** 12.30-
2.30pm, 7.30-11pm Mon-Fri; 1-2.30pm, 7.30-11pm Sat.
Main courses £15.95-£19.50. **Credit** DC, MC, V.
Map p394 B6.
Upstairs from a charming pub, Assaggi is modern,
relaxed and fairly priced. Its reputation as a
pompous hangout for celebrities made tables hard
to book, but the fashion crowd has now moved on
and left others to enjoy well-executed dishes such as
grilled monkfish with wild asparagus.

Rosmarino

*1 Blenheim Terrace, St John's Wood, NW8 (7328
5014). St John's Wood tube.* **Open** noon-2.30pm,
7-10.30pm Mon-Fri; noon-3pm, 7-10.30pm Sat;
noon-3pm, 7-10pm Sun. **Main courses** (Mon-Fri
lunch only) £9.50-£13.50. *Set meals* (dinner, Sat
& Sun lunch) £22.50 2 courses, £27 3 courses, £30
4 courses. **Credit** AmEx, MC, V.
Classic, simple Italian dishes form the backbone of
the menu here. Standards are such that Rosmarino
was winner of the *Time Out* Best Local Restaurant
award in 2001. The colour scheme is a relaxing
cream and green; service is pleasant but can be slow.

Modern European

Clarke's

*124 Kensington Church Street, Kensington, W8
(7221 9225/www.sallyclarke.com). Notting Hill Gate
tube.* **Open** 12.30-2pm, 7-10pm Mon-Fri; 11am-2pm,
7-10pm Sat. *Set dinner* £48 4 courses. **Credit** AmEx, DC, MC, V.
Map p394 B7.
Amicably assured service, discreet surroundings
and peerless ingredients unfussily cooked (in the
Californian manner) keep Sally Clarke's restaurant
in London's premier league. Lunch offers more
flexibility than the no-choice set dinner. For her next-
door bakery, **& Clarke's**, *see p247.*

Eat, Drink, Shop

Rosmarino: upscale Italian in uptown London. *See p217.*

Oriental

Mandarin Kitchen

14-16 Queensway, Bayswater, W2 (7727 9012).
Bayswater or Queensway tube. **Open** noon-11.30pm
daily. **Main courses** £5.90-£25. **Credit** AmEx, DC,
MC, V. **Map** p394 C6.
The Cantonese seafood dishes served at this capacious old restaurant are rarely bettered anywhere in
London: scrumptious deep-fried baby squid in garlic and pepper, succulent lobster, sea-fresh scallops
and razor clams. You may have to queue, even if
you've booked.

Tawana

3 Westbourne Grove, Bayswater, W2 (7229
3785). Bayswater tube. **Open** noon-3pm, 6-11pm
daily. **Main courses** £5.25-£17.95. *Minimum* £10.
Credit AmEx, DC, MC, V. **Map** p394 B6.
A tip-top Thai restaurant decked out in elegant colonial style (bamboo seating, potted palms and the
like). The menu is extensive, offering imaginative
dishes plus a good specials list (fried tofu with black
fungus, for instance).

Polish

Patio

5 Goldhawk Road, Shepherd's Bush, W12 (8743
5194). Goldhawk Road or Shepherd's Bush tube.
Open noon-3pm, 6-11.30pm Mon-Fri; 6-11.30pm
Sat, Sun. **Main courses** £7.50-£8.90. **Credit** AmEx,
DC, MC, V.

Staff at this old-fashioned place are proud of their
home cooking: duck à la polonaise, potato latke and
Polish cheesecake included. The room is eccentrically attired in non-matching crockery and random
samovars. Polish beer and vodka get things lively.

Wódka

12 St Alban's Grove, Kensington, W8 (7937 6513).
Gloucester Road tube. **Open** 12.30-2.30pm, 7-11.15pm
Mon-Fri; 7-11.15pm Sat, Sun. **Main courses** £10.50-
£14. **Credit** AmEx, DC, MC, V. **Map** p396 C9.
Sophisticated, minimalist surroundings provide the
setting for Wódka's modern take on classic Polish
cuisine. Try the barszcz (beetroot soup) with uszka
(baby dumplings). To drink, there's a great choice
of wines, vodka cocktails and glogg (mulled wine).

Vegetarian & organic

The Gate

51 Queen Caroline Street, Hammersmith, W6 (8748
6932/www.gateveg.co.uk). Hammersmith tube. **Open**
noon-3pm, 6-10.45pm Mon-Fri; 6-10.45pm Sat. **Main**
courses £7.95-£10.90. **Credit** AmEx, DC, MC, V.
Through a leafy courtyard, up narrow steps into an
airy converted artist's loft, you'll find one of
London's best vegetarian restaurants. The imaginative, Italian-leaning menu features such delights
as mushroom- and ricotta-filled artichoke hearts
with grilled polenta, followed by pistachio and
lavender brûlée. Service is top-notch, too.
Branch: 72 Belsize Lane, Belsize Park, NW3
(7435 7733).

Pubs & Bars

Raise a glass to London's myriad imbiberies, but be quick: it's nearly 11pm...

Like so many aspects of life in London, drinking culture is dominated by fashion. One smart aleck has a new idea, and before long everyone's trying to imitate. Some trends are to be welcomed. Pubs in London now serve better food than ever after the Eagle-inspired 'gastropub' craze that started in the mid 1990s. It's easier than it was two years ago to find a drinkable cocktail. And even real ale, dismissed as old hat in the 1980s and 1990s as everyone switched to generic bottled lager and glowing alcopops, is again growing in popularity.

Other changes have been less beneficial. London is now full of characterless chain pubs: the bland, flat-packed sophistication of the Pitcher & Piano, All Bar One and Slug & Lettuce chains, the loud and lairy Aussie-themed Walkabout Inns and Irish-slanted O'Neill's. Many corner locals are being bought up by developers and converted into flats. It seems every new bar in London is required by law to feature a DJ playing conversation-killing music four nights a week. Still, some pubs carry on as if nothing's changed, their history written in the memorabilia on the walls and etched in the faces of the customers who've been coming here since before you were born.

There's not an adult in London who hasn't been frustrated by the arcane law that means pubs need a special licence to open outside the hours of 11am-11pm (noon-10.30pm on Sundays). In November 2002, the government

Anchor Bankside.

promised to reform the law, but as yet nothing's changed. Still, those in search of a later drink will be able to find one in central London; *see p230*. And for a full survey of London pubs – this section is the tip of the iceberg – see the *Time Out Pubs & Bars Guide* (£6.99).

Central London

The South Bank & Bankside

Anchor Bankside
34 Park Street, SE1 (7407 1577). London Bridge tube/rail. **Open** 11am-11pm Mon-Sat; noon-10.30pm Sun. **Credit** AmEx, DC, MC, V. **Map** p404 P8.
This riverfront boozer positively creaks with its past. A labyrinthine layout holds countless bars and alcoves – including the Johnson Room, where the great man wrote parts of his dictionary. The terrace is always busy in summer, and understandably so.

Market Porter
9 Stoney Street, SE1 (7407 2495). London Bridge tube/rail. **Open** 6-8.30am, 11am-11pm Mon-Fri; noon-11pm Sat; noon-10.30pm Sun. **Credit** AmEx, MC, V. **Map** p404 P8.
A smashing little hideaway, this, recommendable not just for its early opening hours (it unlocks early for the benefit of traders at Borough Market) but for its genial atmosphere and terrific beer choices.

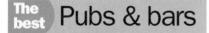

The best Pubs & bars

For cocktails to die for
Townhouse. *See p224.*

For a great British pint
Royal Oak. *See p220.*

For staying in with the in-crowd
Sosho. *See p228.*

For a summer afternoon
Ship. *See p228.*

For genetically unmodified food and drink
Duke of Cambridge. *See p225.*

Mint on Montague

Montague Close, 8-10 Borough High Street, SE1 (7089 5710/www.mintbar.co.uk). London Bridge tube/rail. **Open** noon-midnight Mon-Fri; noon-1am Sat. **Credit** AmEx, MC, V. **Map** p404 P8.

Tucked away in the shadow of hulking Southwark Cathedral, this outpost of the Clerkenwell staple (182-6 St John Street, EC1; 7253 8368) offers cultural modernity in a neighbourhood where trad pubs dominate. Settle in with a cocktail.

Royal Oak

44 Tabard Street, SE1 (7357 7173). Borough tube/London Bridge tube/rail. **Open** 11.30am-11pm Mon-Fri. **Credit** MC, V. **Map** p404 P9.

Recently restored (the mahogany gleams once again, the etched glass sparkles like new), this is a strong candidate for London's best pub. The full range of Harvey's cask-conditioned canon is on offer, from Mild to Old, including seasonal brews.

The City

Black Friar

174 Queen Victoria Street, EC4 (7236 5474). Blackfriars tube/rail. **Open** 11.30am-11pm Mon-Fri. **Credit** AmEx, MC, V. **Map** p404 O6.

An extraordinary wedge-shaped pub with an art nouveau façade, and Edwardian marble, mosaics and pillared fireplaces inside. There's also some decent beer and, more often than not, a sizeable crowd of City suits on hand to enjoy it.

Jamaica Wine House

St Michael's Alley, off Cornhill, EC3 (7929 6972). Bank tube/DLR. **Open** 11am-11pm Mon-Fri. **Credit** AmEx, DC, MC, V. **Map** p405 Q6.

London's first coffee house, this premises was rebuilt after the Great Fire and converted into a pub at the end of the 19th century, hence the nicely aged mahogany interior. Despite the 'wine house' moniker and theming, you'll find the beer's better.

Nylon

1 Addle Street, EC3 (7600 7771/ www.styleinthecity.co.uk). Moorgate tube/rail. **Open** 5pm-midnight Mon-Thur; 4.30pm-midnight Fri. **Credit** MC, V. **Map** p405 Q6.

Be wary of any establishment with a URL as crass as this one. Still, Nylon is as close to Shoreditch cool as you're likely to find in the City: all sleek decor, imaginative cocktails, imported vodkas and the requisite nightly DJs.

Twentyfour

Level 24, Tower 42, 25 Old Broad Street, EC2 (7877 2424/www.twenty-four.co.uk). Bank tube/DLR/ Liverpool Street tube/rail. **Open** 11.45am-11pm Mon-Fri (last admission 10pm). **Credit** AmEx, DC, MC, V. **Map** p402 N5.

The decor might be nice and modish and the cocktails might be immaculately mixed, but everyone's here for the views, 24 floors above London. Drinkers are mostly puffed-up City suits with more money than you.

Bradley's Spanish Bar. *See p221.*

Ye Olde Cheshire Cheese

145 Fleet Street, EC4 (7353 6170). Blackfriars tube/rail. **Open** 11.30am-11pm Mon-Fri; noon-3pm, 5.30-11pm Sat; noon-3pm Sun. **Credit** AmEx, DC, MC, V. **Map** p404 N6.

It might look closed but it probably isn't: a dark frontage conceals the unprepossessing alleyway entrance. Inside, it's a warren of wooden settles, bare boards and sawdust, known to Dickens, Thackeray and Johnson. Perfect for a historical pint.

Holborn & Clerkenwell

Bleeding Heart Tavern

Bleeding Heart Yard, off Greville Street, EC1 (7242 8238). Chancery Lane tube/Farringdon tube/rail. **Open** noon-11pm Mon-Fri. **Credit** AmEx, DC, MC, V. **Map** p402 N5.

With its gory past safely behind it, this City yard plays host to claret of a different kind. The wine list is extensive, the surroundings are warm and comfortable, and the food is modern, French and tasty.

Café Kick

43 Exmouth Market, EC1 (7837 8077/www.cafekick. co.uk). Farringdon tube/rail. **Open** noon-11pm Mon-Sat; noon-10.30pm Sun. **Credit** MC, V. **Map** p402 N4.

A little slice of continental Europe in hearty Clerkenwell, Café Kick's thing is football, both televised (it's a great place to watch a game) and played on a table (there are three lovely *baby foot* tables here). Beer and coffee accompany the action.

Eagle

159 Farringdon Road, EC1 (7837 1353). Farringdon tube/rail. **Open** noon-11pm Mon-Sat; noon-5pm Sun. **Credit** MC, V. **Map** p402 N4.

The pub that kick-started the gastropub revolution has spawned many imitators/competitors – examples nearby include the **Peasant** (240 St John Street, EC1; 7336 7726/www.thepeasant.co.uk) and the **Well** (180 St John Street, EC1; 7251 9363/www.downthewell. com) – but still lives up to the high standards it set for itself and others in both food and wine.

Fluid

40 Charterhouse Street, EC1 (7253 3444/ www.fluidbar.com). Barbican tube/Farringdon tube/rail. **Open** noon-midnight Mon-Wed; noon-2am Thur, Fri; 7pm-2am Sat. **Credit** AmEx, DC, MC, V. **Map** p402 O5.

Japanese theming, slinky tunes and laid-back leather sofas make Fluid a favourite among clubbers and fashionistas. Snacks such as miso soup, and crisp, cool beers complete the picture.

Jerusalem Tavern

55 Britton Street, EC1 (7490 4281/ www.stpetersbrewery.co.uk). Farringdon tube/ rail. **Open** 11am-11pm Mon-Fri; noon-10pm Sat. **Credit** AmEx, MC, V. **Map** p402 O5.

This small, intimate tavern looks as if it's been preserved from the days of the Young Pretender. The sole London outpost of St Peter's Brewery out in Suffolk, Jerusalem Tavern also has half a dozen of its great beers on draught.

Bloomsbury & Fitzrovia

Bradley's Spanish Bar

42-4 Hanway Street, W1 (7636 0359). Tottenham Court Road tube. **Open** noon-11pm Mon-Sat; 3-10.30pm Sun. **Credit** MC, V. **Map** p399 K6.

Tucked away on one of central London's most charmingly shabby streets, Bradley's is a bar out of time: the furniture is worn, the two floors are both tiny and the jukebox is all-vinyl. Among the best bars in town.

CVO Firevault

36 Great Titchfield Street, W1 (7580 5333). Oxford Circus tube. **Open** 9.30am-10.30pm Mon-Fri; noon-6pm Sat. **Credit** AmEx, MC, V. **Map** p398 J5.

No, it's not a fireplace shop. Or, at least, it's not *only* a fireplace shop: in the basement is a luxurious bar. It's fantastically posh, fantastically pretentious and, in the evenings, fantastically precious (you'll need to book at night). For all that, though, it's unique.

Lamb

94 Lamb's Conduit Street, WC1 (7405 0713). Holborn or Russell Square tube. **Open** 11am-11pm Mon-Sat; noon-4pm, 7-10.30pm Sun. **Credit** MC, V. **Map** p399 M4.

One of London's most celebrated pubs, the Lamb is a central London flagship for the Young's brewery (based in Wandsworth). The decor is carefully

Eat, Drink, Shop

restored Victorian, with three wood-panelled drinking areas, the beer is immaculately kept, and the atmosphere is delightfully convivial.

Mash
19-21 Great Portland Street, W1 (7637 5555). Oxford Circus tube. **Open** 11am-midnight Mon,Tue; 11am-2am Wed-Sat. **Credit** AmEx, DC, MC, V. **Map** p398 J5.
If you believe that irony is second only to sarcasm as the lowest form of wit, you'll hate the knowingly retro decor here. Happily, the beers (brewed on site) are no joke – and the food's usually pretty darn good too. DJs play four nights a week.

Nordic
25 Newman Street, W1 (7631 3174). Tottenham Court Road tube. **Open** noon-11pm Mon-Fri; 6-11pm Sat. **Credit** AmEx, MC, V. **Map** p398 J5.
A Scandinavian bar with Scandinavian food (meatballs! yay!), Scandinavian drinks (including Danish lager Red Erik) and Scandinavian prices. No matter, though: it might be a stylish, hip place, but it's by no means unwelcoming.

Marylebone

Queen's Head & Artichoke
30-32 Albany Street, NW1 (7916 6206/ www.theartichoke.net). Great Portland Street tube. **Open** 11am-11pm Mon-Sat; noon-10.30pm Sun. **Credit** AmEx, DC, MC, V. **Map** p398 H4.
Downstairs is a terrific restoration of a late Victorian boozer: buzzy, loud and lively. Upstairs is a dining room, dishing up above-par gastropub food. Taken together, a fine establishment – and handily near Regent's Park too.

Windsor Castle
29 Crawford Place, W1 (7723 4371). Edgware Road tube. **Open** 11am-11pm Mon-Sat; noon-10.30pm Sun. **Credit** MC, V. **Map** p395 F5.
Leaving aside the Thai food, the Windsor is as British as boozers get. Royal memorabilia fills the walls, with pictures of Winston Churchill and wartime crooner Vera Lynn also on display. Somehow, it avoids being the tackiest pub in town.

Mayfair & St James's

Guinea
30 Bruton Place, W1 (7409 1728). Green Park tube. **Open** 10.30am-11pm Mon-Fri; 6.30-11pm Sat. **Credit** AmEx, DC, MC, V. **Map** p400 H7.
The Guinea, a cosy little wood-soaked boozer, is a Young's pub, so the beers are lovely. This being Mayfair, though, the wine list's outstanding. You'll need to book to eat in the acclaimed Grill here.

Red Lion
23 Crown Passage, off Pall Mall, SW1 (7930 4141). Green Park tube. **Open** 11am-11pm Mon-Sat. **Credit** MC, V. **Map** p400 J8.
Both the pub and its regulars are old-fashioned sorts. The saloon bar is all dark woods and velvet-effect banquettes; the sandwiches are sturdy and stomach-packing; the staff are genial and rightly proud of their cirrhosis-inducing range of whiskies. A joy.

CVO Firevault: a glass of white, a G&T and a £4,000 fireplace please, barman. *See p221.*

It's curtains

The ritual is well practised. No bells will ring and no 'last call' will be hollered. Instead, on the final bong of 11pm, the bartender will leave his post to lock the door, draw the curtains and dim both music and lights. Congratulations. You are now a part of a Great British Tradition.

The pub lock-in is born from necessity: English pubs are not permitted to serve alcohol beyond 11pm (10.30pm on Sunday). Change is on the way – the government has promised to reform the arcane law – but as of early 2003, it still stood. Some bars have obtained licences to serve beer beyond 11pm (*see p230*), but they tend to be horribly oversubscribed; supply can't match demand.

Still, if you get lucky, you'll find a regular boozer that simply, secretly, carries on serving after the law says it must stop. Few pubs have lock-ins, and those that do tend to be outside central London: the risk of being caught is too great. But keep your ear to the ground and your fingers crossed.

There are two rules to the lock-in. The first is basic: you must be in the pub by the time 11pm rolls around. It is no use banging on the door and pleading in questionable language to be let in after the cut-off. You are locked out.

The second? Tell no one what you have seen or heard. The lock-in is against the law, sure. But more than that, a regular lock-in at a good pub is a club every bit as exclusive as Soho House or Brooks, but with far fewer arseholes. It is a private party that comes with the illicit thrill that only illegality can provide. It is magnificent.

Once you have found your dream lock-in, treasure it and tell only your most trusted confidantes. We don't want no riff-raff in here, you know. Failure to observe this principle can result in social ostracism, physical abuse and, worst of all, having nowhere to drink after 11pm. But live by the rules – not by the law – and you'll be one of us in no time. Cheers.

Soho & Leicester Square

Akbar
*77 Dean Street, W1 (7437 2525/www.redfort.co.uk/
akbar). Leicester Square tube.* **Open** noon-1am Mon-Fri; 5pm-1am Sat; 6-10.30pm Sun. **Credit** AmEx,
MC, V. **Map** p399 K6.
Located beneath the classy Red Fort restaurant,
Akbar is an exotic den of cool cocktails and subdued
lighting. Cocktails are Indian- and Arabic-influenced, and the snacks are from the Red Fort's
kitchen. Cool but not too cool.

Coach & Horses
*29 Greek Street, W1 (7437 5920). Leicester Square
tube.* **Open** 11am-11pm Mon-Sat; noon-10.30pm Sun.
Credit MC, V. **Map** p399 K6.
A shambolic Soho boozer blessed – if that's the right
word – with a shambolic clientele of chancers,
bores, wannabes, geniuses and, above all, serious
drinkers. Don't come here expecting brushed pine
furniture and rocket salad; this is a proper pub.
Long may it thrive.

Cork & Bottle
*44-6 Cranbourn Street, WC2 (7734 6592/
www.donhewitsonlondonwinebars.com). Leicester
Square tube.* **Open** 11am-midnight Mon-Sat;
noon-10.30pm Sun. **Credit** AmEx, DC, MC, V.
Map p401 K7.
A nondescript doorway is all that's visible at street
level of this cosy underground burrow. There's a

big, juicy wine list, along with blackboards and
flyers announcing assorted bin ends, wines of the
month, and the like.

French House
*49 Dean Street, W1 (7437 2799). Leicester Square
tube.* **Open** noon-11pm Mon-Sat; noon-10.30pm Sun.
Credit AmEx, DC, MC, V. **Map** p399 K6.
The restaurant above it has gone, but this Soho institution remains. During the war, it was a meeting
place for the French Resistance; later, it was a home
from home to the Soho bohos of the 1950s and 1960s.
In continued opposition to British boorishness, staff
still refuse to serve pints (halves only).

Lab
*12 Old Compton Street, W1 (7437 7820/www.lab-
bar.com). Leicester Square or Tottenham Court Road
tube.* **Open** 4pm-midnight Mon-Sat; 4-10.30pm Sun.
Credit AmEx, MC, V. **Map** p399 K6.
The cocktail list at this Soho bar is as weighty as
your average computer manual, but fortunately it's
much more comprehensible and makes for lip-
smacking reading. Sit at the space-age bar to watch
the mixologists at work.

Covent Garden & St Giles's

Freedom Brewing Company
*41 Earlham Street, WC2 (7240 0606). Covent
Garden tube.* **Open** noon-11pm Mon-Sat; noon-
10.30pm Sun. **Credit** AmEx, MC, V. **Map** p399 L6.

Eat, Drink, Shop

The highlight of a visit to this surprisingly large Covent Garden hangout is, of course, the beer: we especially like the pale ale, which goes most of the way towards compensating for the so-so bar food and noisy atmosphere.

Gordon's
47 Villiers Street, WC2 (7930 1408). Covent Garden or Embankment tube/Charing Cross tube/rail. **Open** 11am-11pm Mon-Sat; noon-10pm Sun. **Credit** MC, V. **Map** p401 L7.
Large on atmosphere, light on spring-cleaning, and perennially busy, this basement wine bar is a London landmark. Wine, cheese, candlelight and chaos: this is less a place for a romantic dinner with your wife than for an illicit rendezvous with your mistress.

Lamb & Flag
33 Rose Street, WC2 (7497 9504). Covent Garden tube. **Open** 11am-11pm Mon-Thur; 11am-10.45pm Fri, Sat; noon-10.30pm Sun. **No credit cards**. **Map** p401 L7.
Built in 1623, this is one of London's last wooden-framed buildings, and one of the very few bearable boozers in Covent Garden. No matter the time of day, it'll be busy and noisy.

Lowlander
36 Drury Lane, WC2 (7379 7446/ www.lowlander.com). **Open** 11am-11pm Mon-Sat; 11am-10.30pm Sun. **Credit** AmEx, DC, MC, V. **Map** p399 L6.
Drink and food from Belgium and the Netherlands is the gimmick at this understandably popular spot. The beers are good, but for a real treat try a small sip of jenever or two. If the Indonesian food isn't especially authentic, it's at least very tasty.

Westminster

Boisdale
15 Eccleston Street, SW1 (7730 6922/ www.boisdale.co.uk). Victoria tube/rail. **Open** *Back Bar* noon-11pm Mon-Fri. *Macdonald Bar* noon-1am Mon-Fri; 7pm-1am Sat. **Credit** AmEx, DC, MC, V. **Map** p400 H10.
If you don't mind the ridiculously over-the-top interior – almost everything in sight is tartan – then the Boisdale is worth a visit purely for its range of whiskies: some 250 of them in total. Distinctly un-Cuban ranges of cigars and wine complete the picture. Entry after 10pm costs £10.

Red Lion
48 Parliament Street, SW1 (7930 5826). Westminster tube. **Open** 11am-11pm Mon-Sat; noon-7pm Sun. **Credit** MC, V. **Map** p401 L9.
There's been a tavern here since 1434, but this incarnation has existed since 1900, hence the mahogany and etched-glass fittings. The silent TV screens are tuned to the BBC Parliamentary Channel, which gives a good indication of who the regulars are.

Knightsbridge & South Kensington

Nag's Head
53 Kinnerton Street, SW1 (7235 1135). Hyde Park Corner tube. **Open** 11am-11pm Mon-Sat; noon-10.30pm Sun. **No credit cards**. **Map** p400 G9.
Perhaps the floor of this pint-sized saloon has been raised or that of the bar lowered, but the net result is that staff address your navel. Still, the superbly eccentric decor and the diminutive downstairs snug make this one of SW1's loveliest watering holes.

Townhouse
31 Beauchamp Place, SW3 (7589 5080/ www.lab-townhouse.com). Knightsbridge tube. **Open** noon-midnight Mon-Sat; noon-10.30pm Sun. **Credit** AmEx, MC, V. **Map** p397 F10.
The comfortable, quietly stylish Townhouse comes from the people who brought you Lab (*see p223*), which may be recommendation enough. If not, one of the myriad house Martinis will convert you in no time. A word of warning, though: drinks can only be served with food after 11pm.

Chelsea

Lots Road Pub & Dining Room
114 Lots Road, SW10 (7352 6645). Fulham Broadway or Sloane Square tube then 11, 19, 22 bus. **Open** 11am-11pm Mon-Sat; 11am-10.30pm Sun. **Credit** AmEx, MC, V. **Map** p396 C13.
The gastropub cult reached its apogee with this pleasant if fairly generic refurbishment, and while the location isn't ideal for visitors – it's quite a way from the nearest tube – the effort it takes to get here is just about worth it for the excellent beer and food.

Phene Arms
9 Phene Street, SW3 (7352 3294). Sloane Square or South Kensington tube. **Open** 11am-11pm Mon-Sat; noon-10.30pm Sun. **Credit** AmEx, DC, MC, V. **Map** p397 E12.
For years, the Phene Arms was footballer George Best's local, though alcoholism isn't a prerequisite for those wanting to drink at this democratic Chelsea boozer. It gets busy in summer, but with a terrace this terrific that's no surprise.

North London

Albion
10 Thornhill Road, Islington, N1 (7607 7450). Angel tube. **Open** 11am-11pm Mon-Sat; noon-10.30pm Sun. **Credit** MC, V. **Map** p402 N1.
When people refer to 'leafy Islington' – and they do, especially the ones who live there – this is the kind of place they mean. The Albion is determinedly villagey, preternaturally quaint and an absolute joy. Come in winter for Sunday lunch, and in summer for the gorgeous garden.

Clifton

96 Clifton Hill, St John's Wood, NW8 (7372 3427).
St John's Wood tube. **Open** noon-11pm Mon-Sat;
noon-10.30pm Sun. **Credit** AmEx, MC, V.
Blending in perfectly with the surrounding houses,
the Clifton can be hard to spot (except in summer,
when its outside tables are packed to overflowing).
Inside is all manner of carved wood, a Gothic-
looking bar, ornate fireplaces and snug corners.

Duke of Cambridge

30 St Peter Street, Islington, N1 (7359 3066/
www.singhboulton.co.uk/duke). Angel tube.
Open 5-11pm Mon; noon-11pm Tue-Sat; noon-
10.30pm Sun. **Credit** AmEx, MC, V. **Map** p402 O2.
London's first organic pub – the owners have since
opened two others: the **Crown** on Victoria Park (223
Grove Road, E3; 8981 9998) and Westbourne Grove's
Pelican (45 All Saints Road, W11; 7792 3073) –
enjoys a lovely corner location. All the beers and
food are organic and lovely with it, though prepare
to pay above-average prices for the privilege.

Elbow Room

135 Finchley Road, Swiss Cottage, NW3 (7586
9888/www.theelbow-room.co.uk). Swiss Cottage tube.
Open noon-midnight Mon-Thur; noon-1am Fri-Sat;
noon-10.30pm Sun. **Credit** MC, V.
One of several London branches of this decidedly
upscale pool hall, Swiss Cottage's Elbow Room follows the formula established in Islington with live
DJs, cocktails and pricey pool tables.
Branches: 89-91 Chapel Market, Islington, N1
(7278 3244); 103 Westbourne Grove, Notting Hill,
W2 (7221 5211).

Embassy

119 Essex Road, Islington, N1 (7359 7882). Angel
tube. **Open** 5-11pm Mon-Thur; 5pm-1am Fri, Sat;
5-10.30pm Sun. **Credit** MC, V. **Map** p402 O1.
The **Medicine Bar** (181 Upper Street, N1; 7704
9536) rolls on, the **Salmon & Compasses** (58
Penton Street, N1; 7837 3891) is more popular than
ever, but this is the best DJ bar in Islington, beautifully decorated (halfway between old-school
American lounge and style-mag wet dream) and
offering some splendid music (call to see what's
on, as the schedule changes frequently and special
guests are not uncommon).

Flask

77 Highgate West Hill, Highgate, N6 (8348 7346).
Archway or Highgate tube. **Open** 11am-11pm Mon-
Sat; noon-10.30pm Sun. **Credit** MC, V.
Purportedly dating back to 1663 and preserved pretty well by a series of sympathetic refurbishments,
this is one of north London's loveliest old pubs, and
also one of its busiest. Don't confuse it with the
rather earthier – but just, in its own way, as enjoyable – **Flask** nearby in Hampstead (14 Flask Walk,
NW3; 7435 4580).

Hollybush

22 Holly Mount, Hampstead, NW3 (7435 2892).
Hampstead tube. **Open** noon-11pm Mon-Sat;
noon-10.30pm Sun. **Credit** MC, V.
One of the oldest and most picturesque drinking
haunts in the area, the Hollybush is well hidden up
a tiny backstreet. It has four bars, low ceilings, wood
and plaster walls, and a real coal fire that is great
for toe-warming after winter walks.

Home Swede home: **Nordic**. *See p222.*

Monkey Chews

2 Queen's Crescent, Camden, NW5 (7267 6406/ www.monkeychews.com). Chalk Farm tube.
Open 4-11pm Mon-Fri; noon-midnight Sat; noon-10.30pm Sun. **Credit** MC, V.
Situated at the right end of Camden – as far from the market and the High Street as possible – this is a visually stunning bar, a wild cross between opium den and beach hut. Cocktails are cheap, and the regular DJs don't hurt the ears: try the excellent Moon Palace every first Sunday of the month.

Queen's

49 Regent's Park Road, Camden, NW1 (7586 0408). Chalk Farm tube. **Open** 11am-11pm Mon-Sat; noon-10.30pm Sun. **Credit** MC, V.
A north London gastropub that's a cut above the rest in every department. Food, served in the upstairs dining room, is terrific; drinks come from the Young's brewery. The Queen's oozes civility; it may be the nicest pub in Primrose Hill.

Shakespeare

57 Allen Road, Stoke Newington, N16 (7254 4190). Bus 73. **Open** 5-11pm Mon-Fri; noon-11pm Sat; noon-10.30pm Sun. **Credit** MC, V.
The best boozer in Stokey has retained its homey atmosphere thanks to a location just a little off the beaten track, a terrific and ever-changing range of beers, a friendly vibe and one of the best jukeboxes you'll find in London.

East London

Cantaloupe

35-42 Charlotte Road, Shoreditch, EC2 (7613 4411/ www.cantaloupe.co.uk). Old Street tube/rail. **Open** 11am-midnight Mon-Fri; noon-midnight Sat; noon-11.30pm Sun. **Credit** AmEx, MC, V. **Map** p403 R4.
Credit where it's due: this bar opened before the Shoreditch area got turned into style-mag central. It's no longer as cutting edge as it was, but thank

London loves Beer

First of all, we're not talking lager. You know what that tastes like, and you have your favourites. No. You are welcome to them. No. What we are talking about is real ale. This is proper, living beer that continues to mature in the cask and is served without gas pressure… as opposed to lagers, which are pasteurised, filtered and pumped full of carbon dioxide before being served. The difference is huge.

There is a particular routine to which London real ale fanciers must accustom themselves. Enter pub/bar. Scan for ale pumps: inconclusive (by no means every pub serves it). Ask publican what ales are on offer. Tetley's/John Smith's smoothflow (both pale imitations – literally – of the originals) and Guinness comes the reply. If you're lucky.

So how best to navigate the Smoke's ale conundrum? Best to start at the **Beer Shop** in Hoxton (14 Pitfield Street, N1; 7739 3701). Here you'll find a stupendous cornucopia of bottled ales from all over the world and, next door, the Pitfield Organic Brewery, which emerged in 1980 as herald to the first of many Real Ale Revivals. Nip into the nearby **Foundry** (84-6 Great Eastern Street, EC2; 7739 6900) to sample one of Pitfield's wonders in the former bank's anarchic decor and frank conviviality.

Other boozers are even more welcoming to the ale lover, and offer brews you won't find elsewhere. Take the **Jerusalem Tavern** (55 Britton Street, EC1; 7490 4281),

Clerkenwell's proud old-skool provider of beers from Suffolk's mighty St Peter's Brewery. The old-fashioned wooden premises date from 1720, when – pity the flagon-wielding 18th-century gentlemen – it was a coffee house. Get yourself a pint of fruit beer and score the prize mezzanine-level table.

More hard-to-find beers can be found at marvellous Harvey's pub the **Royal Oak** (*see p220*) and, for the geographically adventurous, the **William the Fourth** (816 Leyton High Road, E10; 8556 2460). This foliage and artefact-packed Victorian pub is the sole venue to offer the wonderful ales brewed downstairs in the Sweet William microbrewery, with E10 Red being the pick of a scintillating selection.

You needn't travel, of course: chain pubs run by the enigmatic Sam Smith's brewery and JD Wetherspoons both serve commendably large ranges of real ale. Smith's pubs are everywhere, while Wetherspoons are rapidly proliferating across the city, with huge swanky premises alongside smaller, peculiarly greasy outlets largely populated by older daytime quaffers. Both provide mighty fine ales at a nice price.

Beer in London comes from all corners of the country, but two large local brewers dominate the landscape and run many pubs in the city. **Young's** have around 150 boozers in London, and also offers a fine tour of its Wandsworth brewery premises (68 Wandsworth High Street, SW18; 8875 7005),

Christ for that: it's now 'just' a nice, buzzy place to have a drink and something to eat in an area where nice, buzzy places are few and far between.

Charlie Wright's International Bar

45 Pitfield Street, Hoxton, N1 (7490 8345). Old Street tube/rail. **Open** noon-1am Mon-Wed; noon-2am Thur-Sun. **Credit** AmEx, MC, V. **Map** p403 Q3.
Mr Wright is a Ghanaian powerlifter. His bar is an institution. DJs play Thursday to Sunday and the beer's exceptional, but you come to Charlie Wright's for the other customers, a gloriously eccentric cavalcade of chancers and wits, locals and travellers, all in search of A Good Time. Most find it here.

Ferry House

26 Ferry Street, Docklands, E14 (7537 9587). Island Gardens DLR. **Open** 2-11pm Mon-Fri; 11am-11pm Sat; noon-10.30pm Sun. **Credit** AmEx, MC, V.
As the name suggests, the Ferry House began life as the ferry master's residence, with the present

where ale has been created on the same site since 1581. Chiswick-based **Fullers** taints itself by continuing to retail its flagship brew, the bafflingly popular London Pride, but that's not the extent of its generally enticing bunch. If you can try but one beer from each, pick Young's Double Chocolate Stout and Fullers Organic Honey Dew.

After a period when all anyone here did was suck down bottles of gassy but fashionable lager and sickly alcopops, the kidz seem to be taking to real beer in a big way again. Do be sure to join them in raising a frothy pint pot and toasting the wonders of the hop. Here's to the death of bland lager's dominion!

building going up in 1823. These days it's an old-fashioned family boozer, with cheap booze and a traditional London Fives dartboard.

Grapes

76 Narrow Street, Limehouse, E14 (7987 4396). Limehouse or West Ferry DLR. **Open** noon-3pm, 5.30-11pm Mon-Fri; noon-11pm Sat; noon-10.30pm Sun. **Credit** AmEx, DC, MC, V.
This superb little pub is steeped in Dickensian charm, and is a real treat in summer if you can find space on the small riverside deck. Best of all, there's no music to disturb the convivial hubbub.

Home

100-106 Leonard Street, Shoreditch, EC2 (7684 8618/www.homebar.co.uk). Old Street tube/rail. **Open** noon-midnight Mon-Fri; 6pm-midnight Sat. **Credit** AmEx, DC, MC, V. **Map** p403 Q4.
It's not quite as welcoming as its name suggests – not least because you wouldn't want to arrive back at your flat to find some of its customers in your living room – but sink into one of the comfy armchairs with a cocktail and you'll find it terribly hard to leave. There are DJs most nights.

Mother Bar

333 Old Street, Shoreditch, EC1 (7739 5949/ www.333mother.com). Old Street tube/rail. **Open** 8pm-2am daily. **Credit** AmEx, MC, V. **Map** p403 R3.
With the **Shoreditch Electricity Showrooms** (39A Hoxton Square, N1; 7738 6934) having seemingly become something of a cliché for the fashionistas, this cosy bar above the 333 club is currently the boozer's bar of choice down Shoreditch. Beware, though, the hideous queues and erratic door policy.

Pride of Spitalfields

3 Heneage Street, Spitalfields, E1 (7247 8933). Aldgate East tube. **Open** 11am-11pm Mon-Sat; noon-10.30pm Sun. **Credit** AmEx, MC, V. **Map** p403 S5.
A genial family-run pub that's resisted the local trend towards DJ nights; unsurprising, given its fantastically mixed clientele (from businessmen and medical students to builders and OAPs). The beer's good, as it should be.

Prospect of Whitby

57 Wapping Wall, Wapping, E1 (7481 1095). Wapping tube. **Open** 11.30am-11pm Mon-Sat; noon-10.30pm Sun. **Credit** AmEx, DC, MC, V.
Built in 1520 and last remodelled in 1777, this historic pub has aged gracefully. The pewter-topped counter, stone-flagged floors, giant timbers and pebbled windows have all been preserved. Enjoy the river views but beware the coach parties.

Sir Alfred Hitchcock Hotel

147 Whipps Cross Road, Leytonstone, E11 (8530 3724). Leytonstone tube. **Open** 11am-11pm Mon-Sat; noon-10.30pm Sun. **Credit** MC, V.
Hitchcock was from around these parts, and portraits of the old curmudgeon line the walls here. In summer, you'd do well to grab one of the outside tables, which afford enticing views of Epping Forest.

Eat, Drink, Shop

Sosho

*2 Tabernacle Street, Shoreditch, EC2 (7920 0701/
www.sosho3am.com). Moorgate or Old Street tube/
rail.* **Open** 11am-10pm Mon; 11am-midnight
Tue,Wed; 11am-2am Thur; 11am-3am Fri; 7pm-3am
Sat. **Admission** £3-£5 after 9pm Fri; £5 after 9pm
Sat. **Credit** AmEx, DC, MC, V.
Peerlessly discerning, Sosho comes into its own as
soon as the cocktail shaker appears, wielded by bar
tenders of rare dexterity. The spacious lounge is decorated with glam touches, while DJs mix it up as con-
fidently as their colleagues working the bar above.

South London

Bread & Roses

*68 Clapham Manor Street, Clapham, SW4 (7498
1779/www.breadandrosespub.com). Clapham
Common or Clapham North tube.* **Open** 11am-11pm
Mon-Sat; noon-10.30pm Sun. **Credit** MC, V.
An excellent, spacious hostelry with a minimalist
interior that somehow manages to retain a traditional pub atmosphere. There's good beer, music,
poetry and comedy events, and a tasty, affordable
African buffet on Sundays.

Dogstar

*389 Coldharbour Lane, Brixton, SW9 (7733 7515/
www.dogstarbar.co.uk). Brixton tube/rail.* **Open**
noon-2am Mon-Thur, Sun; noon-4am Fri, Sat.
Credit AmEx, MC, V.
Where the Brixton revival began, offering late bev-
erages and loud sounds to twentysomethings bored
with the prices and pretensions of the West End.
Less hip than it was, but no less busy.

Fire Stables

*27-9 Church Road, Wimbledon, SW19 (8946 3197/
www.thespiritgroup.com). Wimbledon tube/rail then
200, 93 bus.* **Open** 10am-11pm Mon-Sat; 10am-
10.30pm Sun. **Credit** AmEx, MC, V.
It used to be a dire boozer called the Castle, but these
days the Fire Stables is an upmarket, minimalist bar
with sophisticated cooking. Well worth the schlep it
takes to get here; try to book if you're eating.

Inigo

*642 Wandsworth Road, Battersea, SW8 (7622 4884/
www.inigobar.com). Clapham Common tube.* **Open**
6pm-2am Mon-Fri; noon-2am Sat, Sun. **Credit** MC, V.
The punters at this revamped pub will groove anywhere they can find the space. There are plenty of
them, too, with queues out front every weekend after
11pm. DJs kick off at 8pm daily; turn up between
6pm and 10pm (6-9pm Fri-Sun) and you can snack
on decent pizza as well.

Mayflower

*117 Rotherhithe Street, Rotherhithe, SE16
(7237 4088). Rotherhithe tube/188, P11, P13 bus.*
Open noon-11pm Mon-Sat; noon-10.30pm Sun.
Credit AmEx, DC, MC, V.
A historic seafaring inn with rackety wooden floors,
small wood-partitioned areas and narrow settles

Mother Bar. *See p227.*

(the timbers are reputed to have come from the
Mayflower ship). Greene King bitters are on offer, as
is a short but varied wine list.

Sand

*156 Clapham Park Road, Clapham, SW4 (7622
3022/www.sandbarrestaurant.co.uk). Clapham
Common tube.* **Open** 5pm-2am Mon-Sat; 5pm-1am
Sun. **Credit** MC, V.
The decor's easy on the eye, the listening (Sinatra,
Bacharach) easy on the ear, and candles, spotlights
and intimate (usually reserved) alcoves make it all
very cosy. Add DJs at weekends, miniature movies
and the obligatory sharp Antipodean staff.

Ship

*41 Jew's Row, Wandsworth, SW18 (8870 9667).
Wandsworth Town rail.* **Open** 11am-11pm Mon-Sat;
noon-10.30pm Sun. **Credit** AmEx, MC, V.
The summer pub to end all summer pubs: there's a
lovely riverside beer garden and a barbecue when
the sun comes out. On the other 363 days of the year,
dine on solid pub food and sup on Young's ales or,
on Sundays, a knockout Bloody Mary.

Sultan

*78 Norman Road, Colliers Wood, SW19 (8542
4532). Colliers Wood tube.* **Open** noon-11pm Mon-
Sat; noon-10.30pm Sun. **Credit** MC, V.
Fact #1: this is the only mention, in the 416 pages
of this book, of the nondescript south-west suburb
of Colliers Wood. Fact #2: it's worth coming down

Eat, Drink, Shop

here for the ales alone, chiefly from Salisbury's Hop Back brewery. Drink enough of them and the ride back to civilisation will positively fly by.

Tongue & Groove
50 Atlantic Road, Brixton, SW9 (7274 8600/ www.tongueandgroove.org). Brixton tube/rail. **Open** 8pm-3am Tue-Sun. **Admission** £3 after 11pm Fri, Sat. **Credit** AmEx, MC, V.
This wanton, hip bar is packed most nights of the week, and while it's not worth queuing outside, as many do on weekends, it's great if you're inside. Pornographic murals adorn the walls, cocktails fill the stomachs.

Trafalgar Tavern
6 Park Row, Greenwich, SE10 (8858 2437/ www.trafalgartavern.co.uk). Cutty Sark DLR/ Greenwich or Maze Hill rail. **Open** 11.30am-11pm Mon-Sat; noon-10.30pm Sun. **Credit** MC, V.
This historic pub on the site of the Old George Inn was built in 1837 as a tribute to naval hero Horatio Nelson. There's mahogany panelling, stone fireplaces and the like, plus a riverside terrace.

West London

Albertine
1 Wood Lane, Shepherd's Bush, W12 (8743 9593). Shepherd's Bush tube. **Open** 11am-11pm Mon-Fri; 6.30-11pm Sat. **Credit** MC, V.
It's not about gimmicks at this unassuming hangout: it's purely about wine. It gets busy with the post-work crowd, but the friendly owner is often on hand to help navigate the lengthy menu.

Anglesea Arms
35 Wingate Road, Shepherd's Bush, W6 (8749 1291). Goldhawk Road or Ravenscourt Park tube. **Open** 11am-11pm Mon-Sat; noon-10.30pm Sun. **Credit** MC, V.
Dark wooden floors, exposed brick walls, big leather sofas. You've probably seen it all before, but the Anglesea is still an attractive, comfortable boozer serving fine food with a splendid wine list.

Archery Tavern
4 Bathurst Street, Paddington, W2 (7402 4916). Lancaster Gate tube. **Open** 11am-11pm Mon-Sat; noon-10.30pm Sun. **Credit** AmEx, MC, V. **Map** p395 D6.
This genteel pub sticks to most traditional formulae: plates on the walls, bunches of dried hops, and regulars who commandeer their favourite seat and ask the staff by name to turn the music down.

Canvas
177 Portobello Road, Ladbroke Grove, W11 (7727 2700). Ladbroke Grove or Notting Hill tube. **Open** 5-11pm Tue-Sat; 5-10.30pm Sun. **Credit** MC, V.
Canvas is cool when this review was written but, such is the short attention span of the Notting Hill style-mag posse, it may be over before you arrive. No matter: its 21st-century take on 1970s retro chic is nicer than most.

Churchill Arms
119 Kensington Church Street, Kensington, W8 (7727 4242). High Street Kensington or Notting Hill Gate tube. **Open** 11am-11pm Mon-Sat; noon-10.30pm Sun. **Credit** MC, V. **Map** p394 B8.
Lepidopterists will want to check out the boxed butterflies on display at the back of this pub; others can sink a few ales and tuck into good, cheap Thai food.

Dove
19 Upper Mall, Hammersmith, W6 (8748 5405). Hammersmith tube. **Open** 11am-11pm Mon-Sat; noon-10.30pm Sun. **Credit** AmEx, MC, V.
More than 300 years old and gloriously dishevelled, the Dove has three small split-level rooms around a

Rotherhithe's **Mayflower**. *See p228.*

central bar – one room, at 3.35sq ft (3.12sq m), is the smallest bar in England – and a pretty ivy-clad riverside terrace. A gem, all told.

Grand Union
45 Woodfield Road, Westbourne Park, W9 (7286 1886). Westbourne Park tube. **Open** noon-11pm Mon-Sat; noon-10.30pm Sun. **Credit** MC, V.
A dramatic refurb has cleared out the bus drivers from the nearby depot who used to drink here, and ushered in a decidedly middle-class, self-consciously stylish clientele. The gastropub food is good; the jukebox is better.

Westbourne
101 Westbourne Park Villas, Notting Hill, W2 (7221 1332). Royal Oak tube. **Open** 5-11pm Mon; noon-11pm Tue-Fri; noon-11pm Sat; noon-10.30pm Sun. **Credit** AmEx, DC, MC, V. **Map** p394 B5.
The only way to get an outside table at this terminally hip and almost invariably ram-jammed pub is to turn up when it's chucking it down. A good range of wines and beers, as well as smoothies, make it worth the squeeze.

White Horse
1-3 Parsons Green, Fulham, SW6 (7736 2115/ www.whitehorsesw6.com). Parsons Green tube. **Open** 11am-11pm Mon-Sat; 11am-10.30pm Sun. **Credit** AmEx, MC, V.
This imposing multi-bar Victorian boozer has been pleasantly modernised and comfortably decked out with sofas and chunky wooden furniture. More than 100 fine wines are stocked, plus real ale and every available Trappist brew.

White Swan
Riverside, Twickenham, Middx (8892 2166). Twickenham rail. **Open** *Apr-Sept* 11am-11pm Mon-Sat; noon-10.30pm Sun. *Oct-Mar* 11am-3pm, 5.30-11pm Mon-Thur; 11am-11pm Fri, Sat; noon-10.30pm Sun. **Credit** MC, V.
This characterful riverside pub attracts connoisseurs from miles around. Some come for the beer, which is well kept; on matchdays at nearby Twickenham, the place gets overrun with rugby fans. Raised to avoid flooding, the White Swan overlooks Eel Pie Island, the one-time 1960s rock hangout and still a last refuge for keepers of alternative culture.

Eat, Drink, Shop

After hours

Finding a legal place to drink after 11pm in London is not as tough as it once was. However, until the licensing laws changes – in 2003, if we're lucky – it's tricky to find a late-opening spot that's both decent and free to enter. A few pockets of London – Shoreditch, Soho – are packed with late-licensed bars, but most levy an admission charge after 11pm, from the reasonable (£1.50 at the ICA's bar on the Mall, open until 1am Tue-Sat) to the pricey (Opium on Dean Street in Soho charges a sickening £15 after 10pm). All the places listed below are free at all times.

Admission charge or no, as a rule, you can expect any legal late-opening bar in central London to be eardrum-burstingly loud, packed to the gills with drunks and generally verging on nightclub territory. For taking the quieter, illegal option, *see p223*; and for more on late DJ bars and clubs, *see p322*.

Akbar *77 Dean Street, Soho, W1 (7437 2525).* **Open** noon-1am Mon-Fri; 5pm-1am Sat; 6-10.30pm Sun.
Amber *6 Poland Street, Soho, W1 (7734 3094).* **Open** 5pm-1am Mon-Fri; 4pm-1am Sat.
Atlantic Bar & Grill *20 Glasshouse Street, Covent Garden, W1 (7734 4888).* **Open** noon-3am Mon-Fri; 6pm-3am Sat.
Bar Soho *23-5 Old Compton Street, Soho, W1 (7439 0439).* **Open** 4pm-1am Mon-Thur; 4pm-3am Fri, Sat; 4pm-12.30am Sun.

Café Bohème *13 Old Compton Street, Soho, W1 (7734 0623).* **Open** 8am-2.30am Mon-Sat; 8am-11pm Sun.
Café Lazeez *21 Dean Street, Soho, W1 (7434 9393).* **Open** 11am-1am Mon-Sat.
Cuba *11-13 Kensington High Street, Kensington, W8 (7938 4137).* **Open** noon-2am Mon-Sat; 3-10.30pm Sun.
Eclipse *113 Walton Street, South Kensington, SW3 (7581 0123).* **Open** 5.30pm-1am Mon-Fri; 2pm-1am Sat; 2pm-12.30am Sun.
Hakkasan *8 Hanway Place, Fitzrovia, WC2 (7907 1888).* **Open** *Bar* noon-midnight Mon-Wed; noon-2am Thur-Sat; noon-11.30pm Sun.
The Langley *5 Langley Street, Covent Garden, WC2 (7836 5005).* **Open** 4.30pm-1am Mon-Sat; 3-10.30pm Sun.
Mash *19-21 Great Portland Street, W1 (7637 5555).* **Open** 11am-midnight Mon, Tue; 11am-2am Wed-Sat.
Point 101 *101 New Oxford Street, St Giles's, WC1 (7379 3112).* **Open** 11am-2.30am Mon-Sat; noon-2.30am Sun.
Sevilla Mia *22 Hanway Street, Fitzrovia, W1 (7637 3756).* **Open** 7pm-1am Mon-Sat; 7pm-midnight Sun.
Steam *1 Eastbourne Terrace, Marylebone, W2 (7850 0555).* **Open** 9am-1am Mon-Wed; 9am-2am Thur, Fri; 11am-2am Sat; 11am-11pm Sun.

Shops & Services

Shoppers be glad, credit cards beware: anything buyable can be bought on the streets of London.

Case out **Alfie's Antique Market**.

In introduction to London's shopping pleasures, there's simply not much to say, apart from what you probably already know: whatever you want, you'll find it here. It might be expensive – the price of goods in London doesn't compare favourably with other large cities in either Europe or the US – but someone, somewhere will have what you're after.

Head to **Oxford Street** for the best selection of high street chains, department stores and stifling crowds. Try **Covent Garden** or **Knightsbridge** for fashion (cool and chi-chi respectively). **Soho** and **Notting Hill** are good for music, **Charing Cross Road** is book central and the **King's Road** is your best bet for homewares and kids' stuff. Only resort to **Camden** when desperate.

Central London shops are open late one night a week, usually till 7pm or 8pm. Those in the West End (Oxford Street to Covent Garden) are open until late on Thursdays, while Wednesday is late opening in Chelsea, Knightsbridge and Kensington. In addition, some shops extend their hours in the weeks before Christmas.

For further listings and reviews, the *Time Out Shopping Guide* is available in good bookshops and newsagents. For information on consumer rights, *see p362*.

Antiques

Islington, Kensington and Chelsea are the three antiques centres in London. *Antiques Trade Gazette* (www.antiquestradegazette.com), *The Collector* (www.artefact.co.uk) and *Antique Collecting* (www.antique-acc.com) have listings on London and regional dealers, plus details of auctions and antiques fairs. A variety of merchandise is available at the antiques markets listed below. **Greenwich Market** (*see p255*) also has a sizeable antiques section, as does **Portobello Road Market** (*see p256*).

Alfie's Antiques Market
13-25 Church Street, Marylebone, NW8 (7723 6066/ www.ealfies.com). Baker Street tube. **Open** 10am-6pm Tue-Sat. **Credit** varies. **Map** p395 E4.
Alfie's is a bit of warren, with too many staircases and rows of stalls that look the same, so to keep your bearings it's a good idea to start in the basement, where furniture (especially 20th century) is the mainstay, and work your way up. Otherwise it's Arts and Crafts, kitchenware, textiles, prints, ceramics and glass, militaria, silver and jewellery.

The best Shops

For one-stop shopping
Selfridges. See p236.

For second-hand books
Any Amount of Books. See p233.

For cheese lovers
Neal's Yard Dairy. See p248.

For sexy undies
Agent Provocateur. See p243.

For classy cosmetics
SPAce.NK. See p252.

Camden Passage Antiques Market

Camden Passage, off Upper Street, Islington, N1 (7359 0190). Angel tube. **Open** *Shops hours vary. Market 7am-4pm Wed; 8am-5pm Sat.* **Credit** varies. **Map** p402 O2.

With its charming narrow pedestrian street lined with old shopfronts and its Regency-style arcades, this is an enjoyable place to browse for everything from jewellery to furniture. Stalls are primarily aimed at dealers and wealthy buyers, so casual browsers aren't always given the warmest welcome. Many close earlier than advertised, at around 3pm.

Grays Antiques Market & Grays in the Mews

58 Davies Street & 1-7 Davies Mews, Mayfair, W1 (7629 7034/www.emews.com/www.egrays.com). Bond Street tube. **Open** *10am-6pm Mon-Fri (books also 10am-6pm Sat).* **Credit** varies. **Map** p398 H6.

The main Grays market has probably the best selection of antique jewellery in London, as well as other bijou antiques. The Mews has specialists in many areas, including sporting collectibles, ceramics, dolls/children's toys and Victorian glass.

Books

General

Blackwell's

100 Charing Cross Road, St Giles's, WC2 (7292 5100/www.blackwell.co.uk). Tottenham Court Road tube. **Open** *9.30am-8pm Mon-Sat; noon-6pm Sun.* **Credit** AmEx, MC, V. **Map** p399 K5.

Cinema Bookshop: for film fans.

An excellent general branch of the academic bookseller. What: no coffee shop? Extraordinary. Just lots and lots of books and informed staff.

Books Etc

263 High Holborn, Holborn, WC1 (7404 0261/ www.booksetc.co.uk). Holborn tube. **Open** *9am-7pm Mon-Fri.* **Credit** AmEx, MC, V. **Map** p399 M5.

This extremely popular shop, part of the Borders empire (*see below*), has a good general stock. **Branches**: throughout the city.

Borders

203 Oxford Street, St Giles's, W1 (7292 1600/ www.borders.com). Oxford Circus tube. **Open** *8am-11pm Mon-Sat; noon-6pm Sun.* **Credit** AmEx, MC, V. **Map** p398 J6.

The vast range of books includes some US imports you won't find elsewhere, while the choice of magazines remains impressively eclectic, from quality literary publications to the glossies. The in-store café has been rebranded and expanded by Starbucks. **Branches**: throughout the city.

Foyles

113-19 Charing Cross Road, Soho, WC2 (7437 5660/www.foyles.co.uk). Tottenham Court Road tube. **Open** *9.30am-8pm Mon-Sat; noon-6pm Sun.* **Credit** AmEx, DC, MC, V. **Map** p399 K6.

The reinvention and refurbishment of the formerly musty and unuseable Foyles continues apace. Within its walls now are Silver Moon Women's Bookshop and Ray's Jazz Shop, but its core business remains serious bibliophiles: this is still the best shop in London to find out-of-print titles.

Waterstone's

203-6 Piccadilly, St James's, W1 (7851 2400/ www.waterstones.co.uk). Piccadilly Circus tube. **Open** *10am-11pm Mon-Sat; noon-6pm Sun.* **Credit** AmEx, DC, MC, V. **Map** p400 J7.

This flagship store of the Waterstone's chain is Europe's biggest bookshop, and a great environment in which to browse or attend author signings and readings. There's a gallery space, an event room and even a restaurant. **Branches**: throughout the city.

Specialist

Books for Cooks

4 Blenheim Crescent, Notting Hill, W11 (7221 1992/ www.booksforcooks.com). Ladbroke Grove tube. **Open** *10am-6pm Tue-Sat.* **Credit** AmEx, MC, V.

Two decades old but still going strong, Books for Cooks sells recipe books and books about food from around the world. A café at the rear is as popular with casual shoppers as it is with the cognoscenti.

Cinema Bookshop

13-14 Great Russell Street, Fitzrovia, WC1 (7637 0206). Tottenham Court Road tube. **Open** *10.30am-5.30pm Mon-Sat.* **Credit** MC, V. **Map** p399 K5.

Fred Zentner's shop was the first in Europe to deal exclusively with film material: Peter Cushing was his first customer. The shop sells lobby cards, posters and stills, plus new and out of print books.

Daunt Books
83 Marylebone High Street, Marylebone, W1 (7224 2295). Baker Street tube. **Open** 9am-7.30pm Mon-Sat; 11am-6pm Sun. **Credit** MC, V. **Map** p398 G5.
The rear of this beautiful shop holds a magnificent selection of travel literature, maps and guides. It also has good general stock and a fine kids' section. **Branch**: 193 Haverstock Hill, Hampstead, NW3 (7794 4006).

Edward Stanford
12-14 Long Acre, Covent Garden, WC2 (7836 1321/ www.stanfords.co.uk). Covent Garden or Leicester Square tube. **Open** 9am-7.30pm Mon, Wed-Fri; 9.30am-7.30pm Tue; 10am-7pm Sat; noon-6pm Sun. **Credit** MC, V. **Map** p401 L6.
The first stop for map and globe hunters, Stanford also stocks general travel literature and more guides than you can fit in your rucksack. The basement is devoted to maps and guides to the British Isles.

Forbidden Planet
71-5 New Oxford Street, St Giles's, WC1 (7836 4179/www.forbiddenplanet.com). Tottenham Court Road tube. **Open** 10am-6pm Mon-Wed, Sat; 10am-7pm Thur, Fri. **Credit** AmEx, MC, V. **Map** p399 L5.
The ground floor is a treasure trove of comics, videos, magazines and models. Head down to the basement for books and magazines, where sci-fi, fantasy, horror and slipstream are all well represented.

Gay's the Word
66 Marchmont Street, Bloomsbury, WC1 (7278 7654/www.gaystheword.co.uk). Russell Square tube. **Open** 10am-6.30pm Mon-Sat; 2-6pm Sun. **Credit** AmEx, DC, MC, V. **Map** p399 L4.
This excellent gay and lesbian bookshop has been operating on this little street since 1979. Fiction, travel, counselling, sex manuals, biography, even second-hand books: it's all here.

Helter Skelter
4 Denmark Street, St Giles's, WC2 (7836 1151/ www.skelter.demon.co.uk). Tottenham Court Road tube. **Open** 10am-7pm Mon-Fri; 10am-6pm Sat. **Credit** MC, V. **Map** p399 K6.
The world's only rock 'n' roll bookstore stocks a wild array of publications on bands both famous and forgotten (some published by its own imprint), plus stacks of magazines and fanzines.

Magma
117-19 Clerkenwell Road, Clerkenwell, EC1 (7242 9503/www.magmabooks.com). Farringdon tube/rail. **Open** 10am-7pm Mon-Sat. **Credit** AmEx, MC, V. **Map** p402 N4.
A superb shop for art, photography, design, illustration, animation, posters and postcards. **Branch**: 8 Earlham Street, Covent Garden, WC2 (7240 8498).

Murder One
71-3 Charing Cross Road, Chinatown, WC2 (7734 3483/www.murderone.co.uk). Leicester Square tube. **Open** 10am-7pm Mon-Wed; 10am-8pm Thur-Sat. **Credit** AmEx, MC, V. **Map** p401 K6.
Writer Maxim Jakubowski owns this superb shop for genre fans. Crime, mystery, horror, fantasy, science fiction and, a little incongruously, romance are catered for over two floors.

Zwemmer
72 Charing Cross Road, Covent Garden, WC2 (7240 4158/www.zwemmer.com). Leicester Square tube. **Open** 10am-6.30pm Mon-Wed, Fri; 10am-8pm Thur; 10am-6pm Sat. **Credit** AmEx, MC, V. **Map** p401 K6.
Zwemmer has numerous branches, each with a different specialisation. This one has books on design, graphics and architecture; others deal with subjects including contemporary art, fashion and film. **Branches**: throughout the city.

Used & antiquarian
The **Riverside Walk Market** (10am-5pm Sat, Sun and irregular weekdays) on the South Bank under Waterloo Bridge has cheap paperbacks. If you're after hard-to-find titles, try www.alibris.com or www.bibliofind.com.

Any Amount of Books
56 Charing Cross Road, Covent Garden, WC2 (7836 3697/www.anyamountofbooks.com). Leicester Square tube. **Open** 10.30am-9.30pm Mon-Sat; 11.30am-7.30pm Sun. **Credit** AmEx, MC, V. **Map** p401 K6.
This is what second-hand book buying is all about: hand-drawn maps to (theoretically) guide you through the rooms, a shabby charm diametrically opposed to the likes of Borders (*see p232*). Fiction, sci-fi, lit-crit, lit-biog, military and history upstairs; science, architecture, medicine, religion and occult, sexuality, poetry and reference downstairs.

Skoob Russell Square
10 Brunswick Centre, Bloomsbury, WC1 (7278 8760/www.skoob.com). Russell Square tube. **Open** 11am-7pm Mon-Sat; noon-5pm Sun. **Credit** AmEx, MC, V. **Map** p399 L4.
One of London's most comprehensive second-hand bookshops, Skoob caters for students, academics and those with special interests. Prices are low and students are given a discount. The video and DVD section is pretty extensive too.

Ulysses
40 Museum Street, Bloomsbury, WC1 (7831 1600). Holborn tube. **Open** 10.30am-6pm Mon-Sat. **Credit** AmEx, MC, V. **Map** p399 L5.
One of the best places in London for 20th-century first editions. The really valuable books (prices head into the thousands) are in glass cabinets, but there are plenty of beauties in the £30-£100 range. Rare kids' books, biography and prints are also stocked.

Eat, Drink, Shop

Fortnum & Mason: a regal setting for high-class comestibles.

Department stores

Fortnum & Mason

181 Piccadilly, St James's, W1 (7734 8040/ www.fortnumandmason.co.uk). Green Park or Piccadilly Circus tube. **Open** 10am-6.30pm Mon-Sat. **Credit** AmEx, MC, V. **Map** p400 J7.

Few can resist Fortnum's moving character clock, with its little costumed footmen tolling the hour, or the peppermint-green façade with its tiny windows dressed up with food in inventive ways. Britain's most famous food store is positively regal: red carpets, marbled pillars, chandeliers. Few visitors make it beyond the ground floor, but in the blissful hush of the other levels there's (very) fine china (Limoges, Hermès), fashion (Paul Smith, Caroline Charles, Jean Muir, MaxMara), a gem of a children's department and an unpressured perfumery (Creed, Acqua di Parma and F&M's own brand).

Harrods

87-135 Brompton Road, Knightsbridge, SW1 (7730 1234/www.harrods.com). Knightsbridge tube. **Open** 10am-7pm Mon-Sat. **Credit** AmEx, DC, MC, V. **Map** p397 F9.

Few locals stray beyond the magnificent food halls of the world's most famous department store, while tourists are bedazzled by the ground-floor Luxury Room's watches and bags, or the Egyptian Hall's expensive gifts of brass, bronze and crystal. There's a theme-park feel to Harrods World (tea tins, golf balls and teddies bearing the gold logo), but browsing the conservative fashion floors (Joseph, Armani, Moschino) can be a calming pleasure. Furniture is of the repro/rococo variety, but there is a whole room of grand pianos, and the cookware department is excellent. Stylish refreshment, from oysters to tapas, is provided in venues dotted around the food halls, and a new spa and hairdressing salon has just opened on the fifth floor.

Harvey Nichols

109-25 Knightsbridge, Knightsbridge, SW1 (7235 5000/www.harveynichols.com). Knightsbridge tube. **Open** 10am-7pm Mon, Tue, Sat; 10am-8pm Wed-Fri; noon-6pm Sun. **Credit** AmEx, DC, MC, V. **Map** p397 F9.

Harvey Nicks no longer stands out from the crowd of spruced-up department stores: the much-admired window displays have been lacklustre of late, and the new Beyond Beauty section of the cosmetics department is not as groundbreaking as some have claimed. The fashion floors are better (hot labels such as Dries van Noten and Stella McCartney tussle with the dependable Jean Muir) and the Playground is fun for flatscreen TVs, but the best floor is the fifth: the stylishly packaged and expensive groceries taste fabulous, and the café is suffused with light.

John Lewis

278-306 Oxford Street, Marylebone, W1 (7629 7711/www.johnlewis.co.uk). Bond Street or Oxford Circus tube. **Open** 9.30am-7pm Mon-Wed, Fri, Sat; 9.30am-8pm Thur. **Credit** MC, V. **Map** p398 H6.

John Lewis's deservedly loyal customer base speaks with fondness and reverence about the range of products, but we're not talking cutting-edge design. John Lewis means rock solid, middle-of-the-road stuff that does the job, free delivery for the tiniest item, and the 'never knowingly undersold' price guarantee. There's a good new men's department, while women's fashions mix bourgeois (Betty Barclay, Liz Claiborne) with vaguely funky (Monsoon, Mexx).
Branches: Brent Cross Shopping Centre, NW4 (8202 6535); Wood Street, Kingston, Surrey (8547 3000).

Liberty

210-20 Regent Street, Soho, W1 (7734 1234/ www.liberty.co.uk). Oxford Circus tube. **Open** 10am-6.30pm Mon-Wed; 10am-8pm Thur; 10am-7pm Fri, Sat; noon-6pm Sun. **Credit** AmEx, DC, MC, V. **Map** p398 J6.

Its uniqueness, its often wayward design sense and its rich trading history (encompassing strong oriental connections, the British Arts and Crafts movement and, of course, an enviable archive of the famous Liberty prints) are what draw visitors to Liberty. Enter via Great Marlborough Street for a sweet-scented brush with Paula Pryke's floristry conces-sion before emerging among the Liberty print gifts. The old toiletries department is still here, but its wares have been split with the new Regent Street building, which also sells women's shoes and men's shirts and ties. Distinctive fashions (Dries van Noten, Issey Miyake, Balenciaga) are sold upstairs.

Marks & Spencer
458 Oxford Street, Marylebone, W1 (7935 7954/www.marksandspencer.co.uk). Marble Arch tube. **Open** 9am-9pm Mon-Fri; 8.30am-7.30pm Sat; noon-6pm Sun. **Credit** AmEx, DC, MC, V. **Map** p398 G6.
Seemingly back on track after a period in the dol-drums, Marks & Sparks is now attempting to keep pace with the high street by mixing stylish clothes with sensible prices. Clear signs ('Silk', 'Leather', 'Linen' and so on) point to smart basics: linen shirts, black leather jackets and T-shirts in any neck shape and sleeve length you care to name. Childrenswear is cute and sticks to multi-pack economies, and the food hall is good for lazybones who are happy to splash out on a TV dinner (it also sells reasonably priced flowers and plants).
Branches: throughout the city.

Selfridges
400 Oxford Street, Marylebone, W1 (0870 837 7377/www.selfridges.com). Bond Street or Marble Arch tube. **Open** 10am-7pm Mon-Wed; 10am-8pm Thur, Fri; 9.30am-7pm Sat; noon-6pm Sun. **Credit** AmEx, DC, MC, V. **Map** p398 G6.
Selfridges is an empire as much as a department store, doing for W1 what Harrods tries to do for Knightsbridge. Come over all international gourmet in the food hall; get your eyesight checked, your teeth fixed and your back rubbed; head for the new techno department to be wowed by huge plasma screens. As well as wacky lifestyle concessions, a decent bookshop, a cookshop and an above-average glass department, the fashion offering is vast: from Kookaï to Miu Miu. The ground-floor accessories offers the best range of handbags in London.

Classy department store **Liberty**. *See p225.*

Electronics

Tottenham Court Road, W1, has a glut of electronics and computer shops. It's best to know what you're after and shop around for the best prices: staff are notoriously pushy.

Computers & games

Two other good stockists of video and computer games are **Virgin Megastore** and **HMV** (for both, *see p256*).

Apple Centre
78 New Oxford Street, Fitzrovia, WC1 (7692 9990/www.squaregroup.co.uk). Tottenham Court Road tube. **Open** 9am-5.30pm Mon-Wed, Fri; 9am-6.30pm Thur. **Credit** MC, V. **Map** p399 L5.
A shrine to all things Mac, with everything from PowerBooks to software on offer, and staff on hand to order Mac-related accessories. Repairs, printing and digital scanning are also offered.

Computer Exchange
70 Tottenham Court Road, Fitzrovia, W1 (7916 3110/www.cex.co.uk). Tottenham Court Road tube. **Open** 10am-7pm daily. **Credit** MC, V. **Map** p399 K5.
Used computers and printers at cut-rate prices; machines come with a 12-month warranty. The Rathbone Place branch specialises in video games. **Branch**: 32 Rathbone Place, Fitzrovia, W1 (7636 2666).

Gultronics
264-7 Tottenham Court Road, Fitzrovia, W1 (7436 4120/www.gultronics.co.uk). Tottenham Court Road tube. **Open** 10am-7pm Mon-Sat; 10am-5pm Sun. **Credit** AmEx, MC, V. **Map** p399 K5.
Gultronics is crammed with top-of-the-line Toshiba and Sony laptops, plus a wealth of PC accessories. **Branches**: throughout the city.

DVDs

Laser Disc Shop
15 Needham Road, Bayswater, W11 (7243 3142). Bayswater, Queensway or Notting Hill Gate tube. **Open** 10am-5pm Mon-Sat. **Credit** AmEx, MC, V. **Map** p394 A6.

This tiny Bayswater hideaway doesn't carry laser discs any more, but it does have a 40,000-strong DVD collection: everything from Hitchcock to Cheech & Chong.

Hi-fi

Hi-Fi Experience

227 Tottenham Court Road, Fitzrovia, W1 (7580 3535/www.hifilondon.co.uk). Tottenham Court Road tube. **Open** 10am-7pm Mon-Fri; 9am-6pm Sat. **Credit** AmEx, MC, V. **Map** p399 K5.

The elegant, gallery-like entrance to this shop is reflected in the sophistication of its stock – Mission, Marantz, Denon, NAD and Bang & Olufsen. The staff, however, are pretty down to earth.

Richer Sounds

2 London Bridge Walk, Bankside, SE1 (7403 1201/www.richersounds.co.uk). London Bridge tube/ rail. **Open** 10am-6pm Mon-Wed, Fri; 10am-7pm Thur; 10am-5pm Sat. **Credit** AmEx, MC, V. **Map** p405 Q8.

Richer Sounds has many prestigious brands – Marantz, Arcam, Sherwood, Cambridge Audio – at highly discounted prices. Staff claim they can set up a package of separate components for under £200. **Branches**: throughout the city.

Photography

City-wide chemist **Boots** (*see p252*) also offers developing and sells camera film.

Jessops

63-9 New Oxford Street, St Giles's, WC1 (7240 6077/www.jessops.co.uk). Tottenham Court Road tube. **Open** 9am-6pm Mon-Wed, Sat; 9am-8pm Thur; 9am-7pm Fri; 11am-5pm Sun. **Credit** AmEx, DC, MC, V. **Map** p399 L5.

The largest of Jessop's 20-odd London outlets, this branch sells everything from darkroom equipment, and retouching dye sets to projectors, scanners and Adobe Photoshop; there are also 35mm, APS, digital and medium-format cameras, plus a second-hand department with a nationwide database. And a wide range of camera film, of course.
Branches: throughout the city.

Fashion

Boutiques

Browns

23-7 South Molton Street, Mayfair, W1 (7514 0000/ www.brownsfashion.com). Bond Street tube. **Open** 10am-6.30pm Mon-Wed, Fri, Sat; 10am-7pm Thur. **Credit** AmEx, DC, MC, V. **Map** p398 H6.

This legendary emporium has a reputation for new labels. The roster includes Diane von Furstenberg, Marc Jacobs, Dries van Noten, Carlos Miele, Dolce & Gabbana and Hussein Chalayan; there's also a personal shopper service. Browns Focus (Nos.38-9) caters for the young and fashion-conscious; Labels for Less (No.50) is for the bargain hunters.
Branch: 6C Sloane Street, Chelsea, SW1 (7514 0040).

Designer fashion

London's high-fashion clothing emporia tend to be concentrated in and around two main areas: Mayfair, and Chelsea/South Kensington/Knightsbridge. Most shops are open 10am-6pm six days a week, with many Knightsbridge and South Ken stores opening until 7pm on Wednesdays and West End shops opening until 7pm on Thursdays.

If you're looking for a wide range of labels under one roof, try department stores **Harrods**, **Harvey Nichols**, **Liberty** (for all, *see p235*) or **Selfridges** (*see p236*).

Chelsea, SW3

Sloane Square tube.
King's Road: Joseph (sale shop), World's End (Vivienne Westwood).

Knightsbridge, SW1, SW7

Knightsbridge tube.
Sloane Street: Alberta Ferretti, Armani, Chanel, Christian Dior, Gucci, Hermès, MaxMara, Tommy Hilfiger.

Mayfair, W1

Bond Street tube.
Avery Row: Paul Smith (sale shop).
Brook Street: Comme des Garçons, Pleats Please (Issey Miyake).
Conduit Street: Issey Miyake, Moschino, Krizia, Vivienne Westwood, Yohji Yamamoto.
Davies Street: Vivienne Westwood.
New Bond Street: Burberry, Calvin Klein, Donna Karan, Collezioni Armani, Emporio Armani, Fenwick, Gianni Versace, Louis Vuitton, Miu Miu, Nicole Farhi, Ralph Lauren.
Old Bond Street: Dolce & Gabbana, DKNY, Joseph, Prada.

South Kensington, SW1, SW3

South Kensington tube.
Brompton Road: Emporio Armani, Issey Miyake, Betty Jackson.
Draycott Avenue: Betsey Johnson, Galerie Gaultier.
Sloane Avenue: Paul Smith.

Eat, Drink, Shop

Browns: always up to date with the latest labels. *See p237.*

The Cross

141 Portland Road, Holland Park, W11 (7727 6760). Holland Park tube. **Open** 10.30am-6pm Mon-Sat. **Credit** AmEx, MC, V.

This boutique contains a wealth of carefully selected labels, among them Boyd, Gharani Strok, Anna Sui, Chloé, Alice Lee, Dosa and Easton Pearson. Among the accessories are Elisa John belts, Anya Hindmarch shoes and Kaos bags.

Koh Samui

65-7 Monmouth Street, Covent Garden, WC2 (7240 4280). Covent Garden tube. **Open** 10am-6.30pm Mon, Tue, Sat; 10.30am-6.30pm Wed, Fri; 10.30am-7pm Thur; 11am-5.30pm Sun. **Credit** AmEx, DC, MC, V. **Map** p399 L6.

This perennial favourite boasts an eclectic collection of clothes by established and newer designers, with a unique mix of current trends and more avant-garde individual styles including Antonio Berardi, AF Vandevorst, Marjan Pejoski, Clements Ribeiro, Julien McDonald, Sophia Kokosalaki, Matthew Williamson and Earl Jeans.

Branch: 28 Lowndes Street, Belgravia, SW1 (7838 9292; womenswear only).

Budget

H&M

261-71 Regent Street, Marylebone, W1 (7493 4004/www.hm.com). Oxford Circus tube. **Open** 10am-7pm Mon-Wed, Sat; 10am-8pm Thur, Fri; noon-6pm Sun. **Credit** AmEx, MC, V. **Map** p400 J7.

Trendies, from teenagers to 30-year-olds, know they can score a hit at H&M. Its largest London store, at Oxford Circus, is home to fantastic fashion at a snip. **Branches**: throughout the city.

Mango

8-12 Neal Street, Covent Garden, WC2 (7240 6099/www.mango.es). Covent Garden tube. **Open** 10am-8pm Mon-Sat; noon-6pm Sun. **Credit** AmEx, DC, MC, V. **Map** p396 B9.

A godsend for budget shoppers with an eye for style, this Spanish company's clothes are, miraculously, both cheap and good quality.

Branches: 225-35 Oxford Street, Marylebone, W1 (7434 3694); 106-12 Regent Street, Soho, W1 (7434 1384).

Miss Selfridge

325 Oxford Street, Marylebone, W1 (7927 0188). Oxford Circus tube. **Open** 9am-8pm Mon-Wed, Fri, Sat; 9am-9pm Sat; noon-6pm Sun. **Credit** AmEx, MC, V. **Map** p398 G6.

Miss Selfridge's cavernous store is great for cheap trends. It also recently launched a new range of footwear: funky shoes and tassle boots.

Branches: throughout the city.

New Look

175-9 Oxford Street, Marylebone, W1 (7534 2005/ www.newlook.co.uk). Oxford Circus tube. **Open** 9am-8pm Mon-Wed, Fri; 9am-9pm Thur; 9am-7pm Sat; noon-6pm Sun. **Credit** AmEx, MC, V. **Map** p398 J6.

A recent success story, with top designer Luella Bartley acting as consultant to ensure the in-house designers get the clothing range just right. The Inspire range offers great choice for sizes 16-24.

Branches: throughout the city.

Topshop

36-8 Great Castle Street (entrance on Oxford Street), Marylebone, W1 (7636 7700/www.topshop.co.uk). Oxford Circus tube. **Open** 9am-8pm Mon-Wed, Fri, Sat; 9am-9pm Thur; noon-6pm Sun. **Credit** MC, V. **Map** p398 J6.

The fashion junkie's secret weapon, Topshop has established long and highly successful collaborations with diverse designers. The quality is not as high as the originals, but with most prices under £40, only the strong-willed can resist.
Branches: throughout the city.

Uniqlo
Collier House, 163-9 Brompton Road, Knightsbridge, SW3 (7584 8608/www.uniqlo.co.uk). Knightsbridge tube. **Open** 10am-7pm Mon, Tue, Fri, Sat; 10am-8pm Wed, Thur; 10am-6pm Sun. **Credit** AmEx, MC, V. **Map** p397 E9.
Uniqlo has over 500 stores in its native Japan, and its flagship Knightsbridge store is always busy with buyers who don't believe what they're seeing: polo shirts for £12 and men's shorts for £7, plus a whole range of shirts for less than £30.
Branches: throughout the city.

Zara
118 Regent Street, Mayfair, W1 (7534 9500/ www.zara.com). Oxford Circus or Piccadilly Circus tube. **Open** 10am-7pm Mon-Wed, Fri, Sat; 10am-8pm Thur; noon-6pm Sun. **Credit** AmEx, DC, MC, V. **Map** p400 J7.
Another Spanish success story, Zara stocks an ever-changing range of cheap, stylish clothes, with tamer and more wearable catwalk copies in the shops only a few weeks after the shows. High quality and a good range suits everyone, whether teen, career woman or fashionista.
Branches: 242-8 Oxford Street, Marylebone, W1 (7318 2700); 48-52 Kensington High Street, Kensington, W11 (7368 4680).

Children
The department stores (*see p235*), especially **Selfridges**, have good selections of children's clothes. *See also p259* **Cheeky Monkeys**.

Daisy & Tom
181-3 King's Road, Chelsea, SW3 (7352 5000/ www.daisyandtom.com). Sloane Square tube then 11, 19, 22 bus/49 bus. **Open** 10am-6pm Mon-Wed, Fri, Sat; 10am-7pm Thur; 11am-5pm Sun. **Credit** AmEx, MC, V. **Map** p397 E12.
A children's wonderland, with a traditional carousel, rocking horses, a colouring table, a play train and, best of all, a big book room, where children can lounge on cushions or sit and read. Upstairs are the clothes and shoes: gorgeous and expensive designer labels such as Petit Bateau and Kenzo, as well as Daisy & Tom's own-brand baby clothing.

Jigsaw Junior
190 Westbourne Grove, Notting Hill, W11 (7229 8654/www.jigsaw-junior.com). Notting Hill Gate tube. **Open** 10.30am-6.30pm Mon; 10am-6.30pm Tue, Wed, Sat; 10am-7pm Thur, Fri; noon-6.30pm Sun. **Credit** AmEx, MC, V. **Map** p394 A6.
Jigsaw sells gear for everyone from toddling chicks right up to lanky pre-teens.
Branches: throughout the city.

Trotters
34 King's Road, Chelsea, SW3 (7259 9620/ www.trotters.co.uk). Sloane Square tube. **Open** 9am-6.30pm Mon, Tue, Thur-Sat; 9am-7pm Wed; 10am-6pm Sun. **Credit** AmEx, MC, V. **Map** p397 F11.

Eat, Drink, Shop

Haircuts, clothes and more kiddy delights at **Trotters**.

Clothes, shoes, haircuts and all-round fun at this lively children's shop. Kids can climb aboard the yellow Trotters Express train to have shoes properly fitted, or get togged up in Baby Dior, Oilily, Elle and Chipie, plus some seriously funky swimsuits.
Branch: 127 Kensington High Street, Kensington, W8 (7937 9373).

Mid-range

French Connection

396 Oxford Street, Marylebone, W1 (7629 7766/ www.frenchconnection.com). Bond Street tube. **Open** 10am-8pm Mon-Wed, Fri; 10am-9pm Thur; 10am-7pm Sat; noon-6pm Sun. **Credit** AmEx, MC, V. **Map** p398 G6.
Still a cut above most high street fashion in style and quality (with prices to match), this chain has everything from basic T-shirts to slinky party dresses.
Branches: throughout the city.

Gap

30-31 Long Acre, Covent Garden, WC2 (7379 0779/ www.gap.com). Covent Garden tube. **Open** 10am-7.30pm Mon-Sat; 11am-6pm Sun. **Credit** AmEx, MC, V. **Map** p401 L6.
Perhaps not the commercial giant it once was, Gap remains many shoppers' first port of call for good-value T-shirts, colourful sweaters and jeans.
Branches: throughout the city.

Jigsaw

126-7 New Bond Street, Mayfair, W1 (7491 4484/ www.jigsaw-online.com). Bond Street tube. **Open** 10am-6.30pm Mon-Wed, Fri, Sat; 10am-7.30pm Thur; noon-6pm Sun. **Credit** AmEx, MC, V. **Map** p398 H6.
Great fabrics, a good basic colour range and wearable but sexy items define the Jigsaw look.
Branches: throughout the city.

Karen Millen

262-4 Regent Street, Soho, W1 (7287 6158/www. karenmillen.com). Oxford Circus tube. **Open** 10am-6.30pm Mon-Wed, Fri, Sat; 10am-8pm Thur; noon-6pm Sun. **Credit** AmEx, DC, MC, V. **Map** p398 J6.
The kind of clothing little girls dream about: lots of sequins, diamantés, beads and ruffles adorn figure-hugging dresses and tops.
Branches: throughout the city.

Kookaï

Unit 13, Covent Garden Piazza, Covent Garden, WC2 (7379 1318/www.kookai.co.uk). Covent Garden tube. **Open** 10am-7pm Mon-Sat; noon-6pm Sun. **Credit** AmEx, MC, V. **Map** p401 L7.
For dedicated followers of catwalk fashion who can't afford the real thing – especially twentysomething party girls – Kookaï is a good bet.
Branches: throughout the city.

Oasis

13 James Street, Covent Garden, WC2 (7240 7445/ www.oasis-stores.com). Covent Garden tube. **Open** 10am-7pm Mon-Wed, Fri, Sat; 10am-8pm Thur; noon-6pm Sun. **Credit** AmEx, DC, MC, V. **Map** p401 L6.

The kinks

There are plenty of jokes to be made about the repressed British, and their kinks and perversions. Many's the childhood attachment to rubber sheets or severe schoolmarms that fuelled a grown-up love of dressing-up and roleplay. However, London's theatrical tradition and obsession with fashion also give the city's fetishists an impressive way with uniforms, top hats and drop-dead make-up. Fetish clothing shops cater to this demand very well. And with at least one kinky club every week, it's always a good time to go shopping.

For some reason, Holloway Road, N7, has turned into a discreet strip for purveyors of the perverse. **Showgirls** (No.64; 7697 9072) does designer rubber – think cheongsam-style dresses and *Barbarella*-look bustiers – while **Zeitgeist** (No.66; 7607 2977/www.zeitgeist.co.uk) focuses on the basic black and PVC end of the street. **House of Harlot** (Nos.88-90; 7700 1441/www.houseofharlot.com) sells ready-to-wear rubber, from gowns and catsuits to baby-doll dresses; complete your outfit with some harrowingly high heels from **Little Shoe Box** (No.89; 7607 1247/www. thelittleshoebox.com). Men are catered for in nearby Islington: at **Regulation** (17A St Alban's Place, N1; 7226 0665/www. regulation-ltd.com) for heavy rubber, leather and B&D equipment, and at **Hard Wear** (70 Essex Road, N1; 7359 8667/ www.hard-wear.co.uk) for an intimidating selection of military and institutional gear.

In central London, **Paradiso** in Soho (60 Dean Street, W1; 7287 6913) and **Bizarre** near Piccadilly Circus (4A Peter Street, W1; 7287 7666/www.abs-direct. com) open late and offer rubber, PVC and toys. South of the river, **Honour** (86 Lower Marsh, SE1; 7401 8219/www.honour. co.uk) has a similarly wide selection, while top-name **Skin Two** (Unit N306, Westminster Business Square, 1-45 Durham Street, SE11; 7840 0146/ www.skintwo.com) stocks a well-designed latex range. But if you're a first-timer in need of ideas and Dutch courage, the **London Fetish Fair** – held on the first Sunday of each month (Shillibeers, Carpenter's Yard, North Road, N7; 7916 8360/www.londonfetishfair.co.uk) – has 40 stalls and a bar to steady your nerves.

Eat, Drink, Shop

Duffer of St George.

Catwalk trends at high street prices, with the constantly changing stock ensuring there's always something new to tempt customers. Oasis is also excellent for cheap bags, shoes and jewellery.
Branches: throughout the city.

Whistles
12 St Christopher's Place, Marylebone, W1 (7487 4484). Bond Street tube. **Open** 10am-6pm Mon-Wed, Fri, Sat; 10am-7pm Thur; noon-5pm Sun. **Credit** AmEx, MC, V. **Map** p398 H6.
Whistles outlets stock a core range of (consistently superb) own-brand clothes that sits well beside the Tocca, Holly, Philosophy di Alberta Ferretti, Gharani Strok and Matthew Williamson.
Branches: throughout the city.

Street

Carhartt
56 Neal Street, Covent Garden, WC2 (7836 5659/ www.thecarharttstore.co.uk). Covent Garden tube. **Open** 11am-6.30pm Mon-Wed, Fri, Sat; 11am-7pm Thur; noon-5pm Sun. **Credit** MC, V. **Map** p399 L6.
Everyone's favourite US workwear specialist continues to plough its popular and lucrative furrow. The association of its functional clothing with skating and hip-hop styles has generated a healthy following among the streetwise.
Branch: 13 Newburgh Street, Soho, W1 (7287 6411).

Diesel
43 Earlham Street, Covent Garden, WC2 (7497 5543/www.diesel.com). Covent Garden tube. **Open** 10am-7pm Mon-Wed, Fri, Sat; 10am-8pm Thur; noon-6pm Sun. **Credit** AmEx, MC, V. **Map** p399 L6.

This innovative Italian label sells clothes in abundance but keeps an air of elitist cool. The current collections incorporate vibrant colours into fairly familiar separates. Faded jeans are prominent too.
Branches: throughout the city.

Duffer of St George
29 Shorts Gardens, Covent Garden, WC2 (7379 4660/www.thedufferofstgeorge.com). Covent Garden tube. **Open** 10.30am-7pm Mon-Fri; 10.30am-6.30pm Sat; 1-5pm Sun. **Credit** AmEx, MC, V. **Map** p399 L6.
Some bemoan the lack of innovation in Duffer's recent collections, but that hasn't stopped punters snapping up jeans by Evisu and Levi's Vintage, sweats by Oeuf and Duffer's own-label shirts, knitwear and jackets. Besides, Duffer still has the best selection of sloganned T-shirts in the capital.

Maharishi
19A Floral Street, Covent Garden, WC2 (7836 3860/www.maharishi.co.uk). Covent Garden tube. **Open** 10am-7pm Mon-Sat; noon-5pm Sun. **Credit** AmEx, MC, V. **Map** p399 L6.
Maharishi's unisex embroidered combat trousers ('snow pants', apparently) have developed something of a cult status.

Quiksilver
Units 1 & 23, Thomas Neal Centre, Earlham Street, Covent Garden, WC2 (7836 5371/www.quiksilver. com). Covent Garden tube. **Open** 10am-7pm Mon-Sat; noon-6pm Sun. **Credit** AmEx, MC, V. **Map** p399 L6.
This Aussie surf brand has been going for more than 30 years. Its streetwear includes loose shirts and drawstring trousers for men, and skinny T-shirts and cargo pants for women.
Branches: throughout the city.

and one with nipple-revealing demi-cups. Satin mules – or a leather collar – complete the picture. Branch: 6 Broadwick Street, Soho, W1 (7439 0229).

Rigby & Peller

2 Hans Road, Knightsbridge, SW3 (7589 9293/ www.rigbyandpeller.com). Knightsbridge tube. **Open** 9.30am-6pm Mon, Tue, Thur-Sat; 9.30am-7pm Wed. **Credit** AmEx, MC, V. **Map** p397 F9.

The uniformed doorman reminds you that R&P is corsetière to the Queen, but inside there's a lot more than regal girdles: slips and camisoles in delicate silks, for example, or bikini sets with fluorescent splashes. Famous for its fitting and alteration service. **Branch**: 22A Conduit Street, Mayfair, W1 (7491 2200).

Vintage

Annie's Vintage Clothes

12 Camden Passage, Islington, N1 (7359 0796). Angel tube. **Open** 11am-6pm Mon, Tue, Thur, Fri; 9am-6pm Wed, Sat. **Credit** AmEx, DC, MC, V. **Map** p402 O2.

Annie's is the kind of elegant place you might go to for a pre-war outfit for a special event. Velvet coats, lace petticoats and trimmings are specialities.

The Girl Can't Help It/ Cad van Swankster

Alfie's Antiques Market, 13-25 Church Street, Marylebone, NW8 (7724 8984/www.sparklemoore. com). Edgware Road tube/Marylebone tube/rail. **Open** 10am-6pm Tue-Sat. **Credit** MC, V. **Map** p395 E4.

Sparkle Moore and her partner Jasja often pop to the States to stock up on high-quality Americana. Their shop is full of '30s, '40s, '50s and '60s designs, with plenty of accessories and curious collectibles.

Shop

4 Brewer Street, Soho, W1 (7437 1259). Piccadilly Circus tube. **Open** 10.30am-6.30pm Mon-Fri; 11am-6.30pm Sat. **Credit** AmEx, MC, V. **Map** p400 J7.

The funky womenswear here is always glamorous but rarely over-the-top. Hysteric Glamour, Tocca and Earl Jeans feature, along with the store's own highly regarded label ShopGirl.

Urban Outfitters

36-8 Kensington High Street, Kensington, W8 (7761 1001/www.urbanoutfitters.com). High Street Kensington tube. **Open** 10am-7pm Mon-Wed, Fri, Sat; 10am-8pm Thur; noon-6pm Sun. **Credit** AmEx, MC, V. **Map** p396 A9.

The stock here really is impressive, incorporating just about everything you need for self-consciously cool urban living, from the best streetwear labels (Levi's Red, Fake London, Mandarina Duck, Duffer, Final Home) to the latest wind-up nun gadget.

Underwear

Marks & Spencer (*see p236*) is well known for its range of quality affordable undies.

Agent Provocateur

16 Pont Street, Knightsbridge, SW1 (7235 0229/ www.agentprovocateur.com). Knightsbridge or Sloane Street tube. **Open** 10am-6pm Mon-Sat. **Credit** AmEx, MC, V. **Map** p397 F10.

Corsets, bras, nightwear and accessories are displayed against a backdrop of red, pink and purple. The feel is somewhere between Betty Page and *Playboy* centrefold: trademark bra styles include one in red tulle with black embroidery and satin bows,

Fashion accessories & services

General

Accessorize

22 The Market, Covent Garden, WC2 (7240 2107/ www.accessorize.co.uk). Covent Garden tube. **Open** 9am-8pm Mon-Fri; 10am-8pm Sat; 11am-7pm Sun. **Credit** AmEx, DC, MC, V. **Map** p401 L6.

Probably the best of the high street chains specialising in top-to-toe necessities: hats, bags, scarves and jewellery. Prices start at just a few pounds, and most shops have a children's stand and cosmetics bar. **Branches**: throughout the city.

Dry cleaning & laundry

Buckingham Dry Cleaners

83 Duke Street, Mayfair, W1 (7499 1253). Bond Street tube. **Open** 8am-6pm Mon-Fri; 9.30am-12.30pm Sat. **Credit** AmEx, MC, V. **Map** p398 G6.

Sexy **Agent Provocateur**. *See p243.*

A locally renowned dry cleaners with very reasonable prices: shirts from £3.50, jackets from £10.50 and suits from only £15.50.

Jewellery

Berganza

88-90 Hatton Garden (entrance in Greville Street), Clerkenwell, EC1 (7404 2336/www.berganza.com). Chancery Lane tube. **Open** 10am-5.30pm Mon-Sat. **Credit** AmEx, MC, V. **Map** p402 N5.
Specialising in antique jewellery, Berganza has a large range of diamond, emerald and ruby rings. Staff can advise on remodelling existing jewellery.

Electrum Gallery

21 South Molton Street, Mayfair, W1 (7629 6325). Bond Street tube. **Open** 10am-6pm Mon-Fri; 10am-5pm Sat. **Credit** AmEx, DC, MC, V. **Map** p398 H6.

More like an art gallery than a shop, Electrum has been displaying the work of 100-plus contemporary designers and craftsmen for over 30 years.

Frontiers

37 & 39 Pembridge Road, Notting Hill, W11 (7727 6132). Notting Hill Gate tube. **Open** 11am-6.30pm Mon-Sat; noon-4pm Sun. **Credit** MC, V. **Map** p394 A7.
One shop houses a collection of antique and tribal jewellery from Asia and North Africa, from delicate Indian silver jewellery to big chunks of amber; the other offers terracotta potware and garden furniture.

Garrard

24 Albemarle Street, Mayfair, W1 (7758 8520/ www.garrard.com). Bond Street or Green Park tube. **Open** 10am-5.30pm Mon-Sat. **Credit** AmEx, DC, MC, V. **Map** p400 J7.
Garrard is fast shaking off its old-fashioned image: Jade Jagger is the new creative director and ad campaigns feature Rupert Everett and Missy Elliot. The jewellery runs the gamut from delicate diamond rings and tiaras to the brash and funky.

Lesley Craze Gallery/Craze Two

34-5 Clerkenwell Green, Clerkenwell, EC1 (Lesley Craze Gallery 7608 0393/Craze Two 7251 0381/ www.lesleycrazegallery.co.uk). Farringdon tube/rail. **Open** 10am-5.30pm Mon-Sat. **Credit** AmEx, MC, V. **Map** p402 N4.
The Craze Gallery hosts two major designer exhibitions a year, while Craze Two specialises in mixed media jewellery and includes designs by recent graduates – always worth a look.

Tiffany & Co

25 Old Bond Street, Mayfair, W1 (7409 2790/ www.tiffany.com). Green Park tube. **Open** 10am-6pm Mon-Fri; 10am-5.30pm Sat. **Credit** AmEx, MC, V. **Map** p400 J7.
Though Tiffany has some very expensive, very chic jewellery, it also specialises in affordable little knick-knacks. Also sold in Harrods (*see p235*).
Branch: The Courtyard, Royal Exchange, the City, EC3 (7495 3511).

Wright & Teague

1A Grafton Street, Mayfair, W1 (7629 2777/ www.wrightandteague.com). Green Park tube. **Open** 10am-6pm Mon-Wed, Fri, Sat; 10am-7pm Thur. **Credit** AmEx, MC, V. **Map** p400 J7.
Visit Wright & Teague for stylish contemporary jewellery, mostly made from silver and 18ct gold. Part of the collection can also be seen at Liberty, Harrods and Harvey Nichols (*see p235*).

Leather goods

Bill Amberg

10 Chepstow Road, Notting Hill, W2 (7727 3560/ www.billamberg.com). Notting Hill Gate tube. **Open** 10am-6pm Mon-Wed, Fri, Sat; 10am-7pm Thur. **Credit** AmEx, MC, V. **Map** p394 A5.

Amberg sells thick-skinned, luxurious classics: impressive signature briefcases with stainless steel or coloured glass handles, and sheepskin-lined papooses so great they'll having you wishing for a baby to put in them.

Mulberry
41-2 New Bond Street, Mayfair, W1 (7491 3900/ www.mulberry-england.co.uk). Bond Street tube. **Open** 10am-6pm Mon-Wed, Fri, Sat; 10am-7pm Thur. **Credit** AmEx, DC, MC, V. **Map** p398 H6.
Mulberry are purveyors of delicious luggage and accessories, everything from a washbag to a suit carrier, a blanket roll to a golf bag.
Branches: throughout the city.

Shoes

If you want to treat your feet, try two of the biggest names in fashion: **Jimmy Choo** (169 Draycott Avenue, SW3; 7235 0242) and **Manolo Blahnik** (49-51 Old Church Street, SW3; 7352 3863). For something trad, try **John Lobb** (88 Jermyn Street, St James's, SW1; 7930 8089).

Camper
8-11 Royal Arcade, 28 Old Bond Street, Mayfair, W1 (7629 2722/www.camper.com). Green Park tube. **Open** 10am-6pm Mon-Wed, Fri, Sat; 10am-6.30pm Thur. **Credit** AmEx, MC, V. **Map** p400 J7.
Still attracting a loyal following, this Majorcan company creates cute, funky and comfortable shoes.
Branches: 39 Floral Street, Covent Garden, WC2 (7379 8678); 35 Brompton Road, Knightsbridge, SW1 (7584 5439).

Church's Shoes
201 Regent Street, Mayfair, W1 (7734 2438/ www.church-footwear.com). Oxford Circus tube. **Open** 10am-6.30pm Mon-Wed, Fri, Sat; 10am-7.30pm Thur; noon-6pm Sun. **Credit** AmEx, MC, V. **Map** p398 J6.
Traditional English designs – calfskin brogues, suede ankle boots, tasselled leather slip-ons – are Church's speciality. Standards are impeccably high.

Natural Shoe Store
21 Neal Street, Covent Garden, WC2 (7836 5254). Covent Garden tube. **Open** 10am-6pm Mon, Tue; 10am-7pm Wed-Fri; 10am-6.30pm Sat; noon-5.30pm Sun. **Credit** AmEx, MC, V. **Map** p399 L6.
Ergonomic enough for old hippies, the wooden-soled clogs, round-toed suede slip-ons and leather flip-flops sold at the Natural Shoe Store are up-to-the-minute fashionable too.
Branch: 325 King's Road, Chelsea, SW3 (7351 3721).

Office
57 Neal Street, Covent Garden, WC2 (7379 1896/ www.officelondon.co.uk). Covent Garden tube. **Open** 10am-7.30pm Mon-Wed, Fri, Sat; 10am-8pm Thur; noon-6pm Sun. **Credit** AmEx, MC, V. **Map** p399 L6.
A wide choice of hip and contemporary styles for men and women at affordable prices.
Branches: throughout the city.

Poste
10 South Molton Street, Mayfair, W1 (7499 8002). Bond Street tube. **Open** 10am-7pm Mon-Sat; noon-6pm Sun. **Credit** AmEx, MC, V. **Map** p398 H6.

Suits you, sir... for traditional tailors, head to **Savile Row**. *See p247.*

This smart men's shoe shop in smart Mayfair focuses on one-offs and exclusive lines from top-end designers: think Prada and Unit, though loafers, brogues and slipper-type styles in soft leather and suede are also popular.

Poste Mistress

61-3 Monmouth Street, Covent Garden, WC2 (7379 4040). Covent Garden tube. **Open** 10.30am-7.30pm Mon-Fri; 10am-7pm Sat; noon-6pm Sun. **Credit** AmEx, MC, V. **Map** p399 L6.

Girls get their own version of Poste. Elegant and eccentric shoes from the own-brand line are joined by stock from Marc Jacobs, Dries van Noten, Vivienne Westwood and Buddahood, plus imported sneakers and rare Japanese brands to drool over.

Shellys

266-70 Regent Street, Marylebone, W1 (7287 0939/ www.shellys.co.uk). Oxford Circus tube. **Open** 10am-7pm Mon-Wed, Fri, Sat; 10am-8pm Thur; noon-6pm Sun. **Credit** AmEx, MC, V. **Map** p398 J6.

Shellys' fun and funky footwear has become a high street favourite. Shoes are characterised by club-friendly platform heels and bright colours. **Branches**: throughout the city.

Tailors

Since the middle of the 19th century, **Savile Row**, Mayfair, W1, has been the traditional home of men's tailoring.

Ozwald Boateng

9 Vigo Street, Mayfair, W1 (7437 0620). Green Park or Piccadilly Circus tube. **Open** 10am-6pm Mon-Wed, Fri, Sat; 10am-7pm Thur. **Credit** AmEx, MC, V. **Map** p400 J7.

Wearing a Boateng suit is not for the faint-hearted he inclines towards bright colours and a softer silhouette – which may be why many of his clients, from Robbie Williams to Will Smith, are in the entertainment industry.
Branch: 9 Wimpole Street, W1 (7487 4875).

Timothy Everest

32 Elder Street, Spitalfields, E1 (7377 5770). Liverpool Street tube/rail. **Open** 9am-6pm Mon-Fri; 9am-4pm Sat. **Credit** AmEx, MC, V. **Map** p403 R5.

Perhaps the most successful of the new generation of London tailors, Everest is the suitmaker of choice to David Beckham and Jarvis Cocker. A bespoke suit will set you back a reasonable £1,000.

Flowers

You can pick up bouquets galore at **Columbia Road Market** *(see p256)*.

Paula Pryke Flowers

20 Penton Street, Islington, N1 (7837 7336/ www.paula-pryke-flowers.com). Angel tube. **Open** 8am-6.30pm Mon-Fri; 8am-6pm Sat; 10am-2pm Sun. **Credit** AmEx, DC, MC, V. **Map** p402 N2.

One of the most spacious and elegant flower shops in town provides subtle mixes of colour: a bouquet of salmon pink sweet peas, tightly packed creamy roses and crinkled pink celosia, for example. Pryke has concessions at Liberty and Michelin House.

Wild Bunch

17-22 Earlham Street, Covent Garden, WC2 (7497 1200). Covent Garden or Leicester Square tube. **Open** 10am-7pm Mon-Sat. **Credit** AmEx, DC, MC, V. **Map** p399 K6.

It's hard to walk past this bustling flower stall without stopping to buy. The choice is vast, the quality high and prices are very competitive: you can get something pretty extraordinary for just ten quid.

Food & drink

The department stores *(see p235)* have food halls crammed with goodies.

Bakeries & pâtisseries

Soho, W1, is home to various pâtisseries worth checking out for their scrumptious cakes and pastries. These include **Maison Bertaux** *(see p201)*, and, on Old Compton Street, **Amato Caffe/Pasticceria** (No.14, 7734 5533) and **Pâtisserie Valerie** *(see p201)*; both make cakes to order.

& Clarke's

122 Kensington Church Street, Kensington, W8 (7229 2190/www.sallyclarke.com). Notting Hill Gate tube. **Open** 8am-8pm Mon-Fri; 9am-4pm Sat. **Credit** AmEx, MC, V. **Map** p394 B8.

This bakery-cum-deli nestles alongside owner Sally Clarke's restaurant *(see p217)*. The 30-plus varieties of bread include oatmeal and honey, and fig and fennel versions, as well as traditional favourites such as rye and ciabatta. There are also tarts, croissants, brownies, truffles and a glut of cheeses, chutneys and jams.

Neal's Yard Bakery

6 Neal's Yard, Covent Garden, WC2 (7836 5199). Covent Garden tube. **Open** 10.30am-5pm Mon-Sat. **No credit cards. Map** p399 L6.

Tucked in the corner of this boho courtyard, the health-conscious Neal's Yard Bakery makes only vegetarian food. All the bread is organic, most cakes are vegan, and cakes and biscuits are made using apple juice or malt concentrate instead of sugar.

Paul Bakery & Tearoom

115 Marylebone High Street, Marylebone, W1 (7224 5615). Bond Street tube. **Open** 7am-7pm Mon-Fri; 9am-7pm Sat, Sun. **Credit** V. **Map** p398 G4.

The look at this tearoom is resolutely French, with a café at the back and retail space at the front. Check out the savoury tarts, and the signature chocolate éclairs with chocolate filling. Breads and brioches are made with traditional Camp Rémy wheat.

Eat, Drink, Shop

Pick up a picnic

Of course, you'll need to get lucky with the weather. But assuming you stumble upon a lovely day in London town, do as the locals do and enjoy a picnic in one of the city's myriad parks, gardens and squares. Check the **Sightseeing** section (starting on p71) for details of where to find the loveliest ones... And once you've settled on a spot, go about compiling the perfect picnic hamper from London's gazillion specialist food shops.

The basic requirement for any picnic is bread. The tempting range at **& Clarke's** (*see p247*) includes a fig and fennel loaf so delicious you'll be tearing off chunks to eat before leaving the shop. The traditional French breads at **Poilâne** (46 Elizabeth Street, SW1; 7808 4910) are pricey but much praised, while the organic breads at **Neal's Yard Bakery** (*see p247*) are simply fab.

With bread goes cheese. **Neal's Yard Dairy** (*see p248*), mere yards from the Neal's Yard Bakery, sources its quality cheeses from independent English and Irish producers. Classic cheddars and rarer, smellier varieties are found at revered cheesemongers **Paxton & Whitfield** (93 Jermyn Street, SW1; 7930 0259), while **La Fromagerie** (30 Highbury Park, N5; 7359 7440) sells a vast range, alongside mouth-watering salamis, hams, own-made pâtés and pastries.

Man cannot live by bread (and cheese) alone, of course. And nor should they, given the array of delis around town offering picnic-friendly finger foods. To push the boat out, try the smoked salmon and caviar from **Caviar Kaspia** (18 Bruton Place, W1; 7493 2612); to stay GM-free, head for **Planet Organic** (42 Westbourne Grove, W1; 7221 7171) and **Fresh & Wild** (49 Parkway, NW1; 7428 7575). For traditional British nosh – pork pies, smoked kippers and the like – try **A Gold** (42 Brushfield Street, E1; 7247 2487). And chickens, quiches and pies can

all be found at **Villandry** (170 Great Portland Street, W1; 7631 3131), **Flâneur Food Hall** (41 Farringdon Road, EC1; 7404 4422) and **Butlers Wharf Gastrodome** (36D Shad Thames, SE1; 7403 4030).

Alternatively, take advantage of London's assortment of ethnic food shops. Pick up Portuguese sardines, anchovies and custard tarts at **Lisboa** (54 Golborne Road, W10; 8969 1052), or stroll to Portobello Road for Iberian goods – Serrano ham, olives, palm hearts – at **De Le Feuente** (No.288; 8960 5687) and **Garcia & Sons** (No.248; 7221 6119). Head to Dalston for authentic houmous and halloumi at the **Turkish Food Centre** (89 Ridley Road, E8; 7254 6754), or to **Green Lanes** in Haringey for Greek shops packed with olives, halva and stuffed vine leaves. Banglatown's **Brick Lane** and Chinatown's **Gerrard Street** are good places for authentic Indian and Chinese snacks.

Looking for something with which to wash it all down? Classy **Corney & Barrow** (194 Kensington Park Road, W11; 7221 5122) specialises in French wines, and the excellent **Oddbins** chain (*see p249*) has a wide range of New World wines. With over 100 varieties of champagne at **Roberson** (348 Kensington High Street, W14; 7371 2121), there's plenty of bubbly to complement your comestibles, though those after more simple (and affordable) pleasures should head for the **Beer Shop** (14 Pitfield Street, N1; 7739 3701). Guess what it sells.

Of course, compiling your fantasy picnic from this list of shops is a time-consuming exercise. If you're too lazy to pack your own, the food halls at **Fortnum & Mason**, **Harrods** (for both, *see p235*) and **Bluebird** (350 King's Road, SW3; 7559 1153) sell lavish, costly, pre-prepared hampers. All set? Then the only thing you need now is the sun. Keep your fingers crossed.

Cheese shops

Neal's Yard Dairy

17 Shorts Gardens, Covent Garden, WC2 (7240 5700). Covent Garden tube. **Open** 9am-7pm Mon-Sat. **Credit** MC, V. **Map** p399 L6.
Neal's Yard is still one of the city's finest cheesemongers, with most cheeses sourced directly from small, independent producers and British cheeses a speciality. Sidelines include organic olive oils, jams and own-brand vinegars, mustards and chutneys.

Coffee & tea

Algerian Coffee Stores

52 Old Compton Street, Soho, W1 (7437 2480/www. algcoffee.co.uk). Leicester Square tube. **Open** 9am-7pm Mon-Sat. **Credit** AmEx, DC, MC, V. **Map** p399 K6.
Not an inch of space is wasted here. Behind the narrow counter are 60-odd blends of coffee and a selection of teas; in front, shelves are stacked with confectionery, toasters and coffee machines, and every kind of spirit and flavouring imaginable.

R Twining & Co

216 Strand, Covent Garden, WC2 (7353 3511/ www.twinings.com). Temple tube. **Open** 9.30am-4.30pm Mon-Fri. **Credit** AmEx, MC, V. **Map** p399 M6.
Twinings has traded from the same premises since 1706; a small museum at the back charts the company's history. The huge choice of teas includes several hard-to-find blends and some that are exclusive to the company. There are green teas, herbal and fruit infusions, and organic blends too.

Confectioners

Charbonnel et Walker

1 The Royal Arcade, 28 Old Bond Street, Mayfair, W1 (7491 0939/www.charbonnel.co.uk). Green Park tube. **Open** 10am-6pm Mon-Sat. **Credit** AmEx, MC, V. **Map** p400 J7.
This celebrated confectioner was founded in 1875, and has followed the same traditional recipes ever since. It's particularly renowned for its rose and violet crèmes, and luxurious drinking chocolate.

Godiva

247 Regent Street, Mayfair, W1 (7495 2845/ www.godiva.com). Oxford Circus tube. **Open** 9.30am-7pm Mon-Sat; noon-5.30pm Sun. **Credit** AmEx, MC, V. **Map** p398 J6.
This elegant Belgian chocolatier was established over 75 years ago. It caters very much for the adult palate, using 75% pure cocoa for luxurious taste and smooth texture. Honey and almond truffles are top sellers, but everything's hard to resist.
Branches: throughout the city.

Delicatessens

Bluebird

350 King's Road, Chelsea, SW3 (7559 1153/ www.conran.co.uk). Sloane Square tube then 11, 19, 22 bus. **Open** 8am-8pm Mon-Wed; 8am-9pm Thur-Sat; 11am-5pm Sun. **Credit** AmEx, DC, MC, V. **Map** p397 D12.
Cool jazz plays as you enter Terence Conran's gourmet food hall. Central islands display packaged and tinned goods from around the world, with fresh food on the periphery. There's a fishmonger, butcher, deli, cheese counter and bakery, plus a florist, a café and the Bluebird restaurant.

Carluccio's

28A Neal Street, Covent Garden, WC2 (7240 1487/ www.carluccios.com). Covent Garden tube. **Open** 11am-7pm Mon-Sat; noon-6pm Sun. **Credit** AmEx, MC, V. **Map** p399 L6.
A highlight at Carluccio's is the marvellous selection of seasonal wild funghi and truffles. Pasta and olive oil are in abundant supply, and the shop does great sandwiches, traiteur dishes and pastries.
Branches: throughout the city.

Wines & spirits

For everyday use, **Oddbins**, with branches all over London (see www.oddbins.co.uk), is hard to beat. Supermarkets such as Sainsbury's and Safeway have also improved their alcohol selections in recent years.

Choose from 650 types of whisky at **Milroy's of Soho**. *See p250.*

Eat, Drink, Shop

Gerry's

74 Old Compton Street, Soho, W1 (7734 4215).
Leicester Square tube. **Open** 9am-6.30pm Mon-Fri;
9am-5.30pm Sat. **No credit cards. Map** p399 K6.
Purveyors of all that's weird and wonderful in the
spirit and liqueur world: an Eiffel Tower-shaped
bottle of absinthe, for example, or more than 100
different vodkas, including a cannabis-flavoured one.

Milroy's of Soho

3 Greek Street, Soho, W1 (7437 9311/
www.milroys.co.uk). Tottenham Court Road tube.
Open 11am-7pm Mon-Sat. **Credit** AmEx, MC, V.
Map p399 K6.
London's most famous whisky specialist has been
around for almost 40 years, and stocks around 650
different types. The basement – being revamped as
we went to press – may become a tasting room.

Gifts & stationery

See also p251 **Museum pieces**.

Paperchase

213-15 Tottenham Court Road, Fitzrovia, W1
(7467 6200/www.paperchase.co.uk). Goodge Street
tube. **Open** 9.30am-7pm Mon, Wed, Fri, Sat; 10am-
7pm Tue; 9.30am-8pm Thur; noon-6pm Sun. **Credit**
AmEx, MC, V. **Map** p399 K5.
A stationery superstore. The ground floor holds
cards, wrapping paper, ribbon and funky notepads;
the first floor houses storage files and boxes, frames,
bags, Filofaxes, pens, gadgets and stationery; and
on the top floor you'll find artists' materials.
Branches: throughout the city.

Queens

Shop 111B, Gate 14, Spitalfields Market, Spitalfields,
E1 (7426 0017). Liverpool Street tube/rail. **Open**
11am-6pm Mon-Fri; 9am-6.30pm Sun. **Credit** MC, V.
Map p403 R5.
If the name gives a clue, the carnivalesque dark pink
baroque interior says it all. This homage to camp
specialises in teddy bears with an extravagant
streak (ballerina teddies, Elvis teddies), but also sells
snowstorms, collectable dolls, fairy wings, boas...

Space EC1

25 Exmouth Market, Clerkenwell, EC1 (7837 1344).
Bus 19, 38, 341. **Open** 10.30am-6pm Mon-Fri; 11am-
5pm Sat. **Credit** AmEx, MC, V. **Map** p402 N4.
A stylish and humorous paean to kitsch, Space's fantastic range includes a plastic singing-and-dancing
birthday cake. Plus Mathmos lamps, handcrafted
Vietnamese lacquerware and delicate silver jewellery.

Health & beauty

Beauty services

Porchester Spa

Porchester Centre, Queensway, Bayswater, W2
(7792 3980). Bayswater tube. **Open** *Women only*
10am-10pm Tue, Thur, Fri; 10am-4pm Sun. *Men only*
10am-10pm Mon, Wed, Sat. *Mixed* 4-10pm Sun.
Credit MC, V. **Map** p394 C6.
This atmospheric, shabbily grand facility offers
Turkish hot rooms, Russian steam rooms, a sauna
and a plunge pool, plus a glorious art deco hall in
which to relax afterwards. A range of treatments is

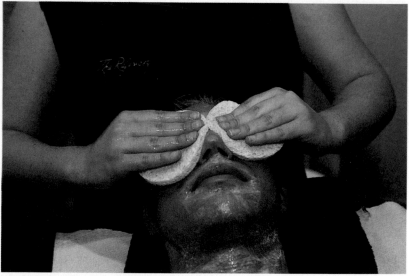

Pampering for men at the **Refinery**. *See p251.*

Museum pieces

Many museum shops in London are little more than an opportunity for the museum in question to front-load their bank balance from the pockets of tired tourists. However, a number are impressive trading posts in their own right, stocking shelves of gifts that won't make you cringe when you unpack them upon your return home. For Londoncentric gifts, *see p39*; for everything else, read on.

Want art prints, postcards and posters? The expected sources all deliver the goods. The **National Gallery**, the **National Portrait Gallery** (for both, *see p129*), **Tate Britain** (*see p134*), **Tate Modern** (*see p79*), the **Royal Academy of Arts** (*see p114*) and the **British Library** (*see p105*) have well-stocked gift shops. However, a less likely source of wall decoration is the excellent shop at **London's Transport Museum** (*see p123*), whose stock of handsome reproduction advertising posters (£2.50-£7.95) is complemented by mouse mats, boxer shorts, T-shirts, shot glasses and fridge magnets with the famous London Underground roundel.

As you may know, **Shakespeare's Globe** on the South Bank (*see p78*) is a delightful reconstruction of the 17th-century theatre where many of the Bard's works were first performed. It's a largely authentic re-creation, although it's doubtful that in Shakespeare's day theatre-goers were given the option of buying Shakey T-shirts, olde worlde leather bottles and Elizabethan-style jewellery. History buffs will also love the **Tower of London**'s many shops (*see p95*): pricey (£34.95) but

colourful and amusing are its Christmas tree ornaments of Henry VIII and his six wives, resplendent in Tudor costume.

Yet it's the smaller museums whose stock can be the most inspired. The **Freud Museum**'s 'action pen' (£3.25) floats Freud's famous psychoanalysis couch along its side when tipped (*see p149*). The **Bramah Museum of Tea & Coffee** (*see p76*) sells a two-cup sized replica of the world's largest teapot for £12.50 (the original, held in the museum, serves 800 people). Horticulturalists can pick up packets of 'Gardener's Gamble' seeds from the **Museum of Garden History** (*see p75*): all seeds are from plants in the museum gardens, but you won't know what you've sown until the shoots appear.

Cash to splash? The Time and Tide shop at the **National Maritime Museum** in Greenwich (*see p171*) sells elegant pocket watches and timepieces (£45 to an eye-watering £700), but kids will be happier with the fun potato clock (a mere £15). For curious or classy gifts, the **British Museum** (*see p102*) can't be beat. Replicas and casts from its global collections include ancient Egyptian cats, Celtic and medieval jewellery, classical busts and wall plaques. And Conan Doyle fans won't want to leave London without a visit to the **Sherlock Holmes Museum** (*see p110*). However, remember that the Customs limit on goods purchased in the UK is £145, so you'll have to make it past airport officials wearing your brand new tweed cape-and-deerstalker Holmes outfit (£450)...

Eat, Drink, Shop

available (book in advance), as well as therapists on women-only days; the men, many regulars, are happy to sit around sweating and playing cards.

The Refinery

60 Brook Street, Mayfair, W1 (7409 2001/www.the-refinery.com). Bond Street tube. **Open** 10am-7pm Mon, Tue; 10am-9pm Wed-Fri; 9am-6pm Sat; 11am-5pm Sun. **Credit** MC, V. **Map** p398 H6.

A five-storey, oak-panelled Georgian townhouse that's home to London's hippest men's salon. A 'club lounge' room has huge TVs. Experts armed with Dermalogica hydrating body wraps and Phytomer anti-pollution facials pamper the stressed execs. **Branch**: 38 Bishopsgate, EC2 (7588 1006).

The Sanctuary

12 Floral Street, Covent Garden, WC2 (08700 630300/www.thesanctuary.co.uk). Covent Garden tube. **Open** 9.30am-6pm Mon, Tue, Sun; 9.30am-

10pm Wed-Fri; 10am 8pm Sat. **Credit** AmEx, DC, MC, V. **Map** p401 L6.

A favourite with stressed-out gals since it opened 25 years ago, the Sanctuary has just completed a £2 million refurb. With a new café/restaurant and lounge, whirlpool, exercise machines, wet treatment rooms, a sanarium and sauna, you can easily while away the day. There's a range of treatments too.

SPAce.NK

127-31 Westbourne Grove, Notting Hill, W2 (7727 8002/www.spacenk.co.uk). Notting Hill Gate tube. **Open** 10am-7pm Mon, Fri; 9am-9pm Tue-Thur; 9am-7pm Sat; 10am-5pm Sun. **Credit** AmEx, DC, MC, V. **Map** p394 B6.

This hip but friendly hangout has all sorts of tempting treatments. A new addition is the Gisele Delorme Full Body Treat (£80): 75 minutes to unwind, with a back exfoliation and lymphatic drainage. Melt your credit card by stocking up on products.

Cosmetics, skincare & perfume

Department stores (*see p235*) are the places to buy well-known upmarket brands of make-up and skincare products.

Aveda Lifestyle Institute

174 High Holborn, Holborn, WC1 (7759 7355/ www.aveda.com). Holborn tube. **Open** 9.30am-7pm Mon-Fri; 9am-6.30pm Sat. **Credit** AmEx, MC, V. **Map** p398 G5.

An all-round emporium of all things Aveda, selling essences, infusions and oils: all natural and organic where possible. There are also treatment rooms, a hairdressing salon and an organic café on site.

Boots

75 Queensway, Bayswater, W2 (7229 9266/ www.wellbeing.com). Bayswater or Queensway tube. **Open** 9am-10pm Mon-Sat; 2-10pm Sun. **Credit** MC, V. **Map** p394 C6.

With a wide range of everyday products, Boots is still the best high street beauty store. Larger branches have a good make-up selection; some even have in-store dental clinics.
Branches: throughout the city.

Jo Malone

150 Sloane Street, Chelsea, SW1 (7730 2100/ www.jomalone.co.uk). Sloane Square tube. **Open** 10am-6pm Mon, Tue, Fri, Sat; 10am-7pm Wed, Thur. **Credit** AmEx, MC, V. **Map** p397 E10.

As if her gorgeous bath, body and home ranges weren't enough, Jo Malone now has an equally luxurious skincare range. Prices aren't bargain basement, but the ingredients are top of the range.

MAC Cosmetics

109 King's Road, Chelsea, SW3 (7349 0022/ www.maccosmetics.com). Sloane Street tube. **Open** 10am-6.30pm Mon-Sat; noon-6pm Sun. **Credit** AmEx, MC, V. **Map** p397 F11.

This shop has a great vibe. Dance music buzzes in the background, staff are friendly and the products are highly covetable.
Branches: throughout the city.

Neal's Yard Remedies

15 Neal's Yard, Covent Garden, WC2 (7379 7222/ www.nealsyardremedies.com). Covent Garden tube. **Open** 10am-7pm Mon-Sat; 11am-6pm Sun. **Credit** AmEx, MC, V. **Map** p399 L6.

Alternative health and beauty products using natural and, wherever possible, organic ingredients. Check out the baseline range: you buy a pure base of, say, massage oil, and add your own essential oils.
Branches: throughout the city.

SPAce.NK

37 Earlham Street, Covent Garden, WC2 (7379 7030/ www.spacenk.co.uk). Covent Garden tube. **Open** 10am-7pm Mon-Wed, Fri, Sat; 10am-7.30pm Thur; noon-5pm Sun. **Credit** AmEx, MC, V. **Map** p399 L6.

SPAce.NK still has the edge over the (admittedly improving) department stores. Staff are friendly and willing to explain products, and the company never lets up when it comes to introducing new ones.
Branches: throughout the city.

Hairdressers

Fish

30 D'Arblay Street, Soho, W1 (7494 2398/ www.fishweb.co.uk). Leicester Square, Piccadilly Circus or Tottenham Court Road tube. **Open** 10am-7pm Mon-Wed, Fri; 10am-8pm Thur; 10am-5pm Sat. **Credit** MC, V. **Map** p399 K6.

Fish is small and cramped, but its lively atmosphere makes it very popular with trendy Soho folk. Cuts and colours are up-to-date and of a high standard.

Geo F Trumper

9 Curzon Street, Mayfair, W1 (7499 1850/ www.trumpers.com). Green Park tube. **Open** 9am-5.30pm Mon-Fri; 9am-1pm Sat. **Credit** AmEx, DC, MC, V. **Map** p400 H8.

This delightful Mayfair barber and perfumery offers much more than a short back and sides: there's a resident chiropodist, pedicures, a hot towel shave and moustache trimming.
Branch: 20 Jermyn Street, St James's, SW1 (7734 1370).

Toni & Guy

8 Marylebone High Street, Marylebone, W8 (7935 7900/www.toniandguy.co.uk). Marylebone tube/rail. **Open** 9am-6.30pm Mon; 9am-8pm Tue-Fri; 9am-6.30pm Sat. **Credit** AmEx, MC, V. **Map** p398 H6.

High-fashion styles for men and women at affordable prices and in a friendly atmosphere. There are various beauty services on offer downstairs.
Branches: throughout the city.

Opticians

Specsavers

6-17 Tottenham Court Road, Fitzrovia, W1 (7580 5115/www.specsavers.com). Tottenham Court Road tube. **Open** 10am-8pm Mon-Fri; 10am-7pm Sat; noon-6pm Sun. **Credit** AmEx, DC, MC, V. **Map** p399 K5.

This branch of the UK's biggest optical retailer keeps half of its eye-testing slots free, so you can generally expect to get an appointment the same day, if not on the spot. Prices for own-brand no-frills plastic and metal frames range from £30 to £169.
Branches: throughout the city.

Homewares

Conran Shop

Michelin House, 81 Fulham Road, Chelsea, SW3 (7589 7401/www.conran.com). South Kensington tube. **Open** 10am-6pm Mon, Tue, Fri; 10am-7pm Wed, Thur; 10am-6.30pm Sat; noon-6pm Sun. **Credit** AmEx, MC, V. **Map** p397 E10.

When you shop (or eat) at Conran, you buy into a lifestyle: just about everything here is clean-lined and unobtrusively stylish, with enough of a humorous edge to save it from being too tasteful and restrained for its own good. Conran 2, in Bluebird (*see p249*), sells Conran gear at reduced prices.

Branches: 55 Marylebone High Street, Marylebone, W1 (7723 2223); 12 Conduit Street, Mayfair, W1 (7399 0710).

Designers Guild
267-71 & 275-7 King's Road, Chelsea, SW3 (7351 5775/www.designersguild.com). Sloane Square tube then 11, 19, 22 bus. **Open** 10am-6pm Mon-Sat; (Nos.267-71 only) noon-5pm Sun. **Credit** AmEx, MC, V. **Map** p397 E10.

Interiors junkies will find more than 2,000 fabrics and 600 wallpapers here. There's funky, original furniture too, plus glassware, ceramics and rugs.

Eat My Handbag Bitch
Old Truman Brewery, 6 Dray Walk, 91-5 Brick Lane, Spitalfields, E1 (7375 3100/www.eatmyhandbag bitch.co.uk). Liverpool Street tube/rail. **Open** 10am-6pm daily. **Credit** AmEx, MC, V. **Map** p403 S5.

Ignore the comedy name: Georgina Stead and George Enoch's shop takes its classic design items seriously. It's a great place for unusual post-war furniture; the stock is a mix of Italian, British and Scandinavian items.

Freud
198 Shaftesbury Avenue, St Giles's, WC2 (7831 1071). Tottenham Court Road tube. **Open** 10.30am-6.30pm Mon-Fri; 11am-6pm Sat; noon-5pm Sun. **Credit** MC, V. **Map** p399 K6.

Interesting items with clean lines is Freud's hallmark: in-house designers produce simple glass vases and porcelain bowls (from £15), sold alongside 1930s-style Cinni Fans and replica Mackintosh chairs.

General Trading Company
2-4 Symons Street, Belgravia, SW3 (7730 0411/ www.general-trading.co.uk). Sloane Square tube. **Open** 10am-6.30pm Mon, Tue, Thur-Sat; 10am-7pm Wed. **Credit** AmEx, MC, V. **Map** p397 F10-11.

Now ensconced in new premises, GTC's enlarged range of modern and traditional homewares is more adventurous and eclectic than ever. You'll find rugs and cushions, furniture, boxes, books, bags, garden items, stationery and gifts, plus a basement full of kitchen- and tableware.

Habitat
196 Tottenham Court Road, Fitzrovia, W1 (7631 3880/www.habitat.net). Goodge Street tube. **Open** 10am-6pm Mon-Wed; 10am-8pm Thur; 10am-6.30pm Fri; 9.30am-6.30pm Sat; noon-6pm Sun. **Credit** AmEx, MC, V. **Map** p399 K5.

An essential stop-off for hip young things looking to kit out their urban pads on a shoestring, Habitat provides simple but striking designs at affordable prices. There's a constantly evolving and innovative furniture collection, and top-quality lighting, kitchen- and tableware departments too.

Branches: throughout the city.

Heal's
196 Tottenham Court Road, Fitzrovia, W1 (7636 1666/www.heals.co.uk). Goodge Street tube. **Open** 10am-6pm Mon-Wed; 10am-8pm Thur; 10am-6.30pm Fri; 9.30am-6.30pm Sat; noon-6pm Sun. **Credit** AmEx, DC, MC, V. **Map** p399 K5.

More grown-up (and expensive) than its next-door neighbour Habitat, Heal's offers a more exclusive take on modern furniture, plus stunning decorative items, especially the glassware. The kitchen department is full of lovely stuff too.

Head east for post-war furniture classics at **Eat My Handbag Bitch**.

Muji

157 Kensington High Street, Kensington, W8 (7376 2484/www.muji.co.jp). High Street Kensington tube.
Open 10.30am-7pm Mon-Wed; 10am-7.30pm Thur, Fri; 10am-7pm Sat; noon-6pm Sun. **Credit** AmEx, DC, MC, V. **Map** p396 B9.

The Japanese store that brings no-brand homeware, clothes, toiletries and stationery to the high street also has a tempting array of table- and kitchenware. **Branches**: throughout the city.

Purves & Purves

220-24 Tottenham Court Road, Fitzrovia, W1 (7580 8223/www.purves.co.uk). Goodge Street tube.
Open 9.30am-6pm Mon, Wed, Fri, Sat; 10am-6pm Tue; 9.30am-7.30pm Thur; 11.30am-5.30pm Sun. **Credit** AmEx, DC, MC, V. **Map** p399 K5.

More playful and colourful than Habitat or Heal's, but unashamedly aimed at those who take their furniture seriously. It's also great for gifts, such as the fun Inflate plastics; there's also a fine in-house café. **Branch**: Canada Place, Canary Wharf Shopping Centre, Docklands, E14 (7719 1169).

Markets

General

Brick Lane Market

Brick Lane (north of railway bridge), Cygnet Street, Sclater Street, E1; Bacon Street, Cheshire Street, Chilton Street, E2. Aldgate East or Shoreditch tube.
Open 8am-1pm Sun. **Map** p403 S5.

Over the past couple of years, Brick Lane Market has gone through a gentrification of sorts, with traders in the Cheshire Street arches cottoning on to the fact that they can overcharge massively and chances are that someone will still pay the asking price. The Brick Lane of old is still here; it's just been pushed to the sidelines. Further down Cheshire Street you'll find every type of tool imaginable, old magazines, new stereos, broken sinks, old cots and even a range of wheelchairs. There's also a butcher, a fishmonger, bikes, video games, clothes, chocolates, books, CDs, fridge-freezers... You name it, in other words.

London loves Car boot sales

They were once a well-kept secret among the nation's bargain hunters, a shady if cheerful world of cash-only transactions signposted at suburban roundabouts. But now, thanks to innumerable TV shows and magazine articles, the secret of the car boot sale is out.

Each year, one million Britons spend £1 billion on unwanted junk sold from car boots and trestle tables in car parks and fields. Anything and everything is fair game at these weekend events, from the predictable (furniture, books, bicycles, vinyl) to the positively crazed (plastic dinosaurs, gas lanterns, 1920s gramophones). Try to imagine a flea market on the scale of Harrods (only cheaper), and you'll be getting there.

Prices for goods sold at car boot sales are lower than at antiques fairs or auctions, in part due to the fact that not all the sellers know what they're selling. Although some car boot sales feature stalls selling new goods, the purest and best involve simply members of the public selling off stuff they don't want any more. That said, some sellers have got wise to the potential profits, while the buyers are led by professional vultures who arrive at 6am, desperate to snatch a bargain before the casual shopper shows up.

The increased popularity of car boot sales can be laid at the door of TV. Brits have always loved a bargain, as the continuing popularity of the BBC's smart, middle-class

Sunday-night staple *Antiques Roadshow* demonstrates. But the earthier *Boot Sale Challenge* and *Bargain Hunt* have taken off in the past few years (the latter making a household name of its over-excitable permatanned presenter David Dickinson).

It's easy to see the appeal of the car boot sale. For one, buyers really can still find a bargain, whether book collectors, musicians or DIY enthusiasts (Victorian tiles and roll-top baths can be snapped up for a fraction of their price at architectural reclamation yards). For two, sellers get to swap their trash for cash. But most alluring of all is the treasure hunt nature of the affair: most people just enjoy spending a morning browsing for bric-a-brac and nosing through other people's stuff, nostalgically buying back childhood toys and records they've discarded over the years.

There aren't many inner London boot sales: most are held in suburban car parks, school playgrounds and fields, located at the edge of town. Check www.carbooting.co.uk and www.carbootcalendar.com for details of your nearest, but among the regular sales worth checking out are those at the BBC's overflow car park in Wood Lane, W12 (from 11am each Saturday and Sunday), Beasford Square in Woolwich (7am-1pm Sundays), the car park at Walthamstow Central station (11am-4pm Sundays) and Edgware Hospital's car park (7am-1pm Sundays). Bring cash...

Brixton Market

Electric Avenue, Pope's Road, Brixton Station
Road, Atlantic Road, Brixton, SW9. Brixton
tube/rail. **Open** 8am-6pm Mon, Tue, Thur-Sat;
8am-3pm Wed.

Traditional fruit and veg stalls are interspersed with
African and Caribbean produce at this market as
multicultural as its neighbourhood, while dozens of
fishmongers sell everything from trout to red snap-
per and butchers display goat's meat alongside the
beef. Apart from food, you'll find household wares,
cheap clothes, Afro hair products, votive candles,
African womenswear and jewellery, plus cheap soul
and R&B CDs, luggage and electrical odds and ends.
On Saturdays there are second-hand clothes and
book stalls along Brixton Station Road.

Camden Market

(7284 2084). Camden Town or Chalk Farm tube.
Camden Market *Camden High Street, junction*
with Buck Street, NW1. **Open** 9am-5.30pm Thur-
Sun. **Camden Lock** *Camden Lock Place, off Chalk*
Farm Road, NW1. **Open** 10am-6pm Sat, Sun
(indoor stalls 10am-6pm Tue-Sun). **Stables Market**
off Chalk Farm Road, opposite junction with
Hartland Road, NW1. **Open** 8am-6pm Sat, Sun.
Camden Canal Market *off Chalk Farm Road,*
south of junction with Castlehaven Road, NW1.
Open 10am-6pm Sat, Sun. **Electric Market**
Camden High Street, south of junction with
Dewsbury Terrace, NW1. **Open** 9am-5.30pm Sun.

It's past its prime, but Camden Market isn't quite
ready to surrender to the hordes of tourists and
teenagers. An afternoon's browsing can still throw
up a few surprises. The original Electric Market on
the High Street isn't too exciting and Camden Canal
seems to have devoted itself exclusively to tourist-
oriented tat, but things get more interesting among
the arts and crafts at Camden Lock, and the nicely
varied Stables Yard, where you'll find interesting
second-hand clothes, old jazz records and some
antique furniture. The crowds are hideous.

Greenwich Market

Cutty Sark DLR or Greenwich DLR/rail. **Antiques**
Market *Greenwich High Road, SE10.* **Open**
9am-5pm Sat, Sun. **Central Market** *off Stockwell*
Street, opposite Hotel Ibis, SE10. **Open** *Outdoor*
7am-6pm Sat; 7am-5pm Sun. *Indoor (Village Market)*
10am-5pm Fri, Sat; 10am-6pm Sun. **Crafts market**
College Approach, SE10. **Open** *Antiques* 7.30am-
5pm Thur. *General* 9.30am-5.30pm Wed, Fri-Sun.
Food market *off Stockwell Street, opposite Hotel*
Ibis, SE10. **Open** 10am-4pm Sat.

Less frenetic and cheaper than Camden and
Portobello, Greenwich Market is perfect for a relaxed
afternoon's outing. The main market provides hand-
icrafts ranging from the chi-chi to the tatty, while
the Compendia shop and a stall sell hand-painted
wooden toys, traditional games and puzzles. For
clothing, including some good second-hand stalls,
records, books and furniture, head to the Village
Market. In between, snack on falafels, curries, crêpes
and burgers in the Food Court.

Old-style **Brick Lane Market**. *See p254.*

Petticoat Lane Market

Middlesex Street, Goulston Street, New Goulston
Street, Toynbee Street, Wentworth Street, Bell Lane,
Cobb Street, Leyden Street, Strype Street, Old Castle
Street, Cutler Street, the City, E1. Liverpool Street
tube/rail. **Open** 9am-2pm Sun (Wentworth Street
also open 10am-2.30pm Mon-Fri). **Map** p405 R6.

Petticoat Lane shows no signs of following in the
footsteps of gentrified Brick Lane: it's resolutely traditional and about as East End as they come. Apart
from a couple of fruit and veg stalls, the market's all
about cheap clothes and consumer durables: electronics, men's and women's clothing, leather goods.
East End Cosmetics at the start of Middlesex Street
has the cheapest beauty products, while Jelly Tots
at the other end is good for all your infant's needs.

Eat, Drink, Shop

Portobello Road Market

Portobello Road, Notting Hill, W10, W11; Golborne Road, W10. Ladbroke Grove, Notting Hill Gate or Westbourne Park tube. **Open** *Antiques* 4am-6pm Sat. *General* 8am-6pm Mon-Wed; 9am-1pm Thur; 7am-7pm Fri, Sat. *Organic market* 11am-6pm Thur. *Clothes & bric-a-brac* 7am-4pm Fri; 8am-5pm Sat; 9am-4pm Sun. *Golborne Road market* 9am-5pm Mon-Sat. **Map** p394 A6.

There are some great finds at this west London staple, from off-the-back-of-a-truck bargains to original designer clothing and unusual antiques. The latter predominate at the Notting Hill end, tending towards expensive jewellery and Victoriana, while fruit and veg stalls start by the Duke of Wellington pub. Then come cheap clothes and some CD stalls, before the second-hand and young designer clothes stalls under the Westway. Traders on the walkway stretching to Ladbroke Grove are often quickest to pick up on new trends, and smart semi-permanent boutiques occupy Portobello Green Arcade.

Flowers

Columbia Road Market

Columbia Road, between Gosset Street & the Royal Oak pub, Bethnal Green, E2. Bus 26, 48, 55. **Open** 8am-1pm Sun. **No credit cards. Map** p403 S3.

Every Sunday, hundreds of London gardeners make an early-morning pilgrimage to Columbia Road. The keenest gardeners arrive at the crack of dawn, but there's plenty still here later on. Half the stalls are dedicated to cut flowers, and the rest offer potted plants, bedding plants and trees, and everything from pak choi to purple basil at £1 a pot.

Food

For details on London's various farmers' markets, call 01225 787914 or visit website www.farmersmarkets.net.

Berwick Street Market

Berwick Street, Rupert Street, Soho, W1. Piccadilly Circus tube. **Open** 8am-6pm Mon-Sat. **Map** p398 J6.
One of London's most authentic, most famous and least expensive fruit and veg markets is situated in the seedy part of Soho. Other stalls sell bread and flowers, among other items.

Borough Market

Between Borough High Street, Bedale Street, Stoney Street & Winchester Walk, South Bank, SE1 (www.boroughmarket.org.uk). London Bridge tube/ rail. **Open** noon-6pm Fri; 9am-4pm Sat; best on 3rd Sat of mth. **Map** p404 P8.
At the best and most interesting food market in London, cottage industry-type producers sell mainly organic food in a beautiful old fruit market (it's still used for fruit and veg storage). There are exotic Chinese teas, Italian cheeses, wild boar, fine pies and sausages, potted shrimps, traditional dry-cured bacon and sundry Spanish delights.

Music

Megastores

HMV

150 Oxford Street, Fitzrovia, W1 (7631 3423/ www.hmv.co.uk). Oxford Circus tube. **Open** 9am-8pm Mon-Wed, Fri, Sat; 9am-9pm Thur; noon-6pm Sun. **Credit** AmEx, DC, MC, V. **Map** p398 J6.
Oxford Street's three-floor emporium offers pretty much everything: CDs, DVDs, videos, books, games, posters, T-shirts and mags are here in their thousands. More attention is paid to underground trends and to dance, trance and hip hop (often on vinyl). **Branches:** throughout the city.

Tower Records

1 Piccadilly Circus, Mayfair, W1 (7439 2500/ www.towerrecords.co.uk). Piccadilly Circus tube. **Open** 8.30am-midnight Mon, Sat; 9am-midnight Tue-Fri; noon-6pm Sun. **Credit** AmEx, DC, MC, V. **Map** p400 J7.
Corporate flagship it may be, but few music lovers come away disappointed from this Piccadilly Circus behemoth: the jazz, classical, world music, folk and opera departments are all impressive. The focus is mainly on CDs, but there are also books, games and magazines, plus dance choons on vinyl. **Branches:** throughout the city.

Virgin Megastore

14-16 Oxford Street, Fitzrovia, W1 (7631 1234/ www.virgin.com). Tottenham Court Road tube. **Open** 9.30am-9.30pm Mon-Sat; noon-6pm Sun. **Credit** AmEx, MC, V. **Map** p399 K6.
Negotiate your way past the hordes milling around the huge Top 40 section and you should be able to find most things you want. Videos and DVDs have

Indie specialist **Rough Trade**. *See p257.*

Top toy emporium **Hamleys**. *See p259.*

their own floor, with world cinema and art house
fairly well represented, and the range of music
extends from relatively obscure indie, dance, hip hop
and soul to jazz, folk, classical and opera.
Branches: throughout the city.

Specialist music shops

Soho's Berwick Street is a music mecca –
Selectadisc (No.34) and **Sister Ray** (No.94)
are strong on indie, **Reckless** (No.30) is good
for mainstream, there's Jamaican music at
Daddy Kool (No.12) and cut-price CDs at **Mr
CD** (No.80). **Ray's Jazz Shop** has moved from
Shaftesbury Avenue into Foyles (*see p232*).

Blackmarket
*25 D'Arblay Street, Soho, W1 (7437 0478/
www.blackmarket.co.uk). Oxford Circus tube.* **Open**
noon-7pm Mon; 11am-7pm Tue, Wed, Sat; 11am-8pm
Thur, Fri. **Credit** AmEx, MC, V. **Map** p399 K6.
Not quite the all-powerful dance nerve centre it
once was, this is still a honeypot for DJs. Pros can
take advantage of a website that's updated every
half-hour. The hottest UK and worldwide house
releases are stocked, and the 'drum and bassment'
is internationally renowned.

Harold Moores Records & Video
*2 Great Marlborough Street, Soho, W1 (7437 1576/
www.hmrecords.co.uk). Oxford Circus tube.* **Open**
10am-6.30pm Mon-Sat; noon-6.30pm Sun. **Credit**
MC, V. **Map** p398 J6.
London's finest classical music store. Downstairs is
a huge variety of chamber and classical music on
second-hand LP, most of it in near-mint condition,
while standards remain lofty in the CD section too.
Classical concerts are available on video.

Honest Jon's
*276 & 278 Portobello Road, Notting Hill, W10
(8969 9822). Ladbroke Grove tube.* **Open** 10am-6pm
Mon-Sat, 11am-5pm Sun. **Credit** AmEx, DC, MC, V.
Map p394 A6.
Honest Jon's has one of London's best choices of jazz
on CD and vinyl. Also here in force are reggae, soul,
funk and Latin sounds, and solid portions of house,
downbeat and breaks.

Intoxica!
*231 Portobello Road, Notting Hill, W11 (7229 8010/
www.intoxica.co.uk). Ladbroke Grove tube.* **Open**
10.30am-6.30pm Mon-Sat; noon-5pm Sun. **Credit**
AmEx, DC, MC, V. **Map** p394 A6.
Soundtracks, funk, jazz, Hammond, gospel, soul,
punk, hip hop, breakbeats: it's all available at this
prince among record stores. But the '60s gems – rare
albums and rarer seven-inchs from big boys like the
Kinks and the Faces – really make it worth the visit.

MDC Classic Music
*437 Strand, Covent Garden, WC2 (7240 2157/
www.mdcmusic.co.uk). Embankment tube or Charing
Cross tube/rail.* **Open** 9am-7pm Mon-Sat; noon-6pm
Sun. **Credit** AmEx, MC, V. **Map** p401 L7.
The commercial end of classical music is represented
well here. It's worth popping in for promotions of
new mainstream releases, but it's probably not the
place for quirkier selections.
Branches: throughout the city.

Rough Trade
*130 Talbot Road, Notting Hill, W11 (7229 8541/
www.roughtrade.com). Ladbroke Grove tube.*
Open 10am-6.30pm Mon-Sat; 1-5pm Sun. **Credit**
AmEx, MC, V. **Map** p394 A5.
Rough Trade offers alternative and underground
cuts. Stock varies wildly according to crazes, but you
can expect insanity, with Japanese thrash lining up
with electro and 'bootleg' oddities. More conventional
stock includes an outstanding range of underground
indie and mainstream rarities.
Branch: 16 Neal's Yard, WC2 (7240 0105).

Pharmacies

For details of emergency health services in
the capital, *see p365*. Several branches of
Boots (*see p252*) in the city centre operate
late-night pharmacies.

Bliss Chemist
*5-6 Marble Arch, Marylebone, W1 (7723 6116).
Marble Arch tube.* **Open** 9am-midnight daily.
Credit AmEx, MC, V. **Map** p395 F6.

Sport & adventure

Lillywhites
*24-36 Lower Regent Street, St James's, SW1 (0870
3339 6000). Piccadilly Circus tube.* **Open** 10am-9pm
Mon-Sat; noon-6pm Sun. **Credit** AmEx, DC, MC, V.
Map p401 K7.

Eat, Drink, Shop

The mother of all sports shops recently changed hands and has ditched some of its specialist stock in favour of focusing on equipment for popular sports such as cricket, football, golf and tennis.

SweatyBetty

21 Beak Street, Soho, W1 (7287 5128/www.sweaty betty.com). Oxford Circus tube. **Open** 11am-7pm Mon-Fri, Sat; 11am-8pm Thur; noon-6pm Sun. **Credit** DC, MC, V. **Map** p400 J6.
A brilliant mini-chain for funky exercise, swim and yoga gear, with the likes of Seafolly, Venice Beach, Nike, Puma, Danskin and SB's own range.
Branches: throughout the city.

YHA Adventure Shop

152-60 Wardour Street, Soho, W1 (7836 8541/ www.yhaadventure.com). Oxford Circus or Tottenham Court Road tube. **Open** 10am-7pm Mon, Tue, Fri; 10.30am-7pm Wed; 10am-8pm Thur; 10am-6pm Sat; noon-6pm Sun. **Credit** AmEx, DC, MC, V. **Map** p398 J6.
Recently moved to this Soho location, the YHA is one of the city's main outdoor equipment suppliers, with better prices than some of its rivals. You'll find everything here from clothing, tents, sleeping bags and cooking equipment to maps, compasses and global positioning systems.
Branches: throughout the city.

Shops by area

The South Bank & Bankside

Borough Market (Markets, *p256*); **Richer Sounds** (Electronics, *p237*); **Riverside Walk Market** (Books, *p233*).

The City

Petticoat Lane Market (Markets, *p255*).

Holborn & Clerkenwell

Aveda Lifestyle Institute (Health & beauty, *p252*); **Berganza** (Fashion accessories, *p244*); **Books Etc** (Books, *p232*); **Lesley Craze Gallery/Craze Two** (Fashion accessories, *p244*); **Magma** (Books, *p233*); **Space EC1** (Gifts & stationery, *p250*).

Bloomsbury & Fitzrovia

Apple Centre (Electronics, *p236*); **Cinema Bookshop** (Books, *p232*); **Computer Exchange** (Electronics, *p236*); **Gay's the Word** (Books, *p233*); **Gultronics** (Electronics, *p236*); **HMV** (Music, *p256*); **Habitat** (Homewares, *p252*); **Heal's** (Homewares, *p252*); **Hi-Fi Experience** (Electronics, *p237*); **Paperchase** (Gifts & stationery, *p250*); **Purves & Purves** (Homewares, *p254*); **Skoob Russell Square** (Books, *p233*); **Specsavers** (Health & beauty, *p252*); **Ulysses** (Books, *p233*); **Virgin Megastore** (Music, *p256*).

Marylebone

Alfie's Antiques Market (Antiques, *p231*); **Bliss Chemist** (Pharmacies, *p257*); **Daunt Books** (Books, *p233*); **French Connection** (Fashion, *p241*); **The Girl Can't Help It/ Cad van Swankster** (Fashion, *p243*); **H&M** (Fashion, *p238*); **John Lewis** (Department stores, *p235*); **Marks & Spencer** (Department stores, *p236*); **Miss Selfridge** (Fashion, *p238*); **New Look** (Fashion, *p238*); **Paul Bakery & Tearoom** (Food & drink, *p247*);

Selfridges (Department stores, *p236*); **Shellys** (Fashion accessories, *p247*); **Toni & Guy** (Health & beauty, *p252*); **Topshop** (Fashion, *p238*); **Whistles** (Fashion, *p242*).

Mayfair & St James's

Browns (Fashion, *p237*); **Buckingham Dry Cleaners** (Fashion accessories, *p243*); **Camper** (Fashion accessories, *p245*); **Charbonnel et Walker** (Food & drink, *p249*); **Church's Shoes** (Fashion accessories, *p245*); **Electrum Gallery** (Fashion accessories, *p244*); **Fortnum & Mason** (Department stores, *p235*); **Garrard** (Fashion accessories, *p244*); **Geo F Trumper** (Health & beauty, *p252*); **Godiva** (Food & drink, *p249*); **Grays Antiques Market & Grays in the Mews** (Antiques, *p232*); **Jigsaw** (Fashion, *p241*); **Lillywhites** (Sport & adventure, *p257*); **Mulberry** (Fashion accessories, *p245*); **Ozwald Boateng** (Fashion accessories, *p247*); **Poste** (Fashion accessories, *p245*); **The Refinery** (Health & beauty, *p251*); **Tiffany & Co** (Fashion accessories, *p244*); **Tower Records** (Music, *p256*); **Waterstone's** (Books, *p232*); **Wright & Teague** (Fashion accessories, *p244*); **Zara** (Fashion, *p239*).

Soho & Chinatown

Algerian Coffee Stores (Food & drink, *p248*); **Berwick Street Market** (Markets, *p256*); **Blackmarket** (Music, *p257*); **Foyles** (Books, *p232*); **Gerry's** (Food & drink, *p250*); **Fish** (Health & beauty, *p252*); **Hamleys** (Toys & games, *p259*); **Harold Moores Records & Video** (Music, *p257*); **Karen Millen** (Fashion, *p241*); **Liberty** (Department stores, *p235*); **Milroy's of Soho** (Food & drink, *p250*); **Murder One** (Books, *p233*); **Shop** (Fashion, *p243*); **SweatyBetty** (Sport & adventure, *p258*); **YHA Adventure Shop** (Sport & adventure, *p258*).

Eat, Drink, Shop

Toys & games

Also check out the toy and game sections of the department stores (*see p235*). For computer games, *see p236*.

Cheeky Monkeys

38 Cross Street, Islington, N1 (7288 1948/ www.cheekymonkeys.com). Angel tube. **Open** 9.30am-5.30pm Mon-Fri; 10am-5.30pm Sat; 11am-5pm Sun. **Credit** MC, V. **Map** p402 O1.
The more covetable stock – mini wooden domestic appliances by Elka, enchanting dressing-up kit – is

far from cheap, but there's also a thoughtfully selected table of pocket-money-priced toys.
Branches: throughout the city.

Hamleys

188-96 Regent Street, Soho, W1 (0870 333 2455/ www.hamleys.com). Oxford Circus tube. **Open** 10am-8pm Mon-Fri; 9.30am-8pm Sat; noon-6pm Sun. **Credit** AmEx, MC, V. **Map** p400 J7.
Children love this perennially busy five-floor wonderland. All the big-brand toys are present and correct, plus a whole jungle of stuffed animals, magic tricks, computer games and gizmos, dolls, dressing-up clothes, Hornby train sets and Scalextric.

Covent Garden & St Giles's

Accessorize (Fashion accessories, *p243*); **Any Amount of Books** (Books, *p233*); **Blackwell's** (Books, *p232*); **Borders** (Books, *p232*); **Carhartt** (Fashion, *p242*); **Carluccio's** (Food & drink, *p249*); **Diesel** (Fashion, *p242*); **Duffer of St George** (Fashion, *p242*); **Edward Stanford** (Books, *p233*); **Forbidden Planet** (Books, *p233*); **Freud** (Homewares, *p253*); **Gap** (Fashion, *p241*); **Helter Skelter** (Books, *p233*); **Jessops** (Electronics, *p237*); **Koh Samui** (Fashion, *p238*); **Kookaï** (Fashion, *p241*); **MDC Classic Music** (Music, *p257*); **Maharishi** (Fashion, *p242*); **Mango** (Fashion, *p238*); **Natural Shoe Store** (Fashion accessories, *p245*); **Neal's Yard Bakery** (Food & drink, *p247*); **Neal's Yard Dairy** (Food & drink, *p248*); **Neal's Yard Remedies** (Health & beauty, *p252*); **Oasis** (Fashion, *p241*); **Office** (Fashion accessories, *p245*); **Poste Mistress** (Fashion accessories, *p246*); **Quiksilver** (Fashion, *p242*); **R Twining & Co** (Food & drink, *p249*); **The Sanctuary** (Health & beauty, *p251*); **SPAce.NK** (Health & beauty, *p251*); **Wild Bunch** (Flowers, *p247*); **Zwemmer Design & Architecture** (Books, *p233*).

Knightsbridge & South Kensington

Agent Provocateur (Fashion, *p243*); **General Trading Company** (Homewares, *p253*); **Harrods** (Department stores, *p235*); **Harvey Nichols** (Department stores, *p235*); **Rigby & Peller** (Fashion, *p243*); **Uniqlo** (Fashion, *p239*).

Chelsea

Bluebird (Food & drink, *p249*); **Conran Shop** (Homewares, *p252*); **Daisy & Tom** (Fashion, *p239*); **Designers Guild** (Homewares, *p253*); **Jo Malone** (Health & beauty, *p252*); **MAC**

Cosmetics (Health & beauty, *p252*); **Trotters** (Fashion, *p239*).

North London

Annie's Vintage Clothes (Islington, Fashion, *p243*); **Camden Market** (Camden, Markets, *p255*); **Camden Passage Antiques Market** (Islington, Antiques, *p232*); **Paula Pryke Flowers** (Islington, Flowers, *p247*); **Cheeky Monkeys** (Islington, Toys & games, *p259*).

East London

Brick Lane Market (Spitalfields, Markets, *p254*); **Columbia Road Market** (Bethnal Green, Markets, *p256*); **Eat My Handbag Bitch** (Spitalfields, Homewares, *p253*); **Queens** (Spitalfields, Gifts & stationery, *p250*); **Timothy Everest** (Spitalfields, Fashion accessories, *p247*).

South London

Brixton Market (Brixton, Markets, *p255*); **Greenwich Market** (Greenwich, Markets, *p255*).

West London

& Clarke's (Kensington, Food & drink, *p247*); **Bill Amberg** (Notting Hill, Fashion accessories, *p244*); **Books for Cooks** (Notting Hill, Books, *p232*); **Boots** (Bayswater, Health & beauty, *p252*); **The Cross** (Holland Park, Fashion, *p238*); **Frontiers** (Notting Hill, Fashion accessories, *p244*); **Honest Jon's** (Music, *p257*); **Intoxica** (Music, *p257*); **Jigsaw Junior** (Notting Hill, Fashion, *p239*); **Laser Disc Shop** (Bayswater, Electronics, *p236*; **Muji** (Kensington, Homewares, *p254*); **Porchester Spa** (Bayswater, Health & beauty, *p250*); **Portobello Road Market** (Notting Hill, Markets, *p256*); **Rough Trade** (Notting Hill, Music, *p257*); **SPAce.NK** (Notting Hill, Health & beauty, *p251*); **Urban Outfitters** (Kensington, Fashion, *p243*).

Arts &
Entertainment

Festivals & Events

From pearly kings to priests on ponies, London's no slouch when it comes to celebrations.

Celebrate in colour at **Chinese New Year**.

If the idea of social events in London summons up images of po-faced tradition, think again. This is a city that does silly every bit as well as it does sober; indeed, it rarely does sober without throwing in a bit of silliness on top. Royal and governmental events are still an important part of the city's packed roster of annual events, but the diversity of cultures and the sheer number of people living here ensure that the widest possible range of interests is catered for.

We've focused on the best of London's regular annual events; scores more irregular events are advertised in *Time Out* magazine each week. Some events need to be booked in advance, some charge admission on the day/night, while others are free; it's a good idea to phone and check. All the dates given below were correct at the time of going to press, but it's always wise to call and double-check nearer the time.

Details of cultural festivals are listed elsewhere: for **dance**, *see p282*; for **film**, *see p287*; and for **music**, *see p305*. Many of the big museums and galleries, such as the **British Museum** (*see p102*), often hold talks and discussions; call them for details. For public holidays in the UK, *see p375*.

January-March 2003

London International Boat Show
Earl's Court Exhibition Centre, Warwick Road, Earl's Court, SW5 (01784 472222/www.bigblue.org.uk). Earl's Court tube. **Map** p396 A11. **Date** 2-12 Jan 2003.
Now in its 49th year, the ever-popular Boat Show includes everything from dinghies to luxury yachts. This is the final show at Earl's Court; it moves to ExCeL in Docklands in time for 2004.

London International Mime Festival
various venues (7637 5661/www.mimefest.co.uk). **Date** 10-26 Jan 2003.
Anyone who thinks mime is all about people standing around Covent Garden pretending to be statues has a surprise in store: this visual theatre festival also includes animation, puppetry and other hybrid forms.

Chinese New Year Festival
around Gerrard Street, Chinatown, W1 (7439 3822/www.chinatown-online.co.uk). Leicester Square or Piccadilly Circus tube. **Map** p401 K7. **Date** 1-3 Feb 2003 (tbc).
One of London's most thrilling festivals: you can't help but get caught up in the surging crowds that follow the 'dragons' as they snake their way through the streets, gathering gifts of money and food.

Art2003
Business Design Centre, Islington, N1 (0870 739 9500/www.londonartfair.co.uk). Angel tube. **Map** p402 N2. **Date** 15-19 Jan 2003.
More than 100 galleries are expected to show at this contemporary art fair. Its £12 million sales in 2001 placed it among the top five art fairs in Europe.

Great Spitalfields Pancake Day Race
Spitalfields Market, entrance on Commercial Street or Brushfield Street, Spitalfields, E1 (7375 0441). Liverpool Street tube/rail. **Map** p403 R5. **Date** 4 Mar 2003.
This traditional tomfoolery starts at 12.30pm, with teams of four tossing pancakes as they run. Call several days in advance if you want to take part.

Ideal Home Show
Earl's Court Exhibition Centre, Warwick Road,
Earl's Court, SW5 (box office 0870 606 6080/
groups 0870 241 0272/www.idealhomeshow.co.uk).
Earl's Court tube. **Map** p396 A11. **Date** 13 Mar-
6 Apr 2003.
Britain's biggest consumer show has everything from
kitchen utensils to full-scale houses (last year's show
included four cottages on a village green with a
medieval tower). Experts are on hand to give advice.

Chelsea Antiques Fair
Chelsea Old Town Hall, King's Road, Chelsea,
SW3 (01444 482514/www.penman-fairs.co.uk).
Sloane Square tube. **Open** 11am-8pm Mon-Fri;
11am-7pm Sat; 11am-5pm Sun. **Map** p397 E12.
Date 14-23 Mar 2003.
Held twice a year (it's also happening 19-28 Sept),
the fair caters to casual browsers and collectors.
Expert committees ensure the goods are authentic.

St Patrick's Day
Date 17 Mar 2003.
With the third biggest Irish population of any city
in the world, it's surprising that there are no organised St Patrick's Day events in London. Not to worry:
there's plenty of craic across town, and enthusiastic
jubilations are guaranteed up in Kilburn (NW6).

Head of the River Race
Thames, from Mortlake, SW14, to Putney, SW15
(01932 220401/www.horr.co.uk). Mortlake rail
(start), Hammersmith tube (mid-point) or Putney
Bridge tube (finish). **Date** 29 Mar 2003.
As impressive as the Oxford & Cambridge race (*see*
below) but less well known, the Head of the River is
raced over the same 4¼-mile (6.8km) course, in the
opposite direction, by more than 400 crews. The best
views are from Hammersmith Bridge or at Putney.
The race starts from Mortlake at 9.45am.

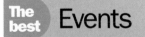

The best **Events**

For pomp and circumstance
State Opening of Parliament. *See p268*.

For going out with a bang
Bonfire Night (*see p268*) or the **Mayor's**
Thames Festival (*see p267*).

For London's hidden architecture
London Open House. *See p267*.

For more pomp and circumstance
Beating Retreat. *See p265*.

For a pint or nine
Great British Beer Festival. *See p266*.

Oxford & Cambridge Boat Race
Thames, from Putney, SW15, to Mortlake, SW1
(www.theboatrace.org). Putney Bridge tube (start),
Hammersmith tube (mid-point) or Mortlake rail
(finish). **Date** 6 Apr 2003.
The 149th Boat Race, contested by Oxford (the Dark
Blues) and Cambridge (the Light Blues) universities,
should start at 4.30pm, with the reserves race held
half an hour earlier. Huge crowds line the course
from Putney to Mortlake, with the riverside pubs
in Mortlake and Hammersmith the most popular
vantage points.

London Marathon
Greenwich Park to Westminster Bridge via the Isle
of Dogs, Victoria Embankment & St James's Park
(7620 4117/hotline 7902 0189/www.london-
marathon.co.uk). **Date** 13 Apr 2003.
The world's biggest road race attracts some 35,000
starters. Would-be runners must apply by the previous October to be entered in the ballot.

London Harness Horse Parade
Battersea Park, Albert Bridge Road, Battersea, SW11
(01733 234451). Battersea Park or Queenstown
Road rail/97, 137 bus. **Date** 21 Apr 2003.
A traditional Easter Monday parade of working nags
with their various commercial and private carriages.

Museums & Galleries Month 2003
various venues (7233 9796/www.may2003.org.uk).
Date 1 May-31 May 2003.
A welter of special events, activities, exhibitions and
welcome days, many and varied, are held at museums and galleries around the country.

May Fayre & Puppet Festival
St Paul's Church Garden, Covent Garden, WC2
(7375 0441/www.alternativearts.co.uk). Covent
Garden tube. **Map** p401 L7. **Date** 11 May 2003.
Celebrating the first recorded sighting of Mr Punch
in England (by Pepys, in 1662), this free event offers
puppetry galore from 10.30am to 5.30pm. *See also*
p267 Punch & Judy Festival.

Chelsea Flower Show
Grounds of Royal Hospital, Royal Hospital Road,
Chelsea, SW3 (7649 1885/www.rhs.org.uk). Sloane
Square tube. **Map** p397 F12. **Date** 20-23 May 2003.
The first two days of this world-famous gardening
extravaganza are only open to Royal Horticultural
Society members; the show closes at 5.30pm on the
final day, with display plants sold off from 4.30pm.

Coin Street Festival
various venues on the South Bank, SW1 (7401 2255/
www.coinstreetfestival.org). Southwark tube/Waterloo
tube/rail. **Date** May-July 2003.
London's biggest free festival of music, dance and
performance is now in its 12th year. Events include
Community Celebration, held on the South Bank
between the National Theatre and Tate Modern.

Arts & Entertainment

Horses come second to hats at **Royal Ascot**'s Ladies Day. *See p265.*

London Wildlife Week

various locations (7261 0447/www.wildlondon. org.uk). **Date** 1-8 June 2003.
Free seasonal activities take place across the nature reserves and urban woodland areas of Greater London as part of a week-long national event.

Victoria Embankment Gardens Summer Events

Victoria Embankment Gardens, Villiers Street, Westminster, WC2 (7375 0441/www.alternativearts. co.uk). Embankment tube. **Map** p399 L7.
Date 1 June-19 Aug 2003.
A packed series of free open-air events, including the Latin American Fiesta da Cultura (1 June), the Open Dance Festival (7-8 June), the Move It Mime Festival (15 June), the Midsummer Poetry Festival (22 June), the Summer Season of Street Theatre (1 July-19 Aug), Out of Africa (6 July) and Out of Asia (20 July).

Royal Academy Summer Exhibition

Royal Academy of Arts, Burlington House, Piccadilly, Mayfair, W1 (7300 8000/www.royalacademy.org.uk). Green Park or Piccadilly Circus tube. **Map** p400 J7.
Date 3 June-11 Aug 2003.
An exuberant annual showcase drawn from around 12,000 works submitted by artists of all styles and standards. A panel of eminent Academicians boils the choice down to around 1,000 entries for display.

Derby Day

Epsom Downs Racecourse, Epsom Downs, Surrey (01372 470047/www.epsomderby.co.uk). Tattenham Corner rail then shuttle bus. **Date** 7 June 2003.
The most important flat race of the season has a carnival mood. If you want comfort and a good view, be prepared to pay for it. *See also p330.*

Fleadh Music Festival

Finsbury Park, N4 (8963 0940/www.meanfiddler. com). Finsbury Park tube/rail. **Date** 7 June 2003.
The nominal Irish slant seems less and less prominent with the passing years, but the annual Fleadh did provide a rare outing for the Pogues *with* Shane MacGowan in 2002.

London Garden Squares Day

various venues (7839 3969/www.londongardenstrust. org.uk). **Date** June 2003 (tbc).
This eminently civilised event offers the chance to discover normally inaccessible green oases all over London (from Japanese gardens to secret 'children-only' play areas), as well as putting on concerts, cream teas, Pimms tastings and Scottish dancing.

Meltdown

South Bank Centre, Belvedere Road, South Bank, SE1 (7960 4242/www.sbc.org.uk). Embankment tube/ Waterloo tube/rail. **Map** p401 M8. **Date** June 2003.
A festival of contemporary culture with a guest curator each year. Among the recent bosses have been Scott Walker, Nick Cave and David Bowie, and the line-ups usually tend towards the unpredictable.

Trooping the Colour

Horse Guards Parade, Whitehall, Westminster, SW1 (7414 2479). Westminster tube/Charing Cross tube/rail. **Map** p401 K8. **Date** 15 June 2003.
Though the Queen was born on 21 April, this is the official celebration. At 10.45am she makes the 15-minute journey from Buckingham Palace to Horse Guards Parade, then scurries back home to watch a midday Royal Air Force flypast and receive a gun salute from Green Park. Crowds gather on the Mall and cheer until they're red, white and blue in the face.

Beating Retreat

Horse Guards Parade, Whitehall, Westminster, SW1 (7414 2271). Westminster tube/Charing Cross tube/rail. **Map** p401 K8. **Date** 17-19 June 2003.
This ineffably patriotic ceremony begins at 7pm, with the 'Retreat' beaten on drums by the Mounted Bands of the Household Cavalry and the Massed Bands of the Guards Division.

Royal Ascot

Ascot Racecourse, Ascot, Berkshire (01344 622211/ www.ascot-authority.co.uk). Ascot rail. **Date** 17-22 June 2003.
This society bash, held at the best flat-racing course in the country, even has some races thrown in. Tickets are most in demand for Ladies' Day (19 June), when the Queen swings by. *See also p330.*

Architecture Week

various venues (7973 6469/www.architectureweek. org.uk). **Date** 20-29 June 2003.
A huge range of previews, tours, lectures, exhibitions and installations designed to fuel public debate about the urban environment.

Wimbledon Lawn Tennis Championships

PO Box 98, Church Road, Wimbledon, SW19 (8944 1066/recorded information 8946 2244/ www.wimbledon.org). Southfields tube/Wimbledon tube/rail. **Date** 23 June-6 July 2003.
The world's most prestigious tennis tournament and, when it's not raining, the best. *See also p331.*

City of London Festival

venues in the City, EC2 (information 7377 0540/ box office 7638 8891/www.colf.org). **Date** 23 June-10 July 2003.
Taking place in some of the City's finest buildings, the festival offers music, dance, theatre, visual art and literature events. This year's theme is 'Trading Places', focusing on the interrelationships between London, New York and Shanghai.

Covent Garden Flower Festival

Covent Garden Market, Covent Garden, WC2 (7735 1518/www.cgff.co.uk). Covent Garden tube. **Map** p401 L7. **Date** last wk of June (tbc).
Installations, demonstrations, floral fashion shows, giant fruit and street performers, all free to the public, in the sixth annual flower show on the Piazza.

July-September 2003

Mardi Gras

www.londonmardigras.com. **Date** July 2003.
London's annual gay and lesbian extravaganza features a march during the day and a huge party in the evening.

Rhythm Sticks

South Bank Centre, Belvedere Road, South Bank, SE1 (7960 4242/www.sbc.org.uk). Embankment tube/ Waterloo tube/rail. **Map** p401 M8. **Date** July 2003.

Each year, Rhythm Sticks takes a week to celebrate everything that bangs, crashes and tinkles. Performers come from all corners of the world and play in the widest possible range of styles.

Henley Royal Regatta

Henley Reach, Henley-on-Thames, Oxfordshire (01491 572153/www.hrr.co.uk). Henley-on-Thames rail. **Date** 2-6 July 2003.
First held in 1839, Henley is now a five-day affair, and about as posh as it gets. Races range from open events for men and women through club and student crews to junior boys.

Greenwich & Docklands International Festival

various venues near the Thames at Greenwich & Docklands (8305 1818/www.festival.org). **Date** 3-13 July 2003.
A host of theatrical and musical events by the river, combining community arts with grander projects.

Soho Festival

St Anne's Gardens & part of Wardour Street, W1 (7439 4303/www.thesohosociety.org.uk). Tottenham Court Road tube. **Map** p401 K7. **Date** 13 July 2003 (tbc).
The famous Waiter's Race, a spaghetti-eating competition and an alpine horn blowing contest bring locals and visitors together in aid of the Soho Society.

Swan Upping on the Thames

various points along the Thames (7236 1863/ 7197/www.royal.gov.uk). **Date** mid July 2003; phone for details.
An archaic ceremony in which groups of herdsmen round up, divide up and mark all the cygnets on particular stretches of the Thames as belonging to the Queen, the Vintners' or the Dyers' livery companies. The route and departure times change daily.

BBC Sir Henry Wood Promenade Concerts

Royal Albert Hall, Kensington Gore, South Kensington, SW7 (box office 7589 8212/www.bbc.co.uk/proms). Knightsbridge or South Kensington tube/9, 10, 52 bus. **Map** p397 D9. **Date** 18 July-13 Sept 2003.
It's a shame the Proms is famed for its jingoistic Last Night, as it consistently programmes an impressive range of (mostly classical) concerts. *See also p306.*

Respect Festival

venue tbc (7983 4274/www.respectfestival.org.uk). **Date** 3rd Sat in July (tbc).
This free anti-racist music and entertainment festival was revived at Finsbury Park in 2001, before moving to Victoria Park in 2002.

South East Marine Week

various locations in south-east London (7261 0447/ www.wildlondon.org.uk). **Date** 2-10 Aug 2003.
A week dedicated to introducing urban tykes to the marine environment. There were 50 free events in 2002, including a beach party on the Hammersmith foreshore and pirate boat trips from King's Cross.

Arts & Entertainment

Great British Beer Festival

Olympia, Hammersmith Road, Kensington, W14 (01727 867201/www.camra.org.uk). Kensington (Olympia) tube/rail. **Date** 5-9 Aug 2003.

Last year 44,000 visitors sampled over 300 British ales and ciders at this boozetastic event. Hiccups and belches are guaranteed. As are hangovers.

Notting Hill Carnival

Notting Hill, W10, W11 (8964 0544/www.thecarnival. tv). Ladbroke Grove, Notting Hill Gate or Westbourne Park tube. **Date** 24-25 Aug 2003.

Europe's biggest street party draws more than a million revellers, so you'll be lucky if you get to see the costume parade, live music and sound systems close up. Terrible loos and continuing bad press about street crime fail to deter the crowds.

Thames Barrier Full Tidal Closure

Thames Barrier Information & Learning Centre, 1 Unity Way, Woolwich, SE18 (8305 4188). Charlton rail. **Date** Sept (depends on tides; call for details).

Watch the engineering marvel of the Thames Barrier (*see p168*), built as the first line of defence against surge tides, go through its yearly full test.

Great River Race

River Thames, from Ham House, Richmond, Surrey, to Island Gardens, Greenwich, E14 (8398 9057/ www.greatriverrace.co.uk). **Date** 6 Sept 2003.

The Great River Race, now in its 15th year, sees more than 250 'traditional' boats, from Chinese dragon boats and shallops to Viking longboats and Cornish gigs, vie for the UK Traditional Boat Championship over a 22-mile (35km) course.

Frequent events

Ceremony of the Keys

Tower of London, the City, EC3 (7709 0765/ www.hrp.org.uk). Tower Hill tube. **Date** daily. **Maximum** *Apr-Oct* party of 7. *Nov-Mar* party of 15. **Map** p405 R7.

Dating back 700 years, the ceremony of locking the entrances to the Tower of London starts at 9.53pm every evening (the public need to assemble at the West Gate by 9pm). It's all over by 10pm, when the last post is sounded. To watch, you have to apply in writing for free tickets, giving a choice of three dates (Ceremony of the Keys Office, HM Tower of London, EC3 4AB) with a stamped self-addressed envelope (UK only, international stamps are not accepted) at least two months in advance.

Changing of the Guard

Buckingham Palace, Horse Guards & St James's Palace, SW1 (0906 866 3344/www.royal.gov.uk). Green Park or St James's Park tube/Victoria tube/rail. **Ceremonies** Buckingham Palace *Apr-Aug* 11.15am daily. *Sept-Mar* alternate days (may be cancelled in very wet weather). **Map** p400 H9. Horse Guards 11am Mon-Sat; 10am Sun. **Map** p401 K8.

Every other day, the new guard – usually one of the five regiments of Foot Guards in their scarlet coats and bearskin hats – line up in the forecourt of Wellington Barracks, Birdcage Walk, from 10.45am; at 11.27am they march, accompanied by their regimental band, to Buckingham Palace for the changing of the sentries, who stand guard in the palace forecourt. At Horse Guards in

Whitehall, which is the official entrance to the royal palaces, it's the Household Cavalry who mount the guard (10am-4pm daily); they then ride to Whitehall via the Mall from Hyde Park for the daily changeover.

Funfairs

Alexandra Park *Muswell Hill, N22 (8365 2121/www.alexandrapalace.com). Wood Green tube/Alexandra Palace rail/W3 bus.* **Dates** selected public holidays (*see p375*); phone for details.

Hampstead Heath *NW3 (7485 4491 for a leaflet detailing events in the park). Belsize Park or Hampstead tube/Gospel Oak or Hampstead Heath rail/24, C11 bus.* **Dates** selected public holidays (*see p375*); phone for details.

Gun Salutes

Green Park, W2, & Tower of London, EC3. **Dates** 6 Feb (Accession Day); 21 Apr (Queen's birthday); 2 June (Coronation Day); 15 June (Trooping the Colour; *see p265*); State Opening of Parliament (Nov/Dec; *see p268*). If the date falls on a Sun, salutes are fired the following Mon. **Map** p400 H8/p405 R7.

On royal occasions, cannons are primed for gun salutes. The King's Troop of the Royal Horse Artillery makes a mounted charge through Hyde Park, sets up the guns and fires a 41-gun salute (at noon, except for on the occasion of the State Opening of Parliament) opposite the Dorchester Hotel. Not to be outdone, the Honourable Artillery Company fires a 62-gun salute at the Tower of London at 1pm.

The Last Night of the **Proms** is broadcast live in Hyde Park. *See p265*

Brick Lane Festival
Brick Lane Market, Brick Lane, E1 (7655 0906/
www.bricklanefestival.org). Aldgate East tube.
Map p404 S5/6. **Date** 14 Sept 2003 (tbc).
This annual celebration of Spitalfields' multicultural communities past and present involves food, music, dance and performance, rickshaw rides, stiltwalkers, clowns and jugglers. The main stage showcases world music acts, while the children's area has funfair rides, inflatables and workshops.

Regent Street Festival
Regent Street, W1 (7491 4429/www.regent-
street.co.uk). Oxford Circus or Piccadilly Circus tube.
Map p399 J6. **Date** 7 Sept 2003.
Fairground attractions, theatre, street entertainers and storytelling, as well as a variety of live music.

Mayor's Thames Festival
between Waterloo Bridge & Blackfriars Bridge
(7928 8998/www.thamesfestival.org). Blackfriars
tube/rail/Waterloo tube/rail. **Date** 20-21 Sept 2003.
Always fun and occasionally spectacular, this waterfest is highlighted by the lantern procession and firework finale on Sunday evening. Prior to it, there are food and crafts stalls in a riverside market, environmental activities and creative workshops, and assorted performances.

London Open House
various venues in London (0900 160 0061/
www.londonopenhouse.org). **Date** 20-21 Sept 2003.
An annual event that allows architecture lovers free access to more than 500 fascinating buildings all over the capital, from palaces to pumping stations. Part of the European Heritage Days initiative, the weekend-long event is the highlight of year-round activities organised by the architectural education charity London Open House.

Horseman's Sunday
Church of St John & St Michael, Hyde Park
Crescent, Paddington, W2 (7262 1732). Edgware
Road tube/Paddington tube/rail. **Map** p395 E6.
Date Sept 2002 (tbc).

A surreal event in which a horseback vicar blesses more than 100 horses before they all trot through Hyde Park. You'd imagine it was an ancient rite, but the ceremony actually dates back to 1969, when local riding stables held an open-air service to protest against threats of closure.

Soho Jazz & Heritage Festival
various venues in Soho, W1 (7434 3995/
www.sohojazzfestival.co.uk). Oxford Circus,
Leicester Square or Piccadilly Circus tube.
Date Sept-Oct 2003.
Hours of (mostly free) live jazz in Soho. The 18th annual festival will be held in a variety of well-known jazz venues, including the 100 Club, Ronnie Scott's and Pizza Express (*see also p314*), plus assorted smaller bars, clubs and restaurants.

October-December 2003

Punch & Judy Festival
Covent Garden Piazza, Covent Garden, WC2 (7836
9136/www.coventgardenmarket.co.uk). Covent
Garden tube. **Map** p401 L7. **Date** early Oct 2003.
More of the crocodile, policeman and Punch punching Judy (and, happily, vice versa). See *also p263*
May Fayre & Puppet Festival.

Pearly Kings & Queens Harvest Festival
St Martin-in-the-Fields, Trafalgar Square,
Westminster, WC2 (7766 1100/www.pearlies.co.uk).
Charing Cross tube/rail. **Map** p401 L7.
Date 5 Oct 2003.
Pearly kings and queens have their origins in the 'aristocracy' of London's early Victorian costermongers, who elected their own royalty to safeguard their interests. Now charity representatives, today's pearly monarchy gathers for this 3pm thanksgiving service in their traditional 'flash boy' outfits.

Trafalgar Day Parade
Trafalgar Square, Westminster, WC2 (7928 8978/
www.sea-cadets.org). Charing Cross tube/rail.
Map p401 K7. **Date** 19 Oct 2003.

Arts & Entertainment

To commemorate Nelson's victory at the Battle of Trafalgar (21 Oct 1805), 500 sea cadets parade with marching bands and musical performances. The culmination is the laying of a wreath at the foot of Nelson's Column.

London Film Festival

National Film Theatre, South Bank, SE1 (7928 3232/www.lff.org.uk). Embankment tube/Waterloo tube/rail. **Map** p401 M8. **Date** Nov 2003.

Attracting big name actors and directors and offering the public the chance to see around 150 new British and international features, the LFF centres on the NFT (*see p286*) and the Odeon West End (*see p284*). For other London film festivals, *see p287*.

State Opening of Parliament

House of Lords, Palace of Westminster, Westminster, SW1 (7219 4272/www.parliament.uk). Westminster tube. **Map** p401 L9. **Date** mid Nov-early Dec 2003.

In a ceremony that has changed little since the 16th century, the Queen officially reopens Parliament after its summer recess. You can only see what goes on inside on telly, but if you join the throngs on the streets, you can watch HRH arrive and depart in her Irish or Australian State Coach, attended by the Household Cavalry.

London to Brighton Veteran Car Run

From Serpentine Road, Hyde Park, W2 (01753 681736/www.msauk.org). Hyde Park Corner tube. **Map** p395 E8. **Date** 2 Nov 2003.

You'll need to be up at the crack of dawn to catch the start of this procession of vintage motors: they set off from Hyde Park at 7.30am, aiming to reach Brighton before 4pm. Otherwise join the crowds lining the rest of the route, which wends down via Westminster Bridge.

Bonfire Night

Date 5 Nov 2003.

This annual pyrotechnic frenzy sees Britons across the country gather – usually in inclement weather – to burn a 'guy' (an effigy of Guy Fawkes, who notoriously failed to blow up James I and his Parliament in the Gunpowder Plot of 1605) on a giant bonfire and set off loads of fireworks. Most public displays are held on the weekend nearest 5 Nov; among the best in London are those at Primrose Hill, Alexandra Palace and Crystal Palace. Alternatively, try to book a late ride on the relevant nights on the British Airways London Eye (*see p72*).

Lord Mayor's Show

various streets in the City (7606 3030/ www.lordmayorsshow.org). **Date** 8 Nov 2003.

Today's the day when, under the conditions of the Magna Carta of 1215, the newly elected Lord Mayor of London has to be presented to the monarch or to their justices for approval. Amid a procession of about 140 floats, the Lord Mayor leaves Mansion House at 11am and travels through the City to the Royal Courts of Justice on the Strand, where he makes some vows before returning to Mansion House by 2.20pm. The event is rounded off by a firework display from a barge moored on the Thames between Waterloo and Blackfriars Bridges.

Remembrance Sunday Ceremony

Cenotaph, Whitehall, Westminster, SW1. Westminster tube/Charing Cross tube/rail. **Map** p401 L8. **Date** 9 Nov 2003.

In honour of those who lost their lives in World Wars I and II, the Queen, the Prime Minister and other dignitaries lay wreaths at the Cenotaph, Britain's memorial to 'the Glorious Dead'. After a minute's silence at 11am, the Bishop of London leads a service of remembrance.

Christmas Lights & Tree

Covent Garden, WC2 (7836 9136/ www.coventgardenmarket.co.uk); Oxford Street, W1 (7629 2738/www.oxfordstreet.co.uk); Regent Street, W1 (7491 4429/www.regent-street.co.uk); Bond Street, W1 (7821 5230/ www.bondstreetassociation.com); Trafalgar Square, SW1 (7983 4234/www.london.gov.uk). **Date** Nov-Dec 2002.

Though the Christmas lights on London's main shopping streets are an increasingly commercialised proposition (those on Regent Street are switched on by a jobbing celeb in early November), some of the childhood wonder remains in the lights on St Christopher's Place, Marylebone High Street and Bond Street, W1, and Kensington High Street, W8. The giant fir tree that's put up in Trafalgar Square each year is a gift from the Norwegian people, in gratitude for Britain's role in liberating their country from the Nazis.

International Showjumping Championships

Olympia, Hammersmith Road, Kensington, W14 (7370 8202/www.olympiashowjumping.com). Kensington (Olympia) tube/rail. **Date** 19-23 Dec 2003.

This annual jamboree for equestrian enthusiasts has more than 100 trade stands. The events include everything from international riders' competitions to the Shetland Pony Grand National.

New Year's Eve Celebrations

Date 31 Dec 2003.

Celebratory events in London tend to be local in nature, though Trafalgar Square (*see p128*) has traditionally been an unofficial gathering point at the turn of the year for those without party invites. Otherwise, many of the city's nightclubs (*see p317*) hold expensive New Year parties.

If you're feeling up to it the next morning, the extremely raucous New Year's Day Parade through central London includes more than 10,000 performers, from marching bands to clowns. The parade starts at Parliament Square, SW1, at noon, and finishes at Berkeley Square, W1, taking in Whitehall, Trafalgar Square, Lower Regent Street and Piccadilly along the way.

Children

Junior's choice.

The Children pages in *Time Out* give weekly listings, while *Time Out London for Children* (£8.99) is a comprehensive guide.

Grand days out

The following attractions are listed in walkable groups, have green spaces for picnics and – best of all – avoid the worst of the traffic.

The South Bank to Bankside p71

The South Bank has a rich seam of family-friendly attractions. Start at Westminster Bridge with the **British Airways London Eye** (*see p72*). It's wise to book in advance, but even if you go on a whim and end up queuing, the views are worth the wait. The nearby **London Aquarium** (*see p72*) has tanks and touch pools – kids love the toothy sharks and piranhas – while ten minutes' walk east, the **BFI London IMAX Cinema** (*see p287*) shows 3D films year-round. Summertime here is lively, thanks to alfresco arts laid on free by the **Coin Street Festival** (*see p263*) and the **National Theatre**'s open-air extravaganza Watch This Space (*see p333*). There's music-making in the National and **Royal Festival Hall** (*see p304*) foyers on weekends and school holidays, plus children's shows and concerts.

Further along, you'll find the superbly child-friendly **Tate Modern** (*see p79*) and the wattle-and-daub walls of **Shakespeare's Globe** (*see p78*), which runs a busy youth and schools programme. You can then skitter down the riverside steps for a spot of stone-skimming and beachcombing, or keep on eastwards to cobbled Clink Street and the **Golden Hinde**

(*see p77*). Round the corner are **Southwark Cathedral** (*see p78*), a good picnic spot, and **Borough Market** (Fri, Sat; *see p256*).

Take the underpass beneath London Bridge Road and get to Tooley Street and the **London Dungeon** (*see p81*). Perhaps too gory for under-tens, it will have been a must-see for your kids ever since they saw the posters. Retreat via Hays Galleria and strike east for the hulking grey **HMS Belfast** (*see p77*). Many of these attractions organise parties and sleepovers: call for details.

The City p84

From the South Bank, it's now easy to get to **St Paul's Cathedral** (*see p87*) by clattering over the formerly wobbly Millennium Bridge. The cathedral's Whispering Gallery offers the essential game of 'catch the mumble' – it's just a shame you have to pay so much to play. Also expensive, but good value given the brilliant Beefeaters and their ravens, the **Tower of London** (*see p95*) will keep you busy all day. There's also the **Tower Bridge Experience** (*see p95*), which offers the best views since the Eye. The other side of St Paul's, the **Museum of London** (*see p94*) can also fill a day; it's close to the **Barbican Centre** (*see p283 and p303*), which has a terrific children's library and kids' films on Saturdays, plus cafés, ducks, picnic spots and free foyer events.

Covent Garden p122

Touristy, yes, but that means there's plenty to see and do in Covent Garden, most of it for free. Children adore street performances on the

The best Child-pleasers

For boats, goats and an adventure
Battersea Park. *See p271.*

For revving up and burning rubber
Playscape. *See p274.*

For dinosaurs that roar
Natural History Museum. *See p139 & p270.*

For itchy trigger fingers
Firepower!. *See p167 & p271.*

For the world in miniature
Legoland. *See p272.*

For the child-friendliest dinners
Smollensky's. *See p276.*

piazza, while the **Royal Opera House** (*see p305*) is fabulously ritzy for a quick free visit. East of the covered market are the excellent **Theatre Museum** (*see p123*), with free events and workshops in the school holidays, and **London's Transport Museum** (*see p123*), always a winner. South, **Somerset House** (*see p98*) has free weekend family activities and an open courtyard with dancing fountains to play in; it doubles as an ice rink come December.

Trafalgar Square p128

With Mayor Ken's plans to pedestrianise the north side of Trafalgar Square in full swing, visiting the symbolic centre of London will be a more pleasurable experience than ever in 2003. The main event is the **National Gallery** (*see p128*), with excellent (and free) trails of paintings and artist-led, drop-in 'Second Weekend' activities (so-called because they happen the second Saturday and Sunday of the month). Next door, the **National Portrait Gallery** (*see p129*) has famous faces for children to identify, an interactive IT gallery and weekend 'Talk and Draw' activities. Children can also create masterpieces across the road in the Brass Rubbing Centre of **St Martin-in-the-Fields** (*see p129*), with its fine café. From Trafalgar Square, head down the Mall to **Buckingham Palace** (*see p130*) and pretty **St James's Park** (*see p130*) – make sure you take the kids to see the pelicans there.

South Kensington p139

Millions of children have beaten a path from South Kensington tube through the foot tunnel to the Natural History, Science and Victoria & Albert museums. Possibly the best is the **Natural History Museum** (*see p139*), with 68 million plants, animals, fossils, rocks and minerals. Highlights include the animatronic *Tyrannosaurus rex* in the Dinosaurs Gallery, the Creepy Crawlies gallery with live ant colony, and the earthquake in the Earth Galleries. The Darwin Centre is also now open, with some 22 million zoological specimens.

Launch Pad, at the **Science Museum** (*see p139*), is a technological adventure playground with hands-on activities for all ages; the museum also hosts popular Science Nights and sleepovers (book well ahead), and boasts an IMAX cinema (*see p287*). At the weekend, free children's workshops and activities are run by the beautiful **V&A** (*see p139*).

When you're done with the museums, herd the kids up Exhibition Road, across Kensington Gore to **Hyde Park**: there's space to run around, and rowing on the Serpentine.

Camden p144

You know the kids are becoming teenagers when they get obsessed with Camden Market (*see p255*), which has hoodies, jewellery, unfeasibly large trousers, skateboard gear, CDs and all the other treasures pocket money can buy. Fear not, though, for Camden has other attractions, too: the excellent **Jewish Museum** (*see p146*) and, for boat trips, the **Regent's Canal** (phone the London Waterbus Company on 7482 2550 or Jason's Trip on 7286 3428).

Greenwich p167

It might be quicker getting the train to Greenwich from Charing Cross or the DLR through Docklands (*see p357*), but it's most fun by boat (*see p359*). From Greenwich Pier, it's a short walk to the brilliant **National Maritime Museum** (*see p171*) and the **Cutty Sark** (*see p169*), which has costumed storytelling and workshops on summer weekends. Between these and the **Royal Observatory** (*see p171*) lie the rolling acres of the Royal Greenwich Park; free children's events take place at the playground during the summer. Other attractions include **Queen's House** and the splendid **Old Royal Naval College** (for both, *see p171*). You can also walk from the *Cutty Sark* through the spooky Victorian tunnel under the Thames to come out in Island Gardens.

Museums & galleries

The biggest noises in the art world, especially where events for children are concerned, are the Tates. Resident artists at **Tate Modern** (*see p79*) run Arts Mixx workshops each Saturday for children aged five and over, while Sunday's Start activity provides each kid with a map, bag and puzzle kit for a madcap exploration of the galleries. Every third Saturday, a poet or storyteller leads an improvised performance based around a work of art. On Sundays (and Thursdays during school holidays), **Tate Britain** (*see p135*) hosts Art Space's sculpture games and Art Trolley fun. When Millbank pier is complete, there'll be a boat link between the two galleries; until then, take the Jubilee line between Southwark and Westminster.

The world-famous **British Museum** is another favourite: Young Friends of the British Museum (YFBM; *see p102*) can enjoy any number of school holiday and weekend activities, including the occasional spooky sleepover with Egyptian mummies.

In east London, the **Museum of Childhood** at Bethnal Green (*see p159*) contains toys from dolls' houses to Game Boys, plus a café and shop.

Swingin'! **Coram's Fields**. See p272.

There are art and craft workshops, games and soft play sessions at weekends and during holidays. The **Ragged School Museum** (*see p160*) has a recreated Victorian classroom, plus activities from workshops to treasure hunts.

The **Horniman Museum** (*see p173*) has finally been refurbished, with a new shop, garden access and exhibition galleries. The Living Waters exhibition and garden animal enclosure are the best, but the main gallery's stuffed animals are eerily compelling. There are free shows for children during summer, and a Music Gallery due to open in late 2002.

Way up north, the excellent **Royal Air Force Museum Hendon** (*see p153*) has a most imaginative programme for young visitors; events at **Firepower!** (*see p167*) in the south-east include paintballing and target practice; and in the far south the **Wimbledon Lawn Tennis Museum** (*see p177*) conducts an award-winning tour and offers an inspired range of school holiday activities.

Parks & green spaces

The loveliest green space in town, **Regent's Park** (*see p109*), has two boating lakes (one for children), three playgrounds and an open-air theatre, as well as **London Zoo** (*see p109*). Kids love **Kensington Gardens** (*see p136*) for the Princess Diana playground (*see p273*).

Hampstead Heath (*see p148* **The wanderers**) is great for views and kite-flying. So is **Alexandra Park** (*see p153*), but it ups

the ante with an ice rink. Also north, **Golders Hill Park**, one of London's best local parks, has a lovely café, play equipment and animal enclosures, as well as flamingos and ducks. **Highbury Fields** has a fantastic playground and is famous for its Bonfire Night fireworks.

Down south, **Battersea Park** (*see p176*) has a good adventure playground and a small kids' zoo (*see p274*). **Crystal Palace Park** (*see p173*) has huge model dinosaurs, a maze and a playground (all undergoing refurbishment), while **Dulwich Park** (*see p172*) offers a wonderful café, bikes for hire and a terrific playground. South-west, the kids can cycle past deer in **Richmond Park** (*see p178*), or explore riverside gardens at **Syon House** (*see p187*).

In east London, **Victoria Park** (*see p160*) has a playground, tennis courts, a bowling green and an animal enclosure. Neighbouring **Mile End Park** (*see p159*) has go-karts, a state-of-the-art children's playground and the famous 'Green Bridge' over Mile End Road. **West Ham Park** runs children's sporting events and free summer activities.

Camley Street Natural Park

12 Camley Street, King's Cross, NW1 (7833 2311/www.wildlondon.org.uk). King's Cross tube/rail. **Open** *Summer* 9am-5pm Mon-Thur; 11am-5pm Sat, Sun. *Winter* 9am-5pm or dusk Mon-Thur; 10am-4pm Sat, Sun. **Admission** free. **Map** p399 L2.
The London Wildlife Trust's flagship reserve has a pond for dipping, meadows and woods for minibeast hunting, and green-minded staff to spread the environmental message to frog-obsessed children.

Arts & Entertainment

Coram's Fields

*93 Guilford Street, Bloomsbury, WC1 (7837 6138).
Russell Square tube.* **Open** 9am-dusk daily.
Admission free (adults only admitted with an
under-16). **Map** p399 M4.

The adventure playground – with a climbing tower,
helter-skelter, swings and assault-course pulley – is
the focus here, but there are huge sandpits, footie
pitches, a basketball court, a toddlers' gym, fenced-
off play areas and a café too. For under-threes, the
drop-in centre provides daily painting sessions and
occasional summer visits by clowns.

Theme parks

All the theme parks listed here are outside
London. If you don't want to spend the whole
day queuing, try to visit on a rainy day outside
normal school holidays (and check online for
advance booking allowing fast-track entry).

Chessington World of Adventures

*Leatherhead Road, Chessington, Surrey (0870 444
7777/www.chessington.com). By train: Chessington
South rail. By car: M25 or A3 (Junction 9).* **Open**
late Mar-end Nov times vary. **Height restrictions**
vary with rides. **Admission** *On the day* £21-£23;
£17-£18 4-12s; £14 concessions; £58-£63 family.
Credit MC, V. **Map** p389.

Jump on the Safari Skyride to see the animals (tigers,
leopards, gorillas and seals) at this zoo-cum-theme
park. Young entomologists enjoy the Creepy Caves,
Beanoland is a hit with under-tens and preschoolers
love Berry Bouncers. Thrill seekers will head for

Rameses Revenge, Samurai's gyrating rotor arms or
the tree-top rollercoaster Vampire, while Tomb
Blaster lets 'em loose in cars armed with laser guns.

Legoland

*Winkfield Road, Windsor, Berks (0870 504 0404/
www.legoland.co.uk). By train: Windsor & Eton
Riverside or Windsor Central rail. By car: B3022
Windsor–Ascot Road.* **Open** *mid Mar-early Nov*
10am-closing time varies. **Admission** £18.95-
£22.95; £15.95-£19.95 3-15s; £12.95-£16.95
concessions. **Credit** AmEx, MC, V. **Map** p389.

The theme park parents approve of... which means
high prices. Although the food is decent, bring a
packed lunch and avail yourself of the many pretty
picnic spots (actually, this goes for all theme parks).
Youngsters can pan for gold, take in some Legoland
theatre or waterplay at Duploland, or drive the boats
and cars; older kids like the miniature cityscapes,
Pirate Falls and Dragon rollercoaster. Truth is, no
one grows out of Lego, so Legoland is irresistible.

Thorpe Park

*Staines Road, Chertsey, Surrey (0870 444 4466/
www.thorpepark.co.uk). By rail: Staines rail then bus.
By car: M25 (Junction 11 or 13).* **Open** *late Mar-
early Nov* 9/10am-5/6pm daily. *Late July-early Sept*
9/10am-7.30pm daily. **Height restrictions** vary
with rides. **Admission** *On the day* £17-£23; £14.50-
£18 4-12s, concessions; free-under 4s; £52-£65
family. **Credit** AmEx, MC, V. **Map** p389.

Some of the star rides at Thorpe leave you a soggy,
rumpled, gibbering wreck. The Colossus rollercoaster will help you lose your lunch, whereas
Detonator merely drops you from 100ft (30m) in the

Swimming in the ball ponds at **Clown Town**. *See p273.*

air at a speed of 75mph (120kph). Amity Cove is the newest attraction, and the wettest: it's a mock-up of a New England village about to be hit by an 85ft (26m) tidal wave. To calm down, there's the 19th-century working farm with duck pond, rare breeds and petting area or, for the youngest, the banana swingboats and carousel of the Ranger County play area.

Playgrounds

To find out about safe, supervised play areas get in touch with **Kidsactive Info** (7736 4443/ www.kidsactive.org.uk), which has a total of six playgrounds across London where disabled and able-bodied children aged 5-15 can play safely, supervised by fully trained staff.

Outdoors

Diana, Princess of Wales Memorial Playground

nr Black Lion Gate, Broad Walk, Kensington Gardens, W8 (7298 2117/recorded information 7298 2141). Bayswater or Queensway tube. **Open** 10am-8pm (or 1hr before dusk if earlier) daily. **Admission** free (adults only admitted with child, or 9.30-10am daily. **Map** p394 C7.

Watchful rangers make sure this enchanting playground (which cost £1.7 million just to build) stays pristine and that no unaccompanied adults get in. A pirate ship dominates: youngsters can play in the fine white sand while their older siblings shin up the rigging to the crow's nest. The cooling mermaids' fountain, wigwams and tree-house encampment all have fans, and much of the equipment has been adapted for children with special needs. The scented shrubs, metal chimes and touchy-feely sculpture make the place a delight for the senses.

Kimber Adventure Playground & BMX Track

King George's Park, Kimber Road, SW18 (8870 2168). Earlsfield Road. **Open** *Termtime* 3.30-7pm Tue-Fri; 11am-6pm Sat. *School holidays* 11am-6pm Mon-Sat. **Admission** free.

Possibly the best equipped and most efficently run adventure playground in town, Kimber has a BMX track, basketball and the usual rope swings and platforms, as well as arts-and-crafts rooms, kitchens and ping pong. It's the only one of three excellent Wandsworth Council adventures (the others are Battersea Park and York Gardens) with a bike track.

Indoors

These adventure playgrounds arrange parties on request.

Bramley's Big Adventure

136 Bramley Road, W10 (8960 1515/ www.bramleysbig.co.uk). Latimer Road tube. **Open** 10am-6pm Mon-Fri; 10am-6.30pm Sat, Sun.

Admission *Weekends and holidays* £3.50-£4.50 1hr 30mins. *Term-time* £3-£4 1hr 30mins. Babies and adults free. **Credit** AmEx, MC, V.

A big, bright, popular indoor playground with three separate play areas for babies/toddlers, small children and older adventurers. There are slides, monkey swings, ball ponds and climbing frames.

Clown Town

222 Green Lanes, Palmers Green, N13 (8886 7520). Palmers Green rail. **Open** 10am-7pm daily. **Height restrictions** children must be under 4ft 9in. **Admission** £3.50 child; free adult. **No credit cards**.

Always busy – and rather sweaty – this play centre in north London boasts ball ponds, net climbs, slides and a toddler area.

Playhouse

Old Gymnasium, Highbury Grove School, Highbury Grove, N5 (7704 9424). Highbury & Islington tube/ rail/4, 19, 236 bus. **Open** 10am-6pm Mon-Thur; 10am-7pm Fri-Sun. **Admission** *1hr30min* £3 over-2s; £2.50 under-2s; £1.50 non-walking babies. **No credit cards**.

A good-value, well-ventilated play centre, so no one has to get steamed up as children scramble up ropes and bounce down slides like billy-o.

Spike's Madhouse

Crystal Palace National Sports Centre, Ledrington Road, Crystal Palace, SE19 (8778 9876/ www.crystalpalace.co.uk). Crystal Palace rail. **Open** *Holidays* noon-4pm Mon-Fri; 10am-5pm Sat, Sun. **Admission** £2/hr; £1/30mins. **Credit** (over £5) MC, V.

Specifically designed for 2-13-year-olds, the four storeys of facilities here include ball pools, scramble nets, slides, rope swings and biff 'n' bash bags.

Swimming

For flumes, slides and splashing about, a selection of leisure pools are listed below, but the **Dolphin Swimming Club** (8349 1844) and **Swimming Nature** (0870 900 8002/ www.swimmingnature.co.uk) are best for swimming lessons. The best lidos for children are Finchley (*see below*) or the **Brockwell Evian** (*see p327*).

Britannia Leisure Centre *40 Hyde Road, Hoxton, N1 (7729 4485). Old Street tube/rail.* **Open** 9am-6.45pm Mon-Fri; 9am-6pm Sat, Sun. **Admission** £2.10-£2.90 adult; £1.40 child. **Credit** MC, V.

Finchley Lido *Great North Leisure Park, High Road, Finchley, N12 (8343 9830). East Finchley or Finchley Central tube.* **Open** 6.45-8.30am, 9am-6.30pm Mon; 6.45-8.30am, 9am-9.30pm Tue, Thur, Fri; 6.45-8.30am, 9am-8pm Wed; 8am-4.30pm Sat, Sun. **Admission** £2.80; £1.60 5-16s, concessions; free under-5s. **Credit** (over £5) MC, V.

Latchmere Leisure Centre *Burns Road, Battersea, SW11 (7207 8004). Clapham Common tube then 345 bus/Clapham Junction rail then 49,*

319, 344 bus. **Open** 7am-9.30pm Mon-Thur, Sun; 7am-6pm Fri; 7am-7.30pm Sat. **Admission** £2.95; £2.35 parent & baby; £2.05 5-16s; £1.30 concessions; free under-5s. **Credit** (over £5) MC, V.
Waterfront Leisure Centre *High Street Woolwich, Woolwich, SE18 (8317 5000). Woolwich Arsenal rail/177, 180, 472 bus.* **Open** 7am-11pm Mon-Fri; 9am-10pm Sat; 9am-9.30pm Sun. *Wet & Wild Adventure Park* 3-8pm Mon-Fri; 9am-5pm Sat; 9am-5pm, 6-8pm Sun. **Admission** £2.15-£4.40; 85p-£3.15 3-16s; free under-3s; additional charge for activities. **Credit** MC, V.

Animal encounters

London Zoo (*see p109*) might have lost many of its most exotic inhabitants, but it still offers all kinds of activities, including an ace petting zoo and party packages. **Battersea Park** (*see p176*) is a smaller, cheaper alternative, as are London's city farms: we've listed our favourites below, but contact the **Federation of City Farms and Community Gardens** (0117 923 1800/www.farmgarden.org.uk) for a full list.

Battersea Park Children's Zoo
Battersea Park, SW11 (zoo 8871 7540/Splodge 7350 1477). Sloane Square tube then 19, 137 bus/Battersea Park or Queenstown Road rail. **Open** *Apr-Sept* 10am-5pm (last entry 4.30pm daily). *Oct-Mar* 11am-3pm Sat, Sun. **Admission** £2; £1 2-15s, concessions; free under-2s. **No credit cards.**
The exotics at this dear little zoo are limited to marmosets, a sleepy pot-bellied pig, meerkats, some birds and a few reptiles, but there are otters, rabbits and lively goats too. Weekend pony rides are available, and Splodge runs parties (call for details).

Freightliner's City Farm
Paradise Park, Sheringham Road, off Liverpool Road, Barnsbury, N7 (7609 0467). Holloway Road tube/Highbury & Islington tube/rail. **Open** 10am-5pm Tue-Sun. **Admission** free; donations appreciated.
Plenty of chickens, ducks, geese, sheep, goats and cows that children can touch and help care for.

Mudchute City Farm
Pier Street, Isle of Dogs, E14 (7515 5901). Crossharbour, Mudchute or Island Gardens DLR. **Open** 9am-4pm daily. **Admission** free; donations appreciated.
Domestic farm animals live serenely here with llamas and parakeets against the backdrop of Canary Wharf tower. Urban rustic? Potty, if you ask us.

Surrey Docks Farm
Rotherhithe Street, Rotherhithe, SE16 (7231 1010). Canada Water or Surrey Quays tube. **Open** 10am-5pm Tue-Thur; 10am-1pm, 2-5pm Sat, Sun. **Admission** free; donations appreciated.
A delightful riverside location and terrific London honey (best in the world, we say), plus the full range of farm animals, regular holiday activities and, of course, plenty of bees.

Entertainment

The **Barbican, Clapham Picture House, Electric, Everyman, NFT, Rio** and **Ritzy** cinemas all have special holiday or weekend film screenings. For details, *see p283*.

Playscape Pro Racing
390 Streatham High Road, SW16 (8677 8677/ www.playscape.co.uk). Streatham rail. **Open** 10am-10pm daily. *Children's practice* 10am-5pm Mon-Fri. **Admission** from £30/hr; £20/30mins.
The raceway can be booked for children's parties (aged eight-plus) or for half-hour taster sessions. Those who become addicted can find out about the Playscape Cadet School.

Polka Theatre
240 The Broadway, SW19 (8543 4888/ www.polkatheatre.com). **Open** *Box office* 9.30am-4.30pm Mon; 9am-6pm Tue-Fri; 10am-5pm Sat. **Admission** £6-£13; £5-£13 children; £5-£8 concessions. **Credit** AmEx, MC, V.

Stringing 'em up

The world of puppet theatre is by definition a small one, but it has many fans in London – of all ages. This came as a relief to the **Little Angel Theatre**. Forced to close by lack of funding in spring 2002, it was salvaged after a successful campaign by enthusiasts, and in October 2002 it was back in business (though its survival was far from certain).

Founded in 1961 by John and Lyndie Wright, the Little Angel developed a worldwide reputation for puppetry and became an important training ground for British puppeteers. The tiny proscenium-arch stage is the only permanent performance space in Britain on which puppeteers can manipulate traditional long-stringed marionettes while remaining hidden. Its programme this year includes *King Arthur and the Quest for the Holy Grail* (scheduled for spring), plus regular 'family days' and Saturday clubs for children.

London's other dedicated puppet stage floats off to Berkshire every June, but the **Puppet Theatre Barge** (*pictured*) does stay safely moored at Little Venice during the autumn and winter months. The intimacy of the place demands advance booking and an attentive audience, but the thrill of seeing a show afloat keeps children agog. The new year kicks off with *The Further Adventures of Punch*.

This dedicated children's theatre has been staging top-quality shows for 22 years. The main theatre, for over-5s, shows homegrown and visiting productions, while preschoolers have the Adventure Theatre downstairs. There's also a playground, café and beautiful rocking horses. Clubs, courses, workshops and competitions are run in holidays and at weekends.

Royal Gunpowder Mills

Beaulieu Drive, Waltham Abbey, Essex (01992 767022/www.royalgunpowdermills.com). Waltham Cross rail then 211, 212, 213, 240, 250, 505, 517 bus. **Open** *Mar-Oct 10am-6pm daily (last entry 5pm). Nov-Feb pre-bookings only (min 10 people).* **Admission** £5.90; £5.25 concessions; £3.25 5-16s; free under-5s; £17 family. **Credit** MC, V.

The story of gunpowder is told with ingenuity at this singular attraction. The watermills, powered by the River Lea, produced the explosive stuff from the 1660s until 1981, but now host a visitors' centre and fine educational programme. When the centre is shut for winter, you can explore the surrounding parkland and the River Lea Country Park.

Unicorn Theatre for Children

Unicorn at the Pleasance Theatre, Carpenter's Mews, North Road, N7 (7700 0702/www unicorntheatre.com). Caledonian Road tube. **Open** *Box office 10am-6pm Mon-Fri.* **Tickets** £5-£10. **Credit** AmEx, MC, V.

The famous Unicorn Theatre, established in 1947, is still lodging at the Pleasance, eagerly awaiting planning permission for its new Tooley Street site. The proposed new theatre may be ready in 2004 (£4.5 million of lottery funding has already been earmarked), but the theatre's exemplary programme of productions for four-year-olds and over will continue regardless.

Childcare & advice

For specific advice and assistance, **Parentline** (0808 800 2222/www.parentlineplus.org.uk) is confidential and free; **Simply Childcare** (7701 6111/www.simplychildcare.com) offers fortnightly childcare listings.

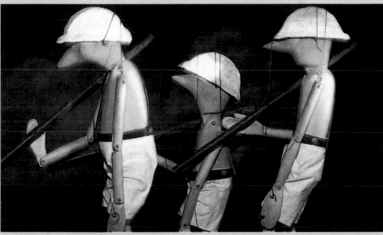

Outside the theatres, Sue Buckmaster proves puppets don't have to be wooden. Daughter of a puppet-maker and now leader of the **Theatre-rites** company, she's created enchanting characters for shows at the Young Vic and Lyric. Theatre-rites shows are often site-specific: for *Millworks*, inspired by the old House Mill at Bromley-by-Bow, her intricate puppets were made from sacks of grain, bread and sheaves of corn. Its next site-specific show, *Shopworks*, is due in spring.

Puppet fans can also head to the resource centre at the **Battersea Arts Centre** (aka BAC; *see p336*). Staff are experts on making and manipulating all sorts of puppets (kids can have a go themselves on Saturday afternoons), and gladly point out upcoming London gigs to visitors.

Little Angel Theatre *14 Dagmar Passage, N1 (7226 1787/www.littleangeltheatre.com). Angel tube.*
Puppet Theatre Barge *opposite 35 Blomfield Road, Little Venice, W9 (7249 6876). Warwick Avenue tube.*
Theatre-rites *8946 2236/ www.theatre-rites.co.uk.*

Arts & Entertainment

Academy Childcare

Family Zone, Victoria Station forecourt (7983 7219). **Open** 8am-6pm Mon-Fri. **Rates** vary. **Credit** MC, V. **Map** p400 H10.

This crèche welcomes children (three months to four years on weekdays; two to 12 years at weekends) for up to four hours, and offers all-day nursery places. Call for details of Academy-run crèches elsewhere.

Childminders

6 Nottingham Street, Marylebone, W1 (7935 3000/2049/www.babysitters.co.uk). **Open** 8.45am-5.30pm Mon-Thur; 8.45am-5pm Fri; 9am-4.30pm Sat. **Rates** £5.20-£6.90/hr. **Credit** AmEx, MC, V. **Map** p398 G5.

A large agency with more than 1,500 babysitters, mainly nurses, nannies and infant teachers (all with references), who live in London or the suburbs.

Pippa Pop-ins

430 Fulham Road, Chelsea, SW6 (7385 2458/ www.pippapopins.com). **Open** 8.15am-6pm Mon-Fri. **Fees** *Sessions* £37-£75 session. **Credit** MC, V. **Map** p396 B13.

A friendly, well-respected nursery school and kindergarten. The fully qualified staff host parties, holiday activities and a very popular crèche.
Branch: 165 New King's Road, Chelsea, SW6 (7731 1445).

Universal Aunts

Daytime childminding 7738 8937/evening babysitting 7386 5900. **Open** 9.30am-5pm Mon-Thur; 9.30am-4pm Fri. **Rates** *Childminding* from £7/hr. *Babysitting* from £5/hr. **No credit cards**.

This London agency, founded in 1921, provides reliable people to babysit, to meet children from trains, planes or boats, or to take them sightseeing.

Eating & drinking

The following are child-friendly joints; **Belgo Centraal** (*see p203*), **Wagamama** (*see p199*) and **Yo! Sushi** (branches throughout the city; www.yosushi.com) are all also worth a visit.

Boiled Egg & Soldiers

63 Northcote Road, Battersea, SW11 (7223 4894). *Clapham Junction rail.* **Open** 9am-6pm Mon-Sat; 10am-5pm Sun. **No credit cards**.

The food here – boiled eggs (yes, with soldiers), beans on toast, fishfingers, glorious home-made cakes – is comforting stuff, and the café often crowded with buggies and attractive young parents.

Bread & Roses

68 Clapham Manor Street, Clapham, SW4 (7498 1779/www.breadandrosespub.com). *Clapham Common or Clapham North tube.* **Open** 11am-11pm Mon-Sat; noon-10.30pm Sun. *Food served* noon-3pm, 7-9.30pm Mon-Fri; noon-4pm, 6-9.30pm Sat, Sun (African buffet only Sun lunch). **Credit** MC, V.

This veteran family haunt (non-smoking until 6pm) has a small back room with kids' toys and games,

an outside space for fine weather and, on Sundays, a larger activities room upstairs (films, games and art workshops). The food's great value.

Carluccio's Caffè

8 Market Place, Marylebone, W1 (7636 2228/ www.carluccios.co.uk). *Oxford Circus tube.* **Open** 8am-11pm Mon-Fri; 10am-11pm Sat; 11am-10pm Sun. **Credit** AmEx, DC, MC, V.

The Carluccio's chain (see the website for branches) could teach its rivals a thing or two about catering for families: there's fine, attractively priced Italian cooking, small portions for kids and glorious puddings, plus indulgent service for the *bambinos*.

Giraffe

46 Rosslyn Hill, Hampstead, NW3 (7435 0343). *Hampstead tube.* **Open** 8am-4pm, 5-11pm Mon-Fri; 9am-5pm, 6-11pm Sat, Sun. **Credit** AmEx, MC, V.

You can drop into this *Time Out* award-winner at any time of day, and each branch has a great location: Hampstead's good for kite-flying on the heath; Marylebone's handy for Madame Tussaud's and the park; Islington's good if you fancy some shopping. The eclectic menu includes veggie options for kids, plus huge shakes and juices.

Smollensky's

O² Centre, 255 Finchley Road, West Hampstead, NW3 (7431 5007/www.smollenskys.co.uk). *Finchley Road tube/rail.* **Open** noon-11pm Mon-Fri; noon-11.15pm Sat; noon-10.30pm Sun. **Credit** AmEx, DC, MC, V.

Providing the same quality US diner fare as its sister restaurant on the Strand, Smollensky's gives families space to spread out. On Sunday afternoons the kids can enjoy computer games, clowns, a raffle and face painting, while parents climb into half-price cocktails. Check the website for other branches.

Strada

11-13 Battersea Rise, Battersea, SW11 (7801 0794/www.strada.co.uk). *Clapham Junction rail.* **Open** noon-11pm Mon-Sat; noon-10.30pm Sun. **Credit** AmEx, DC, MC, V.

This expanding chain (the website lists other branches) serves delectable pizzas from wood-fired ovens and handmade pasta. There's no special kids' menu, but the hospitality and comfy banquette seats make for unhurried and family-friendly meals.

Tiger Lils

16A Clapham Common South Side, Clapham, SW4 (7720 5433/www.tigerlils.com). *Clapham Common tube.* **Open** noon-3pm, 6-11.30pm Mon-Thur; noon-3pm, 6pm-midnight Fri; noon-midnight Sat; noon-11pm Sun. **Credit** AmEx, MC, V.

At Tiger Lils, you're given a bowl of prawn crackers, a plate and the chance to choose from a huge wall of ingredients. You then take them to the wok-wielding chefs, who fire up and douse with your sauce of choice. Children adore it, but will most likely create a right dog's dinner… then insist it's delicious. Branches are listed on the website.

Arts & Entertainment

Comedy

It's a laugh a minute. No, really.

Speak to London's comedy promoters, and you'll find many bemoaning lower-than-average audience turnouts and fly-by-night clubs providing unwelcome competition. Still, that London is a victim of its own success can only be good news for punters: saturation does, after all, imply a spectrum of choice.

For big name acts, head to the self-styled 'National Theatre' of comedy, the **Comedy Store**, the pair of **Bound & Gagged** venues, **Lee Hurst's Backyard** or **Jongleurs**. But cheap laughs and newer acts often do a good night make, and can be garnered from the **Bearcat**, the **Comedy Café** or **Downstairs at the King's Head**. Those in London for June and July can catch comics testing new material for August's Edinburgh Festival (when the scene is at its driest). Look out, too, for the 2003 London Comedy Festival in May (0870 011 9611/www.londoncomedyfestival.com).

Major venues

See also *p337* the **Soho Theatre**.

Amused Moose Soho

Barcode, 3-4 Archer Street, Soho, W1 (8341 1341/ www.amusedmoose.co.uk). Piccadilly Circus tube. **Shows** 8.30pm Mon, Wed, Thur; 8pm Sat, Sun. **Admission** £5-£9. **No credit cards**.
Newish stand-ups, double acts, sketch shows, the odd unannounced secret gig and a number of showcase nights from the 'graduates' of the club's comedy course. The Amused claims to 'only book first-date friendly comedians', which means it's safe, so they reckon, to sit in the front row...

Banana Cabaret

The Bedford, 77 Bedford Hill, Balham, SW12 (8673 8904/www.bananacabaret.co.uk). Balham tube/rail.

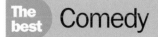

The best Comedy

For political tomfoolery
Canal Café Theatre. *See p277.*

For comedy fledglings
Downstairs at the King's Head. *See p278.*

For expressing displeasure
Up the Creek. *See p279.*

Shows 9pm Fri, Sat; 8.30pm 2nd Sun of mth. **Admission** £10-£14; £7-£10 concessions. **No credit cards**.
This fine club, held in a drum-shaped venue in south London, continues to roll on much as it has done for the last 20 years: with great comics and a friendly atmosphere. Its popularity means you should arrive early (by 8.30pm on Fridays and 7.30pm on Saturdays). A post-laughter DJ entertains until 2am.

Bearcat Club

Turk's Head, 28 Winchester Road, Twickenham, Middx (8891 1852/www.bearcatcomedy.co.uk). St Margaret's rail. **Shows** 8.45pm Sat. **Admission** £8; £7 concessions. **No credit cards**.
The Bearcat was the first club to let 2002 Perrier Award-nominee and Hollywood 'rent-an-Arab' Omid Djalili loose back in 1996. Nowadays, this 18-year-old club entertains a posh south-west London crowd with lively music, continued open spots and sophisticated humour (this is Twickers, after all).

Bound & Gagged

Palmers Green *The Fox, 413 Green Lanes, N13 (8450 4100/www.boundandgaggedcomedy.com). Palmers Green rail.* **Tufnell Park** *Progress Bar, 162 Tufnell Park Road, N7 (8450 4100). Tufnell Park tube.* **Shows** *Palmers Green* 9.15pm Fri. *Tufnell Park* 9.15pm Sat. **Admission** Both £7; £5 concessions. **No credit cards**.
The 200-seater venue in Palmers Green is a lively, classy affair, while the smaller Tufnell Park venue has seen a refurbishment both upstairs (where the comedy takes place) and downstairs (where a DJ entertains until 2am). The bills here are strong ones.

Canal Café Theatre

Bridge House, Delamere Terrace, Little Venice, W2 (7289 6054/www.newsrevue.com). Warwick Avenue tube. **Shows** 7.30pm, 9.30pm Mon-Sat; 7pm, 9pm Sun. **Admission** £5-£10; £4-£8 concessions. **Credit** MC, V. **Map** p394 C4.
The headline act at this welcoming fringe venue is Newsrevue (Thur-Sun), a topical satire of sketches and songs that's been running for 23 years.

Chuckle Club

Three Tuns Bar, London School of Economics, Houghton Street, Holborn, WC2 (7476 1672/ www.chuckleclub.com). Holborn tube. **Shows** 7.45pm Sat. **Admission** £10; £8 concessions. **No credit cards. Map** p399 M6.
The Chuckle Club has spent some 17 years pulling in the punters with the offer of cheap beer, a matey atmosphere and terrific bills of comedy. Don't miss the Chuckle Club song, a warm-up courtesy of resident host Eugene Cheese (real name Paul).

Arts & Entertainment

Comedy Café

66 Rivington Street, Shoreditch, EC2 (7739 5706/ www.comedycafe.co.uk). Old Street tube/rail. **Shows** 9pm Wed-Sat. **Admission** free-£14. **Credit** MC, V. **Map** p403 R4.

The fact that the management team here looks after 2002 Perrier Award-winner Daniel Kitson will give you some idea of the calibre of comedy at this joint, one of only a few purpose-built comedy clubs in the capital. Wednesday's long-established try-out night is cruel but compelling entertainment (and it's free).

Comedy Store

1A Oxendon Street, St James's, SW1 (Ticketmaster 7344 0234/www.thecomedystore.co.uk). Leicester Square or Piccadilly Circus tube. **Shows** 8pm Tue-Thur, Sun; 8pm, midnight Fri, Sat. **Admission** £12-£15; £8 concessions. **Credit** MC, V. **Map** p401 K7.

When Don Ward set up the Comedy Store above a Soho strip joint in 1979, it ushered in an era of fresh, alternative comedy that lasted through the 1980s. Those days have gone, but what remains is one of the best clubs on the circuit. The Comedy Store Players improv team (Wed, Sun) and the satirical Cutting Edge crew (Tue) are both well worth a look.

Downstairs at the King's Head

2 Crouch End Hill, Crouch End, N8 (pub 8340 1028/ office 01920 823265). Finsbury Park tube/rail then W7 bus/Crouch Hill rail. **Shows** 8.30pm Thur, Sat, Sun. **Admission** free-£7. **No credit cards**.

This intimate and down-to-earth long-running club has been a popular haunt for many of today's big names in their early days: come here on Thursdays for try-out night or for bigger acts on Saturdays.

Ha Bloody Ha

Ealing Studios, St Mary's Road, Ealing, W5 (8566 4067). Ealing Broadway tube/rail. **Shows** 8.45pm Fri, Sat. **Admission** £8. **No credit cards**.

A west London institution, on the site that was made famous for its production of a succession of British comedy films. Expect a mix of big name stand-ups alongside some lesser-known but experienced ones, plus a sprinkling of double acts and sketch shows.

Hampstead Clinic

Downstairs at the White Horse, 154 Fleet Road, Hampstead, NW3 (7485 2112). Belsize Park tube/ Hampstead Heath rail. **Shows** 9pm Sat. **Admission** £7; £5 concessions. **Credit** *Food & drink only* MC, V.

This popular haunt, now in its ninth year, defies expectations: intimacy and atmosphere abound, as does a decent array of stand-ups (though don't come expecting double acts or sketch shows).

Headliners

The George IV, 185 Chiswick High Road, Chiswick, W4 (8566 4067). Turnham Green tube. **Shows** 8.30pm Fri, Sat. **Admission** £10. **No credit cards**.

West London's first purpose-built comedy club arrived in September 2002, and is situated in a building that brewers Fullers have spent close to £400,000 converting. The club comes with help from experienced Ha Bloody Ha promoter Simon Randall.

Jongleurs Comedy Club

Battersea *Bar Risa, 49 Lavender Gardens, SW11. Clapham Junction rail.* **Bow** *221 Grove Road, E3. Mile End tube.* **Camden** *Dingwalls, Camden Lock, Chalk Farm Road, NW1. Chalk Farm tube.* **Watford** *76 The Parade, Watford, Herts. Watford tube/Watford Junction rail.* **All** *Information 0870 787 0707/box office 7564 2500/www.jongleurs.com.* **Shows** *Battersea* 8.45pm Fri; 7.15pm, 8.45pm, 1.15pm Sat. *Bow* 8.15pm Fri, Sat. *Camden* 8.45pm Fri; 7.15pm, 8.45pm, 11.15pm Sat. *Watford* 8pm Fri, Sat. **Admission** £6-£14. **Credit** AmEx, MC, V.

Comedy chain Jongleurs is spreading like wildfire (the most recent branch just opened in Majorca), a fact that has seen it dubbed the McDonald's of comedy. True, its mantra 'eat, drink, laugh, dance' doesn't make for immaculately attentive audiences, but the bills at all London's branches are big. Booking is advisable.

Now playing Comedy

The Edinburgh Festival's Perrier Awards have launched the careers of a host of actors and comedians: Stephen Fry and Emma Thompson were among the first to triumph. The winners and nominees from 2002 are an equally sought-after bunch on the London circuit... at least until the next awards are given out this August.

Luckily for his fans, 2002 winner and über-nerd **Daniel Kitson** prides himself on his refusal to bring second-rate versions of his stand-up material to the small screen, preferring instead to ply his trade at live venues. Former psychotherapist **Jimmy Carr** stands out for his smooth image,

and netted a nomination on his first outing to Edinburgh. His management claims he plays some 300 gigs a year, so you should catch him when you're here.

You'll have seen another 2002 nominee, **Omid Djalili**, in *The Mummy* and *Gladiator*. He's Iranian and has a sideline in Hollywood in 'short, fat, Arab parts'. Like Djalili, Aussie Perrier nominee **Adam Hills** uses September 11 in his material, though his prosthetic foot also forms the basis for many well-delivered gags. And other comics to look out for in London include lively Canadian **Phil Nichol** and surreal Brit **Noel Fielding**, who rounded out the 2002 shortlist.

They're selling: are you buying?
The **Comedy Store**. See p278.

Lee Hurst's Backyard Comedy Club

231 Cambridge Heath Road, Bethnal Green, E2 (7739 3122/www.leehurst.com). Bethnal Green tube/rail. **Shows** 8.30pm Fri, Sat. **Admission** £10-£12; £7 concessions. **Credit** AmEx, MC, V.

This purpose-built club was set up in 1998 by comic Lee Hurst, and benefits from his industry clout and desire to treat comics with respect. The bills often include big names, and the food's not bad either.

Meccano Club

Slug & Lettuce, 1 Islington Green, Islington, N1 (7813 4478/www.themeccanoclub.co.uk). Angel tube. **Admission** £7; £5 concessions. **No credit cards.**

The Meccano's recently moved to this big Islington boozer. The comedy, however, remains as good as it has ever been: from practised up-and-comers and older hands, with no open spots.

Red Rose Comedy Club

129 Seven Sisters Road, Finsbury Park, N7 (7281 3051/www.redrosecomedy.co.uk). Finsbury Park tube/rail. **Shows** 9pm Sat. **Admission** £7; £5 concessions. **No credit cards.**

The Red Rose, situated in the back of a Labour club, celebrated its 15th birthday in September 2002. Its outspoken founder and host Ivor Dembina attributes the club's success to his no-frills policy (no meals, no disco, pub-price drinks, cheap admission) and, quite rightly, its top-notch comedy.

Up the Creek

302 Creek Road, Greenwich, SE10 (8858 4581/ www.up-the-creek.com). Greenwich DLR/rail. **Shows** 8.30pm Sat; 9pm Fri, Sun. **Admission** £6-£14; £4-£10 concessions. **Credit** AmEx, MC, V.

This noisy bearpit was set up by eccentric London legend Malcolm Hardee. Entertainment is guaranteed, but new acts will probably find the atmosphere unforgiving. There's also food and a disco until 2am on Fridays and Saturdays.

Other venues

London is home to many smaller clubs that come, go (in the case of the late Aztec Comedy Club, burn down) and shift venues with alarming rapidity. Phone before setting out.

Comedy Brewhouse *Camden Head, 2 Camden Walk, Camden Passage, Islington, N1 (7359 0851).* **Shows** 9pm Fri, Sat. **Map** p402 O2.

Covent Garden Comedy Club *Upstairs at the Essex Serpent, 6 King Street, Covent Garden, WC2 (07960 071340).* **Shows** 8.30pm Fri, Sat.

Hackney Empire Bullion Rooms *117 Wilton Way, Hackney, E8 (8985 2424/www.hackneyempire. co.uk).* **Shows** days vary.

Hampstead Comedy Club *The Washington, England's Lane, Hampstead, NW3 (8299 2601/ www.hampsteadcomedy.co.uk).* **Shows** 9pm Sat.

Hen & Chickens Theatre *109 St Paul's Road, Highbury Corner, Highbury, N1 (7704 2001/ www.henandchickens.com).* **Shows** days vary.

Laughing Horse Camden *Liberties Bar, 100 Camden High Street, Camden, NW1 (7485 4019).* **Shows** 8.30pm Wed. *Cabaret* 8.30pm Thur.

Laughing Horse Greenwich *Spanish Galleon, 48 Greenwich Church Street, Greenwich SE10 (8293 0949). Greenwich tube/rail.* **Shows** 8.30pm Mon.

Laughing Horse Richmond *Britannia, 5 Brewers Lane, Richmond, Surrey (8940 1071).* **Shows** 8.30pm Sun.

Laughing Horse Soho *Coach & Horses, 1 Great Marlborough Street, Soho, W1 (07796 171190).* **Shows** 8.30pm Tue.

Mirth Control West Hampstead *Lower Ground Bar, 269 West End Lane, West Hampstead, NW6 (7431 2211).* **Shows** 8pm Wed.

Pear-Shaped in Fitzrovia *Fitzroy Tavern, 16 Charlotte Street, Fitzrovia, W1 (7580 3714).* **Shows** 8pm Wed.

Soho Laughter Lounge *John Snow, 39 Broadwick Street, Soho, W1 (7437 1344).* **Shows** 8.45pm Sat.

Well Hard Comedy Club *Distillers Arms, 64 Fulham Palace Road, Hammersmith, W6 (8748 2834).* **Shows** 9pm Thur, Sat.

Arts & Entertainment

Dance

... the night away, whether in frou-frou tutus or clacking tap shoes.

London's status as a dance mecca is rivalled only by that of New York City, and some experts claim that London now has the edge. Sharp-eyed programming at a range of smartly refurbished venues will satisfy those hungry to sample the most accomplished, entertaining dance performances from around the globe. At the same time, study options – from one-off workshops to ongoing classes held in studios, halls and arts centres throughout the capital (*see p282*) – can cater to the most eclectic tastes.

As well as the performances and venues below, check the dance pages in *Time Out* magazine. For up-to-the-minute dance information, see www.londondance.com.

Major venues

Barbican Centre
Silk Street, the City, EC2 (7638 8891/ www.barbican.org.uk). Barbican tube/Moorgate tube/rail. **Box office** 10am-8pm daily. **Tickets** £5-£30. **Credit** AmEx, MC, V. **Map** p402 P5.
This arts centre (*see p303*) has become a major dance venue. The sixth Barbican International Theatre Event (BITE) season will be the first to run year-round. Highlights include the bird-like intensity of Italy's Emio Greco (26-29 March) and German choreographer Sasha Waltz's sensational investigation into the workings of the human body, *Körper* (11-14 June).

London Coliseum
St Martin's Lane, WC2 (box office 7632 8300/ textphone 7836 7666/www.eno.org). Leicester Square tube/Charing Cross tube/rail. **Box office** 10am-8pm Mon-Sat. **Tickets** £3-£66; day tickets to personal callers after 10am Mon-Sat; by phone from 12.30pm Mon-Sat. **Credit** AmEx, DC, MC, V. **Map** p401 L7.
The beautiful, spacious Coliseum is home to the English National Opera (ENO) for most of the year. The venue was usually visited by major dance companies over summer and at Christmas, but no dance is scheduled between mid January and late 2003 because of ongoing restoration work.

The Place
17 Duke's Road, WC1 (7387 0031/www.theplace. org.uk). Euston tube/rail. **Box office** 10.30am-6pm Mon-Fri; noon-6pm Sat. **Tickets** £5-£15. **Credit** MC, V. **Map** p399 K3.
This internationally recognised dance venue provides top-notch professional training, as well as classes in all genres for all levels. The 300-seat theatre programmes high-quality contemporary dance from around the world and opens 2003 with the annual Resolution!, a platform for up-and-coming artists (3 Jan-15 Feb). Other highlights are the effervescent Scottish Dance Theatre (27-29 Mar), the risky, frisky talents of UK-based Protein Dance (10-14 June) and Dance Umbrella (*see p282* **Dance festivals**).

Royal Opera House
Bow Street, Covent Garden, WC2 (box office 7304 4000/enquiries 7240 1200/textphone 7212 9228/ www.royaloperahouse.org). Covent Garden tube. **Box office** 10am-8pm Mon-Sat. **Tickets** £3-£155. **Credit** AmEx, DC, MC, V. **Map** p401 L7.
This magnificent theatre is no longer strictly the preserve of ballet classics and the moneyed elite. The main stage is home to the Royal Ballet: standards are variable, but you can still see stars of the calibre of Darcey Bussell and Johan Kobborg.

In autumn 2002 Ross Stretton made an abrupt departure from the director's office after only 13 months in charge. His brief regime was criticised for its lack of understanding of the company's distinct image and heritage. Royal Ballet veteran Monica Mason was put in charge, and it is partly her taste and choices that are reflected in the first half of 2003. The season includes tributes to two deceased artists who enjoyed some of their greatest successes at Covent Garden: legendary dancer Rudolf Nureyev (Apr) and choreographer Kenneth MacMillan (his masterpiece *Manon* plays 31 Jan-6 Mar, then there's a triple bill Apr-May and *Romeo and Juliet* in June).

Though ticket prices were cut following the refurbishment, the best seats remain horrendously pricey. However, the building now houses two more affordable spaces: the Linbury Studio Theatre, a handsome 420-capacity room fast earning a reputation as a leading mid-scale West End venue for music and dance, and the Clore Studio Upstairs, used for rehearsals, workshops and small-scale or experimental performances. Programming responsibility for both lies with ex-Royal dancer Deborah Bull.

The best Venues

For the classics
Royal Opera House. *See p280.*

For the contemporary
Dance Umbrella. *See p282* **Dance festivals**.

For a lesson or two
Danceworks. *See p282.*

This must be **The Place**... *See p280.*

Sadler's Wells

*Rosebery Avenue, Islington, EC1 (7863 8000/
textphone 7863 7863/www.sadlers-wells.com). Angel
tube.* **Box office** 10am-8.30pm Mon-Sat. **Tickets**
£7-£35. **Credit** AmEx, MC, V. **Map** p402 N3.
Peacock Theatre *Portugal Street, off Kingsway,
Holborn, WC2 (7863 8222/www.sadlers-wells.com).
Holborn tube.* **Box office** noon-8.30pm performance
days; otherwise 10am-6pm Mon-Sat. **Tickets** £8.50-
£30. **Credit** AmEx, MC, V. **Map** p399 M6.

Sadler's Wells attracts world-class companies to its
ultra-modern facilities. Early highlights for 2003
include the UK debut of Russia's dramatic Eifman
Ballet (10-15 Feb) and Lyon Opera Ballet with
Maguy Marin's dolls' house version of *Cinderella*
plus a triple-bill (18-22 Feb). Other exciting prospects
include *Lion King* choreographer Garth Fagan's
eponymous company (Mar), the great Paul Taylor's
troupe (Apr) and American Twyla Tharp (June). The
considerably smaller Lilian Baylis Theatre showcases younger or smaller-scale companies.

The Wells retains a second venue, the Peacock
Theatre in Holborn, for runs of more populist fare.

South Bank Centre

*Belvedere Road, South Bank, SE1 (box office 7960
4242/recorded information 7921 0682/www.sbc.
org.uk). Embankment tube/Waterloo tube/rail.*
Box office 10am-9pm daily. **Tickets** £5-£60.
Credit AmEx, DC, MC, V. **Map** p401 M8.

This huge complex (*see also p304*) hosts regular
shows by British and international dance companies
at its three venues: the massive Royal Festival Hall,
the medium-sized Queen Elizabeth Hall and the
smaller Purcell Room. Highlights for 2003 include
Vivisector, a stunning mix of dance and video from
Austria (28 Feb-2 Mar), the UK's George Piper
Dances (25-29 Mar) and brilliant SBC resident
choreographer Akram Khan with an evening of
traditional classical Indian moves (11-15 Apr). Each
January the SBC is one of the prime venues for the
London International Mime Festival, now in its

25th year; later in the year, it hosts Summer on
the South Bank and some higher-profile Dance
Umbrella events (*see p282* **Dance festivals**).

Other venues

Chisenhale Dance Space

*64-84 Chisenhale Road, Bow, E3 (8981 6617/
www.chisenhaledancespace.co.uk). Bethnal Green/
Mile End tube.* **Open** *Enquiries* 10am-6pm Mon-Sat.
Tickets free-£4. **No credit cards**.

This seminal research centre for contemporary dance
and movement-based disciplines of an experimental
nature also runs workshops and a summer school.

Hoxton Hall

*130 Hoxton Street, Hoxton, N1 (box office 7739
5431/www.hoxtonhall.co.uk). Old Street tube/rail.*
Box office *in person* 1hr before performance start-
30mins after. **Tickets** £4-£10. **Membership** £8.
Credit *In person only* AmEx, MC, V. **Map** p403 R2.

This small former music hall schedules some of the
most interesting experimental dance, physical theatre and performance groups in London.

ICA

*The Mall, Westminster, SW1 (box office 7930 3647/
www.ica.org.uk). Piccadilly Circus tube/Charing Cross
tube/rail.* **Box office** noon-9.30pm daily. **Tickets**
prices vary. Membership Daily £1.50, £1 concessions
Mon-Fri; £2.50, £1.50 concessions Sat, Sun; free
under-14s. **Credit** AmEx, DC, MC, V. **Map** p401 K8.

This intimate space hosts experimental, movement-
based theatre and performance with an avant-garde
flavour. The London International Mime Festival is
a regular visitor (*see p262*), as is Dance Umbrella
(*see p282* **Dance festivals**).

Jacksons Lane Dancebase

*269A Archway Road, Highgate, N6 (8341
4421/www.jacksonslane.org.uk). Highgate
tube.* **Open** 10am-11pm daily. **Tickets** £5-£9.
Credit MC, V.

Dance festivals

Held over a six-week stretch from late September, **Dance Umbrella** (8741 5881/ www.danceumbrella.co.uk) is one of the world's top contemporary dance festivals. Now in its 25th year, it features a stimulating mix of proven British and international companies, as well as a number of lesser-known discoveries, at a range of venues. The 2003 roster is topped by certified American dance genius Merce Cunningham's company in a special appearance at Tate Modern (*see p79*).

The **BITE** programme brings a wide range of dance, music and theatre to the Barbican Centre (*see p280*). Among this year's treats are the giddy, multicultural delights of France's Compagnie Montalvo-Hervieu (13-17 May).

Each August the South Bank Centre (*see p281*) presents **Summer on the South Bank**, Britain's biggest and most diverse community dance festival, plus a cornucopia of free dance performances, lectures and workshops.

The Place (*see p280*) is the place to be in January and February, for **Resolution!**, a six-week showcase of nightly triple-bills. It's a hit-and-miss yet lively affair. The Friday/Saturday gigs incorporate Aerowaves, a strand featuring top European artists and companies.

This community centre puts on lots of performances and activities, including contemporary dance. Each autumn there's Zone 3, a showcase of commissioned work by some of the UK's brightest emerging choreographers.

Laban Centre

Creekside, Lewisham, SE8 (8691 8600/ www.laban.org). Deptford/Greenwich DLR. **Open** 9am-5.30pm daily; until 8pm on performance days. **Tickets** £10-£15; £7 concessions. **Credit** MC, V.
This independent conservatory for contemporary dance training and research runs undergraduate and postgrad courses, dance classes, short courses and Easter and summer schools, and regularly presents performances by Transitions, its resident company, and other contemporary choreographers. Its new £22 million home, designed by Herzog & de Meuron, opens this year. The two-week launch of its 300-seat theatre begins 17 Feb and features double-bills by such UK artists as Jonathan Burrows and Wendy Houstoun. For the rest of the season, expect a programme of dance, music and physical theatre performances by professional artists, students and community groups.

Riverside Studios

Crisp Road, Hammersmith, W6 (8237 1000/ box office 8237 1111/www.riversidestudios.co.uk). Hammersmith tube. **Box office** noon-9pm daily. **Tickets** £4.50-£25. **Credit** MC, V.
This leading arts and media centre occasionally hosts British contemporary dance and physical theatre in three auditoria.

Stratford Circus

Theatre Square, E15 (8279 1000/www.stratford-circus.org.uk). Stratford tube/rail/DLR. **Box office** 11am-6pm or 30mins after show starts Mon-Sat. **Tickets** £10; £3-£5 concessions. **Credit** MC, V.
Dance is a key part of this arts centre's programme, which utilises three performance spaces and presents British and international artists. The 2003 schedule includes work by the cutting-edge Random Dance Company and Robert Hylton's Urban Classicism, an engaging blend of street and contemporary styles.

Dance classes

Aside from its all-rounders – Danceworks, Dance Attic, the Drill Hall, Greenwich Dance Studio and Pineapple – London has a number of specialists. Cecil Sharp House offers classes in a variety of folk dance styles, while the London School of Capoeira teaches (you guessed it) capoeira, a fusion of dance, gymnastics and martial arts.

Cecil Sharp House *English Folk Dance and Song Society, 2 Regent's Park Road, NW1 (7485 2206/ www.efdss.org). Camden Town tube.* **Open Enquiries** 9.30am-5.30pm Mon-Fri. **Classes** £5-£8.50. **No credit cards.**
Dance Attic *368 North End Road, Fulham, SW6 (7610 2055). Fulham Broadway tube.* **Open** 9am-10pm Mon-Fri; 10am-5pm Sat, Sun. **Classes** £4-£6. *Membership* £1.50/day; £30/6mths; £50/yr. **Credit** MC, V. **Map** p396 A12.
Danceworks *16 Balderton Street, Mayfair, W1 (7629 6183/www.danceworks.co.uk). Bond Street tube.* **Open** 8am-10.15pm Mon-Fri; 9am-6.15pm Sat, Sun. **Classes** £4-£7. *Membership* £1-£4/day; £40/mth; £120/yr. **Credit** MC, V. **Map** p398 G6.
Drill Hall *16 Chenies Street, Fitzrovia, WC1 (7307 5060/www.drillhall.co.uk). Goodge Street tube.* **Open** 10am-9.30pm daily. **Classes** *Courses* £20-£100. **Credit** AmEx, MC, V. **Map** p399 K5.
Greenwich Dance Agency *Borough Hall, Royal Hill, Greenwich, SE10 (8293 9741/www.greenwich. org.uk). Greenwich DLR/rail.* **Open Enquiries** 9.30am-5.30pm Mon-Fri.
London School of Capoeira *Units 1 & 2, Leeds Place, Tollington Park, Finsbury Park, N4 (7281 2020). Finsbury Park tube/rail.* **Fees** *Beginners' course* (4 lessons) £80; £60-£70 concessions. **No credit cards.** **Map** p399 K3.
Pineapple Dance Studio *7 Langley Street, Covent Garden, WC2 (7836 4004/www.pineapple. uk.com). Covent Garden tube.* **Open** 9am-9.30pm Mon-Fri; 9.30am-6pm Sat. **Classes** £5-£7. *Membership* £2/day; £4/evening; £60-£100 /yr. **Credit** AmEx, MC, V. **Map** p399 L6.

Arts & Entertainment

Film

Lights, camera, action…

If you're from the US, you'll have seen it all before. Not the movies, silly. Well, not *just* the movies: like everywhere in Europe, the UK gets the majority of big flicks up to six months after their stateside release. No: what you'll have seen before are the cinemas. London is overrun by cookie-cutter, US-style multiplexes, designed by committee and about as enticing as a season ticket to a retrospective of films starring Macaulay Culkin. It'll be like you never left.

The **Odeon**s, **Warner**s, **UGC**s and **UCI**s of this world thus taken care of, we can move on to London's more unusual first-run cinemas. And there are a fair few of them, too, bravely holding out against the chains and – in many cases – thriving. The **Barbican**, the **Renoir** and the **Everyman** are enjoyably plush, while the **Screen on the Green** and the **Metro** are both nicely raffish. The two screens at the **ICA** flicker with some of the rarest films to hit town. But for variety, friendliness and choice of films, it's hard to pip the **Curzon Soho** or the **Ritzy**.

For old films, the picture's a little bleaker than it was a few years ago: a few repertory cinemas have closed, and others have morphed into first-run houses. Nonetheless, that still leaves the **Riverside**, perhaps London's purest rep screen since the estimable **National Film Theatre** chose to lay greater emphasis on its many special themed seasons. And then there's the **Prince Charles**, where you can catch recent releases at knockdown rates.

For cinema news and reviews, see *Time Out* each week. Films released in the UK are classified under the following categories: **U** – suitable for all ages; **PG** – open to all, parental guidance is advised; **12A** – under-12s only admitted with an over-18; **15** – no one under 15 is admitted; **18** – no one under 18 is admitted.

Cinemas

First-run cinemas

First-runs range from multiplexes, such as the **Warner Village West End** and **UCI Whiteleys**, to the **Metro** and **Renoir**, which devote themselves to artier releases. Prices vary greatly, but in general the closer you are to Leicester Square, the more you pay. Many cinemas charge less if you go on Mondays or before 5pm from Tuesday to Friday; call them

for the times of their 'Early shows' in the listings below. Book ahead if you're planning to see a blockbuster on the weekend of its release: new films emerge in the UK on Fridays.

The City

Barbican *Silk Street, EC2 (information 7382 7000/bookings 7638 8891/www.barbican.org.uk). Barbican tube/Moorgate tube/rail.* **Screens** 2. **Tickets** £6.50; £5 concessions. *Monday shows £4.* **Credit** AmEx, MC, V. **Map** p402 P5.

Bloomsbury & Fitzrovia

Odeon Tottenham Court Road *Tottenham Court Road, W1 (0870 505 0007/www.odeon.co.uk). Tottenham Court Road tube.* **Screens** 3. **Tickets** £8.20; £5 concessions. *Early shows £5.50.* **Credit** AmEx, MC, V. **Map** p399 K5.
Renoir *Brunswick Centre, Brunswick Square, WC1 (7837 8402). Russell Square tube.* **Screens** 2. **Tickets** £6.80. *Early shows £4.50; £3 concessions.* **Credit** MC, V. **Map** p401 L4.

Marylebone

Odeon Marble Arch *10 Edgware Road, W2 (0870 505 0007/www.odeon.co.uk). Marble Arch tube.* **Screens** 5. **Tickets** £8.50; £5.50 concessions (select times). *Early shows £5.50.* **Credit** AmEx, MC, V. **Map** p395 F6.

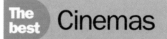

The best Cinemas

For a big screen
The **Odeon Leicester Square** for new releases (*see p284*); the **BFI London IMAX Cinema** for films on the grandest scale (*see p287*).

For a small screen
The teensy **Odeon Mezzanine**. There are some lovely screens in Leicester Square. None of them are here. *See p284.*

For something old
The **Riverside Studios**: rep programming at its most charmingly old-fashioned. *See p286.*

For something new
The **Curzon Soho** (*see p284*) and the **Ritzy** (*see p286*). There's *always* something good on.

Head to **Leicester Square** for the biggest screens – and the biggest billboards – in London.

Screen on Baker Street *96 Baker Street, NW1 (information 7486 0036/bookings 7935 2772/ www.screencinemas.co.uk). Baker Street tube/ Marylebone tube/rail.* **Screens** 2. **Tickets** £6.80. *Early shows* £4. **Credit** MC, V. **Map** p398 G5.

Mayfair & St James's
Curzon Mayfair *38 Curzon Street, W1 (7465 8865). Green Park or Hyde Park Corner tube. Note: scheduled to reopen early 2003.* **Screens** 1. **Tickets** £7.50; £4-£5 concessions (select times). *Early shows* £5. **Credit** AmEx, MC, V. **Map** p400 H8.
ICA Cinema *Nash House, The Mall, SW1 (information 7930 6393/bookings 7930 3647/ www.ica.org.uk). Piccadilly Circus tube/Charing Cross tube/rail.* **Screens** 2. **Tickets** £6.50; £5.50 concessions. *Early shows* £4.50. *Membership* £20-£30/yr. **Credit** AmEx, DC, MC, V. **Map** p401 K8.
Odeon Panton Street *Panton Street, SW1 (0870 505 0007/www.odeon.co.uk). Piccadilly Circus tube.* **Screens** 4. **Tickets** £8; £5 concessions (select times). *Early shows* £5. **Credit** AmEx, MC, V. **Map** p401 K7.
UGC Haymarket *63-5 Haymarket, W1 (0870 907 0712). Piccadilly Circus tube.* **Screens** 3. **Tickets** £7.90; £5 concessions (select times). *Early shows* £4-£5. **Credit** AmEx, MC, V. **Map** p401 K7.
UGC Shaftesbury Avenue *Trocadero, WC2 (0870 907 0716). Leicester Square or Piccadilly Circus tube.* **Screens** 7. **Tickets** £7.90; £5 concessions (select times). *Early shows* £4. **Credit** AmEx, MC, V. **Map** p401 K7.

Soho & Leicester Square
Curzon Soho *93-107 Shaftesbury Avenue, W1 (information 7439 4805/bookings 7734 2255). Leicester Square or Piccadilly Circus tube.* **Screens** 3. **Tickets** £8; £5 concessions (select times). *Early shows* £5. **Credit** AmEx, MC, V. **Map** p401 K6.
Empire *Leicester Square, WC2 (0870 010 2030/ www.uci-cinemas.co.uk). Leicester Square or Piccadilly Circus tube.* **Screens** 3. **Tickets** £8-£10; £5-£5.50 concessions (select times). *Early shows* £5.50-£6.50. **Credit** AmEx, MC, V. **Map** p401 K7.

Odeon Leicester Square *Leicester Square, WC2 (0870 505 0007/www.odeon.co.uk). Leicester Square tube.* **Screens** 6. **Tickets** £10-£11. *Early shows* £6-£6.50. **Credit** AmEx, MC, V. **Map** p401 K7.
Odeon Mezzanine *next to Odeon Leicester Square, WC2 (0870 505 0007/www.odeon.co.uk). Leicester Square tube.* **Screens** 5. **Tickets** £8. *Early shows* £5. **Credit** AmEx, MC, V. **Map** p401 K7.
Odeon Wardour Street *10 Wardour Street, W1 (0870 505 0007/www.odeon.co.uk). Leicester Square or Piccadilly Circus tube.* **Screens** 4. **Tickets** £7.50; £4.50 concessions (select times). *Early shows* £5. **Credit** AmEx, MC, V. **Map** p401 K7.
Odeon West End *Leicester Square, WC2 (0870 505 0007/www.odeon.co.uk). Leicester Square tube.* **Screens** 2. **Tickets** £10; £6 concessions (select times). *Early shows* £6. **Credit** AmEx, MC, V. **Map** p401 K7.
The Other Cinema *11 Rupert Street, W1 (information 7437 0757/bookings 7734 1506/ www.picturehouse-cinemas.co.uk). Leicester Square tube.* **Screens** 2. **Tickets** £7; £4 concessions (select times). *Early shows & Mon* £4. **Credit** MC, V. **Map** p401 K7.
Warner Village West End *Leicester Square, WC2 (0870 240 6020/www.warnervillage.co.uk). Leicester Square tube.* **Screens** 9. **Tickets** £10-£11; £5-£7 concessions (select times). *Early shows* £7.50. **Credit** MC, V. **Map** p401 K7.

Covent Garden & St Giles's
Odeon Covent Garden *135 Shaftesbury Avenue, WC2 (0870 505 0007/www.odeon.co.uk). Leicester Square or Tottenham Court Road tube.* **Tickets** £8.50; £5 concessions (select times). *Early shows* £5. **Screens** 4. **Credit** AmEx, MC, V. **Map** p399 K6.

Chelsea & South Kensington
Chelsea Cinema *206 King's Road, SW3 (7351 3742). Sloane Square tube.* **Screens** 1. **Tickets** £7-£8. *Early shows* £5; £3 concessions. **Credit** AmEx, MC, V. **Map** p397 E12.
UGC Chelsea *279 King's Road, SW3 (0870 907 0710). Sloane Square tube then 11, 19, 22 bus.* **Screens** 4. **Tickets** £8.20; £4.50-£4.80 concessions. **Credit** AmEx, MC, V. **Map** p397 E12.

North London

Everyman Hampstead *5 Hollybush Vale, Hampstead, NW3 (information 7431 1818/bookings 7431 1777/www.everymancinema.com). Hampstead tube.* **Screens** 1. **Tickets** £7.50 (luxury £12); £6 concessions (select times). **Credit** MC, V.

Odeon Camden Town *14 Parkway, Camden, NW1 (0870 505 0007/www.odeon.co.uk). Camden Town tube.* **Screens** 5. **Tickets** £7; £4-£5 concessions (select times). **Credit** AmEx, MC, V.

Odeon Holloway Road *419-27 Holloway Road, Holloway, N7 (0870 505 0007/www.odeon.co.uk). Holloway Road tube.* **Screens** 8. **Tickets** £6.70; £4.50 concessions. *Early show* £4.50. **Credit** AmEx, MC, V.

Odeon Swiss Cottage *96 Finchley Road, Swiss Cottage, NW3 (0870 505 0007/www.odeon.co.uk). Swiss Cottage tube.* **Screens** 6. **Tickets** £7.20; £4.50-£5.20 concessions (select times). *Early show* £4.50-£4.70. **Credit** AmEx, MC, V.

Phoenix *52 High Road, Finchley, N2 (information 8883 2233/bookings 8444 6789/www.phoenixcinema. co.uk). East Finchley tube.* **Screens** 1. **Tickets** £4-£6; £3.50-£4 concessions (select times). *Early shows* £3.50-£4.50. **Credit** MC, V.

Screen on the Green *83 Upper Street, Islington, N1 (7226 3520/www.screencinemas.co.uk). Angel tube.* **Screens** 1. **Tickets** £6.80. *Early shows* £4.50. **Credit** MC, V. **Map** p402 O2.

Screen on the Hill *203 Haverstock Hill, Belsize Park, NW3 (7435 3366/www.screencinemas.co.uk). Belsize Park tube.* **Screens** 1. **Tickets** £6.80. *Early shows* £4.50. **Credit** MC, V.

Tricycle Cinema *269 Kilburn High Road, Kilburn, NW6 (information 7328 1900/bookings 7328 1000/www.tricycle.co.uk). Kilburn tube.* **Screens** 1. **Tickets** £7; £6 concessions (select times). *Early shows* £4.50; £3.50 concessions. **Credit** MC, V.

Warner Village Finchley Road *255 Finchley Road, Swiss Cottage, NW6 (0870 240 6020/www. warnervillage.co.uk). Finchley Road tube.* **Screens** 8. **Tickets** £8.10. *Early shows* £5.80. **Credit** MC, V.

Warner Village Islington *Parkfield Street, Islington, N1 (0870 240 6020/www.warnervillage.co.uk). Angel tube.* **Screens** 8. **Tickets** £8.10. *Early shows* £5.80. **Credit** MC, V.

London loves Singing along

We like to be furtive, us Brits. We like our pleasures secret and a little shameful. So it comes to pass that on a dull Sunday, a crowd shuffles into a cheap second-run cinema off Leicester Square, avoiding the glances of passers-by, seeking a fleeting escape from their ordinary lives. Only once they reach the foyer, among friends, can they relax. Drinks are bought, small talk is made, and coats are shrugged off. Under them are a nun's outfit, an animal costume, a gaudy dress, and, perhaps most disturbingly, one person wrapped tightly from head to toe in brown paper.

Excitement builds. Before long, seats are taken, and a hostess of questionable gender takes the stage for an introduction. And then showbusiness's most innocent star crests the brow of the greenest hill in a ring of mountains. Pan out to glorious Alpine Austria. Cue orchestra. The crowd is on its feet. All together, now: 'The hiiiiiiiiilllls are alive, with… '

The *Sound of Music*. This is the **Prince Charles** cinema (*see p286*), and this is another screening of the *Sing-a-long-a Sound of Music*, wherein willing crowds whose childhood Christmases were forever Maria relive the singing-nun-makes-good story. Fancy dress is optional – there's a competition for the best – but singing (to subtitled lyrics) is compulsory, and boos, hisses and audience participation is zealously encouraged. A goody bag contains props. Wave your edelweiss as the Captain sings! Flap your square of curtain material as Maria seeks sartorial inspiration! Brandish your ball invitation as the Countess sulks! And, most of all, sing your little heart out.

It's good-hearted, it's lovely and it now comes in two more flavours: *Sing-a-long-a Joseph and the Amazing Technicolor Dreamcoat* and *Sing-a-long-a Abba Live in Concert*. Shows are usually on Friday nights and Sunday afternoons and cost £13.50 (£18.50 for Abba; but, hey, there's a band). For more, see www.singalonga.co.uk. Go, enjoy, but – unless they know their edelweiss from their elbow – just don't tell your friends.

East London

Rio Cinema *107 Kingsland High Street, Dalston, E8 (7254 6677/www.riocinema.org.uk). Dalston Kingsland rail/30, 38, 56, 76, 149, 242, 243, 277 bus.* **Screens** 1. **Tickets** £6.50; £5 concessions. *Early shows* £4.50; £3.50 concessions. **Credit** AmEx, MC, V.

South London

Clapham Picture House *76 Venn Street, Clapham, SW4 (information 7498 2242/bookings 7498 3323/www.picturehouse-cinemas.co.uk). Clapham Common tube.* **Screens** 4. **Tickets** £6.50. *Early shows* £4-£5. **Credit** MC, V.

Ritzy *Brixton Oval, Coldharbour Lane, Brixton, SW2 (information 7737 2121/bookings 7733 2229). Brixton tube/rail.* **Screens** 5. **Tickets** £6.50; £4 concessions. *Early shows* £4.50. **Credit** MC, V.

UCI 9 Surrey Quays *Surrey Quays Leisure Centre, Redriff Road, Surrey Quays, SE16 (0870 010 2030/ www.uci-cinemas.co.uk). Surrey Quays tube.* **Screens** 9. **Tickets** £6.25; £4.25-£5 concessions. *Early shows* £5.25. **Credit** AmEx, MC, V.

West London

Electric Cinema *191 Portobello Road, Ladbroke Grove, W11 (information 7727 9958/bookings 7229 8688/www.the-electric.co.uk). Ladbroke Grove or Notting Hill Gate tube.* **Screens** 1. **Tickets** £10-£12.50. *Early shows* £5-£7.50. **Credit** MC, V.

Gate Cinema *87 Notting Hill Gate, Notting Hill, W11 (7727 4043/www.gatecinema.co.uk). Notting Hill Gate tube.* **Screens** 1. **Tickets** £7; £3.50 concessions (select times). *Early shows* £4. **Credit** MC, V. **Map** p394 A7.

Notting Hill Coronet *103-5 Notting Hill Gate, Notting Hill, W11 (7727 6705). Notting Hill Gate tube.* **Screens** 2. **Tickets** £7; £4.50 concessions (select times). *Early shows* £4.50. **Credit** MC, V. **Map** p394 A7.

Odeon Kensington *263 Kensington High Street, Kensington, W8 (0870 505 0007/www.odeon.co.uk). High Street Kensington tube.* **Screens** 6. **Tickets** £8.50; £5.20 children. *Early shows (before 3pm)* £5.20. **Credit** AmEx, MC, V. **Map** p396 A9.

UCI 8 Whiteleys *2nd floor, Whiteleys Shopping Centre, Queensway, Bayswater, W2 (0870 010 2030/www.uci-cinemas.co.uk). Bayswater or Queensway tube.* **Screens** 8. **Tickets** £8; £4-£5 concessions (select times). *Early shows* £5.75. **Credit** AmEx, MC, V. **Map** p394 C6.

UGC Fulham Road *142 Fulham Road, Chelsea, SW10 (0870 907 0711). South Kensington tube.* **Screens** 6. **Tickets** £8.20; £4.50 concessions (select times). *Early shows* £4.50. **Credit** AmEx, MC, V. **Map** p397 D11.

UGC Hammersmith *207 King Street, Hammersmith, W6 (0870 907 0718). Ravenscourt Park tube.* **Screens** 4. **Tickets** £6; £4-£4.90 concessions. *Early shows* £4.90. **Credit** AmEx, MC, V.

Warner Village Shepherd's Bush *West 12 Centre, Shepherd's Bush Green, Shepherd's Bush, W12 (0870 240 6020/www.warnervillage.co.uk). Shepherd's Bush tube.* **Screens** 12. **Tickets** £6.90; £4.20-£5 concessions. *Early shows* £5. **Credit** MC, V.

Repertory cinemas

Can't get tickets for *The Mummy Returns*? *Dude, Where's My Car II* not out yet? No matter: London's rep cinemas offer selections of oldies and rarities that put modern-day Hollywood to shame. In addition to the spots listed below, several cinemas detailed earlier offer a more limited selection of rep-style fare, including the **Curzon Soho**, the **Electric**, the **Phoenix**, the **Rio**, the **ICA** and the **Ritzy**.

Ciné Lumière *Institut Français, 17 Queensberry Place, South Kensington, SW7 (7073 1350/ www.institut.ambafrance.org.uk). South Kensington tube.* **Screens** 1. **Tickets** £6; £4.50 concessions; £4 members. *Membership* £18/yr. **Credit** MC, V. **Map** p397 D10.

National Film Theatre (NFT) *South Bank, SE1 (information 7633 0274/bookings 7928 3232/ www.bfi.org.uk/nft). Embankment tube/Waterloo tube/rail.* **Screens** 3. **Tickets** £7.20; £5.50 concessions. *Membership* £13-£20/yr, allows £1 off all tickets. **Credit** AmEx, MC, V. **Map** p401 M7.

Prince Charles *7 Leicester Place, Leicester Square, WC2 (today 7734 9127/this week 0901 272 7007 premium rate/www.princecharlescinema.com). Leicester Square tube.* **Screens** 1. **Tickets** £1.99-£3.50 non-members; £1.50-£2.50 members. *Membership* £5/yr. **Credit** MC, V. **Map** p401 K7.

Riverside Studios *Crisp Road, Hammersmith, W6 (8237 1111/www.riversidestudios.co.uk). Hammersmith tube.* **Screens** 1. **Tickets** £5.50; £4.50 concessions. **Credit** MC, V.

Watermans Arts Centre *40 High Street, Brentford, Middx (8232 1010/www.watermans.org.uk). Brentford or Kew Bridge rail.* **Screens** 1. **Tickets** £6.50 non-members; £5.85 members; £4.50 concessions. *Membership* from £30/yr. **Credit** MC, V.

Bollywood cinemas

Boasting what some contend is the biggest film industry in the world, Bollywood is famous for its racy potboilers and all-singing, all-dancing romances. Among the following cinemas, the Grade II-listed Himalaya Palace, restored to its 1920s glory, is especially noteworthy.

Boleyn Cinema *11 Barking Road, Newham, E10 (8471 4884).* **Tickets** £5; £3.50 Tue. **No credit cards.**

Cineworld Feltham *Leisure West, Air Park Way, Feltham, Middx (8867 0555/www.cineworld.co.uk). Feltham rail.* **Tickets** £6-£6.20; £4.50 concessions. *Early shows* £2.50-£4.50; £1 Kids Club (Sat). **Credit** MC, V.

Cineworld Wood Green *High Street, Wood Green, N22 (8829 1400/ www.cineworld.co.uk). Wood Green tube.* **Tickets** £5.50; £3.70 concessions. *Early shows* £3.20; £1 Kids Club (10am Sat). **Credit** MC, V.

Himalaya Palace *14 South Road, Southall, Middx (8813 8844/www.himalayapalacecinema.com). Southall rail.* **Tickets** £3 Mon-Thur; £5.50 Fri-Sun; £3.50 concessions. **Credit** MC, V.

Take it to the **BFI London IMAX Cinema**.

Safari Cinema, Croydon *193 London Road, Croydon, Surrey (8688 3422/www.safaricinema.com). West Croydon rail.* **Tickets** £3.50; £2.50 Wed. **Credit** AmEx, MC, V.
Safari Cinema, Harrow *Station Road, Harrow, Middx (8426 0303/www.safaricinema.com). Harrow & Wealdstone tube/rail.* **Tickets** £6; £4 concessions. *Early show* £4. **Credit** AmEx, MC, V.
Uxbridge Odeon *The Chimes Shopping Centre, Uxbridge, Middx (0870 505 0007/www.odeon.co.uk).* **Tickets** £6; £5 concessions. *Early show* £5. **Credit** AmEx, MC, V.

IMAX

Screens don't get much bigger than at London's two IMAX cinemas: the IMAX in the **Science Museum** (*see p140*), and the 480-seater **BFI London IMAX Cinema** on the South Bank, which boasts the biggest screen in the country.

BFI London IMAX Cinema *1 Charlie Chaplin Walk, South Bank, SE1 (7902 1234/www.bfi.org.uk/imax). Embankment tube/Waterloo tube/rail.* **Screens** 1. **Tickets** £7.10; £4.95-£5.95 concessions; free under-3s. **Credit** AmEx, MC, V. **Map** p401 M8.
Science Museum IMAX Theatre *Exhibition Road, South Kensington, SW7 (0870 870 4868/www.sciencemuseum.org.uk). South Kensington tube.* **Screens** 1. **Tickets** £6.95; £5.95 concessions. **Credit** AmEx, MC, V. **Map** p397 D9.

Festivals

London Lesbian & Gay Film Festival
National Film Theatre, South Bank, SE1 (7928 3232/www.llgff.org.uk/www.bfi.org.uk). Embankment tube/Waterloo tube/rail. **Dates** 2-16 April 2003. **Map** p401 M7.

More than 186 new and restored films from around the world, plus a range of special events.

Rushes Soho Shorts Festival
Venues around Soho, W1 (7851 6207/www.sohoshorts.com). Leicester Square, Piccadilly Circus or Tottenham Court Road tube. **Dates** 26 July-1 Aug 2003. **Map** p398, p399.
Around 60 short films, music videos and idents by new directors are screened for free at venues across Soho, from cafés to cinemas.

BFM International Film Festival
Venues around London (8531 9199/www.bfmfilmfestival.com). **Dates** call for details.
The *Black Filmmaker*-programmed festival shows a variety of work from both inside and outside the cinematic mainstream.

Latin American Film Festival
The Other Cinema, Rupert Street, Chinatown, W1 (7851 7042/www.latinamericanfilmfestival.com). Leicester Square tube. **Dates** 5-18 Sept 2003. **Map** p401 K7.
This festival offers a range of new movies from Latin America each autumn.

Raindance
Venues around London (7287 3833/www.raindance.co.uk). Leicester Square tube. **Date** Oct 2003. **Map** p401 K7.
Britain's largest indie film festival concentrates on first-time directors.

London Film Festival
Venues around London (7928 3232/www.lff.org.uk). **Date** Nov 2003.
The biggest film festival in the UK, now in its 47th year, is a broad church; for further details, *see p267*.

Arts & Entertainment

Passionate about Art? We are.

Galleries

Small and ingenious, London's many galleries are thriving.

Expansion and relocation were key features of 2002 for London's commercial galleries. Jay Jopling's White Cube in St James's closed after a decade spent making household names of Damien Hirst, Tracey Emin and Sam Taylor-Wood, but he reopened its Hoxton branch in September with an extra 750 square metres. In the same month, Nicholas Logsdail's Lisson Gallery opened a space in Bell Street. If a publicity war was the aim, Logsdail won hands down: Spanish artist Santiago Sierra boarded up the gallery with corrugated iron, causing consternation among those who turned up to the private view expecting free drinks. Other openings of 2002 included Haunch of Venison, in a space once home to Admiral Lord Nelson, while the westward relocation of Flowers East was one of the more notable changes.

While this activity attests to the continued health of the commercial gallery scene, the capital's alternative, non-profit-making and artist-run spaces are disappearing rapidly. Spiralling rents have ensured that those few that still exist are getting pushed further out of town. That said, London continues to be blessed with an abundance of galleries: those listed below are only a representative sample.

Bigger spaces are listed in the Sightseeing chapter. They include the **Barbican** (*see p96*), **Camden Arts Centre** (*see p148*), the **Courtauld Gallery** (*see p98*) and **Hermitage Rooms** (*see p99*), the **Dulwich Picture Gallery** (*see p173*), the **Hayward Gallery** (*see p76*), the **ICA** (*see p130*), the **National Gallery** (*see p128*), the **Royal Academy of Arts** (*see p114*), the **Saatchi Gallery** (*see p78*), the **Serpentine Gallery** (*see p138*), **Tate Britain** (*see p134*), **Tate Modern** (*see p79*) and the **Whitechapel Art Gallery** (*see p157*).

Some galleries close in August; many also have little to see (if they open at all) between shows: phone ahead or consult *Time Out* magazine. A free brochure, *New Exhibitions of Contemporary Art*, can be picked up at most galleries or online at www.newexhibitions.com.

Central

aspreyjacques
4 Clifford Street, Mayfair, W1 (7287 7675/ www.aspreyjacques.com). Green Park or Piccadilly Circus tube. **Open** 10am-6pm Tue-Fri; 10am-1pm Sat. **No credit cards. Map** p400 J7.

Charles Asprey and Alison Jacques opened this elegant space in 1998, with the aim of looking outside London to emerging centres of contemporary art such as Berlin. The 2002 programme included German artists such as Christian Flamm and Michel Majerus, though the gallery also represents Brits such as photographer/filmmaker Catherine Yass (her 2002 exhibition here was nominated for the Turner Prize).

Corvi-Mora
22 Warren Street, Fitzrovia, W1 (7383 2419). Warren Street tube. **Open** 11am-6pm Tue-Sat. **No credit cards. Map** p398 J4.

Italian gallerist Tommasso Corvi-Mora brings a wealth of international art to this small space. The flavour continues in 2003 with drawings by LA-based artist Jim Isermann (whose work is a permanent fixture in the window) and politically themed paintings by Italian artist Andrea Salvino.

Entwistle
6 Cork Street, Mayfair, W1 (7734 6440/ www.entwistlegallery.com). Green Park or Piccadilly Circus tube. **Open** 10am-5.30pm Tue-Sat. **Credit** MC, V. **Map** p400 J7.

One of the few consistently interesting spaces on Cork Street, Entwistle shows a mixed bag of overseas and homegrown talent. Typical of the eclectic programme were shows in 2002 of young Glasgow-based painter Alan Michael, an installation of mesmeric counting LEDs by Japanese artist Tatsuo Miyajima, and Michael Stubbs' glossy abstractions.

Frith Street
60 Frith Street, Soho, W1 (7494 1550/www. frithstreetgallery.com). Tottenham Court Road tube. **Open** 10am-6pm Tue-Fri; 11am-4pm Sat. **No credit cards. Map** p399 K6.

Arts & Entertainment

Frith Street, Soho's finest. *See p289.*

Frith Street's interlinked rooms have hosted some truly excellent shows in recent years. The gallery represents a growing band of international figures, including Marlene Dumas, Tacita Dean and Callum Innes, who won the 2002 Jerwood Painting Prize. Abstract paintings by endlessly inventive Frenchman Bernard Frize should be a highlight of 2003.

Gagosian

8 Heddon Street, Mayfair, W1 (7292 8222/ www.gagosian.com). Oxford Circus or Piccadilly Circus tube. **Open** 10am-6pm Tue-Sat; by appointment Mon. **No credit cards. Map** p400 J7.
US superdealer Larry Gagosian, 'Go-Go' to his friends, opened this London branch in 2000, and has since brought over a wealth of big names – work by Warhol and Francesco Clemente appeared in 2002 – as well as lesser-known US and European artists. Brits represented include Peter Davies, who won the prestigious John Moores Painting Prize in 2002.

Haunch of Venison

6 Haunch of Venison Yard, Mayfair, W1 (7495 5050/www.haunchofvenison.com). Bond Street tube. **Open** 10am-6pm Mon-Wed, Fri; 10am-8pm Thur; 10am-5pm Sat. **Credit** MC, V. **Map** p398 H6.
One of the most eagerly anticipated openings of 2002. Previously leased as a project space by Anthony d'Offay, who announced his retirement in 2001, Haunch is run by Harry Blain, a founder of nearby Blains Fine Art, and Graham Southern, an ex-director of the Anthony d'Offay Gallery. First up was an exhibition by sculptor Rachel Whiteread.

Lisson

29 & 52-4 Bell Street, Marylebone, NW1 (7724 2739/www.lissongallery.com). Edgware Road tube. **Open** 10am-6pm Mon-Fri; noon-5pm Sat. **Credit** MC, V. **Map** p395 E5.
Tony Fretton's 1991 building is one of London's most beautiful spaces and a superb platform for artists including Douglas Gordon, Dan Graham and the 'Lisson Sculptors': Anish Kapoor, Richard Wentworth, Tony Cragg and Richard Deacon. Names new to the stable, such as Roddy Buchanan, Ceal Floyer and Jemima Stehli, prove that founder Nicholas Logsdail isn't resting on his laurels.

Sadie Coles HQ

35 Heddon Street, W1 (7434 2227/ www.sadiecoles.com). Oxford Circus or Piccadilly Circus tube. **Open** 10am-6pm Tue-Sat. **No credit cards. Map** p400 J7.
Sarah Lucas, Elizabeth Peyton, John Currin… Sadie Coles represents some of the hippest artists from both sides of the Atlantic. Must-sees for 2003 will be Currin's new paintings of pneumatic babes and alarming matriarchs, Richard Prince's 'Naughty Nurse' pictures and new films by TJ Wilcox.

Stephen Friedman

25-8 Old Burlington Street, Mayfair, W1 (7494 1434/www.stephenfriedman.com). Green Park or Piccadilly Circus tube. **Open** 10am-6pm Tue-Fri; 11am-5pm Sat. **No credit cards. Map** p400 K6.
From this shopfronted space, Friedman shows an interesting variety of international artists, including Yinka Shonibare, Vong Phaophanit and Stephan Balkenhol. A Corey McCorkle installation inspired by Roger Anger's architecture was the best of 2002; look forward to Helen Mirra's fabric transcriptions of geographical forms and Yoshitomo Nara's rather malevolent cartoon characters in 2003.

Waddington Galleries

11 Cork Street, Mayfair, W1 (7437 8611/ www.waddington-galleries.com). Green Park or Piccadilly Circus tube. **Open** 10am-5.30pm Mon-Fri; 10.30am-1.30pm Sat. **No credit cards. Map** p400 J7.
If it's a selection of blue-chip stock you're after, head to Waddington Galleries. You're likely to find a smörgåsbord of British and American modernism in the gallery's changing displays, as well as solo shows by UK and US big guns; John Chamberlain and Robert Rauschenberg appeared in 2002.

East

Anthony Wilkinson Gallery

242 Cambridge Heath Road, Bethnal Green, E2 (8980 2662/www.anthonywilkinsongallery.com). Bethnal Green tube. **Open** 11am-6pm Thur-Sat; noon-6pm Sun; also by appointment.
No credit cards.
A series of smallish rooms over three floors, this excellent gallery represents mainly British and European artists, including Bob & Roberta Smith

(aka Patrick Brill) whose knockabout text pieces and sculptures poke gentle fun at the art world, the artist duo BANK and peripatetic artist/writer/curator Matthew Higgs. It also hosts a video programme of work from the 1960s to the present.

The Approach

1st floor, Approach Tavern, 47 Approach Road, Bethnal Green, E2 (8983 3878). Bethnal Green tube. **Open** noon-6pm Wed-Sun; also by appointment. **No credit cards**.

An extremely pleasant, airy room located above an equally pleasant pub, and one of the more prominent commercial galleries in town, representing Michael Raedecker, Tim Stoner – a winner of the Beck's Futures prize – and Evan Holloway. A salon-style painting show called 'Dirty Pictures' kicks off the 2003 programme, followed by watercolours by LA-based David Muller and sculpture by Gary Webb.

Chisenhale Gallery

64 Chisenhale Road, Bow, E3 (8981 4518/ www.chisenhale.org.uk). Bethnal Green or Mile End tube/D6, 8, 277 bus. **Open** 1-6pm Wed-Sun. **No credit cards**.

This former factory contains a dance space, artists' studios and a large gallery. One of the few truly independent spaces in the East End and a vital part of the scene, Chisenhale has a reputation for spotting the stars of tomorrow and continues to give one-person shows to young or lesser-known artists.

Flowers East

82 Kingsland Road, Hoxton, E2 (7920 7777/ www.flowerseast.com). Old Street or Liverpool Street tube. **Open** 10am-6pm Tue-Sat; 11am-5pm Sun. **Credit** AmEx, MC, V. **Map** p403 R3.

Painting dominates at Flowers East, and at its two other spaces: Flowers Central (21 Cork Street, W1) and Flowers West (beyond our remit in Santa Monica, LA). Renny Tait, Carol Robertson, David Hepher and Trevor Sutton were among those shown in 2002, though it relocated from London Fields to these new Shoreditch premises near the year's end.

Interim Art

21 Herald Street, Bethnal Green, E2 (7729 4112). Bethnal Green tube. **Open** 11am-6pm Thur-Sun; also by appointment. **No credit cards**. **Map** p403 R3.

Here since 1999, Maureen Paley's Interim Art represents Turner Prize-winners Wolfgang Tillmans and Gillian Wearing, Paul Noble (best known for drawings of his fictitious town, Nobson) and collagist David Thorpe, whose foray into sculpture wowed audiences in 2002. Maureen Gallace's Connecticut paintings kick off 2003, with a rare Wearing solo show following later in the year.

Matt's Gallery

42-4 Copperfield Road, Mile End, E3 (8983 1771/www.mattsgallery.org). Mile End tube. **Open** noon-6pm Wed-Sun; also by appointment. **No credit cards**.

The graduates

Every summer, thousands of art students graduate from London's art colleges. Each student and college is desperate for attention. There are reputations to be upheld, names to be made and – of course – money to be earned. Galleries, collectors, journalists, agents, posh ladies, men in suits: anyone interested in buying art descends in the hope of finding the next Tracey Emin or Damien Hirst.

There are nearly 30 art colleges in London, and you'll usually find something of note at all of them, but there are a few heavies who get the most media attention year in, year out. It is a matter of debate as to which is the best horse in the race: each jostles for glory every year.

Goldsmiths Colleges (7919 7282/ www.goldsmiths.ac.uk) became popular and trendy after most of the Young British Artists (or YBAs) came out of there in the 1980s. The **Royal College of Art** (Kensington Gore, SW7; 7590 4444/www.rca.ac.uk) still sees itself as the one and only serious contender, while the **Royal Academy Schools** (Piccadilly,

W1; www.royalacademy.org.uk/7300 5920) has recently brought in new blood in the form of new artist/tutors. All the above colleges do only postgraduate courses. However, students on both MA and BA courses exhibit at other shows, and undergraduates shouldn't be ignored for the sake of postgrads.

Among the more intriguing of the other colleges is the **London Institute**, an amalgam of five old art schools: Camberwell, Central St Martin's, Chelsea College of Art and Design, the London College of Printing and the London College of Fashion (see www.linst.ac.uk). Despite being vulnerable to the bureaucratic merging and renaming of courses, each college still keeps to its specific areas of study, and has a strong reputation of its own.

These, though, are just the tip of the iceberg. For a full list of London colleges, see www.arteutile.net/schoolslondon.htm, and check *Time Out* each summer for details on the exact wheres and whens for the graduate shows.

Arts & Entertainment

There are few galleries in town as well respected as Matt's. Over two decades, it has commissioned installations as memorable as *20:50*, Richard Wilson's expanse of sump oil, and Mike Nelson's *The Coral Reef*. Installation continues to be the gallery's forte, though Jo Bruton showed a series of glitzy, Las Vegas-inspired paintings here in 2002.

Nylon
10 Vyner Street, Bethnal Green, E2 (8983 5333/ www.nylongallery.com). Bethnal Green tube. **Open** noon-6pm Thur-Sun. **No credit cards**.
Artists from New York and London. Run by Mary-Jane Aladren, the gallery represents a diverse range of artists – including Kate Belton and John Strutton – working across all media. Every January, an up-and-coming curator is invited to take over the space.

The Showroom
44 Bonner Road, Bethnal Green, E2 (8983 4115/ www.theshowroom.org). Bethnal Green tube. **Open** 1-6pm Wed-Sun. **No credit cards**.
The Showroom has gained a reputation for its commitment to young artists, often commissioning large-scale works at early stages in their careers. The triangular space isn't easy to fill successfully, but it responded well to video projections by the Finnish artist Gun Holmström last year.

Victoria Miro
16 Wharf Road, Islington, N1 (7336 8109/ www.victoria-miro.com). Angel tube/Old Street tube/ rail. **Open** 10am-6pm Tue-Sat. **Credit** MC,V. **Map** p402 P3.
This huge converted Victorian factory is one of the most fabulous art spaces anywhere, and is responsible for launching the careers of Chris Ofili, Jake and Dinos Chapman, and Peter Doig. Last year's emphasis on painting – with architect David Adjaye, Ofili created a stunning chamber in which to show his *Last Supper* series – looks set to continue with works by Denmark-based Tal R.

Vilma Gold
66 Rivington Street, Shoreditch, EC2 (7613 1609). Liverpool Street or Old Street tube/rail. **Open** noon-6pm Thur-Sun. **No credit cards**. **Map** p403 R4.
Rachel Williams and Steven Pippet have a magic touch. The cognoscenti flock here for such fashionable fare as the neo-neo-expressionist paintings of Sophie von Hellermann and Markus Vater, or Andrew Mania's conglomerations of drawings, paintings, sculpture and found photographs.

Wapping Project
Wapping Hydraulic Power Station, Wapping Wall, Wapping, E1 (7680 2080/www.wapping-wpt.com). Wapping tube. **Open** 10am-6pm Tue-Sat; noon-6pm Sun. **Credit** AmEx, DC, MC, V.
This magnificent converted hydraulic power station was intended to attract those working with film, video and the digital arts. Magnum photos of New York before, during and after September 11 2001 was a hard-hitting highlight of 2002.

White Cube
48 Hoxton Square, Hoxton, N1 (7930 5373/ www.whitecube.com). Old Street tube/rail. **Open** 10am-6pm Tue-Sat. **Credit** AmEx, MC, V. **Map** p403 R3.
Jay Jopling's eastern outpost reopened in September with new paintings by Gary Hume. The rooftop extension includes 'Inside the White Cube', a project space with its own curator, Louise Neri, who plans to commission work by less well-known international artists. Plans are afoot to convert a nearby electricity substation into a larger venue.

South

Essor Gallery
1 America Street, Southwark, SE1 (7928 3388). Southwark or Borough tube. **Open** 9am-6pm Mon-Fri; 10am-5pm Sat. **No credit cards**. **Map** p404 P8.
Before opening this space, Sharon Essor worked at the Lisson Gallery for ten years, so it's hardly surprising that she's quickly established a reputation for high-calibre solo shows and thoughtful, themed group exhibitions here. Three large rooms constitute the main gallery, with a large project space a few blocks away opposite the Jerwood Space.

Hales Gallery
70 Deptford High Street, Deptford, SE8 (8694 1194/ www.halesgallery.com). New Cross tube/Deptford Bridge DLR/Deptford rail. **Open** 10am-5pm Mon-Sat. **Credit** AmEx, DC, MC, V.
It might be off the beaten track, but Hales repays the trek with high-standard shows. Run by Paul Hedge and his team, the gallery represents Spencer Tunick, Judith Dean, Danny Rolph and Ben Ravenscroft, whose kaleidoscopic abstract paintings were aired in a solo show here in 2002.

Jerwood Space
171 Union Street, Bankside, SE1 (7654 0171/ www.jerwoodspace.co.uk). Borough or Southwark tube. **Open** 10am-6pm daily (during exhibitions; phone to check). **No credit cards**. **Map** p404 O8.
Just when we'd given up hope of ever again seeing cutting-edge contemporary art at the Jerwood Space, a new initiative was announced: a platform for young artists based on nominations by critics and curators. First up last year was Alan Currall, whose playful videos test our systems of belief and toy with our credulity. Looks like the Jerwood's back on track.

Percy Miller Gallery
39 Snowsfields, SE1 (7207 4578/ www.percymillergallery.com). London Bridge tube/rail. **Open** 11am-6pm Tue-Fri; noon-4pm Sat. **No credit cards**. **Map** p405 Q9.
This likeable little gallery is divided into two distinct spaces: the ground floor is used for exhibitions, such as 'In Your Time' (figurative paintings by Tom Ellis, Paul Ryan and others); in the basement you'll find individual works including, if you're lucky, photographs by Philippine Hoegen and David Spero.

Arts & Entertainment

The power-packed **Wapping Project**. *See p293.*

South London Gallery

65 Peckham Road, Camberwell, SE5 (7703 9799/
www.southlondongallery.org). Oval tube then 36
bus/Elephant & Castle tube/rail then 12, 171 bus.
Open 11am-6pm Tue, Wed, Fri; 11am-7pm Thur;
2-6pm Sat, Sun. **No credit cards.**
Built in 1891 as a philanthropic venture, this cathedral of a space has become one of the capital's foremost venues for contemporary art. 0worth a visit, the
SLG is host to a remarkably varied programme. In
2002 it included 'Supercollider', an epic production by
Turner Prize-nominee Keith Tyson.

Other spaces

Further spaces listed in the Sightseeing chapter
include the **Design Museum** (*see p83*), the
Geffrye Museum (*see p158*), the **Museum
of London** (*see p94*) and the **V&A** (*see p141*).

Architectural Association

36 Bedford Square, Fitzrovia, WC1 (7887 4000/
www.aaschool.ac.uk). Tottenham Court Road
tube. **Open** 10am 7pm Mon-Fri; 10am-3pm Sat.
Credit *Shop* MC, V. **Map** p399 K5.
Talks, events, discussions and exhibitions: four
good reasons for visiting these elegant premises.
During the summer, the gallery shows work by
graduating students of the AA School.

Crafts Council

44A Pentonville Road, Islington, N1 (7278 7700/
www.craftscouncil.org.uk). Angel tube. **Open** 11am-
6pm Tue-Sat; 2-6pm Sun. **Credit** AmEx, MC, V.
Map p402 N2.
The Council showcases the nation's craft output.
Shows often take a theme and demonstrate work in
that area – in 2002, 'Pattern Crazy' filled the space
with textiles, paintings, sound patterns and com-
puter-generated images. The finalists of the Jerwood
Applied Art Prize: Jewellery are shown in autumn.

Royal Institute of British Architects

66 Portland Place, Marylebone, W1 (7580 5533/
www.architecture.com). Oxford Circus or Regent's
Park tube. **Open** 9am-6.30pm Mon-Fri; 9am-5pm Sat.
Credit MC, V. **Map** p398 H5.
Based on a monumental edifice built by Grey
Wornham in 1934, the Royal Institute of British
Architects (aka RIBA) has a gallery that celebrates

the profession's great and good and checks emerging architecture from around the world. The building also hosts a programme of discussions.

Photography

Photofusion

17A Electric Lane, Brixton, SW9 (7738 5774/
www.photofusion.org). Brixton tube/rail. **Open** 10am-
6pm Tue, Thur-Sat; 10am-8pm Wed. **Credit** MC, V.
The gallery at Photofusion, the largest independent
photography resource centre in town, puts on regular shows: among 2002's impressive exhibitions were
Stephen Hughes' desolate, European landscapes.

Photographers' Gallery

5 & 8 Great Newport Street, Covent Garden,
WC2 (7831 1772/www.photonet.org.uk). Leicester
Square tube. **Open** 11am-6pm Mon-Sat; noon-6pm
Sun. **Credit** AmEx, DC, MC, V. **Map** p401 K6.
A giant among photography galleries, this space
hosts a huge range of diverse shows each year, while
doing tons of work to promote photography around
the country. With its long opening hours and excellent programme, the gallery's always a good bet for
a spontaneous visit.

Shine Gallery

3 Jubilee Place, Chelsea, SW3 (7352 4499/
www.shinegallery.co.uk). Sloane Square tube.
Open noon-6pm Tue-Sat; by appointment Mon.
Credit AmEx, MC, V. **Map** p397 E11
This small second-floor studio space, located above
the Hulton Getty Picture Library (7376 4525) and
Michael Hoppen Photography (7352 3649), specialises in cutting-edge photography. Top-drawer
exhibitions in 2002 included a retrospective of controversial Japanese photographer Nobuyoshi Araki.

Zelda Cheatle Gallery

99 Mount Street, Mayfair, W1 (7408 4448/
www.zcgall.demon.co.uk). Bond Street or Green Park
tube. **Open** 10am-6pm Tue-Fri; 11am-4pm Sat.
Credit AmEx, MC, V. **Map** p400 G7.
The Eve Arnold show in 2002 was typical of the
high standards set and met by this specialist in the
exhibition and sale of vintage and contemporary
photography. Exhibitions for 2003 include a retrospective of photos by the late, great Helen Chadwick.

Gay & Lesbian

With so many bars, clubs and saunas, there's no point playing it straight.

The London gay scene stands accused of losing its edge. In the mid '90s, the indie scene kicked off, while Fiction and Up blazed a trail at the turn of the millennium. Since then? Exclusive Soho venues with member privileges for those with excess cash (*see p300* **Hangin' with the A-Gays**) and little else. On the plus side, lesbians in London have more choice than ever before. But otherwise, the scene is a victim of its own success; the fact that it's money-oriented and has run out of ideas is only to be expected. London's Mardi Gras, usually the first weekend in July, is a case in point. The morning march, once a headline-grabbing political event, is now firmly separated from (and relegated behind) the money-spinning music bash in the afternoon and evening.

Still, berating London for being commercial is a slightly pointless exercise. Only the strong survive here, and this is still the most cosmopolitan gay scene in the world. **Soho** is the scene's mecca and Old Compton Street its main drag: the road is lined with gay shops and bars, its pavements overflowing with outdoor tables in summer. Other gay enclaves include **Earl's Court** and **Vauxhall**, though there's a local gay pub in many neighbourhoods. Contrary to reputation, friendly venues and people aren't hard to track down. You may find attitude and superficiality, but then that's what some people are looking for.

The national pulse is pinker than ever. Gay characters are beamed into the nation's living rooms in just about every television drama and reality TV show. The 2001 *Big Brother* winner Brian Dowling was openly gay, and Will Young came out in the national tabloids after his *Pop Idol* triumph of 2002. These days, the concept of gay celebs is as likely to induce a yawn as it is outrage. On the political stage, homophobic rhetoric is passé, though there remain bastions of prejudice in the right-wing press.

Online resources are strong. For those after no-strings sex, **www.gaydar.co.uk** is hugely popular; it now caters for the girls as well as boys. However, its chatrooms cater to wider interests, as do those of **www.uk.gay.com**, while **www.gingerbeer.co.uk** is highly recommended for dyke visitors.

Culture vultures shouldn't have a problem. The highlight for gay movie-goers is the annual **London Lesbian & Gay Film Festival** (*see p287*), with the main competition in 2002 a low-profile yet excellent Mardi Gras film season at the Curzon Soho (*see p284*) and a two-week Mardi Gras Arts Festival at Lauderdale House in Highgate. And if you don't find anything of interest in the theatre listings, chances are you're not looking hard enough.

For information on gay events in London, pick up *Time Out* magazine. Freesheets *Boyz* and *QX* are available in most gay venues and will give you a detailed rundown of where to find what, while on newsagents' shelves, gay lifestyle is adequately covered by *Gay Times*, men's mag *Attitude* and dyke bible *Diva*.

Accommodation

For more accommodation, *see p45*.

Accommodation Outlet
32 Old Compton Street, Soho, W1D 4TP (7287 4244/www.outlet.co.uk). Leicester Square tube. **Open** 10am-6pm Mon-Fri; noon-5pm Sat. **Map** p399 K6. This service for lesbian and gay flat-seekers, landlords and people looking for short-term holiday accommodation can find rooms in the West End from £55 per night.

Restaurants & cafés

You're unlikely to encounter prejudice in any London restaurant. There's plenty of choice out there, but if you're looking for somewhere with a gay slant, try one of the following places.

The best Gay stuff

For girl-watching
Candy Bar. *See p296.*

For guy-watching
Crash. *See p300.*

For a funky bar
Friendly Society. *See p297.*

For a funky club
Fiction. *See p301*

For a giggle
Duckie. *See p300.*

Balans

*60 Old Compton Street, Soho, W1 (7437 5212/
www.balans.co.uk). Leicester Square or Piccadilly
Circus tube.* **Open** 8am-5am Mon-Thur; 8am-6am Fri,
Sat; 8am-2am Sun. **Admission** £5 midnight-3am
Mon-Sat, midnight-2am Sun. **Credit** AmEx, MC, V.
Map p399 6K.
Stylish Soho brasserie Balans remains the premier
London restaurant for queens and company. The food
is adequate, while the staff – usually out-of-work gay
actors – provide the eye candy.

First Out

*52 St Giles High Street, St Giles's, WC2 (7240
8042/www.firstoutcafebar.com). Tottenham Court
Road tube.* **Open** 10am-11pm Mon-Sat; 11am-
10.30pm Sun. **No credit cards. Map** p399 6K.
A friendly and popular lesbian café that's welcoming to all (except for 'Girl Friday' each week, where
men are welcome as guests only). It's a good daytime destination and a popular pre-club venue, with
plenty of healthy options on the menu.

Old Compton Café

*34 Old Compton Street, Soho, W1 (7439 3309/
www.balans.com). Leicester Square tube.* **Open** 24hrs
daily. **Credit** AmEx, MC, V. **Map** p399 6K.
Now owned by the folks behind Balans, the Old
Compton Café is the Soho institution that never
sleeps. Pre- or post-clubbers fill up on sandwiches,
soups or snacks. Buzzy and friendly, it's the best
place on this stretch to people-watch, especially on
the outdoor seating in summer.

Keep your **Balans** in Soho.

Black Cap

*171 Camden High Street, Camden, NW1 (7428
2721). Camden Town tube.* **Open** noon-2am
Mon-Thur; noon-3am Fri, Sat; noon-12.30am Sun.
Credit AmEx, MC, V.
Camden's gay drinking den is a north London institution. The upstairs bar and beer garden offer
typical pub surroundings, then in the evenings the
basement opens up for drag shows and partying. It's
particularly popular on Sunday night.

The Box

*Seven Dials, 32-4 Monmouth Street, Covent
Garden, WC2 (7240 5828). Leicester Square tube.*
Open 11am-11pm Mon-Sat; noon-10.30pm Sun.
Credit AmEx, MC, V. **Map** p399 L6.
A busy bar and café serving drinks, coffee and food
to scene queens. Pretty, flirtatious staff make it pop-
ular with straight women, too, but of an evening, it's
clubby boys who rule the roost.

Brompton's

*294 Old Brompton Road, Earl's Court, SW5
(7370 1344). Earl's Court tube.* **Open** 8.30pm-
2am Mon-Sat; 5pm-12.30am Sun. **Admission**
£3 after 11pm Mon-Thur; £5 after 10.30pm Fri,
Sat; £2 after 10.30pm Sun. **Credit** MC, V.
Map p396 B11.
Two bars and a cabaret stage make Brompton's a
popular destination for the Earl's Court male set.
Thursdays offer midnight cabaret, and there are
strippers on Sunday.

Candy Bar

*4 Carlisle Street, Soho, W1 (7494 4041/
www.candybar.easynet.co.uk). Tottenham Court
Road tube.* **Open** 5-11.30pm Mon-Thur, Sun; 5pm-
2am Fri-Sat. **Admission** £5 after 9pm Fri, Sat.
Credit *Bar only* MC, V. **Map** p399 K6.
London's flagship gay women's establishment is
popular with lesbians, bisexual women and their
male guests. Back at its original address, regular DJs
and extended hours keep the clientele upbeat.

Compton's of Soho

*51-3 Old Compton Street, Soho, W1 (7479 7961/
www.comptons-of-soho.co.uk). Piccadilly Circus tube.*
Open noon-11pm Mon-Sat; noon-10.30pm Sun.
Credit MC, V. **Map** p399 K6.

Pubs & bars

Most of London's bars are open to gay men and
lesbians. In our reviews, we've tried to indicate
where a given place has less to offer either male
or female drinkers.

Admiral Duncan

*54 Old Compton Street, Soho, W1 (7437 5300).
Leicester Square tube.* **Open** noon-11pm Mon-Sat;
noon-10.30pm Sun. **Credit** AmEx, MC, V.
Map p399 K6.
The location of a homophobic bomb attack on a
busy Friday night in 1999, this doughty Old
Compton Street survivor sails on, perhaps slightly
enlivened by the sense of solidarity that horror
induced. Expect a slightly older male crowd in the
darkened surroundings.

Barcode

*3-4 Archer Street, Soho, W1 (7734 3342/
www.bar-code.co.uk). Piccadilly Circus tube.*
Open 1pm-1am Mon-Sat; 1-10.30pm Sun.
Admission £3 after 11pm Fri, Sat. **Credit** MC, V.
Map p401 K7.
Barcode combines cheap prices, a masculine clientele and an expectant atmosphere. The cruisy basement, which puts on comedy in the week and funky
house and disco at weekends, becomes quite a
pick-up spot later on.

Fancy a bit of rough? Compton's is the place if you like your blokes to be blokey. Shaved heads and bomber jackets predominate. Thumping house and disco from the basement soundtrack the cruising.

The Edge

11 Soho Square, Soho, W1 (7439 1313/ www.edge.uk.com). Tottenham Court Road tube. **Open** noon-1am Mon-Sat; 1-10.30pm Sun. **Credit** AmEx, MC, V. **Map** p399 K6.
A multi-floored Soho drinking den for men and women, the Edge is relaxed and sociable, and a good place to meet friends and hang out. Fine food is served downstairs, and for summer there's the park right on the doorstep.

Escape Bar

10A Brewer Street, Soho, W1 (7734 2626/ www.kudosgroup.com). Leicester Square tube. **Open** 3pm-3am Mon-Sat; 4-10.30pm Sun. **Admission** £2 after 11pm Tue-Sat. **Credit** AmEx, MC, V. **Map** p401 K7.
A friendly crowd drink, chat and jiggle to music videos. Escape's male and female clientele are free of attitude and up for a good time.

Freedom Café-Bar

60-6 Wardour Street, Soho, W1 (7734 0071). Leicester Square, Oxford Circus or Tottenham Court Road tube. **Open** noon-midnight Mon-Wed; noon-2am Thur; noon-3am Fri, Sat; 2-10.30pm Sun. **Admission** £3 after 11pm Mon, Tue; £5 after midnight Fri, Sat. **Credit** MC, V. **Map** p399 K6.
Once the destination for London's A-gays and then increasingly straight, well-located Freedom is still stylish – albeit pricey, and getting a little scuffed – and crammed with reckless hedonists.

Friendly Society

79 Wardour Street (entrance in Tisbury Court), Soho, W1 (7434 3805). Leicester Square, Oxford Circus or Tottenham Court Road tube. **Open** 4-11pm Mon-Fri; 2-11pm Sat; 2-10.30pm Sun. **Credit** MC, V.
This hip yet friendly designer bar with retro-futuristic decor is popular with gay men and women. DJs play in the evenings.

Glass Bar

West Lodge, Euston Square Gardens, 190 Euston Road, Bloomsbury, NW1 (7387 6184/ www.glassbar.ndo.co.uk). Euston tube/rail.

Cruise control

George Michael was in the wrong city when he flashed his bits in an LA public toilet. If Michael had been caught in London, the Old Bill barely would have raised an eyebrow. For while cottaging – picking up strangers for gay sex in a public place – happens around the world, nowhere does it seem to occur on such a grand scale as it does in London.

Far from being a by-product of the sexual revolution, cottaging was common as early as the 1700s in public gardens, where 'mollies' would wave white hankies as part of a secret code. Police paid agent provocateurs to trap men on 'Sodomite's Walk', an area of drained marshland in Moorfields, during the 19th century. And in 1810, the Home Secretary even proposed locking the gates of Hyde Park and St James's Park at night to prevent the practice. But the Victorian boom in building public lavatories provided fertile ground for the practice to flourish.

Sad closet cases and married men – that's the old cliché about cottaging. But an NHS AIDS Education Unit survey reveals that 75 per cent of those who seek sex in public loos and parks are openly gay men who also frequent gay pubs and clubs. Joe Orton's sister Leoni Orton-Barnett explained the appeal: 'It wasn't just the cheap sex: Joe liked to be a fly on the wall. You don't get to know what life is really like by knocking

about with BBC directors and Oxford dons. The crudity and sparseness of life is to be found in public lavatories.'

Among them were the 105-year-old toilets in South End Green, Hampstead, as featured in Orton biopic *Prick Up Your Ears*; if you believe Orton's diaries, a visit to the urinal could quickly descend into an orgy. The toilets of Brockwell Park were the subject of a recent TV documentary, *The Truth About Gay Sex*, which introduced the Great British Public to the curious 'glory holes' in cubicle partitions. Who said romance was dead?

Checking the cruising directory at www.gaytoz.com, it would seem London is one big cottage, from the Epping Forest car park ('sound action most nights') to Streatham Common ('heaving after dark'), from the legendarily cruisey Hampstead Heath to West Brompton Cemetery – really, guys, is nowhere sacred? – where police have been known to set up sting operations. But cottaging could soon be legalised, if David Blunkett's recent government white paper 'Setting the Boundaries' becomes law. The paper advocates sweeping away the Victorian offences of gross indecency and soliciting by men, arguing than in some cases, similar behaviour between men and women would be seen as 'no more than chatting up'. So *that's* what George was doing...

It's not all Old Compton Street swankiness, you know: head north to **Krystals**. *See p298.*

Open 5pm-late Mon-Fri; 6pm-late Sat (closing hours can vary). **Admission** £1. **No credit cards**. **Map** p398 J4.

No, your eyes do not deceive you. This friendly and stylish women-only venue is located in one of the old stone lodges outside Euston Station. Knock on the door if you're not sure, and dress smart-casual.

The Hoist

Railway Arch, 47B&C South Lambeth Road, Vauxhall Cross, Vauxhall, SW8 (7735 9972/ www.thehoist.co.uk). Vauxhall tube/rail. **Open** 10pm-3am Fri; 10pm-4am Sat; 9pm-2am Sun. **Admission** £5-£8. **No credit cards**.

London's premier leather, rubber and uniform bar. Adhere to the dress code and relax with a pint before indulging in whatever takes your fancy.

King William IV

77 Hampstead High Street, Hampstead, NW3 (7435 5747). Hampstead tube. **Open** noon-11pm Mon-Sat; noon-10.30pm Sun. **Credit** AmEx, DC, MC, V.

An old-fashioned, popular local in the heart of Hampstead. A relaxed mix of ages take advantage of the beer garden while music plays inside (loud enough, but less than threatening).

Krystals

97 Stoke Newington Road, Stoke Newington, N16 (7254 1967/www.krystals.org). Dalston Kingsland rail/149, 156, 243 bus. **Open** 5-11pm Mon-Fri; 1-11pm Sat; 1-10.30pm Sun. **Credit** *Bar only* MC, V.

This friendly local up on the edge of Stoke Newington offers drag acts, occasional karaoke and quiz nights.

Kudos

10 Adelaide Street, Covent Garden, WC2 (7379 4573/www.kudosgroup.com). Charing Cross tube/rail. **Open** 11am-11pm Mon-Sat; noon-10.30pm Sun. **Credit** AmEx, MC, V. **Map** p401 L7.

Two floors of fun for fashionable scene queens and suits, with music videos blaring in the basement on Mondays and Tursdays to get the week off to a trashy start. It promises to get you in the mood for Heaven on Wednesdays and Saturdays with cheap booze and other antics. There's a kitchen here, too, recently refurbished and its menu rethought.

Retro Bar

2 George Court, off Strand, Charing Cross, WC2 (7321 2811). Charing Cross tube/rail. **Open** noon-11pm Mon-Sat; noon-10.30pm Sun. **Credit** MC, V. **Map** p401 L7.

Unpretentious, relaxed and friendly, the Retro Bar's two floors are a respite from the style-conscious bars of Soho just under a mile away. The music is '70s, '80s and alternative, and there are regular theme nights and quizzes.

Rupert Street

50 Rupert Street, Soho, W1 (7292 7141). Leicester Square or Piccadilly Circus tube. **Open** noon-11pm Mon-Sat; noon-10.30pm Sun. **Credit** AmEx, MC, V. **Map** p401 K7.

An upmarket, pricey Soho bar for the image-conscious and professional sets. The glass frontage makes certain that those who see can also be seen, which becomes increasingly important as day turns into evening.

Arts & Entertainment

Two Brewers

*114 Clapham High Street, Clapham, SW4
(7498 4971). Clapham Common tube.*
Open 4pm-2am Mon-Thur; 4pm-3am Fri, Sat;
2pm-12.30am Sun. **Admission** free before 11pm,
£2 after 11pm Tue-Thur; free before 9.30pm,
£3 9.30-11pm, £4 after 11pm Fri, Sat. **Credit**
AmEx, MC, V.
Drag queens do their thing nightly on the tiny corner stage, with the lighting kept high enough for you
to see anything else that might take your fancy. The
camp disco of the main bar gives way to harder
sounds in the larger back room.

Vespa Lounge

*Upstairs at the Conservatory Bar, 15 St Giles
High Street, St Giles's, WC2 (7836 8956).
Tottenham Court Road tube.* **Open** 6-11pm
Mon-Sat; 6-10.30pm last Sun of mth. **No credit
cards. Map** p399 K6.
A centrally located, easy-to-find bar for laid-back
girls and their male guests. Thai food is served until
closing, and the Laughing Cows comedy night happens on the last Sunday of the month.

Village Soho

*81 Wardour Street, Soho, W1 (7434 2124).
Piccadilly Circus tube.* **Open** 11.30am-1am Mon-Sat;
11.30am-midnight Sun. **Admission** £2 after
10.30pm Fri, Sat. **Credit** MC, V. **Map** p398 J6.
Village Soho offers three floors of mostly male bar
action for fun-loving young guys. The main bar features go-go boys pole-dancing on busy evenings.
Upstairs is chilled, and offers a superb view over the
gay strip, while the basement has a busy dancefloor.

West Central

*29-30 Lisle Street, Soho, WC2 (7479 7981). Leicester
Square tube.* **Open** *Ground floor bar* 2-11pm Mon-Sat;
2-10.30pm Sun. *Basement bar* 10.30pm-1am Mon, Wed,
Thur; 10.30pm-3am Fri, Sat; 2-7pm Sun. **Admission**
Basement bar £2-£5. **Credit** MC, V. **Map** p401 K7.
Unashamedly camp, this fun bar plays showtunes
to theatrical types upstairs and pop tunes for a more
up-for-it crowd on the ground floor. The small club
in the basement is cheap and cheerful.

The Yard

*57 Rupert Street, Soho, W1 (7437 2652/
www.yardbar.co.uk). Piccadilly Circus tube.*
Open noon-11pm Mon-Sat; noon-10.30pm Sun.
Credit AmEx, MC, V. **Map** p401 K7.
Summer's choice for relaxed drinking, the Yard has
a courtyard and a comfortable loft in addition to its
small, buzzy main bar. It's mainly for men, who tend
to be mainstream thirtysomethings, though the
upstairs is pretty mixed.

Clubs

Club nights come and go often, so check *Time
Out* for the latest news. However, there are
plenty of evergreens, the pick of which are
listed below. For more on nightlife, *see p317*.

Action

*Mayfair Works, off Miles Street, SW8 (07973
233377). Vauxhall tube.* **Open** 11pm-6am
1st & 3rd Sat of mth. **Admission** £14;
£10 members.

No-no-no: it's shirt first, then tie second... **Popstarz**. *See p301.*

Hangin' with the A-Gays

Soho's always been a bit of a sniffy place. Though there are some relaxed venues here, the bars tend to try and out-cool each other, catering to a homogenous crowd that do the same. Lately, though, a more insidious trend has come to the fore. Exclusivity is the thing these days, and if your name's not down, you're not coming in.

First to arrive in 2001 was the **Shadow Lounge** (*pictured*; 5 Brewer Street, W1; 7287 7988/www.theshadowlounge.co.uk). In a previous life as the Astral, it was a sex cinema and a pole-dancing emporium, but it's now out with the dirty mac brigade and in with monied, dressed-up queens.

According to the press blurb, 'On entering the club you are greeted by one of the attractive and friendly hosts who will whisk you down the stairs.' If you've paid the £300 annual membership fee, that is. Otherwise, you're just going to have to plead with the aggressive door staff. If you're a middle-aged guy going alone, don't reckon on your chances.

Once in, you'll find air-conditioning and snazzy decor, including a dancer's pole: a hangover from the Astral, no doubt. Suspiciously tanned people congregate in roped-off seating areas as hassled waiters do the rounds. The bar staff smile politely as they explain the tenner you've offered for two gin and tonics isn't enough. And it's a huge success. By 11.30pm on a Friday or Saturday, the place is heaving, as the lounge bar becomes a club and, like most other venues, a sweaty, messy affair. Getting a drink becomes a nightmare. Still, if you're lucky, you might get a glimpse of Julian Clary.

The bar was the brainchild of promoter Paul Richardson, who tried to replicate its success with the even more exclusive **Sweet Suite** on Wardour Street. Members were called 'Sweeties' and at their disposal was the 'Suite Mobile', a house Rolls-Royce done out in shocking pink with blacked-out windows. It was taking the '80s revival too far. Richardson had left by the summer of 2002, the Sweet Suite was undergoing a name change, and the future wasn't looking so, uh, pink.

Entrepreneur-turned-politico Ivan Massow, never one to miss out on publicity, then joined in on the act. A founder of Sweet Suite, he held the launch for his online social network, called **Jake**, at the venue in winter 2001. Jake's website, www.jaketm.org, promises 'appropriate match-making between companies/individuals' among its 10,000 members, with a social event

---

A sweaty, happy and largely male event for muscle boys, scene queens and party animals. A big dance arena offers pumped-up turbo house; there's also a cruise room and a heated outdoor terrace.

Beyond

Club Colosseum, 1 Nine Elms Lane, SW8 (07905 035682). Vauxhall tube. **Open** 4.30am-noon Sat night. **Admission** £8 with flyer, otherwise £10 before 6am, then £12.

This Sunday morning shindig brought to you by the Crash team offers funky sounds in three rooms for those who can't stop dancing. The venue specialises in after-hours events for a pumped-up crowd.

Club Kali

Dome, 1 Dartmouth Park Hill, Tufnell Park, N19 (7272 8153). Tufnell Park tube. **Open** 10pm-3am 1st & 3rd Fri of mth. **Admission** £6 with flyer before 11pm, then £7. **No credit cards**.

The world's biggest gay Asian club night is a fortnightly affair, with the barn-like venue echoing to bhangra, Bollywood and Western sounds. You'll find a friendly, mixed crowd and, if you're lucky, some amazing displays of South Asian dancing.

Crash

Arch 66, Goding Street, Vauxhall, SE11 (7636 7630/www.crashlondon.co.uk). Vauxhall tube/rail. **Open** *Club* 10.30pm-6am Sat. **Admission** £10; £8 members. **Credit** AmEx, DC, MC, V.

Crash, down near Vauxhall, is where the Muscle Marys head for a night of hard beats and beefcake (check the go-go dancers). The subterranean setting comprises four bars, two dancefloors and two chill-out areas. Recommended.

Dolly Mixtures

Candy Bar, 4 Carlisle Street, Soho, W1 (7494 4041/www.candybar.easynet.co.uk). Tottenham Court Road tube. **Open** *Club* 9pm-2am Sat. **Admission** free before 9pm, then £5. **Credit** *Bar only* MC, V.

A girls' party night, with DJ Slamma spinning house and garage in London's premier lesbian venue. R&B plays in the basement.

DTPM

Fabric, 77A Charterhouse Street, Clerkenwell, EC1 (7439 9009/www.dtpm.net). Barbican tube/ Farringdon tube/rail. **Open** *Club* 10pm-late Sun.

every Wednesday at Soho club 23 Romilly Street (sister organisation Jackie, at www.jackietm.org, launched in October 2002 and promises the same service for girls, with a social at the same spot on Thursdays).

For now, £75 buys you a six-month membership and use of Jake Bar London from 5pm to 11.30pm, Monday to Friday. If the gallery on the website is anything to go by, it's a great opportunity to meet a bunch of suits. But then if that's your fetish, you can indulge it for free at Rupert Street bar any night of the week.

Admission £14, £10 concessions, members or before 10.30pm with flyer. **Credit** *Bar only* MC, V. **Map** p402 O5.

DTPM is tops for R&B, house, hip hop and disco. A mixed set of dedicated clubbers gather at one of London's biggest and best nightclubs.

Duckie

Royal Vauxhall Tavern, 373 Kennington Lane, Vauxhall, SE11 (7582 0833). Vauxhall tube. **Open** *Club* 9pm-2am Sat. **Admission** £5. **No credit cards.**

This eccentric long-runner can still be relied on for a good laugh. The eclectic playlist, cabaret and diverse clientele prove a happy combination in this endearing south London fleapit.

Exilio Latino

Houghton Street, Holborn, WC2 (07956 983230/ www.exilio.co.uk). Holborn tube. **Open** *Club* 10pm-3am Sat. **Admission** £6 before 11.30pm, £7 after. **No credit cards.** **Map** p399 M6.

If you're a Latino lover, look no further. The studenty venue plays host to a popular, relaxed gay salsa night with a Latin-enthused, mixed clientele of all ages.

Fiction

The Cross, King's Cross Goods Yard, off York Way, King's Cross, N1 (7439 9009/www.dtpm.net). King's Cross tube/rail. **Open** *Club* 11pm-late Fri. **Admission** £9 before 11.30pm with flyer, then £13; £10 members. **Credit** *Bar only* MC, V. **Map** p399 L2.

A trendy affair, with three dancefloors offering varying degrees of house to a glamorous, mixed set. It gets very busy, especially in summer when the outdoor terrace comes into its own.

Fist

Imperial Gardens, 299 Camberwell New Road, Camberwell, SE5 (7252 6000/www.fist.co.uk). Bus 36, 185. **Open** *Club* 10pm-6am 2nd Sat of mth. **Admission** £13; £10 members. **No credit cards.**

A monthly fetish institution with a darkroom, a gallery and a fully stocked playroom for S&M-loving gay men and women. The dress code is strict: leather, rubber, skin gear and uniform.

G-A-Y

Astoria & Mean Fiddler, 157-65 Charing Cross Road, Soho, WC2 (7734 6963/premium rate 0906 100 0160/www.g-a-y.co.uk). Tottenham Court Road tube. **Open** *Club* 10.30pm-4am Mon, Thur; 11pm-4am Fri; 10.30pm-5am Sat. **Admission** £3-£10; discounts with flyer. **No credit cards.** **Map** p399 K6.

The big one for the young, pink and fluffy. The huge venue leaves something to be desired (for more, *see p307*), but it doesn't stop the hordes dancing their socks off to Kylie, S Club 7 et al. Mondays and Thursdays are Pink Pounder nights with cheap drinks and entry, Friday is the larger-scale Camp Attack, and Saturdays feature guest appearances from big chart acts. Check the venue is still the same before setting out, though: in late 2002, the Astoria was battling with Westminster council to retain its licence.

Ghetto

5-6 Falconberg Court, Soho, W1 (7287 3726/ www.ghetto-london.co.uk). Tottenham Court Road tube. **Open** 10pm-3am Mon, Sun; 10.30pm-3am Tue-Thur; 10.30pm-4.30am Fri; 10.30pm-5am Sat. **Admission** £3-£7; discounts with flyer, concessions. **No credit cards.** **Map** p399 K6.

This intimate, central club has an array of nights: indie and nu-metal (Monday), pop (Tuesday), electro (Wednesday) and early '90s (Thursday). The Cock puts the spunk back into Soho on Fridays, and on Saturday there's long-running trash night Wig Out. On the day of rest? Funky house, natch.

Heaven

off Villiers Street, Charing Cross, WC2 (7930 2020/ www.heaven-london.com). Embankment tube/Charing Cross tube/rail. **Open** 10.30pm-3am Mon, Wed; 10.30pm-5am Fri; 10pm-5am Sat. **Admission** £1-£12. **Credit** AmEx, DC, MC, V. **Map** p401 L7.

London's most famous gay venue has three main rooms. Popcorn (Mondays) and Fruit Machine (Wednesdays) offer upbeat early-week fun and

Fridays are house-focused and very mixed, but Heaven really comes alive on Saturdays, with commercial house played to a packed set of gay revellers.

Popstarz
Scala, 275 Pentonville Road, King's Cross, N1 (7738 2336/www.popstarz.org). King's Cross tube/rail. **Open** *Club* 10pm-5am Fri. **Admission** free before 11pm with flyer or website printout, then £8; £7 with flyer; £5 concessions. **Credit** MC, V. **Map** p399 L3.

It's renowned as a big indie night popular with students, but there's much more to Popstarz. A diverse, attitude-free crowd lap up indie classics on the main floor, R&B/funk in the Love Lounge, and pop in the Trash Room. It's deservedly still packing them in, as the queues testify, so get there early.

Substation South
9 Brighton Terrace, Brixton, SW9 (7737 2095/ www.substationsouth.com). Brixton tube/rail/N2, N3, N37, N109 bus. **Open** 10pm-2.30am Mon; 10.30pm-2.30am Tue, Thur; 10.30pm-3am Wed; 10.30pm-5am Fri; 10.30pm-6am Sat; 10pm-late Sun. **Admission** £4-£8. **No credit cards**.

A cruisey venue that doesn't mess around. Monday is underwear-only night with Y Front; Tuesday is for hot and hard cruising; Wednesday is uniform night with Boot Camp; and Friday is Dirty Dishes,

with funky house attitude. The weekend is more music-oriented with Queer Nation's New York-style house and garage on Saturday, and popular indie night Marvellous on Sunday.

Saunas

Chariots I
1 Fairchild Street, Shoreditch, EC2 (7247 5333/ www.gaysauna.co.uk). Liverpool Street tube/rail. **Open** noon-9am daily. **Admission** £13; £11 concessions. **Credit** AmEx, MC, V. **Map** p403 4R.

Two steam rooms, two saunas, a jacuzzi, a Roman-style pool, dozens of private rooms, an extensive dark area, a bar, a snack bar and a gym. It's a popular destination, especially with nearby City workers. **Branches**: 57 Cowcross Street, Clerkenwell, EC1 (7251 5553); 292 Streatham High Road, Streatham, SW16 (8696 0929).

Sauna Bar
29 Endell Street, Covent Garden, WC2 (7836 2236/ www.thesaunabar.com). Covent Garden tube. **Open** noon-11.30pm Mon-Sat; noon-11pm Sun. **Admission** £13; £10 concessions. **Credit** MC, V. **Map** p399 L6.

A relatively small men-only sauna with a comfortable bar area, a steam room, a sauna, a splash pool and showers, plus some private rooms if you can get to them first.

Music

Take note: you won't find many music scenes on the planet to better this one.

Classical & Opera

It's arguable whether any city needs four major orchestras. But this is London, and London doesn't do things by halves. And so it goes that London's catch-all music scene boasts a quartet of notable orchestras. All except the roving **Royal Philharmonic Orchestra** are tied to a venue: the impressive **London Symphony Orchestra** to the **Barbican** (*see below*), the **London Philharmonic Orchestra** and the **Philharmonia** to the South Bank Centre (*see p304*). And that's leaving aside the **BBC Symphony Orchestra**, the majority of whose London concerts are at the Barbican.

Of course, the city also enjoys the attentions of countless smaller groups, from the largely traditionalist **City of London Sinfonia** to the joyously esoteric **London Sinfonietta**, from big bands to string quartets. The town's two opera houses – the Royal Opera and the English National Opera – are both troubled in their own way, but both still capable of brilliance (*see p305*). Mix in the international ensembles who visit London's many venues and the many festivals that dot the calendar, and it becomes obvious that the choice of entertainment is ridiculously large. Check *Time Out* magazine each week for advice on narrowing it down.

TICKETS AND INFORMATION

With the exception of roving festivals and the occasional special outdoor event, tickets for classical and opera events in London are available from the venues: book ahead for good seats. Many major venues have online booking systems in addition to the telephone box offices.

A number of major venues, such as the Barbican and the South Bank, operate standby schemes, whereby unsold tickets for some shows are sold off at cut prices hours before the show to students, seniors and others eligible for discounted rates. Call the venues for full details.

Classical venues

Barbican Centre
Silk Street, the City, EC2 (7638 4141/box office 7638 8891/www.barbican.org.uk). Barbican tube/ Moorgate tube/rail. **Box office** 9am-8pm daily. **Tickets** £6.50-£35. **Credit** AmEx, MC, V. **Map** p402 P5.

First, the bad news. This 20-year-old complex is aesthetically disgusting and chaotically laid out. The good news is that its events are often excellent. It helps that the resident orchestra is the London Symphony Orchestra: the best in town, it plays around 90 concerts a year. But there's rarely much drop in quality with the English Chamber Orchestra and the BBC Symphony Orchestra, who also play regularly. The Great Performers series, which in 2003 stars the likes of Yo-Yo Ma and Murray Perahia, is a joy, while the modern music programming, taking in jazz, rock, world and country, has come on in leaps and bounds in the last five years. There's free music in the foyer, and the centre also holds cinemas, galleries, theatres, restaurants and a library.

Bush Hall
310 Uxbridge Road, Shepherd's Bush, W12 (8222 6955/www.bushhallmusic.co.uk). Shepherd's Bush tube. **Box office** 9.30am-5pm Mon-Fri. **Tickets** £6-£25. **Credit** AmEx, MC, V.
Opened in 1904 as the Carlton Ballroom (the plasterwork is dotted with musical motifs) and then a snooker hall, the Bush Hall was refurbished and reopened as a plush music venue in 2000. And a delightful place it is, too, hosting a fairly even spread of small-group classical concerts and recitals and low-key, often acoustic, rock shows.

Royal Albert Hall
Kensington Gore, South Kensington, SW7 (information 7589 3203/box office 7589 8212/ www.royalalberthall.com). South Kensington tube/ 9, 10, 52 bus. **Box office** 9am-9pm daily. **Tickets** £4-£50. **Credit** AmEx, MC, V. **Map** p397 D9.

The best Live music

For the classics
Barbican Centre. See p303.

For the next Coldplay
Barfly. See p311.

For a trip to the country
Borderline. See p310.

For the smallest stage in town
12 Bar Club. See p313.

For homegrown jazz
606 Club. See p314.

Arts & Entertainment

Outside the Proms, this grand monument to Queen Victoria's husband stages everything from grand-scale opera to all-in wrestling via rock, jazz and the occasional convention. The closer you can get to the stage, the better: the acoustics are a little murky and the hall is so huge that the top balcony is in a different postal district to the stage. We jest.

St James's Church Piccadilly

197 Piccadilly, St James's, W1 (7734 4511/ www.st-james-piccadilly.org). Piccadilly Circus tube. **Open** 8am-6.30pm daily. **Admission** free-£17; tickets available at the door 1hr before start of performance. **No credit cards. Map** p400 J7.
This little-known Wren church was flattened during World War II and subsequently rebuilt to its original form. Nowadays it hosts free lunchtime recitals (Mon, Wed, Fri) and a less regular programme of evening concerts. The church also hosts such varied events as participatory Taizé singing, a homeless help-group and the William Blake Society.

St John's, Smith Square

Smith Square, Westminster, SW1 (7222 1061/ www.sjss.org.uk). St James's Park or Westminster tube. **Box office** 10am-5pm Mon-Fri, or until start of performance on concert nights; from 1hr before start of performance Sat, Sun. **Tickets** £5-£30. **Credit** MC, V. **Map** p401 K10.
This former church, rebuilt after bomb damage in World War II, hosts a variety of recitals and concerts featuring a surprising variety of performers, from Sir Thomas Allen to London university orchestras. The crypt is home to a wonderfully secluded bar and restaurant.

St Martin-in-the-Fields

Trafalgar Square, Westminster, WC2 (concert information 7839 8362/www.stmartin-in-the-fields. org). Charing Cross tube/rail. **Box office** 10am-5pm Mon-Sat, or until start of that evening's performance. **Admission** *Lunchtime concerts* donations requested. *Evening concerts* £6-£17. **Credit** MC, V. **Map** p401 L7.
Tucked away on the edge of Trafalgar Square, St Martin's classical music programme is pleasant enough, if surprise-free. Free lunchtime recitals (Mon, Tue, Fri) come courtesy of music students, while evening concerts (Thur, Fri, Sat, occasional Tue) tend to be of the Vivaldi-by-Candlelight variety.

South Bank Centre

Belvedere Road, South Bank, SE1 (7960 4242/ www.sbc.org.uk). Embankment tube/Waterloo tube/ rail. **Box office** 9am-9pm Mon-Sat; 9.30am-9pm Sun. **Tickets** £5-£75. **Credit** AmEx, DC, MC, V. **Map** p401 M8.
Home to two major orchestras, the Philharmonia and the London Philharmonic, and boasting close links with a number of other ensembles (such as the London Sinfonietta, the country's leading ensemble for new music), the South Bank is a major global venue. There's still plenty of interest here in the centre's three halls: the 2,600-capacity **Royal Festival**

Leonard Slatkin leads the BBC Symphony Orchestra at the **Barbican Centre**. *See p303.*

Hall, which stages mainly symphony concerts and those of a more popular bent; the **Queen Elizabeth Hall**, a third of the size, which offers chamber groups, dance and some rock and jazz events; and the **Purcell Room**, which hosts everything from solo recitals to spoken word events. Aside from this triumvirate, there's free foyer music, a decent bookshop, a record store, a poetry library and performance room, and a number of cafés, bars and restaurants, including the People's Palace.

Wigmore Hall

36 Wigmore Street, Marylebone, W1 (7935 2141/ www.wigmore-hall.org.uk). Bond Street tube. **Box office** *In person Apr-Oct* 10am-8.30pm Mon-Sat; 10.30am-6.30pm Sun. *Nov-Mar* 10am-5pm Mon-Sat; 10.30am-4pm Sun. *By phone Apr-Oct* 10am-7pm Mon-Sat; 10.30am-6.30pm Sun. *Nov-Mar* 10am-7pm Mon-Sat; 10.30am-4pm Sun. **Tickets** £5-£35. **Credit** AmEx, DC, MC, V. **Map** p398 G6.
The century-old Wigmore Hall is many concertgoers' favourite London venue. They do things the old-fashioned way here; unsurprising, as the venue is an entirely old-fashioned place. We like it exactly

Arts & Entertainment

how it is, though, especially since a refurbishment at the turn of the century returned the interior to its former glories. The acoustics are the best anywhere in town, and the programme of recitals and small-ensemble concerts is extremely impressive. The Monday lunchtime concerts, recorded for Radio 3, are especially good value.

City lunchtime concerts

Among London's best-kept musical secrets are the lunchtime concerts held in the City's old churches. Many of these buildings have fascinating histories and a couple are stunning buildings in their own right, even before you add in the regular chamber concerts and recitals performed, usually to a high standard, by London's young musicians. Admission is usually free or by donation, and *City Events*, available from the City Information Centre by St Paul's Cathedral, will have details of what's on. In addition to the venues listed below, organ recitals are held at **Temple Church** (off Fleet Street, EC4, 7353 8559), **Grosvenor Chapel** (South Audley Street, W1, 7499 1684) and **St James's** (Clerkenwell Close, EC1, 7251 1190).

St Anne & St Agnes *Gresham Street, EC2 (7606 4986). St Paul's tube.* **Performances** 1.10pm Mon, Fri. **Map** p404 P6.
St Bride's *Fleet Street, EC4 (7427 0133). Blackfriars tube/rail.* **Performances** 1.15pm Tue, Fri (except Aug, Advent, Lent). **Map** p404 N6.
St Lawrence Jewry *Guildhall, EC2 (7600 9478). Mansion House, Bank or St Paul's tube.* **Performances** 1pm Mon, Tue. **Map** p404 P6.
St Magnus the Martyr *Lower Thames Street, EC3 (7626 4481). Monument tube.* **Performances** 1pm occasional Tue; phone to check.
St Margaret Lothbury *Lothbury, EC2 (7606 8330). Bank tube.* **Performances** 1.10pm Thur. **Map** p405 Q6.
St Martin within Ludgate *Ludgate Hill, EC4 (7248 6054). St Paul's tube/Blackfriars tube/rail.* **Performances** 1.15pm Wed. **Map** p404 O6.
St Mary-le-Bow *Cheapside, EC2 (7248 5139/www.stmarylebow.co.uk). Bank, Mansion House or St Paul's tube.* **Performances** 1.05pm Thur. **Map** p404 P6.
St Michael Cornhill *Cornhill, EC3 (7626 8841). Bank or Monument tube.* **Performances** 1pm Mon. **Map** p405 Q6.

Opera houses

English National Opera
The Coliseum, St Martin's Lane, Covent Garden, WC2 (box office 7632 8300/fax credit card bookings 7379 1264/minicom 7836 7666/www.eno.org). Leicester Square tube/Charing Cross tube/rail. **Box office** *By phone* 24hrs daily. **Tickets** £3-£61. *Day tickets* to personal callers after 10am Mon-Sat & by phone from 12.30pm Mon-Sat. **Credit** AmEx, DC, MC, V. **Map** p401 L7.

For years, ENO has looked on smugly as the Royal Opera endured a beating from press and public. Now it's ENO's turn to take the flak. The company has long styled itself as the accessible, hip cousin of its Covent Garden comrade, and with good reason: all productions are sung in English, and stagings are more adventurous than at the ROH. However, a slew of poor productions and falling sales resulted in general director Nicholas Payne leaving his post, and the company has been dogged by rumours of huge job cuts and mounting debts. Its impressive venue, the Coliseum, will be closing for a seven-month renovation in mid 2003, during which time the company will relocate to the Barbican. Whether anyone will be listening remains to be seen.

Royal Opera
Royal Opera House, Covent Garden, WC2 (7304 4000/www.royaloperahouse.org). Covent Garden tube. **Box office** 10am-8pm Mon-Sat. **Tickets** £3-£175. **Credit** AmEx, DC, MC, V. **Map** p399 L6.
The Covent Garden soap opera rolls on, though things do seem to be improving under chief exec Tony Hall. Figures published by London's grandest opera house in 2002 illustrated that audiences are now younger and less well-off than popular cliché suggests, while the troubles at ENO (*see above*) meant that critics have turned their sights away from Covent Garden Piazza for a change. A recent (and very pricey) refurbishment gave the place a much-needed facelift. That said, there's still a way to go: prices are still high, the standard of performance is variable (expect traditional operas, traditionally staged), and the house's public image remains hopeless. Hall's aim is to change all that. Good luck.

Festivals

In addition to the major annual festivals listed chronologically below, the Barbican (*see p303*), the South Bank and the Wigmore Hall (for both, *see p304*) all present a variety of themed events and seasons throughout the year.

Spitalfields Festival
Various venues (7377 1362/www.spitalfieldsfestival. org.uk). Date 9-27 June 2003; 10-19 Dec 2003. **Tickets** free-£27. **Credit** MC, V. **Map** p403 S5.
This delightful twice-yearly festival of music old and new has traditionally been held in the imposing Christ Church Spitalfields. However, while the church is renovated the festival will become itinerant, surfing through venues including the 1740 St Leonard's Church in Shoreditch, Wilton's Music Hall and the Dutch Church on Austin Friars. There'll be a Huguenot flavour to the June event.

Holland Park Theatre
Holland Park, Kensington High Street, Kensington, W8 (7602 7856/www.operahollandpark.com). High Street Kensington or Holland Park tube. **Date** June-early Aug 2003. **Tickets** £26-£29. **Credit** AmEx, MC, V. **Map** p394 A8.

Arts & Entertainment

This open-air theatre hosts opera for around a month each summer. A canopy covering the stage and the audience ensures that the British summer doesn't ruin things (and it had a damn good go in 2002).

Hampton Court Palace Festival

Hampton Court, East Molesey, Surrey (Ticketmaster 7344 4444/www.hamptoncourtfestival.com). Hampton Court rail/riverboat from Westminster or Richmond to Hampton Court Pier (Apr-Oct). **Date** June 2003. **Tickets** £15-£85. **Credit** AmEx, MC, V.

School's in

Those music students who aren't touting their talents at City churches (*see p304*) are usually preparing to give a concert at their own college. With four top-notch music colleges in town, there's plenty of choice. The **Royal Academy of Music** (Marylebone Road, Marylebone, NW1, 7873 7300/www.ram.ac.uk), the **Royal College of Music** (Prince Consort Road, Knightsbridge, SW7, 7589 3643/www.rcm.ac.uk), **Trinity College of Music** (*pictured*; King Charles Court, Old Royal Naval College, Greenwich, SE10, 8305 4444/www.tcm.ac.uk) and the **Guildhall School of Music & Drama** (Silk Street, the City, EC2, 7628 2571/www.gsmd.ac.uk) all run programmes of regular concerts and recitals, some in the evenings but many during the day.

More of a social occasion than a musical event, the Hampton Court Palace Festival offers an assortment of unchallenging classics for the picnicking hordes (the event's even sponsored by a supermarket).

City of London Festival

Venues in & around the City (information 7377 0540/box office 7638 8891/www.colf.org). **Date** 23 June-10 July 2003. **Tickets** free-£40. **Credit** AmEx, MC, V.

A splendid annual event, this, and a near-perfect fusion of art and location. The City of London Festival utilises a number of venues around the City, from cathedrals to street corners, for its admirably eclectic and inclusive programme of music. Some events sell out.

BBC Sir Henry Wood Promenade Concerts

Royal Albert Hall, Kensington Gore, South Kensington, SW7 (information 7765 5575/box office 7589 8212/www.bbc.co.uk/proms). South Kensington tube/9, 10, 52 bus. **Date** 18 July-13 Sept 2003. **Tickets** £3-£35. **Credit** AmEx, MC, V. **Map** p397 D9.

Over a century old, the Proms remains the world's finest music festival, mixing old favourites with modern works, premières and the odd wild card (late-night jazz, poetry readings). Buy a festival programme from a bookshop and plan ahead: the choice is overwhelming. You can buy reserved seats in advance, but many prefer to continue the tradition that gave the festival its name: queuing up on the day and buying cheap tickets for the seatless 'promenade' area by the stage. Tickets for the Last Night, still dominated by a triumphalist and jingoistic display of flag-waving and singalongs, are impossible to get hold of, but – if you really must see it – it's beamed on to a big screen in Hyde Park for free.

Kenwood Lakeside Concerts

Kenwood House, Hampstead Lane, Highgate, NW3 (information 8233 7435/box office 7413 1443/www.picnicconcerts.com). Golders Green or East Finchley tube then courtesy bus on concert nights. **Date** July, Aug 2003. **Tickets** £12.50-£30 (approx). **Credit** AmEx, MC, V.

A pleasant programme of tried-and-tested acts in the expansive grounds of Kenwood House, from Mozart standards to – in 2002 – an Abba tribute band and an evening of music from Bond films. It's best enjoyed on a fireworks night.

Marble Hill Concerts

Marble Hill Park, Richmond Road, Twickenham, Middx (information 8233 7435/box office 7413 1443/www.picnicconcerts.com). St Margaret's rail or Richmond tube/rail then 33, 90, 290, H22, R70 bus. **Date** July, Aug 2003. **Tickets** £10-£20 (approx). **Credit** AmEx, MC, V.

Like Kenwood, the key's in the URL: picnic first, concert second. Still, if you're expecting nothing more than unthreatening classics competently played in a lovely setting, you'll go away fulfilled.

Resources

British Music Information Centre

10 Stratford Place, Marylebone, W1 (7499 8567/www.bmic.co.uk). Bond Street tube. **Open** noon-5pm Mon-Fri. **Concerts** 7.30pm Tue, Thur (except Aug). **Tickets** £3-£7. **No credit cards. Map** p398 H6.

A mine of information on British music: books, scores and recordings (audio and video). The BMIC also runs twice-weekly concerts and recitals of modern British music at nearby St Cyprian's Church (on Glentworth Street, W1).

National Sound Archive

British Library, 96 Euston Road, NW1 (7412 7440/ www.bl.uk/collections/sound-archive). Euston or King's Cross tube/rail. **Open** 10am-8pm Mon; 9.30am-8pm Tue-Thur; 9.30am-5pm Fri, Sat. **Map** p399 K3.

From music to drama and from vox pops to wildlife sounds, it's all here, along with a wide range of books, magazines and journals covering every aspect of recorded sound. Listening is free, though membership of the British Library is required and it's advisable to call ahead with your request.

Rock, Dance, Roots & Jazz

You want it? We got it. London has long had one of the richest live music scenes in the world, and that state of affairs shows no sign of letting up. No matter that great homegrown bands and musicians have been thin on the ground of late: every act from home and abroad who wants to make it big has to pass through, and every act who's already made it big returns to consolidate their position and cash in on their fame.

Check *Time Out* weekly and you'll see the overwhelming volume and variety of live shows every night. January and July/August are both fairly quiet, but otherwise, it's no exaggeration to suggest you could find a worthwhile gig here five nights out of every week. And that's before factoring in nightclubs, for which *see p317*.

TICKETS AND INFORMATION

Like the quality of Oasis albums, prices for gigs in London vary from the sublime (you'll *Definitely Maybe* want to check out free shows at the South Bank and the in-store PAs at shops such as Rough Trade and Virgin) to the ridiculous (if you want to *Be Here Now* for gigs from the likes of Elton John, you'll pay upwards of £50). As a rule of thumb, though, shows at the 1,200-12,000-capacity spots listed below under major venues go for £10-£25, gigs at the 300-1,000-capacity club venues are usually

£5-£12, while pub venues rarely charge more than a fiver. Most shows at roots venues are under £10; jazz gigs vary from £2 up to £20.

Most pub venues – the Water Rats and Barfly are the main exceptions – don't sell advance tickets, and for most roots and some jazz venues (such as the Bull's Head and the Vortex) you can just pay on the night. For everywhere else, buy tickets in advance if possible. Not all shows sell out by any means, but it's tough to predict which ones will. And whether heavy metal or trad jazz, headline acts usually come on around 9-10pm.

Always try to buy tickets direct from the venue if you want to avoid paying a raft of often crippling booking fees and handling charges. If the venue has sold out, try an agency: the big three are **Ticketmaster** (7344 4444/www.ticketmaster.co.uk), **Stargreen** (7734 8932/www.stargreen.co.uk) and **Ticketweb** (7771 2000/www.ticketweb.co.uk). Avoid at all costs buying from the scamming chancers with violent tendencies – otherwise known as ticket touts – who hang around outside bigger venues: you'll pay a fortune for what may be a forged ticket.

Rock venues

Major venues

In addition to the venues listed below, the **South Bank Centre** (*see p304*), the **Royal Albert Hall** and the **Barbican Centre** (for both, *see p303*) all stage major gigs.

Astoria

157 Charing Cross Road, Soho, WC2 (information 8963 0940/box office 7344 0044/www.meanfiddler. com). Tottenham Court Road tube. **Box office** *In person* 11am-7pm Mon-Sat. *By phone* 24hrs daily. **Tickets** £8-£19.50. **Credit** AmEx, MC, V. **Map** p399 K6.

The Mean Fiddler has taken on this careworn venue, but it hasn't yet done much to improve it: the vile stairwell mural remains, as does the murky sound. Sightlines are good, but as punters at a recent Counting Crows show can testify, when it's busy, it can get very uncomfortable. As of late 2002, it was in a battle with Westminster council to retain its licence.

Blackheath Halls

23 Lee Road, Blackheath, SE3 (8463 0100/ www.blackheathhalls.com). Blackheath rail/54, 89, 108, 202, N53 bus. **Box office** 10am-7pm Mon-Sat; 11am-5pm Sun. **Tickets** £2.50-£18.50. **Credit** AmEx, MC, V.

South-east London's premier music venue presents a variety of different styles, from classical to rock. Though not as easily accessible as other major venues, it still attracts top performers, and it's worth the trek for the right occasion.

Brixton Academy

*211 Stockwell Road, Brixton, SW9 (information
7771 3000/box office 0870 771 2000/www.brixton-
academy.co.uk). Brixton tube/rail.* **Box office** *By
phone* 24hrs daily. **Tickets** £10-£20. **Credit** MC, V.
One of London's biggest venues (it holds upwards
of 4,000) is also one of its best. A pronounced slope
in the stalls means everyone can see the stage, and
the sound is usually surprisingly good for a venue
this size. Unless the hall's not that full, that is, in
which case there's a ruinous reverb.

Earl's Court Exhibition Centre

*Warwick Road, Earl's Court, SW5 (7385 1200/box
office 7370 8078/www.eco.co.uk). Earl's Court tube.*
Box office *By phone* 24hrs daily. **Tickets** £17-£50.
Credit AmEx, MC, V. **Map** p396 A11.
As a rule of thumb, when a band's gotten big enough
to play this 12,000-capacity hangar, they're probably not worth seeing anyway. Bruce Springsteen
and the E Street Band made it work for them a couple of years ago; few others ever have.

Electric Ballroom

*Camden High Street, Camden, NW1 (7485 9006/
www.electricballroom.co.uk). Camden Town tube.*
Box office 9am-5pm Mon-Thur; 10.30am-1am
Fri, Sat; 10.30am-5pm Sun. **Tickets** £7-£10.
No credit cards.
This slightly scuzzy but surprisingly large hall
is right next door to Camden tube, and offers a mix
of live shows and club nights each week. It's currently under threat from London Underground,
which wants to expand the tube station; sad to say,
few will really miss it if it eventually vanishes.

Forum

*9-17 Highgate Road, Kentish Town, NW5
(information 7284 1001/box office 7344 0044/
www.meanfiddler.com). Kentish Town tube/rail/N2
bus.* **Box office** *In person* from the Astoria or the
Jazz Café. *By phone* 24hrs daily. **Tickets** £5-£15.
Credit AmEx, MC, V (phone bookings only).
In the last half-decade or so, the Forum's been
usurped by the Shepherd's Bush Empire (*see p310*)
as London's top mid-sized venue. It's something
of a pity: despite its grimy location, it's arguably
the best of the Fiddler halls. Grand yet intimate,
with decent sound and above-par views, it's an
altogether splendid place to catch your favourite
guitar-toting stars-in-the-making.

Hammersmith Apollo

*Queen Caroline Street, Hammersmith, W6 (0870
400 0700). Hammersmith tube.* **Box office** *In
person* 10am-6pm Mon-Sat. *By phone* 24hrs daily.
Tickets £10-£40. **Credit** AmEx, MC, V.
The one-time Hammersmith Odeon seems to now
be through its identity crisis, and is back to hosting
big name mainstream acts – James Taylor, Paul
Simon, Dolly Parton – alongside the occasional theatrical spectacular and comedy stage show. It's a
little shabby, sure, but its name is usually prefixed
with the phrase 'much-loved' for good reason.

London Arena

*Limeharbour, Isle of Dogs, E14 (7538 1212/
www.londonarena.co.uk). Crossharbour & London
Arena DLR.* **Box office** *In person* 9am-6pm
Mon-Fri; 10am-2pm Sat. *By phone* 24hrs daily.
Tickets £5-£75. **Credit** AmEx, MC, V.

For sound, sightlines and atmosphere, *see p308* Earl's Court Exhibition Centre. Yup, it's another vast venue, wedged in the middle of nowhere and boasting few redeeming features save the doors marked 'exit'.

Marquee

16 Parkfield Street, Islington, N1 (information 7288 4400/box office 0870 120 2221/ www.themarquee.com). **Box office** noon-5pm Mon-Fri. **Tickets** £4-£18. **Credit** (phone bookings only) MC, V.

Re-established in late 2002, after nigh on a decade away, by one-time Eurythmic Dave Stewart and flamboyant London restaurateur Mark Fuller, the latest incarnation of the Marquee – gleaming metal everywhere, buzzy restaurant downstairs, bouncers galore – is a long way from its edgy 1960s Soho roots and is perhaps the least rock 'n' roll rock venue in London. No matter: what it may lack in atmosphere (it's in a shopping mall, for Chrissakes), it makes up for with fine views and impeccable sound.

Now playing **Rock & roots**

The British music industry having an attention span rivalled in its brevity only by the average goldfish, London's rock scene changes rapidly. Today's Next Big Things are soon either Tomorrow's Stars or Yesterday's News. The mind-boggling turnover of indie acts at Camden pub venues is only rivalled by the indecent haste with which bands are thrust spotlight-wards and then shunted out of it by a music press hungry to stay ahead of the game.

However, a few bands live outside short-termist strategies, and can be relied upon to deliver a smattering of smashing shows year-round. Gigs by cult London act **Menlo Park** (named, brilliantly, for the town in which Edison first recorded sound) are usually memorable: fans still talk in hushed tones about one especially theatrical show at Shoreditch Town Hall a while back. **Simian** are less worthwhile musically, but make up for it with some try-hard live shows, often in unique locations.

Husband-and-wife duo **The Arlenes** (*pictured*) play it straighter, but draw good crowds with their sweet-natured, winsome take on country music; Big Steve also co-runs a splendidly convivial country music club at the Golden Lion pub (4pm Sundays, Royal College Street, NW1; www.comedownandmeetthefolks.co.uk). In many ways, they're a north London counterpoint to south London's **Hank Dogs**, another country-tinged act who host their own acoustic club: Easycome, Wednesdays at Peckham's Ivy House (40 Stuart Road, SE15; 7732 0222/www.the-ivyhouse.co.uk).

Indie acts are ten a penny, but a few names sporadically surface in the listings (not just around record release dates, when any act worth their salt will be constantly playing live). Among them are veteran garage rock nutjob Billy Childish with his band the **Buff Medways**, lovelorn popsters the **Free French**, po-faced punkers **Sona Fariq**, no-tech electronica act **Max Tundra** and the brilliantly intense **Byrne**.

Arts Café at Toynbee Hall. *See p311*.

Ocean

270 Mare Street, Hackney, E8 (switchboard 8986 5336/box office 8533 0111/24hr bookings 7314 2800/www.ocean.org.uk). Hackney Central or Hackney Downs rail. **Box office** *In person 11am-7pm daily; later on performance nights. By phone 24hrs daily.* **Tickets** *£3-£30.* **Credit** MC, V.

This dazzling new complex out in Hackney hasn't really found its feet yet. The basic infrastructure is superb: all three halls here boast great sightlines and terrific sound quality. But the decor is a little sterile (when it's not busy, it resembles nothing if not a provincial leisure centre) and the programming is a messy ragbag of dance shows, rock gigs, jazz events and other oddities. Give it time.

Shepherd's Bush Empire

Shepherd's Bush Green, Shepherd's Bush, W12 (7771 2000/www.shepherds-bush-empire.co.uk). Shepherd's Bush tube. **Box office** *In person noon-5pm Mon-Fri. By phone 24hrs daily.* **Tickets** *£5-£25.* **Credit** MC, V.

In a nutshell, this is London's top mid-sized venue. The sound here is usually great (unless you're in the low-ceilinged alcove behind the stalls bar, where it's dreadfully muffled), the atmosphere is cosy but not cramped, and the staff are among London's friendliest. For the best views, get tickets for one of the (non-smoking) balconies: sightlines from the all-standing stalls are poor.

Union Chapel

Compton Terrace, Islington, N1 (7226 1686/box office 0870 120 1349/www.unionchapel.org.uk). Highbury & Islington tube/rail/N19, N65, N92 bus. **Open** *Gigs 7.30pm, nights vary.* **Tickets** *£3-£25.* **Credit** MC, V.

This impressive Islington construction leads an intriguing double existence as both church and gig venue. It's a beautiful room, certainly, though you're best off sticking to small and/or acoustic ensembles: the pronounced and rather muddy echo is a real distraction when there's a full band making the noise, though sitting in the stalls under the balconies to the left and right of the stage can work as a surprisingly effective reverb-ridder.

Wembley Arena

Empire Way, Wembley, Middx (8902 0902/www. wembleyticket.com). Wembley Park tube/Wembley Central tube/rail. **Box office** *By phone 24hrs daily.* **Tickets** *£5-£100.* **Credit** AmEx, MC, V.

Competition is stiff, but this might be the worst music venue in London. Sure, very few halls this size (it holds over 10,000) are appealing places, but this joyless aircraft hangar – pricey concessions, horrible sound, zero atmosphere – really is the pits.

Club venues

Among other smaller venues that host regular live shows are the **Bush Hall** (*see p303*), **Cargo** (*see p318*) and the **ICA** (The Mall, SW1; 7930 3647/www.ica.org.uk).

Borderline

Orange Yard, Manette Street, Soho, W1 (7734 2095/www.borderline.co.uk). Tottenham Court Road tube. **Box office** *10am-6pm Mon-Sat.* **Open** *Gigs 8-11pm Mon-Sat. Club 11.30pm-3am Mon-Sat.* **Admission** *Gigs £6-£16. Club £3-£8.* **Credit** MC, V. **Map** p399 K6.

For our money, London's best music venue. The sound is immaculate, the atmosphere is homey, and the music programme is an inviting mix of young British indie acts (albeit usually very mediocre ones), wizened singer-songwriters, terrific Americana and alt-country outfits, and the occasional wild card (Mexican party band Los de Abajo, for example).

Dingwalls

Middle Yard, Camden Lock, Chalk Farm Road, Camden, NW1 (information 7267 1577/box office 7428 5929/Ticketmaster 7344 4040/www.dingwalls. com). Camden Town or Chalk Farm tube. **Box office** *In person tickets from Rhythm Records, 281 Camden High Street, NW1 (7267 0123). By phone 24hrs daily.* **Open** *Gigs 7.30pm-midnight, nights vary.* **Admission** *£5-£15.* **Credit** AmEx, MC, V.

Dingwalls is primarily a comedy venue (for the twice-weekly Jongleurs nights, *see p278*), but it still hosts gigs regularly enough to merit inclusion here. However, it's hardly suited to it: the multi-level layout is fine for sit-down comedy shows, but somewhat messy for all-standing music events.

Garage

*20-22 Highbury Corner, Highbury, N5 (information
8963 0940/box office 7344 0044/www.meanfiddler.
com). Highbury & Islington tube/rail.* **Box office** *In
person* 4-11pm show nights. *By phone* 24hrs daily.
Open *Gigs* 8pm-midnight Mon-Thur, some Suns;
8pm-3am Fri, Sat. **Admission** £4-£10. **Credit** MC, V.
The Garage is home to indie-leaning acts too big to
play the Barfly (*see below*) but not famous enough
to fill the Astoria (*see p307*). And the sooner they go
one way or the other, the better. The sound at this
low-ceilinged venue is usually below average, and
it can get unbearably hot if it's more than about
two-thirds full. Smaller sister venue Upstairs at the
Garage (guess where it is) is a little nicer.

100 Club

*100 Oxford Street, Fitzrovia, W1 (7636 0933/
www.the100club.co.uk). Oxford Circus or Tottenham
Court Road tube.* **Open** *Gigs* 7.30pm-midnight Mon-
Thur; noon-3pm, 8pm-1am Fri; 7.30pm-1am Sat; 7.30-
11pm Sun. **Admission** £6-£12. **Credit** AmEx, JCB,
MC, V. **Map** p399 K6.
Established 60 years ago, the 100 Club was once frequented by Glenn Miller, before morphing into a
leading trad-jazz joint ('50s), a blues and R&B hangout ('60s) and the home of punk ('70s). These days, a
mix of spunky indie and old-school jazz can be heard
in the awkward-shaped room (though, happily, not
at the same time). A London treasure, truly.

Alt-country and anti-folk
at the **Windmill**.
See p312.

Mean Fiddler

*165 Charing Cross Road, Soho, WC2 (information
7434 9592/box office 7344 0044/www.meanfiddler
com). Tottenham Court Road tube.* **Box office**
In person 10am-6pm Mon-Sat. *By phone* 24hrs
daily. **Tickets** £8-£18.50. **Credit** AmEx, MC, V.
Map p399 K6.
A sadly underused little brother to the adjacent
Astoria, the Fiddler stages precious few gigs. A pity,
as both sound and sightlines are better than they are
next door. If the band's rubbish, head up to the
glassed-off bar to the left of the balcony.

Spitz

*Old Spitalfields Market, 109 Commercial Street,
Spitalfields, E1 (7392 9032/www.spitz.co.uk).
Aldgate East tube/Liverpool Street tube/rail.*
Open 11am-11pm Mon-Sat; 11am-10.30pm Sun.
Admission £4-£10. **Credit** MC, V. **Map** p403 R5.
On the edge of Spitalfields and opposite the imposing Christ Church (*see p155*), the Spitz is all things
to all people: gallery, restaurant, café and, upstairs,
live music venue. Expect anything from experimental electronica to gutsy country and most things
in between.

Underworld

*174 Camden High Street, Camden, NW1 (7482
1932). Camden Town tube.* **Open** *Gigs* 7pm-3am,
nights vary. **Admission** £3-£12. **No credit cards.**
A maddening underground space, a maze of corridors and pillars and bars and, eventually, a decent
live room. Expect indie and metal.

University of London Union (ULU)

*Malet Street, Bloomsbury, WC1 (7664 2000/
www.ulu.lon.ac.uk). Euston Square or Goodge Street
tube.* **Open** *Gigs* 8-11pm, nights vary. **Admission**
£5-£10. **Credit** MC, V. **Map** p399 K4.
… And you can pretty much expect the same thing
here: British students are not known for their sophisticated tastes in music, and the acts who fill this
anonymous hall will invariably have been featured
heavily in the *NME* not long before their show.

Pub & bar venues

Arts Café at Toynbee Hall

*28 Commercial Street, Spitalfields, E1 (7247 5681).
Aldgate East tube.* **Open** 10am-9pm Mon-Wed; 10am-
11pm Thur; 10am-midnight Fri, Sat. *Gigs* 8.30pm,
nights vary. **Admission** £3-£5. **Credit** MC, V.
A nice spot, this, a fairly recent addition to the
London circuit. The music is generally good – expect
acts from the more non-conformist end of the alternative rock field – and the pizza isn't bad either.

Barfly

*49 Chalk Farm Road, Camden, NW1 (7691 4244/
box office 0870 907 0999/www.barflyclub.com).
Chalk Farm tube.* **Open** 7.30-11pm Mon-Thur;
7.30pm-2am Fri, Sat; 7.30-10.30pm Sun. *Gigs* 8.15pm
daily. **Admission** £4-£6. **Credit** *Ticketline only*
AmEx, MC, V.

Arts & Entertainment

The Barfly club sure knows how to churn 'em out: around 20 indie acts – three a night – play here weekly. A few go on to bigger things, the rest vanish. Your best bets for catching one of the former are probably the regular nights hosted by the *NME* (On) and radio station Xfm (Exposure), both of which deal in alt-rock, and Club Kerrang!, a metal showcase.

Betsey Trotwood

56 Farringdon Road, Clerkenwell, EC1 (7253 4285). Farringdon tube. **Open** 8am-11pm Mon-Fri; 11am-11pm Sat; noon-10.30pm Sun. *Gigs* 9pm Mon-Thur. **Admission** £4-£5. **Credit** MC, V.

The lovely chaps from the Water Rats (*see p312*) promote various nights of indie-kid bliss in the 70-capacity upstairs room at this boozer, an ideal place for checking out lo-fi underground celebs (and staff at the *Guardian* newspaper, for whom the pub is a local).

Boston Arms

178 Junction Road, Tufnell Park, N19 (7272 8153/www.dirtywaterclub.com). Tufnell Park tube. **Open** 11am-midnight Mon-Wed, Sun; 11am-1am Thur-Sat. *Gigs* 10pm, day varies. *Club* 9pm every other Fri. **Admission** £4-£6. **No credit cards.**

This briefly became the trendiest venue in Britain when the White Stripes rolled into town in 2001. On alternate Fridays, the Dirty Water club turns it into a swinging-'60s retro-bash: expect DJs playing R&B, classic beats and mod grooves, plus bands of the trashy garage punk variety.

Bull & Gate

389 Kentish Town Road, Kentish Town, NW5 (7485 5358). Kentish Town tube/rail. **Open** 11am-11pm Mon-Sat; noon-10.30pm Sun. *Gigs* 8.30pm daily. **Admission** £3-£5. **No credit cards.**

Recent renovations have smartened up what used to be a real toilet of a venue, but the bills are the same as ever: guitar-toting hopefuls in search of a big break. In the pantheon of pub venues, this one sits below Barfly but above the Dublin Castle.

Dublin Castle

94 Parkway, Camden, NW1 (7485 1773/ www.dublincastle.co.uk). Camden Town tube. **Open** noon-1am Mon-Sat; noon-midnight Sun. *Gigs* 8.45pm Mon-Sat; 8.30pm Sun. **Admission** £4.50-£6. **No credit cards.**

Despite the music-packed back room, the Castle is still better used as a pub than as a music venue. Bands are of the struggling indie variety; you won't come here unless you know someone in the band.

Hope & Anchor

207 Upper Street, Islington, N1 (7354 1312). Highbury & Islington tube/rail. **Open** noon-1am daily. *Gigs* 8pm daily. **Admission** £4-£6. **No credit cards. Map** p402 O1.

This minuscule cellar was a pub rock and punk legend a quarter-century ago. These days, the pub upstairs is considerably smarter and the acts are less noteworthy. Again, it's mostly indie up-and-comers.

Notting Hill Arts Club

21 Notting Hill Gate, Notting Hill, W11 (7460 4459/www.nottinghillartsclub.com). Notting Hill Gate tube. **Open** 6pm-1am Mon-Wed; 6pm-2am Thur, Fri; 4pm-2am Sat; 4pm-midnight Sun. *Gigs* times vary. **Admission** £3-£6. **Credit** MC, V.

This tidy little venue can get wildly busy – it's in Notting Hill, so expect the hipsters to show up in droves if the style mags tell them they should – but the programme of clubs and gigs interesting and eclectic enough to rise above its neighbourhood. Saturday afternoons see Rough Trade's Rota sessions, with a hand-picked assortment of indie acts kicking off at 5pm.

Public Life

82A Commercial Street, Spitalfields, E1 (7375 2425/www.publiclife.org). Liverpool Street tube/rail. **Open** noon-midnight Tue-Sun. *Gigs* 8pm daily. **Admission** free-£2 (voluntary donation). **Credit** MC, V.

This swish basement – a converted public toilet on a grimy East End thoroughfare – is the kookiest venue in town. Doubling as a bar/café/exhibition space, it offers various nights of off-kilter acts (lo-fi indie, electronica and dance).

Verge

147 Kentish Town Road, Camden, NW1 (7284 1178/www.theverge.co.uk). Camden Town or Kentish Town tube. **Open** 8pm-midnight Mon-Wed, Sun; 8pm-2am Thur-Sat. **Admission** £3-£15. **Credit** AmEx, MC, V.

A pleasant boozer, with a late licence at weekends and a roster of live music that's perhaps just a little above average. Expect guitary indie a cut above that found further towards the centre of Camden, and assorted rootsier acts.

Water Rats

328 Gray's Inn Road, Bloomsbury, WC1 (7837 7269/www.plumpromotions.co.uk). King's Cross tube/rail. **Open** *Gigs* 8.30-11pm Mon-Sat. **Admission** £4-£6. **No credit cards. Map** p399 M3.

Bob Dylan played his first UK gig in the quietly impressive back room of this King's Cross boozer four decades ago. These days, the line-ups tend to be a little noisier: alt-rock and metal types, sometimes on the edge of big things or secretly showcasing new material.

Windmill

22 Blenheim Gardens, Brixton, SW2 (8671 0700). Brixton tube. **Open** *Gigs* 7-11pm Mon-Sat; 7-10.30pm Sun. **Admission** free-£3. **No credit cards.**

A typically shambling Brixton boozer with an atypically decent selection of live music. There are free barbecues on Sunday afternoons in summer, indie acts from time to time, and – best of all – journalist Tim Perry's country-infused Twisted AM Lounge, held here most Sundays.

Dance the night away at **Cecil Sharp House**.

Roots venues

Don't miss Mwalimu Express, a weekly world music event at the **Bread & Roses** (*see p228*).

Africa Centre

38 King Street, Covent Garden, WC2 (7836 1973/ www.africacentre.org.uk). Covent Garden tube.
Open *Gigs* 11.30pm Fri. *Club* 9.30pm-3am Fri, Sat. **Admission** £6-£10. **Credit** MC, V. **Map** p401 L7.
Situated in the heart of Covent Garden, the Africa Centre offers top African bands most Friday nights, plus occasional gigs on other nights.

Cecil Sharp House

2 Regent's Park Road, Camden, NW1 (7485 2206/www.efdss.org). Camden Town tube.
Open *Gigs* 7pm, nights vary. **Admission** £3-£8. **No credit cards**.
This is the centre of the English Folk Dance and Song Society. The folk club on Tuesdays is fun and totally untouched by the modern era, while there are regular cajun nights and all sorts of classes (from flamenco to clog-dancing) to be sampled.

Hammersmith & Fulham Irish Centre

Blacks Road, Hammersmith, W6 (8563 8232/ www.lbhf.gov.uk/irishcentre). Hammersmith tube.
Open *Gigs* nights vary. **Admission** £4-£10. **No credit cards**.
You'll find all kinds of Irish music events, from free ceilidhs to biggish-name Irish acts such as the Popes, on offer at this small, friendly craic dealer.

12 Bar Club

22-3 Denmark Place, St Giles's, WC2 (information 7916 6989/box office 7209 2248/www.12barclub. com). Tottenham Court Road tube. **Open** 8pm-1am daily. *Gigs* 8.30pm daily. **Admission** £5-£10. **Credit** MC, V. **Map** p399 K6.
A hidden gem, literally: this cupboard is tucked away around the back of Denmark Street. It's tiny: you can't get more than three people on stage without it being a ridiculous crush. Still, the line-ups, often singer-songwriters, are usually worthwhile, the atmosphere's pleasant, and a recent expansion has opened the bar area up nicely.

Jazz venues

Bull's Head

373 Lonsdale Road, Barnes, SW13 (8876 5241/ www.thebullshead.com). Barnes Bridge rail.
Open 11am-11pm Mon-Sat; noon-10.30pm Sun. *Gigs* 8.30pm Mon-Sat; 2-4.30pm, 8-10.30pm Sun. **Admission** £3-£10. **Credit** AmEx, DC, MC, V.
This delightful riverside pub (and Thai bistro) is something of a jazz landmark, staging gigs by musicians from both here and the States. In true jazz tradition, it also has a particularly well-stocked bar: check out the selection of malt whiskies.

Jazz Café

5 Parkway, Camden, NW1 (information 7916 6060/ box office 7344 0044/www.jazzcafe.co.uk). Camden Town tube. **Open** 7pm-1am Mon-Thur; 7pm-2am Fri, Sat; 7pm-midnight Sun. *Gigs* 9pm daily. **Admission** £8-£20. **Credit** AmEx, MC, V.

The name doesn't the whole story: jazz is a small piece in the jigsaw of events here. It also takes in funk, hip hop, soul, R&B, singer-songwriters and more besides. Pray that the expense-accounters who pack the balcony don't talk through the entire set.

Pizza Express Jazz Club

10 Dean Street, Soho, W1 (restaurant 7437 9595/ Jazz Club 7439 8722/www.pizzaexpress.co.uk). Tottenham Court Road tube. **Open** *Restaurant 11.30am-midnight daily. Jazz Club 7.45pm-midnight daily. Gigs 9pm daily.* **Admission** £15-£20. **Credit** AmEx, DC, MC, V. **Map** p399 K6.

Now playing Jazz

Life is not exactly a picnic for a jazz musician in London. There's never been much money in the industry for all but the top players, but with so many musicians competing for gigs and attention, it's hard to get noticed and make a reasonable living. Of course, while it's no fun for the musician, it's terrific news for the casual jazz fan, overwhelmed by high-calibre musicians who play more or less nightly.

Of the singers who play regularly in London, **Christine Tobin** and newcomer **Niki King** are probably the pick of the female vocalists, with **Ian Shaw** – whose showy style may not appeal to purists – the best of an underwhelming collection of men. The scene's better served for saxophonists in particular: veteran **Stan Sulzmann**, former lawyer **Tim Whitehead**, the wilfully eccentric **Iain Ballamy** and the firebreathing **Mornington Lockett** all consistently impress.

London's two finest regular-gigging jazz pianists come from opposite ends of the age spectrum. **Stan Tracey**'s now 76 years old but is still thriving, touting his mannered, inventive music on the circuit regularly (often in the company of drummer son **Clark Tracey**). **Gareth Williams**, young enough to be his grandson, works regularly with singer **Claire Martin**, but is best observed in his own fearsome trio.

Completing our trip around the tip of the iceberg are a pair of guitar players. Scotsman **Jim Mullen** is from the old school, but that's no knock: his playing is still vital and feisty. As for south London's **Billy Jenkins**... well, there's no school on earth that would let him enlist, but his chaotic, satiric, fevered improvisations and garbled stage banter are invariably entertaining in the extreme.

The food takes second billing in the basement of this eaterie: this is all about the (non-challenging, largely contemporary) jazz. Audiences are, pleasingly, respectful: there's no talking through the sets here. Other Pizza Express branches offer live jazz, albeit more as background noise than anything else.

Pizza on the Park

11 Knightsbridge, Knightsbridge, SW1 (7235 5273). Hyde Park Corner tube. **Open** *8.30am-midnight Mon-Fri; 9.30am-midnight Sat, Sun. Gigs 9.15pm, 10.45pm daily.* **Admission** £10-£20. **Credit** AmEx, DC, MC, V. **Map** p400 G8.

Pizza on the Park used to be owned by the same company as Pizza Express, and takes a similar tack with the jazz programming in its basement: music here is pleasing and professional, if totally mainstream.

Ronnie Scott's

47 Frith Street, Soho, W1 (7439 0747/www. ronniescotts.co.uk). Leicester Square or Tottenham Court Road tube. **Open** *8.30pm-3am Mon-Sat. Gigs 9.30pm Mon-Sat.* **Admission** (non members) £15 Mon-Thur; £25 Fri, Sat. **Credit** AmEx, DC, MC, V. **Map** p399 K6.

Scott died in 1996 after running one of the world's most famous jazz clubs for almost four decades. It's still there, but it's struggled since his demise. The roster of acts, who play two sets a night for runs of at least a week, is not as interesting (or as jazzy) as it was, and the crowds are brasher and chattier than ever. Still, after hours, when the tourists have headed home and only the diehards remain, it's as atmospheric as it gets. Call ahead to book a table.

606 Club

90 Lots Road, Chelsea, SW10 (7352 5953/www. 606club.co.uk). Earl's Court or Fulham Broadway tube/11, 22 bus. **Open** *7.30pm-1.30am Mon-Wed; 8pm-1.30am Thur; 8pm-2am Fri, Sat; 8pm-midnight Sun. Gigs 8pm-1am Mon-Wed; 9.30pm-1.30am Thur; 10pm-2am Fri, Sat; 9.30pm-midnight Sun.* **Admission** *Music charge (non-members) £6 Mon-Thur; £8 Fri, Sat; £7 Sun.* **Credit** MC, V. **Map** p396 C13.

A restaurant, late-night club and popular musicians' hangout, this Chelsea joint has the laudable policy of booking British-based jazz musicians. There's no entry fee: the musicians are funded from a music charge that is added to your bill at the end of the night. Alcohol is only served with meals.

Vortex

139-41 Stoke Newington Church Street, Stoke Newington, N16 (7254 6516/www.palay.ndirect. co.uk/vortex.jazz). Stoke Newington rail/67, 73, 76, 106, 243 bus. **Open** *10am-5pm & 8pm-midnight Mon-Sun. Gigs 9pm daily.* **Admission** free-£10. **Credit** MC, V.

After a period of flux – a proposed move to the Ocean complex fell through and left the venue in all sorts of financial trouble – things have happily settled down at this splendid enterprise. Expect live jazz nightly, invariably from British musicians, in a matey and convivial atmosphere.

Arts & Entertainment

Bobby Wellins blows at the **606 Club**. *See p314.*

Terminus Place, London SW1
Telephone: 020 7834 4440
info@pachalondon.com
www.pachalondon.com

PACHA LONDON

Nightlife

Hey, Mister DJ, put a record on.

Londoners have always liked to be at the cutting edge. As the big name superclubs have waned over the last couple of years, there's been a fresh injection of new joints working on creative and inspiring ways to pull in the punters. In addition to the basic *DJ + sound system + lights = club* formula, many venues now feature live music, artworks and complex visuals. Clubbers may indeed be grateful: it keeps pressure on well-established venues that might be tempted to rest on their laurels.

This doesn't mean, though, that there's a dearth of tried-and-tested favourites: plenty of club nights keep on keeping on with their own particular favourites for their own particular fanbases. Breakbeat, hip hop, funk and drum 'n' bass may be the current flavour of the month, but those up for house, garage, techno or trance won't be disappointed. If it sounds too cool, there are plenty of relaxed retro nights around: the school uniform and cheesy disco fest that is SchoolDisco.com (check online for venues) is still massively popular.

The areas with the most concentrated nightlife scenes are Soho, Brixton and Shoreditch/Hoxton. Around these areas you can hardly move for clubs and DJ bars (*see p322*). It's also worth wandering north and west, though, where some gems await you amid the shadows. And bear in mind that some of the best nights, such as Soul Jazz's long-running 100% Dynamite, take place in venues that are not normally clubs.

In these reviews, we've highlighted some nights worth looking out for; for full details as to what's on when, check the weekly *Time Out* magazine. It's also worth picking up flyers in record shops, cafés, bars and on the street, looking in specialist club magazines, and listening out for radio ads. Nights quickly come and go, venues change and close, and new places are always springing up, so always check before trekking halfway across town.

Clubs

For gay-oriented clubbing, such as **Heaven** or **Popstarz**, *see p299*; for live venues that also run popular club nights, *see p307*.

Aquarium
256 Old Street, Hoxton, EC1 (7251 6136/ www.clubaquarium.co.uk). Old Street tube/rail. **Open** 10pm-3am Thur, Sun; 10pm-4am Fri; 10pm-5am Sat. **Admission** £10-£15. **Map** p403 R3.
This place is definitely worth a visit, if only for the novelty value of having a swimming pool in a nightclub. It ain't a bog-standard dipper, either: the large T-shaped Roman pool has a mirrored wall and a six-person jacuzzi with a window looking on to the dancefloor. The music is less refreshing: mainly house, garage and the requisite 'club classics'.

Bagley's Studios
King's Cross Freight Depot, off York Way, King's Cross, N1 (7278 2777/www.bagleys.net). King's Cross tube/rail. **Open** 10.30pm-6am Fri, Sat. **Admission** £10-£20. **Map** p399 L2.
The labyrinthine warren of rooms in this pioneering warehouse often throbs to the beat of monster drum 'n' bass, old skool and UK garage extravaganzas such as United Dance and Pure Silk, when hordes of teens and the (so) glam crew turn up to go large. Get your skates on at the irregular, retrotastic Rollerdisco (ring for details).

Bar Rumba
36 Shaftesbury Avenue, Soho, W1 (7287 2715/ www.barrumba.co.uk). Piccadilly Circus tube. **Open** 9pm-3am Mon, Wed; 6pm-3am Tue, Thur, Fri; 9pm-5am Sat; 8pm-2am Sun. **Admission** £3-£12. **Map** p401 K7.
Some of the best dancing in town is to be had in this long-established basement club. Gilles Peterson's long-running jazzy, funky Monday-nighter THIS! (That's How It Is) has a large and loyal following, Movement is a storming drum 'n' bass blowout, and there are excellent one-nighters all through the week.

The best Clubs

For the high life
Café de Paris. *See p318.*

For the low life
333. *See p321.*

For a bit of everything
Cargo. *See p318.*

For a religious experience
Mass. *See p319.*

For a dip
Aquarium. *See p317.*

Play your imaginary ukulele from 7pm nightly at Shoreditch's **Bridge & Tunnel**.

Bridge & Tunnel

*4 Calvert Avenue, Shoreditch, E2 (7729 6533/
www.bridgeandtunnel.co.uk). Liverpool Street or Old
Street tube/rail.* **Open** 7pm-midnight Mon-Thur, Sun;
7pm-2am Fri, Sat. **Admission** free-£3. **Map** p403 R4.
The futuristic industrial interior design of this place
could make it feel a little clinical were it not for the
excellent music, awesome sound system, (fairly)
unpretentious crowd and cosy dancefloor. Run by
the guys from Nuphonic, it's no surprise the music
(monthly residencies from Groove Armada, Ninja
Tunes and Gilles Peterson) is consistently brilliant.

Café de Paris

*3-4 Coventry Street, St James's, W1 (7734 7700/
www.cafedeparis.com). Leicester Square or Piccadilly
Circus tube.* **Open** 6pm-3am Wed, Thur; 6pm-4am
Fri, Sat. **Admission** free-£15. **Map** p401 K7.
Both top and tragic nights have taken place over the
years in this art deco ballroom, a popular haunt for
dressy punters. Twisted cabaret night Merkin Does
Vegas, with Pam Hogg and Boy George DJ, is worth
a peek; Saturday nights are more conventional.

Camden Palace

*1A Camden High Street, Camden, NW1 (09062
100200/www.camdenpalace.com). Camden Town or
Mornington Crescent tube.* **Open** 10pm-2.30am Tue;
10pm-6am Fri, Sat. **Admission** £3-£25.
This former music hall was transformed into a massive, multi-level extravaganza in the early '80s. The
tiered bars and plush seating are looking a little
weary these days, but indie-rock night Feet First on
Tuesdays and Friday's trance, tribal house and
garage gig Peach show there's life in the old dog yet.

Cargo

*83 Rivington Street, Shoreditch, EC2 (7739 3440/
www.cargo-london.com). Old Street tube/rail.*
Open noon-1am Mon-Thur; noon-3am Fri; 6pm-
3am Sat; noon-midnight Sun. **Admission** free-£8.
Map p403 R4.

Set in the heart of super-cool Shoreditch, Cargo is a
stylish urban-industrial under-the-arches kind of
place, serving up good food, decent drink and a
whole host of fresh and frequently innovative music.
A mixture of DJ sets and live bands mean variety's
the name of the game. Be prepared for a hefty queue
if there are big names on the bill, but it'll almost certainly be worth it.

Colosseum

*1 Nine Elms Lane, Nine Elms, SW8 (7627 1283/
www.clubcolosseum.com). Vauxhall tube/rail.*
Open 10pm-noon Mon, Sat, Sun; 10pm-5am Fri.
Admission £8-£10.
Looking good after its refurb last year, Colosseum
boasts a new chill-out room and a riverside bar with
great views over the Thames. But the facelift hasn't
turned the place soft: Traffic is a pounding drum 'n'
bass night, there's a huge new UK hip hop night, and
you can get out your fetish gear, drag duds and body
art for the regular Torture Garden nights.

The Cross

*Arches, 27-31 King's Cross Goods Yard,
off York Way, King's Cross, N1 (7837 0828/
www.the-cross.co.uk). King's Cross tube/rail.* **Open**
11pm-5am Fri; 10pm-6am Sat; 11pm-5am every
other Sun. **Admission** £12-£15. **Map** p399 L2.
Another hip brick-and-arches venue, this one has a
garden area – all lush plants and comfy sofas – that
becomes another dancefloor in summer. Well known
for glam house nights such as Renaissance and
Serious, the Cross can also get funky. The friendly,
sussed crowd whip up a great atmosphere: just get
there early to avoid queuing for hours.

The End

*18 West Central Street, St Giles's, WC1 (7419 9199/
www.the-end.co.uk). Holborn or Tottenham Court
Road tube.* **Open** 10pm-3am Mon, Wed; 10pm-4am
Thur; 10pm-5am Fri; 10pm-7am Sat; phone for
details Sun. **Admission** £4-£15. **Map** p399 L6.

This place is fly right across the board: the minimalist design, the quality sound system, the monthly rotation of funky techno, drum 'n' bass, garage and deep house parties... hell, even the toilets rock. Crowds of eager clubbers show their appreciation at Darren Emerson's Underwater or Trash's glam, electronica, punk, pop and disco mixmash on Mondays.

Fabric

77A Charterhouse Street, Farringdon, EC1 (7336 8898/advance tickets for Fri 7344 4444/ www.fabriclondon.com). Farringdon tube/rail. **Open** 9.30pm-5am Fri; 10pm-7am Sat. **Admission** £12-£15. **Map** p402 O5.
Once a meat cellar, these days Fabric is one of London's biggest clubs, with a diverse selection of music and a cool but unpretentious crowd. The music policy is eclectic, revolving around underground DJ talent, live acts and inspiring new beats (all cranked through the scary Bodysonic dancefloor). Still unsure? Check the massive queues...

Fridge

1 Town Hall Parade, Brixton Hill, Brixton, SW2 (7326 5100/www.fridge.co.uk). Brixton tube/rail. **Open** 10pm-6am Fri, Sat. **Admission** £8-£15.
For those who like their nights hard, uplifting and seamlessly flowing into morning, Brixton's biggest venue has been delivering the goods for years. Flocks of techno heads and dreadlocked ravers descend on this former theatre for Escape from Samsara and Logic, while Love Muscle remains one of London's most popular gay party nights.

Herbal

10-14 Kingsland Road, Shoreditch, E2 (7613 4462/www.herbaluk.com). Old Street tube/rail. **Open** 7.30pm-2am Mon; 8pm-2am Wed, Thur; 8pm-3am Fri, Sat; 9pm-2am Sun. **Admission** free-£5. **Map** p403 R3.
Sparse and industrial, this joint manages to maintain a warm and cosy vibe, although it does get dead sweaty. Bang in the middle of Coolsville, the punters are laid-back, friendly and up for fun. The music is usually funky and urban (the monthly Ninja Tunes night Red Alert is a scorcher), with a sprinkling of live gigs to showcase newcomers.

Madame Jo Jo's

8 Brewer Street, Soho, W1 (7734 3040/ www.madamejojos.com). Leicester Square or Piccadilly Circus tube. **Open** 10.30pm-3am Wed, Fri; 9.30pm-3am Thur; 10pm-3am Sat. **Admission** £5-£8. **Map** p401 K6.
This great venue is enhanced by a touch of Soho cabaret sleaze. There are some promising midweek funk and hip hop nights, but the big draw is Keb Darge's Deep Funk, where blindingly funky chickens move furiously to obscure '60s and '70s cuts.

Mass

The Brix, St Matthew's Church, Brixton Hill, Brixton, SW9 (7737 1016/www.massclub.com). Brixton tube/rail. **Open** 10pm-6am Fri, Sat. **Admission** £12-£20.
When the party goes off, it's far from holy at this three-room club high up in a converted church. The sound system is less than spectacular and the lack of air-conditioning means the hot, sticky air won't

Cargo. Scary. *See p318.*

Arts & Entertainment

smell of ros(ari)es, but Mass is a great space with cutting-edge monthly line-ups (including the award-winning drum 'n' bass and hip hop night Dekefex).

Ministry of Sound

103 Gaunt Street, Walworth, SE1 (7378 6528/ www.ministryofsound.com). Elephant & Castle tube/rail. **Open** 10.30pm-5am Fri; 11pm-8am Sat. **Admission** £12-£15. **Map** p404 O10.
For many clubbers, it's cooler to slag off the Ministry than actually go there, but London's best-known club still draws huge crowds of all-night dancers. Big name guest DJs from the US and UK spin house, garage and R&B anthems at this clubland giant.

93 Feet East

150 Brick Lane, Spitalfields, E2 (7247 3293/ www.93feeteast.co.uk). Aldgate East tube. **Open** 6-11pm Mon-Wed, Sun; 6pm-2am Thur-Sat. **Admission** £5-£10. **Map** p403 S5.
This large three-room venue has gained a solid reputation for its variety of discriminating nights and exciting music. No prizes for the sound system, but a stylish downstairs bar, kitschy upstairs bar and main dancefloor conspire to create winning nights (Mish Mash, the Bemerton Resort). In summer, the outdoor tables and terrace buzz to deep funky house.

Notting Hill Arts Club

21 Notting Hill Gate, Notting Hill, W11 (7460 4459/ www.nottinghillartsclub.com). Notting Hill Gate tube. **Open** 6pm-1am Mon-Wed; 6pm-2am Thur-Fri; 4pm-2am Sat; 4pm-midnight Sun. **Admission** free-£6. **Map** p394 A7.
A hangout for cool Westsiders, where artists, DJs and musicians swap ideas, and the music and visual arts here are all about cultural diversity and innovation. But just because they're thoughtful and arty doesn't mean they don't know how to party: Sunday's Lazy Dog has punters queuing round the block.

Pacha London

Terminus Place, Victoria, SW1 (7834 4440/ www.pachalondon.com). Victoria tube/rail. **Open** 10pm-6am Fri, Sat. **Admission** £15-£20. **Map** p400 H10.
This lavish outpost of the global club giant that has dominated Ibiza for years was made for lording it: chandeliers, oak panels and a stained-glass ceiling ensure a chic clubbing experience. Glammed-up clubbers dress in keeping with the sumptuous decor, shaking their beautiful booty to kickin' house beats.

Plastic People

147-9 Curtain Road, Shoreditch, EC2 (7739 6471/ www.plasticpeople.co.uk). Old Street tube/rail. **Open** 10pm-2am Mon-Thur; 10pm-3.30am Fri, Sat; 7pm-midnight Sun. **Admission** £3-£7. **Map** p403 R4.
Plastic People is a good place to come for after-hours drinks without breaking the bank, but that's not all this tiny downstairs club has to offer. Music ranges from percussive Afro-jazz and hip hop to Latin and deep house: just watch the little dancefloor get rammed with a chilled but funky crowd.

This is **The End**. *See p318.*

Propaganda

201 Wardour Street, Soho, W1 (7424 3820). Tottenham Court Road tube. **Open** call for details. **Admission** call for details. **Map** p399 K6.
This stylish club is the latest venue of hugely popular '70s party Carwash – dig out that glamorous, glitzy discowear (leaving the wigs at home) and get funked on a Saturday. Propaganda sings a few other tunes, too, including Candy Box on a Wednesday, a confection of indie classics, '60s soul, pop and rock with an enthusiastic Anglo and Euro following.

Rouge

144 Charing Cross Road, Soho, WC2 (7836 4324/ www.rouge-club.com). Tottenham Court Road tube. **Open** call for details. **Admission** call for details. **Map** p399 K6.
This ace four-room Soho venue is a baby on the West End, but could grow up to be a favourite son. Combining beautifully decorated boudoir bars with cool warehousey dance areas, the well-designed space is a treat for anyone despairing of the cheesefest around Leicester Square. The music is vocal-led house, the crowd appropriately glamorous.

Scala

275 Pentonville Road, King's Cross, N1 (7833 2022/www.scala-london.co.uk). King's Cross tube/rail. **Open** 7.30pm-midnight Mon-Thur (promotion nights only); 10pm-5am Fri, Sat. **Admission** £6-£14. **Map** p399 L3.

The Scala's main room might be cavernous, but this doesn't mean the atmosphere's hollow. The Scala pulls in a relaxed, (usually) trainer-friendly clientèle who rock out to a variety of beats: as well as Popstarz (*see p302*), there's monthly hip hop institution Scratch and UK garage stalwart Cookies and Cream.

Sound

Swiss Centre, Leicester Square, W1 (7287 1010/ www.soundlondon.com). Leicester Square or Piccadilly Circus tube. **Open** 5pm-4am Mon-Sat; 6pm-2am Sun. **Admission** free-£12. **Map** p401 K7.
Credit where it's due: Sound is at least trying to put on decent nights, despite its deeply uncool Leicester Square location. Trevor Nelson's bump 'n' grind R&B night (Fridays) is mighty popular with the laydeez, though Kerrang! Club's weekly goth-metal fest attracts a somewhat different crowd. However, '80s retro night Love Shack keeps the place in touch with its surroundings.

Subterania

12 Acklam Road (under the Westway), Ladbroke Grove, W10 (8960 4590/www.meanfiddler.com). Ladbroke Grove tube. **Open** 8pm-2am Mon-Sat. **Admission** £5-£8.
Humming on Wednesdays to the sounds of the reggae, ska and dub institution known as Rodigan's Reggae, this small, dark club has a great vibe. Weekends have a different flavour, with DJs spinning funky house, classic soul and R&B to dressier punters. Friday's Rotation and Saturday's Soulsonic fill up fast, so get there early.

333

333 Old Street, Hoxton, EC1 (7739 5949/ www.333mother.com). Old Street tube/rail. **Open** 10pm-3am 1st Thur of mth; 10pm-5am Fri, Sat; 10pm-4am Sun. **Admission** £5-£8. **Map** p403 Q4.
This three-storey club makes up for what it lacks in interior decoration with excellent music and friendly, lively punters (a whole lot of 'em, too: beware the queues). The basement usually bounces to drum 'n' bass and hip hop, while the main room heaves to funky soul and US garage. The top-floor bar, Mother (*see p226*), is plusher: a great hangout for yakkin' and boozin', it runs good nights of its own.

Turnmills

63B Clerkenwell Road, Clerkenwell, EC1 (7250 3409/www.turnmills.com). Farringdon tube/rail. **Open** 6.30pm-midnight Tue; 10.30pm-7.30am Fri; 10pm-5am Sat. **Admission** £5-£15. **Map** p402 N4.
Turnmills' nooks and crannies are a hedonist's playground. Offering pretty much the full musical spectrum, from hip hop and soul to salsa and house, it also attracts a varied and agreeable crowd. Anexo, its sister venue, opened next door in 2002.

Velvet Room

143 Charing Cross Road, Soho, WC2 (7734 4687/ www.velvetroom.co.uk). Tottenham Court Road tube. **Open** 10pm-3am Mon-Thur; 10pm-4am Fri, Sat; 7.30pm-midnight Sun. **Admission** £5-£10. **Map** p399 K6.

Clubbed to death

Remember the Last Days of Disco? Well, it's happening again. But this time, instead of Disco Sucks, it's more a case of Hang the DJ. Superclubs such as the Ministry of Sound may have attracted thousands of clubbers during the '90s, but the backlash has begun. Many landmark northern clubs are in steep decline, and in London the once-mighty Ministry is concentrating on dreary compilations amid rumours that it plans to sell off its club. Pacha, an Ibiza-style superclub that opened in 2001, has failed to set London on fire.

So what went wrong? Not long ago, clubbers were shelling out a fortune every weekend to hear their gods behind the decks – Paul Oakenfold, Judge Jules, Pete Tong – spinning their 12-inches. But gradually kids cottoned on to the fact that, with a couple of decks and a bit of practice in your bedroom, anyone could do it. The rampant egomania of the superstar DJs didn't help either, and nor did their complacency: one big name allegedly showed up at a gig with just three records in his bag.

The corporatisation of clubbing saw the superclubs descend into parody. DJs asked for laughable fees and clubs, in turn, charged extortionate covers. High-street shops became saturated with superclub compilations and ridiculous brand extensions. Ministry – the Starbucks of club culture – was the worst offender, with a range of merchandise that ranged from T-shirts to towels. Clubbing in these monstrous venues became about as cutting edge as clubbing at Asda.

Not that club culture is dead: far from it. In a backlash against corporate blandness, clubbers are flocking to smaller, more eclectic venues, where good DJs can be heard on the cheap in settings that are more intimate and less cheesy. The superclub looks set to be consigned to *I ♥ 1996* television specials, until the inevitable revival in 2020 when Christmas concerts at Wembley Arena starring the by-now pensionable Jeremy Healy and Roger Sanchez will pack in the office parties.

Arts & Entertainment

Fabric. *See p319.*

Plush becomes, er, velvety at this luxurious club. A good bet for a midweek night out in the West End, Wednesdays go off with top drum 'n' bass night Swerve, while other nights focus on deep house and techno. For a change, Forward on Sundays will assail you with phat beats, breaks, b-lines and fresh dub party flavas. Dress is stylish club clobber.

DJ bars

It's not a great surprise that DJ bars have been all the rage in recent years. They're generally free (or cheap) – to get into and offer a fine selection of DJs, yet they have an intimate, friendly atmosphere that draws both those wanting to dance and those keener on shooting the shit with pals. It's a winning formula, and funky new spots are sprouting rapidly.

Listed below are a selection of London's finest DJ bars; unless stated, admission is free. Plenty of other bars feature regular DJs, and some are listed in the Pubs & Bars chapter. Among the finest are the **Elbow Room** and the **Embassy** in Islington (for both, *see p225*), **Monkey Chews** in Camden (*see p226*), **Home** and **Sosho** in Shoreditch (*see p227*), Clapham's **Sand** (*see p228*) and **Tongue & Groove** in Brixton (*see p229*).

AKA

18 West Central Street, WC1 (7836 0110/ www.akalondon.com). Holborn or Tottenham Court Road tube. **Open** 6pm-3am daily. **Admission** £3 after 11pm Wed; £5 after 11pm Thur; £7 after 10pm Fri; £10 after 9pm Sat. **Map** p399 L6.

Joined at the hip – physically as well as musically – to the End next door (*see p318*), this popular hang-out attracts top international DJs, who entertain friendly punters as they chow down on good food, drink mouth-watering cocktails and merrily loosen up. The venue is incorporated into the End's club nights on Fridays and Saturdays; be prepared to queue at weekends.

Bug Bar

The Crypt, St Matthew's Church, Brixton Hill, Brixton, SW2 (7738 3366/www.bugbar.co.uk). Brixton tube/rail. **Open** 7pm-2am Wed; 8pm-2am Thur, Sun; 8pm-3am Fri, Sat. **Admission** £4-£5 Wed; £3 after 10pm Thur; £4 before 11pm, £6 after 11pm Fri, Sat; £3 after 10pm Sun.

It may be a converted crypt, but Bug Bar is always alive and kicking, all the more so since refurbishments were completed in May 2002. Live music, top-quality DJs and competitively priced drinks ensure the place maintains its kudos.

Cherry Jam

58 Porchester Road, Bayswater, W2 (7727 9950/www.cherryjam.net). Royal Oak tube. **Open** 6-11pm Tue; 10pm-2am Wed; 6pm-2am Thur-Sat; 6pm-midnight Sun. **Admission** £5-£7 after 8pm Mon-Fri; £6 7-10pm, £8 after 10pm Sat; £5 after 7pm Sun. **Map** p394 C5.

Part-owned by Notting Hill Arts Club (*see p312*) aficionados Alan Grant and Everything But the Girl's Ben Watt (who's often seen down here, if star-spotting's your thing), there's a rich calendar of exhibitions, live music and DJ nights to elevate and entertain the vibrant west London clientele in this atmospheric and intimate setting.

Dragon Bar

*5 Leonard Street, Shoreditch, EC2 (7490 7110) Old
Street tube/rail.* **Open** noon-11pm Mon-Thur; noon-
midnight Fri, Sat; 2-11pm Sun. **Map** p403 Q4.

Oozing urban cool, the bare-brick walls, candles,
worn sofas and tagged-out schoolyard outside make
this a cosy, hip and decidedly suit-free zone. As the
night wears on, hip hop, reggae and rare funk tunes
get the laid-back, arty skate-crowd busting mean
moves wherever they can find the space.

Form

*4-5 Greek Street, Soho, W1 (7434 3323).
Tottenham Court Road tube.* **Open** 5pm-3am Mon-
Sat; 5-10.30pm Sun. **Admission** £3 Fri; £7 Sat.
Map p399 K6.

Dark, retro and very funky, Form is a great place to
go for both quiet sofa chats and groovy dance sessions. Wednesday's hip hop nights are always worth a
look, while Thursdays mix up disco and house.

Fridge Bar

*1 Town Hall Parade, Brixton Hill, Brixton, SW2
(7326 5100/www.fridge.co.uk). Brixton tube/rail.*
Open 6pm-2am Mon-Thur; 6pm-4am Fri; 6-11am,
6pm-4am Sat; 6-11am, 6pm-2am Sun. **Admission**
£5-£8 Fri-Sun.

A chilled, spacious hangout with mellow global beats,
or a packed-out, feverish party going off: the Fridge
Bar does it how you like it. Although it hosts a chill-
down session (6-11am) on behalf of the club next door
(*see p319*), it makes the most of its dark basement
dancefloor to throw decent parties all by itself.

Ion

*161-5 Ladbroke Grove, Ladbroke Grove, W10
(8960 1702/www.meanfiddler.com). Ladbroke Grove
tube.* **Open** noon-midnight daily. **Admission** £5
after 9pm Fri, Sat; £5 after 7pm Sun.

Feeling lazy? Hop out of the tube and on to one of
the red and brown velvet sofas in this trendy lounge
bar. The music is varied and soulful, the vibe is west
London cool. Be prepared for a goldfish-in-bowl
sensation if you're self-conscious, though: there's a
whole lotta glass in front.

Market Place

*11 Market Place, Marylebone, W1 (7079 2020)
Oxford Circus tube.* **Open** 11am-midnight Mon-
Wed; 11am-1am Thur-Sat; noon-11pm Sun.
Admission £7 after 11pm Fri, Sat (redeemable
against food and drink). **Map** p398 J6.

Another new recruit, the wooden chalet-style basement of Market Place oozes a warmth and cosiness,
while the global cuisine and dynamic music line-ups
make it an essential stop-off. Just off Oxford Circus,
it tends to attract a post-work crowd in the week,
but weekends have more of a party spirit.

Medicine Bar

*181 Upper Street, Islington, N1 (7704 9536).
Highbury & Islington tube/rail.* **Open** 5pm-midnight
Mon-Thur; 5pm-2am Fri; noon-2am Sat; noon-
10.30pm Sun. **Map** p402 O1.

Stylish but comfortable, this funky and popular
Islington hangout fills with pre-clubbers as the after-
work drinkers fade away. With its newly added upper
floor, it's a great place to hear classic soul, disco and
funk. Membership may be required on busy nights.
Branch: 89 Great Eastern Street, Shoreditch, EC2
(7739 5173).

Redstar

*319 Camberwell Road, Camberwell, SE5 (7737
0831/www.redstarbar.co.uk). Oval tube then 36, 185
bus.* **Open** 5pm-2am Mon-Thur; 5pm-4am Fri, Sat;
5pm-midnight Sun. **Admission** £4 after 10pm Fri;
£6 after 10pm Sat.

With consistently great DJs, an easygoing loungey
ambience, decent prices and views over Camberwell
Green, it's not surprising this place is so popular,
especially with students from the local art college.

Salmon & Compasses

*58 Penton Street, Islington, N1 (7837 3891). Angel
tube.* **Open** 5pm-midnight Mon-Wed; 5pm-2am Thur;
2pm-2am Fri, Sat; 2pm-10.30pm Sun. **Admission** £3
after 9pm Thur-Sat. **Map** p402 N2.

Islington's lairiest, most no-nonsense DJ bar packs
in an up-for-it crowd on weekends with a rotating
back of themed nights. Early in the week, it's chilled,
and it actually becomes possible to use the pool table.

Social Bar

*5 Little Portland Street, Marylebone, W1 (7636
4992/www.thesocial.com). Oxford Circus tube.*
Open noon-midnight Mon-Fri; 1pm-midnight Sat.
Map p398 J5. **Map** p398 J5.

Established by Heavenly Records in 1999, the Social
is popular with music industry workers, minor alt-
rock celebs and other sassy trendies, but a fantastic
sound system and great music roster mean it pulls
in anyone who's up for a quality time.

Vibe Bar

*Old Truman Brewery, 91-5 Brick Lane, Shoreditch,
E1 (7377 2899/www.vibe-bar.co.uk). Liverpool Street
tube/rail or Aldgate East tube.* **Open** 11am-11.30pm
Mon-Thur; 11am-1am Fri, Sat; 11am-10.30pm Sun.
Admission £3 after 8pm Fri, Sat. **Map** p403 S5.

The lively crowd make whoopee in the massive
fairy-lighted courtyard to diverse tunes: you'll be
hard pressed walking past without being tempted
to pop in. Near the ace 93 Feet East (*see p320*), the
Bar is packed at weekends and no one's surprised.

Casinos

It's only since 1999 that British casinos have
been allowed to advertise in any form. Even
now, advertisements have to be 'informative'
rather than 'promotional'. However, the law
does allow visitors to apply for membership of
a casino in advance, rather than having to turn
up in person. Legally speaking, all casinos have
to be notified of your intention to play at least
24 hours in advance, and you must be either a
member or the guest of a member.

Arts & Entertainment

While British law forbids us to list casinos in this guide, a check in the *Yellow Pages* or a chat to the concierge of your hotel will yield a few pointers as to the gaming establishments nearest you. Most casinos are open from mid-afternoon through to around 4am every night, and the vast majority are in central London (not least in and around the traditional rich gents' playground of Mayfair. Check with the casino if you're worried about a dress code. However, as a rule of thumb, while casual attire – though not jeans or trainers – may be acceptable for the afternoons, in the evenings gentlemen almost always have to don a jacket and tie.

The naked truth

As Shoreditch rises, so Shoreditch falls. In recent years, this grimy pocket of London just north-east of the City has undergone unprecedented change. Where once stood deserted warehouses and derelict shopfronts are now style bars and smart restaurants; buildings formerly boarded up have been converted into achingly fashionable nightclubs. It's all a far cry from the pubs that, until only a few years ago, provided the only after-dark entertainment around these parts.

The gradual fading-away of the Shoreditch strip pub scene is unlikely to trouble too many people. The British don't share the liberal attitudes held by their European neighbours to the sex industry, and the prurience with which they tend to regard it is invariably dressed up with gloopy layers of moral indignation. We do sleazy very well here; we just can't bring ourselves to admit it.

These are not glamorous places. Nor are they identikit: they range from the smart (**Browns**, 1 Hackney Road, E2) to the relaxed (the **White Horse**, 66 Shoreditch High Street, E1), from the imposing (the faded Victorian grandeur of **Ye Olde Axe**, 69 Hackney Road, E2) to the seedy (the **Spread Eagle**, 1-3 Kingsland Road, E2). But essentially, all are East End pubs in which you can see women take off their clothes; that simple, that no-nonsense. Generally, there's a stage in the corner, and the girls circulate collecting money from the customers (£1 is standard) before taking to it. In the daytime, it's an agreeably becalmed scene; at night, it can get a little lairier, as the groups of lads from the City descend, cash in hand and beer in belly.

The customers, of course, are almost all men (though in the tidier establishments, it's not out of the ordinary to see a woman lurking, usually with their partner). But unlike in many other corners of the London sex industry – not least on nearby Commercial Street, where a parade of weatherbeaten, drug-addicted prostitutes patrol nightly in desperate search of a trick – a half-hour spent observing the dynamic in any of these pubs reveals that the power rests squarely with the strippers. Appropriate, then, that a 2002 book about the scene, *Baby Oil and Ice*, should have been compiled by women: editor (and stripper) Lara Clifton, who collated stories and reminiscences from both strippers and customers, and photographers Julie Cook and Sarah Ainslie, whose pictures of the girls and the pubs are by turns lavish and bleakly vérité.

If you hadn't already figured it out, this is a world away from the DJ bars down the road; both communities regards the other with indifference at best, antipathy at worst. It is also a world that's gradually vanishing. Several strip pubs have closed in the last few years, while others are doing a less than roaring trade. The pubs are now overshadowed by their more fashionable and respectable neighbours. And the City boys, so long the financial mainstays of the strip pubs, are beginning to turn to newer, pricier, more glamorous and entirely homogenous lap-dance venues in the West End such as **Spearmint Rhino** (161 Tottenham Court Road, Fitzrovia, W1), **Bada Bing!** (62 Parker Street, Covent Garden, WC2) and **For Your Eyes Only** (11 White Horse Street, Mayfair, W1).

If lack of business doesn't get the strip pubs, the proposed extension of the East London tube line right through the area probably will. As building work begins, more of the pubs may shut. The gentrification that's already begun in the area will pick up apace, and another of London's characterfully seedy corners will be lost to the ages. Shame.

Sport & Fitness

Watch the pros slug it out, or pull on the sweats and get physical yourself.

The weekly Sport section of *Time Out* magazine gives a rundown of the main action, while fitness, complementary therapy and alternative living are covered under the Body & Mind heading. For in-depth coverage, check out the *Time Out Sport, Health & Fitness Guide*.

Participation sports

Athletics

The following facilities are open to casual users, but are also home to clubs that can offer a more structured and competitive approach.

Barnet Copthall Stadium *Great North Way, Hendon, NW4 (8457 9915). Mill Hill East tube.* **Cost** £2/day; £75/yr.
Crystal Palace National Sports Centre *Ledrington Road, Crystal Palace, SE19 (8778 0131/www.crystalpalace.co.uk). Crystal Palace rail.* **Cost** £1.25-£2.35/day.
Millennium Arena *Battersea Park, East Carriage Drive, Battersea, SW11 (8871 7537). Battersea Park rail.* **Cost** £1.90/day.
Regent's Park Track *Regent's Park, Outer Circle, Camden, NW1 (7486 7905). Camden Town tube then 274 bus.* **Cost** free.

Baseball & softball

For details of playing opportunities and to find your nearest team, contact BaseballSoftball UK.

BaseballSoftball UK *Ariel House, 74A Charlotte Street, Fitzrovia, London W1T 4QJ (7453 7055/ www.baseballsoftballuk.com).*

Cycling

The oldest cycle circuit in the world, Herne Hill is a venue for serious cyclists. Lee Valley caters for BMX, road racing, time-trials, cyclo-cross and mountain biking on various purpose-built tracks. For bike hire, *see p361*.

Herne Hill Velodrome *Burbage Road, Herne Hill, SE24 (7737 4647). Herne Hill or North Dulwich rail.* **Open** *Summer* 10am-6pm Mon-Fri; 9am-1pm Sat. *Winter* 10am-4pm Mon-Fri; 9am-1pm Sat. **Cost** £5.30; £1.90 under-16s.
Lee Valley Cycle Circuit *Quartermile Lane, Stratford, E15 (8534 6085/www.leevalleypark.com). Leyton tube.* **Open** *Summer* 8am-8pm daily, but check availability. *Winter* 9am-4pm daily. **Cost** *With bike hire* £4.60; £3.60 under-16s. *With own bike* £2.40; £1.30 under-16s.

Golf

Teeing off at the 18-hole public courses listed below won't require membership, though it's wise to book in advance. For more courses, see www.thelondongolfer.com. *See also p328.*

Air Links *Southall Lane, Hounslow, Middx (8561 1418). Hounslow West tube/Hayes & Harlington rail then 195 bus.* **Green fee** £14 Mon-Fri; £20 Sat, Sun.
Birchwood Park *Birchwood Road, nr Dartford, Kent (01322 660554). Swanley rail.* **Green fee** £17 Mon-Fri; £22 Sat, Sun.
Dulwich & Sydenham Hill *Grange Lane, College Road, Dulwich, SE21 (8693 8491). West Dulwich rail.* **Green fee** £30 Mon-Fri; £35 Sat, Sun (limited).
Richmond Park *Roehampton Gate, Priory Lane, Richmond, SW15 (8876 3205). Richmond tube/rail.* **Green fee** £16 Mon-Fri; £19-£20.50 Sat, Sun.
Trent Park *Bramley Road, N14 (8367 4653). Oakwood tube.* **Green fee** £13.50 Mon-Fri; £16.95 Sat, Sun.

Horse riding

Getting saddled up in London will probably cost you a pony for an hour's individual class, unless if you're part of a group. Stables offer classes to suit riders of all ages and abilities.

Hyde Park & Kensington Stables *63 Bathurst Mews, Paddington, W2 (7723 2813/ www.hydeparkstables.com). Lancaster Gate tube.* **Open** *Summer* 7.15am-6.30pm Tue-Fri; 8.30am-5pm

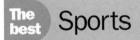

The best Sports

For tradition
The first day of a Test at **Lord's**. See p329.

For action
The **London Knights** ice hockey team. See p330.

For passion
A London football derby: **Tottenham-Arsenal**, say, or **Fulham-Chelsea**. See p329.

For scenery
The ice rink at **Somerset House**. See p326.

For fun
Ten-pin bowling. See p328.

Arts & Entertainment

Sat, Sun. *Winter* 7.15am-sunset Tue-Sat; 8.30am-sunset Sun. **Fees** *Lessons* £39-£59/hr. **Map** p395 D6.
Wimbledon Village Stables
24 High Street, Wimbledon, SW19 (8946 8579/
www.wimbledonvillagestables.co.uk). Wimbledon
tube/rail. **Open** 8am-5pm Tue-Sun. **Fees** *Lessons*
£17-£35/hr.

Ice skating

Aside from the rinks listed below (of which only
Broadgate is outdoors), the courtyard of
Somerset House (*see p98*) has a delightful
outside rink for two months over the Christmas
period (7845 4600/www.somerset-house.org.uk).

Alexandra Palace Ice Rink *Alexandra Palace
Way, N22 (8365 4386). Wood Green tube then W3
bus.* **Open** 11am-1.30pm, 2-5.30pm Mon-Thur; 11am-
1.30pm, 2-5.30pm, 8.30-11pm Fri; 10.30am-12.30pm,
2-4.30pm, 8.30-11pm Sat, Sun. **Admission** (incl
skate hire) £3.90-£5.50; £3.30-£4.20 children.
Broadgate Ice Rink *Broadgate Circle, EC2 (7505
4068/www.broadgateestates.co.uk). Liverpool Street
tube/rail.* **Open** *Late Oct-mid Apr* noon-2.30pm, 3.30-
6pm Mon-Thur; noon-2.30pm, 3.30-6pm, 7-10pm Fri;
11am-1pm, 2-4pm, 5-8.30pm Sat; 11am-1pm, 2-4pm,
5-7pm Sun. **Admission** (incl skate hire) £7; £4
children. **Map** p403 Q5.
Lee Valley Ice Centre *Lea Bridge Road, Lea
Bridge, E10 (8533 3154/www.leevalleypark.org.uk).
Blackhorse Road or Walthamstow Central tube/rail
then 158 bus/48, 55, 56 bus.* **Open** noon-4pm Mon;
noon-4pm, 6.30-9pm Tue, Wed; noon-4pm, 8.30-
10.30pm Thur; noon-4pm, 4.30-6.30pm, 8.30-11pm
Fri; noon-4pm, 7-9.30pm Sun. **Admission** (incl skate
hire) £6.10; £5.10 children.
Leisurebox *First Bowl, 17 Queensway, Bayswater,
W2 (7229 0172). Bayswater tube.* **Open** 10am-
1.45pm, 2-4.45pm, 5-6.45pm, 8-10.45pm Mon-Thur;
10am-1.45pm, 3-4.45pm, 5-6.45pm, 7.30-10.45pm Fri,
Sat. 10am-1.45pm, 2-4.45pm, 5-6.45pm, 8-10pm Sun;
Admission (incl skate hire) £6-£6.50. **Map** p394 C6.
Streatham Ice Arena *386 Streatham
High Road, Streatham, SW16 (8769 7771/
www.streathamicearena.co.uk). Streatham rail.* **Open**
10am-4pm, 4.15-7pm, 7.30-10pm Mon-Fri; 10am-5pm,
5.30-7.30pm, 8-11pm Sat; 10.30am-5pm Sun.
Admission (incl skate hire) £6.80; £5.80 under-12s.

Sport & leisure centres

Many of the city's parks have 'trim trails'
(circuits of outdoor exercise stations) that can
help keep blubber at bay, but for a more serious
workout, London's sports centres offer indoor
sports, plus pools, gyms and classes. The
centres below are open to all for short-term use.

Eqvvs Personal Training

*43A Cheval Place, Knightsbridge, SW7 (7838 1138/
www.eqvvs.com). Knightsbridge tube.* **Open** 6am-
9pm daily.
Eqvvs offers personalised one-to-one programmes
in state-of-the-art surroundings. Prices are high.

Hyde Park & Kensington Stables. *See p325.*

Jubilee Hall Leisure Centre

*30 The Piazza, Covent Garden, WC2 (7836 4835/
www.jubileehallclubs.co.uk). Covent Garden tube.*
Open 7am-10pm Mon-Fri; 9am-9pm Sat; 10am-5pm
Sun. Last entry 45mins before closing. **Map** p401 L7.
A brace of decent exercise studios, plus a range of
weights machines, free weights and CV equipment.

Michael Sobell Leisure Centre

*Hornsey Road, Holloway, N7 (7609 2166/
www.aquaterra.org). Holloway Road tube.* **Open**
7am-10pm Mon-Fri; 9am-6pm Sat; 9am-9.30pm Sun.
Activities at this north London centre also include
ice skating and ice hockey.

Porchester Centre

Queensway, W2 (7792 2919/www.courtneys.co.uk).
Open 7am-10pm Mon-Fri; 8am-8pm Sat, Sun.
Next door to the wonderful art deco spa are some
great fitness facilities and a decent enough pool.

Queen Mother Sports Centre

*223 Vauxhall Bridge Road, Victoria, SW1 (7630
5522). Victoria tube/rail.* **Open** 6.30am-10pm
Mon-Fri; 8am-8pm Sat, Sun. **Map** p400 J10.
A no-nonsense venue for enthusiasts, with three
pools plus lifting, running and sweating activities.

Seymour Leisure Centre

*Seymour Place, Marylebone, W1 (7723 8019).
Marble Arch tube.* **Open** 6.30am-10pm Mon-Fri;
7am-8pm Sat; 8am-8pm Sun. **Map** p395 F5.

Glamorous it ain't, but the friendly and well-equipped Seymour is nonetheless a popular pit stop for fitness freaks of all ages.

Westway Sports Centre

1 Crowthorne Road, Ladbroke Grove, W10 (8969 0992). Latimer Road tube. **Open** 8am-10pm Mon-Fri; 8am-8pm Sat; 10am-10pm Sun.
A £10 million investment has brought sparkle and shine to the facilities here, which include everything from a climbing wall to Eton Fives.

Street sports

The PlayStation Skate Park (Bays 65-6, Acklam Road, W10; 8969 4669) is the city's most popular street sports venue, while those in search of a more underground edge might want to check out Stockwell Skate Park (Stockwell Road, next to Brixton Cycles, SW9). Meanwhile, rollerbladers are free to make use of London's many parks; a click on www.londonskaters.com will bring you up to speed with events in town.

Swimming

To find your nearest pool, try the *Yellow Pages*. For pools in leisure centres, *see p326*; for pools particularly suited to children, *see p273*.

Indoor pools

Highbury Pool *Highbury Crescent, Highbury, N5 (7704 2312/www.aquaterra.org). Highbury & Islington tube/rail.* **Open** 6.30am-9pm Mon-Fri; 7.30am-7pm Sat; 7.30am-9pm Sun. *Women only* 7-9pm Tue. **Admission** £2.80; £1.20 5-16s; free under-4s.

Ironmonger Row Baths *Ironmonger Row, Finsbury, EC1 (7253 4011/www.aquaterra.org). Old Street tube/rail.* **Open** 6.30am-9pm Mon; 6.30am-8pm Tue-Thur; 6.30am-7pm Fri; 9am-5.30pm Sat; noon-5pm Sun. **Admission** £2.80; £1.20 4-16s; free under-3s. **Map** p402 P4.

Oasis Sports Centre *32 Endell Street, Covent Garden, WC2 (7831 1804).Holborn tube.* **Open** *Indoor pool* 6.30am-6.30pm Mon-Fri; 9.30am-5pm Sat, Sun. *Outdoor pool* 7.30am-9pm Mon-Fri; 9.30am-5pm Sat, Sun. **Admission** £3; £1.10 5-16s; free under-5s. **Map** p399 L6.

Outdoor pools

Brockwell Lido *Dulwich Road, Herne Hill, SE24 (7274 3088/www.thelido.co.uk). Herne Hill rail.* **Open** *May-Sept* 6.45-10am, noon-7pm Mon-Fri; 11am-7pm Sat, Sun. *Oct-Apr* closed. **Admission** £2-£4; £1.50-£2.50 5-16s; free under-5s.

Hampstead Heath Ponds *Hampstead Heath, NW3 (7485 4491). Hampstead tube/Gospel Oak or Hampstead Heath rail/C2, C11, 214 bus.* **Open** 7am-dusk daily. **Admission** free.

Oasis Sports Centre *See above.*

Parliament Hill Lido *Hampstead Heath, Gordon House Road, NW5 (7485 3873). Gospel Oak rail/C11 bus.* **Open** *May-Sept* 7-9.30am, 10am-6pm daily. *Oct-Apr* 7-9.30am daily. **Admission** £1.50-£3.50; free 7-9.30am.

Serpentine Lido *Hyde Park, W2 (7298 2100). Knightsbridge or South Kensington tube.* **Open** usually for two months over summer; phone for times and prices. **Map** p395 E8.

Tooting Bec Lido *Tooting Bec Road, Tooting Bec Common, Tooting, SW17 (8871 7198). Tooting Bec tube/Streatham rail.* **Open** *Jun-Sept* 10am-7.30pm daily. *Oct-May* closed except for club members. **Admission** £2.60-£3.10; £2.10-£2.25 children.

London loves Darts

For a time, it was huge. Its big finals drew TV audiences of millions, its top players were household names. But the glory days of darts are behind it, and the sport only has itself to blame. In the early 1990s the world's best players fell out with the sport's governing body, the British Darts Organisation (BDO), and left to start the World Darts Council (now the Professional Darts Council, or PDC). A decade on, and the sport is still riven with disharmony, with two sets of rankings and two separate world championships. It's no way to promote a sport at the margins of public interest.

None of this is of particular import to the casual player, mind. Dartboards are not as common as they once were in London pubs, but the game still thrives at a grassroots level among a sizeable hardcore of enthusiasts.

Find a pub with a board, and you've done well. And once you have, you'll find the game's attractions are manifold.

For one, the rules are simple: start at 301 or 501 and take three darts a turn, with the winner the first to count down to zero by ending on a double (so if your remaining score is 40, you must hit double 20). For two, you can play while drinking and smoking. And for three, throwing sharp objects is fun.

There are a number of amateur leagues throughout London, with teams based at local pubs. However, if there's no league action going on, the board will probably be free and the bar staff should have some darts you can use. It's not as easy as it looks – you could be there all night shooting for a double – but you'll have plenty of (alcohol-fuelled) fun trying. So what are you waiting for?

Watersports

Of the companies listed, Putney specialises in rowing, Docklands deals in jet ski and wet bike hire, and Lea Valley has windsurfing, sailing, wake-boarding, water-skiing and canoeing.

Docklands Watersports Club *Tereza Joanne, Gate 14, King George V Dock, Woolwich Manor Way, Woolwich, E16 (7511 7000/www.tereza-joanne.com). Gallions Reach DLR/North Woolwich rail.* **Open** 10am-1hr before dusk Wed-Sun.
Lea Valley Watersports Centre *Banbury Reservoir, Harbet Road, Chingford, E4 (8531 1129/www.leevalleypark.org.uk). Angel Road rail.* **Open** 9.30am-5.30pm daily.
Putney *Thames Rowing Club, Putney Embankment, SW15 (8788 0798/www.thamesrc.demon.co.uk).* **Open** by appointment.
Queen Mary Sailing Club & Sailsports *Queen Mary Centre, Ashford Road, Ashford, Middx (01784 248881).* **Open** 9am-5pm Mon, Tue; 9am-1hr before sunset Wed-Sun.

Spectator sports

Basketball

This increasingly popular sport has a number of teams in the capital. The Towers and the Leopards both play in the British Basketball League. For more, contact the **English Basketball Association** (0113 236 1166/www.basketballengland.org.uk).

DG London Leopards Kool Kats *Brentwood Leisure Centre, Doddinghurst Road, Brentwood, Essex (01277 230231).* **Admission** £7.50-£8.50; £5.50-£6.50 concessions.
Kinder London Towers *Crystal Palace National Sports Centre, Ledrington Road, Crystal Palace, SE19 (8776 7755/www.london-towers.co.uk). Crystal Palace rail.* **Admission** £7-£8; £5-£6 concessions.

Boxing

Most London boxing promotions take place at York Hall Leisure Centre on Old Ford Road, Bethnal Green, E2 (8980 2243), though major fights are staged at bigger venues such as Earl's Court Arena, Wembley Arena, London Arena (for both, *see p332*) and the Royal Albert Hall (*see p303*). Seats can cost from £10 to £200. For more, contact the **British Boxing Board of Control** (029 203 67000/www.bbbofc.com).

Cricket

If time is of the essence, catch a one-day match in the C&G Trophy or Norwich Union League rather than a four-day County Championship match. For regular county games (everything except the semi-finals and finals of knockout

Winter at **Somerset House**. *See p326.*

Tennis

Many public parks have courts that cost little or nothing to use. For lessons in tennis and golf, try the **Regent's Park Golf & Tennis School** (7724 0643; www.rpgts.co.uk). For grass courts, phone the **Lawn Tennis Association**'s Information Department or check its website (7381 7000/www.lta.org.uk).

Islington Tennis Centre *Market Road, Barnsbury, N7 (7700 1370/www.aquaterra.org). Caledonian Road tube.* **Open** 7am-11pm Mon-Thur; 7am-10pm Fri; 8am-10pm Sat, Sun. **Fees** *Outdoor* £7.20/hr. *Indoor* £16/hr.

Ten-pin bowling

For more lanes, call the **British Ten-pin Bowling Association** (8478 1745/www.btba.org.uk). The average price is around £5 a game, including shoes. *See also p326* **Leisurebox**.

Rowans Bowl *10 Stroud Green Road, Finsbury Park, N4 (8800 1950/www.rowans.co.uk). Finsbury Park tube/rail.* **Open** 10.30am-1am Mon-Thur, Sun; 10.30am-3am Fri, Sat. **Lanes** 24.
Streatham MegaBowl *142 Streatham Hill, Streatham, SW2 (8678 6007/www.megabowl.co.uk). Streatham Hill rail.* **Open** noon-midnight Mon; noon-1am Tue-Fri; 10am-1am Sat; 10am-midnight Sun. **Lanes** 36.

competitions), tickets cost around £10. Lord's (home to Middlesex) and the Oval (Surrey's home ground) also host Test matches and one-day internationals, for which you should book ahead. The season runs April to September.

AMP Oval *Kennington Oval, Kennington, SE11 (7582 7764/www.surreyccc.co.uk). Oval tube.*
Lord's *St John's Wood Road, St John's Wood, NW8 (MCC 7289 1611/tickets 7432 1066/ www.lords.org.uk). St John's Wood tube.*

Football

Tickets for Barclaycard Premiership matches are now virtually impossible to come by for casual spectators. Yet London clubs also feature in all three divisions of the Nationwide League, and at this level tickets are cheaper and easier to get. The prices quoted below are for adult non-members buying on a match-by-match basis.

Clubs
Arsenal *Arsenal Stadium, Avenell Road, Highbury, N5 (7704 4000/www.arsenal.com). Arsenal tube.* **Tickets** £23.50-£43.50. **Premiership.**
Brentford *Griffin Park, Braemar Road, Brentford, Middx (8847 2511/www.brentfordfc.co.uk). South Ealing tube/Brentford rail.* **Tickets** £12 standing; £15 seated. **Division 2.**

Tee off in **Regent's Park**. *See p328.*

Charlton Athletic *The Valley, Floyd Road, Charlton, SE7 (8333 4010/www.cafc.co.uk). Charlton rail.* **Tickets** £15-£30. **Premiership.**
Chelsea *Stamford Bridge, Fulham Road, Chelsea, SW6 (7386 7799/www.chelseafc.co.uk). Fulham Broadway tube.* **Tickets** £28-£40. **Premiership.** **Map** p396 B13.
Crystal Palace *Selhurst Park, Whitehorse Lane, Selhurst, SE25 (8771 8841/www.cpfc.co.uk). Selhurst rail.* **Tickets** £19-£25. **Division 1.**
Fulham *Craven Cottage, Stevenage Road, Fulham, SW6 (7893 8383/www.fulhamfc.co.uk). Putney Bridge tube.* **Tickets** £23-£40. **Premiership.**
Leyton Orient *Matchroom Stadium, Brisbane Road, Leyton, E10 (8926 1111/www.leytonorient. com). Leyton tube.* **Tickets** £12-£16. **Division 3.**
Millwall *The Den, Zampa Road, Bermondsey, SE16 (7231 9999/www.millwallfc.co.uk). South Bermondsey rail.* **Tickets** £16-£25. **Division 1.**
Queens Park Rangers *Loftus Road Stadium, South Africa Road, Shepherd's Bush, W12 (8740 2575/www.qpr.co.uk). White City tube.* **Tickets** £14-£20. **Division 2.**
Tottenham Hotspur *White Hart Lane, Bill Nicholson Way, High Road, Tottenham, N17 (0870 011 2222/www.spurs.co.uk). White Hart Lane rail.* **Tickets** £25-£55. **Premiership.**
Watford *Vicarage Road, Watford, Herts (01923 496010/www.watfordfc.com). Watford Junction rail.* **Tickets** £10-£25. **Division 1.**
West Ham United *Boleyn Ground, Green Street, West Ham, E13 (8548 2700/www.whufc.com). Upton Park tube.* **Tickets** £26-£46. **Premiership.**
Wimbledon *Selhurst Park, Whitehorse Lane, Selhurst, SE25 (8771 8841/www.wimbledon-fc.co.uk). Selhurst rail.* **Tickets** £18-£27. **Division 1.**

Golf

Two of the UK's most famous courses lie within easy reach of London. Wentworth hosts the World Matchplay tournament every October.

Sunningdale *Ridgemount Road, Sunningdale, nr Ascot, Berks (01344 621681/www.sunningdale-golfclub.co.uk). Sunningdale rail.*
Wentworth *Wentworth Drive, Virginia Water, Surrey (01344 842201/www.wentworthclub.com). Virginia Water rail.*

Greyhound racing

See also p330 **London loves**, and www.thedogs.co.uk.

Catford Stadium *Adenmore Road, Catford, SE6 (8690 8000). Catford or Catford Bridge rail.* **Races** 7.30pm Thur-Sat. **Admission** £4.50.
Romford Stadium *London Road, Romford, Essex (01708 762345). Romford rail.* **Races** 7.30pm Mon, Wed, Fri; 7.30pm Sat. **Admission** £1.50-£6.
Walthamstow Stadium *Chingford Road, Chingford, E4 (8531 4255/www.wsgreyhound.co.uk). Walthamstow Central tube/rail then 97, 215 bus.* **Races** 7.30pm Tue, Thur, Sat. **Admission** free (lunchtimes Mon, Fri); £6 eves.

Arts & Entertainment

Wimbledon Stadium *Plough Lane, Wimbledon,
SW17 (8946 8000/www.wimbledondogs.co.uk).
Tooting Broadway tube/Wimbledon tube/rail/
Haydons Road rail.* **Races** 7.30pm Tue, Thur-Sat.
Admission £5.50.

Horse racing

The horse-racing year is divided into the flat
racing season (Apr-Sept) and the National Hunt
season over jumps (Oct-Apr). Evening meetings
are held in summer.

Ascot

*High Street, Ascot, Berks (01344 622211/
www.ascot.co.uk). Ascot rail.* **Admission** £6-£49.
The Royal Meeting in June is the high point, but the
event (in particular, the flummery of Ladies Day) is
regarded with derision by many hardcore race-goers.

Epsom

*Epsom Downs, Epsom, Surrey (01372 726311/
www.epsomderby.co.uk). Epsom, Epsom Downs or
Tattenham Corner rail.* **Admission** £5-£18.
Home to the Derby, Epsom draws the crowds. The
race takes place in June, with around ten other meetings scheduled for the rest of the year.

Kempton Park

*Staines Road East, Sunbury-on-Thames, Middx
(01932 782292/www.kempton.co.uk). Kempton Park
rail.* **Admission** £6-£18.
Kempton makes up for what it lacks in glamour with
excellence. There are meetings year-round, with the
themed summer nights especially popular.

Sandown Park

*Portsmouth Road, Esher, Surrey (01372 463072/
www.sandown.co.uk). Esher rail.* **Admission** £11-£18.
Sandown is generally considered the best-equipped
track in the south-east. Its major occasions include
the Whitbread Gold Cup in April and the Coral
Eclipse Stakes in July.

Windsor

*Maidenhead Road, Windsor, Berks (01753 865234/
www.windsorracing.co.uk). Windsor & Eton
Riverside rail.* **Admission** £5-£18.
A pleasant Thameside location and views of the
nearby Castle make this track a relaxing place to
spend a day at the races.

Ice hockey

Created in 1998 to spearhead British ice
hockey's expansion, the London Knights play
(with some success) in the Superleague. For
further information on London's ice hockey
fixtures, contact Ice Hockey UK (0115 924
1441/www.icehockeyuk.co.uk).

London Knights *London Arena, Limeharbour,
Docklands, E14 (7538 1212/www.knightice.co.uk).
Crossharbour & London Arena DLR.* **Admission**
£12-£18; £7 concessions.

Motor sport

Every Sunday, a range of bangers, hot rods and
stock cars provide a bout of family-oriented
mayhem in Wimbledon.

Wimbledon Stadium. *Plough Lane, Wimbledon,
SW17 (stadium 8946 8000/stock car information
01420 588020/www.wimbledonstadium.co.uk).
Tooting Broadway tube/Wimbledon
tube/rail/Earlsfield or Haydons Road rail.*
Admission £10; £5 concessions.

Rugby league

At present, the Broncos – who may move
grounds in mid-2003; check online for more –
are the only pro rugby league team outside the
game's traditional northern heartland. The
Super League season runs March to September.

London loves The dogs

Some British institutions, like Parliament or
the FA Cup Final, are grand, elegant treasures
that need little introduction. Others, such as
a night out at the dogs in London, are just
a little too lively and unique to pass over
without comment. Sure, greyhound racing
isn't exclusive to these shores, but there is
something innately British about it, and in
London's weather-worn stadia the sport has
found its spiritual home.

The attractions of the dogs are threefold:
cheap entertainment, gambling and beer.
Unlike horse racing, its more gentrified
relation, the dogs knows no class barriers

and – at least on the surface – doesn't take
itself too seriously. With 12 races spread over
a few hours (*see p329* for details of tracks
in London), there isn't time for the casual
punter to stay in the doldrums too long:
there's always another sprint just minutes
away, another collection of hounds to pore
over in the form book, and another round of
drinks to buy. Consequently, the euphoria
after you've shouted yourself hoarse for six
races and finally bagged a win is unrivalled.

What you see is what you get at the dogs...
unless, of course, you're referring to the
occasional propensity of your odds-on

London Broncos *The Valley, Floyd Road, Charlton, SE7 (8853 8800/www.londonbroncos.co.uk). Charlton rail.* **Admission** £10-£15; £3-£5 children.

Rugby union

With a capacity of more than 60,000, Twickenham is the home of English rugby union, playing host to most internationals and domestic cup finals. Tickets for matches in the Six Nations Championship (January to March) are almost impossible to obtain for casual spectators, but those for cup finals and other matches are easier to come by; call for details.

Many leading internationals play their club rugby in London, notably with Harlequins, London Wasps and Saracens. The Zurich Premiership and the three-division National League run from August to May; most games are played on Saturday and Sunday afternoons.

Twickenham *Whitton Road, Twickenham, Middx (information 8892 2000/tickets 8831 6666/ www.rfu.com). Twickenham rail.*

Clubs

Esher *369 Molesey Road, Hersham, Surrey (01932 220295/www.esherrfc.org). Hersham rail.* **Admission** £5; free under-16s. **Division 2.**
London Wasps *Twyford Avenue Sports Ground, Twyford Avenue, Acton, W3 (8740 2545/ www.wasps.co.uk). Ealing Common tube.* **Admission** £6-£16. **Premiership.**
London Welsh *Old Deer Park, Kew Road, Richmond, Surrey (8940 2368/www.london-welsh. co.uk). Richmond tube/rail.* **Admission** £10 standing; £14 seated. **Division 1.**
NEC Harlequins *Stoop Memorial Ground, Langhorn Drive, Twickenham, Middx (8410 6000/www.quins.co.uk). Twickenham rail.* **Admission** £12-£25. **Premiership.**
Rosslyn Park *Priory Lane, Upper Richmond Road, Roehampton, SW15 (8876 6044/*

www.rosslynpark.co.uk). *Barnes rail.* **Admission** £8; £4 concessions. **Division 3 South.**
Saracens *Vicarage Road Stadium, Watford, Herts (01923 496000/www.saracens.com). Watford High Street rail.* **Admission** £12-£35. **Premiership.**

Tennis

Britain's most famous tournament runs from 23 June to 6 July 2003. Seats on Centre and Number One courts are allocated by ballot and must be applied for the preceding year. However, if you're prepared to queue on the day, you can get into the outer courts, where the freedom to wander means you're never far from the action. Late in the day, you can buy returned show-court tickets for a fraction of their face value.

Wimbledon is preceded by the Stella Artois tournament, at which stars from the men's circuit warm up for the main event. The 2003 event will be held 9-15 June at Queen's Club.

All England Lawn Tennis Club (Wimbledon)
PO Box 98, Church Road, Wimbledon, SW19 (8944 1066/information 8946 2244/www.wimbledon.org). Southfields tube.
Queen's Club *Palliser Road, Hammersmith, W14 (7385 3421/www.queensclub.co.uk). Barons Court tube.*

Major venues

Crystal Palace National Sports Centre

Ledrington Road, Crystal Palace, SE19 (8778 0131/www.crystalpalace.co.uk). Crystal Palace rail.
Now a Grade II-listed building, this sizeable centre has managed to dodge countless threats of closure. Still, no refurbishment has managed to banish the air of bygone glory that continues to cling to the place. There's a Grand Prix athletics meeting every summer, plus a huge variety of activities and competitions, including basketball, netball, martial arts, hockey and weightlifting.

London Arena

Limeharbour, Docklands, E14 (7538 1212/ www.londonarena.co.uk). Crossharbour & London Arena DLR/D8, D9 bus.
Not exactly a jewel in our architectural crown, the London Arena still provides a comfortable setting for major indoor sports. As well as being home to ice hockey's London Knights (*see p330*), it also plays host to big boxing promotions (*see p328*).

Wembley Arena/Conference Centre

Empire Way, Wembley, Middx (8902 0902/ www.wembley.co.uk). Wembley Park tube/Wembley Stadium rail.
Since the closure of Wembley Stadium in 2000, sporting activity here has diminished significantly. You can still see showjumping and basketball at the Arena, however, and the nearby Conference Centre hosts boxing and snooker.

favourite to – and you're sure you saw it, especially after your sixth pint – suddenly start limping halfway round, thus seeing to another fiver. Down the years, the dogs has garnered a reputation for being a tad shady. It's a reputation not rooted in fact (such observations are only made by whiningly bad losers) and one its scrupulously clean organisers are understandably keen to avoid, yet the shadowy image is actually part of the charm. And if you see any shifty men laying down a wad of tenners on an unfancied mutt seconds before the race, do the same: you may just beat the odds.

Arts & Entertainment

Theatre

From the bright lights of the West End to the backrooms of Islington boozers.

Mark one up for the quality controllers. In theatrical terms, the aftermath of September 11 sorted out the men from the boys in London's West End. A tiny handful of shows carried on not quite like nothing had happened, but with relative comfort. Many long-runners hung on grimly amid the inevitable downturn in ticket sales, but hung on they did. Other big shows, which had long been playing to less than packed houses but that had been doing just enough business to keep afloat, capitulated in a hurry, safe in the knowledge that without the tourist dollar, they didn't stand a chance.

Things improved quicker than expected. At Christmas 2001 Ken Livingstone brokered an inventive ticket-discounting deal with West End theatres that safeguarded the futures of a number of shows. As a result, while it wasn't business as usual in 2002, London's theatres were fuller than anyone had hoped.

As regards the quality of London's mainstream theatre, you can argue both ways. On the one hand, this autumn, there were three times as many Chekhov plays in the West End than there were Lloyd Webber musicals. Yet on the other, the failure of *Kiss Me Kate*, a brilliant production of a sparkling Cole Porter musical at the Victoria Palace Theatre, while queues were forming outside the hopeless *We Will Rock You* hardly showed London in the best light.

Truth be told, there's good and there's bad stuff out there. While there'll always be a market for blockbusting musicals, and while some of them deliver the goods in spades (hello, *Les Misérables* and *The Lion King*), we could certainly live without the witless, gutless and ultimately plotless shows themed around greatest-hits albums by the likes of Madness (*Our House*), Abba (*Mamma Mia!*) and Queen (*We Will Rock You*). Yet, conversely, not all straight dramas in the West End succeed: too many are reliant solely on the presence of a Hollywood name to draw crowds. If in doubt, check reviews in the press and in *Time Out* – which runs reviews on more or less every play running in the city – before you sign up.

WHERE TO GO AND WHAT TO SEE

The **West End** is a cultural term, rather than a geographic one. Some of its leading theatres lie well outside the traditional boundaries of London's theatreland. The most reliable of West End venues, with an exciting repertory of new plays and classics rather than fixed, long-running programmes, are the building-based companies such as the South Bank's **Royal National Theatre** and **Shakespeare's Globe** (for both, *see p333*).

Off-West End refers to the next rung down in terms of financial means, and offers the best mix of quality and originality. These theatres are usually heavily subsidised; top writers, directors and actors are lured by the prospect of artistic liberty. Still, they have a pecking order: wealthier theatres such as the **Young Vic** (*see p338*) and the **Almeida** (*see p337*) lead the pack, with the likes of the **Gate** and the **King's Head** (for both, *see p338*) often dependent on hopefuls prepared to work for nothing.

The **Fringe**, meanwhile, is scattered all over London, and is a theatrical underclass where standards are more variable. Among the most reliable venues are the **New End Theatre** (27 New End, NW3; 7794 0022) and the **Grace Theatre** (503 Battersea Park Road, SW11; 7794 0022), all three struggling in adverse financial circumstances to develop bold artistic policies.

Tickets & information

The first rule to observe when buying tickets for London shows is to book ahead. The second rule is to go direct to the theatre's box office. Booking agencies such as **Ticketmaster** (7344 4444, www.ticketmaster.co.uk) and **First Call** (7420 0000, www.firstcalltickets.com) sell tickets to many shows, but you'll get hit with booking fees that could top 20 per cent.

In a late bid to fill their venues, many West End theatres offer reduced-price tickets for shows that have not sold out. These seats,

The best Theatres

For new writing
Royal Court. See p333.

For old writing
Shakespeare's Globe. See p333.

For a bit of both
Almeida. See p337.

Take the tour, sure, but try to also catch a play at **Shakespeare's Globe**.

available only on the night, are known as 'standby' tickets, and usually sell for about half what a top-priced ticket would cost. Always call to check both availability and conditions: some standby deals are limited to those with student ID, and it varies as to when tickets go on sale.

Alternatively, try **tkts**, a non-profit-making organisation run from the Clock Tower building in Leicester Square by the Society of London Theatres that sells tickets for West End shows on a first-come, first-served basis on the day of the performance. Each ticket is subject to a fee of £2.50 and a maximum of four are allowed per customer, but tickets for many shows can be snapped up for as much as 50 per cent off face value. Be aware that the other gaudy booths advertising cheap seats around Leicester Square are unofficial, expensive and, often, dodgy.

tkts

Leicester Square, WC2 (www.officiallondontheatre. co.uk). Leicester Square tube. **Open** 10am-7pm Mon-Sat; noon-3pm Sun. **Credit** AmEx, DC, MC, V. **Map** p401 K7.

West End

Repertory companies

For the **Royal Shakespeare Company**, *see p335* **No great Shakes**.

Royal Court

Sloane Square, Chelsea, SW1 (7565 5000/ www.royalcourttheatre.com). Sloane Square tube. **Box office** 10am-6pm Mon-Sat. **Tickets** 10p-£26; all tickets £7.50 Mon. **Credit** AmEx, MC, V. **Map** p400 G11.

The Royal Court is the undisputed centre of new writing in Britain, and has been since it opened its doors in 1956: among the first productions here was John Osborne's *Look Back in Anger*. Now back in its long-time Sloane Square home after a £25 million refurbishment, it boasts two performing spaces – the imaginatively titled Upstairs (a small studio theatre) and Downstairs (a proscenium arch main stage) – plus a snazzy restaurant and bar.

Royal National Theatre

South Bank, SE1 (information 7452 3400/box office 7452 3000/www.nationaltheatre.org.uk). Embankment or Southwark tube/Waterloo tube/rail. **Box office** 10am-8pm Mon-Sat. **Tickets** *Olivier & Lyttelton* £10-£33. *Cottesloe* £10-£27. *Standby* £8, £16. **Credit** AmEx, DC, MC, V. **Map** p401 M7.

It's all change at the National. Trevor Nunn's on his way out as the company's artistic director, with Nicholas Hytner taking to the hot seat from April. And while radical change is unlikely, neither is it necessary: Nunn is leaving this South Bank stalwart in good shape. The revamped Lyttelton Theatre is an improvement on the unloved space that was there before; the 2002 season was marked by a perfect balance between new work and classics (including a spellbinding *Streetcar Named Desire* starring Glenn Close); and the programme of various extra-curricular activities (live music, DJs) has brought more people into the building than ever. In short, the future looks bright.

Shakespeare's Globe

21 New Globe Walk, Bankside, SE1 (7401 9919/ www.shakespeares-globe.org). Blackfriars or Mansion House tube. **Box office** *Off season* 10am-6pm Mon-Fri. *Theatre season* 10am-8pm daily. **Tickets** £5-£29. **Credit** AmEx, MC, V. **Map** p404 O7.

Partly a tourist attraction, but only partly. Under adventurous artistic director Mark Rylance, the reconstructed Globe has nailed itself a deserved reputation as a serious theatre as well as its daytime role as a presenter of neatly packaged Britlit history to coach parties of Americans (*see p78*). The season runs only from April to October (it's open-air, of course) and is no friend of artistic nuance, but it does offer interesting insights into how Will dealt with mob dynamics. That said, it's unlikely he had to contend with planes flying overhead every few minutes.

Long-runners & musicals

Most theatres have evening shows Monday to Saturday (starting 7.30-8pm) and matinées on one weekday (usually Wednesday) and Saturday. Check *Time Out* magazine for details.

Blood Brothers

Phoenix Theatre, Charing Cross Road, St Giles's, WC2 (7369 1733/www.theambassadors.com). Tottenham Court Road tube. **Box office** *In person* 10am-7.45pm Mon-Sat. *By phone* 9am-9pm Mon-Sat; 10am-6pm Sun. *Ticketmaster* 24hrs daily. **Tickets** £14.50-£37.50. *Standby* £15. **Credit** AmEx, MC, V. **Map** p399 K6.

Scouse sentiment and toe-tapping songs in Willy Russell's likeable, long-running melodrama about two brothers separated at birth and exiled to opposite ends of the social ladder.

Bombay Dreams

Apollo Victoria, Wilton Road, Pimlico, SW1 (0870 4000 650/www.clearchannel.co.uk). Victoria tube/rail. **Box office** *In person* 9am-8pm Mon-Sat. *Ticketmaster* 24hrs daily. **Tickets** £10-£40. **Credit** AmEx, MC, V. **Map** p400 H10.

No great Shakes

The recent furore over the plans for the future of the **Royal Shakespeare Company** illustrates the high regard in which this pioneering theatrical group is held. It also points to the heavy burden of tradition that has an overarching influence on the company's direction. The directorship of the group can be likened to a stint as England football manager: the cooing and congratulations are quickly replaced with catcalls the minute you're perceived to have taken your eye off the ball. Why this eagle-eyed attention, then, and why all the fuss?

Set up as a repertory company in 1960 by Sir Peter Hall – its parent theatre, the Shakespeare Memorial (now Royal Shakespeare) Theatre, was established in Stratford-upon-Avon 80 years earlier – the RSC has since stood at the forefront of world theatre. It's long been a tourist attraction of which to be proud, an educator that is many people's only point of contact with the Bard, a nurturer of British acting talent (Dame Judi Dench, Kenneth Branagh and Ralph Fiennes all furnished their CVs here). Still these things and more, the RSC is now also in chaos.

Change is hard to instigate in any business this rooted in tradition. Yet the problem with artistic director Adrian Noble's recent plans for the RSC wasn't so much that they were too progressive, as that they weren't very sensible. In Noble's proposals, Stratford's famous playhouse would be demolished and replaced with an all-new 'Shakespeare village', and the RSC would sever all ties with its London theatre, at the Barbican Centre.

Certainly, there's widespread agreement that the RSC's Stratford theatre needs redeveloping. Yet not everyone agrees that the building should be flattened: many believe that the RSC would do just as well to refurbish the existing structure, saving both money and a building many see as important and noteworthy.

Noble's decision to leave the Barbican, though, has met with widespread opposition. The company moved into the complex in 1982 and staged plays in its two theatres year-round until, in the late 1990s, Noble decided to leave for six months a year to tour RSC shows. This scheme met with marginal success, but didn't justify his 2001 decision to ditch two perfectly suitable London theatres and a permanent home in the capital, and leave the RSC bumbling around town looking for new theatres for each new production. Its 2002 season saw ticket sales fall.

Soon after announcing his plans for Stratford, however, and seemingly stung by the furious criticism they received, Noble announced he was quitting. Michael Boyd, associate director of the company since the mid 1990s, takes over from Noble this spring, and it'll be interesting to see how he'll tackle the mess. The RSC should endure if it continues to stage great productions of ancient and modern works performed by a repertory of highly talented actors. But Boyd's got his work cut out if he wants this storied company to get its act together sooner rather than later.

Bombay Dreams. *See p335.*

Meera Syal's rags-to-Bollywood-riches script misses, but AR Rahman's wonderfully sensual score and some thrilling choreography both hit it big.

Chicago

Adelphi Theatre, Strand, Covent Garden, WC2 (Ticketmaster 7344 0055). Charing Cross tube/rail. **Box office** *In person* 10am-8pm Mon-Sat. *By phone* 24hrs daily. **Tickets** £15-£40. **Credit** AmEx, MC, V. **Map** p401 L7.
Kander and Ebb's Easy Street has established itself as a West End staple.

Chitty Chitty Bang Bang

London Palladium, Argyll Street, W1 (0870 890 1108/www.chittythemusical.co.uk). Oxford Circus tube. **Box office** *In person* 10am-7.30pm Mon-Sat. *Ticketmaster* 24 hours daily. **Tickets** £15-£40. **Credit** AmEx, MC, V. **Map** p398 J6.
The car's great, the cast's great, the kids will enjoy themselves… but there's precious little here for adults to enjoy.

Les Misérables

Palace Theatre, Shaftesbury Avenue, Soho, W1 (7434 0909/www.lesmis.com). Leicester Square tube. **Box office** 10am-8pm Mon-Sat. *Ticketmaster* 24hrs daily. **Tickets** £7-£40. *Standby* £17.50. **Credit** AmEx, MC, V. **Map** p399 K6.
Boubil and Schonberg's 15-year-old money-spinner idealises the struggle between paupers and villains in Victor Hugo's revolutionary Paris.

The Lion King

Lyceum Theatre, Wellington Street, Covent Garden, WC2 (0870 243 9000). Covent Garden tube/Charing Cross tube/rail. **Box office** *In person* 10am-6pm Tue-Sat. *Ticketmaster* 24hrs daily. **Tickets** £17.50-£42.50. **Credit** AmEx, MC, V. **Map** p401 L7.
This Disney extravaganza about a lion cub struggling to grow up has been wildly acclaimed.

Mamma Mia!

Prince Edward Theatre, 30 Old Compton Street, Soho, W1 (7447 5400/www.mamma-mia.com). Leicester Square or Tottenham Court Road tube. **Box office** *In person* 10am-7pm Mon-Sat. *By phone* 24hrs daily. **Tickets** £18.50-£40. **Credit** AmEx, MC, V. **Map** p399 K6.
This musical links Swedish supergroup Abba's greatest hits into a continuous but spurious story.

My Fair Lady

Theatre Royal Drury Lane, Catherine Street, Covent Garden, WC2 (7494 5000/www.rutheatres.com). Covent Garden tube. **Box office** 10am-8pm Mon-Sat. **Tickets** £7.50-£40. **Credit** AmEx, MC, V.
A strong cast succeeds in extracting the comedy and pathos from Lerner and Loewe's musical of George Bernard Shaw's class-conscious romance *Pygmalion*.

The Mousetrap

St Martin's Theatre, West Street, Covent Garden, WC2 (7836 1443). Leicester Square or Tottenham Court Road tube. **Box office** 10am-8pm Mon-Sat. **Tickets** £11.50-£30. **Credit** MC, V. **Map** p399 K6.
An absurdly long-running mystery (50 years and still going strong) written by Agatha Christie.

Our House

Cambridge Theatre, Covent Garden, WC2 (7494 5399/www.ourhousethemusical.com). Covent Garden tube. **Box office** *In person* 10am-8pm Mon-Sat. *Ticketmaster* 24 hours daily. **Tickets** £12.50-£40. **Credit** AmEx, MC, V. **Map** p399 L6.
A la *Mamma Mia*, a patchwork quilt of songs by 1980s popsters Madness. Reviews have been kind.

Phantom of the Opera

Her Majesty's Theatre, Haymarket, St James's, SW1 (7494 5400/www.thephantomoftheopera.com). Piccadilly Circus tube. **Box office** *In person* 10am-7.45pm Mon-Sat. *By phone* 24hrs daily. **Tickets** £10-£40. **Credit** AmEx, MC, V. **Map** p401 K7.
Lloyd Webber's best musical, this long-runner concerns a deformed theatre-goer who becomes obsessed with a beautiful opera singer. Autobiographical?

We Will Rock You

Dominion Theatre, Tottenham Court Road, Fitzrovia, W1 (7413 1713/www.london-dominion.co.uk). Tottenham Court Road tube. **Box office** *In person* 9am-7.30pm Mon-Sat. *Ticketmaster* 24 hours daily. **Tickets** £22.50-£42.50. **Credit** AmEx, MC, V. **Map** p399 K5.
All your favourite Queen hits, unconvincingly rendered and stitched together by a deeply feeble Ben Elton plot. Freddie would've hated it.

The Woman in Black

*Fortune Theatre, Russell Street, WC2 (7836
2238/www.thewomaninblack.com). Covent
Garden tube.* **Box office** 10am-8pm Mon Sat.
Tickets £10-£29.50. *Standby* £10. **Credit** AmEx,
MC, V. **Map** p399 L6.

A persistently popular West End spine-chiller
written by Susan Hill.

Off-West End

Almeida

*Almeida Street, Islington, N1 (7359 4404/
www.almeida.co.uk). Angel tube.* **Box office**
In person 5-7pm Mon-Fri; 10am-7pm Sat.
By phone 24hrs daily. **Tickets** £5-£27.50.
Credit AmEx, MC, V. **Map** p399 L2.

It's all change at the Almeida, after some golden
years under artistic directors Ian McDiarmid and
Jonathan Kent. The duo left the theatre in mid 2002,
leaving former Royal Shakespeare Company man
Michael Attenborough to take charge of the
Almeida's move back into its Islington theatre after
renovations (the building should finally reopen in
spring 2003). Kent and McDiarmid raised the
Almeida's profile immeasurably by pairing famous
actors with a classy line-up of plays. Attenborough
has a lot to live up to.

BAC (Battersea Arts Centre)

*Lavender Hill, Battersea, SW11 (7223 2223/
www.bac.org.uk). Clapham Common tube/Clapham
Junction rail/77, 77A, 345 bus.* **Box office** *In person*
10.30am-6pm Mon; 10.30am-9pm Tue-Sun. *By phone*
10.30am-6pm Mon-Sat; 3.30-6pm Sun. **Tickets** £3.50-
£12.75; 'pay what you can' Tue. **Credit** MC, V.

The BAC has three theatres (a main house and two
studios) that together carry much of the capital's
very best fringe work. Their innovative and laudable Scratch programme allows the public to see
work at various stages of its development.

The Bush

*Shepherd's Bush Green, Shepherd's Bush, W12
(7610 4224/www.bushtheatre.co.uk). Goldhawk
Road or Shepherd's Bush tube.* **Box office** *In
person* 5-8pm Mon-Sat. *By phone* 10am-7pm Mon-Sat.
Tickets £7-£13.50. **Credit** AmEx, MC, V.

Imagine the Royal Court without the glamour or the
money, and you have the Bush. That's no slight,
mind: this underfunded pub theatre is one of the
most important venues for new writing in London.

Donmar Warehouse

*41 Earlham Street, Covent Garden, WC2 (7369
1732/www.donmar-warehouse.com). Covent Garden
tube.* **Box office** *In person* 10am-7.30pm Mon-Sat.
By phone 9am-9pm Mon-Sat; 10am-6pm Sun.
Ticketmaster 24hrs daily. **Tickets** £5-£29.
Credit AmEx, MC, V. **Map** p399 L6.

Director Sam Mendes hauled the Donmar from the
doldrums in the early 1990s and turned it into one
of London's most exciting and visible theatres with
a mix of classic revivals and new plays performed
by starry casts. Mendes, though, departed at the end
of 2002 to pursue his cinematic career, leaving
Michael Grandage to take over as artistic director.
As with Attenborough at the Almeida (*see above*),
it'll be fascinating to see how he shapes up.

Talkin' 'bout a revolution:
Les Misérables. *See p336.*

Drill Hall

16 Chenies Street, Fitzrovia, WC1 (7307 5060/www.drillhall.co.uk). Goodge Street tube. **Box office** *In person* 10am-7.30pm Mon-Fri; 11am-6pm Sat. *By phone* 10am-9pm Mon-Fri; 10am-10pm Sat; 10am-6pm Sun. **Tickets** £5-£10. **Credit** AmEx, MC, V. **Map** p399 K5.

London's biggest gay and lesbian theatre is not generally a separatist venue, though Mondays are women only from 6pm and Thursdays are non-smoking days.

The Gate

above Prince Albert Pub, 11 Pembridge Road, Notting Hill, W11 (7229 0706). Notting Hill Gate tube. **Box office** 10am-6pm Mon-Fri. **Tickets** £6-£12; 'pay what you can' Mon. **Credit** MC, V. **Map** p394 A7.

Another west London pub theatre – this one in Notting Hill – the Gate presses ever-onwards with its programme of script-driven entertainment in a plain and usually setless black box space.

Hampstead Theatre

98 Avenue Road, Swiss Cottage, NW3 (7722 9301/www.hampstead-theatre.co.uk). Swiss Cottage tube. **Box office** 10am-7pm Mon-Sat. **Tickets** £8-£19. **Credit** MC, V.

The Hampstead Theatre is widely respected for its contemporary drama. And at long last, it will get the venue it deserves in 2003, when its gleaming new £10 million theatre opens for business. It remains to be seen whether the increased capacity (from the present 175 up to 325) will result in a dramatic change of programming policy, but let's hope not.

King's Head

115 Upper Street, Islington, N1 (7226 1916/ www.kingsheadtheatre.org). Angel tube/Highbury & Islington tube/rail. **Box office** 10am-8pm Mon-Sat; 10am-4pm Sun. **Tickets** £5-£18. **Credit** MC, V. **Map** p402 O1.

The oldest pub theatre in the city shuffles on, despite Islington council shamefully cutting back its funding. The programme here is a real mishmash, from straight drama to musical revue, with quality similarly varied. Still, the pub out front is always great.

Lyric Hammersmith

King Street, Hammersmith, W6 (8741 2311/ www.lyric.co.uk). Hammersmith tube. **Box office** *In person* 10am-8pm Mon-Sat. *By phone* 10am-7pm Mon-Sat. **Tickets** £5-£20. **Credit** AmEx, DC, MC, V.

From the outside, the Lyric looks purely modern, yet its main stage is gloriously old fashioned, with plush seats and a proscenium arch. This stage, and the smaller studio space, specialise in work that, while alternative in nature, is by no means inaccessible.

Open Air Theatre

Regent's Park, NW1 (7486 2431/www.open-air-theatre.org.uk). Baker Street tube. **Repertory season** June-Sept; phone for details. **Tickets** £9-£26. *Standby* £9 (approx). **Credit** AmEx, DC, MC, V. **Map** p398 G3.

It's all in the name: the Open Air Theatre sits outside in London's loveliest park, bare to the elements. The productions here tend to be mainstream, but the quality is far higher than you might expect from a venue that's more than just a tourist sop.

Orange Tree

1 Clarence Street, Richmond, Surrey (8940 3633/ www.orangetreetheatre.co.uk). Richmond tube/rail. **Box office** 10am-7pm Mon-Sat. **Tickets** £5.50-£15.50. **Credit** MC, V.

It's very definitely a locals' theatre, the Orange Tree, and is something of a haul to get to from central London. Still, the usually impressive performances make the trek worthwhile, as does the uniqueness of the space: this is London's only theatre set up permanently in the round.

Soho Theatre

21 Dean Street, Soho, W1 (7478 0100/ www.sohotheatre.com). Tottenham Court Road tube. **Box office** 10am-9.30pm Mon-Sat. **Tickets** £5-£15. **Credit** AmEx, MC, V. **Map** p399 K6.

One of the real success stories of London theatre in the last few years, the once homeless Soho Theatre opened in these swanky premises in early 2000 and has since served up an enticing mix of new plays (2002 saw Tim Fountain's *Julie Burchill is Unwell* hit headlines), foreign imports (including several from South Africa and Australia) and an ever-increasing volume of stand-up comedy.

Theatre Royal Stratford East

Gerry Raffles Square, Stratford, E15 (8534 0310/ www.stratfordeast.com). Stratford DLR/tube/rail. **Box office** 10am-7pm Mon-Sat. **Tickets** £3.50-£16. **Credit** MC, V.

This powerhouse of popular community-oriented drama, musicals, revues and panto (each Christmas, and usually one of the best in London) reopened in December 2001 after an impressive three-year refurbishment programme, but still boasts the same well-loved Victorian auditorium.

Tricycle

269 Kilburn High Road, Kilburn, NW6 (7328 1000/ www.tricycle.co.uk). Kilburn tube. **Box office** 10am-9pm Mon-Sat; 2-9pm Sun. **Tickets** £9-£20.50. **Credit** MC, V.

Tilting its programme squarely at its local population, the Tricycle specialises in high-quality black and Irish shows. The centre also incorporates its own art gallery and super-comfortable cinema, plus one of Kilburn's few agreeable bars.

Young Vic

66 The Cut, Waterloo, SE1 (7928 6363/ www.youngvic.org). Southwark tube/Waterloo tube/rail. **Box office** 10am-7pm Mon-Sat. **Tickets** £9.50-£19. **Credit** MC, V. **Map** p404 N8.

Like the Old Vic, only younger? Well, not far off. The Young Vic stages a variety of theatrical entertainments in its two spaces, from home and abroad in runs both long and short.

Trips Out
of Town

Trips Out of Town

Tired of London, tired of life? Piffle: you just need an excursion.

Map p389

Busy, smelly, tiring. Sometimes the secret for enjoying London is knowing when to escape and where. Just as well, then, that there's a plethora of little-known but easily accessible attractions just beyond the M25. Most of the places we've listed are within an hour and a half's train journey from London, though some require a further bus or taxi ride.

For a more in-depth look at getaways within easy reach of London, pick up a copy of *Time Out Weekend Breaks from London* (£12.99). Many of the destinations in this chapter are great for families, particularly the castles. For details of theme parks within easy reach of London, *see p272*.

PLANNING A TRIP

The **Britain Visitor Centre** (*see below*) stocks guidebooks and free leaflets and offers advice on any destination in the UK and Ireland; you can also book rail, bus, air or car travel, reserve tours, theatre tickets and accommodation, and there's even a bureau de change, a branch of Thomas Cook, a ticket agency and a bookshop. Travellers should also visit the tourist information centre as soon as they arrive in a town; these can provide leaflets, further information about accommodation and where to eat, and details of local attractions.

Britain Visitor Centre

1 Regent Street (south of Piccadilly Circus), SW1 (www.visitbritain.com). Piccadilly Circus tube. **Open** *Oct-May* 9.30am-6.30pm Mon; 9am-6.30pm Tue-Fri; 10am-4pm Sat, Sun. *June-Sept* 9.30am-6.30pm Mon; 9am-6.30pm Tue-Fri; 9am-5pm Sat; 10am-4pm Sun. **Credit** AmEx, MC, V. **Map** p401 K7.
This centre is open to personal callers only, but the website contains masses of useful information and advice on destinations across the country.

OPENING TIMES & PRICES

For the main entries below, we've included full details of opening times, admission and transport details, but be aware that these can change without notice: always phone to check that a particular sight is open if you're planning a visit around it. Major sights are open all through the year, but many minor attractions close in winter (Nov-Mar).

The accommodation prices listed in the 'Where to stay' sections are the range for a double room.

Getting there

By train

For information on train times and ticket prices, call **08457 484950**. (To reserve tickets in advance by credit card, ask for the appropriate number.) Make sure you ask about the cheapest ticket for the journey you are planning, and be aware that for longer journeys, the earlier you book, the cheaper the ticket. The **rail travel centres** in all London's main-line stations, as well as in Heathrow and Gatwick airports and the Britain Visitor Centre (*see above*), will also be able to help with timetable information and ticket booking. The train journey times we give are the fastest available.

The website www.virgintrains.co.uk gives online timetable information for any British train company, while www.thetrainline.com allows you to buy tickets online for any train operator in the UK.

London main-line rail stations

Charing Cross *Strand, Covent Garden, WC2.* **Map** p401 L7.
For trains to and from south-east England (including Dover, Folkestone and Ramsgate).
Euston *Euston Road, Euston, NW1.* **Map** p399 K3.
For trains to and from north and north-west England and Scotland, and a suburban line north to Watford.
King's Cross *Euston Road, King's Cross, N1.* **Map** p399 L2.

The best Days out

For beach, blankets and bingo
Brighton. *See p343.*

For a glass of water
Bath. *See p341.*

For getting lost
The maze at **Leeds Castle**. *See p349.*

For keeping the kids quiet
Legoland. *See p272.*

For a simple stroll
Epping Forest. *See p348.*

Stately Roman **Bath**.

For trains to and from north and north-east England and Scotland, and suburban lines to north London and Hertfordshire.
Liverpool Street *Liverpool Street, the City, EC2.* **Map** p403 R5.
For trains to and from the east coast (including Harwich) and Stansted Airport; also for trains to East Anglia and suburban services to east and north-east London.
Paddington *Praed Street, Paddington, W2.* **Map** p395 D5.
For trains to and from south-west and west England, south Wales and the Midlands.
Victoria *Terminus Place, Victoria, SW1.* **Map** p400 H10.
For fast trains to and from the Channel ports (Folkestone, Dover, Newhaven); also for trains to and from Gatwick Airport, plus suburban services to south and south-east London.
Waterloo *York Road, Waterloo, SE1.* **Map** p401 M8.
For fast trains to and from the south and south-west of England (Portsmouth, Southampton, Dorset, Devon), and suburban services to south-west London.

By coach

Coach and bus travel is almost always cheaper than rail travel, but more often than not it's also slower. **National Express** (0870 580 8080) runs routes to most parts of the country; its coaches depart from Victoria Coach Station on Buckingham Palace Road, five minutes' walk

from Victoria rail and tube stations. **Green Line** (0870 608 7261) operates within an approximate 40-mile (64-kilometre) radius of London. Most buses depart from Eccleston Bridge, SW1 (Colonnades Coach Station, behind Victoria Station).

Victoria Coach Station

164 Buckingham Palace Road, Victoria, SW1 (7730 3466). Victoria tube/rail. **Map** p400 H11.
Britain's most comprehensive coach company **National Express** (*see above*) and **Eurolines** (01582 404511), which travels to the Continent, are based at Victoria Coach Station. There are many other companies operating to and from London (some departing from Marble Arch).

By car

If you're in a group of three or four, it may be cheaper to hire a car (*see p361*), especially if you plan to take in several sights within an area. The road directions given in the listings below should be used in conjunction with a map. (Note that, for example, 'J13 off M11' means 'exit the M11 motorway at junction 13'.)

Town & city breaks

Bath

Dickens, Sir Walter Scott, Gainsborough and Handel were all fans of Bath, Daniel Defoe called the city 'a particular favour of heaven', but waspish Jane Austen is justly Bath's most famous literary scion. 'Oh, who can ever be tired of Bath?' sighed the heroine of her novel *Northanger Abbey*, echoing the sentiment of many a social butterfly who flitted from the Pump Room to the new Theatre Royal, between the promenades, balls and assemblies that confirmed the city as high society's favourite watering hole in the 1800s.

In the 1880s the cellars of the Pump Room finally gave up their pagan secret: site of the Great Roman Bath and a temple to Minerva, it was just too much ungodliness for good old Queen Victoria, who is said to have snapped shut the curtains of her carriage when being driven through the city, for fear of clapping eyes on half-naked bathers. Today, the **Roman Baths Museum** (01225 477785) is the city's most famous attraction and the most impressive non-military Roman remains in Britain. The restoration of the baths as a spa is nearing completion, with the opening of five listed buildings and a new four-storey complex – complete with an enticing rooftop pool – expected to take place in spring 2003 (call 01225 477710 for details). In the meantime, the waters are still bubbling up at a rate of 250,000 gallons

Bath's greatest attraction is its streets. The grandest of them all is the much-photographed **Royal Crescent**, a breathtaking sweep of 30 houses designed by John Wood the Younger between 1767 and 1775. **No.1 Royal Crescent** (01225 428126), designated a World Heritage building, is furnished in authentic period style with a fully restored Georgian garden (closed Dec-mid Feb). Nearby is the magnificent **Circus**, designed by the elder John Wood and completed by his son in 1767. Composed of three crescents forming a circle, its three tiers of columns have led it to be described as 'the Colosseum turned outside in'. In many ways it's finer than the Royal Crescent.

The **River Avon**, which adds greatly to the appeal of the city, is spanned by the shop-lined **Pulteney Bridge**, an Italianate masterpiece by Robert Adam. There are walks beside the river and the adjacent Kennet and Avon Canal, and in summer boats can be hired from the Victorian **Bath Boating Station** (Forester Road; 01225 466407).

Further information
Where to eat & drink Sally Lunn's **Refreshment House & Museum** (01225 461634) in North Parade Passage is the oldest house in Bath; here you can sample the famous buns made fashionable by Sally Lunn in the 1680s. The best of

Sucking up the spa: Bath's **Pump Room**.

(over a million litres) a day; you can taste them in the adjoining **Pump Room**, though most prefer the Earl Grey. Overlooking the baths is **Bath Abbey** (01225 422462), a 15th-century reworking of a Norman structure. Built on the site of the Saxon church where Edgar, first king of a united England, was crowned back in 973, it's a beautifully harmonious building, boasting some fine fan vaulting and stained glass.

Bath has close on 20 museums, most of them excellent. These include the **Building of Bath Museum** on Lansdown Road (01225 333895), the highlight of which is a spectacular model of the city, and the **Museum of East Asian Art** (01225 464640) in Bennett Street, which contains a fine collection of Chinese jade carvings. Opposite, in the grand Assembly Rooms (the social focus of high society in Georgian times), there's the renowned **Museum of Costume** (01225 477789), with the oldest of the posh togs on display dating back to the 1660s. The **Victoria Art Gallery** (01225 477233) on Bridge Street houses the region's permanent collection of British and European art from the 15th century to the present day, and the **American Museum & Gardens** (01225 460503) at Claverton Manor offers a fascinating series of reconstructed 17th- to 19th-century US domestic interiors.

The wonderful Woods' sublime **Circus**.

Bath's many restaurants are top-rank curry house **Jamuna** at 9-10 High Street (01225 464631) and the classy, cosy **Moody Goose** (01225 466688) with its Modern British cuisine on Kingsmead Square. Popular pubs include the **Bell** in Walcot Street, the **Old Green Tree** on Green Street, and the **Cross Keys** on the corner of Midford Road and Southstoke Road – its garden and aviary make it great for kids. **Where to stay** Harington's Hotel (8-10 Queen Street, 01225 461728, £88-£118) is the best-value central hotel. **Holly Lodge** (8 Upper Oldfield Park, 01225 424042, £79-£97) is a classy B&B perched high above the city. The **Queensberry Hotel** (Russell Street, 01225 447928, £120-£225) provides Regency elegance in the centre of town. **Royal Crescent** (16 Royal Crescent, 01225 823333, £165-£330) has possibly the best address of any hotel in Britain and is the place to come for a splurge. **Getting there** *By train* from Paddington (1hr 25mins). *By coach* National Express (3hrs 20mins). *By car* J18 off M4 then A46, use park 'n' rides to get into the centre.

Tourist information centre *Abbey Chambers, Abbey Churchyard (01225 477101/ www.visitbath.co.uk).* **Open** *May-Sept* 9.30am-6pm Mon-Sat; 10am-4pm Sun. *Oct-Apr* 9.30am-5pm Mon-Sat; 10am-4pm Sun.

Brighton

Whether you're here for the political party conferences or a party of a different feather, saucy old Brighton looks after its visitors. Here you'll find countless hotels, guesthouses and restaurants, lots of intriguing shops, and a vibrant and sophisticated cultural scene and nightlife that all thrive on close connections to the capital. Relatively sunny, Brighton provides the gaudy fun of a typical British beach town (even if the shoreline is full of pebbles rather than sand and the 'town' has technically been a city since December 2000). A constant influx of coach parties and daytrippers soak up beer, buy sticks of rock and play on dodgems on the pier.

A lot of these weekenders catch a dose of Brighton fever and in the end find themselves settling here. The city is of famously liberal persuasion and greets outsiders, new agers, artists, freaks and eccentrics with open arms and a warm heart. These persecuted hipsters, along with an array of absconders from the big city rat race, relocate to Brighton's pebbly shore to tune in, turn on and drop out. A thriving gay and lesbian scene has also put Brighton on the map, with even the local authorities having to acknowledge the power of the pink pound.

Nowhere in Brighton better reflects this diversity, extravagance and exuberance than its best-known landmark, the outrageous **Royal Pavilion** (01273 290900). Built by John Nash in 1823 for the Prince Regent (later George IV), it none too subtly blends elements of Indian,

Chinese and Islamic architecture. Next door, the **Brighton Museum & Art Gallery** (01273 290900) has a good crop of 19th-/20th-century and ethnic art, as well as a fine array of art nouveau and art deco.

Down at the waterfront, the gaudy **Palace Pier** is packed with archetypal seaside attractions: slot machines, funfair, fish and chips. On a clear day you can gaze west from the top of the helter-skelter to the Isle of Wight, or along the shore to the derelict, skeletal but Grade I-listed **West Pier** (as we went to press, long-awaited restoration work was being held up by local planning objections) and genteel Hove. Ocean lovers should visit the **Brighton Fishing Museum** (01273 723064) on the lower prom between the piers and the **Sea-Life Centre** (01273 604234), housed in a beautiful 19th-century aquarium on Marine Parade.

When the sea loses its fascination, duck into the **Lanes** (between West Street and the Old Steine), a warren of old fishermen's cottages that now house a variety of antiques and specialist shops, punctuated by pubs and cafés. If these prove too expensive, cross North Street and explore the vibrant **North Laine** area for vintage clothing, street fashion, records, kitsch and cafés of every kind, or visit the **Duke of York's** (01273 626261) at Preston Circus, quite possibly the cosiest indie cinema in the UK.

If you fancy taking your new glad rags out for the evening, you're in the right place: Brighton is a clubbers' mecca too. Located on the seafront, the **Zap** (01273 202407) is the grandaddy of the city's clubs, though also worth checking out in King's Road Arches are the **Honey Club** (01273 202807), **Beach** (01273 722272) and the **Funky Buddha Lounge** (01273 725541).

Further information

Where to eat & drink For food, try the enticing Anglo-Asian dishes at the unpromisingly sited **Black Chapati** (12 Circus Parade, New England Road, 01273 699011), the famous vegetarian fare at **Terre à Terre** (71 East Street, 01273 729051), the magnificent French food at **La Fourchette** (101 Western Road, 01273 722556), or the Modern European dishes in Blanch House hotel (*see below*) at the ultra-cool **C Restaurant** (01273 645755). The most charming trad boozers are the **Cricketers** in Black Lion Street, the **Eastern** in Trafalgar Street and the **Battle of Trafalgar** in Guildford Road. For something trendier, try the **St James** in Madeira Place, the **Sidewinder** in Upper St James Street or, for camping it up large-style, the **Regency Tavern** in Russell Square.
Where to stay Blanch House (17 Atlingworth Street, 01273 603504, £100-£220) is petite but seriously funky. **Hotel Pelirocco** (10 Regency Square, 01273 733845, £85-£115) offers kitschy decor to a party-hard crowd. **Hotel Twenty One** (21

Charlotte Street, 01273 686450, £60-£95) is a well-run B&B with Victorian furniture, while **Nineteen** (19 Broad Street, 01273 675529, £95-£150) is chic, stylish and intimate. The **Oriental** (9 Oriental Place, 01273 205050, £50-£140) is a bohemian budget option that's close to the sea too.

Events The **Brighton Festival** (01273 700747) fills the first three weeks of May with theatre, comedy, art, music and literature. On Sundays throughout the year Madeira Drive on the seafront hosts a range of diverse events – notably the **London to Brighton Bike Ride** in June and the **London to Brighton Veteran Car Run** in November. Monthly listings guides *Impact* and *The List* are available from newsagents, or you can find out what's going down by tuning in to Surf 107FM from 6.30pm to 7pm (Mon-Fri). **Brighton Pride** takes place each year in August; for other gay events, see the monthly *G Scene* or visit www.scene22.com.

Getting there *By train* from Victoria (from 50mins), or from King's Cross (1hr 10mins). *By coach* National Express (1hr 50mins). *By car* M23 then A23.

Tourist information centres *10 Bartholomew Square (0906 711 2255/www.visitbrighton.com). Open Jan-June, Sept-Dec* 9am-5pm Mon-Fri; 10am-5pm Sat; 10am-4pm Sun. *July, Aug* 9am-5.30pm Mon-Fri; 10am-6pm Sat; 10am-4pm Sun. *Hove Town Hall, Church Road, Hove (0906 711 2255). Open Jan-June, Sept-Dec* 9am-5pm Mon-Fri. *July, Aug* 11am-5pm Mon-Fri.

Cambridge

One of the great things about Cambridge is that its historic centre, and most of its sights, can easily be covered on foot, even though the city stretches out surprisingly far across commons and pastures. Many of the red-brick roads in the central area are semi-pedestrianised, encouraging the naïve to wander with carefree abandon. This, of course, is just what the cyclists are waiting for: stealthy, silent, they will mow down the unwary, chiming their little bells in celebration.

Most of these free-wheeling bell-ringers are students of the **university**, which has dominated Cambridge life since the 14th century. The oldest college is **Peterhouse** on Trumpington Street, endowed in 1284. The original hall survives, though most of the present buildings are 19th century. Just up the road is **Corpus Christi**, founded in 1352. Its Old Court dates from that time and is linked by a gallery to the 11th-century **St Bene't's Church**, the oldest building in town. Next head down Silver Street to 15th-century **Queens';** most of its original buildings remain, including the beautiful timbered president's lodge, and the inner courts are wonderfully picturesque.

Further north up King's Parade, **King's** was founded by Henry VI in 1441 and is renowned for its **chapel** (01223 331155), built between 1446 and 1515. Considered one of the greatest

Gothic buildings in Europe, it boasts a breathtaking interior with the original stained glass still intact. If you visit in term-time, be sure to attend a service, when the choirboys' other-worldly voices provide a sublime counterpoint to the beauty of the building.

Still heading north, you'll find **Trinity**, founded in 1336 by Edward III and refounded by Henry VIII in 1546. A fine collection of Tudor buildings surrounds the Great Court where, legend has it, Lord Byron used to bathe naked in the fountain with his pet bear. Wittgenstein studied and taught here; the library, designed by Wren, where he occasionally worked is open to visitors at certain times (noon-2pm Mon-Fri, 10.30am-12.30pm Sat term-time only; 01223 338400). Further on, at the corner of Bridge and St John's Streets, is the **Round Church**, the oldest of the four remaining round churches in England. Behind this main group of colleges is the **Backs**, a series of beautiful meadows, some still grazed by cows, bordering the willow-shaded **River Cam**, which is spanned by several fine footbridges. It's a perfect spot for summer strolling, or you can hire a punt and drift lazily along the river.

Among Cambridge's non-collegiate attractions are the **Fitzwilliam Museum** on Trumpington Street (01223 332900), which has outstanding collections of antiquities and Old Masters; **Kettle's Yard** (Castle Street; 01223 352124), which has fine displays of 20th-century art; and the university's **Botanic Gardens** (01223 336265) on Bateman Street.

Unsurprisingly, Cambridge is an excellent place to buy books – new, second-hand and antiquarian – and the daily market in **Market Square** is always a pleasure to browse, whether for books, clothes, antiques, flowers or just good things to eat.

Further information

Where to eat & drink For posh nosh, try the inventive French cooking at **Midsummer House** (01223 369299) on Midsummer Common, the global cuisine at tiny, candlelit **Restaurant 22** (01223 351880) or the bargain goodies at **Dojo Noodle Bar** in Miller's Yard, Mill Lane (01223 363471). Pub-wise, though the **Eagle** on Bene't Street receives all the plaudits, there are many other pubs of equal merit, including the **Pickerel** on Magdalene Street, **Fort St George** by the river on Midsummer Common, and the **Mill** and the **Anchor**, practically next door to each other, between Granta Place and Silver Street. **Where to stay** Cambridge is notoriously short on characterful accommodation. The newish **Meadowcroft Hotel** (16 Trumpington Road, 01223 346120, £130-£150) is head and shoulders above the competition, while the simple modern cells of the **Sleeperz Hotel** (Station Road, 01223 304050, £55) betray Scandinavian and Japanese influences.

Trips Out of Town

Sand or no sand, **Brighton** beach is the business. *See p343.*

Events The **Cambridge Shakespeare Festival** is held annually in July and August, with plays performed in college gardens. Also in July, the recently revived and surprisingly prestigious **Cambridge Film Festival** takes place; as does the ever-popular **Cambridge Folk Festival**.
Getting there *By train* from King's Cross (50mins) or Liverpool Street (1hr 15mins). *By coach* National Express (1hr 50mins). *By car* J11 or J12 off M11.
Tourist information centre *Old Library, Wheeler Street (01223 322640/www.tourismcambridge.com).* **Open** *Apr-Oct* 10am-6.30pm Mon-Fri; 10am-5pm Sat; 11am-4pm Sun. *Nov-Mar* 10am-5.30pm Mon-Fri; 10am-5pm Sat.

Canterbury

England has many medieval cathedral cities, some better preserved and others in more idyllic settings than Canterbury. But the major events of Canterbury's early history – the coming of Christianity with St Augustine in the sixth century and the murder of the Archbishop of Canterbury in 1170 – were so significant they continue to reverberate in its narrow streets and landmark **cathedral** (01227 762862).

With its superb stained glass, stone vaulting and vast Norman crypt, Canterbury Cathedral is now the mother church of Anglicans worldwide. A plaque near the altar marks the spot where Archbishop Thomas à Becket was murdered in 1170 by four overzealous knights. They had overheard King Henry II moan, 'Will no one rid me of this turbulent priest?' and decided to do

the troubled king a favour. Becket's tomb has been a site of pilgrimage ever since. **Trinity Chapel** contains the site of the original shrine, plus the tombs of Henry IV and the Black Prince.

Though it gets overcrowded in summer, the small city centre is charming. **Eastbridge Hospital** (01227 471688) on the High Street was founded to meet the growing kipping needs of pilgrims in the wake of Becket's murder and retains the smell and damp of ages past. There are also the remains of a Roman townhouse and mosaic floor at the **Roman Museum** on Butchery Lane (01227 785575), and the **Museum of Canterbury** (01227 452747) on Stour Street gives the best version of the history of the city. Meanwhile, **Canterbury Tales** (01227 479227) clunkily but endearingly recreates the experience of Chaucer's 14th-century pilgrims.

Further information
Where to eat & drink Tue e Mio at 16 The Borough (01227 761471) is a stylish Italian with matching food; on St Dunstan's Street, **Café des Amis du Mexique** (No.95, 01227 464390) is upbeat and deservedly popular, while **Lloyds** (Nos.89-90, 01227 768222) offers ambitious international cuisine. Further afield on St Dunstan's Street, you can drink in the pretty and peaceful **Unicorn** with its charmingly kitsch garden; there's also the ancient and sedate **Thomas Becket** in Best Lane.
Where to stay Acacia Lodge & Tanglewood (39-40 London Road, 01227 769955, £40-£48) is a well-priced B&B formed from 1880s farm cottages

Trips Out of Town

and run by a former town guide. The **Coach House** (34 Watling Steet, 01227 784324, £40-£48) is a fresh, new B&B with fleamarket decor. The **Falstaff** (8 10 St Dunstan's Street, 01227 462138, £105) is Canterbury's loveliest historic hotel.

Getting there *By train* from Victoria to Canterbury East (1hr 20mins), or from Charing Cross to Canterbury West (1hr 30mins). *By coach* National Express (1hr 50mins). *By car* A2 then M2 then A2 again.

Tourist information centre *34 St Margaret's Street (01227 378100/www.canterbury.co.uk).* **Open** *Jan-Mar* 9.30am-5pm Mon-Sat. *Apr-Oct* 9.30am-5.30pm Mon-Sat; 10am-4pm Sun. *Nov, Dec* 9.30am-5pm Mon-Sat; 10am-4pm Sun.

Oxford

Oxford city centre is dominated by the university and its colleges; the first students began to gather here in the early 12th century, and by the end of the century Oxford was firmly established as England's first university town. Of the city's 118,000 inhabitants, approximately 15 per cent are reckoned to be the transient university population; in addition, the streets throb all year round with tourists and rucksacked European school parties.

The university's architecturally spectacular buildings are usually open to the public. Among the finest is **Christ Church**, with its Wren-designed Tom Tower. While Oxford's origins are Saxon, the roots of the city's development can be traced back to an early eighth-century priory settlement that once stood on this site, and Christ Church's chapel serves as Oxford's cathedral. Nearby **Merton**, founded in 1264, boasts a marvellous medieval library and garden. **Magdalen** (pronounced 'maudlin'), often said to be the loveliest Oxford college, has a deer park and a meadow where the rare snakeshead fritillary still blooms every April. Other centres of academia include the **Bodleian Library** (01865 277000), begun in 1598, and the dinky, elegant **Radcliffe Camera**, England's earliest example of a round reading room (1737).

Oxford's attractions don't end with the university. **Carfax Tower** (01865 792653), the only surviving part of the 14th-century church of St Martin, is notable for its two 'quarter-boy' clocks that chime every quarter-hour; it also provides great views of the city if you climb the 99 steps to the top. There's a wealth of museums, too, ranging from the quirky **Pitt Rivers** (Parks Road; 01865 270927), with its voodoo dolls, shrunken heads and other ethnological delights, to the all-embracing **Ashmolean** (Beaumont Street; 01865 278000), the country's oldest museum housing the university's collection of art and antiquities. There's also the recently revamped **Modern**

Art Oxford (Pembroke Street; 01865 722733), which has established an international reputation for pioneering temporary exhibitions of contemporary and 20th-century work.

If you've had too much culture, a browse around the city's boutiques is a pleasant diversion. Little Clarendon Street and Gloucester Green offer some interesting specialist shops, while the classy **Covered Market** (opened in 1774), linking Market Street and the High, is a foodie's delight.

Other parts of town – notably Jericho and Summertown to the north, and Headington and Cowley (once more a thriving centre for British car-manufacturing with the new Mini) to the east – have their own distinct identities and considerably fewer sightseers, while the **Oxford Canal**, the **River Thames** (sometimes called the Isis, from the Latin 'Tamesis') and the **Cherwell** (pronounced 'Char-well') provide fine strolling and punting opportunities. Out beyond Jericho you can picnic watching wild horses on Port Meadow, one of the country's largest remaining commons, but for the classic view of Matthew Arnold's 'dreaming spires' head to Boar's Hill, three miles (two kilometres) south-west of the city.

Further information

Where to eat & drink Cherwell Boathouse (01865 552746) off Bardwell Road offers upmarket fare, while Raymond Blanc's swish, metropolitan brasserie **Le Petit Blanc** (71-2 Walton Street, 01865 510999) is excellent value. **Branca Bar Italian Brasserie** (111 Walton Street, 01865 556111) is a funky newcomer. Oxford has loads of pubs, but few are cheap or quiet – the busy 16th-century **King's Arms** in Holywell Street is a studenty choice with good beer and decent pub grub; the **White House** behind the station is a gastropub offering live trad jazz at Sunday lunchtime; and the part-thatched **Perch** on Binsey Lane has a big garden and a children's play area.

Where to stay Burlington House (374 Banbury Road, 01865 513513, £70-£80) is an outstanding small hotel with B&B prices. The 17th-century **Old Parsonage** (1 Banbury Road, 01865 310210, £165-£200), home to Oscar Wilde when he was an undergraduate, is classy, and the **Old Bank Hotel** (92-4 The High, 01865 799599, £135-£300) sleek, modernist and arty.

Getting there *By train* from Paddington (1hr), then use your rail ticket for a free ride into the centre on one of Oxford's pioneering electric buses (every 10mins). *By coach* frequent, cheap, fast services from several London departure points; details from National Express (1hr 40mins), Stagecoach (01865 727000) and Oxford Bus Company (01865 785410). *By car* J8 off M40 then A40; use the park 'n' rides.

Tourist information centre *The Old School, Gloucester Green (01865 726871/www.visitoxford.org).* **Open** *Easter-Oct* 9.30am-5pm Mon-Sat; 10am-3.30pm Sun. *Nov-Easter* 9.30am-5pm Mon-Sat.

Stratford-upon-Avon

Stratford's cutesy half-timbered architecture, cobbled mews and teashop culture aren't for everyone, and local proprietors aren't shy when it comes to milking Shakespeare's connection with the town. Sheep Street, in particular, has fallen prey to pricey boutiques and restaurants, and ghastly souvenir shops.

Yet it's worth braving if you're a genuine Shakespeare junkie. In the town centre are **Shakespeare's Birthplace** (01789 204016) on Henley Street, which underwent major restoration in 2000, adding period room-settings to the hall, parlour, kitchen and bedchambers; **Hall's Croft** (01789 292107) on Old Town, named after Dr John Hall, who married the Bard's daughter Susanna; and **Nash's House** (01789 292325) on Chapel Street, which belonged to the first husband of Shakespeare's granddaughter, Elizabeth. In the garden of the latter are the foundations of **New Place**, the writer's last home, demolished in 1759.

A mile and a half (2.5 kilometres) away at Shottery, and accessible from Stratford by public footpath, is **Anne Hathaway's Cottage** (01789 292100), where Shakespeare's wife lived before she married. The girlhood home of his mother, **Mary Arden's House** (01789 293455), is at Wilmcote, a pleasant four-mile (6.5-kilometre) stroll along the Stratford Canal. Both may also be reached by bus; there are also trains to Wilmcote.

Shakespeare was educated at **Stratford Grammar School**, which you can see on Church Street, and buried in **Holy Trinity Church**. The latter has a fine riverside setting and supposedly the playwright's tomb. But, of course, his most meaningful memorials are his plays, and the **Royal Shakespeare Theatre** (01789 403403; *see also p338* **No great Shakes**) is the place to see them. If you can't get a ticket (they sell out fast), take a backstage tour and visit the **RSC Collection** museum of props and costumes (for tours, call 01789 403405).

Stratford has been a market town since 1169 and, in a way, that's still what it does best. See it on a Friday, when the awnings go up over the stalls at the top of Wood Street and locals flock in from outlying villages. In the town centre, which still maintains its medieval grid pattern, many fine old buildings survive, among them **Harvard House** (open around June-Oct; 01789 204507) on the High Street. Dating from 1596, it was home to Katharine Rogers, mother of John Harvard, founder of Harvard University, and now houses an important collection of pewter.

Trips Out of Town

Primeval pastimes

If you fancy a day out of London without actually leaving the metropolis, take up a stout walking stick and get on the Central line to Loughton. Once there, you'll soon find yourself in **Epping Forest**. It's thanks to the Victorians that this particular green lung of London survives: in 1878 Parliament granted the City of London Corporation power to buy land within 25 miles (40 kilometres) of the Square Mile, so that urbanites could continue to enjoy it in its natural state.

Some 6,000 acres (2,430 hectares) remain of the primeval forest that once covered most of East Anglia; they're perfect for walking, cycling, horse riding, picnicking and blackberrying. The **visitors' centre** (phone 8508 0028 for opening times), adjacent to wheelchair- and pushchair-friendly paths among the 300-year-old hornbeams, has friendly staff who can suggest walks or supply leaflets and maps. The centre is a two-mile (three-kilometre) uphill walk from **Loughton** station, so you might prefer to buy a map of the forest beforehand (try Edward Stanford;

see p233) and get there through the forest rather than along main roads. **Theydon Bois** – only a couple of tube stops further on – offers an alternative route into the forest. It's a pretty village with a green and duck pond.

Within the forest, there are two Iron Age earthworks: the 6.5 acres (2.5 hectares) of **Loughton Camp**, enclosed by a curved rampart and 45-foot (14-metre) ditch, and **Ambresbury Banks**, which is 12 acres (five hectares) of rectangular hill fort, with ramparts reaching seven feet (two metres). Boudicca is said to have sallied forth from Ambresbury Banks, only to be defeated by the Romans. She's thought to have then killed herself with a handful of poisonous berries on Epping Upland. The forest didn't do King Harold, who rebuilt **Waltham Abbey** in 1060, much good either. He stopped off to say his prayers at the abbey in the middle of a three-week yomp south to Hastings after duffing up the Vikings, and his mortal remains duly returned for burial after his defeat at Hastings.

The town's charms are enhanced by the waterways running through it. Both the **River Avon** and the **Stratford Canal** have walks beside them, and the canal basin is usually crammed with narrowboats. The long-established **Avon Boating** (01789 267073) can provide punts, rowing boats, Canadian canoes and other passenger vessels, but many tourists prefer just to loll under the willows.

Further information

Where to eat & drink The **Opposition** (01789 269980) on 13 Sheep Street is a great bistro, **Russon's** (01789 268822) at 8 Church Street specialises in imaginative fish dishes, and **Desport's** (01789 269304) at 13-14 Meer Street offers eclectic modern cooking. Drink with the thesps at the **Dirty Duck** (aka the **Black Swan**) on Stratford Way. **Where to stay** Caterham House Hotel (01789 267309, £80-£85) at 58 Rother Street is close to the Royal Shakespeare Theatre and popular with both audience and actors. Another good choice, **Victoria Spa Lodge** (01789 267985, £65) on Bishopton Lane has the feel of a grand country house; Queen Victoria stayed here before ascending the throne in 1837. **Tourist information centre** *Bridgefoot (01789 293127)*. Open *Easter-Oct* 9am-6pm Mon-Sat; 11am-5pm Sun. *Nov-Easter* 9am-5pm Mon-Sat. **Getting there** *By train* from Paddington (2hrs 10mins). *By coach* National Express (2hrs 45mins) or Guide Friday (01789 294466) from Euston. *By car* J15 off M40 then A46.

Henry VIII put Epping to a more sporting use: hunting. He completed a grand timber-framed temple to the pastime in 1543. Repaired by his daughter in 1589, **Elizabeth I's Hunting Lodge** (6 Ranger's Road, Chingford; 8529 6681; open 1-4pm Wed-Sun) still provides splendid views of Chingford Plain, where Tudor hounds bayed and their masters view-halloed. Restored in 1993, the lodge is thought to be the last royal hunting grandstand in the world, and boasts a recreated Tudor kitchen complete with authentic (though not, happily, actual 16th-century) food. Those lacking a horse and hounds can reach the lodge by foot from Chingford railway station. You might still catch a glimpse of the fallow deer that roam the forest to this day.

You might also spot the chanterelle smuggler, who's alleged to be shipping carloads of wild mushrooms out of Epping. The rumoured destination is a restaurant in Sicily, so it's best not to disturb him.

Castles

Arundel

Arundel, West Sussex (01903 882173/ www.arundelcastle.org). **Getting there** *By train* from Victoria (1hr 30mins). *By car* A24 then A280 and A27. **Open** *Apr-Oct* noon-5pm Mon-Fri, Sun (last entry 4pm). **Admission** £8.50; £7 concessions; £5.50 5-16s; £24.50 family. **Credit** MC, V.

This wonderful, imposing pile has its origins in the 11th century. The original castle was heavily damaged during the Civil War, then extensively remodelled in the 18th and 19th centuries. Inside is a fine collection of 16th-century furniture, and paintings by Van Dyck, Gainsborough and Reynolds, among others. Don't miss the 14th-century Fitzalan Chapel, a Roman Catholic chapel tucked inside an Anglican church so that the dukes and their families could worship according to Catholic rites. Home to a clutch of tombs of Dukes of Norfolk past, it mercifully shows no signs of the time when Oliver Cromwell used it as a stable.

Arundel also has its own neo-Gothic 19th-century **cathedral**, which is actually more impressive outside than inside, plus a number of agreeable shops and some decent alehouses.

Hever

Hever, nr Edenbridge, Kent (01732 865224/ www.hevercastle.co.uk). **Getting there** *By train* Victoria to Edenbridge (1hr), then 5min taxi journey, or Victoria to Hever (1hr), then 1-mile walk. *By car* J5 off M25 then B2042 and B269, or J6 off M25 then A22, A25 and B269. **Open** *Mar-mid Oct* 11am-6pm daily. *Mid Oct-Nov* 11am-dusk daily. **Admission** *House & gardens* £8.20; £4.50 5-14s; £7 over-60s; free under-5s; £20.90 family. *Garden only* £6.50; £4.30 5-14s; £5.60 over-60s; £17.30 family. **Credit** MC, V.

The childhood home of Henry VIII's ill-fated second wife Anne Boleyn, this 13th-century castle is surrounded by a double moat and has a splashing water maze with water jets for visitors to negotiate. Hever was bought and restored by William Waldorf Astor in 1903; it was he who built the 'Tudor' village that lies behind it and created the magnificent gardens and lake. Attractions inside the house include an exhibition of miniature model houses and a fairly gruesome display of instruments of execution and torture that date back over the past few hundred years. Special events include Easter egg trails, jousting demonstrations and music festivals.

Leeds Castle

Broomfield, nr Maidstone, Kent (01622 765400/ www.leeds-castle.com). **Getting there** *By train* Victoria to Bearsted (1hr), then 10min bus transfer. *By car* J8 off M20. **Open** *Mar-Oct* 10am-7pm daily (last entry 5pm). *Nov-Feb* 10am-5pm daily (last entry 3pm). **Admission** *Castle & park (peak season)* £12; £10.50 concessions; £8.50 4-15s; £35 family. **Credit** MC, V.

A Boleyn alley at **Hever Castle**. *See p349*.

Stunningly sited on two small islands in the middle of a lake, Leeds was built by the Normans shortly after 1066 on the site of a Saxon manor house. Converted into a royal palace by Henry VIII, it now contains a mishmash of medieval furnishings, paintings, tapestries and, bizarrely, the world's finest collection of antique dog collars. The castle's greatest attractions, though, are external. Apart from the flower-filled gardens, there's the Culpeper Garden (an outsize cottage garden), a duckery and an aviary containing more than 100 rare bird species. Best of all is the maze, which centres on a spectacular underground grotto adorned with stone mythical beasts and shell mosaics. There are good facilities for disabled visitors and special events through the year, including spectacular Guy Fawkes' night fireworks.

Windsor

High Street, Windsor, Berkshire (01753 831118/24hr recorded information 01753 831118/www.royalresidences.com). **Getting there** *By train* Paddington to Slough then change for Windsor Central (45mins); Waterloo to Eton & Windsor Riverside (1hr). *By car* J6 off M4. **Open** *Mar-Oct* 9.45am-4pm (last entry) daily. *Nov-Feb* 9.45am-3pm (last entry) daily. *Changing of the Guard* (weather permitting) Apr-June 11am daily; July-Mar call ahead. **Admission** £11.50; £9.50 concessions; £6 4-15s; £29 family. **Credit** AmEx, MC, V.
Admission to Windsor Castle normally includes entry to the state apartments, St George's Chapel, Queen Mary's Dolls' House, the Albert Memorial Chapel, the castle precincts and the gallery. The state rooms, destroyed by the 1992 fire, have now been fully restored and are open to the public: they include the opulent Waterloo Chamber, which was built to celebrate the famous victory over the French in 1815. The gorgeous 15th-century St George's

Chapel is the burial place of ten monarchs, including Henry VIII (note that it's closed to visitors on Sunday, although worshippers are welcome). The amazing Dolls' House, designed by Edward Lutyens and complete with flushing loos and electricity, took some 1,500 men three years to complete.

Country houses & gardens

Althorp – the burial place of Diana, Princess of Wales – is in Northamptonshire, a 90-minute drive from London (contact 0870 167 9000/ www.althorp.com for details). The house is only open during July and August.

Audley End

Saffron Walden, Essex (01799 522399). **Getting there** *By train* Liverpool Street to Audley End (1hr) then 1-mile (1.5km) walk or 2min taxi ride. *By car* J8 off M11 then B1383. **Open** *Apr-Sept* 11am-5pm Wed-Sun; tours by appointment. **Admission** £8; £4 5-16s; £6 concessions; £20 family. **Credit** MC, V.
This magnificent Jacobean mansion was the largest house in the country when it was built for Thomas Howard, 1st Earl of Suffolk, way back in 1614. It was later owned by Charles II, but was given back to the Howards in the 18th century. The latter demolished two-thirds of it in order to make the place more manageable. More than 30 rooms are open to the public today, many of them restored to Robert Adam's 1760s designs. 'Capability' Brown landscaped the gardens. You can book a tour by calling ahead.
   Saffron Walden (1 mile/1.5km from Audley End) is an appealing market town containing many timber-framed houses with decorative plastering ('pargeting'). Eight miles (13km) south-west of here is the village of **Thaxted**, where Gustav Holst

wrote much of *The Planets*; it's also the site of a superb three-tiered, half-timbered Guildhall (01371 831339), dating from the 15th century. There are many other fine villages and much great walking in the area.

Blenheim Palace

Woodstock, Oxfordshire (24hr recorded information 01993 811325/www.blenheimpalace.com). **Getting there** *By train* Paddington to Oxford (1hr) then 30-40min bus ride. *By car* J9 off M40 then A34 and A44. **Open** *Palace & gardens* mid Mar-Oct 10.30am-4.45pm (last entry) daily. *Park* 9am-4.45pm daily. **Admission** *Palace, park & gardens* £10; £8 concessions; £5 5-15s. *Park only* £7 per car (incl occupants), pedestrian £2.50; £1 5-15s. **Credit** AmEx, DC, MC, V.

Waddesdon Manor. *See p352.*

After defeating the French at the Battle of Blenheim in 1704, John Churchill, first Duke of Marlborough, was so handsomely rewarded that he could afford to build this fabulous palace. Designed by Sir John Vanbrugh and set in huge grounds landscaped by 'Capability' Brown, it's the only non-royal residence in the country grand enough to be given the title 'palace'. Even if you decided not to tour the palace itself – with its remarkable long library, gilded state rooms and Churchill exhibition (Sir Winston was born here, and is buried at nearby Bladon) – there's plenty to keep you occupied in the grounds, including a butterfly house, miniature railway, adventure playground, lake for boating and fishing, and the world's biggest symbolic hedge maze).

The handsome, well-scrubbed Oxfordshire town of **Woodstock** has a long history of royal connections but now chiefly services visitors to Blenheim and the Cotswolds (*see p353*).

Groombridge Place Gardens

Groombridge, nr Tunbridge Wells, Kent (01892 863999/www.groombridge.co.uk). **Getting there** *By rail* Charing Cross to Tunbridge Wells (53mins) then 10min taxi ride. *By car* J5 off M25 then A21, A26 and B2176. **Open** *Easter-Oct* 9am-6pm/dusk daily. **Admission** £8.30; £7 concessions; £6.80 5-15s; £27.50 family. **Credit** MC, V.

The Manor of Groombridge has passed through many hands since its early life as a medieval pig pasture, flourishing and wilting along with its owners' fortunes. Much of what can be seen today is down to barrister and academic Philip Packer, who in the mid 17th century demolished the old manor house, constructed Groombridge Place and enlisted the help of diarist John Evelyn to design brand new gardens.

Having inspired artists and writers for several centuries (Sir Arthur Conan Doyle and Peter Greenaway among them), the gardens finally opened to the public in 1994. Visitors can now watch peacocks strut around the spring-fed pools and waterfalls, wonder at the strange topiary, play giant chess, take a canal boat to the award-winning 'Enchanting Forest' or simply stroll through the vineyard.

Hatfield House

Hatfield, Hertfordshire (01707 287010/ www.hatfield-house.co.uk). **Getting there** *By train* from King's Cross to Hatfield (25mins). *By car* J4 off A1(M). **Open** *House* noon-4pm daily. *Tours* noon-4pm Mon-Fri. *West Gardens* 11am-5.30pm daily. *East Gardens* 11am-5.30pm Fri. Closed Oct-Easter. **Admission** *House, park & gardens* £7.50; £4 5-15s. *Park & gardens* £4.50; £3.50 5-15s. *Park only* £2; £1 5-15s. **Credit** MC, V.

Built by Robert Cecil, Earl of Salisbury, in 1611, this superb Jacobean mansion oozes history. In the grounds stands the remaining wing of the Royal Palace of Hatfield, the childhood home of Queen Elizabeth I: she held her first Council of State here in 1558. The gardens include herb terraces, orchards and fountains restored to their former glory by the present-day marchioness.

Sissinghurst Castle Garden

*Sissinghurst, Cranbrook, Kent (01580 712850/
www.nationaltrust.org.uk).* **Getting there** *By train*
Charing Cross to Staplehurst (53mins) then 10min
taxi ride. *By car* J5 off M25 then A21 and A262.
Open *22 Mar-2 Nov* 11am-6.30pm Mon, Tue, Fri
(last entry 5.30pm); 10am-6.30pm Sat, Sun (last entry
5.30pm). **Admission** £6.50; £3 5-15s. **Credit** AmEx,
MC, V.

Sissinghurst is famous not only for its wonderfully
inspirational garden but also for its celebrity cre-
ators, poet and novelist Vita Sackville-West and the
historian and diplomat Harold Nicolson, her husband. Devised around what was left of an
Elizabethan mansion, there's tremendous individuality evident in the varied gardens, which have
something to offer whatever the season. Visitors can
also see Vita's study, the 15th-century long library
and the central prospect tower.

Stowe

*Buckinghamshire (gardens 01280 822850/house
01280 818282/www.nationaltrust.org.uk).* **Getting
there** *By train* Euston to Milton Keynes (40mins)
then bus to Buckingham (30mins) then 5min taxi
ride. *By car* J10 off M40 then A43 and A422, or J14
off M1 then A5 and A422. **Open** *Mar-Oct* 10am-
5.30pm (last entry 4pm) Wed-Sun. *Nov-Dec* 10am-
4pm (last entry 3pm) Wed-Sun. **Admission**
Gardens £5; £2.50 5-15s; £15 family. *House* £3;
£1.50 5-15s. **Credit** MC, V.

Three miles (5km) north-west of Buckingham,
Stowe is quite possibly the most important and
spectacular 18th-century landscaped garden in the
country. Its 325 acres (132 hectares) were first laid
out in 1680 but were transformed over the following century by the addition of trees, six lakes and
32 temples. To 'Capability' Brown's naturalistic
landscaping were added monuments by almost
every big name architect of the time, among them
James Gibbs and John Vanbrugh. The overall effect
is beautiful, idyllic and quintessentially English.
Little of the house can be seen because it's occupied
by Stowe School.

Waddesdon Manor

*Waddesdon, nr Aylesbury, Buckinghamshire (01296
653226/www.waddesdon.org.uk).* **Getting there** *By
train* Marylebone to Aylesbury (53mins) then bus. *By
car* J9 off M40 then A41. **Open** *House* 2 Apr-3 Nov
11am-4pm Wed-Sun. *Grounds* 5 Mar-23 Dec 10am-
5pm Wed-Sun. **Admission** *House & grounds* £11;
£8 5-16s; free under-5s. *Grounds only* £4; £2 5-16s;
free under-5s. **Credit** MC, V.

Baron Ferdinand de Rothschild's truly magnificent
French Renaissance-style château was constructed
in the 1870s and houses one of the world's foremost
collections of 18th-century French decorative art,
together with some important English paintings.
The garden is famous for its specimen trees, seasonal bedding displays and rococo-style aviary of
exotic birds. The website gives details of seasonal
events held here, including wine tastings and talks
on paintings and textiles.

There's wonderful walking country within easy
reach of the city, particularly in the North
Downs, which lie south of London; the Chilterns
to the north-west; and the Cotswolds to the
west. You can also try **Epping Forest** (*see
p348* **Primeval pastimes**) or the **Thames
Path**, which follows a 180-mile (288-kilometre)
stretch of river from its source near Kemble in
Gloucestershire via the Cotswolds, Oxford, the
Chilterns, Windsor and through London to the
Thames Barrier at Woolwich (leaflets are
available at tourist information centres).

Country Lanes *9 Shaftesbury Street,
Fordingbridge, Hampshire SP6 1JF (01425
655022/www.countrylanes.co.uk).*

Representatives from Country Lanes will meet you
off your train from London and lead you on cycling
or walking tours of the New Forest and the
Cotswolds. There are day trips, short breaks and six-
day tours. Visit the website or phone for a brochure.

The Chilterns

Getting there: *By train* from Paddington to Henley
(55mins); Paddington to Bourne End then change for
Marlow (1hr 5mins). *By car* Henley/Marlow J8 off M4
then A404(M) and A4130, or J4 off M40 then A404
and A4155. *Wendover* J20 off M25 then A41 and
A4011, or A40 and A413.

Stretching in a broad arc around the north-west of
London, the Chilterns rarely receive more than a cur-
sory glance out of the window from the coachloads
of tourists powering through to Oxford and
Stratford. Yet this gently hilly region has some great
walking and excellent pubs (despite some charmless
towns) and is easily accessible from the capital.

At the place where Oxfordshire, Berkshire and
Buckinghamshire meet sits cocky little **Henley**
(tourist office 01491 578034). This wealthy commuter burgh becomes the epicentre of braying-toff
life for five loud days at the tail-end of June, when
the **Royal Regatta** is in full swing (*see p265*). It's
otherwise most useful as a base from which to
explore the wonderful villages and countryside
nearby. Some of the best walking in the Chilterns
can be found around **Frieth** and **Nettlebed**, as well
as further north around **Wendover**.

Another good (if very popular) place from which
to explore the southern Chilterns and the Thames
Valley, **Marlow** is a relaxed little town with some
good Georgian architecture and a fine pub – the Two
Brewers on St Peter's Street – where author Jerome
K Jerome is said to have penned much of *Three Men
in a Boat*. Other notable literary residents of Marlow
have included the Romantics Percy Bysshe and
Mary Shelley and Nobel laureate TS Eliot.

The cutesy village of **Cookham**, four miles (7km)
east of Marlow, is famed as the home of one of
20th-century Britain's greatest and most idiosyncratic painters, Stanley Spencer. Several of his
deceptively naïve works are displayed in the

Derek Jarman's garden at **Dungeness**: beauty out of adversity. *See p354.*

Stanley Spencer Gallery (01628 471885) on the High Street, and exhibit the artist's characteristic obsession with sex and God.

The Cotswolds

Getting there *By train* Paddington to Moreton-in-Marsh (1hr 20mins). *By car* M40 then A40 and A44.

Nowhere in England is there such a harmonious relationship between buildings and landscape as there is in the Cotswolds. The enchanting stone villages and incomparable 'wool churches' that characterise the area were built by medieval merchants who had grown rich from the profits of the local wool trade. The stone here, routinely described as 'honey-coloured', is actually very variable, but its ubiquity helps unify a region that sprawls over six counties.

Certain parts of the Cotswolds suffer horrible congestion during summer weekends, but this problem is always localised. While crowds tend to buzz around **Bourton** and **Bibury**, equally charming villages such as **Stanton** and **Stanway** slumber on, remaining relatively undisturbed. The small Cotswold towns are often even more memorable than the villages: the elegant 17th-century houses in **Stow-on-the-Wold** (where you'll find the area's tourist information centre; 01451 831082), the gargoyle-encrusted church at **Winchcombe**, cottage gardens full of wisteria, clematis and old roses spilling out on to **Broadway** High Street.

Best of all, though, are the 600-year-old houses and glorious church of **Chipping Campden**. Chipping Campden is also the starting point of the **Cotswold Way** long-distance path. Fortunately, Cotswold footpaths are as suitable for Sunday strollers as they are for hardened hikers. Well-maintained and way-marked, they converge on every town and village. The ancient **Eight Bells Inn** (01386 840371) and the **Cotswold House Hotel** (01386 840330) in Chipping Campden, as well as the **Malt House Hotel** (01386 840295) in Broad Campden, are recommended as bases. For **Stratford-upon-Avon**, *see p348.*

The North Downs

Getting there *By train* Waterloo to Boxhill & Westhumble or Dorking (40-50mins) then 10min taxi ride. *By car* A3 then A243 and A24.

The bones of the landscape of England south of London are the Downs – long chalk ridges facing each other across the Weald. The South Downs are the more spectacular of the two, but the North Downs are far closer to the capital; so close, in fact, that you can enjoy some of the south-east's best views just 20 miles (32km) from the heart of London.

A long-distance footpath, the **North Downs Way**, runs for 140 miles (224km) from Farnham in Surrey to the White Cliffs of Dover. Opportunities for shorter walks are plentiful, and the ancient market town of **Dorking** is a good centre. There's easy access from here to **Box Hill**, which has been a popular picnic spot since the days of Charles II – avoid weekends if you can. Not far away is **Ranmore Common**, which offers good walks on the south slopes of the Downs. Another good spot for walking, six miles (9km) south-west of Dorking, is **Leith Hill**, the highest point in south-east England.

More than just oysters: **Whitstable** beach.

Seaside towns

See also p343 **Brighton**.

Hastings & Battle

Getting there *By train* Charing Cross to Hastings (1hr 20mins). *By car* M25 then A21.

Hastings is an odd combination of fading resort, still-active fishing port and bohemian outpost (fittingly, the **Hastings Museum and Art Gallery** is on Bohemia Road). The well-situated ruins of William the Conqueror's **Norman castle** hold **The 1066 Story** (01424 781112), but the **Smugglers' Adventure** (01424 422964) in St Clement's Caves is more grisly and more exciting. Smuggling was one of Hastings' major industries until the early 19th century, but tourism keeps more of the locals busy these days – the tourist office is to be found in Queens Square (01424 781111).

While they could be said to lack imagination, the founders of **Battle** couldn't be accused of inaccuracy: five miles (8km) inland from Hastings, it's where William and Harold slugged it out for the English crown. To thank God for his victory, William built **Battle Abbey** (01424 773792) on the spot where Harold was killed. The abbey is now reduced to wonderfully evocative ruins, but an audio-visual display fills in the details. The town is rather touristy, but the 14th-century **Almonry** on the High Street is worth a look for the 300-year-old Guy Fawkes effigy in the hallway. A new museum is scheduled to open in spring 2003.

Rye & Dungeness

Getting there *By train* Charing Cross to Ashford then change for Rye (1hr 40mins). *By car* J10 off M20 then A2070 and A259.

Rye was one of the original Cinque Ports, but its river silted up, the sea retreated and the town found itself two miles inland. Nowadays its narrow cobbled streets and skew-whiff little houses draw hordes of snap-happy visitors (it's best to visit out of season). Novelist Henry James lived here at **Lamb House** (01797 890651), and **Rye Castle** (01797 226728) and **Rye Art Gallery** (01797 222433) are also worth a peek. Two of the best B&Bs in town are **Jeake's House** (01797 222828; £63-£130) on Mermaid Street and **Little Orchard House** (01797 223831; £64-£90) on West Street; eating options include the **Landgate Bistro** (01797 222829) and the **Mermaid Inn** (01797 223065). The **tourist information centre** (01797 226696) for the area is also here.

A few miles east of Rye, **Dungeness** is remote and gloriously desolate. The promontory on which it sits (actually, the world's biggest accumulation of shingle) has been built up by longshore drift over 1,000 years. You can investigate the area's fragile ecology at the **Dungeness RSPB Nature Reserve** (01797 320588), enjoy the views from the **Old Lighthouse** (01797 321300) or watch the **miniature railway**, built in 1927 by millionaire racing driver Captain Howey, puff across the bleak landscape. It was here that **Derek Jarman**, during the latter stages of his life, created his surreal and intoxicatingly beautiful garden against the backdrop of massive **Dungeness Nuclear Power Station** (01797 321815). Visitors are free to wander in the garden, but don't be intrusive: it's still a private residence. The **Britannia** (01797 321959) will provide sustenance and shelter.

Whitstable

Getting there *By train* Victoria to Whitstable (1hr 15mins). *By car* J7 off M2 then A99.

Whitstable has a superb, ramshackle seafront cluttered with toy-like cottages, fishermen's huts and sailmakers, but this gently bohemian town is really famous for its succulent, uniquely flavoured native oysters. If you can, time your visit to coincide with the annual week-long **Oyster Festival** at the end of July: there are races between old working yawls and the pre-season oyster catch is paraded round town by locals doing the Fish Slapping Dance (a kind of maritime morris dance with seaweed and shell costumes). In season (Sept-Apr), the best places for oysters are the **Whitstable Oyster Fishery Company** (01227 276856), an upmarket choice offering simple, unfussy dishes, or the more basic **Wheeler's** (01227 273311), which is the town's oldest oyster bar. You can learn more about the oysters at the excellent **Whitstable Museum & Gallery** (01227 276998), which also has a Peter Cushing display (who was a big fan of the town). If you want to spend a night or two here, you can bed down in one of the restored 1860s **Fishermen's Huts** (01227 280280; £75-£115). Whitstable's **tourist office** (01227 275482) is on Oxford Street.

Directory

Features

Directory

Getting Around

Arriving & leaving

For London's domestic rail and coach stations, *see p340*.

By air

Gatwick Airport

01293 535353/www.baa.co.uk/ gatwick. About 30 miles (50km) south of central London, off the M23.
Of the three rail services that link Gatwick to London, the quickest is the **Gatwick Express** (08705 301530, www.gatwickexpress.co.uk) to Victoria Station, which takes about 30 minutes and runs 4.30am to 12.30am daily: on the hour and half-hour between 4.30am and 6am, every 15 minutes between 6am and 7.45pm, then half-hourly until 12.30am. Tickets cost £11 for a single, £11.70 for a day return (after 9.30am) and £21 for a period return (valid for 30 days). Under-15s get half-price tickets; under-5s travel for free.

Connex South Central (08457 484950, www.connex.co.uk) also runs a rail service between Gatwick and Victoria, with trains around every 15 minutes (or hourly 1-4am). It takes up to eight minutes longer than the Gatwick Express but tickets are cheaper: £8.20 for a single, £8.30 for a day return (after 9.30am) and £16.40 for a period return (valid for one month). Under-15s get half-price tickets, and under-5s go for free.

If you're staying in Bloomsbury or catching a train at King's Cross, take the **Thameslink** service (08457 484950, www.thameslink.co.uk). It runs through Blackfriars, City Thameslink, London Bridge, Farringdon and King's Cross; frequency and journey times vary. Tickets to King's Cross cost £9.80 single, £14.50 for a day return and £19.60 for a 30-day period return.

If you want your hand held from airport to hotel and have £20 spare, try **Hotelink** (01293 552251, fax 01293 531131, www.hotelink.co.uk). Give staff your flight details when you book, and someone will meet your plane and escort you all the way to your hotel.

Sadly, there's no real **coach** service from Gatwick to London. Even worse, a **taxi** into town will cost close to £100 and will take an age.

Heathrow Airport

0870 000 0123/www.baa.co.uk/ heathrow. About 15 miles (24km) west of central London, off the M4.
The **Heathrow Express** (0845 600 1515, www.heathrowexpress.co.uk), which runs to Paddington every 15 minutes between 5am and midnight daily, takes 15-20 minutes. The train can be boarded at one of the airport's two tube stations. Tickets cost £12 each way or £23 return (£11.70 or £22.50 return if booked online); under-16s go half-price. Many airlines have check-in desks at Paddington for both hand and hold luggage.

A longer but considerably cheaper journey is by tube on the **Piccadilly line**. Tickets for the 50- to 60-minute ride into central London cost £3.60 one way (£1.50 under-16s). Trains run every few minutes from about 5am-11.45pm daily except Sunday, when they run 6am-11pm.

National Express (08705 808080/www.gobycoach.com) runs daily coach services to London Victoria between 5.30am and 9.30pm daily, leaving Heathrow Central bus terminal every 30 minutes. For a 40-minute journey to London, you'll pay £7 for a single (£3.50 under-15s) or £10 return (£5 under-15s).

As at Gatwick, **Hotelink** (*see above*) offers a hand-holding service for £14 per person each way.

Don't think about taking a **taxi**: fares into town are high (around £45) and the journey time will be at least 45 minutes, far longer in rush hour.

London City Airport

7646 0000/www.londoncityairport.com. About 9 miles (14km) east of central London, Docklands.
Silvertown & City Airport rail station, on the Silverlink line, offers a service that runs around every 20 minutes via Stratford, where you can pick up a Central line tube.

Most people, though, head to London on the blue **Shuttlebus** (7646 0088), whose 25-minute ride to Liverpool Street Station goes via Canary Wharf. It leaves every ten minutes (6.50am-10pm during the week; 6.50am-1.15pm on Saturdays; and 11am-10pm on Sundays). Tickets to Liverpool Street Station cost £6 one-way, or £3 to Canary Wharf.

The journey by **taxi** to the City takes about 30-40 minutes and will cost around £20.

Luton Airport

01582 405100/www.london-luton. co.uk. About 30 miles (50km) north of central London, J10 off the M1.
Luton Airport Parkway Station is close to the airport, but not in it: there's still a short shuttle-bus ride. The **Thameslink** service (*see above*) calls at many stations (King's Cross among them) and has a journey time of 30-40 minutes. Trains leave every 15 minutes or so, and cost £9.50 single and £9.60 for a cheap day return (available after 9.30am Monday to Friday).

The journey from Luton to Victoria takes 60-90 minutes by coach. **National Express** (*see above*) runs a 24-hour service with a frequency of around 30 minutes at peak times. An adult single costs £7, £3.30 for under-15s, while returns cost £10 and £5 respectively.

Again, taking a **taxi** will prove a waste of time (allow at least an hour) and money (upwards of £50).

Stansted Airport

0870 000 0303/www.baa.co.uk/ stansted. About 35 miles (60km) north-east of central London, J8 off the M11.
The quickest way to get to London from Stansted is on the **Stansted Express** train (08457 484950) to Liverpool Street Station; the journey time is 40-45 minutes. Trains leave every 15-30 minutes depending on the time of day, and tickets cost £13 for a single and £23 for a period return; under-15s travel half-price.

The **Airbus A6** (08705 808080) coach service from Stansted to Victoria takes at least an hour and 40 minutes and runs from 12.05am to 11.05pm. Coaches run roughly every 30 minutes, more frequently during peak times. An adult single costs £8 (£4 for under-15s), a return is £12 (£5.50 for under-15s).

The hour-plus **taxi** ride to central London will cost around £80.

By rail

Eurostar

Waterloo International Terminal, SE1 (08705 186186/www.eurostar.com). Waterloo tube/rail. **Map** p401 M8.
Eurostar trains arrive into the central Waterloo Station; you can then take a tube, bus or taxi to your hotel.

Public transport

Information

Details on public transport in London can be found online at www.thetube.com and/or www.londontransport.co.uk, or on 7222 1234.

Travel Information Centres

TfL's Travel Information Centres provide maps and information about the tube, buses and Docklands Light Railway (DLR; *see below*). You can find them in the stations listed below.

Euston 7.15am-6pm Mon-Sat; 8.30am-5pm Sun.
Heathrow Airport *Terminals 1, 2 & 3 Underground station* 6.30am-7pm Mon-Sat; 7.15am-7pm Sun. *Terminal 4 Arrivals Hall* 6am-3pm Mon-Sat; 7.15am-3pm Sun.
King's Cross *Underground station* 8am-6pm Mon-Sat; 8.30am-5pm Sun.
Liverpool Street 8am-6pm Mon-Fri; 8.45am-5.30pm Sat, Sun.
Victoria 7.45am-7pm Mon-Sat; 8.45am-7pm Sun.
Waterloo *Eurostar Arrivals Hall* 8am-11pm daily.

Fares & tickets

Bus and tube fares are based on a zone system. There are six zones stretching 12 miles (20 kilometres) out from the centre of London. For most visitors, the Travelcard (*see below*) is the cheapest way of getting around. Beware of on-the-spot £10 penalty fares for anyone caught without a ticket.

Adult fares

The single underground fare for adults within zone 1 is £1.60. For zones 1 and 2 it's £2, while an all-zones single fare is £3.70. Single bus fares are 70p for a journey outside zone 1 and £1 for a trip within zone 1 or crossing the zone 1 boundary.

Buying individual tickets is the most expensive way to travel. If you're likely to make three or more journeys in one day, it's cheaper to buy a Travelcard (*see below*).

Child fares

On all buses, tubes and local trains, under-16s are classified as children; under-5s travel free. Under-16s pay a child's fare until 10pm; after 10pm (buses only) they pay an adult fare. Fourteen- and 15-year-olds must carry child rate photocards, available from any post office: take a passport-size photo and proof of age (passport or birth certificate) with you. The single Underground fare for children in zone 1 is 60p, or 80p for zones 1 and 2, rising to £1.50 for an all-zone ticket. Single child bus fares are 40p anywhere in London.

One-Day LT Cards

One-Day LT Cards will only be of interest if you intend to travel before 9.30am on weekdays and make several journeys during the day. They're valid for travel throughout Greater London on tube, Tramlink and Docklands Light Railway services, but not on National Rail or on the Bakerloo line between Kenton and Harrow & Wealdstone. They are also valid for travel across the London bus network, but not on special bus services or excursions. A one-day LT card costs £8 and £3.50 for children (5-15s), and are valid from midnight on the date of validity and for any journey that starts before 4.30am the following day.

Travelcards

If you wish to start travelling before 9.30am (Mondays-Fridays), you can purchase a One-Day Travelcard. Zones 1-2 costs £5.10 and £2.50 for children, with prices rising to £10.70 (£5.30 children) for an all-zones card. If you need a zones 1-5 or 1-6 card and are not using National Rail services, it is cheaper to buy an LT Card. All tickets are valid for journeys before 4.30am the next day.

Carnet

If you're planning on making a lot of short-hop journeys within zone 1 over a period of several days, it makes sense to buy a Carnet of ten tickets for £11.50 (£5 for children). This brings down the cost of each journey to £1.15 rather than the standard £1.60. Note that if you exit a station outside of zone 1 and are caught with only a carnet ticket, you'll be liable to a £10 penalty fare.

Photocards

Photocards are required for all bus passes and Travelcards except the One-Day and Weekend versions. Child-rate photocards are required for five- to 15-year-olds using child-rate Travelcards and bus passes. Fourteen- and 15-year-olds need a child-rate photocard in order to buy any ticket at the discounted rate.

London Underground

There are frequent delays. Escalators are often out of action. Some lines close at weekends for engineering. It's unbearably hot and crowded in rush hour (8-9.30am and 4.30-7pm Mon-Fri). Still, London's underground rail system – aka the tube – is still the quickest way to get around London.

Using the system

Tube tickets can be purchased from a ticket office or from self-service machines. Unfortunately, staff rarely speak foreign languages and can be unhelpful. You can buy most tickets, including Carnets and One-Day LT Cards, from self-service machines, but for anything covering a longer period you'll need to show a valid photocard to a ticket officer. Ticket offices in some stations close early (around 7.30pm), but it's best to keep change with you at all times: using a ticket machine is quicker than queuing at a ticket office.

To enter the tube, insert your ticket in the automatic checking gates with the black magnetic strip facing down, then pull it out of the top to open the gates. Exiting the system at your destination is done in much the same way, though if you have a single journey ticket, it will be retained by the gate as you leave.

There are 12 Underground lines, colour-coded on the tube map for ease of use. There's a full map of the London Underground on the back page of this book.

Underground timetable

Tube trains run daily from around 5.30am (except Sunday, when they start an hour or two later, depending on the line). The only exception is Christmas Day, when there is no service. Generally, you won't have to wait more than ten minutes for a train, and during peak times the service should run every two or three minutes. Times of last trains vary, though they're usually around 11.30pm-1am daily except Sunday, when they finish 30 minutes to an hour earlier. The only all-night public transport is by night bus.

Docklands Light Railway (DLR)

7363 9700/www.dlr.co.uk.
The DLR is administered as part of the tube system. Its driverless trains run on a raised track from Bank (Central or Waterloo & City lines) or Tower Gateway, close to Tower Hill tube (Circle and District lines), to Stratford, Beckton and down the Isle of Dogs to Island Gardens, Greenwich and Lewisham. Trains run from 5.30am-12.30am Monday to Friday, 6am-12.30am Saturday and 7.30am-11.30pm Sunday.

Get this feeling.

And experience London with a class of service second to none.

Europcar are proud to offer you a fleet of vehicles and range of offers specifically designed to make your stay in London a stay to remember.

For Reservations and Sales, call **0870 607 5000**, or visit our website at **www.europcar.co.uk**

Europcar

Docklands Shuttle South (Lewisham to Canary Wharf) tickets cost £1.60; Docklands Shuttle East (valid between Beckton/Stratford and Island Gardens via Westferry) tickets are £2.20; City Flyer South (valid between Bank and Lewisham) tickets are £3; and City Flyer East (valid between Beckton/Stratford and Bank) tickets are £3.30. Expect to pay around half-price for child tickets (under-16s; photocard required for 14-15s).

The DLR also offers one-day 'Rail & River Rover' tickets that combine unlimited DLR travel with a riverboat trip between Greenwich, Tower and Westminster Piers (boats run from 10am-6pm; call City Cruises on 7740 0400 for exact round-trip times). Starting at Tower Gateway, trains leave on the hour (from 10am), with a DLR guide giving passengers the lowdown on the area as the train glides along. Tickets cost £8.30 for adults, £4.20 for kids and £22 for a family pass (two adults and up to three kids); under-5s travel free. Note that family tickets may only be purchased in person from the piers.

Buses

What it lacks in speed, it *really* lacks in speed. Thanks to the shocking traffic, travelling by bus in London can be awfully slow. Still, the fares are cheap – £1 for journeys that take in zone 1, 70p for others – and if you can spare the time, there are few better spots from which to get acquainted with the streets of London than the top deck of a traditional red bus. But hurry: if Ken gets his way, they're going to be phased out in favour of more practical but considerably uglier single-decker models.

Night buses

Night buses are the only form of public transport that runs all night, operating from 11pm-6am around once an hour on most routes (more often on Fridays and Saturdays). All pass through central London and the majority stop at Trafalgar Square, so head there if you're unsure which bus to get. Night buses have the letter 'N' before their number, and are free to holders of One-Day Travelcards, Weekend Travelcards, Family Travelcards and One-Day LT Cards. You'll find free maps and timetables at LT Travel Information Centres (*see p357*). Fares for night buses are now the same as for day buses.

Green Line buses

Green Line buses (0870 608 7261, www.greenline.co.uk) serve the suburbs and towns within a 40-mile (64km) radius of London. Their main departure point is Eccleston Bridge, SW1 (Colonnades Coach Station, behind Victoria).

Routes 205 & 705

Bus routes 205 and 705 (7222 1234) connect all the main London rail termini (except Charing Cross) on circular trips. These express services are convenient for the disabled, the elderly, people laden with luggage or those with small children. Bus 205 runs from Whitechapel station to Euston Square station via Aldgate, Aldgate East, Liverpool Street, Moorgate, Old Street, Angel, King's Cross, St Pancras and Euston. Starting at around 5am (6am on Sunday) to just after midnight every day, they run around every 10-15 minutes; check the timetable. Route 705 starts at Paddington around 7.50am (8.15am from Liverpool Street) and runs around every 30 minutes until 7.50pm (8.15pm from Liverpool Street), stopping at Victoria, Waterloo, London Bridge and Fenchurch Street. The fare is £1 for adults, 40p for five- to 15-year-olds.

Rail services

Independently run commuter services leave from the city's main rail stations (*see p340*). Travelcards are valid on these services within the right zones. Perhaps the most useful is **Silverlink** (01923 207258, www.silverlink-trains.com; or National Rail Enquiries on 08457 484950), which runs from Richmond in the south-west to North Woolwich in the east, via London City Airport. Trains run about every 20 minutes daily except Sunday, when they run every half-hour.

For more information about train travel, *see p340*. For lost property, *see p368*.

Water transport

The times of London's chaotic assortment of river services vary, but most operate every 20 minutes to one hour between 10.30am and 5pm. Services may be more frequent and run later in summer.

Journey times are longer than by tube, but it's a nicer way to travel. Call the operators listed below for schedules and fares, or see www.tfl.gov.uk. The names in bold below are the names of piers.

Embankment–Tower (30mins)– **Greenwich** (30mins); Catamaran Cruises 7987 1185.

Greenland Dock–Canary Wharf (8mins)–**St Katharine's** (7mins)– **London Bridge City** (4mins)– **Bankside** (3mins)–**Blackfriars** (3mins)–**Savoy** (4mins); Collins River Enterprises 7977 6892.

Greenwich–(Thames) Barrier Gardens (25mins); Campion Launches 8305 0300.

Savoy–Cadogan (15-20mins)– **Chelsea** (2mins); Riverside Launches 07831 574774.

Westminster–(Thames) Barrier Gardens (1hr 30mins); Thames Cruises 7930 3373/ www.thamescruises.com.

Westminster–Festival (5mins)– **London Bridge City** (20mins)–**St Katharine's** (5mins); Crown River 7936 2033/www.crownriver.com.

Westminster–Greenwich (1hr); Westminster Passenger Services 7930 4097/ www.westminsterpier.co.uk.

Westminster–Kew (1hr 30mins)– **Richmond** (30mins)–**Hampton Court** (1hr 30mins); Westminster Passenger Service Association 7930 2062.

Westminster–Tower (25-30mins); City Cruises 7740 0400/www.citycruises.com.

Taxis

Black cabs

Licensed London taxis are known as black cabs – even though they now come in a variety of colours thanks to on-cab advertising – and are a quintessential feature of London life. Drivers of black cabs must pass a test called the Knowledge to prove they know the name of every street in central London, where it is and the shortest route to it.

When a taxi's yellow 'For Hire' sign is switched on, it can be hailed in the street. If a taxi stops, the cabbie must take you to your destination, provided it's within seven miles. In reality, some turn

Directory

their noses up at south London, or, indeed, anywhere they don't fancy going. Thanks to a huge price hike in 2001 aimed at getting more cab drivers out after dark, you'll pay 50 per cent more after 8pm on weekdays and all weekend.

You can book black cabs in advance. Both **Radio Taxis** (7272 0272; credit cards only) and **Dial-a-Cab** (7253 5000) run 24-hour services for black cabs (there'll be a booking fee in addition to the regular fare). Enquiries or complaints about black cabs should be made to the Public Carriage Office. Note the badge number of the offending cab, which should be displayed in the rear of the cab as well as on its back bumper. For lost property, *see p368.*

Public Carriage Office *200 Baker Street, Marylebone, NW1 5RZ (7918 2000). Baker Street tube.* **Open** *By phone* 9am-4pm Mon-Fri. *In person* 9pm-2am Mon-Fri.

Minicabs

Minicabs (saloon cars) are generally cheaper than black cabs, but be sure to only use licensed firms and avoid minicab drivers who tout for business on the street (common at Victoria Station, in Soho, and outside many nightclubs). They'll be unlicensed and uninsured, almost certainly won't know how to get around, and charge extortionate fares.

There are, happily, plenty of trustworthy and licensed local minicab firms. Among Londonwide firms are **Lady Cabs** (7254 3501), which employs only women drivers (great for women travelling alone), and **Addison Lee** (7387 8888). Whoever you use, ask the price when you book and confirm it with the driver when the car arrives.

Driving

If you can avoid driving in London while you're here, do so. The traffic is horrendous,

the parking is worse, and the situation will be complicated by the scheduled introduction on 17 February 2003 of the Congestion Charge. This will mean every driver driving in central London – an area defined as within King's Cross (N), Old Street roundabout (NE), Aldgate (E), Old Kent Road (SE), Elephant and Castle (S), Vauxhall (SW), Hyde Park Corner (W) and Edgware Road tube (NW) – between 7am and 6.30pm Monday to Friday will have to pay a £5 fee. Passes can be bought from newsagents, garages and the like, and the scheme will be enforced by countless CCTV cameras.

Breakdown services

If you're a member of a motoring organisation in another country, check to see if it has a reciprocal agreement with a British organisation. Both the AA and the RAC offer schemes that cover Europe in addition to the UK.

AA (Automobile Association)
Information 08705 500600/ breakdown 0800 887766/members 0800 444999/www.theaa.co.uk. **Open** 24hrs daily. **Membership** £43-£192/yr. **Credit** MC, V.

ETA (Environmental Transport Association) *68 High Street, Weybridge, Surrey KT13 8RS (01932 828882/www.eta.co.uk).* **Open** *Office* 8am-6pm Mon-Fri; 9am-4pm Sat. *Breakdown service* 24hrs daily. **Membership** £25/yr. **Credit** MC, V.

RAC (Royal Automobile Club) *RAC House, 1 Forest Road, Feltham, Middx TW13 7RR (breakdown 0800 828282/office & membership 08705 722722/www.rac.co.uk).* **Open** *Office* 8am-9pm Mon-Fri; 8.30am-5pm Sat; 10am-4pm Sun. *Breakdown service* 24hrs daily. **Membership** £33-£193. **Credit** AmEx, DC, MC, V.

Parking

Central London is scattered with parking meters, but finding a free one could take several hours, and when you do it'll cost you up to £1 for every 15 minutes to park there, and you'll be limited to two

hours on the meter. Parking on a single yellow line, a double yellow line or a red line at any time during the day is illegal, and you're likely to end up being fined, clamped or towed.

However, in the evening (from 6pm or 7pm in much of central London) and at various times at weekends, parking on single yellow lines is legal and free. If you find a clear spot on a single yellow line during the evening, check a nearby sign before you leave your car: this sign should tell you at which times parking is legal on this particular yellow line, as times vary from street to street. It's a similar story with meters, which become free after a certain time in the evening and at various times on weekends: check before paying, as it could save you several quid. Parking on double yellow lines and red routes is, by and large, illegal at all times.

NCP 24-hour car parks (7499 7050/www.ncp.co.uk) in and around central London are numerous but phenomenally expensive. Prices vary with location, but expect to pay £6-£10 for two hours and £30-£50 for 24 hours. Among its central car parks are those at Arlington House, Arlington Street, St James's, W1; Upper Ground, Southwark, SE1; and 2 Lexington Street, Soho, W1.

A word of warning: almost all NCPs in central London are underground, and a few – such as the car park on Adeline Place behind Tottenham Court Road – are frequented by drug users looking for a quiet place in which to smoke, snort or inject. Take care.

Clamping

The immobilising of illegally parked vehicles by attaching a clamp to one wheel is commonplace in London. There will be a label attached to the car telling you which payment centre to phone or visit. Some boroughs let you pay over the phone with a credit card, others insist you go in person. Either way, you'll have to stump up an £80 clamp release fee and show a valid licence (there's a 50% discount on the fine if you pay within two weeks). If you can't show a valid licence, you'll have to pay a release fee of £120 for motorcycles and cars, £600 for any other vehicle.

Staff at the payment centre will promise to de-clamp your car some time within the next four hours, but they won't tell you exactly when. You are also warned that if you don't remove your car immediately, they might clamp it again. This Kafkaesque system means you may have to spend quite some time waiting by your car.

If you feel you've been clamped unfairly, look for the appeals procedure and contact number on the back of your ticket. If your appeal is turned down and you still wish to take things further, call the Clamping and Vehicle Section (7747 4700), an independent governing body.

Vehicle removal

If your car has mysteriously disappeared, chances are that, if it was legally parked, it's been nicked; if not, it's probably been hoisted on to the back of a truck and taken to a car pound, and you're facing a stiff penalty: a fee of £160 is levied for removal, plus £15 per day from the first midnight after removal. To add insult to injury, you'll probably get a parking ticket of £40-£80 when you collect the car (there's a 50% discount if you pay within 14 days). To find out where your car has been taken and how to retrieve it, call the Trace Service hotline (7747 4747).

Vehicle hire

To hire a car, you must have at least one year's driving experience with a full current driving licence; in addition, many car hire firms refuse to hire vehicles out to people under the age of 23. If you're an overseas visitor, your current driving licence is valid in Britain for a year.

Prices for car hire vary wildly; always ring several competitors for a quote (see the *Yellow Pages* or www.yell.com). As well as the companies listed below – call or check online to find the location of your nearest office – Easycar's online-only service, at www.easycar.com, offers competitive rates, just so long as you don't mind driving a heavily branded car around town.

Alamo *0870 400 4508/www.alamo. com*. **Open** 8am-7pm Mon-Fri; 8am-6pm Sat; 9am-4pm Sun. **Credit** AmEx, MC, V.

Avis *08705 900500/www.avis.co.uk*. **Open** 24hrs daily. **Credit** AmEx, DC, MC, V.

Budget *0800 181181/ www.gobudget.com)*. **Open** 9am-5.30pm Mon-Fri; 8am-4pm Sat. **Credit** AmEx, DC, MC, V.

Enterprise *01252 353620/ www.enterprise.com*. **Open** 8am-6pm Mon-Fri; 8am-noon Sat. **Credit** AmEx, MC, V.

Europcar *0870 607 5000/ www.europcar.com*. **Open** 24hrs daily. **Credit** AmEx, DC, MC, V.

Hertz *0870 599 6699/ www.hertz.com*. **Open** 24hrs daily. **Credit** AmEx, MC, V.

Motorbike hire

HGB Motorcycles *69-71 Park Way, Ruislip Manor, Middx (01895 676451/www.hgbmotorcycles.co.uk)*. Ruislip Manor tube. **Open** 9am-6pm Mon-Fri; 9am-4pm Sat. **Credit** MC, V. **Map** p399 M3.

It costs £75 a day or £385 a week to hire an ST1100 Pan European. All rental prices include 250 miles (402km) a day, with excess mileage at 10p a mile, AA cover, insurance and VAT. Bikes can only be hired with a credit card and a deposit (£350-£850, depending on bike size). There's no crash helmet hire.

Cycling

The traffic being what is it, London is an unfriendly town for cyclists, but thanks to the many blackspot-avoiding cycle routes – contact the London Cycle Network (7974 2016/ www.londoncyclenetwork.org) or the London Cycling Campaign (*see below*) to order one or more of the 19 area maps illustrating said routes – it's not as bad as many make out. A safety helmet, a filter-mask and a determined attitude are advisable.

London Cycling Campaign

30 Great Guildford Street, South Bank, SE1 0HS (7928 7220/ www.lcc.org.uk). **Open** *Phone enquiries* 10am-5pm Mon-Fri. Individual membership (£23.50 a year) allows discounts at selected bike shops, advice and information on bike maintenance, insurance deals, route maps and a subscription to *London Cyclist* magazine.

Cycle hire & storage

Bikepark

11-13 Macklin Street, Covent Garden, WC2 (7430 0083/ www.bikepark.co.uk). Covent Garden or Holborn tube. **Open** 8.30am-7pm Mon-Fri; 10am-6pm Sat. **Credit** MC, V. **Map** p399 L6.

This Bikepark allows you to leave your bike in secure parking (£2 for 24 hours, £7.50 for a week, £20 for a month) and a repair service. For bike hire (£12/1st day, £6/2nd day, £4/day thereafter; £200 deposit), try the SW3 branch.

Branch: 67 New King's Road, Chelsea, SW3 (7731 7012).

London Bicycle Tour Company

1A Gabriel's Wharf, 56 Upper Ground, South Bank, SE1 (7928 6838/www.londonbicycle.com). Southwark tube/Blackfriars or Waterloo tube/rail. **Open** *Easter-Oct* 10am-6pm daily. *Nov-Easter* by appointment. **Hire** £2.50/hr; £12/1st day; £6/day thereafter. **Deposit** £100 (unless paying by credit card). **Credit** AmEx, DC, MC, V. **Map** p404 N7.

In addition to bike hire and the increasingly popular rickshaw hire (which costs £12/hour, self-drive), this company, as its name implies, conducts daily bicycle tours covering either west London, east London or the centre of town. All tours cost £14.95 and last around three hours. The firm also offers weekend breaks in the countryside around London.

Walking

The best way to see London is on foot. However, the town is extremely complicated in terms of its street layout – so much so, in fact, that even locals carry maps around with them most, if not all, of the time. This means that you should be prepared to get lost on at least a semi-regular basis.

We've included a selection of street maps covering central London in the back of this book (starting on *p394*), but we recommend that you also buy a separate map of the city: both the standard Geographers' *A–Z* and Collins' *London Street Atlas* versions come in a variety of sizes and are very easy to use.

Resources A-Z

Addresses

London addresses invariably come with a postcode attached. This helps indicate where the street is found, but also helps differentiate between streets with the same name in different parts of London (there are 20 Park Roads in the city, for example).

A London postcode written in its most basic form takes a point of the compass – N, E, SE, SW, W and NW, plus EC (East Central) and WC (West Central) – and then a number; for example, N1, WC2, SE24. With the exception of those numbered 1, which denote the area nearest the centre of London, the numbers are ordered alphabetically by area. Thus, in east London, E1 is Whitechapel (closest to central London), but then E2 is Bethnal Green, E3 is Bow etc.

Age restrictions

You must be 17 or older to drive in the United Kingdom, and 18 to buy cigarettes or be served alcohol (to be safe, carry photo ID if you're under 22 years of age, or look as if you might be). For both hetero- and homosexuals, the age of consent in Britain is 16.

Business

Financial Times and *The Economist* are the best business periodicals (*see p369*).

Conventions & conferences

London Tourist Board & Convention Bureaux

7932 2020/www.londontown.com. The LTB runs a venue enquiry service for conventions and exhibitions. Call or email for an information pack that lists the facilities offered by various venues.

Queen Elizabeth II Conference Centre

Broad Sanctuary, Westminster, SW1 (7222 5000/www.qeiicc.co.uk). St James's Park tube. **Open** 8am-6pm Mon-Fri. *Conference facilities* 24hrs daily. **Map** p401 K9.

This purpose-built centre has some of the best conference facilities in the capital. Rooms have capacities ranging from 40 to 1,100, all with wireless LAN technology installed.

Couriers & shippers

DHL and FedEx offer local and international courier services; Excess Baggage is the UK's largest shipper of luggage.

DHL *181 Strand, Covent Garden, WC2 (08701 100 300/ www.dhl.co.uk). Charing Cross tube/rail.* **Open** 7am-8pm Mon-Fri; 8am-6pm Sat. **Credit** AmEx, DC, MC, V. **Map** p401 L7.

Excess Baggage *168 Earl's Court Road, Earl's Court, SW5 (7373 1977/www.excess-baggage.com). Earl's Court tube.* **Open** 8am-6pm Mon-Fri; 9am-2pm Sat. **Credit** AmEx, MC, V. **Map** p396 B10.

FedEx *0800 123800/www.fedex.com.* **Open** 7.30am-7.30pm Mon-Fri. **Credit** AmEx, DC, MC, V.

Office hire & business centres

ABC rents office equipment, while British Monomarks offers communications services.

ABC Business Machines *59 Chiltern Street, Marylebone, W1 (7486 5634/www.abcbusiness.co.uk). Baker Street tube.* **Open** 9am-5.30pm Mon-Fri; 9.30am-12.30pm Sat. **Credit** MC, V. **Map** p398 G5.

British Monomarks *Monomarks House, 27 Old Gloucester Street, Bloomsbury, WC1 (7419 5000/7404 5011/www.britishmonomarks.co.uk). Holborn tube.* **Open** *Mail forwarding* 9.30am-5.30pm Mon-Fri. *Telephone answering* 9am-6pm Mon-Fri. **Credit** AmEx, MC, V. **Map** p399 L5.

Secretarial services

Reed Employment

143 Victoria Street, Westminster, SW1 (7834 1801/www.reed.co.uk). Victoria tube/rail. **Open** 8am-6pm Mon-Fri. **Map** p400 J10.

Reed supplies secretarial, computing, accountancy and technical services to registered companies. This branch specialises in secretarial and admin. **Branches**: throughout the city.

Translators & interpreters

Central Translations

21 Woodstock Street, Mayfair, W1 (7493 5511/www.centraltranslations. co.uk). Bond Street tube. **Open** 9am-5pm Mon-Fri. **Map** p398 H6.

Be it typesetting, proofreading, translation or the use of an interpreter, Central can work with almost every language under the sun.

Consumer

Most shops will happily offer a full refund for faulty or defective goods. If you do experience any difficulty in obtaining a refund, contact your local council's Trading Standards department for help and legal advice.

Customs

When entering the UK, non-European Union citizens and anyone buying duty-free goods should be aware of the following import limits:

● 200 cigarettes or 100 cigarillos or 50 cigars or 250 grams (8.82 ounces) of tobacco;
● wine plus either 1 litre of spirits or strong liqueurs (more than 22% alcohol by volume) or 2 litres of fortified wine (under 22% abv), sparkling wine or other liqueurs;
● 60cc/ml of perfume;
● 250cc/ml of toilet water;
● other goods to the value of £145 for non-commercial use;
● the import of meat, meat products, fruit, plants, flowers and protected animals is restricted or forbidden.

Since the Single European Market agreement came into force at the beginning of 1993, people over the age of 17 arriving from an EU country have been able to import large quantities of goods for their own personal use, but Customs officials may need convincing that you do not intend to sell any of the goods.

Disabled

Compared to some European cities, London is relatively friendly to the mobility-impaired. But while many of the capital's sights do make provision for wheelchair users, the great headache for them is transport. For information on provision for the disabled on the tube, check out the *Access to the Underground* booklet, available free from ticket offices, TfL's Access to Mobility (42-50 Victoria Street, SW1H 0TL; 7918 3312) and Travel Information Centres (*see p357*). Access to Mobility also has details on buses and Braille maps. All DLR stations have wheelchair access.

Access in London by Gordon Couch, William Forrester and Justin Irwin (Quiller Press, 1997) has detailed maps of step-free routes and accessible tube stations, sections on shopping, accommodation and entertainment, and a guide to adapted toilets. It's available at some bookshops for £7.95, or from Radar (39 Bradley Gardens, W13 8HE; 7250 3222).

For the National Bureau for Students with Disabilities, *see p373*.

Artsline
54 Chalton Street, Somers Town, NW1 (tel/textphone 7388 2227/ www.artsline.org.uk). Euston tube/ rail. **Open** 9.30am-5.30pm Mon-Fri. **Map** p399 K3.
Information on disabled access to entertainment events in London and on adapted facilities in venues.

Can Be Done
7-11 Kensington High Street, Kensington, W8 5NP (8907 2400/ www.canbedone.co.uk). High Street Kensington tube. **Open** *Phone enquiries* 9am-5.30pm Mon-Fri. **Map** p396 A9.
Holidays and tours in London and around the UK that are tailored to the needs of disabled people.

DAIL (Disability Arts in London)
Diorama Arts Centre, 34 Osnaburgh Street, Fitzrovia, NW1 (7916 6351/ textphone 7691 4201/www.ldaf.net). Great Portland Street tube. **Open** 11am-4pm Mon-Fri. **Map** p398 H4.
DAIL produces a monthly magazine with reviews and articles on the arts and the disabled (£10 per year, £30 for overseas subscribers). DAIL is part of **LDAF** (London Disability Arts Forum; 7916 5484), which organises events for disabled people in London.

DAIL UK (National Association of Disablement Information & Advice Lines)
01302 310123/www.dialuk.org.uk. **Open** 9am-5pm Mon-Thur; 9am-4pm Fri.
DIAL UK holds details of local groups in the United Kingdom that can offer free information and advice on all aspects of disability.

Greater London Action on Disability
336 Brixton Road, Brixton, SW9 (7346 5800/information line 7346 5819/textphone 7326 4554/ www.glad.org.uk). Brixton tube/rail. **Open** *Phone enquiries* 9am-5pm Mon-Fri. *Information line* 1.30-4.30pm Mon, Wed, Fri.
A valuable source of information for disabled visitors and residents, GLAD publishes the fortnightly *Update*, containing relevant extracts from national newspapers, and the magazines *London Disability News* (monthly) and, for disabled women, *Boadicea* (bi-monthly).

Holiday Care Service
0845 124 9971/ www.holidaycare.org.uk. **Open** *Helpline* 9am-5pm Mon, Tue; 9am-1pm Wed-Fri.
An advisory service specialising in disabled holiday accommodation.

London Sports Forum for Disabled People
Ground floor, Leroy House, 436 Essex Road, N1 3QP (7354 8666/textphone 7354 9554/ www.londonsportsforum.org.uk).
LSF holds a database of contacts for a broad range of sports, and works with local authorities and individual sports centres to develop facilities for people of all ages with disabilities.

Royal Association for Disability & Rehabilitation
12 City Forum, 250 City Road, Islington, EC1 (7250 3222/textphone 7250 4119/www.radar.org.uk). Old Street tube/rail. **Open** 9am-4pm Mon-Fri. **Map** p402 P3.
A central organisation for disabled voluntary groups gives advice on almost any aspect of life and publishes the monthly newsletter *Bulletin*.

Tripscope
Vassall Centre, Gill Avenue, Fishponds, Bristol BS16 2QQ (tel/textphone 08457 585641/ www.tripscope.org.uk). **Open** *Phone enquiries* 9am-5pm Mon-Thur; 9am-4.30pm Fri.
This phone-based advisory service for the elderly and disabled can help with all aspects of getting around London, the UK and overseas. You can write in or email via the website if you have difficulty with the phone.

Wheelchair Travel & Access Mini Buses
1 Johnston Green, Guildford, Surrey GU2 9XS (01483 233640/ www.wheelchair-travel.co.uk). **Open** 9am-5pm Mon-Fri.

Travel advice

For up-to-date information for travelling to a specific country – including the latest news on safety and security, health issues, local laws and customs – contact your home country government's department of foreign affairs. Most have websites with useful advice for would-be travellers.

Australia
www.dfat.gov.au/travel

Canada
www.voyage.gc.ca

New Zealand
www.mft.govt.nz/travel

Republic of Ireland
www.irlgov.ie/iveagh

UK
www.fco.gov.uk/travel

USA
http://travel.state.gov/travel.

Hires out converted vehicles, including adapted minibuses (with or without driver), plus cars with hand controls and 'Chairman' cars

William Forrester

1 Belvedere Close, Guildford, Surrey GU2 6NP (01483 575401). William Forrester is a London Registered Guide and, since he's a wheelchair user himself, has extensive experience in leading tours in the capital for disabled individuals and groups. Very popular, so make sure you book early.

Electricity

The United Kingdom uses the standard European 220-240V, 50-cycle AC voltage. British plugs use three pins rather than the standard two, so travellers with appliances from mainland Europe should bring an adaptor, as should anyone using US appliances, which run off 110-120V, 60-cycle.

Embassies & consulates

Check the telephone directory and *Yellow Pages* under 'Embassies' for embassies, consulates and high commissions. For individual departmental opening times for the places listed below, check their websites.

American Embassy *24 Grosvenor Square, Mayfair, W1 (7499 9000/ www.usembassy.org.uk). Bond Street or Marble Arch tube.* **Open** 9am-5pm Mon-Fri. **Map** p400 G7.
Australian High Commission *Australia House, Strand, Holborn, WC2 (7379 4334/ www.australia.org.uk). Holborn or Temple tube.* **Open** 9.30am-3.30pm Mon-Fri. **Map** p401 M6.
Canadian High Commission *38 Grosvenor Street, Mayfair, W1 (7258 6600/www.canada.org.uk). Bond Street or Oxford Circus tube.* **Open** 8-11am Mon-Fri. **Map** p400 H7.
Irish Embassy *17 Grosvenor Place, Belgravia, SW1 (7235 2171). Hyde Park Corner tube.* **Open** 9.30am-1pm, 2.30-5.30pm Mon-Fri. **Map** p400 G9.
New Zealand High Commission *New Zealand House, 80 Haymarket, St James's, SW1 (7930 8422/ www.nzembassy.com). Piccadilly Circus tube.* **Open** 9am-5pm Mon-Fri. **Map** p401 K7.

South African High Commission

South Africa House, Trafalgar Square, St James's, WC2 (7451 7299/www.southafricahouse.com). Charing Cross tube/rail. **Open** 8.30am-1pm, 2-5pm Mon-Fri. **Map** p401 K7.

Emergencies

In the event of a serious accident, fire or incident, call **999** – free from any phone, including payphones – and specify whether you require ambulance, fire service or police. For addresses of A&E departments, *see below*; for helplines, *see p367*; and for city police stations, *see p370*.

Gay & lesbian

For help and information, try either of these phone services.
London Friend *(7837 3337).* **Open** 7.30-10pm daily.
London Lesbian & Gay Switchboard *(7837 7324).* **Open** 24hrs daily.

Health

Free emergency medical treatment under the National Health Service (NHS) is available to the following:

● European Union nationals, plus those of Iceland, Norway and Liechtenstein. They are also entitled to specific treatment for a non-emergency condition on production of form E112 or E128.
● Nationals (on production of a passport) of Bulgaria, the Czech and Slovak Republics, Gibraltar, Hungary, Malta, New Zealand, Russia, former Soviet Union states (not Latvia, Lithuania and Estonia) and the former Yugoslavia.
● Residents, irrespective of nationality, of Anguilla, Australia, Barbados, British Virgin Islands, Channel Islands, Falkland Islands, Iceland, Isle of Man, Montserrat, Poland, Romania, St Helena, Sweden, Turks & Caicos Islands.
● Anyone who has been in the UK for the previous 12 months.
● Anyone who has come to the UK to take up permanent residence.
● Students and trainees whose courses require more than 12 weeks in employment during the first year. Others living in the UK for a settled purpose for more than six months may also not be liable to charges.

● Refugees and others who have sought refuge in the UK.
● Anyone formally detained by the immigration authorities.
● People with HIV/AIDS at a special clinic for the treatment of sexually transmitted diseases. The treatment covered is limited to a diagnostic test and counselling associated with that test.

There are no NHS charges for the following services:

● Treatment in Accident & Emergency departments.
● Certain district nursing, midwifery or health visiting.
● Emergency ambulance transport.
● Diagnosis and treatment of certain communicable diseases, including STDs.
● Family planning services.
● Compulsory psychiatric treatment.

Any further advice should be obtained from the Patient Services Manager at the hospital where treatment is to be sought.

Accident & emergency

Below are listed most of the London hospitals that have 24-hour Accident and Emergency departments.

Charing Cross Hospital *Fulham Palace Road, Hammersmith, W6 (8846 1234). Barons Court or Hammersmith tube.*
Chelsea & Westminster Hospital *369 Fulham Road, Chelsea, SW10 (8746 8000). South Kensington tube.* **Map** p396 C12.
Guy's Hospital *St Thomas Street (entrance Snowsfields), Bankside, SE1 (7955 5000). London Bridge tube/rail.* **Map** p404 P8.
Homerton Hospital *Homerton Row, Homerton, E9 (8510 5555). Homerton rail.*
Royal Free Hospital *Pond Street, Hampstead, NW3 (7794 0500). Belsize Park tube/Hampstead Heath rail.*
Royal London Hospital *Whitechapel Road, Whitechapel, E1 (7377 7000). Whitechapel tube.*
St George's Hospital *Blackshaw Road, Tooting, SW17 (8672 1255). Tooting Broadway tube.*
St Mary's Hospital *Praed Street, Paddington, W2 (7886 6666). Paddington tube/rail.* **Map** p395 D5.
St Thomas's Hospital *Lambeth Palace Road, Lambeth, SE1 (7928 9292). Westminster tube/Waterloo tube/rail.* **Map** p401 M9.

Directory

University College Hospital
Grafton Way, Fitzrovia, WC1 (7387 9300). Euston Square or Warren Street tube. **Map** p398 J4.
Whittington Hospital *Highgate Hill, Archway, N19 (7272 3070). Archway tube.*

Complementary medicine

British Homeopathic Association

15 Clerkenwell Close, Clerkenwell, EC1R OAA (7566 7800/ www.trusthomeopathy.org).
Open *Phone enquiries* 9am-5pm Mon-Fri.
The BHA will indicate your nearest homeopathic chemist and/or doctor.

Institute for Complementary Medicine

PO Box 194, SE16 7QZ (7237 5165/www.icmedicine.co.uk).
Send an SAE and two loose first-class stamps for a list of registered practitioners or training advice.

Contraception & abortion

Family planning advice, contraceptive supplies and abortions are free to British citizens on the National Health Service. This also applies to EU residents and foreign nationals living, working and studying in Britain. If you decide to go private, contact one of the organisations listed below. You can also phone the Contraception Helpline on 7837 4044 for your nearest branch of the **Family Planning Association**. The 'morning after' pill, effective up to 72 hours after intercourse, is now available over the counter – but will cost you a hefty £20.

British Pregnancy Advisory Service

08457 304030/www.bpas.org.
Callers are referred to their nearest clinic. Contraception advice and contraceptives are available, as is pregnancy testing.

Brook Advisory Centre

Headquarters: 421 Highgate Studios, 53-79 Highgate Road, Kentish Town, NW5 (7284 6040/helpline

0800 018 5023/www.brook.org.uk).
Open *Helpline* 9am-5pm Mon-Fri.
Map p399 K2.
Advice and referrals on sexual health, contraception and abortion, plus free pregnancy tests for under-25s. Call for your nearest clinic.

Marie Stopes House

Family Planning Clinic/Well Woman Centre *108 Whitfield Street, Fitzrovia, W1 (family planning clinic 7388 0662/ terminations 0845 300 8090/ www.mariestopes.org.uk). Warren Street tube.* **Open** *Clinic* 9am-5pm Mon-Fri. *Termination helpline* 7am-10pm Mon-Fri. **Map** p398 J5.
For contraceptive advice, emergency contraception, pregnancy testing, unplanned pregnancy counselling, an abortion service, cervical and health screening or gynaecological services.

Dentists

Dental care is free under the National Health Service to the following British residents:

● Under-18s.
● Under-19s in full-time education.
● Pregnant women and those with a baby under the age of one when treatment begins.
● People receiving Income Support, Jobseeker's Allowance, Family Credit or Disability Working Allowance.

All other patients must pay. NHS charges start from around £4 for a check-up. To find an NHS dentist, get in touch with the local Health Authority or a Citizens' Advice Bureau (*see p367*), or the following:

Dental Emergency Care Service

Guy's Hospital, St Thomas Street, Bankside, SE1 (7955 2186). **Open** 9am-3pm Mon-Fri (try to arrive before 1.30pm).
The DECS refers callers to a surgery open for treatment (private or NHS).

Guy's Hospital Dental School

Guy's Tower, St Thomas Street, Bankside, SE1 (7955 4317). London Bridge tube/rail. **Open** 9am-3.30pm Mon-Fri. **Map** p405 Q8.
A free walk-in dental emergency service for all-comers.

Doctors

If you're a British citizen or working in the United Kingdom, you can go to any

general practitioner (GP). If you're not visiting your usual GP, you'll be asked for details of the doctor with whom you are registered, in order that your records can be updated. People ordinarily resident in the UK, including overseas students, are also permitted to register with an NHS doctor.

Great Chapel Street Medical Centre

13 Great Chapel Street, Soho, W1 (7437 9360). Leicester Square, Oxford Circus or Tottenham Court Road tube. **Open** 11am-12.30pm, 2-4pm Mon, Tue, Thur; 2-4pm Wed, Fri. **Map** p399 K6.
A walk-in NHS surgery for anyone without a doctor. Phone first, as it operates different clinics each day.

Hospitals

For a list of hospitals with A&E departments, *see p365*; for other hospitals, see the *Yellow Pages*; for what to do in an emergency, *see p365*.

Opticians

For details of opticians in London, *see p252*; you can also consult the *Yellow Pages*.

Pharmacies

Most pharmacies keep regular shop hours (9am-6pm; closed Sun). For London's late-opening pharmacies, *see p257*.

Prescriptions

In the UK, most drugs are only available on prescription. A pharmacist will dispense medicines on receipt of a prescription from a GP. NHS prescriptions cost £6.10, but under-16s and over-60s are exempt, and contraception is free for all. If you're not eligible to see an NHS doctor, you'll be charged cost price for medicines prescribed by a private doctor. Pharmacists, who must be qualified, can advise on the appropriate treatment for minor ailments.

STDs, HIV & AIDS

NHS Genito-Urinary Clinics (such as the Centre for Sexual Health; *see below*) are affiliated to major hospitals. They provide free, confidential treatment of STDs and other problems, such as thrush and cystitis; offer counselling about HIV and other STDs; and can conduct blood tests to determine HIV status.

The 24-hour **National AIDS Helpline** (0800 567123/ textphone 0800 521361) is free and confidential; from 6-10pm, a second helpline (0800 917227) caters for different languages: Bengali (Mon), Urdu (Tue), Arabic (Wed), Gujerati (Thur), Hindi (Fri), Punjabi (Sat) and Cantonese (Sun). For other helplines, *see below*; for abortion and contraception services, *see p366*.

Ambrose King Centre

Royal London Hospital, Turner Street, Whitechapel, E1 (7377 7306). Whitechapel tube. **Open** 9am-4pm Mon, Tue; noon-4pm Wed, Thur; 9am-noon Fri.
The centre provides specific gay (Thur 6.45pm-9pm) and lesbian (Fri 1pm-3pm) health clinics.

Centre for Sexual Health

Genito-Urinary Clinic, Jefferiss Wing, St Mary's Hospital, Praed Street, Paddington, W2 (7886 1697). Paddington tube/rail. **Open** *Walk-in clinic* 8.45am-4.30pm Mon; 8.45am-6pm Tue, Thur; 11.45am-6pm Wed; 8.45am-1pm Fri. *Appointments* 10am-noon Sat. **Map** p395 D5.
A free and confidential walk-in clinic. New patients must arrive at least 30mins before closing.

Mortimer Market Centre for Sexual Health

Mortimer Market Centre, Mortimer Market, off Capper Street, Bloomsbury, W1 (appointments 7530 5050). Goodge Street or Warren Street tube. **Open** 9am-6pm Mon, Tue, Thur; 1-7pm Wed; 9am-2.45pm Fri. **Map** p398 J4.
A clinic for gay and bisexual men and women under 26. There are walk-in clinics for women (Mon 3.45-6pm) and men (Thur 7-9pm), but make an appointment if you can.

Terrence Higgins Trust Lighthouse

52-4 Gray's Inn Road, Holborn, WC1 (office 7831 0330/helpline 0845 122 1200/www.tht.org.uk). Chancery Lane tube. **Open** *Office* 9.30am-6pm Mon-Fri. *Helpline* 11am-10pm daily.
This charity advises and counsels those with HIV/AIDS, their relatives, lovers and friends. It also offers free leaflets about AIDS and safer sex.

Helplines

See also above **STDs, HIV & AIDS**. For gay and lesbian helplines, *see p365*.

Alcoholics Anonymous

7833 0022/www.alcoholics-anonymous.org.uk. **Open** *Helpline* 10am-10pm daily.
Operators put you in touch with a member in your area who can act as an escort to your first meeting.

Childline

Freepost 1111, London N1 0BR (0800 1111/textphone 0800 400 222/7239 1000/www.childline.org.uk). **Open** *Phone lines* 24hrs daily.
Free helpline for children and young people in trouble or danger.

Citizens' Advice Bureaux

The council-run CABs offer free legal, financial and personal advice. Check the phone book for your nearest.

NHS Direct

0845 4647/www.nhsdirect.nhs.uk. **Open** 24hrs daily.
NHS Direct is a first-stop service for medical advice on all subjects.

MIND

Granta House, 15-19 Broadway, Stratford, E15 4BQ (0845 766 0163/www.mind.org.uk). **Open** *Information* 9.15am-5.15pm Mon-Fri.
MIND staff can tell you where to get help for mental distress, and provide more than 60 factsheets on all facets of mental health.

Narcotics Anonymous

7730 0009/www.ukna.org. **Open** 10am-10pm daily (times may vary).
NA offers advice and informs callers of their nearest meeting.

National Missing Persons Helpline

0500 700 700/ www.missingpersons.org. **Open** 24hrs daily.
The volunteer-run NMPH publicises information on anyone reported missing, helping to find missing persons through a network of

contacts. It can artificially age photographs and its 'Message Home' freephone service (0800 700 740) allows runaways to reassure friends or family of their wellbeing without revealing their whereabouts.

Providence Row Charity

41 Spelman Street, Aldgate, E1 (7422 6395). Aldgate East tube. **Open** 10am-6pm Mon-Fri.
This organisation (previously called Just Ask) counsels people aged 35 and under who are homeless, unemployed or on a low income, but will advise anyone with a personal problem.

Rape & Sexual Abuse Support Centre

8683 3300/www.rasasc.org.uk. **Open** noon-2.30pm, 7-9.30pm Mon-Fri; 2.30-5pm Sat, Sun.
Provides support and information.

Refuge Helpline

08705 995443. **Open** 24hrs daily.
Refuge referral for women suffering domestic violence. When phones are not manned, an answerphone will give alternative numbers where you can get immediate help.

Rights of Women

7251 6577. **Open** *Helpline* 2-4pm, 7-9pm Tue-Thur; noon-2pm Fri.
Legal advice for women.

Samaritans

08457 909090/www.samaritans. org.uk. **Open** 24hrs daily.
The Samaritans listen to anyone with emotional problems. It's a popular service, so persevere when phoning.

Victim Support

National Office, Cranmer House, 39 Brixton Road, Brixton, SW9 6DZ (0845 303 0900/www.victim support.com). **Open** *Support line* 9am-9pm Mon-Fri; 9am-7pm Sat, Sun.
Victims of crime are put in touch with a volunteer who provides emotional and practical support, including information and advice on legal procedures. Interpreters can be arranged where necessary.

Insurance

Insuring personal belongings is highly advisable. It's difficult to arrange once you've arrived in London, so do so before you leave.

Medical insurance is often included in travel insurance packages. Unless your country has a reciprocal medical treatment arrangement with

Britain (*see p365*), it's very important to check that you do have adequate health cover.

Internet

Many hotels in London now have modem points in each room; those that don't sometimes offer surfing facilities elsewhere. There are also a huge number of cybercafés around town, of which the biggest are in the **easyEverything** chain.

Massive competition in the ISP sector has meant that prices have plummeted, and there are now a great many ISPs that do not charge a subscription fee, only billing for calls. If you do want to get set up online over here, check one of the UK's many internet publications for details on current deals when you arrive; the best is *Internet* magazine.

For the best London websites, *see p378*.

Internet access

Café Internet *22-4 Buckingham Palace Road, Belgravia, SW1 (7233 5786). Victoria tube/rail.* **Open** 8am-10pm Mon-Fri; 10am-8pm Sat; noon-8pm Sun. **Net access** £2/hr. **Terminals** 22. **Map** p400 H10.
Cybergate *3 Leigh Street, Bloomsbury, WC1 (7387 6560/ www.c-gate.com).* **Open** 9am-9pm daily. **Net access** £1/30min. **Terminals** 24. **Map** p399 L3.
easyEverything *160-66 Kensington High Street, W8 (7938 1841/www.easyeverything.com). High Street Kensington tube.* **Open** 7.30am-11.30pm daily. **Net access** from 50p (credit varies depending on number of other users). **Terminals** 500. **Map** p396 B9. **Branches**: throughout the city.

Left luggage

Airports

Call the following numbers for details on left luggage.

Gatwick Airport *South Terminal 01293 502014/North Terminal 01293 502013.*
Heathrow Airport *Terminals 1-3 8759 3344/Terminal 4 8897 6874.*

London City Airport *7646 0162.*
Luton Airport *01582 395212.*
Stansted Airport *01279 663213.*

Rail & bus stations

The threat of terrorism has meant that London stations tend to have left-luggage desks rather than lockers; to find out whether a train station offers this facility, call 08457 484950.

Legal help

Those in legal difficulties can visit a Citizens' Advice Bureau (*see p367*) or contact the groups below; for details on legal aid, contact the Legal Services Commission (7759 0000/ www.legalservices.gov.uk).

Community Legal Services Directory

0845 608 1122/www.justask.org.uk. **Open** 9am-10pm daily.
This free telephone service guides those with legal problems to government agencies and law firms that may be able to help.

Joint Council for the Welfare of Immigrants

115 Old Street, Hoxton, EC1 (7251 8706). Old Street tube/rail. **Open** *Phone enquiries* 2-5pm Tue, Thur.
JCWI's telephone-only legal advice line offers guidance and referrals.

Law Centres Federation

Duchess House, 18-19 Warren Street, Fitzrovia, W1 (7387 8570/ www.lawcentres.org.uk). Warren Street tube/rail. **Open** *Phone enquiries* 10am-6pm Mon-Fri.
Free legal help for people who can't afford a lawyer. Local centres only offer advice to those living or working in their immediate area; this central office connects you with the nearest.

Release

388 Old Street, Hoxton, EC1 (7729 9904/after-hours 7603 8654). Old Street tube/rail. **Open** 10am-5pm Mon-Fri.
Free addiction counselling and legal advice to those with drug problems or dependency-related legal trouble.

Libraries

Unless you're a London resident, you won't be able to join a lending library. Only the

exhibition areas of the British Library are open to non-members: the other libraries listed can be used for reference, copying and browsing.

British Library *96 Euston Road, Somers Town, NW1 (7412 7000/ www.bl.uk). King's Cross tube/rail.* **Open** 9.30am-6pm Mon, Wed-Fri; 9.30am-8pm Tue; 9.30am-5pm Sat; 11am-5pm Sun. **Map** p399 K3.
Holborn Library *32-8 Theobald's Road, Bloomsbury, WC1 (7974 6345). Chancery Lane tube.* **Open** 10am-7pm Mon, Thur; 10am-6pm Tue, Fri; 10am-1pm, 2-5pm Sat. **Map** p399 M5.
Kensington & Chelsea Central Library *Philimore Walk, Kensington, W8 (7937 2542). High Street Kensington tube.* **Open** 9.30am-8pm Mon, Tue, Thur; 9.30am-5pm Wed, Fri, Sat. **Map** p396 A9.
Victoria Library *160 Buckingham Palace Road, Belgravia, SW1 (7641 4287). Victoria tube/rail.* **Open** 9.30am-7pm Mon, Tue, Thur, Fri; 10am-7pm Wed; 9.30am-5pm Sat. *Music library* 11am-7pm Mon-Fri; 10am-5pm Sat. **Map** p400 H10.
Westminster Reference Library *35 St Martin's Street, Westminster, WC2 (7641 4636). Leicester Square tube.* **Open** 10am-8pm Mon-Fri; 10am-5pm Sat. **Map** p401 K7.

Lost property

Always inform the police if you lose anything, if only to validate insurance claims. *See p370* or the *Yellow Pages* for your nearest police station. Only dial 999 if violence has occurred. Report lost passports both to the police and to your embassy (*see p365*).

Airports

For property lost on the plane, contact the relevant airline or handling agents; for items lost in a particular airport, contact the following:

Gatwick Airport *01293 503162.*
Heathrow Airport *8745 7727.*
London City Airport *7646 0000.*
Luton Airport *01582 395219.*
Stansted Airport *01279 663293.*

Public transport

If you've lost property in an overground station or on a train, call 08700 005151; an operator will connect you to the appropriate station. For property lost on a tube or bus, *see below.*

Transport For London

Lost Property Office, 200 Baker Street, Marylebone, NW1 5RZ (recorded information 7486 2496). Baker Street tube. **Open** 9.30am-2pm Mon-Fri. **Map** p398 G4.

Allow three working days from the time of loss. If you lose something on a bus, call 7222 1234 and ask for the phone numbers of the depots at either end of the route. If you lose something on a tube, pick up a lost property form from any station.

Taxis

Taxi Lost Property

200 Baker Street, Marylebone, NW1 (7918 2000). Baker Street tube. **Open** *Phone enquiries* 9am-4pm Mon-Fri. **Map** p398 G4.

This office deals only with property found in registered black cabs. For items lost in a minicab, contact the office from which you hired the cab.

Media

Magazines

After years of boom, the new millenium saw a heavy downturn in the magazine industry. The market for women's magazines had actually been declining since 1996, while the men's market proved unable to sustain its growth rate of 283 per cent between 1995 and 1999. *Loaded, FHM* and *Maxim* are still the biggest men's titles, while women flock to *Cosmopolitan, Vogue, Marie Claire* and *Elle.* Celebrity magazines thrive, with the glossy *Heat* doing particularly well, and style mags like *i-D* and *Dazed and Confused* have found a profitable niche.

The *Spectator*, the *New Statesman, Prospect* and the *Economist* are about as good as it gets at the serious end of the market, while the satirical fortnightly *Private Eye* adds a little levity. The *Big Issue*, sold on the streets by homeless people, is also worth a look.

Newspapers

For newspapers, at the serious end of the scale is the broadsheet. The right-wing *Daily Telegraph* and *The Times* (which is best for sport) are balanced by the *Independent* and the *Guardian* (best for arts). All have bulging Sunday equivalents bar the *Guardian*, which has a sister Sunday paper, the *Observer*. The pink *Financial Times* (daily) is the best for business facts and figures. In the middle of the market, the leader has long been the odious right-wing *Daily Mail* (and *Mail on Sunday*); its rival, the *Daily Express* (and *Sunday Express*), continues to struggle.

The most popular kind of newspaper is still the tabloid, with the *Sun* (and Sunday's *News of the World*) the undisputed leader. The *Daily Star* and *Mirror* are the main lowbrow contenders. The *People*, the *Sunday Mirror* and a new Sunday *Star* provide weekend sleaze.

London's main daily paper is the right-wing *Evening Standard*, which comes out in several editions during the day (Mon-Fri). There's also the free morning paper *Metro*, which is picked up and then swiftly discarded at tube stations.

Radio

BBC Radio 1 *98.8 FM.* Youth-oriented pop, indie, metal and dance.
BBC Radio 2 *89.1 FM.* Still bland during the day, but good after dark.
BBC Radio 3 *91.3 FM.* Classical music dominates, but there's also discussion, world music and other arts (try Andy Kershaw, 10.15-11.30pm Fri, or Late Junction, 10.15pm-midnight Mon-Thur).
BBC Radio 4 *93.5 FM, 198 LW.* The BBC's main speech station. Today (6-9am Mon-Fri) bristles with self-importance.
BBC Radio 5 Live *693, 909 AM.* Rolling news and sport. Avoid the phone-ins, but Up All Night (1-5am nightly) is terrific.
BBC London *94.9 FM.* A shadow of its former (GLR) self, but Robert Elms (noon-3pm Mon-Fri) is still ace.

BBC World Service *648 AM.* A distillation of the best of all the other BBC stations; transmitted worldwide.
Capital FM *95.8 FM.* London's most popular station suffocates listeners with repetitive playlisting.
Capital Gold *1548 AM.* Where old DJs and old records go to die.
Choice FM *96.9 & 107.1 FM.* The pioneering MOBO station has two schedules, one for south London (96.9) and one for north (107.1).
Classic FM *100.9 FM.* Classical music for people who don't like it.
Heart FM *106.2 FM.* Capital Gold for grown-ups.
Jazz FM *102.2 FM.* Smooth jazz (aka elevator music) now dominates.
Kiss FM *100.0 FM.* Dance music in all its myriad shapes and forms, 24-7.
LBC *1152 AM.* Phone-ins and features. The cabbies' favourite.
Liberty *963 & 972 AM.* Cheesy hits from the '70s and '80s.
Magic *105.4 FM.* Soporific MOR.
News Direct *97.3 FM.* ITN's news channel trails behind 5 Live's success.
Premier Radio *1332 AM.* The south-east's Christian radio channel.
Radio Asia *1458 AM.* Aimed at London's Asian communities.
Resonance FM *104.4 FM.* Art radio. The oddest thing on the airwaves by some distance.
Spectrum *558 AM.* Produced by London's ethnic minorities.
TalkSport *1053 & 1089 AM.* TalkSport puts its focus on phone-ins. Best to stick with 5 Live.
Virgin *105.8 FM, 1215 AM.* Heart with more attitude. Not much more.
XFM *104.9 FM.* Much-improved alt-rock station. Perhaps a little studenty, but a decent variety of sounds.

Television

The next generation of TV in the UK is now here, in the form of Sky Digital, ONdigital and various other digital cable TV companies, so the non-network sector now crammed with stations on a variety of formats (satellite and cable, as well as digital). We've listed the pick of the channels.

Network channels

BBC1 The Corporation's mass-market station. There's a smattering of soaps and game shows, and the odd quality programme. Daytime programming, however, stinks. As with all BBC radio and TV stations, there are no commercials.
BBC2 In general, BBC2 is free of crass programmes. It doesn't mean the output's riveting, but it's not insulting, offering a cultural cross-section and plenty of documentaries.

ITV1 Carlton provides weekday programming for ITV, which means monotonous mass-appeal shows and ad breaks, with any successful formula repeated ad infinitum. LWT (London Weekend Television) takes over at the weekend with more of the same. ITV2 is on digital.

Channel 4 C4's output includes extremely successful US imports (*Friends, ER, The Sopranos* and so on), but it still comes up with some gems, particularly films.

Five Britain's newest terrestrial channel has offered sex, US TV movies, sex, rubbish comedy, sex, more sex and US sport, but has shown signs of moving upmarket of late with some nice docs.

Satellite, digital & cable channels

BBC News 24 The Beeb's rolling news network.
Bravo B-movies and cult TV.
CNN News and current affairs.
Discovery Channel Science and nature documentaries.
FilmFour Channel 4's movie outlet, with 12 hours of programming daily.
History Channel Self-explanatory.
MTV Rock/pop channel that borrows from its US counterpart.
Performance Dance, theatre and opera, plus interviews with the stars.
Sky News Rolling news.
Sky One Sky's version of ITV.
Sky Sports Sports. There are also Sky Sports 2 and Sky Sports 3.
UK Gold Reruns of BBC and ITV successes of yesteryear.
UK Horizon Science documentaries.
VH-1 MTV for grown-ups.

Money

Britain's currency is the pound sterling (£). One pound equals 100 pence (p). Coins are copper (1p, 2p), silver (round: 5p, 10p; seven-sided: 20p, 50p), yellow-gold (£1) or silver in the centre with a yellowy-gold edge (£2). Paper notes are blue (£5), orange (£10), purple (£20) or red (£50). You can exchange foreign currency at banks and bureaux de change (*see below*). If you want to open a bank or building society account, you'll need a passport for identification and probably a reference from your home bank.

Western Union

0800 833833/www.westernunion.com. The old standby for bailing cash-challenged travellers out of trouble. Beware: it's pricey.

ATMs

Aside from inside and outside banks themselves, cash machines can be found in some supermarkets, in certain shops, and in larger tube and rail stations. The vast majority accept withdrawals on major credit cards, and most also allow withdrawals using the Maestro/Cirrus debit system.

Banks

Minimum banking hours are 9.30am to 3.30pm Monday to Friday, but most branches close at 4.30pm (some stay open until 5pm). Exchange and commission rates on currency vary hugely, so it pays to shop around. Commission is sometimes charged for cashing travellers' cheques in foreign currencies, but not for sterling travellers' cheques, provided you cash the cheques at a bank affiliated to the issuing bank (get a list when you buy your cheques); it's also charged if you change cash into another currency. You always need ID, such as a passport, to exchange travellers' cheques.

Bureaux de change

You'll be charged for cashing travellers' cheques or buying and selling foreign currency at a bureau de change. Commission rates, which should be clearly displayed, vary. **Chequepoint, Lenlyn** and **Thomas Cook** have branches all over town. Major rail and tube stations in central London have bureaux de change, and there are many in tourist areas. Most are open 8am-10pm, but those listed below are open 24 hours daily.

Chequepoint *548-50 Oxford Street, Marylebone, W1 (0800 699799). Marble Arch tube.* **Map** p398 G6.
Branches: *2 Queensway, Bayswater, W2 (0800 699799); 71 Gloucester Road, South Kensington, SW7 (0800 699799).*

Credit cards

Many places now accept credit cards. Visa and Mastercard are the most widely accepted, American Express and Diners Club less so.

Report **lost/stolen credit cards** immediately to both the police and the 24-hour services below, and inform your bank by phone and in writing.

American Express *01273 696933.*
Diners Club *01252 513500.*
JCB *7499 3000.*
MasterCard/Eurocard *0800 964767.*
Switch *08706 000459.*
Visa/Connect *0800 895082.*

Tax

With the exception food, books, newspapers, children's clothing and a few other choice items, UK purchases are subject to VAT – value-added tax, aka sales tax – of 17.5 per cent. Unlike in the US, this is included in prices quoted in shops (a price tag of £10 does *not* mean you pay £11.75). Beware: hotels often naughtily quote room rates exclusive of VAT. Be sure to ask whether the rate quoted includes tax.

Opening hours

The following are general guidelines: actual hours can vary in all cases. Times for specific establishments appear in the main listings, while opening hours on public holidays can be erratic.

Banks 9am-4.30pm (some close at 3.30pm) Mon-Fri.
Bars 11am-11pm Mon-Sat; noon-10.30pm Sun.
Businesses 9am-5pm Mon-Fri.
Post offices 9am-5.30pm Mon-Fri; 9am-noon Sat.
Shops 10am-6pm Mon-Sat.

Police stations

The police are a good source of information about the locality and are used to helping visitors. If you've been robbed,

Directory

assaulted or involved in an infringement of the law, go to your nearest police station. (We've listed a handful in central London; you can also look under 'Police' in the phone book or call Directory Enquiries on 192.) If you have a complaint about the police, ensure that you take the offending police officer's identifying number (it should be displayed on his or her epaulette). You can then register a complaint with the **Police Complaints Authority** (10 Great George Street, SW1P 3AE, 7273 6450), contact any police station or visit a solicitor or Law Centre.

Belgravia Police Station *202-6 Buckingham Palace Road, Pimlico, SW1 (7730 1212). Victoria tube/rail.* Map p400 H10.

Charing Cross Police Station *Agar Street, Covent Garden, WC2 (7240 1212). Charing Cross tube/rail.* Map p401 L7.

Chelsea Police Station *2 Lucan Place, Chelsea, SW3 (7589 1212). Sloane Square tube.* Map p397 E10.

Euston Road Police Station *Euston Station, Euston Road, NW1 (7704 1212). Euston tube/rail.* Map p401 K3.

Islington Police Station *2 Tolpuddle Street, Islington, N1 (7704 1212). Angel tube.* Map p402 N2.

Kensington Police Station *72-4 Earl's Court Road, Kensington, W8 (7376 1212). High Street Kensington tube.* Map p396 B11.

King's Cross Police Station *76 King's Cross Road, King's Cross, WC1 (7704 1212). King's Cross tube/rail.* Map p399 M3.

Marylebone Police Station *1-9 Seymour Street, Marylebone, W1 (7486 1212). Baker Street tube/ Marylebone tube/rail.* Map p395 F6.

Paddington Green Police Station *2-4 Harrow Road, Paddington, W2 (7402 1212). Edgware Road tube.* Map p396 E5.

West End Central Police Station *27 Savile Row, Mayfair, W1 (7437 1212). Piccadilly Circus tube.* Map p400 J7.

Postal services

You can buy stamps at all post offices and many newsagents. Current prices are 19p for second-class letters, 27p for first-class letters and 37p for letters to EU countries. Post-

cards cost 37p to send within Europe and 40p to countries outside Europe. Rates for other letters and parcels vary with weight and destination.

Post offices

Post offices are usually open 9am-5.30pm Mon-Fri and 9am-noon Sat, with the exception of **Trafalgar Square Post Office** (24-8 William IV Street, WC2N 4DL; 08457 223344; Charing Cross tube/rail), which is open 8.30am-6.30pm Mon-Fri and 9am-5.30pm Sat. The busiest time of day is usually 1-2pm. Listed below are the other main central London offices. For general post office enquiries, call the central information line on 08457 223344 or consult www.postoffice.co.uk.

43-4 Albemarle Street *Mayfair, W1 (08456 223344). Green Park tube.* Map p400 J7.

111 Baker Street *Marylebone, W1 (08456 223344). Baker Street tube.* Map p398 G5.

202 Great Portland Street *Marylebone, W1 (08456 223344). Great Portland Street tube.* Map p398 H4.

32A Grosvenor Street *Mayfair, W1 (08456 223344). Bond Street tube.* Map p400 H7.

19 Newman Street *Fitzrovia, W1 (08456 223344). Tottenham Court Road tube.* Map p398 J5.

1-5 Poland Street *Soho, W1 (08456 223344). Oxford Circus tube.* Map p398 J6.

Poste restante

If you want to receive mail while you are away, you can have it sent to Trafalgar Square Post Office, where it will be kept at the enquiry desk for a month. Your name and 'Poste Restante' must be clearly marked on the letter, followed by the address given above. You'll need ID to collect it.

Religion

Anglican
St Paul's Cathedral *For listings details, see p89.* Services 7.30am, 8am, 12.30pm, 5pm Mon-Fri; 8am,

8.30am, 12.30pm, 5pm Sat; 8am, 10.15am, 11.30am, 3.15pm, 6pm Sun. Map p404 O6.
Times may vary; phone to check.
Westminster Abbey *For listings details, see p134.* Services 7.30am, 8am, 12.30pm, 5pm Mon-Fri; 8am, 9am, 12.30pm, 3pm Sat; 8am, 10am, 11.15am, 3pm, 5.45pm Sun. Map p401 K9.

Baptist
Bloomsbury Central Baptist Church *235 Shaftesbury Avenue, Covent Garden, WC2 (7240 0544/ www.bloomsbury.org.uk). Tottenham Court Road tube.* Open 10am-4pm Mon-Fri; 10am-8.30pm Sun. *Friendship Centre* noon-2.30pm Tue; 10.30am-8.30pm Sun. Services & meetings phone ahead. Map p399 L6.

Buddhist
Buddhapadipa Thai Temple *14 Calonne Road, Wimbledon, SW19 (8946 1357/www.buddhapadipa.org). Wimbledon tube/rail then 93 bus.* Open *Temple* 1-6pm Sat, Sun. *Meditation retreat* 7-9pm Tue, Thur; 4-6pm Sat, Sun.

Catholic
London Oratory *For listings, see p139.* Services 7am, 8am (Latin mass), 10am, 12.30am, 6pm Mon-Fri; 7am, 8.30am, 10am, 6pm Sat; 7am, 8.30am, 10am (tridentine), 11am (sung Latin), 12.30pm, 3.30pm, 4.30pm, 7pm Sun. Map p397 E10.
Westminster Cathedral *For listings, see p135.* Services 7am, 8am, 9am, 10.30am, 12.30pm, 5pm Mon-Fri; 8am, 9am, 12.30pm, 6pm Sat; 7am, 8am, 9am, 10.30am, noon, 5.30pm, 7pm Sun. Map p400 J10.

Hindu
Swaminarayan Hindu Mission *105-19 Brentfield Road, Church End, NW10 (8961 5031/ www.swaminarayan.org). Neasden tube/Harlesden tube/ rail.* Open 9am-6.30pm daily. Services 11.45am, 7pm daily.
In addition to a large prayer hall, this huge complex contains a conference hall, a marriage suite, sports facilities, a library and a health clinic.

Islamic
London Central Mosque *146 Park Road, St John's Wood, NW8 (7724 3363). Baker Street tube/bus 74.* Open dawn-dusk daily. Services 5.30am, 1pm, 4pm, 7pm, 8.30pm daily.
East London Mosque *82-92 Whitechapel Road, E1 (7247 1357/ www.eastlondon-mosque.org.uk). Aldgate East or Whitechapel tube.* Open 10am-8.30pm daily. Services Friday prayer 1.30pm (1pm in winter). Map p405 S6.

Directory

Jewish

Liberal Jewish Synagogue *28 St John's Wood Road, St John's Wood, NW8 (7286 5181/www.ljs.org). St John's Wood tube.* **Open** *Enquiries* 9am-5pm Mon-Thur; 9am-1pm Fri. **Services** 6.45pm Fri; 11am Sat.

West Central Liberal Synagogue *109 Whitfield Street, Fitzrovia, W1 (7636 7627). Warren Street tube.* **Services** 3pm Sat. **Map** p398 J4.

Methodist

Methodist Central Hall *Westminster Central Hall, Storey's Gate, Westminster, SW1 (7222 8010/www.wch.co.uk). St James's Park tube.* **Open** *Chapel* 9am-6pm Mon-Fri. **Services** 12.45pm Wed; 11am, 6.30pm Sun. **Map** p401 K9.

Quaker

Religious Society of Friends (Quakers) *Friends House, 173-7 Euston Road, Bloomsbury, NW1 (7387 3601/www.quaker.org.uk). Euston tube/rail.* **Open** 8.30am-9.30pm Mon-Fri; 8.30am-4.30pm Sat. **Meetings** 11am Sun. **Map** p399 K3.

Safety & security

Use common sense and follow these basic rules.

● **Keep** wallets and purses out of sight, and handbags securely closed.
● **Don't** leave briefcases, bags or coats unattended, especially in pubs, cinemas or fast-food restaurants, on public transport, or in crowds.
● **Don't** leave bags or coats beside, under or on the back of a chair.
● **Don't** put bags on the floor near the door of a public toilet.
● **Don't** wear expensive jewellery or wrist watches that can be easily snatched.
● **Don't** take short cuts through dark alleys and car parks: stick to well-lit roads.
● **Don't** keep your passport, money, credit cards, etc, together. If you lose one, you'll lose them all.
● **Don't** carry a wallet in your back pocket, and don't flash money or credit cards around.

Smoking

Smoking is permitted in almost all pubs and bars – though an increasing number have non-smoking areas – and in most restaurants, though specify when you book that you'd like a table in the smoking section. Smoking is forbidden in shops and on public transport.

Study

Being a student in London is as expensive as it is exciting; *Time Out*'s *Student Guide*, available from October each year, provides the lowdown on London and how to survive it. In this guide, entry prices for students are usually designated 'concessions'. You'll have to show ID (an NUS or ISIC card) to get these rates. Students, whether EU citizens or not, wanting or needing to find work in the UK as a way of boosting their funds should turn to *p375*.

Language classes

The places listed below offer various courses; call for details.

Aspect Covent Garden Language Centre *3-4 Southampton Place, WC1 (7404 3080/www.aspectworld.com). Holborn tube.* **Map** p399 L5.

Central School of English *1 Tottenham Court Road, W1 (7580 2863/www.centralschool.co.uk). Tottenham Court Road tube.* **Map** p397 K5.

Frances King School of English *77 Gloucester Road, SW7 (070 0011 2233/www.francesking.co.uk). Gloucester Road tube.* **Map** p395 F9.

London Study Centre *Munster House, 676 Fulham Road, SW6 (7731 3549/www.londonstudycentre.com). Parsons Green tube.*

Sels College *64-5 Long Acre, WC2 (7240 2581/www.sels.co.uk). Covent Garden tube.* **Map** p399 L6.

Shane English School *59 South Molton Street, W1 (7499 8533/www.saxoncourt.com). Bond Street tube.* **Map** p398 H6.

Students' unions

Many unions only let in students with relevant ID, so always carry your NUS or ISIC card. We've listed (from the *Time Out Student Guide*) those with the five best student bars, all of which offer a good night out at student-friendly prices.

Imperial College *Beit Quad, Prince Consort Road, SW7 (7589 5111). South Kensington tube.* **Open** noon-2pm, 5-11pm Mon-Fri; noon-11pm Sat; noon-10.30pm Sun (times vary out of term-time). **Map** p397 D9.

International Students House *229 Great Portland Street, W1 (7631 8300). Great Portland Street tube.* **Open** noon-2pm, 5-11pm Mon, Tue; noon-2pm, 5pm-midnight Wed; noon-2pm, 5pm-1am Thur; noon-2pm, 5pm-3am Fri; noon-3am Sat; noon-10.30pm Sun. **Map** p398 H4.

King's College *Macadam Building, Surrey Street, WC2 (7836 7132). Temple tube.* **Open** *Waterfront* noon-11pm Mon-Fri; 7-11pm Sat. *Tutu's* 9pm-3am Fri; 10.30pm-3am Sat. **Map** p401 M7.

London Metropolitan University *166-220 Holloway Road, N7 (7607 2789). Holloway Road tube.* **Open** *Rocket* 11am-11pm Mon, Tue, Thur; 11am-2am Wed; 11am-late Fri; 11am-6am Sat.

University of London Union (ULU) *Malet Street, WC1 (7664 2000). Goodge Street tube.* **Open** 11am-11pm Mon-Thur; 11am-1am Fri, Sat; noon-10.30pm Sun. **Map** p399 K4.

Universities

Brunel University *Cleveland Road, Uxbridge, Middx (01895 274000/students' union 01895 462200). Uxbridge tube.*

City University *Northampton Square, EC1 (7040 5060/students' union 7040 5600). Angel tube.* **Map** p402 O3.

Guildhall University *Calcutta House, Old Castle Street, E1 (7320 1000/students' union 7320 2233). Aldgate East tube.* **Map** p405 S6.

South Bank University *Borough Road, SE1 (7928 8989/students' union 7815 6060). Elephant & Castle tube/rail.* **Map** p104 O9

University of Greenwich *Old Royal Naval College, Park Row, SE10 (8331 8000/students' union 8331 7629). Greenwich DLR.*

University of Middlesex *Trent Park, Bramley Road, N14 (8362 5000/students' union 8411 6450). Cockfosters or Oakwood tube.*

University of North London *166-220 Holloway Road, N7 (7607 2789/students' union 7753 3367). Holloway Road tube.*

University of Westminster *309 Regent Street, W1 (7911 5000/students' union 7915 5454). Oxford Circus tube.* **Map** p398 H4.

University of London

The University consists of 34 colleges, spread across the city; only the seven largest are listed below. All London universities (with the exception of Imperial College) are affiliated to the National Union of Students (NUS; 7272 8900/www.nusonline.co.uk).

Goldsmiths' College *Lewisham Way, SE14 (7919 7171/students'*

union 8692 1406). New Cross/New Cross Gate tube/rail.
Imperial College *Exhibition Road, SW7 (7589 5111/students' union 7594 8060). South Kensington tube.* **Map** p397 D9.
King's College *Strand, WC2 (7836 5454/students' union 7836 7132). Temple tube.* **Map** p401 M7.
Kingston University *Penrhyn Road, Kingston, Surrey (8547 2000/students' union 8547 8868). Kingston rail.*
London School of Economics (LSE) *Houghton Street, WC2 (7405 7686/students' union 7955 7158). Holborn tube.* **Map** p399 M6.
Queen Mary University of London *327 Mile End Road, E1 (7882 5555/students' union 7882 5390). Mile End/Stepney Green tube.*
University College London (UCL) *Gower Street, WC1 (7679 2000/students' union 7387 3611). Euston Square, Goodge Street or Warren Street tube.* **Map** p399 K4.

Useful organisations

For BUNAC and the Council on International Educational Exchange, *see p376.*

National Bureau for Students with Disabilities *Chapter House, 18-20 Crucifix Lane, SE1 (0800 328 5050/textphone 0800 068 2422/ www.skill.org.uk).* **Open** *Phone enquiries* 1.30-4.30pm Mon-Thur.

Telephones

Since 2000, London's dialling code has been 020. If you want to call a London number from within London, you omit the code (020) and dial the last eight digits. We've therefore listed London numbers without their 020 code throughout this book. If you're calling from outside the UK, dial the international access code from the country from which you're calling, then the UK code 44, then the full London number, omitting the first 0 from the code. For example, to make a call to 020 7813 3000 from the US, dial 011 44 20 7813 3000. To dial abroad from the UK, first dial 00, then the relevant country code from the list below.

Australia 61; **Austria** 43; **Belgium** 32; **Brazil** 55; **Canada** 1; **Czech Republic** 420; **Denmark** 45; **France** 33; **Germany** 49; **Greece** 30; **Hong Kong** 852; **Iceland** 354; **India** 91; **Ireland** 353; **Israel** 972; **Italy** 39; **Japan** 81; **Netherlands** 31;

Crime and the city solution

Once upon a time, if you went to New York, you got mugged. Or so went the stereotype. London, in the eyes of the tourist, was a kinder, gentler place, where there was always a bobby walking the beat. How times have changed. According to the latest statistics, you're now six times more likely to be mugged in London than in the Big Apple, with yellow witness appeal signs detailing horrific assaults as common a London sight as double-decker buses.

The media hysteria reached its peak in November 2001, when the number of muggings in London reached 232 a day, with 30 a day in the borough of Lambeth alone. Shortly afterwards, a teenage girl in Walthamstow was shot in the head for her mobile phone. But London's mugging epidemic really made headlines around the world when a robber tried to snatch Liza Minnelli's necklace from her throat.

Clearly, something had to be done. Home Secretary David Blunkett gave Scotland Yard an ultimatum: reduce street crime within six months or face government intervention in police affairs. Operation Safer Streets was launched, scrutinising weekly reports to pinpoint mugging hotspots, and redeploying hundreds of traffic officers to walk the beat.

By August 2002, muggings had dropped 31 per cent. Scotland Yard chief Sir John Stevens announced that 'London has turned the corner' as street robbery fell to its lowest level in 13 months, with offences down to an average of 154 a day. In Lambeth, the monthly average of incidents fell from 622 to 443, while muggings fell 18 per cent in the Borough of Westminster to 320 muggings a month.

Not exactly Pleasantville, you might say, but take heart. Journalist Donal Macintyre filmed a documentary in which he went to Brixton attempting to get mugged. In a reassuring – if ridiculous – programme, Macintyre walked the area's most dangerous streets at night, brazenly flashing around his mobile phone and laptop to every unsavoury character he met. And it took him three days to get robbed.

The majority of the public have not been the victims of street crime and are never likely to be. According to police statistics, late Victorian London was 20 times more dangerous than it is today. One-third of street robberies involve mobile phones only; contrary to stereotypes, the area most afflicted by muggings is outside secondary schools between 2pm and 4pm. More than a third of assaults are carried out by groups of ten- to 17-year-olds, mostly preying on other teenagers.

If you're still really worried, you could always spend your holiday in the capital's safest borough: Richmond-upon-Thames. With a mere 32 street robberies a month, hell, the neighbourhood is almost as safe as New York.

Directory

New Zealand 64; **Norway** 47;
Portugal 351; **South Africa** 27;
Spain 34; **Sweden** 46; **Switzerland**
41; **USA** 1.

Public phones

Public payphones take coins,
credit cards or prepaid phone-
cards (sometimes all three).
The minimum cost is 20p:
this buys a 110-second local
call (11p per minute). But be
careful: some payphones, such
as the counter-top ones found
in many pubs, require more.

Operator services

Operator

Call **100** for the operator if you have
difficulty in dialling; for an early-
morning alarm call; to make a credit
card call; for information about the
cost of a call; and for help with
international person-to-person calls.

Dial **155** if you need to reverse the
charges (call collect) or if you can't
dial direct, but be warned that this
service is very expensive.

Directory enquiries

Dial **192** for any number in Britain,
or **153** for international numbers.
Phoning the service from a private
phone is expensive, and only two
enquiries are allowed per call, but it's
free from public call boxes.

Talking Pages

This 24-hour free service lists the
numbers of thousands of businesses
in the UK. Dial **0800 600900** and
say what type of business you
require, and in what area of London.

Telephone directories

There are three phone
directories for London (two
for private numbers, one
for companies), which are
available at post offices and
libraries. Hotels have them,
too. They are issued free to
all residents, as is the *Yellow
Pages* directory (also accessible
online at www.yell.com), which
lists businesses and services.

Mobile phones

Mobile phones in the UK work
on either the 900 or 1800 GSM
system. As this is used through

much of Europe, it's worth
checking whether your service
provider has a reciprocal
arrangement with a UK-based
service provider. The situation
is more complex for US
travellers. If your service
provider in the US uses the
GSM system, your phone
probably runs on the 1900
band; this being the case,
you'll need a tri-band
handset in addition to your
provider having a reciprocal
arrangement with a UK-based
provider.

The simplest option may be
to buy a 'pay as you go' phone
(about £40-£200). There's
no monthly fee and calls are
charged not by billing but
by buying (widely available)
cards that slot into your phone
in denominations of £10 and
up. Check before you buy
whether the phone is capable
of making and receiving
international calls.

Telegrams

There is no longer a domestic
telegram service, but you can
still send telegrams abroad:
call 0800 190190. This is also
the number to call to send an
international telemessage:
phone in your message and it
will be delivered by post the
next day (at a cost of 92p a
word, including the recipient's
name and address).

Time

London operates on Greenwich
Mean Time, which is five
hours ahead of the US's
Eastern Standard time. In
spring (30 Mar 2003) the UK
puts its clocks forward by one
hour to British Summer Time
(BST). In autumn (26 Oct 2003)
the clocks go back to GMT.

Tipping

In Britain it's accepted that
you tip in taxis, minicabs,
restaurants (some waiting staff

rely heavily on tips), hotels,
hairdressers and some bars
(not pubs). Ten per cent is
normal, with some restaurants
adding as much as 15 per cent.
Always check if service has
been included in your bill:
some restaurants include
service, then leave the space
for a gratuity on your credit
card slip blank.

Toilets

Public toilets are few and far
between in London, and pubs
and restaurants reserve their
toilets for customers only.
However, all main-line rail
stations and a very few tube
stations – Piccadilly Circus, for
one – have public toilets (you
may be charged a small fee).
It's also usually possible to
sneak into a large department
store such as John Lewis.

Tourist information

The **London Tourist
Board** or LTB (7932 2000/
www.londontown.com) runs
the information centres listed,
all of which supply free London
maps. There are also tourist
offices in Greenwich and next
to St Paul's (**Map** p404 O6).
Winter opening times are
given; hours are usually longer
for the rest of the year. If you
require information on travel
elsewhere in Britain, *see p.340*.

Britain Visitor Centre *1 Regent
Street, Piccadilly Circus, W1 (no
phone/www.visitbritain.com).*
Piccadilly Circus tube. **Open** *Oct-May*
9.30am-6.30pm Mon; 9am-6.30pm
Tue-Fri; 10am-4pm Sat, Sun. *June-
Sept* 9.30am-6.30pm Mon; 9am-
6.30pm Tue-Fri; 9am-5pm Sat;
10am-4pm Sun. **Map** p401 K7.
Heathrow Airport *Terminals 1, 2
& 3 tube station, Heathrow Airport,
TW6.* **Open** 8am-6pm daily.
Liverpool Street *Liverpool Street,
the City, EC2.* **Open** 8am-6pm Mon-
Fri; 8am-5.30pm Sat; 9am-5.30pm
Sun. **Map** p401 R5.
London Visitor Centre *Arrivals
Hall, Waterloo International
Terminal, SE1.* **Open** 8.30am-
10.30pm daily. **Map** p405 M9.

Southwark Information Centre
London Bridge, 6 Tooley Street, SE1.
Open *Easter-Oct* 10am-6pm Mon-Sat; 10.30am-5.30pm Sun. *Nov Easter*
10am-6pm Mon-Sat; 11am-4pm Sun.
Map p407 Q8.
Victoria *Station Forecourt, Pimlico, SW1.* **Open** 7.45am-7pm Mon-Sat; 8.45am-7pm Sun. **Map** p400 H10.

Visas & immigration

Citizens of EU countries don't require a visa to visit the United Kingdom; citizens of other countries, including the USA, Canada and New Zealand, require a valid passport for a visit of up to six months in duration. The immigration department of the Home Office (*see below*) deals with queries on immigration, visas and work permits from Commonwealth countries.

To apply for a UK visa or check your visa status **before you travel**, contact the British embassy, consulate or high commission in your own country. The visa allows you entry for a maximum of six months. For information about work permits, *see p377*.

Home Office *Immigration & Nationality Bureau, Lunar House, 40 Wellesley Road, Croydon, Surrey CR9 1AT (0870 606 7766/ application forms 0870 241 0645/ www.homeoffice.gov.uk).* **Open** *Phone enquiries* 9am-4.45pm Mon-Thur; 9am-4.30pm Fri.

Weights & measures

The United Kingdom is gradually moving towards full metrication. Distances are still measured in miles but recent legislation means that all goods are now officially sold in metric quantities, with no legal requirement for the imperial equivalent to be given. The following are some useful conversions.

1 centimetre (cm) = 0.39 inches (in)
1 inch (in) = 2.54 centimetres (cm)
1 yard (yd) = 0.91 metres (m)
1 metre (m) = 1.094 yards (yd)

1 mile = 1.6 kilometres (km)
1 kilometre (km) = 0.62 miles
1 ounce (oz) = 28.35 grammes (g)
1 gramme (g) = 0.035 ounces (oz)
1 pound (lb) = 0.45 kilogrammes (kg)
1 kilogramme (kg) = 2.2 pounds (lb)
1 pint (US) = 0.8 pints (UK)
1 pint (UK) = 0.55 litres (l)
1 litre (l) = 1.75 pints (UK)

When to go

Climate

The British climate is notoriously unpredictable, but **Weathercall** on 09003 444 900 (60p per min) can offer some guidance. *See also p377* **Weather report** and www.met-office.gov.uk.

Spring extends approximately from March to May, though winter often seems to stretch well beyond February. March winds and April showers may be a month early or a month late, but May is often very pleasant.
Summer (June, July and August) can be unpredictable, with searing heat one day followed by sultry greyness and thunderstorms the next. High temperatures, humidity and pollution can create problems for anyone with hayfever or breathing difficulties, while temperatures down in the tube can reach dangerous levels, particularly during rush hour.

Autumn starts in September, although the weather can still have a mild, summery feel. Real autumn comes with October, when the leaves start to fall. When the November cold sets in, you'll be reminded that London is situated on a fairly northerly latitude.
Winter may contain the odd mild day, but don't bank on it. December, January and February are usually pretty chilly, although snow is rare. But a crisp, sunny winter's day in London is hard to beat.

Public holidays

On public holidays (widely known as bank holidays), many shops remain open, but public transport services generally run to a Sunday timetable. The exception is Christmas Day, when almost everything shuts.

New Year's Day Wed 1 Jan 2003; Thur 1 Jan 2004.
Good Friday Fri 18 Apr 2003; Fri 9 Apr 2004.
Easter Monday Mon 21 Apr 2003; Mon 12 Apr 2004.
May Day Holiday Mon 5 May 2003; Mon 3 May 2004.
Spring Bank Holiday Mon 26 May 2003; Mon 31 May 2004.
Summer Bank Holiday Mon 25 Aug 2003; Mon 30 Aug 2004.
Christmas Day Thur 25 Dec 2003; Sat 25 Dec 2004.
Boxing Day Fri 26 Dec 2003; Sun 26 Dec 2004.

Weather report

Average daytime temperatures, rainfall and hours of sunshine in London

	Temp (°C/°F)	Rainfall (mm/in)	Sunshine (hrs/dy)
Jan	6/43	54/2.1	1.5
Feb	7/44	40/1.6	2.3
Mar	10/50	37/1.5	3.6
Apr	13/55	37/1.5	5.3
May	17/63	46/1.8	6.4
June	20/68	45/1.8	7.1
July	22/72	57/2.2	6.4
Aug	21/70	59/2.3	6.1
Sept	19/66	49/1.9	4.7
Oct	14/57	57/2.2	3.2
Nov	10/50	64/2.5	1.8
Dec	7/44	48/1.9	1.3

Directory

Women

London is home to dozens of women's groups and networks, from day centres to rights campaigners; www.gn.apc.org or www.wrc.org.uk provide information and many links.

Visiting women are unlikely to be harassed. Bar the very occasional sexually motivated attack, London's streets are no more dangerous to women than to men, if you follow the usual precautions (*see p372*).

The Women's Library

25 Old Castle Street, Whitechapel, E1 (7320 2222). Aldgate or Aldgate East tube. **Open** *Reading room* 9am-5pm Tue, Wed, Fri; 9am-8pm Thur; 10am-4pm Sat.
Europe's largest women's studies archive has made a £4 million move to larger premises (on the same road). Check www.thewomenslibrary.ac.uk for details of current exhibitions. Staff are usually happy to help with general women-related queries.

Working in London

Finding temporary work in London can be a full-time job in itself. Those with a reasonable level of English who are EU citizens or have work permits should find work in catering, labouring, bars/pubs or shops. Graduates with an English or foreign-language degree could try teaching. If your English isn't great, there's always the mind-numbing task of distributing free magazines or seasonal work in tourist spots. Ideas can be found in *Summer Jobs in Britain*, published by Vacation Work, 9 Park End Street, Oxford OX1 1HJ (£9.99 plus £1.50 p&p). The **Central Bureau for Educational Visits & Exchanges** (*see below*) has other useful publications.

Good sources of job information are the *Evening Standard*, local/national newspapers and newsagents' windows. Vacancies for temporary and unskilled work are often displayed on Jobcentre noticeboards; your nearest Jobcentre can be found under 'Employment Agencies' in *Yellow Pages*. If you have good typing (over 40 wpm) or word processing skills and know how to dress the part, you could sign on with some of the temp agencies. Many of them have specialisms beyond the obvious admin/secretarial roles, such as translation.

Work permits

With few exceptions, citizens of non-European Economic Area (EEA) countries have to have a work permit before they can legally work in the United Kingdom. Employers who are unable to fill particular vacancies with a resident or EEA national must apply for a permit to the Department for Education and Employment (*see below*). Permits are issued only for high-level jobs.

Au Pair Scheme

Only 17- to 27-year-old citizens of the following countries are permitted to become au pairs: Andorra, Bosnia-Herzegovina, Croatia, Cyprus, Czech Republic, Faroe Islands, Greenland, Hungary, Macedonia, Malta, Monaco, San Marino, Slovak Republic, Slovenia, Switzerland and Turkey. Employment as an au pair usually includes free accommodation, but the wages tend to be on the low side.

Sandwich students

Approval for course-compulsory sandwich placements at recognised UK colleges must be obtained for potential students by their college from the DfEE's **Overseas Labour Service** (*see below* **Department for Education & Employment**).

Students

Visiting students from the US, Canada, Australia or Jamaica can get a blue BUNAC card enabling them to work in the UK for up to six months. Either contact the Work in Britain Department of the **Council on International Educational Exchange** or call **BUNAC** (*see below*). BUNAC students should obtain an application form OSS1 (BUNAC) from BUNAC, which is then submitted to the nearest Jobcentre to obtain permission to work.

Working holidaymakers

Citizens of Commonwealth countries aged 17-27 may apply to come to the UK as a working holidaymaker, by contacting their nearest British Diplomatic Post in advance. They are then allowed to take part-time work without a DfEE permit.

Useful addresses

BUNAC

16 Bowling Green Lane, Clerkenwell, EC1 (7251 3472/www.bunac.org.uk). Farringdon tube/rail. **Open** 9.30am-5.30pm Mon-Thur; 9.30am-5pm Fri. **Map** p402 N4.

Council on International Educational Exchange

Work in Britain Department, 20th floor, 633 3rd Avenue, New York, NY 10017, USA (00 1 212 822 7244/www.ciee.org). **Open** 9.30am-5.30pm Mon-Fri.
The Council on International Educational Exchange aids young people to study, work and travel abroad. It's divided into international study programmes and exchanges.

Department for Education & Employment

Work Permits UK helpline (0114 259 4074/www.workpermits.gov.uk). **Open** *Phone enquiries* 9am-5pm Mon-Fri.
Employers seeking work permit application forms should phone 08705 210224 or visit the website.

Home Office

Immigration & Nationality Directorate, Lunar House, 40 Wellesley Road, Croydon, Surrey CR9 2BY (0870 606 7766/ www.ind.homeoffice.gov.uk). **Open** *Phone enquiries* 9am-4.45pm Mon-Thur; 9am-4.30pm Fri.
The Home Office is able to provide advice on whether or not a work permit is required.

Overseas Visitors Records Office

180 Borough High Street, Borough, SE1 (7230 1208). Borough tube/Elephant & Castle or London Bridge tube/rail. **Open** 9am-4.30pm Mon-Fri. **Map** p404 P9.
In a former incarnation this was the Aliens Registration Office run by the Metropolitan Police. These days, though, it's known as the vastly less scary Overseas Visitors Records Office, and it charges £34 to register a person if they have a work permit.

Further Reference

Fiction

Peter Ackroyd *Hawksmoor;
The House of Doctor Dee;
Great Fire of London*
Intricate studies of arcane London.
Martin Amis *London Fields*
Darts and drinking way out east.
Jonathan Coe
The Dwarves of Death
Mystery, music, mirth, malevolence.
Norman Collins
London Belongs to Me
A witty saga of '30s Kennington.
Wilkie Collins
The Woman in White
Spooky goings-on.
Joseph Conrad *The Secret Agent*
Anarchism in seedy Soho.
Charles Dickens
*Oliver Twist; David Copperfield;
Bleak House; Our Mutual Friend*
Four of the master's most London-
centric novels.
Sir Arthur Conan Doyle
The Complete Sherlock Holmes
Reassuring sleuthing shenanigans.
Maureen Duffy *Capital*
The bones beneath our feet and the
stories they tell.
Christopher Fowler *Soho Black*
Walking dead in Soho.
Anthony Frewin *London Blues*
One-time Kubrick assistant explores
'60s porn movie industry.
Neil Gaiman *Neverwhere*
A new world above and below the
streets by *Sandman* creator.
Graham Greene
The End of the Affair
Adultery and catholicism.
Patrick Hamilton *20,000 Streets
Under the Sky; Hangover Square*
A romantic trilogy among Soho
sleaze; love and death in Earl's Court.
Tobias Hill *Underground*
Women are being pushed under tube
trains, and secret tunnels abound.
Alan Hollinghurst
The Swimming Pool Library
Gay life around Russell Square.
**Maria Lexton (vol 1)/
Nicholas Royle (vol 2) (eds)**
*Time Out Book of London Short
Stories Volumes 1 & 2*
Writers pay homage to their city.
Colin MacInnes
City of Spades; Absolute Beginners
Coffee 'n' jazz, Soho 'n' Notting Hill.
Derek Marlowe *A Dandy in Aspic*
A capital-set Cold War classic.
Michael Moorcock
Mother London
A love-letter to London.
Iris Murdoch *Under the Net*
The adventures of a talented but
wastrel writer.

Courttia Newland *The Scholar*
Life is full of choices for a kid on a
west London estate.
Kim Newman *The Quorum*
Docklands-based media intrigue.
George Orwell
Keep the Aspidistra Flying
Saga of a struggling writer.
Derek Raymond
I Was Dora Suarez
The blackest London noir.
Jean Rhys *After Leaving Mr
Mackenzie; Good Morning, Midnight*
Sad, lost women haunt the streets
and squares of Bloomsbury.
Nicholas Royle *The Matter of the
Heart; The Director's Cut*
Abandoned buildings and secrets
from the past.
Will Self *Grey Area*
Short stories.
Iain Sinclair *Downriver;
Radon Daughters; White Chappell,
Scarlet Tracings*
The Thames' own *Heart of Darkness*
by London's laureate; William Hope
Hodgson via the London Hospital;
Ripper murders and book dealers.
Muriel Spark
The Ballad of Peckham Rye
Mayhem in Peckham.
Jane Stevenson *London Bridges*
Greek monks and murder.
Barbara Vine
King Solomon's Carpet; Grasshopper
From the Underground to a rooftop
love story.
Evelyn Waugh *Vile Bodies*
Shameful antics in 1920s Mayfair.
Angus Wilson
The Old Men at the Zoo
London faces down oblivion.
Virginia Woolf *Mrs Dalloway*
A kind of London *Ulysses*.

Non-fiction

Peter Ackroyd
London: The Biography
Wilfully obscurantist city history.
Marc Atkins & Iain Sinclair
Liquid City
Sinclair haunts photographed.
Felix Barker & Ralph Hyde
London as it Might Have Been
Schemes that never happened.
Anthony Burgess
A Dead Man in Deptford
The life and murder of Elizabethan
playwright Christopher Marlowe.
Margaret Cox *Life and Death in
Spitalfields 1700-1850*
The removal and analysis of bodies
from Christ Church Spitalfields.
Daniel Farson *Soho in the Fifties*
An affectionate portrait.
Stephen Halliday
The Great Stink of London
The sewage crisis in London in 1858.

Derek Hanson
The Dreadful Judgement
The embers of the Great Fire re-raked.
Sarah Hartley *Mrs P's Journey*
An affectionate biography of
Phyllis Pearsall, the woman who
singlehandedly created the *A–Z*.
Stephen Inwood
A History of London
A recent, readable history.
Ian Jack (ed) *Granta, London:
the Lives of the City*
Fiction, reportage and travel writing.
**Edward Jones & Christopher
Woodward** *A Guide to the
Architecture of London*
What it says. A brilliant work.
**Rachel Lichtenstein & Iain
Sinclair** *Rodinsky's Room*
The mysterious disappearance of an
East End Jew.
Jack London
The People of the Abyss
Extreme poverty in the East End.
Nick Merriman (ed)
The Peopling of London
2,000 years of settlement.
Tim Moore *Do Not Pass Go*
London, as seen around the
Monopoly board.
Gilda O'Neill *Pull No More Bines;
My East End*
Personal social histories of earthy
east London.
George Orwell
Down and Out in Paris and London
Waitering and starving.
Samuel Pepys *Diaries*
Fires, plagues, bordellos and more.
Lisa Picard *Dr Johnson's London;
Restoration London.*
London past, engagingly revisited.
Patricia Pierce *Old London Bridge*
The story of the world's longest
inhabited bridge.
Roy Porter
London: A Social History
An all-encompassing history.
Jonathan Raban *Soft City*
The city as state of mind; a classic.
Iain Sinclair *Lights Out for the
Territory; London Orbital.*
Time-warp visionary crosses
London; and circles it on the M25.
Derek Sumeray
Discovering London Plaques
A monumental piece of research
detailing commemorative plaques in
the capital.
Adrian Tinniswood
His Invention So Fertile
Illuminating biography of
Christopher Wren.
Richard Trench
London Under London
The subterranean city.
**Ben Weinreb & Christopher
Hibbert (eds)**
The London Encyclopaedia
Fascinating, thorough, indispensable.

Andrew White (ed)
Time Out Book of London Walks
Volumes 1 & 2.
Writers, cartoonists, comedians and
historians take a walk through town.
Jerry White *London in the 20th*
Century: A City and Its People.
The city transforms itself.

Films

Alfie *dir. Lewis Gilbert* (1966)
What's it all about, Michael?
Beautiful Thing *dir. Hettie*
MacDonald (1996)
A tender, amusing coming-of-age flick.
A Clockwork Orange
dir. Stanley Kubrick (1971)
Kubrick's vision still shocks.
Blow-Up *dir. Michelangelo*
Antonioni (1966)
Swingin' London captured in
unintentionally hysterical fashion.
Croupier *dir. Mike Hodges* (1997)
Gambling and drinking dominate
Hodges' terrific flick.
Death Line *dir. Gary Sherman* (1972)
Cannibalism on the tube. Yikes.
Jubilee *dir. Derek Jarman* (1978)
A horribly dated but still interesting
romp through the punk era.
The Krays *dir. Peter Medak* (1990)
The Kemp brothers excel as the
notorious East End gangsters.
Life is Sweet; **Naked**; **Secrets &**
Lies; **Career Girls**; **All or**
Nothing *dir. Mike Leigh* (1990; 1993;
1996; 1997; 2002)
A mocking but affectionate look at
Metroland; a compelling character
study; familial tensions; old friends
meet; a family falls apart.
Lock, Stock & Two Smoking
Barrels; **Snatch** *dir. Guy Ritchie*
(1998; 2000)
Mr Madonna's pair of East End faux-
gangster flicks.
London; **Robinson in Space**
dir. Patrick Keiller (1994; 1997)
Fiction meets documentary.
The Long Good Friday *dir. John*
MacKenzie (1989)
Bob Hoskins stars in the classic
London gangster flick.
Mona Lisa; **The Crying Game**
dir. Neil Jordan (1986; 1992)
Prostitution, terrorism, transvestism.
Mrs Dalloway
dir. Marleen Goris (1997)
Vanessa Redgrave stars in this
adaptation of the Woolf novel.
Nil by Mouth
dir. Gary Oldman (1997)
A violent, uncompromising but truly
compelling tale of working-class life.
Notting Hill
dir. Roger Michell (1999)
Hugh Grant and Julia Roberts get it
on in west London.
Peeping Tom *dir. Michael Powell*
(1960)
Powell's creepy murder flick still
shocks 40 years after release.

Performance *dir. Nicolas Roeg,*
Donald Cammell (1970)
The cult movie to end all cult movies
made west London cool for life.
28 Days *dir. Danny Boyle* (2002)
Post-apocalyptic London.
Wonderland *dir. Michael*
Winterbottom (1999)
A gritty, verité London classic of
love, loss and deprivation.

Music

Albums

Animals that Swim *I Was the*
King, I Really Was the King (1996)
Overlooked geniuses from N16.
Blur *Modern Life is Rubbish* (1993);
Park Life (1994)
Modern classics by the Essex exiles.
The Clash *London Calling* (1979)
Epoch-making punk classic.
Ian Dury & the Blockheads *New*
Boots & Panties (1977)
The late Dury's seminal work.
Handel *Water Music; Music For the*
Royal Fireworks (1717; 1749)
The glory days of the 18th century.
The Jam *This is the*
Modern World (1977)
Paul Weller at his splenetic finest.
Madness *Rise & Fall* (1982)
The nutty boys wax lyrical about
their beloved home.
Morrissey *Vauxhall & I* (1994)
The former Smiths frontman's finest
solo album.
Anthony Newley
The Very Best of… (1997)
Swingin' retrospective of everyone's
favourite Cockney scallywag.
The Rolling Stones *December's*
Children (and Everybody's) (1965)
Moodily cool evocation of the city.
The Sex Pistols
Never Mind the Bollocks (1977)
The best ever punk album.
So Solid Crew
They Don't Know (2001)
Mainstream urban garage.
The Streets
Original Pirate Material (2002)
Straight outta Brixton.
Simon Warner
Waiting Rooms (1997)
Bedsit decadence; a lost gem.

Songs

assorted *A Foggy Day (in London*
Town); A Nightingale Sang in
Berkeley Square; Let's All Go
Down the Strand; London Bridge is
Falling Down; Maybe It's Because
I'm a Londoner
David Bowie *London Boys*
Elvis Costello & the Attractions
(I Don't Want to Go to) Chelsea
Ray Davies *London Song*
Nick Drake *Mayfair*
Eddy Grant *Electric Avenue*

The Kinks *Denmark Street;*
Muswell Hillbillies; Waterloo Sunset
Pet Shop Boys *King's Cross;*
West End Girls
The Pogues *A Rainy Night in Soho;*
Misty Morning, Albert Bridge
Gerry Rafferty *Baker Street*
Roxy Music *Do the Strand*
St Etienne *London Belongs to Me*
Sham 69 *Hersham Boys*
Simple Minds *Chelsea Girl*
Squeeze *Up the Junction*
Sugar Minott *Riot Inna Brixton*
XTC *Towers of London*

Websites

BBC London *www.bbc.co.uk/london*
Online news, travel, weather,
entertainment and sport.
Classic Cafés *www.classiccafes.co.uk*
London's '50s and '60s caffs.
Greater London Authority
www.london.gov.uk
See what Ken and co are up to.
London Active Map
www.uktravel.com
Click on a tube station and find out
which attractions are nearby.
LondonTown *www.londontown.com*
The official tourist board website is
stuffed full of information and offers.
London Underground Online
www.thetube.com
A website devoted to the capital's
beleaguered Underground network.
Meteorological Office
www.met-office.gov.uk
Find out what the Met Office says
before you head out. Not always
accurate, but the best you'll get.
Place Names
www.krysstal.com/londname.html
Where London's neighbourhoods got
their monikers.
Pubs.com *www.pubs.com*
London's traditional boozers.
The River Thames Guide
www.riverthames.co.uk
Places and events along the banks of
the Thames.
Street Map *www.streetmap.co.uk*
Search for a road name or area, then
zoom in, zoom out and find grid
references and postcodes.
This is London
www.thisislondon.co.uk
The online version of the London
Evening Standard.
Time Out *www.timeout.com*
An essential source, of course,
with an online guide and a welter
of reviews.
Transport for London
www.londontransport.co.uk
The official website for buses, DLR,
river services and other forms of
transport in the capital, with real-
time travel information and journey
planning resources.
Yellow Pages Online *www.yell.com*
This business directory can help you
find a specific company or service.

Index

Index

Advertisers' Index

Please refer to the relevant pages for addresses and telephone numbers.

Places of interest or entertainment	⬛
Railway stations	⬛
Underground stations	⊖
Parks	⬜
Hospitals	⬜
Casualty units	✚
Churches	✚
Synagogues	✡
Districts	MAYFAIR

Maps

SAFER STREETS
LONDON AGAINST STREET CRIME

PUBLIC SUBWAY

UNDERGR

OUT OF SIGHT IS SAFER

IF YOU HAVE ANY INFORMATION ABOUT STREET ROBBERS
CALL CRIMESTOPPERS ANONYMOUSLY
0800 555 111

 METROPOLITAN POLICE *Working for a safer London*

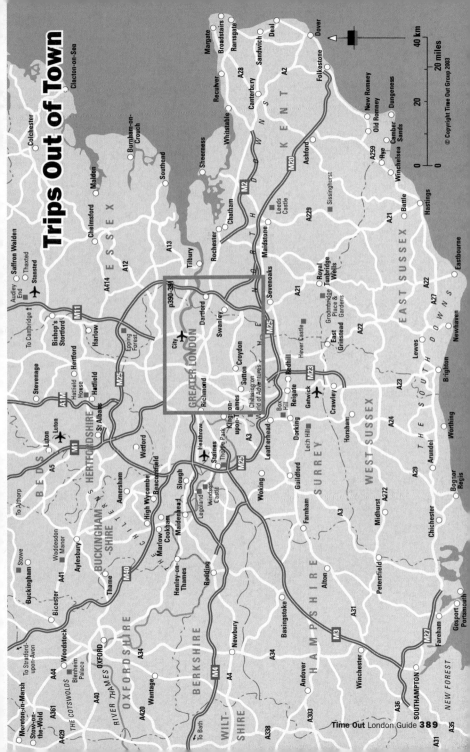

Trips Out of Town

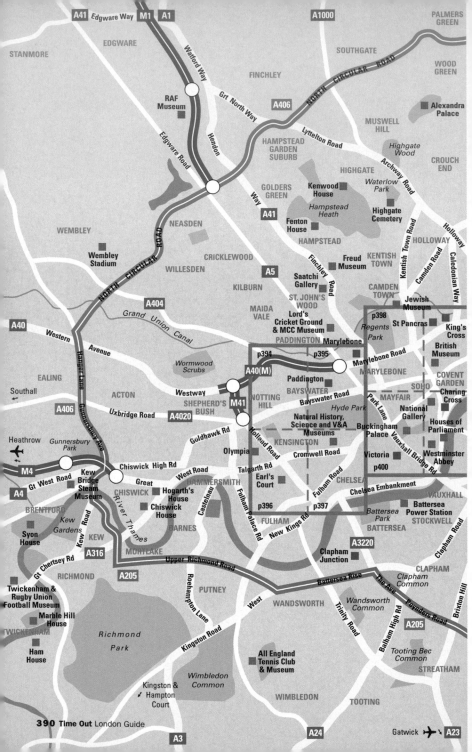

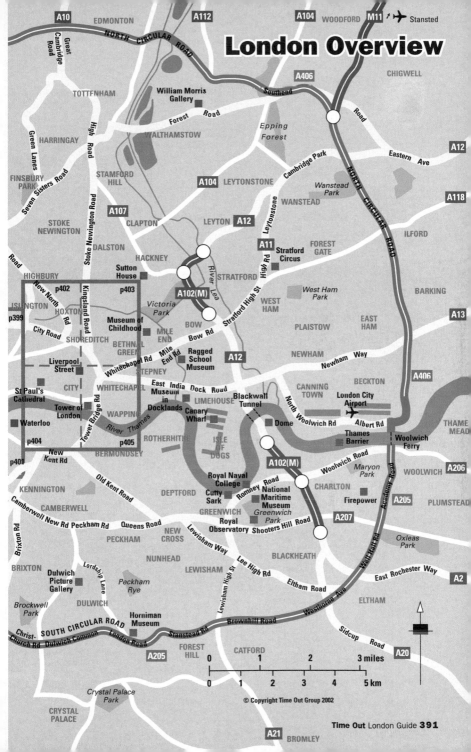

Central London
by Area

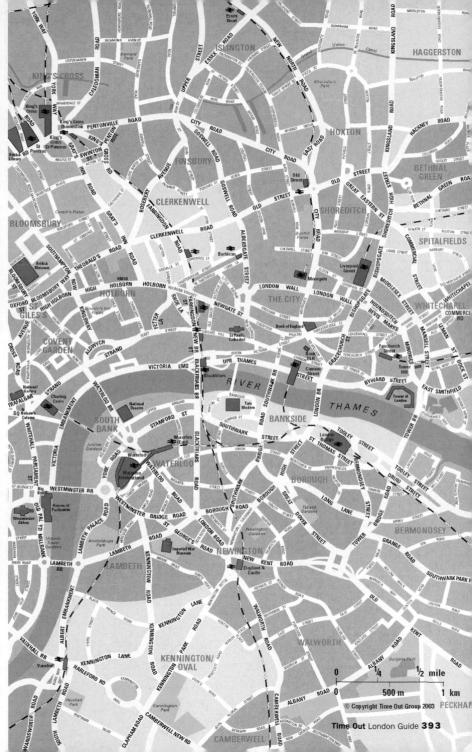

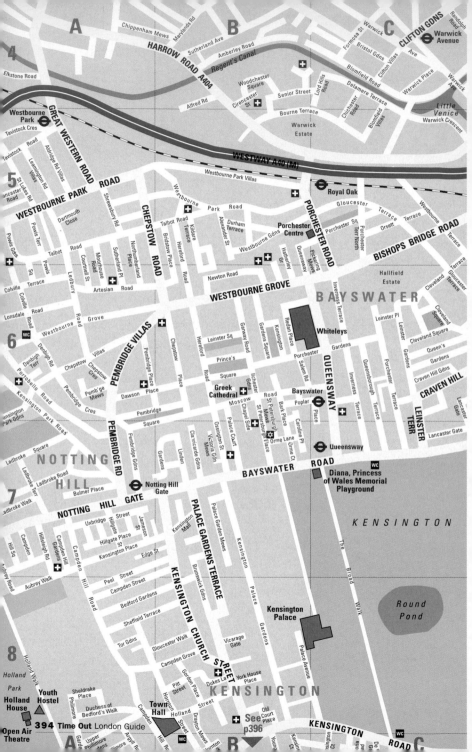

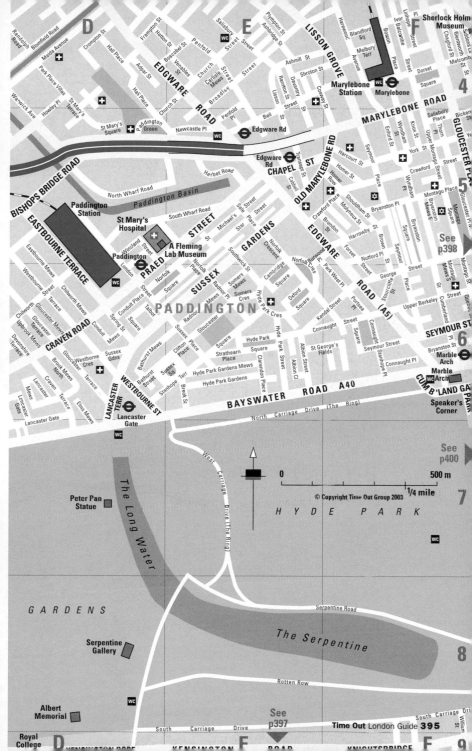

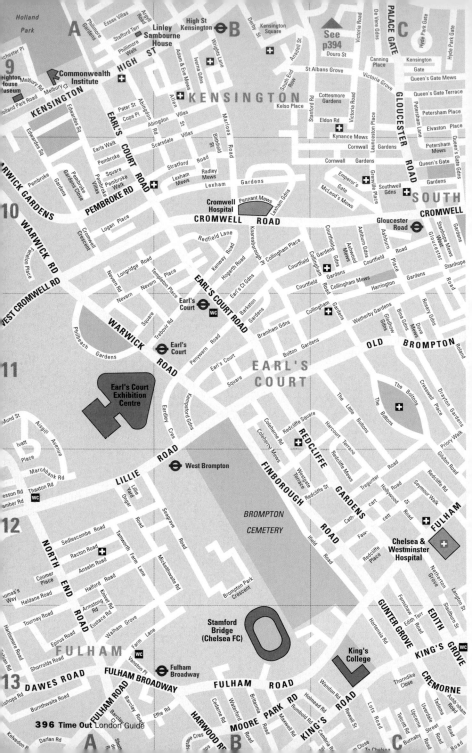

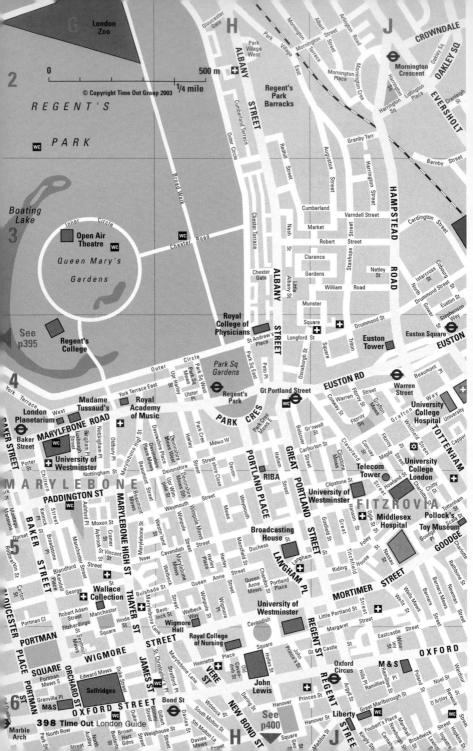

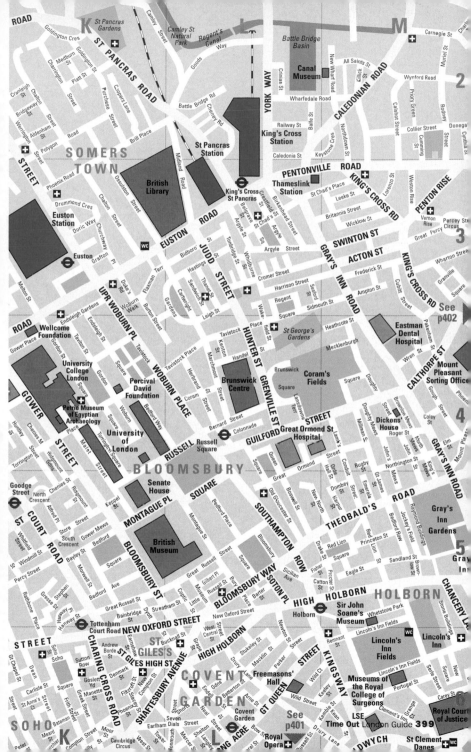

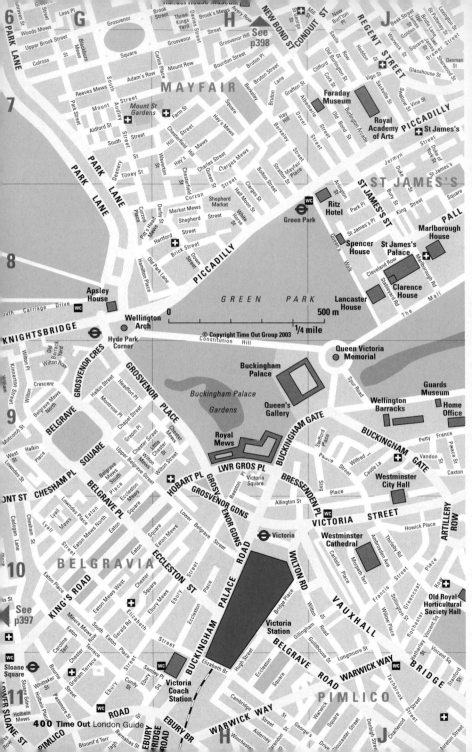

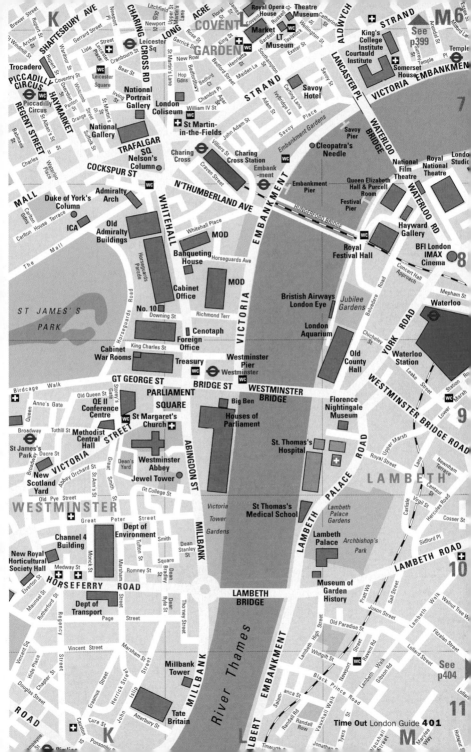

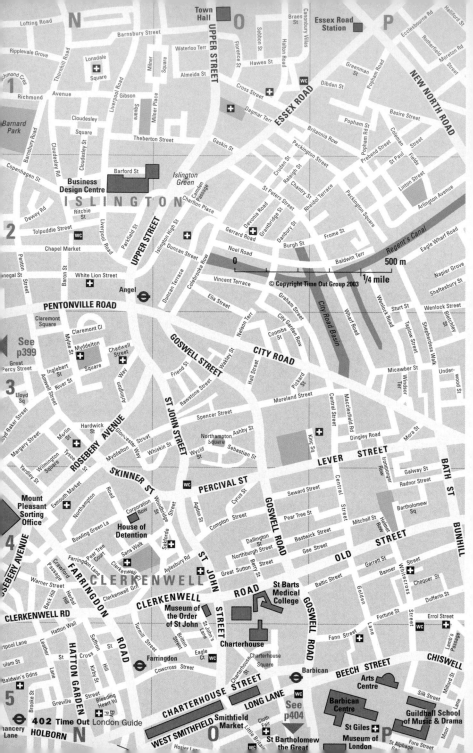

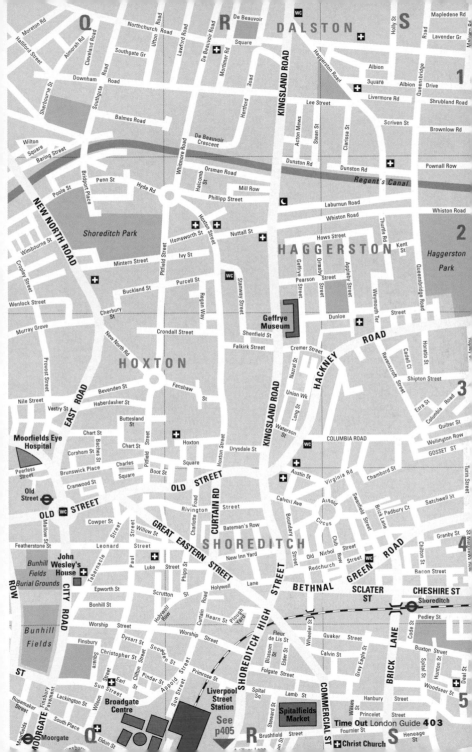

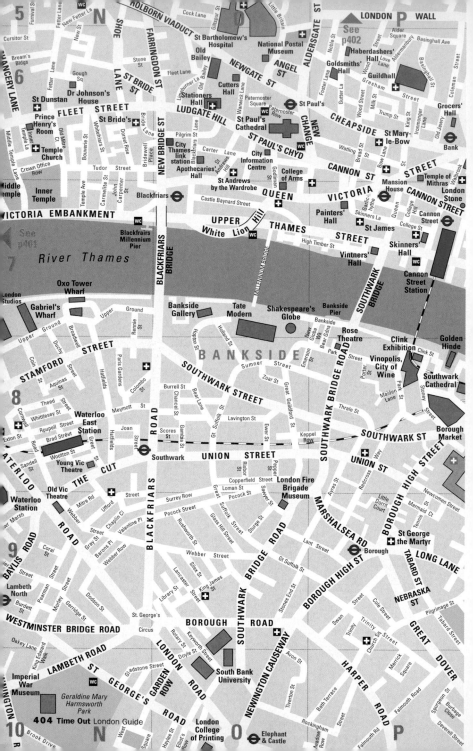

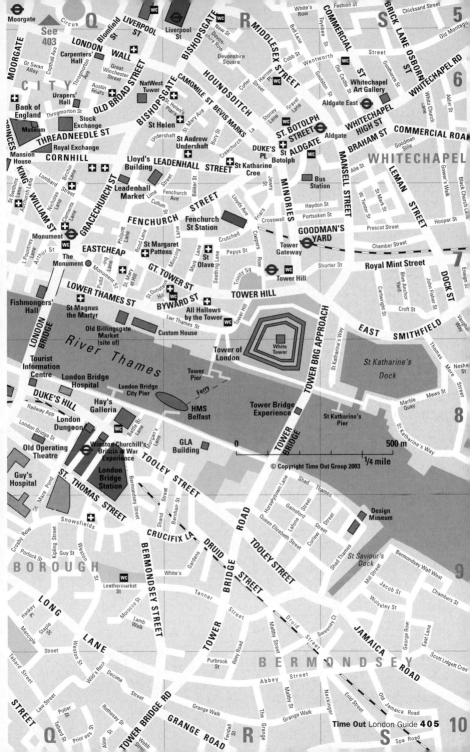

Street Index

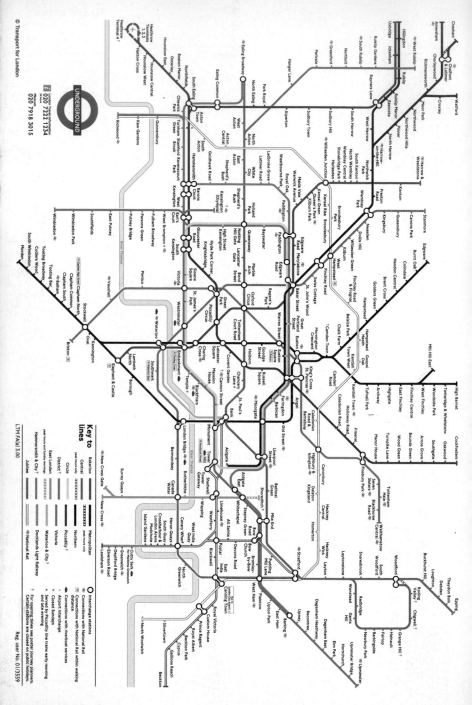